Exotic No More

Exotic No More:

EDITED BY JEREMY MacCLANCY

Anthropology on the Front Lines

The University of Chicago Press / Chicago and London

Jeremy MacClancy is professor in social anthropology at Oxford Brookes University. He is the author or editor of a number of books, including *Consuming Culture, Popularizing Anthropology*, and *The Decline of Carlism*.

The University of Chicago Press, Chicago 60637
The University of Chicago Press, Ltd., London
© 2002 by The University of Chicago
"Fieldwork at the Movies" © 2002 by Faye Ginsburg
All rights reserved. Published 2002
Printed in the United States of America
11   10   09   08   07   06   05   04   03   5   4   3   2

ISBN (cloth): 0-226-50012-8
ISBN (paper): 0-226-50013-6

The University of Chicago Press gratefully acknowledges a subvention from the Royal Anthropological Institute in partial support of the costs of production of this volume.

Library of Congress Cataloging-in-Publication Data

Exotic no more : anthropology on the front lines / edited by Jeremy MacClancy.
    p.   cm.
    Includes bibliographical references and index.
    ISBN 0-226-50012-8 (cloth : alk. paper) — ISBN 0-226-50013-6 (pbk. : alk. paper)
    1. Anthropological ethics.   2. Anthropology—Field work.   3. Philosophical anthropology.   I. MacClancy, Jeremy.
    GN33.6 .E93   2002
    301 — dc21

2001005920

Contents

Acknowledgments

Jonathan Benthall, then director of the Royal Anthropological Institute, initiated this project by asking me to take it on: I accepted gladly. He, his successor, Hilary Callan, and John Davis, who was president of the RAI during most of the development of this book, have been unfailingly supportive. At the University of Chicago Press, David Brent and Amy Collins have acted as exemplary editors throughout. My next set of creditors is the readers, who generously agreed to pass comment on certain chapters. One wishes to remain anonymous: the others are Ian Fowler, Elaine Genders, Abigail Halcli, Catherine Hill, Chris McDonaugh, and Sarah Pink. The next group whose kindness I must (and am happy to) recognize are those who have lent photos or granted permission for reprinting illustrations: Lila Abu-Lughod, Ben Campbell, Igloolik Isuma Productions, Inc., Cambridge University Press, Nicole Klagsbrun Gallery, Fred Panos Pictures, and Survival International for their understanding and generosity. Finally, I am grateful to all the contributors, who rose to the occasion: we are all indebted to the peoples among whom we have lived and who have taught us so much.

I perform the usual rites of absolution. If you have any complaints, cavils, or carps, please do not worry any of the above. Instead direct your comments to

Jeremy MacClancy
Oxford Brookes University

Introduction:
Taking People Seriously

JEREMY MacCLANCY

For far too long, social anthropology has been seen as an academic discipline dedicated to the study of abstruse customs of out-of-the-way tribes. Extraordinary ceremonies in exotic settings, unusual behaviors in isolated communities—these have been seen by many as anthropologists' stock in trade. However, like so many stereotypes, this outdated image of anthropology is more misleading than revealing, for anthropologists have always set the world, and not just its more wondrous corners, as their geographical limit. Since the very beginning of the subject in the late nineteenth century, there have been anthropologists working in Britain as well as Papua New Guinea, in France as well as Niger. It is just that much more work was done beyond the confines of Europe and that the potentially more sensational and more colorful of that work (especially those in particularly distant, even mysterious settings) has received far greater publicity.

Similarly, anthropologists have never restricted themselves to the academic investigation of the odd or the potentially entertaining, leaving the study of anything of any possible practical importance to others. Since the relatively early days of the discipline, some anthropologists have dedicated themselves to research into matters of immediate relevance, such as nutritional practices, attitudinal surveys, and the fallacious presuppositions of racisms. In the 1920s the great American anthropologist Franz Boas played a major role in the intellectual attack on scientific racism. Once again, it is the more eye-catching studies that have gained more of the public's attention, skewing popular perception of the discipline in the process.

A particularly ugly example of this bias occurred in 2000 when an expert on Amazonia published a book accusing a senior anthropologist of grossly exploiting his position among the Indians he had lived with for the sake of his own selfish ends. The author's accusations of the anthropologist's apparent complicity in genocide and his sustained insensitivity towards the Indians made good copy for hungry journalists. The image of an arrogant outsider dangerously overlording it in an exotic setting was too good to resist. At the time of going to press, the debate is continuing and, although some of the accusations might appear well grounded, we must await the replies of the accused before attempting to reach any judgment. But what needs to be avoided right now is that the sensational treatment of a seemingly miscreant anthropologist be allowed to besmirch the whole profession. That many anthropologists are dedicated to research which has socially beneficial ends is evidenced on page after page of this book: exposing the weaknesses in grand policy programs, acting as advocates for the unvoiced, championing the downtrodden, and so on. In these circumstances, should the bad apparently performed by the odd renegade be allowed to overshadow the much greater good performed by the many?

The aim of this book is to reverse this trend in sensationalism and to reemphasize the public value of the discipline. Thus all the contributors strive to demonstrate exactly how today's social anthropology can make a large contribution towards the understanding of a wide range of practical social issues. In a series of essays covering a rich diversity of topics from fundamentalism to food security, from child labor to crack dealing, they seek to show how anthropologists today are committed, to a degree greater than ever before, to investigating contemporary social problems and to studying the West as much as the "rest." Even Aldous Huxley, writing in the mid-1930s during the rise of fascism, was well aware of the need to rebalance anthropological efforts. In *Eyeless in Gaza*, he has one character argue that Europeans are not worse than indigenes: "They've just been badly handled— need a bit of anthropology, that's all!"

The chapters by Bourgois and Scheper-Hughes come first, because they give a taste of what fieldwork is actually like. Compelling accounts, they portray the mundane surrealities anthropologists can encounter, the personal resources they may have to dredge up, and the intellectual twists and turns their investigations may well be forced to take. They are impassioned portraits of research in the field, revealing the commitment sometimes required of fieldworkers and the quotidian dangers or ridicule they may face in the pursuit of their intellectual tasks.

Since human activity cannot be boxed into neatly sealed compartments, the other chapters are very loosely grouped. Any order to their sequence is more apparent than real. We start with trade (Schneider on markets; and see figure 1), progress to politics (Hann on ideologies), descend to violence (Gilsenan), investigate nationalism (Jenkins), check out religion (Beeman on fundamentalisms) examine the topics of "race," genders, and health (in turn, Harrison, Gottlieb, and

FIGURE 1 Consuming culture: trading relations in a Maasai tourist village outside the Maasai Mara Game Reserve, Kenya. (© Dylan Garcia/Survival)

Lock), move on to the land (Leach and Fairhead), and then explore some varieties of human misery (Messer and Shipton on famine, de Waal on aid, Daniel on refugees). Next come the chapters by Messer, Napier, and Ennew which, concentrating on different but overlapping sets of human rights, form a complementary trio. Franklin follows, with her contribution on science.

Since we did not want all the contributions to this book to read like an analytical chronicle of gloom and doom from womb to tomb, we end with four chapters devoted to topics more commonly associated with "high" or popular culture: Ginsburg on the media, Chernoff on musics, Steiner on visual arts, and MacClancy on tourisms. Unlike the other contributors, who focus exclusively on anthropological efforts to increase our understanding about particular social issues, Chernoff's concern is to outline the problems of studying music, whether by anthropologists or by ethnomusicologists. But since the lessons he draws are so instructive and general, his gemlike chapter well deserves its place in this book.

Many anthropologists, despite their best intentions, have hidden their insights and cloaked their findings in the thickest of prose. Their texts, weighed down with recondite terms, ugly neologisms, and an excess of polysyllabic abstract nouns, are usually difficult to read and harder to finish. This is as unnecessary as it is unwanted. If an idea is worth expressing, the chances are it can be most powerfully expressed in a simple manner. All the contributors to this book have done their best to uphold this principle by trying to write in a way that is as clear, unpretentious, and jargon-free as possible. A key purpose of this book is to put the anthropological message across. We want the taxpayers, who ultimately foot most of our bills, to know what we are up to, not dive for the dictionary before they have turned the first page.

The term *anthropology* can have a very broad set of meanings, and for that reason I must stress that this book is exclusively about *social* anthropology. None of the contributors is primarily concerned with the distant past (that's archaeology), nor with comparing languages and their structures (anthropological linguistics), nor with the effect of biological variables on human populations (biological anthropology). So, what exactly is social anthropology and what is so distinctive about it?

FIELDWORK

Anthropology is about taking people seriously. It is about trying to understand how people interpret and act in the world. Anthropologists listen to what people say, watch what they do, and then try to make sense of their words and their deeds by putting them into context.

Since we all interpret the world within the terms of our own particular language, anthropologists have to learn the language of the people they are working with. But learning a language and getting to know people both take time, lots of it. So anthropologists have made *fieldwork* the core method of their discipline. This means living, day and night, with a group of people for a protracted period, usually about two years, at least for the initial study. It also means trying, as much as possible, to live like the locals: participating in daily activities while at the same time observing and asking questions.

The key consequence of adopting this approach is that the vast majority of anthropologists, unlike most social scientists, do not normally try to *measure* things. Usually, they do not try to create quantitative data (numbers, frequencies, percentages, etc.), but strive to gather qualitative information. When starting a new study, their first task is not to devise a questionnaire, but to make friends and to begin speaking in a foreign tongue. The idea is to get to know the locals, before try-ing to learn what they know. For instance, Bourgois, in his chapter on Puerto Ri-can crack dealers in East Harlem, argues that outsiders who breeze in and use quantitative surveys to study local crime tend to collect fabrications, as the people they study don't trust them. As Messer and Shipton mention in their chapter on hunger in Africa, many polite Africans favor "yes" as an answer, just to be agree-able, especially where the questioner is perceived as senior. In these circum-stances, any hurriedly collected data are meaningless mathematically. Further-more, anthropologists' primary concern is to understand what is important to the locals they are studying, rather than to impose their own ideas and categories on others. For instance, once Bourgois had gained the respect of the Harlem drug dealers he lived among, he could begin to learn from them "about the complex ex-perience of extreme social marginalization in the United States." As these two ex-amples imply, to most anthropologists the idea of starting out with a set of pre-formed questions is wrongheaded and completely anathema.

One real strength of fieldwork is that it allows anthropologists to take very little for granted. Since different peoples comprehend the world in different ways, what is common sense for one group may well be deepset prejudice, if not non-sense, for another. Thus an anthropologist, newly arrived in the field, presumes very little and has to be prepared for even her most cherished preconceptions to be overturned. By living for so long with one group of people, she is eventually able to discern their basic beliefs, to apprehend their degree of order, and to put the seemingly irrational into context. Thus de Waal, in his chapter on anthropology and aid, shows that when in March 1985, at the nadir of the Ethiopian famine, a group of refugees insisted on leaving their refugee camp in order to return home, they were acting in a perfectly rational manner. Though relief workers thought them suicidal and about to embark on a "march of death," the anthropologist real-ized that their strong desire to return was in fact part of a logical strategy "which, if successful, would enable them to cultivate for the following year and return to a degree of normalcy after the famine." Consider a second example: Westerners have long regarded the forest-savanna transition in West Africa as undergoing sustained, rapid deforestation. But Leach and Fairhead, in their chapter on envi-ronmentalism, argue convincingly that the West African villagers they worked with are not deforesters but in fact very careful managers of their forests, which they and their forefathers have extended over the last hundred years.

As well as taking very little for granted, an anthropologist on fieldwork may well find that what appeared at first as simply unbelievable is in fact all too true. For ex-ample Scheper-Hughes, in her chapter on the global market in human body or-gans, discusses how in her Brazilian fieldwork she first encountered surreal rumors about the theft, by the almost inhumanly avaricious, of human eyes, hearts, and kidneys. To begin with, like many of her colleagues, she thought these tales reflected the existential insecurities of the marginalized poor. Only after further work did she come to realize how very well-grounded these frightening stories were.

By spending so much time in the field, an anthropologist has the opportunity to establish relations of trust and maybe even something approaching friendship with the people she is living with. This holds the promise of allowing her to discover whether things really are as they seem. Having gained the confidence of her hosts, an anthropologist can attempt to ascertain whether what people initially told her in fact corresponds with what they do and, if not, how they explain the gap between the two. People are usually ready to represent themselves publicly in a certain clear-cut way, while quietly upholding a much more nuanced set of rules. Gilsenan, in his contribution on conflict and violence, writes about his fieldwork in the early 1970s in northern Lebanon. At first he learned about the great landlords of the area, renowned for their ruthlessness and use of force; he heard much boasting about the glorious and fearless deeds committed by these men or in their name. Slowly, however, he began to perceive that much unspoken effort was spent on *avoiding* direct physical violence and conflict. Upholding one's honor had its price, and, as some admitted to Gilsenan, "a man has to live." So, though many would be quick to utter pious phrases of solidarity and outrage, all knew that most action did not go beyond the lip.

A further strength of extended fieldwork is that so much is learned by serendipity. In other words, an anthropologist must try to be always ready for chance events, for unexpected things randomly happening in front of her. These accidental encounters may be surprising and at first incomprehensible. But by inquiring into what is going on and why, an anthropologist may well come to learn something about her hosts which she had never even suspected. In the late 1970s I was carrying out fieldwork in a coastal village on the island of Tanna, in the South Pacific archipelago of Vanuatu. The country was then in the throes of a classical anticolonial struggle, with most villages marked out as dedicated either to pro- or anti-independence parties. People allied to one party claimed not to cooperate in any way with those of another. One day, two months into my work, I was astonished to see a man from a politically opposed village bring his small boat into the bay, where he was met by a local to whom he gave some fish. When I asked what was going on, I was told, "But they are kin. And when these political troubles are over, we can all be brothers once again." Further questions over the next few days showed me that, though most kept up a front of political partisanship, many quietly maintained relationships which had existed long before political parties had ever been introduced to the area.

The summary point of the preceding discussion is that a clipboard-bearing social administrator who simply drops into a community, asks a predetermined list of
questions, collects the answers, and then goes home at the end of the working day
to tabulate his results mathematically is much less likely to have his prejudices un-
settled, to be able to distinguish between local ideology and reality, or to witness an
accidental but revelatory event. Instead, he is much more likely to confirm what he
sought to establish in the first place, even if it is wrong, misguided, or prejudicial.

Of course, no discipline is a harmonious whole unto itself, with all its practitioners in complete agreement about the nature and aims of their subject. Social
anthropology is no exception. Some anthropologists might disagree with my
characterization of the discipline so far. They might wish to argue the plurality of
social anthropologies that exist: comparative mythologists analyzing the stories
people tell; structuralists studying the fundamental structures and operations of
the human mind; sociobiologists trying to integrate social and biological factors in
their approaches to the study of societies; social theorists bent on formulating abstract models of human behavior; and so on. In this book, it is true, the contributors emphasize, in chapter after chapter, the power and value of fieldwork-based
ethnography rather than, for instance, engaging in speculation about the nature of
mental operations. But that is solely in order to achieve the aim of this book: to
demonstrate the relevance of social anthropology to our understanding of the
contemporary social world.

In recent decades, academics in other disciplines have begun to recognize the
power and value of fieldwork as well. For instance, some sociologists and lecturers
in cultural studies have adopted anthropological procedures: in their own terms,
they practice "fieldwork" and they write "ethnography." This cross-disciplinary
borrowing is potentially very flattering. Trouble is, what exactly the borrowers do
is often rather different from (and frequently less than) the anthropological approach of intensive interaction with a particular group of people, including learning their language, for a prolonged period of time. Thus, even though fieldwork
and ethnography are no longer exclusive to social anthropology, they are still central to the anthropological enterprise. And it is this central place of fieldwork-
based ethnography within social anthropology which continues to make it a distinctive discipline, with a distinctive contribution to the understanding of social
concerns.

THE NATURAL, THE CULTURAL, AND THE ANTHROPOLOGIST

Time and again the contributors show how anthropologists do not just make the
strange familiar. They can make the familiar strange as well. In other words, they
can both place seemingly unusual customs in their local cultural logics *and* draw

out the cultural peculiarity of seemingly natural Western ideas. In this reflexive mode, anthropology can act as a very powerful tool for understanding our own position in the world. For example, Schneider, Harrison, and Gottlieb, in their chapters on markets, racisms and sexuality respectively, demonstrate that though common Western ideas about "free" markets, human "races" and genders are made to seem perfectly natural they are in fact thoroughly cultural in their construction. This strategy of "naturalizing" the cultural is as widespread as it is insidious. For instance, as Gottlieb shows, many Westerners still believe that it is a naturally determined fact that there are only two genders. A trawl through ethnographies of other cultures, however, soon demonstrates that there are many societies whose members divide themselves into three or even four genders. Despite what those Westerners who believe in two (and only two) genders might think, the sky does not fall, chaos does not ensue in these societies just because their members perceive a greater number of genders. Indeed, as far we are able to judge, they are all able to live together in as contented and fruitful a manner as people in other societies. As this example suggests, the power of the arguments deployed by Schneider, Harrison, and Gottlieb resides in the fact that since many associate the normative with the natural, exposing the cultural fabrication of what appears natural does away with its normative consequence. To put that another way, the radical shift in position steered by the three contributors is from "because this is the way things are 'naturally,' this is the way things have to be" to "because there is nothing natural about the way things are, there is no natural reason why they have to continue so into the future."

Steiner, in his chapter on art and museums, takes a parallel tack when he argues that the question whether a non-Western cultural artifact is art or not is ultimately sterile. Reflection on this query shows that the fundamental question we should be asking here is a much broader one: What are the social institutions, agents, actions, and cultural frameworks which allow any object, whether non-Western or Western, to be viewed as art? Similarly, Beeman, writing on fundamentalism, notes that it has gained strongly pejorative connotations for many people. Yet, he argues, a deeper, comparative approach to this nearly universal phenomenon may forestall these dismissive attitudes. As he notes, "An adequate understanding of fundamentalism requires us to acknowledge its potential in every movement or cause. . . . We are all of us, to some degree and in some sense, fundamentalists." For Napier, facilitating some awareness of how culturally peculiar are our own property practices is the fundamental contribution anthropology can make to discussions of intellectual property rights. Daniel's work on refugees underlines the fact that Western notions of personhood and of the individual are not universally accepted, and may cause difficulties when officials try to decide whether a displaced person working according to different cultural presuppositions can be treated as a "genuine refugee" or not.

Similar arguments about the thoroughly cultural nature of Western practices can be applied to that supposedly impregnable bastion of Western rationality, science. For though the great majority of scientists uphold their investigations as completely free of cultural bias, work by anthropologists suggests strongly that this is often not the case. Franklin, in her contribution, demonstrates that scientists' pretensions of having a "culture of no culture" is a misleading representation, as work in laboratories is in fact shaped by very distinctive cultural forces. Indeed, a succession of studies by anthropologists has exposed just how very deeply cultural values and beliefs shape the making of scientific knowledge. Leach and Fairhead, in their chapter, show that, despite their universalizing pretensions, global scientific orthodoxies about environmentalism are themselves partial cultural perspectives grounded in particular relations of power, where the views of influential Westerners, supposed "experts," usually prevail over those of locals. What is needed, they contend, is a democratization of expertise in the very definition of environmental issues and problems. Lock argues in a similar vein about the practice of doctors, for she lays bare how much of North American medical approaches is culturally informed. Her line of argument makes it clear that quantification and measurement should not be elevated as the unquestionable gold standards by which medical disorders are understood. Instead, their potential value needs to be continually reexamined.

GLOBALIZING ANTHROPOLOGY, LOCALIZING ISSUES

The groups of people with whom anthropologists work may be small, but the issues they deal with can be enormous. Just because one is studying the lives of a relatively restricted number of people does not mean that the ramifications of the analysis might not be very extensive. For if the world is the ultimate geographical limit of anthropology, then nothing less than the nature of humanity is its ultimate intellectual limit. For instance, Hann, in his chapter on political ideologies, shows that comparative work on a series of small-scale ethnographic studies reveals how a variety of ordinary people, as opposed to party leaders and policymakers, have understood the alternatives of socialism and capitalism and to what extent they have been able to identify these grand programs with their own, local ideologies. In much the same manner, Jenkins, in his contribution on ethnicity, is able to reaffirm, thanks to a plethora of contemporary ethnographic studies, the essentially negotiated nature of ethnicity. Though some politicians or journalists would have us believe it is primordial or natural, repeated anthropological work demonstrates that ethnicity can be negotiable and flexible from one social situation to another (though never *infinitely* so). In other circumstances, it may be non-negotiable. For those trapped within ethnic conflicts, there may be no choice.

Formerly, many anthropologists wrote up their studies of local groups as though they were more or less isolated communities, in contact with their neighbors and aware of what was going on slightly further afield, but essentially ignorant of what occurred much beyond. This once-convenient fiction can no longer be sustained with any conviction. The ever-increasing spread of capitalist practices, the continuing growth of both labor migration and mass tourism, and the rise of worldwide telecommunications have all contributed to the ending of any real sense of isolation (see plate 1). It is all too evident now that peoples are as affected by global forces as by local ones. Anthropologists have shifted their focus accordingly. The majority of contributors to this book emphasize how one cannot understand people's present predicaments without taking broader frames into account. Thus Ginsburg contributes a chapter on mass media that demonstrates how anthropologists study this contemporary cultural force throughout the globe: the ways it can extend the forms and processes of political expression; the ways it may alter already established identities and enable the creation of new ones. Of course, just because peoples throughout the world are subject to similar globalizing tendencies does not mean that they experience or interpret these forces in the same way. MacClancy, in his contribution on tourism, makes it clear that mass tourism need not always have a damaging effect on local cultures. In some cases the arrival of visitors can boost or even revitalize local ways. In parts of central Australia, for instance, the rise of a tourist market in Aboriginal artifacts has freed the locals from year-round dependence on state hand-outs. Fortified with the cash from sales of their creations, they can now afford to re-adopt their "walkabout" lifestyle for several months of the year.

The effects of globalization are perhaps most clearly seen, however, in the created tensions between edicts of universal scope prescribed by agencies with a worldwide reach and the diversity of local realities. Thus Ennew writes about the potential mismatches between the desires of UNICEF officials to establish a universal benchmark for the Rights of the Child and the kaleidoscopic variety of ways in which "childhood" is understood in different cultures, each with its different aims, approaches, and consequences. In such a context, one potential role for anthropologists is as active participants in the high-level debates which lead to the formulation of global guidelines. For example, in the 1990s anthropologists working with Non-Governmental Organizations (NGOs) in the UN development summits helped to negotiate the substantive contents and added a genuinely cross-cultural dimension to the legislation on the human rights for women, children, refugees, indigenous groups and other minorities.

It is relatively easy for the UN and legislators to lay down the principles of human rights. It is much more difficult to ensure that they are put into practice and continue to be upheld. Messer points out that anthropologists can play a significant, activist role here. While on fieldwork or dispatched on assignment by NGOs, they can monitor compliance with codes of human rights and publicly criticize any violations or abuses. They may also help to establish channels through which abused indigenous peoples can make effective protests and directly demand protection. Anthropologists here may act as advocates and enablers for those unused to the special languages of international conventions or the Byzantine intricacies and pitfalls of formalized legal codes. This can be dangerous terrain, as there are always others ready to stifle opposition to their aggressive plans. Advocacy has its own very real risks—deportation, imprisonment, assassination—as some engaged anthropologists have learned, to their personal cost.

When dealing with global concerns, the questions may be large and the problems huge, but the most effective answers may well be surprisingly low-level. A series of small-scale initiatives, sensitive to local approaches, can prove to be much more productive than one very large one, even if it has the loftiest of aims. Thus Napier, after exposing the catch-22s of so many grand projects to safeguard the intellectual property rights of indigenes, argues that it is not high-flying, but ground-level encounters which hold the most promise. If a transnational corporation is genuinely concerned to assist the locals whose intellectual property it is so keen to exploit, then its agents will need to get out of their executive jets and cut their way to the shaman's door. Shipton and Messer make much the same point with respect to development aid projects: most of the successes in this sphere have been small in scale. Usually drawing on local initiatives, they have often involved private or NGO activity. These participatory programs may not be glamorous, but, compared to the grand development projects so beloved by publicity-seeking politicians, they have a much greater chance of achieving their aims.

STUDYING ELITES, ENCOURAGING EMPOWERMENT

Traditionally, anthropologists have tended to "study down." That is, they have worked with people who usually perceive them as coming from more prestigious or more powerful societies than their own. In the last two decades, many anthropologists, realizing how restrictive this focus is, have changed tack and started to "study up." These trendsetters work on previously uninvestigated elite groups, regarding them as cultures unto themselves with their own self-justifying logics and staffed by professionals who evolve their own, ever more elaborate languages in order to legitimate their claims to specialist expertise. Thus, in this book, de Waal examines the various institutions within the aid and development industry, and

Franklin surveys ethnographic work on laboratories, where anthropologists have had to adopt a subordinate position with teams of scientists. This shift in focus was in part necessary because anthropologists had come to recognize that the all-important definitions of the peoples they were studying were being imposed by outsiders, whose own ways had to be investigated if the fuller picture was to emerge. Definition here is so significant because it determines what treatment people receive. This point is made most forcibly by Daniel in his chapter on refugees. There he argues that, to study displaced persons, we need above all to look at the definition of "refugee" used by states and the procedures utilized by their receiving agencies to deal with these new entrants to their countries (figure 2). What is required, he contends, are ethnographies of the state if we wish to better comprehend displacement, if we wish to clarify what exactly constitutes the "homelessness" of the refugee.

Along with this change to studying up, many anthropologists have switched from studying in one particular place to multisite ethnography. If people move, anthropologists follow their movement to a new site, whether refugee camp, center for migrant labor, or tourist destination. Key questions that arise here are How do people organize themselves socially in their new place of residence, however temporary it may be? What senses of culture do they wish to maintain or recreate? What kinds of relations do they negotiate with their host community? Work on

FIGURE 2 Twa (formerly known as "pygmies") displaced by the 1994 violence in Rwanda, staying in a shelter set up by a local Methodist priest, Zaire. (© Adrian Arbib/Survival)

these topics is already helping to show that the long-standing conception of a culture as a fixed, clearly bounded, relatively static entity must now be forsaken for a much more fluid, dynamic sense of culture, conceived as a continuing creation of its members. At the same time, because so many phenomena are now global in scope, anthropologists study their manifestations in different sites wherever they occur in the world. For instance Scheper-Hughes and her colleagues are simultaneously studying the trade in human organs in Brazil, South Africa, and elsewhere precisely in order to better understand this grisly but still developing world market. Investigating the phenomenon in a single place would not have enabled them to answer the wide-ranging questions they need to ask.

To some critics of anthropology, studying down all too often went hand in hand with colonialism or neocolonialism. For many of them, the discipline is still irrevocably tarred with the same "imperialist" brush. This generalization about anthropology is as sweeping as it is misrepresentative. It is true that in colonial times many anthropologists were funded by colonial agencies. Yet that does not necessarily mean that their work assisted the colonial process. Using the example of Sudan during its Anglo-Egyptian days, de Waal argues that although anthropology was used as an adjunct to military intelligence, anthropologists working there frequently ended up with more sympathy and understanding for the subjects of their research and wrote up their reports accordingly. Many British anthropologists who worked in Africa in the postwar decades have since stressed that they acted as liberal critics of the colonial regime, not as its handservants.

De Waal goes on to argue that this critical stance of anthropologists during the colonial period manifests the essentially subversive role that anthropology can so often play. In this book for instance, contributor after contributor emphasizes how anthropology is on the side of the "people," the subalterns. Through the accumulated examples of their writings, they underscore how anthropology helps to empower the alienated and give voice to the otherwise unvoiced. Unlike almost any other discipline, anthropology can humanize institutional process, the effects of politics, and the work of nations. Anthropologists, by listening to and then transmitting the words of the marginalized, the poor, and the ignored, can bring high-flying approaches back down to the ground and reintroduce the concerns of ordinary people into the equations of policymakers. For these reasons, among others, we have included at the end of the book a statement by a leading member of Survival International about its continuing campaigns to defend the threatened rights of tribal peoples. Anthropologists have long supported the work of Survival, and many have assisted in its work.

Of course, there are several other kinds of anthropology, many of which have what at first sight appears to be a much more academically narrow focus: for example, comparative mythology, kinship structures, the nature of symbolism, the intricacies of indigenous cosmologies. However here, above all, we must remember that the boundaries of what is "socially relevant" research are constantly shifting, in tune with changing circumstances. What may appear to be abstruse scholarship one day may become material of great political import the next day. For instance, ethnographic work on the details of Australian Aboriginal conceptions of person and place is now key in a whole range of court cases brought by indigenes against the appropriations of the Australian state. A version of this book published in thirty years' time might well have a very different set of chapters.

In sum, if there is a single point that all the contributors wish to put across, it is that anthropology remains a discipline with the greatest of promise, whose distinctive approach continues to yield a diversity of significant insights into matters of contemporary import, and whose potential value for our understanding of the social world has still not yet been fully tapped.

ACKNOWLEDGMENTS

My thanks to Elaine Genders, Abbey Halcli, and Catherine Hill for comments on an earlier draft.

1.

Understanding Inner-City Poverty: Resistance and Self-Destruction under U.S. Apartheid

PHILIPPE BOURGOIS

I did not run fast enough out the door of the video arcade crackhouse to avoid hearing the lookout's baseball bat thud twice against a customer's skull. I had misjudged the harsh words Caesar, the lookout, had been exchanging with a drug-intoxicated customer to be the aggressive but ultimately playful posturing that is characteristic of much male interaction on the street. Pausing on the curb in front of the crackhouse, I tried to decide from the continued sound of scuffling inside whether or not I should call for medical emergency. Reassured when I saw the beaten young man crawl out the door amidst a parting barrage of kicks and howling laughter, I walked two doors down the block to my tenement where I was living at the time in the primarily Puerto Rican neighborhood of East Harlem, New York. Confused by my impotence in the face of the violence of my crack dealer friends, I ended my fieldwork early that night and tried to recover from my own anger and rushing adrenaline by rocking my newborn son to sleep. My baby's appreciative gurgles, however, did not erase from the back of my mind the sound of Caesar's baseball bat thudding on the drug addict's skull.

The following evening, I forced myself to return to the crackhouse where I was spending much of my time conducting research on inner-city poverty and social marginalization (figure 1). I rebuked Caesar for his "overreaction" to the obnoxious customer the night before. Caesar was only too pleased to engage me in a playful argument. Half way through our verbal jousting, he grabbed my tape recorder out of my shirt pocket, turned it on, and spoke directly into the microphone. He wanted to make sure I had a clear record of his riposte so that it could be included as a direct quote in the book on street culture and the underground economy that I was writing at the time:

FIGURE 1 The Game Room video arcade and crackhouse. (Photo by author)

Nah, Felipe, you just don't understand. It's not good to be too sweet sometimes to people, man, because they're just gonna take advantage of you.

That dude was talking shit for a long time, about how we weak; how he control the block; and how he can do whatever he wants.

I mean, we were trying to take it calm like, until he starts talkin' this'n'that, about how he gonna drop a dime on us [report us to the police].

That's when I grabbed the bat—I looked at the axe that we keep behind the Pac-Man but then I said, "No; I want something that's going to be short and compact. I only gotta swing a short distance to clock him.

[Now shouting out the video arcade doorway for everyone outside to hear] You don't control nothin', because we rocked your bootie. Ha! Ha! Ha!

[Turning back to me] That was right when you ran out the door, Felipe. You missed it. I had gotten wild.

You see, Felipe, you can't be allowing people to push you around in this neighborhood, or else you get that reputation, like: "That homeboy's soft."

Primo, the manager of the crackhouse, further confirmed Caesar's story and raised the credibility of his violent persona by noting with a chuckle that he had only barely managed to subdue Caesar after the second blow of the baseball bat to keep Caesar from killing the offending customer while he lay semiconscious on the floor.

THE LOGIC OF VIOLENCE IN STREET CULTURE

Most readers might interpret Caesar's behavior and public rantings and ravings to be those of a dysfunctionally antisocial psychopath. In the context of the underground economy, however, Caesar's braggadocio and celebration of violence are good public relations. Periodic public displays of aggression are crucial to his professional credibility. They ensure his long-term job security. When Caesar shouted his violent story out the door of the crackhouse for everyone in the vicinity to hear, he was not bragging idly or dangerously; on the contrary, he was advertising his effectiveness as a lookout, and confirming his capacity for maintaining order at his work site. Another side benefit that Caesar derives from his inability to control his underlying rages is a lifelong monthly Social Security Insurance check for being—as he puts it—"a certified nut case." He periodically reconfirms his emotional disability by occasional suicide attempts.

In short, at age nineteen, Caesar's brutality has allowed him to mature into an effective career as crackhouse lookout. Aside from providing him with what he considers to be a decent income, it also allows him on a personal and emotional level to overcome the terrified vulnerability he endured growing up in East Harlem. Born to a sixteen-year-old heroin addict, he was raised by a grandmother who beat him regularly, but whom he loved dearly. Sent to reform school for striking a teacher with a chair, Caesar admitted,

I used to cry every day; be a big sucker. I was thinking suicide. I missed my moms. I mean 'buela [Granma]—you've met her.

Plus I was a little kid back then—like about twelve or thirteen—and I'd get *beat* down by other kids and shit. I was getting my ass kicked. I used to get hurt.

It was a nasty reform school. I used to see the counselors holding down the kids naked outside in the snow.

Being smart and precocious, Caesar soon adapted to the institutionalized violence of his school and developed the skills that eventually allowed him to excel in the underground economy:

So then, I just learned. I used to fight so wild that they wouldn't bother me for awhile. I would go real crazy! Real crazy, every time I would fight. Like I would pick up a chair or a pencil or something and really mess them up. So they'd thought I was wild and real crazy.

I mean, I always got into fights. Even if I lost, I always started fights. That let me relax more, because after that nobody messed with me.

ANTHROPOLOGICAL APPROACHES TO POVERTY
AND THE INNER CITY

Caesar and his immediate supervisor, Primo, were merely two members out of a network of some twenty-five Puerto Rican retail crack sellers whom I befriended in the more than four years that I lived and worked in East Harlem at the height of what politicians and the media called "the crack epidemic," extending roughly from 1985 to 1991. As a cultural anthropologist engaged in the research methodology of "participant-observation fieldwork," or "ethnography," I can only collect "accurate data" by violating the canons of traditional, positivist research. We anthropologists have to become intimately involved with the people we study, striving to establish long-term, respectful, and usually mutually empathetic relationships. We attempt to suspend our value judgments in order to immerse ourselves in the common sense of the people we live with.

Researchers who are not cultural anthropologists have a hard time believing that useful, reliable data can be generated from the small samples of people that we study using participant-observation, qualitative methods. This is because quantitative-oriented researchers who collect data via surveys or by consulting published censuses do not understand the intensity of the relationship one must develop with each individual in one's sample in order to obtain information that addresses the cultural contexts and processual dynamics of social networks in holistic contexts. Anthropologists do not correlate discrete statistical variables; rather, they explain (or evoke) the reasons (or accidents) for why and how social relations unfold within their indigenous (and global) contexts. Ideally, anthropologists develop an organic relationship to a social setting where their presence only minimally distorts indigenous social interaction. We must seek out a legitimate social role within the social scene we are studying in order to develop friendships (and sometimes enmities) that allow us (with informed consent) to observe behavior directly in as unobtrusive a manner as possible. A major task of participant-observers is to put themselves "in the shoes" of the people they study in order to "see local realities" through "local eyes." Obviously, on an absolute level, such an achievement is impossible and possibly even dangerous, as it implies a power imbalance. Indeed, the premise that the "essence" of a group of people or a culture can be understood and described by an outsider and translated into academic analytic categories can lead to stereotyping. Postmodernists have criticized ethnography as being predicated on a totalizing modernist fantasy that is ultimately oppressive. Anthropologists risk imposing ethnocentric, power-laden, analytic categories and exotifying images onto the unsuspecting people they study in the name of an arrogantly assumed ethnographic academic authority. To avoid imposing in the name of science images that "other" the people they study, ethnographers need to be self-reflexively critical and to recognize that no single, simple reality or essence of a culture necessarily exists. Cultures and social processes are inevitably both more—but also less—than what can be captured in one outsider's attempt to reduce them into a coherent ethnographic monograph or article. Nevertheless, for the sake of defining participant-observation in a meaningful way, suffice it to say that cultural anthropologists, for all the problems that cross-cultural reportage implies, try to get as close as possible to local, everyday worlds without disrupting and judging them. The overall goal is to obtain a holistic perspective on the internal logics of and external constraints on the way processes unfold while at the same time recognizing humbly that cultures and social meanings are fragmented and multiplicitous.

In the case of my work with crack dealers in East Harlem, before even being able to initiate my research formally, I had to confront the overwhelming reality of racial- and class-based segregation in urban America. Initially, it felt as if my white skin signaled the terminal stage of a contagious disease sowing havoc in its path. Busy street corners emptied amidst a hail of whistles whenever I walked by as nervous drug dealers scattered in front of me, certain that I was an undercover narcotics agent. Conversely, the police made it clear to me that I was violating unconscious apartheid laws by throwing me spread-eagled against building walls to search me for weapons and drugs when they encountered me on their patrols. From their perspective, the only reason for a "white boy" to be in the neighborhood after dark is to buy drugs. As a matter of fact, the first time the police stopped me, I naively tried to explain to them in a polite voice that I was an anthropologist studying social marginalization. Convinced I was making fun of them, they showered me with a litany of curses and threats. They then escorted me to the nearest bus stop and ordered me to leave East Harlem, "and go buy your drugs in a white neighborhood ya' dirty mother . . ."

It was only through my long-term physical presence, residing in the neighborhood, and my polite perseverance on the street that I was able to overcome these racial and class boundaries and eventually earn the respect and full cooperation of the dealers operating on my block. It helped when they saw me getting married and having a baby. By the time my son was old enough to be baptized in the local church, I was close enough to several of the dealers to invite them to the party at my mother's apartment downtown.

In contrast, I was never able to communicate effectively with the police. I learned, however, always to carry a "picture I.D." showing my correct local ad-

dress, and I always forced myself to stare at the ground politely and mumble effu-
sive "yes sirs" in a white, working-class, New York accent whenever they stopped
me. Unlike most of the crack dealers I spent time with, I was never beaten or arrested—only occasionally threatened and sometimes politely queried and advised
to "find a cheap apartment in Queens instead."

I am convinced that it is only by painstakingly violating urban apartheid that I
was able to collect meaningful data on inner-city poverty. Methodologically, it is
only by establishing lasting relationships based on mutual respect that one can begin to ask provocative personal questions and expect to engage in substantive con-
versations about the complex experience of extreme social marginalization in the
United States. Perhaps, this is why the experience of poverty and social marginalization is so poorly understood. The traditional, quantitative-oriented survey
methodologies of upper-middle-class sociologists or criminologists tend to collect
fabrications. Few people on the margins of society trust outsiders when they ask
invasive personal questions, especially concerning money, drugs, and alcohol. In
fact, nobody—whether rich or poor—likes to answer such indiscrete, incriminat-
ing queries.

Historically, inner-city poverty research has been more successful at reflecting
the biases of an investigator's society than at analyzing the experience of poverty or
documenting race and class apartheid. The state of poverty and social marginalization research in any given country emerges almost as a litmus for gauging contemporary social attitudes towards inequality and social welfare. This is particularly true in the United States, where discussions of poverty almost immediately
become polarized around moralistic value judgments about individual self-worth,
and frequently degenerate into stereotyped conceptions of race. In the final analysis, most people in the United States—rich and poor alike—believe in the Hora-
tio Alger myth of going from rags to riches. They are also intensely moralistic
about issues of wealth; perhaps this stems from their Puritanical/Calvinist heritage. Even progressive leftist academics in the United States secretly worry that
the poor may actually deserve their fate. As a result they often feel compelled to
portray the inner city in an artificially positive manner that is not only unrealistic
but is also theoretically and analytically flawed.

This ideological context for inner-city poverty research in the United States is
probably best epitomized by the best-selling books of the anthropologist Oscar
Lewis in the 1960s. He collected thousands of pages of life-history interviews with
an extended family of Puerto Ricans who migrated to East Harlem and the South
Bronx in search of employment. Some thirty years later, his culture of poverty theory remains at the center of contemporary polemics around the inner city in the
United States. Despite his being a social democrat in favor of expanding govern-

ment poverty programs, his theoretical analysis offers a psychological reduction-ist—almost blame-the-victim—explanation for the transgenerational persistence of poverty. On some level it sounded the death knell for the Great Society dreams of the Johnson administration and helped disabuse the dream of the early 1960s that poverty in America could be eradicated. If anything, thirty years later, his theory resonated more than ever with the campaigns for individual responsibility and family values that were so celebrated by politicians in U.S. national elections during the 1990s. In a 1966 *Scientific American* article, Lewis wrote,

By the time slum children are six or seven, they have usually absorbed the basic attitudes and values of their subculture. Thereafter they are psychologically unready to take full advantage of changing conditions or improving opportunities that may develop in their lifetime. . . .
   It is much more difficult to undo the culture of poverty than to cure poverty itself.

In their anger and frustration over the way Lewis's family-based and Freudian-influenced focus on impoverished Puerto Rican immigrants confirms conservative American biases, liberal social scientists have often fallen into the trap of glorify-ing the poor and denying any empirical evidence of personal self-destruction. When I moved into the same inner-city neighborhood where the Puerto Rican families that Lewis studied had lived more than thirty years ago, I was determined to avoid his failure to examine structural inequality, while at the same time documenting the way oppression is painfully internalized in the day-to-day life of the persistently poor. Striving to develop a political economy perspective that takes culture and gender seriously, and which also recognizes the link between individual actions and social/structural determination, I focused on how an oppositional street culture of resistance to exploitation and social marginalization is contradictorily self-destructive to its participants. In fact, street dealers, addicts, and criminals become the local agents administering the destruction of their surrounding community.

THE DOLLARS AND SENSE OF DRUGS

Given the extraordinary economic importance of illicit drugs and the destructive impact they have on people's lives, inner-city researchers have to address the issue of substance abuse and the role of drugs in the underground economy. The easiest dimension of drug dealing for outsiders to understand is its economic logic. On a worldwide scale, illegal drugs have become an immense, multibillion-dollar business. Tragically, in the United States during the 1980s and through the 1990s, the crack/cocaine and heroin industries have been the only dynamically growing, equal-opportunity employers for inner-city men. For example, the street in front of my tenement was not atypical and within a two-block radius I could obtain heroin, crack, powder cocaine, hypodermic needles, methadone, valium, angel dust (an animal tranquilizer), marijuana, mescaline, bootleg alcohol, and tobacco. Within one hundred yards of my stoop there were three competing crackhouses selling vials at two, three, and five dollars. Two additional retail outfits sold powder cocaine in ten- and twenty-dollar plastic-sealed packages, patented with a neatly carved, rubber stamp logo. Immediately above the particular crackhouse camouflaged as a video arcade where I spent most of my time, two legally registered doctors administered a "pill mill," writing several dozen prescriptions for opiates, stimulants, and sedatives every day. This added up to several millions of dollars worth of drugs per year. In the projects opposite my tenement, the New York City Housing Authority Police arrested a fifty-five-year-old mother and her twenty-two-year-old daughter while they were "bagging" twenty-one pounds of cocaine into ten-dollar, quarter-gram "jumbo" vials of adulterated product worth approximately one million dollars on the street. The police found twenty-five thousand dollars in small-denomination bills in this same apartment.

In other words, many millions of dollars worth of business takes place within a stone's throw of the youths growing up in East Harlem tenements and housing projects. Drug dealing in the underground economy offers youths—primarily males—a career with real possibilities of upward mobility. Like most other people in the United States, drug dealers are merely scrambling to obtain their "piece of the pie" as fast as possible. In fact, in their pursuit of success they are following the minute details of the classical Yankee model for upward mobility: up-by-the-bootstraps via private entrepreneurship. Perversely, they are the ultimate rugged individualists braving an unpredictable frontier where fortune, fame, and destruction are all just around the corner—and where competitors are ruthlessly hunted down and shot.

Despite the obvious economic incentives, most of East Harlem's residents shun drugs and work nine-to-five plus overtime at legal jobs. The problem, however, is that this law-abiding majority has lost control of public space. They have been pushed onto the defensive, living in fear, or even in contempt, of their neighborhood. Worried mothers and fathers are forced to maintain children double-locked behind apartment doors in determined attempts to keep street culture out. Their primary goal is to save up enough money to move to a safe, working-class neighborhood.

The drug dealers in this book, consequently, represent only a small minority of East Harlem's population, but they have managed to set the tone for public life. They force local residents, especially women and the elderly, to live in fear of being assaulted or mugged. Most important, on a daily basis, the street-level drug

FIGURE 2 Vacant lot next to the tenement where the author lived. (Photo by author)

dealers offer a persuasive, even if violent and self-destructive, alternative lifestyle—what I call street culture—to the youths growing up around them. The drug economy is the material base for street culture, and its expansion during the 1980s and 1990s unconsciously rendered street culture even more appealing and fashionable.

On a subtler level, street culture is more than economic desperation or greediness; it is also a search for dignity and a refusal to accept the marginalization that mainstream society imposes on children who grow up in the inner city. As noted earlier, it can be understood as a culture of resistance—or at least of opposition—to economic exploitation and cultural denigration. Concretely, this takes the form of refusing low wages and poor working conditions, and of celebrating marginalization as a badge of pride—even if it is ultimately self-destructive.

Once again, an argument with Caesar clearly illustrates this dynamic. In this particular confrontation, Caesar was responding to the chiding of a legally employed, undocumented, new-immigrant Mexican who was sitting on a stoop near the crackhouse accusing Puerto Ricans of being lazy. Caesar replied,

That's right my man! We is real vermin lunatics that sell drugs. We don't wanna be a part of society. What do we wanna be working for? Puerto Ricans don't like to work. Okay, maybe not all of us, 'cause there's still a lot of strict folks from the old school that still be working. But the new generation, no way!

FIGURE 3 Abandoned tenement repopulated by its former superintendent with stuffed animals. (Photo by author)

We have no regard for nothing. The new generation has no regard for the public. We wanna make easy money, and that's it. *Easy* now mind you. We don't wanna work hard. That's the new generation for you.

Now the old school was for when we was younger, and we used to break our asses. I had all kinds of stupid jobs . . . scrap metal sorting, dry cleaning, advertising agencies.

But not no more [putting his arm around Primo]. Now we're in a rebellious stage. We rather evade taxes; make quick money; and just survive. But we're not satisfied with that either, ha!

HISTORY AND POLITICAL ECONOMY

Caesar's words need to be placed in their historical and structural context lest they serve to confirm racist stereotypes and psychological-reductionist explanations for violence, substance abuse, and ultimately for poverty itself. Indeed, that is one of the weaknesses of ethnographic accounts; they risk becoming voyeuristic constructions of a dehumanized, sensationalized "exotic" other in a political and economic vacuum. Upon closer examination, one can discern that Caesar's celebration of unemployment, crime, and substance abuse is integrally related to labor market forces, historical developments, and even international political confrontations that are well beyond his control.

Most fundamentally, the unfortunate strategic geopolitical location of the island of Puerto Rico in the Caribbean has always made it a military prize for world superpowers, resulting in a particularly distorted legacy of economic and political development. This was as true under Spanish colonialism as it is under the contemporary United States-sponsored political control of the territory. An artifice of the Cold War to check the influence of neighboring Cuba, Puerto Rico continues to bear the ambiguous status of "Free Associated Commonwealth." Puerto Ricans who remain on their native island are forbidden from voting in Federal elections, despite being subject to U.S. military selective service. Soon after the U.S. marines invaded the island in 1898, the economy was taken over by U.S. agro-export corporations and Puerto Rico was subjected to one of the most rapid and dislocating economic transformations that any Third World nation has ever undergone in modern history. To add insult to injury in the post–World War II decades, in an attempt to upstage the Cuban state-run socialist experiment, the United States dubbed Puerto Rico's development strategy "Operation Bootstrap" and declared it to be a magnificent success of free market investment incentives. Perhaps the best index of the human failure of Puerto Rico's economic model, however, is provided by the fact that between a third and half of the island's population have been forced to leave their native island to seek work and sustenance abroad since the late 1940s. More Puerto Ricans live outside Puerto Rico today than inside. Like all new immigrants arriving in the United States throughout history, Puerto Ricans have been confronted by racism and cultural humiliation. This is exacerbated by the phenotypical fact that, unlike the Irish, the Jews, and the Italians who arrived in New York City before them, most Puerto Ricans do not have white skin.

In other words, New York–born Puerto Ricans are the descendants of an uprooted people in the midst of a marathon sprint through economic history propelled by realpolitik forces rather than by humanitarian or even by any straightforward economic logic. In diverse permutations, over the past two or three generations their parents and grandparents went (1) from semisubsistence peasants on private hillside plots or local haciendas (2) to agricultural laborers on foreign-owned, capital-intensive agro-export tropical plantations, (3) to factory workers in export-platform shanty towns, (4) to sweatshop workers in New York City ghetto tenements, (5) to service-sector employees in high-rise, inner-city housing projects. Over half of those who remained on the island are so impoverished today that they qualify for food stamps. Those who made it to New York City endure the highest family poverty rates of all ethnic groups in the nation, except for Native Americans.

FROM MANUFACTURING TO SERVICE
AND THE CRACK ALTERNATIVE

The Puerto Rican experience in New York City has been further exacerbated by the fact that most Puerto Ricans arrived on the U.S. mainland in the post–World War II period in search of factory work precisely at the historical moment when those kinds of jobs were leaving U.S. metropolitan areas. Over the past three decades, multinational corporations have restructured the global economy by moving their factory production facilities overseas to countries with lower labor costs. The personal disruption of living through the structural transformation of New York's economy as an entry-level laborer was clearly articulated by the crack dealers in their life-history tape recordings. Almost all the crack dealers and addicts whom I interviewed over the years—especially the older ones—worked at one or more legal jobs in their early youth. In fact, most entered the labor market at a younger age than the typical middle-class American. This was the case for Primo, the manager of the video arcade crackhouse.

I was like fourteen or fifteen playing hooky and pressing dresses and whatever they were making on the steamer. They was cheap, cheap clothes.

My mother's sister was working there first, and then her son, my cousin Hector—the one who's in jail now—was the one they hired first, because his mother agreed: "If you don't want to go school, you gotta work."

So I started hanging out with him. I wasn't planning on working in the factory. I was supposed to be in school; but it just sort of happened.

Teenage Primo's marginal factory moved out of East Harlem within a year of his employment there. He became merely one more of the half-million manufacturing workers in New York City to lose their livelihood almost overnight as factory employment dropped 50 percent from 1963 to 1983. Of course, instead of understanding himself as the victim of a structural transformation, Primo remembers with pleasure and even pride the extra income he earned for clearing the machines out of the factory space: "Them people had money, man. Because we helped them move out of the neighborhood. It took us two days—only me and my cousin, Hector. Wow! It was work. They gave us seventy bucks each."

Caesar, the crackhouse lookout, had a similar experience working as a high school dropout in a metal-plating, costume jewelry factory. At this stage in their lives, had Caesar and Primo not been confined to the weakest sector of manufacturing in a period of rapid job loss, their teenage working-class dream might have stabilized. Formerly, when most entry-level jobs were found in factories, the contradiction between an oppositional street culture and traditional, working-class, shop-floor culture—especially when it was protected by a union—was less pronounced. In the factory, being tough and violently macho is accepted behavior; a certain degree of opposition to management is expected and is considered masculine.

DISRESPECT AT WORK

Manufacturing jobs have been largely replaced by service-sector employment in New York's expanded, finance-driven economy. At the entry-level, the fastest growing niche for high school dropouts, or even college graduates, is office support work in the administrative headquarters of the multinational corporations that have moved their production plants overseas. The problem, of course, is that the oppositional street identity that is so effective and appealing in the burgeoning underground economy does not allow for the humble, obedient social interaction that professional office workers demand from their subordinates. A qualitative change has occurred in the tenor of social interaction in service-sector employment. Workers in a mail room or behind a photocopy machine cannot publicly maintain their cultural autonomy. Most concretely, they have no union; more subtly, there are few fellow workers surrounding them to insulate them and to provide them with a culturally based sense of class solidarity. Instead they are besieged by supervisors and bosses from an alien, hostile, and obviously dominant culture. When these office managers are not intimidated by street culture, they ridicule it.

Obedience to the norms of high-rise, office-corridor culture is interpreted as overwhelmingly humiliating by street culture standards—especially for males. On the street, the trauma of experiencing a threat to one's personal dignity has been frozen linguistically in the commonly used phrase "to diss," which is short for, "to disrespect." One does not have to dig deeply to obtain stories of deep humiliation due to the loss of personal and cultural autonomy experienced by the dealers in their previous bouts of service-sector employment. This was the case for Primo when he worked as a messenger for a trade publication magazine.

When my boss be talking to people in the office, she would say, "He's illiterate," as if I was really that stupid that I couldn't understand what she was talking about, 'cause I'd be standing right there.

So what I did one day was, I just looked up the word, "illiterate" in the dictionary, and I saw that she's saying to her associates that I'm stupid or something.

I'm stupid! You know like [pointing to himself], "He doesn't know nothin.'"

Well, I am illiterate anyway.

Although Primo resented being called illiterate, the most profound dimension of his humiliation was being obliged to look up in the dictionary the word used to insult him. In contrast, in the underground economy, he does not have to risk this kind of threat to his self-worth: "My boss, Papo [the crackhouse owner], he would never disrespect me that way. He wouldn't tell me that, because he's illiterate too."

When Primo attempted to show initiative and answer the telephone when his supervisors were busy, he was rebuked for scaring away customers with his Puerto Rican accent. Another crack dealer, Leroy, who operated his own independent sales point on a neighboring block (plate 2), had also been profoundly humiliated when he worked as a messenger because a white woman fled from him shrieking down the hallway of a high-rise office building. He had ridden in the elevator with the terrified woman and, coincidentally, had stepped off on the same floor with her to make a delivery. Worse yet, he had been trying to act as a debonair man at the time, allowing her to step off the elevator first.

She went in the elevator first, but then she just waits there to see what floor I press.

She's playing like she don't know what floor she wants to go to, because she wants to wait for me to press my floor. And I'm standing there and I forgot to press the button.

I'm thinking about something else—don't know what was the matter with me. And she's thinking like, "He's not pressing the button; I guess he's following me!"

Leroy struggles to understand the terror that his dark skin inspires in white office workers. He confided this to me early in our relationship, and I noticed that, like most Americans, he becomes uncomfortable when talking across class and ethnic boundaries about race relations:

It's happened before. I mean after awhile you become immune to it. Well, when it first happens, it like bugs you, "That's messed up; how they just judge you."

But I understand a lot of them. How should I say it? A lot of white people . . . [looking nervously at me] I mean Caucasian people [flustered, putting his hand gently on my shoulder]. If I say white, don't get offended, Felipe.

But those other white people, they never even experienced Puerto Rican or black people. So automatically they think something wrong with you. Or you know, they think you out to rob them or something.

It irks me; like, you know, it clicks my mind; makes me want to write a [rap] rhyme. I always write it down.

Of course, as a crack dealer, Leroy no longer has to confront these dimensions of class and racial humiliation.

POLARIZATION AROUND GENDER

In addition to their obvious racial conflict, service-sector confrontations also include a tense gender dynamic. Most of the supervisors at the lowest levels of the service sector are women, and street culture forbids males from accepting public subordination across gender lines. Typically, in their angrier memories of disrespect at work, many of the male crack dealers would refer to their female bosses in explicitly sexist language, often insulting their body parts, and dismissing them with street-slang, sexualized curses. They also specifically describe themselves and the other males around them at work as effeminate. Caesar was particularly incensed:

I lasted in the mail room for like eight months at this advertising agency that works with pharmaceutical stuff. They used to trust me.

But I had a prejudiced boss. She was a ho' [prostitute]. She was white. I had to take a lot of crap from that fat, ugly ho', and be a wimp.

I didn't like it, but I kept on working, because . . . [shrugging] you don't want to mess up the relationship. So you just be a punk.

Oh my God! I hated that head supervisor. That ho' was *really* nasty. She got her rocks off on firing people, man. You can see that on her face, boy. She made this one guy that worked with me cry—and beg for his job back.

This structural workplace confrontation that polarizes relations between young, inner-city men and white-collar, upwardly mobile women parallels another profound transformation in traditional gender power relations occurring within working-poor immigrant families. The loss of decently paid factory jobs that provide union family benefits for health and retirement makes it increasingly impossible for men to fulfill old-fashioned patriarchal dreams of being an omnipotent provider for a wife and several children. At the same time, dramatic increases in labor force participation among Puerto Rican women, as well as the broader cultural redefinitions of increased individual rights and autonomy for women occurring throughout all levels of U.S. society since the late 1960s, have thrown into crisis the traditional family model of the conjugal household dominated by an authoritarian man.

Males, however, are not accepting the new rights and roles that women have been earning over the past few decades; instead, they attempt to reassert violently their grandfather's lost autocratic control over their households and over public space. This is exacerbated in the inner-city Puerto Rican case by the persistence of a rural-based memory of large, male-dominated, farming households "blessed" with numerous children. Males who are no longer effective heads of households often experience the rapid structural transformations of their generation as a dramatic assault on their sense of masculine dignity. In the worst-case scenario, as males become impotent economic failures in the service economy, they lash out against the women and children they can no longer support economically or control ideologically. Concretely, this takes the form of fists in the face at home and gang rape in the crackhouse.

IN SEARCH OF SOLUTIONS

The crisis that has accompanied the complicated historical rearrangement of gender-power relations over the past few decades is glossed by political leaders into superficial slogans such as "the crisis in family values" or "Just say no to drugs." This kind of psychological-reductionist and blame-the-victim moralism obfuscates the structural inequalities around race, class, and gender that must be addressed if real improvements in the lives of the poor are to occur. Politicians and the media expect to find simple, quick-fix solutions to the persistent poverty that is increasingly concentrated in urban cores—whether it be in the teeming shantytowns of nonindustrial nations, the working-class public housing suburbs of European cities, or the postindustrial wastelands of U.S. inner-city neighborhoods.

Of all the industrialized nations, the United States is the most extreme with respect to income inequality and ethnic segregation. By the end of the twentieth century, only Russia and Rwanda imprisoned larger proportions of their populations than the United States. No other wealthy, industrialized country came close to having such a large proportion of its citizens living below the poverty line.

The inner city represents the United States' greatest domestic failing, hanging like a sword of Damocles over the larger society. The only force sustaining this precariously suspended sword is the fact that drug dealers, addicts, and street criminals internalize their rage and desperation. They direct their brutality against themselves and their immediate community rather than against their structural oppression.

If the United States were to serve as an international model for political and economic development at the dawn of the twentieth century it should be as a model for what not to imitate. The balance of structural economic power that penalizes and humiliates the working poor and pushes them into the underground economy serves few people's interests. The public policy response of building bigger and more expensive prisons is irrational from both an economic cost/benefit analysis and also a humanitarian perspective. Finally, the painful and prolonged self-destruction of people like Primo and Caesar and their families and loved ones is cruel and unnecessary.

There are no simple, technocratic formulas for implementing the public policies that might provide equitable access to shelter, employment, sustenance, and health. The first step out of the impasse requires a fundamental ethical and political reevaluation of basic socioeconomic models. Anthropologists, because of their participant-observation methods and their culturally relative sensibilities can play an important role in fostering a public debate over the human cost of poverty. The challenge is clearly in front of us. Do we have the intellectual and political energy to confront it both at home and abroad?

ACKNOWLEDGMENTS

I thank my neighbors, the crack dealers, and their families who invited me into their homes and lives in East Harlem. I changed everyone's name and camouflaged the street addresses to protect individual privacy. The article was written with support from the National Institute on Drug Abuse (grant R01-DA10164). I also want to thank the following institutions for their generous financial support while I conducted fieldwork in East Harlem: the Harry Frank Guggenheim Foundation, the Russell Sage Foundation, the Social Science Research Council, the Ford Foundation, the Wenner-Gren Foundation for Anthropological Research, the United States Bureau of the Census, and the National Institute on Drug Abuse (grant R03 DA06413-01). I thank Harold Otto for transcribing the tape recordings, Joelle Morrow for typing the article with me, and Ann Magruder for inputting the final edits. A preliminary version appeared in French in *Actes de la recherche en sciences sociales* 94 (1992): 59–78.

SUGGESTIONS FOR FURTHER READING

Anderson, Elijah. 1978. *Place on the Corner.* Chicago: University of Chicago Press.

Bourgois, Philippe. 1998. "The Moral Economies of Homeless Heroin Addicts: Confronting Ethnography, HIV Risk, and Everyday Violence in San Francisco Shooting Encampments." *Substance Use and Misuse* 33, no. 11: 2323–51.

———. 1995. *In Search of Respect: Selling Crack in El Barrio.* New York: Cambridge University Press.

Connolly, Deborah. 2000. *Homeless Mothers: Face to Face with Women and Poverty.* Minneapolis: University of Minnesota Press.

Davis, Mike. 1990. *City of Quartz: Excavating the Future in Los Angeles.* London, New York: Verso.

Dehavenon, Anna Lou. 1994. "Monitoring Emergency Shelter for Homeless Families in New York City." *Practicing Anthropology.* 16, no. 4: 12–16.

Devine, John. 1996. *Maximum Security: The Culture of Violence in Inner-City Schools.* Chicago: University of Chicago Press.

Hamid, Ansley. 1990. "The Political Economy of Crack-Related Violence." *Contemporary Drug Problems* 17, no. 1: 31–79.

Katz, Michael. 1995. *Improving Poor People: The Welfare State, the "Underclass," and Urban Schools as History*. Princeton, NJ: Princeton University Press.

Leacock, Eleanor Burke, ed. 1971. *The Culture of Poverty: A Critique*. New York: Simon and Schuster.

Lewis, Oscar. 1966. *La Vida: A Puerto Rican Family in the Culture of Poverty—San Juan and New York*. New York: Random House.

Liebow, Elliot. 1993. *Tell Them Who I Am: The Lives of Homeless Women*. New York: Penguin Books.

Macleod, Jay. 1995 [1987]. *Ain't No Makin' It: Aspirations and Attainment in a Low-Income Neighborhood*. Boulder, CO: Westview Press.

Rigdon, Susan M. 1988. *The Culture Facade: Art, Science, and Politics in the Work of Oscar Lewis*. Urbana: University of Illinois Press.

Rodriguez, Clara. 1989. *Puerto Ricans: Born in the USA*. Boston: Unwin Hyman.

Sassen, Saskia. 1991. *The Global City: New York, London, Tokyo*. Princeton, NJ: Princeton University Press.

Scheper-Hughes, Nancy. 1992. *Death without Weeping: the Violence of Everyday Life in Brazil*. Berkeley: University of California Press.

Steinberg, Stephen. 1981. "The Culture of Poverty Reconsidered." In *The Ethnic Myth: Race, Ethnicity, and Class in America*, 106–28. New York: Atheneum.

Tonry, Michael. 1995. *Malign Neglect: Race, Crime, and Punishment in America*. New York: Oxford University Press.

Wacquant, Loïc. 1997. "Three Pernicious Premises in the Study of the American Ghetto." *International Journal of Urban and Regional Research*. 21, no. 2: 341.

Waterston, Alisse. 1993. *Street Addicts in the Political Economy*. Philadelphia: Temple University Press.

Williams, Terry. 1992. *The Crackhouse: Notes from the End of the Line*. Reading, MA: Addison-Wesley.

Willis, Paul. 1981. *Learning to Labor: How Working Class Kids Get Working Class Jobs*. New York: Columbia University Press.

Wilson, William Julius. 1996. *When the Work Disappears: the World of the New Urban Poor*. New York: Knopf.

Wojcicka Scharff, Jagna. 1998. *King Kong on Fourth Street: Families and the Violence of Poverty on the Lower East Side*. Boulder, CO: Westview Press.

2.

Min(d)ing the Body: On the Trail of Organ-Stealing Rumors

NANCY SCHEPER-HUGHES

For many years I have been documenting the violence of everyday life—the many small wars and invisible genocides—resulting from the structural violence of poverty and the increasing public hostility to the bodies, minds, children, and reproductive capacities of the urban poor. Here I will be addressing an uncanny dimension of the usual story of race and class hatred to which we have become so accustomed. This is the covert violence occurring in the context of a new and thriving global trade in human organs and other body parts for transplant surgery. It is a business that is justified by many—including doctors and bio-ethicists—as serving "altruistic" ends. But for the poorest and most marginalized populations living on the fringes of the new global dis-order, the scramble for fresh organs for transplant surgery increases the already profound sense of ontological insecurity in a world that values their bodies more dead—as a reservoir of spare parts—than alive.

Descend with me for a few moments into that murky realm of the surreal and the magical, into the maelstrom of bizarre stories, fantastic allegations, and a hideous class of rumors that circulate in the world's shantytowns and squatter camps, where this collaborative research project had its origins. The rumors were of kidnapping, mutilation, and dismemberment—the removal of blood and organs—for commercial sale. I want to convey to you the terror and panic that these rumors induce in the nervous and hungry residents of urban shantytowns, tent cities, squatter camps, and other "informal settlements" in the Third World.

I first heard the rumor in the shantytowns of Northeast Brazil in the mid-1980s, when I was completing research for my book, *Death without Weeping*, on maternal thinking and practice in the context of extremely high infant and child mortality. The rumors told of the abduction and mutilation of poor children who were eyed greedily as fodder for an international traffic in organs for wealthy transplant patients in the first world. Residents of the ramshackle hillside *favela* of Alto do Cruzeiro, the primary site of my research, reported multiple sightings of large blue and yellow combi-vans [the so-called "gypsy taxis" used by the poor the world over] driven by Americans or Japanese "agents" said to be scouring poor neighborhoods in search of stray youngsters, loose kids and street children, kids that presumably no one would miss. The children would be grabbed and shoved into the van. Later their discarded and eviscerated bodies—minus certain organs— heart, lungs, liver, kidneys, and eyes—would turn up on roadsides, between rows of sugarcane, or in hospital dumpsters. "They are looking for donor organs. You may think this is just nonsense," said my friend and research assistant, "Little Irene" in 1987. "*But we have seen things with our own eyes in the hospitals and the morgues, and we know better.*"

"Nonsense! These are stories of the poor and illiterate," countered another of my friends, Casorte, the skeptical manager of the municipal cemetery of Bom Jesus da Mata. "I have been working here for over a year and never have I seen any-thing. Where are these bodies?" Yet even as we spoke on the following day, a mu-nicipal truck arrived at the gates of the cemetery with the body of a "desconicido," the remains of an unknown, unclaimed man found murdered in an abandoned field not far from town. The eyes and genitals had been removed. "Death squads," whispered Casorte, by way of explanation, and he made the gesture of a throat be-ing slit.

The body-snatching rumors were picked up by newspapers in Recife and reported on the radio. Most news reports mocked the credulity of illiterate people. But the media coverage, meant to dispel the rumors, actually exacerbated them. "Yes, it is true," wept Dona Aparecida, wringing her hands on the doorstep of her shack on the garbage strewn street called the Vultures' Path. "I even heard them talk about it on the radio." Consequently, a great many toddlers and small children were kept securely locked in at home while their parents were out work-ing. I found one terrified little girl tethered like a goat to a wobbly table leg. Street children believed themselves to be at particular risk of kidnapping for their organs (see figure 1).

Soon after I began writing articles that interpreted the Brazilian organ-stealing rumors in terms of the normal, accepted, everyday violence practiced against the bodies of the poor and the marginal in public medical clinics, in hospitals, and in police mortuaries, where their ills and afflictions were often treated with scorn, neglect, and general disrespect, I began to hear other variants of the organ-theft stories from anthropologists working in Argentina, Colombia, Peru, Guatemala,

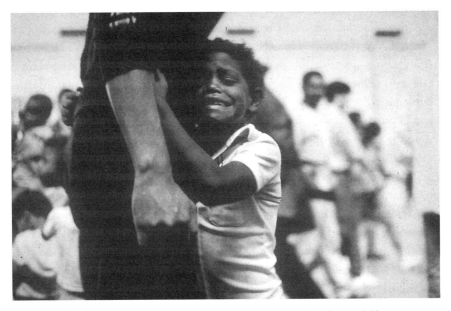

FIGURE I The Real Central Station, Rio de Janeiro, Brazil. In the wake of street child executions, a terrified street child grabs at passers-by for support. (Photo by Viviane Moos)

Honduras, Mexico, India, and Korea. Though most of the stories came from Central and South America, organ-theft rumors were also surfacing in Poland and Russia, where it was reported that poor children's organs were being sold to rich Arabs for transplant surgery. Luise White recorded blood-sucking/blood-stealing vampire stories from East and Central Africa, and South African anthropologist Isak Niehaus recorded blood- and organ-stealing rumors in the Transvaal collected during fieldwork in 1990–1993. The African variants told of "firemen" or paramedics driving *red* combi-vans looking to capture unsuspecting people to drug and to kill in order to drain their blood or remove their organs and other body parts—genitals and eyes in particular—for magical medicine *(muti)* or for more traditional medical purposes. The Italian variants identified a *black* ambulance as the kidnap vehicle.

The rumors had powerful effects, resulting in a precipitous decline in voluntary organ donation in some countries, including Brazil and Argentina. What does it mean when a lot of people around the world begin to tell variants of the same bizarre and unlikely story? How does an anthropologist go about interpreting the uncanny and the social imaginary of poor, third-world peoples? To folklorists like Alan Dundes and Veronique Campion-Vincent, and to oral historians like Luise White, the rumors are seen as constituting a genre, an oral literary form, the "urban legend." The stories are circulated and repeated because they are "good to tell," they entertain by fright just like good old-fashioned ghost stories. The French folklorist Campion-Vincent interprets the organ-theft stories as the literary inventions of semiliterate people who lack the skills to sort out the credible and realistic from the incredible and the fantastic. To members of the global transplant community of surgeons and patient activists, the rumors are groundless, pernicious lies that need to be exposed, refuted, and killed.

To the anthropologist, however, working closely with the urban poor, the rumors spoke to the ontological insecurity of people "to whom almost anything could be done." They reflected everyday threats to bodily security, urban violence, police terror, social anarchy, theft, loss, and fragmentation. Many of the poor imagined, with some reason as it turns out, that autopsies were performed to harvest usable tissues and body parts from those whose bodies had reverted to the state: "Little people like ourselves are worth more dead than alive." At the very least the rumors were (like the scriptures) metaphorically true, operating by means of symbolic substitution. The rumors express the existential and ontological insecurities of poor people living on the margins of the postcolonial global economies where their labor, their bodies, and their reproductive capacities are treated as spare parts to be bought, bartered, or stolen. Underlying the rumors was a real concern with a growing commodification of the body and of body parts in these global economic exchanges.

The organ-stealing stories were told, remembered, and circulated because they were true at that indeterminate level between the real, the surreal and the uncanny. They expressed an intuitive sense that something was amiss, signaling the chronic "state of emergency" of the world's subcitizens living in a negative zone of existence where lives and bodies are experienced as a constant crisis of presence (hunger, sickness, injury) on the one hand, and as a crisis of absence and disappearance on the other.

If one paid attention to the timing and geopolitical distribution of the organ-stealing rumors, certain patterns began to emerge. While rumors of blood and body snatching appear and disappear periodically, the current spate of organ- and child-stealing rumors arose and spread in the late 1980s. In Brazil, Argentina, Guatemala, El Salvador, and South Africa the organ-stealing rumors arose within a specific political context, following a history of military regimes, police states, civil wars, and "dirty wars" in which abductions, "disappearances," mutilations, and deaths were commonplace. Mayan Indian villages in Guatemala sustained military attacks that were nothing less than genocidal over the past decade. The counterinsurgency war, which reached its height between 1978 and 1984, left more than one hundred thousand people dead, thousands mutilated, another one million internally displaced, and caused thousands to flee across the Mexican border. More than 440 rural Indian villages in the highlands were destroyed. Women were widowed, and children were displaced, lost, and orphaned by the tens of thousands. These displaced children became the focus of international adoption efforts, contributing to villagers' mounting sense of panic, terror, and disaster, which they expressed, in part, through child and organ-stealing rumors. The spate of physical attacks on American tourists—especially those seeking to adopt Indian babies—had to be understood in light of that terrifying recent history.

Similarly, in Northeast Brazil—where my research focused for many years on the causes of infant and childhood death, and, later, on the deaths and "disappearances" of older street children—the child- and organ-stealing rumors had to be understood within the context of a transitional postmilitary state in which privatized death squads had taken the place of the military police in launching attacks on "superfluous" and marginalized populations. According to a report issued by the Brazilian Federal Police, more than five thousand children and youths were murdered in Brazil between 1988 and 1990. Few of these deaths have ever been investigated, hardly surprising when off-duty police officers are often the prime suspects. Most of the victims were black males between the ages of fifteen and nineteen. The Medical-Legal Institute (the public morgue) in Recife, the capital of Pernambuco, received an average of fifteen bodies of unidentified children a month in the early 1990s. Eighty percent of the bodies arrived at the morgue already damaged or mutilated. These acts of brutality against the bodies of the poor and socially abandoned provided the missing social and political context within which strange events occurred and even stranger rumors circulated to account for them.

During the Argentine "Dirty War" (1976–1982), university students, journalists, and other suspected subversives were captured, interrogated, tortured, and killed. The babies of imprisoned dissidents were kidnapped and given to reward loyal, childless military families. This reproductive theft was justified in terms of "saving" Argentina's innocent children from the "germ" of Communism. Older children were abducted by security officers, brutalized in detention, and then returned, "transformed," to relatives. Others were tortured in the presence of their captive parents. Much later scientific reports appeared in the *British Medical Journal* of blood, corneas, and organs taken from "executed" political prisoners and from abandoned mental patients during the late military and postmilitary periods (Chaudhary 1994).

Despite the work of official truth commissions, established in the mid-1980s, in documenting the atrocities that had terrorized large segments of the Argentine population, Dr. Felix Cantarovitch, representing the Ministry of Health in

Buenos Aires in 1990, felt compelled to deny any truth behind the "child kidnapping" rumors. In an article published in the international medical journal *Transplantation Proceedings* (1990), Dr. Cantarovitch wrote: "In Argentina between 1984 and 1987 a persistent rumor circulated about child kidnapping. The rumor was extremely troublesome because of its persistence sustained by the exaggerated press that has always been a powerful tool to attract attention of people about the matter. In November 1987 the Secretary of Health gathered the most important authorities of justice, police, medical associations, and also members of Parliament with the purpose of determining the truth. As a result it was stated that all the rumors and comments made by the press were totally spurious." But here we have the fox reporting on the safety of the hen house. In fact, children *were* kidnapped, and my research in 2000 documented that blood and organs were taken from mental patients in public asylums without consent.

Similar allegations of body- and organ-stealing by doctors working in hospitals and in police mortuaries in South Africa began to circulate during the late apartheid years when the country was plunged into a civil war and apartheid's medical bureaucrats sometimes were complicit in the physical and medical abuse of suspected political "terrorists." In each context the body- and organ-stealing rumors arose at a time when members of the military believed that they could do as they pleased to the bodies of subcitizens, people perceived as social and political "waste."

In Latin America the organ-stealing rumors surfaced during or *soon after* the democratization process was initiated and in the wake of human rights reports such as *Nunca Mas* in Argentina and *Brazil Nunca Mas*. They appeared during a time when ordinary people became aware of the magnitude of the atrocities practiced by the state and its military and medical officials. Insofar as the poor of urban shantytowns are rarely called upon to speak before official truth commissions, the body-theft rumors could be seen as a surrogate form of political witnessing. The rumors participated in the spirit of human rights testifying to human suffering on the margins of "the official story." Still, in our "rational," secular world, rumors are one thing, while scientific reports in medical journals are quite another. But in the late 1980s the two distinct narratives began to converge as articles published in *The Lancet, Transplantation Proceedings*, and the *British Medical Journal* began to cite evidence of an illegal global commerce and black market in human organs and other body parts. Indeed, wild rumors, like metaphors, do sometimes harden into ethnographic "facts."

Recognizing the need to define new international standards for human transplant surgery, an international task force from ten countries, comprising fourteen transplant surgeons and transplant specialists, medical human rights professionals, and three social scientists was formed. The "Bellagio Task Force on Securing Bodily Integrity for the Socially Disadvantaged in Transplant Surgery" met in 1995 and 1996 at the Rockefeller Conference Center in Bellagio and several times in smaller groups at medical, public health, and bio-ethics meetings and conferences in Japan; Washington, DC; Berkeley, California; and New York City. We came together to share experiences and data, to discuss, analyze, and recommend new ways of dealing with the vulnerability of certain social groups—the urban poor, cultural minorities, refugees, prisoners, and women—called upon and coerced into serving as organ donors, living and dead. At the top of our agenda were allegations of the use of organs from executed prisoners in China for commercial sale in transplant surgery; the traffic in organs in India; and the truth, if any, behind the rumors and urban legends of body and organ theft and other gross violations in the procurement and distribution of organs.

Finally, in 1996, encouraged by my medical colleagues on the task force, I decided to track down independently the rumors to their most obvious, and yet least studied, source: the routine practices of organ procurement and distribution for transplant surgery. But as soon as I abandoned the more distanced and symbolic analyses of the organ-stealing rumors for anthropological "detective work" to determine whether or not a market in human organs actually existed, my research was both suspect and discredited. "Is this some kind of anthropological detective work?" one anthropological colleague asked. Others charged that I had fallen into the "assumptive world" of my uneducated and gullible informants. Indeed, a great deal is invested in maintaining a social and clinical reality which denies any factual basis for poor people's fears of medical technologies. The transplant community's insistence on the patent absurdity of the organ-stealing rumors offers a remarkably resilient defense and protection against having to respond seriously to allegations of medical abuses in organ procurement, harvesting, and distribution.

For example, a transplantation website *(TransWeb)* posts the "Top Ten Myths about Donation and Transplantation" next to authoritative refutations of each. The myth that "rich and famous people get moved to the top of the waiting list, while regular people have to wait a long time for a transplant" is simply denied: "The organ allocation system is blind to wealth or social status." But our exploratory research in several countries indicates that this and other transplant "myths" have some basis in contemporary transplant practices. And so for example, the director of his region's Transplant Central in São Paulo, Brazil, explained exactly how wealthy clients (especially foreigners) and those with political clout or other social connections managed to bypass established waiting lists, while patients without private insurance were often dropped, *without their knowledge*, from "active status" on the official waiting lists for organs. Even the most far-fetched of the organ rumors ("I heard about a guy who woke up the next morning in a bath-tub full of ice. His kidneys were stolen for sale on the black market"), which the *TransWeb* site states has never been documented anywhere, finds some basis in the uncanny stories told by some of our informants in India (Cohen 1999), South Africa, and Brazil, stories backed up by lawsuits and criminal investigations concerning organ theft at public hospitals. The following section introduces a few scenes from our ongoing and collaborative research.

STRANGER THAN FICTION

During the summer of 1998 I was sitting at a sidewalk cafe in downtown São Paulo with Laudiceia da Silva, an attractive, young mother and office receptionist who had agreed to share her bizarre medical story with me. She had just filed a legal complaint with the city government requesting an investigation of the large public hospital where in June 1997, during a routine operation to remove an ovarian cyst, she had "lost" a kidney. The missing kidney was discovered soon after the operation by the young woman's family doctor during a routine follow-up examination. When confronted with the information, the hospital representative told a highly improbable story: that Laudiceia's missing kidney was embedded in the large "mass" that had accumulated around her ovarian cyst. But the hospital refused to produce either their medical records or the evidence—the diseased ovary and the kidney had been "discarded," she was told. When I called on representatives of the São Paulo Medical Council, which investigates allegations of malpractice, they refused to grant an interview. A representative of the council said that there was no reason to distrust the hospital's version of the story, and they had no intention of launching an independent investigation. Laudiceia insists that she will pursue her case legally until the hospital is forced to account for just what happened, whether it was a gross medical error or a criminal case of kidney theft. To make matters worse, Laudiceia's brother had been killed in a random act of urban violence several weeks earlier and the family arrived at the hospital too late to stop organ retrieval based on Brazil's new "presumed consent" law. "Poor people like ourselves are losing our organs to the state, one by one," Laudiceia said angrily.

Across the globe at roughly the same time (summer 1998), Lawrence Cohen sat in a one-room flat in a municipal housing-project in a Chennai (Madras) slum in South India talking with five local women, each of whom had sold a kidney for 32,500 rupees (about 1,200 dollars at the time of the sale). Each had undergone their "operation" at the clinic of Dr. K. C. Reddy, India's most outspoken advocate of the individual "right to sell" a kidney. Unlike those who ran the more seedy "organs bazaars" that sprang up a decade ago in Bombay, Dr. Reddy prides himself on running an exemplary clinic: the kidney sellers are fully informed about the implications and potential dangers of the operation. They are carefully followed for two years after the organ removal and receive free health care at his clinic during that period, and he carefully avoids contact with intermediaries and organs brokers. The women Cohen interviewed were primarily low-paid domestic workers with husbands in trouble or in debt. Most said that the kidney sale was preceded by a financial crisis: the family had run out of credit and could not get by. Friends had passed on the word that there was quick money to be had through Dr. Reddy's clinic. Cohen asked if the sale had made a difference in their lives, and was told that it had, for a time, but the money was soon swallowed by the usurious interest charged by the local moneylenders, and the families were all in debt again. Would they do it again? Yes, the women answered; what other choice did they have, with the money gone and the new debts piling up? If only they had three kidneys, with two to spare, then things might be better.

Cohen, who has worked in rural towns in various regions of India over the past decade, reports that in a very brief period the idea of trading "a kidney for a dowry" has caught on and become one strategy for poor parents desperate to arrange a comfortable marriage for an "extra" daughter. In other words, a spare kidney for a spare daughter. A decade ago, when townspeople first heard through newspaper reports of kidney sales occurring in the cities of Bombay and Madras, they responded with predictable alarm. Today, Cohen says, some of these same people now speak matter of factly about when it might be necessary to sell a "spare" organ. Cohen argues that it is not that every townsperson actually knows someone who has been tempted to sell a vital part of the self, but that the idea of the "commodified" kidney has permeated the social imaginary. Today the kidney represents "everyman's" last economic resort; the kidney stands as the marker of one's ultimate collateral." Some parents say they can no longer complain about the fate of a dowryless daughter. "Haven't you got a spare kidney?" one or another neighbor is likely to respond. With the appearance of new sources of capital, the dowry system is expanding, along with kidney sales, into areas where it had not been a traditional practice.

Several months later, I sat next to Mrs. Rosemary Sitshetshe on a torn black plastic couch in her small but neat concrete slab house in Guguletu township outside Cape Town, South Africa. On her other side sat Rosemary's mother, a powerful woman, who sustained her daughter as she retold the painful story of how the body of her only son, seventeen-year-old Andrew, had been manhandled and mutilated at the police mortuary in Cape Town, his eyes and possibly other body parts removed without consent and given to doctors to transplant into other people's bodies.

Andrew was caught in the crossfire of township gang warfare during the dangerous period just before the end of apartheid. Badly wounded, he was taken to the local police station where Rosemary found him lying on the floor with a bleeding chest wound. By the time the ambulance attendants arrived, late as usual, Andrew was dead (or very nearly so) and the police advised Rosemary to go home until the morning when she could claim her son's body for burial. But the following morning, the officials at the police mortuary turned Rosemary away saying that the body was not yet ready for identification and viewing. Two days later, when the family was finally allowed to view Andrew's body they were shocked at what they saw (figure 2): the blanket covering the body was bloody and Andrew's head had two deep holes on either side of his forehead "so you could easily see the bone." His face was swollen and there seemed to something was wrong with his eyes. "So, I did the unthinkable, I lifted up his eyelids."

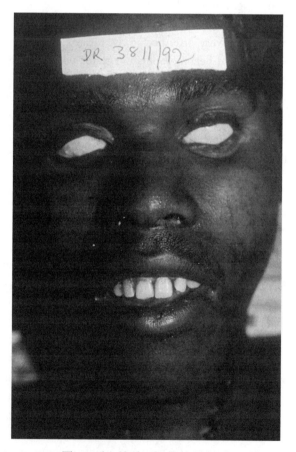

FIGURE 2 The mutilated body of Andrew Sitshetshe, as his mother found it at Salt River Mortuary in Cape Town, South Africa. (Courtesy of Mrs. Rosemary Sitshetshe)

But when Rosemary questioned the people in charge, they denied that anything was wrong and treated Rosemary and her estranged husband abusively. Later, accompanied by her own private pathologist paid for by the African National Congress, Mrs. Sitshetshe learned at the morgue that her son's eyes had been removed and that inside his abdominal cavity the organs found there had all been severed and carefully replaced for viewing. "But were those parts his own?" Mrs. Sitshetshe asked me. "I know my son's eyes by color but not his heart or kidneys."

At the local eye bank Rosemary was told that her son's corneas had been "shaved" (figure 3) and given to two "lucky" patients at the nearby academic hospital. The remains of Andrew's eyes were being kept in the refrigerator and the di-

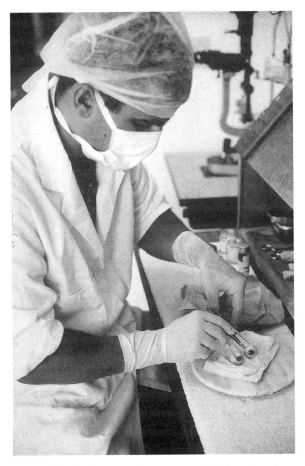

FIGURE 3 Shaving the cornea from two eyes taken from the police mortuary in Cape Town, South Africa. (Photo by Viviane Moos)

rector refused to return them to Andrew's mother for burial. And so, unwilling to argue any further, Andrew Sitshetshe was buried without his eyes. But Rosemary found she could not bury her anger. "Although my son is dead and buried," Mrs. Sitshetshe said, with tears coursing down her cheeks, "Is it good that his flesh is here, there, and everywhere, and that parts of his body are still floating around? Must we be stripped of every comfort ? How could the medical doctor know what was most important for us?" Mrs. Sitshetshe has since taken her complaint against the mortuary and eye bank staff to South Africa's Truth and Reconciliation Commission. She wants her case to be treated as but one example of a practice that was widespread in police mortuaries under apartheid and which may have continued out of habit, even in the "new" South Africa.

Because of the casual disregard of the bodies of those who are brought to police mortuaries, the residents of black townships in Nanga, Langa, and Guguletu townships, just a stone's throw from the famous Groote Schurr teaching hospital where Christian Barnard first pioneered heart transplants, express fearful, suspicious, and negative attitudes toward organ transplantation. Among older people and recent arrivals from the rural homelands, the very idea of organ harvesting bears an uncanny resemblance to traditional witchcraft practices, especially *muti* (magical) murders in which body parts—especially skulls, hearts, eyes, and genitals—are removed and used or sold by deviant traditional practitioners to magically increase the wealth, influence, health or fertility of a paying client. An older Xhosa woman and recent rural migrant a squatter camp on Guguletu commented in disbelief when my assistant, Monga Melwana, and I confronted her with "the facts" of transplant surgery: "If what you are saying is true, that the white doctors can take the beating heart from one person who is dead, but not truly dead, and put it inside another person to give him strength and life, then these doctors are witches just like our own."

Younger and more sophisticated township residents are more knowledgeable about organ transplant but are equally critical of a practice which they see as a legacy of apartheid medicine. "Why is it," I was asked, "that in our township we have never met or even heard of such a person who received a new heart, or eyes, or a kidney? And yet we know a great many people who say that the bodies of their dead have been tampered with in the police morgues?" Township residents are quick to note the inequality of the exchanges in which organs and tissues have been taken from young, productive, black bodies—the victims of excess mortality caused by apartheid's policies of substandard housing, poor street lighting, bad sanitation, and hazardous transportation, in addition to the overt political violence of the apartheid state and the black struggle for freedom—and transplanted to older, debilitated, affluent, white bodies.

Despite the insistence of Cape Town's current generation of heart transplant patients that Dr. Chris Barnard was no racist, race was always at issue in South Africa's organ transplant program, and it continues to haunt the practices of transplant surgery to this day. During the heyday of apartheid, transplant surgeons were not obligated by law to solicit family consent before harvesting organs (and tissues) from cadaveric donors. "Up until 1983 or 1984 the conditions for transplantation were easier," said Dr. Johan Brink, the head cardiac and transplant surgeon from the University of Cape Town. "We didn't worry too much in those early days. We just took the hearts we needed, but it was never really a racial issue." But what Dr. Brink meant was that there was no hesitancy on the part of doctors in transplanting black and colored (mixed race) hearts—sometimes taken without the consent or knowledge of family members—into the ailing bodies of their mostly white, male patients. (Until the early 1990s, 85 percent of South Africa's heart transplant recipients were white males). Surgeons refused to reveal the race of donor hearts to concerned and sometimes racist organ recipients, saying that hearts have no race. "We always used whatever hearts we could get," Dr. Brink said, whether or not the patient feared he might be getting an "inferior" organ. In 1994, the year of the elections, for the first time a significant percentage (36 percent) of all heart transplant patients at the university hospital in Cape Town were assigned to mixed-race, Indian, or black patients. However, by that time, most heart transplant surgery had moved to the private-sector hospitals where patients of means, many of them arriving from foreign countries, were housed in relative luxury while awaiting a scarce organ. Dr. Brink directed my attention to the real "culprit" in the commodification of human organs—the independent organs brokers who solicited patients, doctors, and transplant coordinators, one of whom, Brink said, "comes from your neck of the woods."

Consequently, in September 1999, I sat nursing a cherry Coke in a dilapidated Denny's Restaurant on Sunset Blvd. in Hollywood. Across from me sat a tall, extremely thin, middle-aged man with intensely blue eyes and a nervous, tentative manner. He gulped frequently and seemed ready to flee from our booth at the slightest provocation and put an end to this strange ethnographic interview. Jim Cohan is a notorious "organs broker" who solicits international buyers and sellers from his home office using the telephone, Internet, and fax. No, I could not tape record our conversation, Jim said, though he was willing to be interviewed about his activities on behalf of "matching up people in need."

"There's no reason for anyone to die in this country while waiting for a heart or a kidney to materialize. There are plenty of spare organs to be had in other parts of the world. One can't be choosy. One has to play by my rules and go where I say. And one has to move quickly." Though Jim operates in a gray, nether world, he insists that what he does is not illegal. He deals with doctors, hospitals, and a "soft" commerce in "excess" cadaveric organs. Although he was arrested and jailed in Italy in 1998 for illegally "brokering" organs, the charges were dropped eventually, and Jim maintains his innocence. In fact, he is proud of his newly invented profession. "Don't think of me as an outlaw," he said. "Think of me as a new version of the old-fashioned marriage broker. I locate and match up people in need; people whose suffering can be alleviated on either side."

FOLLOWING THE BODIES: THE TRAFFIC IN HUMAN ORGANS

As these few scenarios plucked out of hundreds of transcribed interviews with transplant specialists, transplant patients, organs brokers, organ buyers, and sellers suggest, transplant surgery today is a blend of altruism and commerce; of science and magic; of gifting, barter, and theft; of choice and coercion. We have found that the "organs trade" is real, spectacularly lucrative, and widespread, even though it is illegal in most countries and unethical according to every governing body of medical, professional life. It is therefore covert. In some of the sites we have explored—India, Brazil, South Africa, and the United States—the trade in organs and other body parts links surgeons and technicians from the upper strata of biomedical practice to "body mafia" from the lowest reaches of the criminal world. The transactions involve police, mortuary workers, pathologists, civil servants, ambulance drivers, emergency room workers, eye bank and blood bank managers, biotechnicians, funeral directors, and transplant coordinators.

Together, we are documenting hard and soft forms of organ sales, investigating rumors of body theft, allegations of human rights violations of the nearly dead, and mutilations of pauper cadavers in police mortuaries. We are trying to pierce the secrecy surrounding organ transplantation and to "make public" all practices regarding the harvesting, selling, and distribution of human organs and tissues. These transactions have been protected, even concealed, by a deadly indifference to the population of organ donors, living and dead, most of them poor, and by an unquestioned acceptance in most industrialized nations of transplant surgery as a social and moral good.

But the entry of "free markets" into the business of organ procurement poses a challenge to the social ethics of organ transplant. By their nature, markets are indiscriminate and inclined to reduce everything—including human beings, their labor, and their reproductive capacity—to the status of commodities—things that can be bought, sold, traded, and stolen. And the global economy has stimulated the movement of mortally sick bodies in one direction and detached "healthy" organs—transported for shorter distances by commercial airlines in ordinary Styrofoam beer coolers conveniently stored in the overhead luggage compartment of the economy section—in another direction, creating a "kula ring" of international trade in surgeries, bodies, and body parts. In general, the flow of organs follows the modern routes of capital: from South to North, from third to first world, from poor to rich, from black and brown to white, and from female to male bodies.

Religious prohibitions in one country or region can stimulate an "organs market" in more secular or pluralistic neighboring areas. Residents of the Gulf States travel to India, the United States, and Eastern Europe to obtain kidneys and other organs made scarce locally due to fundamentalist Islamic teachings that will in some areas allow organ transplantation (to save a life), but draw the line at organ donation. Japanese patients travel to North America and to China for transplant surgery with organs retrieved from brain-dead donors, a definition of death only recently and very reluctantly accepted in Japan. Until the practice was cited and condemned by the World Medical Association in 1994, patients from several Asian countries traveled to Taiwan to purchase organs harvested from executed prisoners. But the ban on using organs from executed prisoners in capitalist Taiwan merely opened up a similar practice in socialist China. The demand for hard currency by strapped governments has no fixed ideological or political boundaries. Turkey comes and goes as an active site of illegal traffic in transplant organs, with both living donors and recipients arriving from other countries for operations organized by illegal organs brokers.

Meanwhile, patients from Israel, which has its own, well-developed, but underused, transplantation centers travel to the West Bank, Turkey, Russia, Moldava, Georgia, and Romania, where kidneys are purchased from living donors, and to the United States, Europe, and South Africa, where transplantation clinics in private hospitals can resemble four star hotels.

In all these transactions, a new profession of organs brokers—ranging from entrepreneurial doctors to criminal "body mafia" and new businesspeople like the elusive Jim Cohan in the United States and Coby Dyan in Israel—are the essential actors. Together, they have generated a "body trade" which promises to certain, select individuals of reasonable economic means living almost *anywhere* in the world—from the Amazon Basin (and I have met a Suya Indian who was flown to São Paulo from Mato Grosso to receive a new kidney) to the deserts of Oman—a "miraculous" extension of what Giorgio Agamben calls "brute" or "naked" life—the life of the species rather than a *consciously* lived human and ethical life.

ANTHROPOLOGISTS ON MARS

Our initial forays have taken us into alien and, at times, hostile and dangerous territory, where we are exploring some of the backstage scenes of organ transplantation. Of the many fieldsites in which I have found myself, none compares to the world of transplant surgery for its mythical properties, its codes of secrecy, its impunity, and its exoticism. Dr. Christian Bernard, the world's first heart transplant surgeon, now comfortably retired and enjoying his later years in the peace and tranquility of the rural western Cape wine lands, spends his time writing science fiction thrillers with a strong autobiographical flavor—for example, *The Donor,* (1996)—which deals with the passions and insatiable "appetites" surrounding the quest for organs for transplant. But Dr. Bernard refused to be interviewed about the real-life struggles that were taking place in the Supreme Court of Cape Town in 1998 among some of his own protégés, heart transplant surgeons operating in competing public and the private sectors, each suing the other for concealing negative data on unacceptably high transplant mortalities, destroying slides and other data, and destroying usable hearts to keep them from "the competition" (see *Vosloo vs. Von Oppel,* Supreme Court of Cape Town, February 1998), a case that was tossed out of court by the judge, who issued a stinging reprimand to both parties to "clean up" their "houses."

Operating in these back ward to back-alley contexts, Cohen and I sometimes feel that Oliver Sack's felicitous phrase, "an anthropologist on Mars" is most apropos. Playing the role of the anthropological court jesters, we have begun our work by raising "foolish" but necessary "first questions": What is going on here? What truths are being served up? Whose needs are being overlooked? Whose voices are being silenced? What unrecognized sacrifices are being made? What secrets lie behind the transplant rhetoric of gifts, altruism, scarcities, and needs?

To date, our initial findings reveal the following: (1) race, class, and gender inequalities and injustices in the acquisition, harvesting, and distribution of organs; (2) widespread violation of national laws and international regulations against the sale of organs; (3) the collapse of cultural and religious sanctions against body dismemberment and commercial use in the face of the enormous market pressures in the transplant industry; (4) the appearance of new forms of debt peonage in which the commodified kidney occupies a critical role; (5) the emergence of soft sales in the form of "compensated gifting" of kidneys within extended families along with "coerced" gifts, as vulnerable workers "donate" organs to their employers in exchange for secure work and other entitlements, and prisoners donate them in exchange for reduction in prison sentences; (6) popular resistance to new laws of presumed consent for organ donation; (7) widespread violations of cadavers in public morgues, organs and tissues being removed without any consent for international sale; (8) the disposal and wasting of viable organs in the context of intense competition of public and private hospitals; (9) the critical importance of transplant surgery and commodified organs to the new economics of privatized health care throughout the world; (10) the circulation of narratives of terror concerning the theft and disappearance of bodies and body parts globally, some of which have a basis in reality; (11) the spread of a lucrative transplant tourism in which patients, doctors, and sellers are serviced by rings of organ brokers. Perhaps what is needed from anthropology is something akin to Donna Haraway's (1985) radical "manifesto" for the cyborg bodies and selves we have already become through the appearance of strange markets, excess capital, advanced biotechnologies, "surplus bodies," and spare body parts.

KEYWORDS: ARTIFICIAL SCARCITIES AND INVENTED NEEDS
Several keywords in organ transplantation require a radical deconstruction: for example: *scarcity, need, donation, gift, bond, life, death, supply,* and *demand.* The "gift" of life, for example, hides the real demand for a "gift of death," insofar as, for a great many people, brain death is still understood as a relinquishing of life before it is time, a false death, as it were, that *precedes real* death.

The "demand" for human organs—and for wealthy transplant patients to purchase them—is driven by the medical discourse on scarcity. The specter of long transplant "waiting lists"—often, we have found, only virtual lists with little material basis in reality—has motivated and driven questionable practices of organ harvesting with blatant sales alongside "compensated gifting"; doctors acting as brokers; and fierce competition between public and private hospitals for patients of means. At its worst, the scramble for organs and tissues has lead to human rights abuses and violations in intensive-care units and in public morgues. But the very idea of organ "scarcity" is what Ivan Illich would call an artificially created need, invented by transplant technicians and dangled before the eyes of an ever-expanding sick, aging, and dying population.

The medical discourse on scarcity has produced what Margaret Lock has called "rapacious demands." Japanese sociologist, Tsuyoshi Awaya (1994) goes even further, referring to transplant surgery as a form of "neo-cannibalism." "We are now eyeing each other's bodies greedily," he says," as a source of detachable spare parts with which to extend our lives." While unwilling to condemn this "human revolution," Awaya wants organ donors and recipients to recognize the kind of social exchange in which they are engaged.

The discourse on scarcity conceals the actual existence of "excess" and "wasted" organs that daily end up in hospital dumpsters throughout those parts of the world where the necessary infrastructure is lacking to use them. But the ill will and competitiveness of hospital workers and medical professionals also contributes to the production of organ wastage. The transplant specialists whom Cohen and I interviewed in our respective field sites scoffed at the notion of organ scarcity given the appallingly high rates of youth mortality, accidental deaths, homicides, and transport deaths that produce a superabundance of young, healthy cadavers. But these precious commodities are routinely wasted in the absence or indifference of trained "organ capture" teams in hospital emergency rooms and intensive care units.

And organ scarcity is reproduced in the increasing competition between public and private hospitals and their competing teams of transplant surgeons who, in the words of one South African transplant coordinator, "order their assistants to dispose of perfectly good organs rather than allow the competition to get their hands on them." The real scarcity, we have found, is not of organs but of transplant patients of sufficient means to pay for the expensive surgery. In India, Brazil, and even in South Africa there is a superabundance of poor people willing to sell a kidney or even a cornea for a pittance.

MEDICAL BIO-PIRACY

While high-quality organs and tissues are scarce, there are plenty of what Dr. S., the director of an Eye Bank in São Paulo, referred to as usable "leftovers" floating around the world. Brazil, he said, has long been a favored "dumping ground" for surplus inventories from the first world, including old, poor-quality or damaged tissues and organs. In extensive interviews with Dr. S. in 1997 and 1998, he complained of a U.S.-based program which routinely sent surplus cornea to his center. "Obviously," he said, "these are not the best cornea. The Americans will only send us what they have already rejected for themselves." "Excess" cornea are shipped in bulk from the United States to other (including Third World) countries. And permissible handling charges constitute sales.

The director of a private eye bank in Pretoria, South Africa, complained that the American company that provided his institution with human cornea charged exorbitant prices, up to $1,000 per cornea. "And where do all these 'excess' cornea come from in the U.S.?" the eye bank director asked pointedly, a question we at Organs Watch are just now beginning to pursue. Meanwhile, in Cape Town, the director of South Africa's largest eye bank, an independent foundation, normally keeps a dozen or more "post-dated" cadaver eyes in her organization's refrigerator. These "poor-quality cornea" (actually *eyes*) would not be used, she said, for transplantation anywhere in South Africa. They could, however, be sent for "handling fees" to less fortunate, neighboring countries in Africa that requested them.

Because commercial exchanges have also contributed to the transfer of transplantation capabilities to previously underserved areas of the world, transplant specialists I interviewed in Brazil and South Africa are deeply ambivalent about them. Surgeons in São Paulo, Brazil told of a controversial plan proposed some years ago by Dr. Thomas Starzl of the University of Pittsburgh Medical School, in which Starzl proposed an exchange of North American "state-of-the-art" transplant expertise for a regular supply of surplus Brazilian human livers. Since Brazil had not yet at that time developed a liver transplant program, it had a surplus of livers that could help meet the needs of American transplant patients. In exchange for those excess livers, Starzl and his colleagues would help surgeons at the major public medical center in São Paulo develop their own liver transplant program. The public outcry in Brazil against this ghoulish exchange fueled in large part by the Brazilian media interrupted the agreement.

Although Brazilian livers were not delivered to Pittsburgh, many other Third World organs and tissues have found their way to the United States. In the files of a town council member in São Paulo, I found results of a police investigation of the local Medical-Legal Institute (police morgue) indicating that several thousand pituitary glands had been taken (without consent) from poor people's cadavers and sold to private medical firms in the United States, where they were used in the production of growth hormones. Similarly, an anatomy professor at the Federal University of Pernambuco in Recife was prosecuted some years ago for having sold thousands of inner ear parts taken from pauper cadavers to NASA for their space training and research programs.

Transplant surgeries reached a peak in Brazil in the late 1970s during the presidency of General Figueiredo, when relations between academic and military hospitals involving criminal organs transactions were flagrant. A retired transplant physician who was attached to a major academic medical center in Brazil told us that doctors and surgeons were under military orders to produce quotas of organs sometimes gotten "on demand" by chemically inducing the appearance of "brain death" in seriously ill patients from the lowest classes who had been abandoned as charity patients and, therefore, seen in every sense as wards of the state. Because of the history of past abuses by some of his own colleagues, this surgeon vehemently opposes Brazil's new law of presumed consent, calling it a law against the poor. "It is not the organs of the super-citizen," he said, "which will disappear, but those of nameless people without resources."

In South Africa, the director of an experimental research science unit of a large public medical school showed me official documents approving the transfer of human heart valves taken (without consent) from the bodies of the poor in the police mortuary and shipped "for handling costs" to medical centers in Germany and Austria. These permissible fees, I was told, helped defray the unit's research program in the face of the austerities and downsizing of advanced medical research facilities in the new South Africa. But to a great many ordinary citizens in India, South Africa, and Brazil, such commercial exchanges are seen as a form of global bio-piracy, and increasingly today one hears demands to "nationalize" dead bodies, tissues, and body parts to protect them from global exploitation. The mere idea of "Brazilian livers" going to American transplant patients gives Dr. O., a Brazilian surgeon, "an attack of spleen." But whatever their destination, the removal of organs, tissues, and other body parts without consent is terrifying for those populations, mostly poor and socially marginalized, who see their bodies at risk of medical bio-piracy—whether in Cape Town, Rio de Janeiro, *or* New York City.

TRANSPLANT ETHICS AND HUMAN SACRIFICE IN THE POSTMODERN ERA

At the heart of this project is an anthropological analysis of postmodern forms of human sacrifice. Though it bears little resemblance to the burnt offerings of the desert Hebrews or to the agony of Christian martyrs thrown to lions at the dawn of the second millennium, human sacrifice is still with us. Organ harvesting carries some trace elements and vestigial images of Aztec hearts ripped—still beating— from the chests of state-appointed, ritual scapegoats. Global capitalism and advanced biotechnology have released new, medically incited "tastes" (a New Age gourmet cannibalism, perhaps) for human bodies, living and dead, for the skin and bones, flesh and blood, tissue, marrow, and genetic material of "the other." Like other forms of human sacrifice, transplant surgery partakes in the really real, the surreal, the magical, and the uncanny. What is different today is that the sacrifice is disguised as a "gift," a donation, and is unrecognized for what it really is. The sacrifice is rendered invisible by its anonymity and hidden within the rhetoric of "life saving" and "gift giving," two of several transplant "key words" we are trying to open to a long overdue public discussion.

Inserting ourselves into transplant surgery theaters that were sometimes more like theaters of the absurd and following transplant patients from dialysis clinics to surgery, and donor bodies from township shabeens to police stations and public mortuaries and from there to the various eye banks, medical clinics, and research laboratories where their parts were harvested and redistributed, we encountered everywhere a kind of *apartheid medicine* that privileged some patients—organ *recipients*—over other patients, organ *donors*, about whom almost nothing is known. Organ donors represent a social and semiotic zero, an ideal place for a critical medical anthropologist dedicated to "following the bodies" to begin. We made the conscious decision to position ourselves on the "other side" of the transplant equation, representing the voice of the silent or silenced organ donors, living and dead, here seen as rights-bearing individuals and as vulnerable patients rather than as fodder for advanced medical technologies.

Two anecdotes convey the origins of this decision for me. After I had begun to write about the fears of the Brazilian shantytown poor following rumors of child kidnapping for organ removal (Scheper-Hughes 1992), my husband, then a medical social worker at a large children's hospital, returned home one day deeply moved by a transplant operation that had just saved the life of a twelve-year-old child. Quite unthinkingly I asked, "Whose organ?" Michael's anger at my "inappropriate" question lead me to realize that here was a question that *had* to be asked. Then, later, in 1996 when I was already deeply involved in this research, a transplant surgeon in Recife, Brazil, who relied heavily on live kidney donors, answered my questions about patient follow-up procedures quite defensively. "Follow up!" he fairly boomed. "With transplant patients it's like a marriage—you are never free of them!" "Yes," I replied. "But what about your *other* patients, your kidney donors. Do you follow *them?*" To which the surgeon replied. "Of course not. They are *not* patients. They are healthy people just like a woman who gives birth." When I spoke of the many kidney donors I met who later encountered medical and psychological difficulties, he replied, "These are neurotic people who want to be heroized for what they have done." But when I countered, "Why *shouldn't* they be?" the doctor had no reply.

Then, during a field trip to Brazil in 1998, I encountered in Salvador, Bahia, a "worst-case scenario" showing just how badly a live kidney donation could turn out in a Third World context. "Josefa," the only girl among eight siblings from a poor, rural family in the interior of the state, developed end-stage kidney disease in her twenties (figure 4). With the help of people from her local Catholic church, Josefa moved to Salvador for dialysis treatments, but there her condition continued to deteriorate. Her only solution, she was told, would be a transplant, but as a "public" patient, her chances of getting to the top of local "waiting lists" was next to nil. At her doctor's suggestion, Josefa sought a kidney donor among her siblings. An older brother, "Tomas," the father of three young children, readily offered to help his "baby" sister (figure 5). But what first seemed like a miraculous transfer of life rather quickly turned problematic. Soon after the "successful" transplant, Josefa suffered a crisis of rejection and lost her new kidney. Meanwhile, Tomas himself fell ill and was himself diagnosed with kidney disease resulting from a poorly treated childhood infection. What the doctors referred to as a "freak accident" and a stroke of "bad luck" struck Josefa (and her brother) as evidence of a larger social disease: "We were poor and ignorant; the doctors didn't really care whether we were properly matched or whether I could afford the drugs I needed to stay alive after the transplant." Josefa's enormous guilt toward her dying brother brought tears to her eyes throughout our interviews. She was committed to doing everything possible to help out his family, to which she felt so miserably indebted. Tomas, a slender, nervous man, looking far older than his years, said ruefully dur-

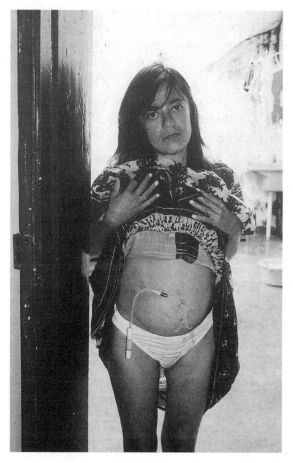

FIGURE 4 "Josefa da Silva," Salvador, Brazil. (Photo by author)

ing a separate interview: "I love my sister and I don't hold her responsible for what has happened. The doctors never asked about my own medical history before the operation. And afterwards it was too late."

Perhaps this last anecdote may serve as a partial response to the following, often-raised challenge: If a living donor can do without the organ, why can't the donor profit and medical science benefit? Transplant surgeons have disseminated an untested hypothesis of "risk-free" live kidney donation in the absence of *any* published, longitudinal studies of the effects of nephrectomy (kidney removal) among the urban poor living anywhere in the world. Live donors from shanty-towns, inner cities, or prisons face extraordinary threats to their health and personal security through violence, injury, accidents, and infectious disease that can all too readily compromise the kidney of last resort. As the use of live kidney

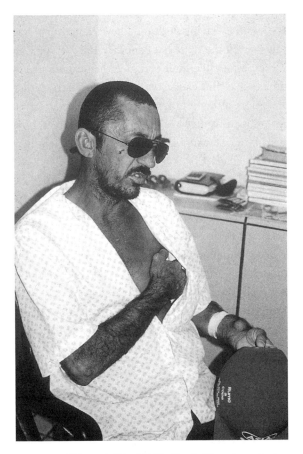

FIGURE 5 "Tomas da Silva," Bahia, Brazil. (Photo by author)

donors has moved from the industrialized West, where it takes place among kin and under highly privileged circumstances, to areas of high risk in the Third World, transplant surgeons are complicit in the needless suffering of a hidden population.

The "preferential option" for the organ donors expressed here does not imply a lack of empathy for transplant recipients or for the expanding queues of wait-listed patients who have been promised a kind of immortality by transplant professionals. Poised somewhere between life and death, their hopes waxing and waning as they are stranded at the middle or the bottom of official waiting lists which are subject in many places to corruption by those with access to private medicine and to powerful surgeons who know how to circumvent or bend the rules, these all-but-abandoned transplant candidates have their own painful stories to contribute to the larger project.

Few organ recipients know anything about the kinds of demands being made on the bodies of "the other," living or dead. They recognize, of course, that their good fortune comes out of the tragedy of another and they pass along the transplant folklore of the permissible guilt and glee they experience on rainy nights when traffic accidents rise. But cadaveric donor anonymity prevents scruples in the recipient population, although organ recipients often do try to learn something about their donors. But they are never privy to the secret negotiations and sometimes the psychological manipulations of the donor's family members while they are in shock and deep grief.

Meanwhile, organs brokers—like any other brokers—try to keep (kidney) buyers and sellers apart. But even when live donation is transacted within families, recipients can be protected from knowing the human cost of donation. In Brazil, for example, kidney donors are cautioned by their doctors that it is wrong, after donation, ever to bring the subject up in front of the recipient. Their act, they are told, must be completely "forgotten." This mandate alone is a burden that forces the donors to carry within themselves a deep "family secret." If the medical and psychological risks, pressures, and constraints on organ donors (and their families) were more generally known, potential transplant recipients might want to consider "opting out" of procedures that presume and demand so much of the other.

WHOSE VALUES ARE THESE?

Amid the contestations between organ givers and organ receivers, between doctors and patients, between North and South, between individuals and the state, between the illegal and the "merely" unethical, anthropologists need to be especially clear about their values in these complex transactions. Indeed, as professional hunters and gatherers of human values, anthropologists are characteristically shy when it comes to discussing their own individual or cultural notions of the good and its opposites. Why would anthropologists regard such "Western" and modernist notions of bodily autonomy and bodily integrity as basic human rights? This would seem particularly ironic given the deconstructionist and relativist impetus that lay behind Margaret Lock's and my earlier "mindful body" essay (1987).

However, we have since found that notions of bodily autonomy and integrity are almost universally shared today. They lie behind "First Peoples" demands for the repatriation and reburial of human remains warehoused in museum archives (as witnessed in the tremendous flack around the recovery of Ishi's brain). They lie behind patients' rights movements demanding access to medicine and medical technology—rights to "medical citizenship" as it were. They lie behind the demands of the wretchedly poor for dignified death and burial. And they certainly lie behind organ-stealing rumors and popular resistance to "presumed consent" laws.

For some of those, however, who live on the margins of the global economy, who are daily assaulted by disease, hunger, and premature death, whose living and working conditions are degrading, and for whom the experience of bodily alienation is already a defining feature of their lives, the possibility of selling an organ can sometimes appear as an act of empowerment. "I prefer to sell it [my body] myself rather than to let the state get it," was a sentiment frequently expressed by shantytown residents in urban Brazil.

In fact, it is in the West where the modernist values of bodily autonomy and integrity are most under assault. As commodification and commercialization have entered almost every sphere of life—from markets in "beauty queen" ova and "genius sperm" to a corrupted "willed body" program at the University of California, Irvine, Medical School—those in the North cannot claim any high moral ground. Meanwhile, the new constitutions and bills of rights adopted by democratic Brazil and post-apartheid South Africa are far more developed than ours with respect to recognizing human rights to bodily integrity.

We are particularly concerned about social and race-based inequities in the selection of candidates for transplant surgery in the United States. While it is true that African-Americans are, at best, reluctant organ donors, we question the biomedical rationale for race-based "matching," a procedure that is not followed in either Brazil or, historically, in South Africa, where black donors provided a great many organs for white recipients. Trust in medicine and in transplant procedures—especially medical definitions of brain death—is low in black, inner-city neighborhoods in the United States, and this contributes to the low incidence of organ donation. Hence, a vicious cycle is created and maintained. Medical exclusions based on poor blood and tissue matches, previous medical and reproductive histories, and exposure to infectious disease disqualify a great many black candidates for transplant surgery. One has to be relatively "healthy," affluent, and *white* in the United States to be a candidate for a cadaveric organ. Under these exclusionary conditions, resistance to organ donation makes perfect sense. One result is that African-Americans are counseled by their doctors more frequently than white Americans to pursue live (kidney) donation. And there is some evidence that African-Americans express more resistance to *making* such demands on their loved ones.

FOUNDING THE BERKELEY ORGANS WATCH

The emergence of death camps, torture camps, and organ-harvesting camps—which came together at certain decisive junctures in the late twentieth century—points to the demise of classical humanism and holism and the rise of "an ethics of parts"—part histories, part truths, and now, it seems, divisible bodies in which detached and free-standing organs function as market commodities. Human organ sales have emerged as a niche market in which certain disadvantaged populations and nations have been demoted and fragmented in the interests of global capitalism. This ghoulish market in bodies and body parts erodes the enormous trust invested in biomedicine by nation states and by transnational corporations. In all, it conjures up the darker side, the anarchy and chaos of the global economy.

In its odd juxtapositions of ethnography, fact-finding, documentation/ surveillance, and human rights advocacy, this project blends genres and transgresses cherished distinctions among anthropology, political journalism, scientific report, moral philosophy, and human rights advocacy. These newer ethnographic engagements with everyday violence and human suffering require the anthropologist to penetrate spaces—that is, the "back alleys and police morgues" of this research—where nothing can be taken for granted and where a hermeneutics of suspicion replaces the earlier fieldwork modes of phenomenological bracketing and suspension of disbelief. That these transgressive uses of anthropology make some of my colleagues uneasy or angry is understandable. Neither are my collaborators and I entirely comfortable with what we have taken on. Yet, is any *other* discipline better situated than anthropology to interrogate human values and practices from a position of epistemological "openness" and to offer alternatives to the limited pragmatic utilitarianism and rational-choice models that dominate medical and bio-ethical thinking today?

Rather than views from the armchair, this research reports on views from over, under, and beyond the operating table and mortuary slab. If peering into surgical slop buckets to document the number of "wasted" organs is not ethno-*graphic* research, then I am afraid to consider what *else* it might be. In bridging the normally discrete boundaries between fieldwork in elite medical centers and in shantytowns and back alleys, our orientation holds to the simple dictum—"Follow the bodies!" Problems remain, however, with respect to the incompleteness of the evidence based on innuendo and fragments of conversation, as well as on hundreds of transcribed formal interviews and structured observations in dialysis clinics and operating rooms in each of our multiple research sites. Multisited research runs the risk of being too thinly spread, but the alternatives to this are unclear, given our mandate to investigate rumors, allegations, and scandals of kidnap, body-part sales, and organ theft, many of which prove are difficult to verify because of the almost impenetrable secrecy surrounding global practices of organ harvesting and transplant surgery. Our research also demands a sacrifice of the normally leisurely pace of traditional ethnographic work. We have to respond, move, and write quickly. We are learning, and rather quickly, as we go along.

In addition to the normal production of scholarly articles, papers, and monographs, we established in Berkeley in 1999 an Organs Watch Project (Monaghan

2000) modeled after human rights surveillance programs such as Amnesty International. From this base, we are coordinating original fieldwork and archival data collection on normative and deviant practices of organ harvesting and distribution worldwide, and we are making our findings available through the Internet [see http://sunsite.berkeley.edu/biotech/organswatch] and through a bi-annual newsletter (Berkeley Organs Watch 2000). The evolving archive is mapping the routes by which organs, doctors, medical capital, and donors circulate; documenting changes in international and national regulations on organ and tissue transfer; and recording and participating in crucial debates, public forums, and governmental hearings regarding the manner in which tissues and organs are harvested and distributed (Scheper-Hughes 2001a). Finally, we are collaborating with investigative reporters from major newspapers and public radio and television—granting interviews, traveling with reporters, and introducing them to our fieldsites, a practice that is, as far as I know, extremely rare (for obvious reasons) among anthropologists. In March 2001 I traveled with Mike Finkel of the *New York Times*, who produced a cover story (Finkel 2001) on organs traffic in the Middle East that had been uncovered by me (in Israel) and by two Organs Watch interns, Jennifer Khan and Aslihan Senal (in Turkey).

In sum, our goal is to bring broader social and social justice concerns to bear on global practices of organ harvesting and distribution as an alternative to the myopic, case-by-case view of transplant surgeons. While most of our field research to date has taken place in the Third World, we are learning the extent to which these global exchanges involve and implicate the United States and Western Europe. The rapacious demand for organs in one area stimulates the market for brokers and organ sellers or body mafia in other nations. For example, during the fall and winter of 2000–2001, several Israeli kidney patients arranged, through brokers, to have transplant surgeries at major hospitals on the East Coast of the United States with kidneys purchased from living donors. Organs Watch contacted the surgical unit directors, who expressed surprise and indignation that these illicit practices were happening "behind their backs." But the rule operating in many U.S. kidney transplant centers at the present time with respect to living kidney donation can be described as an implicit policy of "Don't ask, don't tell," or "Ask, but please don't tell us anything we don't want to hear" (see Scheper-Hughes 2001a). At the very least, the loose and highly localized surveillance (or, more commonly, the lack thereof) of living kidney donation, worldwide, requires serious attention in light of the rapidly growing phenomenon of living unrelated organ donation (Live Organ Donor Consensus Group 2000).

Organ transplantation depends on a social contract and a social trust; it cannot exist without protest and refusal unless the grounds for social trust are explicit. At a very rudimentary level, the ethical practice of organ transplantation requires a reasonably fair and equitable health care system within a reasonably democratic state in which basic human rights are protected and guaranteed. Organ transplantation occurring within the milieu of a police state where political "disappearances" or "dirty wars" are practiced, or where routine police torture and injury and deaths in detention are common, can only generate fears and panics. And organ transplantation occurring within a competitive market economy in which sellers are reduced to "suppliers" of valuable spare parts corrupts the profession of medicine. Under such circumstances, the most vulnerable people will fight back with one of the only resources they have—gossip and rumors which convey, albeit obliquely, the reality of the "situation of emergency" that exists for them.

We in Organs Watch are seeking assurances that the social and medical practices around organ transplantation *include attention to* the needs and wishes of organ donors, both living and dead. We are asking transplant surgeons to pay attention to where organs come from and the manner in which they are harvested. We want assurances that organ donation everywhere is voluntary and based on altruistic motives. And we want the bodies of potential donors—living and dead—to be protected and not exploited by those who are charged with their care. We want the risks and benefits of organ transplant surgery to be more equally distributed among and within nations, and among ethnic groups, genders, and social classes. Finally, we want assurances that the so-called "gift of life" never deteriorates into a "theft of life." We hope that this new project will be seen as an attempt to establish a new ethical blueprint for anthropology and for medicine into the twenty-first century.

ACKNOWLEDGMENTS

I would like to extend a special thanks to the Open Society Institute for their generous support of the project "Medicine, Markets, and Bodies."

REFERENCES AND SUGGESTIONS FOR FURTHER READING

Agamben, Giorgio. 1995. *Homo Sacer: Sovereign Power and Bare Life.* Stanford, CA: Stanford University Press.

Appadurai, Arjun. 1986. *The Social Life of Things: Commodities in Cultural Perspective.* Cambridge, U.K.: Cambridge University Press.

Berkeley Organs Watch. 2000. *Berkeley Organs Watch News: Social Justice, Human Rights, and Organ Transplantation* no. 1 (summer).

Cameron, Jackie. 1995. "Muti Doctor Arrested for Killing Boy." *Cape Times*, August 10, 2.

Campion-Vincent, Veronique. 1990. "The Baby-Parts Story: A New Latin American Legend." *Western Folklore* 49, no. 1 (January): 9–26.

Cantarovitch, Felix. 1990. "Values Sacrificed and Values Gained by the Commerce of Organs: The Argentine Experience." *Transplant Proceedings* 22, no. 3: 925–27.

———. 1992. "Legal Aspects of Transplantation in Argentina." *Transplantation Proceedings* 24, no. 5: 2123–24.

Cantarovitch, F.; L. Casto, and A. M. Cerrajeira. 1991. "Aspects of Argentine Transplant Program: A Twelve-Year Review." *Transplant Proceedings* 23, no. 5: 2521–22.

Chaudhary, Vivek. 1994. "Organ Trade Investigators Seize Hospital Records." *Guardian,* June 22, 10.

Chengappa, Raj. 1990. "The Organs Bazaar." *India Today* (July): 30–37.

Cohen, Lawrence. 1999. "Where It Hurts: Indian Material for an Ethics of Organ Transplantation." *Daedalus* 128, no. 4: 135–65.

Falla, Ricardo. 1982. "The Massacre at the Rural Estate of San Francisco, July 1992." *Cultural Survival Quarterly* 7 (1): 37–42.

———. 1992. *Massacres de la Selva: Ixcan, Guatemala, 1975–1982.* Guatemala: Universidad de San Carlos de Guatemala.

Finkel, Michael. 2001. "Complications: This Little Kidney Went to Market." *New York Times Magazine,* May 27, 26–33, 52.

Fox, Renee, and Judith Swazey. *Spare Parts: Organ Replacement in American Society.* Oxford: Oxford University Press.

Green, Linda. 1998. *Fear as a Way of Life.* New York: Columbia University Press.

Hebert, Hugh. 1994. "Victims of the Transplant Trade." *Guardian,* June 24, 38.

Hogle, Linda. 1999. *Recovering the Nation's Body: Cultural Memory, Medicine, and the Politics of Redemption.* New Brunswick: Rutgers University Press.

"Latest UCI Probe Targets Sale of Body Parts." 1999. *Los Angeles Times,* September 18, 1.

Leventhal, Todd. 1995. "The Illegal Transportation and Sale of Human Organs: Reality or Myth?" Paper presented to conference of the International Association of Chiefs of Police (photocopy). Washington, DC: USIA.

Live Organ Donor Consensus Group. 2000. "Consensus Statement on the Live Organ Donor." *Journal of the American Medical Association* 284: 2919–26.

Lock, Margaret. 1995. "Transcending Mortality: Organ Transplants and the Practice of Contradictions." *Medical Anthropology Quarterly* 9, no. 3: 390–99.

———. 1996. "Deadly Disputes: Understanding Death in Europe, Japan, and North America." *Doreen B. Townsend Center Occasional Papers* 4: 7–25.

———. 1997. "Culture, Technology, and the New Death: Deadly Disputes in Japan and North America. *Culture* 17, no. 1–2: 27–42.

Marcus, George. 1998. *Ethnography through Thick and Thin.* Princeton, NJ: Princeton University Press.

Marshall, P. A.; D. C. Thomas; and A. S. Daar. 1996. "Marketing Human Organs: The Autonomy Paradox." *Theoretical Medicine* 17, no. 1: 5–8.

Max, Arthur. 1995. "Stolen Kidneys Supplying India's Transplant Industry." *San Francisco Chronicle*, April 6.

Monaghan, Peter. 2000. "Scholarly Watchdogs for an Ethical Netherworld." *Chronicle of Higher Education*, October 6, A23–24.

Network of Independent Monitors. 1996. *Breaking with the Past: Reports of Alleged Human Rights Violations by South African Police*. Cape Town: Network of Independent Monitors.

Niehaus, Isak. 1993. "Coins for Blood and Blood for Coins: Toward a Genealogy of Sacrifice in the Transvaal Lowveld." Paper read at the meeting of the Society for South African Anthropology, Johannesburg.

"Researchers to Monitor Trade in Human Organs." 1999. *New York Times*, Nov. 5, A-23.

Rothman, David, et al. 1997. The Bellagio Task Force Report on Transplantation, Bodily Integrity, and the International Traffic in Organs." *Transplantation Proceedings* 29: 2739–45.

Rothman, Sheila. 1998. "Monitoring Kidney Donations from Living Donors: A Pilot Study in the New York Metropolitan Region." Paper read at the World Bioethics Meetings in Tokyo, Japan, November 4–6.

Scheper-Hughes, Nancy. 1990. "Theft of Life." *Society* 27, no. 6: 57–62.

———. 1992. *Death without Weeping: The Violence of Everyday Life in Brazil*. Berkeley and Los Angeles: University of California Press.

———. 1996. "Small Wars and Invisible Genocides." *Social Science and Medicine* 43, no. 5: 889–900.

———. 2000. "The Global Traffic in Organs." *Current Anthropology* 41, no. 2: 191–224.

———. 2001a. "Neo-Cannibalism: The Global Traffic in Human Organs." Report and testimony presented as expert witness before the International Operations and Human Rights Subcommittee Hearings on June 27, 2001. House of Representatives, Washington, DC.

———. 2001b. "The Organ of Last Resort." *UNESCO Courier* (July).

Scheper-Hughes, Nancy, and Margaret Lock. 1987. "The Mindful Body: A Prolegomena to Future Work in Medical Anthropology." *Medical Anthropology Quarterly* 1, no. 1: 1–39.

Sharp, Leslie. 1994. "Organ Transplantation as a Transformative Experience: Anthropological Insights into the Restructuring of the Self." *Medical Anthropology Quarterly* 9, no. 3: 357–89.

Smith, Robert. 1989 "The Trafficking in Central American Children." *Report of Guatemala* 10, no. 3: 4–5.

Suarez-Orozco, Marcelo. 1987. "The Treatment of Children in the Dirty War." In *Child Survival*, ed. Scheper-Hughes, 227–46. Dordrecht, Holland: D. Reidel.

Taussig, Michael. 1980. *The Devil and Commodity Fetishism*. Chapel Hill: University of North Carolina Press.

———. 1987. *Shamanism., Colonialism, and the Wild Man.* Chicago: University of Chicago Press.

———. 1991. *The Nervous System.* New York: Routledge.

USIA. 1994. *The Child Organ Trafficking Rumor: A Modern Urban Legend.* Report submitted to the United Nations Special Rapporteur on the Sale of Children, Child Prostitution, and Pornography, December.

Wallace, Charles. 1992. "For Sale: The Poor's Body Parts." *Los Angeles Times*, August 27, A1, 1.

White, Luise. 1993. "Cars Out of Place: Vampires, Technology, and Labor in East and Central Africa." *Representations* 43 (summer): 27–50.

World Medical Association. 1985. "WMA Statement on Live Organ Trade." Brussels, Belgium (October).

Younger, Stuart; Renee Fox; and Laurence O'Connell, eds. 1996. *Organ Transplantation: Meanings and Realities.* Madison: University of Wisconsin Press.

3.

World Markets: Anthropological Perspectives

JANE SCHNEIDER

From an anthropological perspective, the world is a vastly uneven playing field in which a hegemonic "free market culture" and disruptive "market forces" move outward from centers of concentrated power and wealth to exert pressure on peripheries that are more or less vulnerable to their impact. By "free market culture" is meant a set of dispositions, values, and practices that gravitate around the following principles, associated with market-friendly laws and institutional arrangements. The first is an expectation that the drive for gain is the mainspring of human behavior, so that all humans, if given a chance, will instinctively welcome the opportunities for choice offered by markets and choose "rationally" to maximize individual advantage. The second is a conviction that markets are efficient engines of technological innovation and progress, and should therefore be allowed to operate without cumbersome regulations and controls. Third is a firm belief in the capacity of unfettered markets to deliver human happiness—a decent, even pleasing standard of living not only for society's elites, but also for its middle and working classes. This principle shades into, without being the same as, "consumer culture" and "political democracy." That markets might also create unhappiness, disrupting lives and widening the gap between the haves and the have-nots, is, according to the fourth principle of free market culture, a temporary condition, often explainable by the unworthiness of the have-nots (they are lazy, rent-seeking, risk avoiding, prone to cronyism, profligate, live for the moment, have too many children, and so on).

Rooted in the scientific, technological, and commercial breakthroughs of early modern Europe, then reinforced and disseminated through the intellectual movement of the Enlightenment, the French Revolution, the heady power of industry, and the inventions of advertising and shopping, free market culture was a Western creation, even if markets, and other market cultures, were not. By the late twentieth century, however, we find its dispositions, values, and practices, summarized by the word *capitalism*, to have spread throughout the world. This dispersal corresponds to the independence movements and projects for agricultural and industrial development that have unfolded in Europe's former colonies since the Second World War. And yet, despite these transformations, the world remains a vastly unequal place.

This said, it is important to know that anthropology is the site of continuous, productive disagreement regarding, precisely, the vastness of the gulf between, to use a shorthand expression, "the West and the rest." Are European societies, whose institutions and values already favored free markets before the twentieth century, radically different from societies that have experienced these markets as an intrusion from the outside? Are the differences narrowing? Is there a risk in overstating them in the first place? Will Europeans inevitably continue to spread their culture and institutions throughout the world, or is this a Eurocentric conclusion that blinds us to the precocious development of the Asian Pacific before the nineteenth century, and to its recent spectacular "comeback" after an interlude of European expansion? There is, and has been, little consensus among anthropologists on these questions.

For example, since its inception, the discipline has produced passionate arguments on both sides of the rationality debate: for some, all humans are capable of enlightened self-interest, strategize to maximize benefits and minimize costs, and intrinsically value the expression of rational choice—conforming, thereby, to one of the core principles of free market culture. For others, the very idea of a universal humanity, or a set of motives that are universally human, is dangerous to the recognition and maintenance of valuable cultural differences—alternative rationalities—around the world. Most anthropologists fall between these extremes, yet the fact that both positions have long been represented in the discipline is the source of its considerable ability to self-correct. Anthropologists in general retreat from abstract modeling, document complexity, and are intrigued by the contradictions and unanticipated surprises of human life. This quality, which is enhanced by the tradition of fieldwork, is evident in the following brief review of a succession of anthropological arguments regarding world markets in the different epochs of capitalism.

ANTHROPOLOGISTS AND OTHERS: EARLY ENCOUNTERS

Argonauts of the Western Pacific, written by Bronislaw Malinowski in 1922, is a classic starting place for anthropologists' first reflections on the universality of free market culture. In it Malinowski analyzes the vast network of exchange that he observed in the Trobriand Islands of the South Pacific, in which men dared to travel by canoe over open seas to trade with distant partners for ornamental arm bands and necklaces made of shell. The resulting chain of relations, the "Kula ring," bore no resemblance to a market, he argued, and the shell objects no relation to money. Like Europeans contemplating the crown jewels, Trobrianders related to these objects with reverence, manifesting a keen interest in whom, and how prestigious, the previous owners had been. Although Malinowski laid out the Kula system in a chapter on "tribal economics," he depicted it as simultaneously economic, political, magical, and ceremonial-religious. By contrast, market systems, based on economizing behaviors, were "economic."

Malinowski's Trobriand Islands ethnography led some of his successors to classify objects of exchange as gifts or commodities. Common English usage associates gifts with selfless, disinterested generosity; it associates commodities with wealth accumulation and the satisfaction of individual desires. But although this simple dichotomy, which is isomorphic with the notion of a radical gap between "the West and the rest," surfaces from time to time in anthropological writing, it is consistently challenged. Already in the 1940s, British anthropologist Raymond Firth, observing that Malay fishermen competed with each other for glory or honor by strategically choosing among alternatives, declared that striving to maximize individual advantage is a human universal. One has only to adjust for the desired ends to be able to apply formal economic modeling everywhere. Firth's approach, and critique of Malinowski, inspired many subsequent anthropologists, some of whom attributed the hypothesis of a great divide between capitalist and noncapitalist, Western and non-Western societies, to other anthropologists' overly romantic view of "them" and/or "antimarket mentality."

An especially productive rethinking of these issues derives from the work of French anthropologist Marcel Mauss, whose pathbreaking 1924 essay, *The Gift*, made ample use of Malinowski's data. Mauss minimized the altruistic side of gift giving, stressing instead the side having to do with power. Defining gift exchange as a "total social phenomenon"—at once moral, religious, and economic—and considering gifts to include services, rituals, brides, land, and rank, as well as "things," he argued that the human compunction to give, receive, and repay is also fundamentally political. In a far from voluntary manner, givers lavishly disperse what they have in order to stave off receivers' sentiments of envy or resentment—sentiments that might otherwise lead to magical retribution in the form of evil eye, and even to open war. Once given, gifts compel reciprocity, the spirit of the giver being embodied in them, adding moral weight. Although different from a commodity economy, a gift economy should not be considered its opposite: gift-exchange is neither solidary, harmonious, nor egalitarian. At the same time as it levels wealth, giving fosters indebtedness, allowing creditors to accumulate power, which can then be translated back into wealth.

Mauss developed a similarly qualified picture of market society, based on observations of his native France. Citing his fellow citizens' rivalry to spend on wedding ceremonies and entertaining their friends, he argued that gift exchange was far from banished among the French. Moreover, charity was as much a part of French custom as shopping in department stores. The French would hardly dispute that holders of excessive wealth should seek to neutralize the envy of others by adopting a self-sacrificing, ascetic life-style or indulging in generosity. Obviously influenced by socialist ideology, Mauss saw workers giving life and labor to their communities as well as to their bosses; of course they would make revolutionary demands if denied a share in the profit. Although the laws of the free market might dictate otherwise, solutions to this problem lay in notions of group morality expressed through aristocratic philanthropy, social insurance, and public welfare. Since all of these redistributive measures were evident in France, its market society did not appear to be radically at odds with the moral and economic arrangements of the Trobriands.

Mauss's double-edged solution to reducing the distance between "them and us"—his bridging of the conceptual gap between gifts and commodities—resonates well with recent ethnographic accounts of entrepreneurship in various parts of the world. For example, a study by Italo Pardo of the relatively poor residents of central Naples finds them engaged in "strong, continuous interaction" between moral values of generosity or "good-heartedness" and clever practices for making money, between bestowing favors out of genuine benevolence and using the "favor system" to get ahead, between lovingly tending the shrines of local saints and souls of the dead and presumptuously expecting their blessings and even miracles. More or less moral actors—irreverent and humorously self-deprecating—these small-scale Neapolitan entrepreneurs are above all motivated to construct a "good life" as manifested in the symbolic display of material possessions, a reputation for giving and hosting, and signs that the saints have supported—not undermined—the health of their families.

EUROPEAN COLONIALISM, NEO-COLONIALISM, AND WORLD MARKETS

During the period of European colonial expansion, and in many respects during a neocolonial period following independence, Europe's colonies and dependent regions produced primary products (agricultural and mineral resources) for world markets, importing industrial goods manufactured in metropolitan "core" regions in exchange. The result was a substantially unequal pattern, referred to as "uneven development," which favored the further industrial growth of Western Europe, North America, and eventually Japan. Through market relations as well as out-right plunder, some peripheral regions were actually "de-developed," drawn to specialize in the production of a single crop or mineral, which left them wide open to the disappointment of extremely low value-added returns and the chaotic effects of swings in commodity prices.

How anthropologists approached this situation is reflected in their conflicting reception of the work of Hungarian economist Karl Polanyi in the 1950s and 1960s. In his 1944 book, *The Great Transformation*, Polanyi questioned European capitalism as a unique and strange phenomenon. This was not because of its deep entanglement with markets and money and profits, all of which predated capitalism by centuries and had a well-established historic presence on every continent on earth. The "great" transformation was specific to the eighteenth-century English countryside, where, with the backing of the state and in the name of agricultural improvement, a fiction was created that land, and labor, and capital are nothing but commodities, reducible to quantified measures of cost and benefit. Stripped of their rights to land through Parliamentary Acts of Enclosure and the formation of a land market, former peasants became agricultural or industrial workers, required to sell their labor for a wage in a brand new institution: a market for labor. A forceful moral critic of this historic shift, although less radical in his prescribed remedies than Marx and Engels, Polanyi argued that humans, robbed of the "protective covering" of culturally sensitive definitions of land and labor, would "perish from the effects of social exposure." No wonder that, by the middle of the nineteenth century, new forms of protection (specifically, labor and welfare legislation), were on the horizon.

In a second book, coauthored with anthropologist Conrad Arensberg, Polanyi outlined three stages in the emergence of full-fledged "market societies," defined as having markets for land, labor, and capital as well as goods and services. At the simplest, and presumably the earliest, level of this evolutionist scheme were societies whose economies were structured by reciprocity—the exchange of gifts. A principle of redistribution dominated societies that were more complex and later in time. Here chiefly regimes and state bureaucracies siphoned up the social product, allocating it then to various claimants, based on some combination of need, calculated interest, and the maintenance of patron-client relations. (Socialist command economies might be said to fall under the rubric of "redistribution." Anthropologists have noted a strong continuity between Western discourses about "Oriental" societies, said to have subordinated markets and individual liberties to "despotic" states made tyrannous by the absence of private property, and discourses about both Chinese and Russian variants of Communism. Dramatizing

Western history as dynamic, youthful, and energetic, these discourses caricature the Oriental/Communist "other" as stagnant: bogged down by "dynastic cycles," then stifled by collectivization.) In Polanyi's rendering, systems of reciprocity and redistribution did not lack contact with markets. Within them, however, world markets were restricted to quarantined "ports of trade," such that market forces would not penetrate and dissolve customary relations of land and labor.

Polanyi provoked a lively critique among anthropologists in the Firth tradition, who accused him of fundamentally disliking markets, romantically overplaying the altruism and solidarity of noncapitalist societies, and exaggerating the difference between these societies and the West. Yet others of the profession found his work attractive. At the time of the Vietnam War, American anthropologists attempting to understand the outbreak of peasant revolutions and independence movements in Europe's former colonies were an especially receptive audience. For example, Eric Wolf's comparative study, *Peasant Wars of the Twentieth Century* (1969), traced six instances of peasant unrest (Vietnam among them) to peasants' loss of access to land and engagement with world markets—interrelated consequences of colonial expansion and the worldwide quest for cotton, jute, sugar, rubber, coffee, and other tropical commodities that Europeans desired.

For both the colonial and postcolonial periods, clashing concepts of property— divergent meanings attached to resources—have continued to capture the attention of anthropologists. Thanks to recent archival as well as ethnographic studies, researchers are reconstructing the awkward and contested formation of land and labor markets in the heavily colonized regions of Africa and Asia. There now exists, for example, a fascinating literature on the transformation of the "cattle complex" in eastern and southern Africa. Here, prior to colonialism, cattle-keeping societies rarely ate these animals or put them to tasks that Westerners considered useful, viewing them rather as an important storehouse of wealth (figure 1). As John and Jean Comaroff (1990) propose in discussing the case of Tshidi Barolong, a Tswana people resident along today's South Africa-Botswana border, cattle also served as metaphors for society—the kind of "total social phenomenon" that interested Mauss. Only men had, and herded, cattle. Through cattle, paid out as bridewealth, they garnered access to women's childbearing and food-producing capacities. Chiefly men, who possessed the largest herds, harnessed spiritual powers by sacrificing cattle to ancestors and making cattle payments to ritual specialists. Finally, men who were rich in cattle gained power, for cattle could be deployed in building up loyal, militarily ready clienteles.

Contradicting this pattern, Christian missionaries of the early contact period promoted concepts of private property in land and cattle; of the retention and investment of wealth; of men farming instead of women; of the complete restructur-

FIGURE I Dinka pastoralists watering their cattle at a trough, Thiet, southern Sudan. (© Adrian Arbib/Survival)

ing of farming practice through the use of cattle for traction; and of the reorientation of agricultural production toward world markets. In the context of these changes, Tshidi men with the largest herds acquired the lion's share of the land, while others were dispossessed. Subsequently, the colonial state imposed a head tax, coercing landless men into migration streams that fed the labor markets of agricultural and mining enterprises in South Africa. Former chiefs, no longer recipients of tribute and fines, became tax collectors instead. Although in a much-diminished position, they at least had a respectable money income and could live at home with their families. Poor men, by contrast, had to leave, remitting their meager wages to their womenfolk, who stayed behind to raise subsistence crops and care for children and old people.

Significantly, the Tshidi continue to reckon transactions that concern enduring social relationships—payments for bridewealth, healing, court-imposed fines, and loans between patrons and clients—in terms of nominal cattle known as "cows without legs," cattle whose value does not fluctuate with the price of an ox in the marketplace but instead reflects the quality of the ties between the exchanging parties. Anthropologist James Ferguson has recorded the frustration of Western development experts in Lesotho upon encountering similar practices in the early 1980s. Not even a worsening drought in those years, and the likelihood that many cattle would die, could compel their sale in the market.

The Lesotho communities studied by Ferguson have retained a concept of property that interdicts marketing livestock except in times of emergency or because of a dire need for food and shelter. To do so under other conditions—to cross what is essentially a "livestock-cash barrier"—is to succumb to utter humiliation. This "bovine mystique," as Ferguson calls it, should not be seen as a stubborn remnant of traditionalism, surviving into the present as if by inertia. Rather, it is part of a wider complex in which 70 percent of household income derives from the remitted wages of emigrant men, working in South Africa's mines and industries. The men, for their part, invest some of their earnings in cattle. Unlike cash, this investment is not subject to the constant demands of wives and children for money—demands that are sometimes intensified by wives' suspicion that husbands dissipate their earnings on beer and other women near the place of work.

Protected from women's demands, cattle constitute a retirement fund for the migrant men. By loaning cows to others of the home community to milk, breed, or otherwise use, they earn prestige and a place for themselves, notwithstanding their long-term absence. And the cattle can be sold in old age if necessary. So important are these considerations that Lesotho men in general, and older men in particular, ideologically reinforce the "bovine mystique," even as women ridicule them for being "old-fashioned."

THE GLOBAL FACTORY

Since the 1970s, industrial production for world markets has spread to every continent, incorporating volumes of new workers, some into factories, others into workshops, still others through work that is done by the piece in their homes. Accelerating the flow of rural-to-urban migration, this change undoes the characterization of former colonies and neocolonial dependencies as predominantly agrarian. The old pattern of uneven development, in which dominated peoples produced primary products for an industrialized metropolitan "core," is substantially broken; industrial commodities are manufactured the world over and can flow from the former colonies, often glossed as the Third World, to the first free market societies as frequently as they flow in the other direction.

Anthropologists have been interested in the provenience and condition of laborers in the various worksites of the global factory: their social and geographical distance from a place of origin, their ethnic mix, their composition with regard to gender and age—how many of them are young and female—and the discipline to which they are subjected at work and home. Under some conditions, wage work is liberating—a breath of fresh air when compared to the servile labor that often accompanies monocrop agriculture. For many young women, earning wages has constituted an opportunity to escape patriarchal surveillance. Best of all, perhaps, wages and piece-rates enable the acquisition of markers of modernity. The spread of the global factory has gone hand-in-hand with the transformation of villages and towns, as cash incomes get poured into new or restructured houses for ordinary folk. Boasting a larger size, previously unheard of building materials, and the wonders of electricity, such dwellings justify to their proud owners the sacrifices of hard work. Motivated to obtain them, workers may respond with enthusiasm to a development-oriented government that promotes the concept of a hard work ethic through the schools and mass media.

At the same time, field research into the local effects of the global factory suggests that many new industrial workers experience the labor market as a terrain of constraint and insecurity, from which they have little relief. A problem that has received particular attention is the situation of young women workers in unregulated export-processing zones such as Ciudad Juárez, just over the Mexican border from the United States. Here wage earners, employed by transnational corporations, far from being liberated or allowed to spend on themselves, remit what they earn to their parents. Anthropological studies have also shown that factory managers mobilize parental authority as reinforcement in disciplining the young women at work.

Transnational corporations pose other problems. Assisted by innovations in communications technology, they operate with an ever-wider reach, at the same time maintaining an anchor in the (frequently Western) home country. Yet they do not necessarily own all of the firms that manufacture the goods they market. An anthropological study of a shoe-producing town in rural Taiwan illustrates how the meanings of work, of marketing, and of consumption—interconnected activities that span the continents—can veer off in directions that have virtually nothing to do with one another. In Taiwan, shoes are cut and stitched for the Nike Corporation by a multiplicity of small, independently owned factories and workshops. Religion is everywhere. A traditional network of interconnected temples crisscrosses the island, offering a ready-made communications grid for contracting and subcontracting arrangements between local and parent firms. New religions are also present: Yiguan Dao, for example, emphasizes cultivating the Dao as a way to ward off the imminent destruction of the world.

Yiguan Dao's daily rituals of bowing and kowtowing mimic the motions of machines, while the urgency of its Armageddon-like message reflects the intensity of work. In the peak seasons of heavy deadlines, the workday runs from 8 A.M. to 9 P.M. on weekdays, with an hour's break for lunch and a half hour's break for dinner, and from 8 to 6 on Saturdays and alternate Sundays. Symbols of modernity broadcast the payoff: bowling alleys and stock brokerages commingle with spirit mediums and rice paddies. Women doing piecework, such as silk-screening logos, sit before modest but modernized houses; entrepreneurs enjoy palatial homes and BMWs. Meanwhile, on the other side of the world, the transnational, Nike, conducts marketing research, designs and redesigns shoes to stay ahead of fashion trends (the average life of a shoe style fell from seven years to ten months between 1971 and 1989), and purchases advertising and promotion. Owning the "swoosh" trademark and distribution system, if not the retail stores, it encourages U.S. consumers to believe that athletic prowess, indeed the cult of athleticism, can be accessed through Nike sneakers.

Whether giant transnationals subcontract with foreign manufacturers or establish foreign plants of their own, a driving motivation is often that of escaping high labor costs and environmental regulations at home. This puts the new industrial locales under pressure to keep wages low and turn a blind eye as aquifers disappear and emissions and effluents foul the air and water. Ian Skoggard, the anthropologist who researched shoe production in Taiwan, notes that the images highlighted in Nike's New York shrine to athletes, with its Fifth Avenue address, Greek columns, and videos of sponsored players and teams, would be tarnished if a consumer campaign were to dwell on the oppressive gender relations that contribute to disciplining the labor of women among its Asian suppliers.

In the past, when peripheral regions were reduced to simplified, agrarian forms of production, being a Third World consumer was not much fun. Colonial merchants foisted shoddy and often inappropriate goods off on people through a "truck system" of company stores. Miners and agricultural workers purchased supplies for home and work in these stores, which were located at or near the work site, and were often forced to take part or all of their wage in kind. The storekeepers, who at first were Europeans, advanced them credit, further tying them in to world markets. More than this, they aggressively pushed items for which there was apparently no demand at the behest of wholesalers higher up in the commodity chain.

By contrast, the world of the global factory is a world of global desire. Truck marketing has disappeared, indigenous merchants and shopkeepers have replaced foreigners in local markets, and distributors are highly attentive to consumer demand. Out of this new situation comes an interesting anthropological debate as to how vulnerable and manipulated these new consumers are. Some anthropologists, evoking the pessimism about consumer culture fostered by the Frankfurt school of social theory at the end of World War II, are convinced that market forces retain the upper hand: clever marketers and advertisers coerce people's labor or docility through unnecessarily multiplying their wants and needs.

There is, however, a strong research tradition within anthropology to the contrary. Goods that embellish the house, adorn the body, and serve as gifts to kin and friends, not to mention goods that ease the tasks of everyday living, both resonate with preexisting cultural values and assist people in the creation of new social identities—new projects for life—appropriate to their participation in the modern world. No matter that these goods are produced by distant powers (some, of course, may be produced locally, given the terms of the global factory); no matter even that advertisers promote them to audiences that have been targeted through marketing research. The point is to discover how buyers use, and construct the meanings of, soaps and perfumes, Nikes and jeans, washing machines and televisions sets, and television advertising itself.

There is much to be learned about these issues from Daniel Miller's (1997) ethnography of Trinidad, where, he claims, capitalism is more taken for granted than in Europe. Miller prefers the term *capitalism* to *markets* because it suggests a phenomenon with political and historical dimensions rather than an abstract force of nature, propelled by its own logic, as in "market forces." Trinidadians, it seems, identify with and feel they have a right to what capitalism is famous for giving the world: reliable, high-quality commodities sold under recognized brands at affordable prices.

The qualities that make one brand more attractive than another are not necessarily self-evident—for example, the preference in Trinidad for Chinese shiny peanuts over American salted peanuts remains a mystery. Yet the distributors of commodities, for the most part Trinidadians of African and Indian as well as European descent, can hardly be said to be manipulating demand. On the contrary, Miller (1997) shows that their advertising and promotional campaigns are to a large extent driven by processes of competition and emulation among themselves. Often it is a matter of waiting to see which among a number of competing firms takes the lead in investing in some innovation or other, perhaps an innovation deriving from a U.S. or European trade show. Miller's most developed examples come from the manufacturers and distributors of soft drinks (called sweet drinks), whose flavors, packaging, and labels have proliferated to such a degree under this kind of competitive pressure as to create confusion for those who must load the trucks and stock the shelves. In the fray, foreign brands like Canada Dry and Coca-Cola, made locally under franchise, do extremely well, especially as mixers for rum. (One is reminded of William Roseberry's description of coffee entrepreneurs of the 1980s competing to develop the gourmet coffee market in the United States: every so often one of a multitude of uncharted experiments worked.)

It should finally be noted that commodities manufactured in the First World do not necessarily rob Third World consumers of the autonomy and the joy of producing cultural artifacts of their own. Industrially manufactured yarns have been shown to be a tremendous boon to handloom weavers, enabling them to concentrate their energies on the more artistic and interesting aspects of the textile craft. Chemical dyestuffs are tremendously attractive to dyers who must otherwise labor intensely for decades to get good reds from natural dyes, always, from their point of view, coming up short. By the same token, and in tune with Dick Hebdige's (1979) analysis of punk style in late-twentieth-century London, anthropologists appreciate that people can deploy consumer goods in shocking, theatrical ways to resist consumerism. They reject, in other words, the facile assumption that runaway shopping and purchasing mean a homogenization (or Americanization) of diverse cultural practices or the erosion of cultural creativity altogether. And yet, a few anthropologists have warned of going too far in the direction of celebrating consumers for their capacity to fashion something of their own definition from the goods they buy. For millions of people worldwide, the need and desire for consumer goods seals their participation in labor markets, even at the cost of long-distance migration, the separation of families, and the sense of earning less— for women, far less—than one's worth.

FINANCIAL MARKETS AND STRUCTURAL ADJUSTMENT

The emergence of the global factory both gained from and further encouraged the worldwide liberalization of finance, which dates to the economic downturn of the United States in the late 1960s and early 1970s as Japan, Germany, and the oil-producing countries challenged its dominant position. Out of the resulting crisis came a negotiated end to the post–World War II Bretton Woods monetary system. The Bretton Woods Accords defined economies as national; the movement of money in and out of them was necessarily subject to national controls. In modifying the Accords, a contrary argument was made that if nation-states deregulated money flows and freed up markets from what are called "distortions"—namely, state subsidies and monopolies, price controls, and restrictions on imports—then investment capital would gravitate toward less-developed regions where returns on labor are greater, stimulating these regions toward fuller development with benefits for the whole. In the imagined world that would thus be created, commodities would be produced wherever the conditions for producing them were optimal, with tremendous leaps in manufacturing efficiency and the multiplication of wealth through worldwide trade.

Miller characterizes this vision of the future as "pure capitalism"—a concept that he contrasts with the "organic capitalism" practiced in a place like Trinidad, where firms, including transnational firms, are part of a regional institutional trajectory whose norms and precedents have accumulated over time. The choice of the word "pure" evokes the principles of free market culture outlined at the beginning of this essay, but directs our attention to specific institutions that distill the logic of markets, abstracted from any regional or historical context, and promote the resulting model with missionary zeal. Key examples of promotional institutions are major U.S. schools of business and finance, the central banks and treasury departments of the first industrialized countries, Wall Street firms, and the heavily American-influenced International Monetary Fund, World Bank, and International Financial Corporation, a World Bank subsidiary. In Miller's view, these source-points of "pure capitalism" have played an ideological role in history no less potent than that played by various Communist Parties, whose leaders believed they could shape diverse social realities into conformity with a utopian ideal. If anything, the late 1980s collapse of Communism and its associated command economies has vastly enlarged the terrain in which the free market gospel can be preached.

As liberalization advanced over the 1980s and 1990s, governments around the world created fledgling stock markets in the hope of supplementing bank-based systems of investment and avidly set out to attract private foreign capital, promising its unfettered entry and exit. In glossy brochures, they advertised minimal regulation, tax benefits, low wages, labor peace, free-floating national currencies, extravagantly modern "world trade centers," and gorgeous hotels and beaches— each a bargaining chip in the competitive courtship dance for major money. Meanwhile, in the capital-rich locations, institutional investors like mutual funds with decidedly short-term investment horizons multiplied, as did a series of innovations in financial instruments modeled on commodities futures. Enhanced through information-age technology, these instruments allow transnational investors to speculate on currency spreads, interest rate movements, bond prices, and various swaps and options, in the hopes of hedging their other operations in a world of unhinged values. Significantly, public discourse ceased referring to Europe's former colonies and dependencies as "underdeveloped" or "developing" countries. The new language, invented by officials at the International Finance Corporation in the mid-1980s, is "emerging markets." As the shift implies, world financial markets are not merely about allocating resources for the old, quasi-political goal of development. Speculative profit-seeking activity, encouraged by governments' abdication of the power to regulate, has multiplied astronomically, and with it the danger of downturns becoming crashes.

Although it is too soon for there to be much anthropological writing on this startling new moment in the history of world markets, we can anticipate contributions that follow in the footsteps of research done in Latin America during the 1980s; for that continent, if for somewhat different reasons, offered a preview of the instability of today. As is well known, the first phase of financial liberalization after the oil crisis of 1973–74 saw U.S. banks embark on a lending boom to Asian, African, and above all, Latin American countries—a boom that was already unraveling by 1981. Unable to sustain confidence that the loans and investments would be repaid, the affected governments undertook programs of "structural adjustment," which the IMF mandated as a quid pro quo for negotiating more realistic terms. The main features of the adjustment were to raise interest rates so as to staunch capital flight, reorient production around exports, and drastically cut government services and programs as a step toward lowering the public deficit. State-owned industries were either closed down or privatized; agricultural and industrial enterprises found it difficult to borrow. And, in an unhappy coincidence, millions of people lost both their jobs and the possibility of government-funded "safety net" assistance.

Thrown back on their communities and families, or thrown out into the swelling streams of migrants, these dispossessed people—industrial laborers as well as peasants—caught the attention of ethnographers who charted their course. June Nash's (1994) comparison of Mayan farmers in the highlands of Chiapas, Mexico, with tin miners in Bolivia (figure 2) is exemplary, both because of her long-term familiarity with these two situations dating to the 1960s, and because she also studied the surprisingly parallel instance of laid-off General Electric workers in Pittsfield, Massachusetts. Her writings tell of the intensification of subsistence economies among people who had long depended on the market for most of their daily provisioning. In Bolivia, wives had traditionally kept vegetable gardens and raised guinea pigs for protein, but now they also undertook lengthy trips to visit kinfolk in the rich farming hinterland of Cochabamba. In Pittsfield, men turned to hunting for wild turkey and pheasant, and to fishing, only to discover that encroaching urban sprawl and industrial pollution had jeopardized these resources. Another quite predictable response was intensified out-migration: more highland Mayan men left for the lowland coffee plantations than had been the case before; many Pittsfield families pulled up stakes and scattered. When the Bolivian government closed the tin mines in 1986, thousands of miners departed for the coca-producing areas near the border with Brazil or for Brazil and Argentina.

At first, the tin miners did not take off. Together with their families and sympathetic schoolteachers, they mobilized a "March for Life," and, when that was repressed by government troops, they staged a hunger strike. In Pittsfield, by contrast, neither union nor community generated a collective response. Nash pro-

FIGURE 2 Miners eat breakfast before going down the tin mines high above the town of Llallagua, Bolivia. (Paul Smith/Panos)

poses that these differences reflect contrasts in what Miller would call "organic capitalisms"—the specific regional histories of past engagements with the market. For the highland Maya, Nash's third case, these past engagements involved, on the one hand, male out-migration to coffee plantations and, on the other hand, an inward-turning pattern of conflict in the home communities. Between her first visit in 1957 and 1980, villagers acquired electricity, paved streets, and cement block houses with television aerials on them. In the same period, they lost their sense of control over local ancestral spirits whom they believed had abandoned them to take up residence in a non-Indian town. They also started to level accusations of witchcraft against innovative leaders and entrepreneurs, especially those who did not make generous contributions to the local fiesta cycle. This inward-turning mode of coping with anxiety about change carried over into the 1980s when, as a consequence of debt restructuring, the costs for transport, fertilizer, and credit doubled. Different from the Bolivian tin miners, who directed their anger outward, at state officials, and from Pittsfield's passive unemployed, the Mayan highlanders became embroiled in a rising rate of intracommunity violence. Traditional local authorities, heavily identified with folk-Catholicism, expelled younger men and women, many of whom professed attraction to reform Catholic and Protestant religious movements.

The IMF missionaries of "pure capitalism" present the steps of structural adjustment as a necessary "strong medicine" which, if followed as prescribed, can restore a country's ability to attract investment capital. But in cases where excessive debt is traceable to instability in the economic environment—for example the post-boom collapse of world prices for a strategic export like oil or tin—governments must immediately scramble to find alternative sources of livelihood for their people, or watch them embark on the dangerous path of seeking illegal entry into First World countries. A well-worn alternative in desperate times is the artisan production of indigenous arts and crafts (weavings, embroideries, batiks, carpets, woodcarvings, ironwork, and ceramics), which not only garner income, but also confer pride and prestige. How reliable such production can be in a worldwide context of structural adjustment is another matter, however. Anthropological research points to the challenges of gaining and maintaining a competitive edge.

One issue is how the distribution system is organized. A study of weavings from Oaxaca, Mexico, traces government programs encouraging their manufacture back to the 1940s, when the opening of the Pan-American Highway first brought tourists to the region. In certain designated towns, local merchants began putting out materials to weaving households with whom they had a godparent relation, and in which family labor could be exploited. The strongest merchants were those who had accumulated startup capital during earlier bouts of migration to the United States and who benefited, as well, from U.S. commercial contacts. Then came the 1980s debt crisis and the drastic devaluation of the peso. In this context, U.S. importers flooded into Mexico, advantaged by cheap airfares, hotels, rented cars, and interpreters. The Oaxacan merchants lost ground to these interlopers just as the differential between wholesale and retail prices approached 1,000 times. The Oaxacan weavers lost, too. Whereas the local merchants had recycled their profits into the fiesta system and community public works, the interlopers felt no compulsion to distribute their earnings in Oaxacan weaving towns.

American intermediaries of Oaxacan textiles, wedded to the pure capitalist principle that commodities should be made wherever it is cheapest to make them, tried to get the Oaxacan weavers to incorporate "Oriental" carpet motifs into their designs, just as they had given weavers in India Zapotec motifs to copy. Interestingly, these projects met resistance, for although the resulting textiles might have retained their exotic, handcrafted appearance, the artisans worried that an "inauthentic" product would lose market share.

Anthropologists writing on arts and crafts point out that the word *authenticity* means different things to different people. Governments promoting "commercial" or "tourist" arts, and exporters seeking to market them, often go to great lengths to depict these commodities as faithful to an unchanging, ancestral tradition, laden with cultural meaning. This is because the ultimate consumers, perhaps out of nostalgia for pasts that never were, want to be reassured that what they are buying is "real," not spurious or fake. Indeed, highly educated tourists and collectors covet objects that were not only originally made for "the natives," but used by them as well. Yet this does not mean that arts and crafts defined as "authentic" by those who market and consume them are in fact all that old or unchanged. Art and craft producers have long modified their wares to fit with First World lifestyles, transforming, let us say, indigenous blouses and shawls into alien place mats and pillow covers. More to the point, many apparently "authentic" crafts originated during the first colonial contact, or as "trinkets" to appeal to the earliest tourists and collectors. One can argue, in fact, that all art and craft traditions are hybrids of multicultural interactions and that all of them change through time. Yet if "native" craftsmen and artists are unable to define and maintain a discrete ethnic identity, they risk losing out to more efficient, if "inauthentic," competitors. Hence the recent plea of Inuit carvers to the Canadian government that soapstone sculptures, a relatively new tourist art, are "theirs"; whites and other outsiders should not be carving them (figure 3). In their case, as in countless others, the viability of art and craft production will ultimately rest on the ("distorting") intervention of governmental and nongovernmental (NGO) support.

FIGURE 3 Inuit sculptor, northern Quebec, Canada, 1991. (© Pietro Jovane/Survival)

Tourism is closely intertwined with art and craft manufacture as a moneymaking activity to fall back on or cultivate when the economic order is in disarray. Tourist markets, including "ecotourism" or the marketing of nature, are in some ways the reciprocal of migration, bringing First World people to Third World places, hopefully to boost, not destroy, the local economy. Migrant flows and tourist flows interact in complex ways. A by now well-documented trajectory is that of immigrants not merely remitting wages to family members in the home country, but saving and investing in home-country businesses related to tourist development—hotels, restaurants, guest houses, even street peddling stands. Here, too, competition is daunting, whether from better capitalized international players, from other tourist destinations, or from the inherent contradiction of the tourist industry itself, which is that the more a place attracts visitors, the fewer visitors will eventually want to go there.

And still, the arts and crafts and tourist options seem so much healthier than other alternatives that have been seized upon in recent years by people dispossessed of their livelihood—in particular, narcotics production and trafficking, and the tragic commerce in sex work. In the case of the latter, rural families make ends meet in part through the remitted earnings of one or more daughters, deployed through networks of kin in a city of the same nation or abroad and at risk of contracting the HIV infection.

Meanwhile, recovery through agriculture or industry has been rendered more challenging by some very recent First World developments: bioengineering applied to crops and animals, with the result of vastly increasing agricultural productivity; and the growing presence of truly cheap labor in the form of new immigrants. The latter constitute a wellspring of servants and errand boys in support of the gentrification of professional and managerial elites, and a highly exploitable labor pool for go-getting, immigrant-owned businesses. Among the latter are the infamous sweatshops that signal the return of clothing manufacturing from cheaper locales "off-shore."

Not surprisingly, the anthropological literature offers two quite different perspectives on the renewed assertion of "pure capitalism" in these First World settings. In one, illustrated by Igor Kopytoff's well-known essay, "The Cultural Biography of Things" (1986), market forces are characterized as acultural—as an inexorable march toward ever greater calculation and abstraction in human affairs, facilitated by ever-expanding technological upgrades in the instruments of exchange. At the same time, even in the United States, the most highly commercialized, monetized society on earth, this march, or drive, is held to be counteracted by localized cultural values. Culturally sensitized individuals and groups at times erect barriers to the circulation of commodities, for example, by boycotting goods deemed to have been produced under morally reprehensible conditions. As the word "biography" implies, there is another, more everyday respect in which culture confronts economism. Things, the argument goes, move in and out of commodity status as people redefine their meaning, conferring on them "biographies" that change through time.

Charting a different course, Roger Rouse (1995) suggests that in the United States, the market has *become* the culture. Over the last two decades, the champions of free markets in corporations, advertising firms, and the media have fostered a broad consensus around an ethos of buying and selling, investing and borrowing, shopping and consuming, and around the idea of consumption as a measure of self-worth. Thanks to their hegemony—to their propagation of this ethos through entertainment, persuasion, and the evocation of desire—it is now totally normal for young people to acquire credit cards as a rite of passage. That billboards have invaded more public spaces; that stores are open around the clock; that stock market quotations fill the airwaves; and that prisons are entrusted to franchises are but a few indications of the extent to which commercial values are taken for granted and embedded in everyday life.

TOWARD THE FUTURE

A possible conclusion from this review is that, while the myriad organic capitalisms of the world might be credited with raising standards of living, and enabling the assumption of a modern identity, in many countries the destabilizing consequences of the push to "purify" these capitalisms and compel their conformity with free market culture has wreaked a kind of counterproductive havoc. In light of this, many anthropologists are tempted to "relativize" this culture, to make it strange. Perhaps its strangest feature is a moral one. For beyond celebrating rational-choice behavior as a human universal, and beyond defining markets as the source of all progress, the dispositions, values, and practices of pure capitalism imply a moral economy of good and bad. The good are those who by investing in a resource make it more efficient and productive to the benefit of all; the bad, or potentially bad, are those who interfere with this process. Because investment is inherently destabilizing as well as enhancing, however, not least because it may be followed by disinvestment, this moral economy must go to some lengths to represent the victims of destabilization as merely transitory casualties of change. Disparaged as free-riders or "cronyistic" if they band together to impede progress, such persons are otherwise expected to accept the argument that their society will eventually recover and they will be reabsorbed. Implied is a shallow, exonerative understanding of what dislocation means to families and communities, especially in places that will not easily regain their economic health.

From an anthropological perspective, discourses on the assumed temporariness of market dislocations and the incipient moral or political indictment of those who would protest are interesting for having developed earlier in England than in other places in the West, and for being most forcefully articulated in English and Anglo-American variants of capitalism. Perhaps—an anthropologist might imagine—this radical instance of market culture grew out of the history of English agriculture, in which moves toward the privatization of property were already evident in the Middle Ages, well before the eighteenth-century Enclosure Acts that so troubled Polanyi, and in contrast with medieval agriculture in, for example, France. However it was first established, the "pure" variant of capitalism surely gained support from the English state and from English successes with industrial technology, colonialism, and imperialism—successes that Anglo-Americans built upon in the twentieth century. In the 1980s, the governments of Ronald Reagan in the United States and Margaret Thatcher in England renewed the premises of a moral economy that would purge itself of sentimentalism—the disparaging word for an undue concern with those whose lives are disrupted by market forces. This purging set the stage for the promotion of financial liberalization worldwide.

And this brings us to a final arena of anthropological reflection on the future direction of world markets. If free market culture in its most radical and demanding form indeed had particular historical roots, so that it is experienced by many as alien and in need of modulation, will it forever be the case that the terms of this culture shape the world's most powerful and well-capitalized international institutions? Or, in a context of capital flight and chain-linked global recession, might other values and practices, alternative understandings and discourses, come to the fore, not only within individual states, but also in wider, transnational networks?

Anthropologists typically seek to recognize and question Eurocentric imaginings of the world. The argument recently put forth by Andre Gunder Frank in his provocative book, *ReOrient* (1998), that until the late eighteenth century the Chinese people were more productive and "developed" than Europeans, is one they are prepared to seriously consider. Were China to become a world power again, would its cultural values and practices influence the worldwide values and practices of capitalism? Anthropologists now working in China have proposed that personalized Chinese relations of kinship, friendship, and patronage, known as *guanxi*, have actually facilitated, not sapped, the efficiency of light industrial manufacturing firms, nominally still owned by villages and towns. Perhaps firms of this type will outlive the current pressures for structural adjustment to serve as a future challenge to "pure capitalism" which, despite the chaos that it is known to be capable of creating, is hegemonic today.

SUGGESTIONS FOR FURTHER READING

Blim, Michael. 1997. "Can Not-Capitalism Lie at the End of History, or Is Capitalism's History Drawing to an End?" *Critique of Anthropology* 17, no. 4: 351–63.

Burke, Timothy. 1996. *Lifebuoy Men, Lux Women: Commodification, Consumption, and Cleanliness in Modern Zimbabwe.* Durham, NC: Duke University Press.

Comaroff, Jean, and John L. Comaroff. 1990. "Goodly Beasts, Beastly Goods: Cattle and Commodities in a South African Context." *American Ethnologist* 17, no. 2: 195–217.

Ferguson, James. 1994. *The Anti-Politics Machine: "Development," Depoliticization, and Bureaucratic Power in Lesotho.* Minneapolis: University of Minnesota Press.

Frank, Andre Gunder. 1998. *ReOrient: Global Economy in the Asian Age.* Berkeley and Los Angeles: University of California Press.

Graburn, Nelson H. H. 1999. "Ethnic and Tourist Arts Revisited" In *Unpacking Culture: Art and Commodity in Colonial and Postcolonial Worlds*, ed. Ruth B. Phillips and Christopher B. Steiner, 335–53. Berkeley and Los Angeles: University of California Press.

Hebdige, Dick. 1979. *Subculture: The Meaning of Style.* London: Methuen.

Kopytoff, Igor. 1986. "The Cultural Biography of Things." In *The Social Life of Things: Commodities in Cultural Perspective*, ed. Arjun Appadurai, 64–95. Cambridge: Cambridge University Press.

Miller, Daniel. 1997. *Capitalism: An Ethnographic Approach.* Oxford: Berg.

Nash, June. 1994. "Global Integration and Subsistence Insecurity," *American Anthropologist* 96, no. 1: 7–31.

Ong, Aiwah. 1987. *Spirits of Resistance and Capitalist Discipline: Factory Women in Malaysia.* Albany: State University of New York Press.

Pardo, Italo. 1996. *Managing Existence in Naples.* Cambridge and New York: Cambridge University Press.

Roseberry, William. 1996. "The Rise of Yuppie Coffees and the Reimagination of Class in the United States." *American Anthropologist* 98, no. 4: 762–76.

Rothstein, Frances Abrahamer, and Michael L. Blim, eds. 1992. *Anthropology and the Global Factory: Studies of the New Industrialization in the Late Twentieth Century.* New York: Bergin and Garvey.

Rouse, Roger. 1995. "Thinking through Transnationalism: Notes on the Cultural Politics of Class Relations in the Contemporary United States," *Public Culture* 7: 535–602.

Schiller, Nina Glick; Linda Basch; and Cristina Blanc-Szanton, eds. 1992. *Toward a Transnational Perspective on Migration: Race, Class, Ethnicity, and Nationalism Reconsidered.* Annals of the New York Academy of Sciences, vol. 645. New York: New York Academy of Sciences.

Schneider, Jane. 1978. "Peacocks and Penguins: the Political Economy of European Cloth and Colors." *American Ethnologist* 5, no. 4: 413–37.

Skoggard, Ian. 1998. "Transnational Commodity Flows and the Global Phenomenon of the Brand." In *Consuming Fashion: Adorning the Transnational Body*, ed. Anne Brydon and Sandra Niessen, 57–71. Oxford: Berg.

Smart, Allen. 1997. "Oriental Despotism and Sugar-Coated Bullets: Representations of the Market in China." In *Meanings of the Market: the Free Market in Western Culture*, ed. James G. Carrier, 159–95. Oxford: Berg.

Stephen, Lynn. 1993. "Weaving in the Fast Lane: Class, Ethnicity, and Gender in Zapotec Craft Commercialization." In *Crafts in the World Market: the Impact of Global Exchange on Middle American Artisans*, ed. June Nash, 25–59. Albany: State University of New York Press.

Wolf, Eric R. 1969. *Peasant Wars of the Twentieth Century*. New York: Harper and Row.

4.

Political Ideologies: Socialism and Its Discontents

Why do we have to have rich and poor? Why? Why can't everybody have a little bit? What's wrong with that? That motherfucking Gorbachov is to blame for this mess.
Bulgarian villager in 1992

CHRIS HANN

When the American anthropologist Gerald Creed began his research in Bulgaria in the mid-1980s, Comrade Todor Zhivkov had held power unchallenged for more than thirty years, and the Balkan states seemed as stable as other socialist regimes in the vast region known as the Soviet bloc or the Second World. Creed investigated transformations at village level. There were good economic as well as ideological reasons for bringing peasants together to form larger farming units, but collectivization was imposed crudely from above and was therefore unwelcome to villagers. As elsewhere in Eurasia, it obliterated earlier forms of cooperation and created new structures of bureaucratic and political power.

Creed goes on to tell a more complex and less familiar tale of how these same villagers accomplished a further revolution in the following decades. They "domesticated" socialism through their everyday activities, focused on personal plots and family contracting. Collective farm ideology was progressively modified, and the villagers reaped the material benefits. Creed was able to revisit "his" village after the momentous political changes of 1989–90 and to hear local people discuss the respective merits of socialism and capitalism. Opinions differed, as they do in most human groups, but the majority held a positive view of socialism. They wanted to retain the security and relative equality that socialist policies had brought them. Villagers who were critical of socialism while it lasted nonetheless identified strongly not only with its ideals as they understood them (primarily in terms of equality) but also with the actual accomplishments of decades of socialist rule. Some Western observers have seen this as testimony to the continued force of socialist ideology, long after the demise of one-party rule.

I begin with this concrete example because I suggest that this is the hallmark of an anthropological approach to political ideology in the sense treated here. Ideology can be studied in any human community (for some "traditional" cases, see Bloch 1989; Wolf 1999). It is arguably most effective when it merges into the realms we call religion, cosmology, or even "culture," and is hard to disentangle from them. However, certain forms of the modern state have developed new techniques to mobilize their populations through public rituals and to inculcate specific doctrines through their control over education and the mass media. Fascism and many varieties of nationalism conform to this pattern, but the paradigmatic case remains Marxist-Leninist socialism.

Many books have been written about socialism by philosophers, political theorists, and other intellectuals. There are fewer accounts of what socialism has meant in practice. Most of the literature falls into one of four categories. In the socialist countries themselves, the ideology was reproduced through endless propaganda texts, including hagiographies of the founding fathers and contemporary leaders. In the nonsocialist countries academic studies tended to give socialism a bad press: political scientists applied concepts such as totalitarianism, and economists had little trouble in proving that centrally planned economies would never work. Third, there was a charitably disposed Western left, but this orientation, too, largely overlooked actual conditions in the socialist countries. Fourth, dissident movements and their successors were good at attracting Western attention, but not always successful in representing the views and aspirations of ordinary consumers of socialist ideology. Consequently the images that most Westerners held of socialism were a mixture of journalistic caricature and myth. In contrast, anthropological fieldwork offers a means of understanding how socialist ideology interacted with distinctive local traditions to shape human lives.

The term *ideology* is of relatively recent origin and has been adapted in different ways by different academic disciplines (see Eagleton 1991; McClellan 1995). Marx and Engels themselves made important contributions to the theory of ideology, but this chapter cannot enter into those intellectual debates. Instead, proceeding from the most common popular understanding that an ideology is a body of political doctrines pertaining to the organization of society in some fundamental sense, I shall first outline some of the basic ways in which ideologies were promoted under socialism. Extreme models of Marxism-Leninism aimed at nothing less than the creation of a new belief system, a new, future-oriented world view for new people. Other models of socialism, however, paid more attention to the past—for example, to the evocation of traditions of social harmony in an age when modern markets did not yet threaten. Whichever cases one looks at, we are less interested in the doctrinal discussions of political elites than in the interactive processes that accompanied the dissemination of the ideology in society. We shall therefore explore encounters between the universalizing and homogenizing tendencies of ideologists, and the localizing tendencies motivating other social actors; sometimes these encounters were conducive to realizing the goals of the ideology, but often they were subversive of it.

In contrast to the assertion of Marx and Engels (in *The German Ideology*, 1845–46) that the "ideas of the ruling class are in every epoch the ruling ideas," anthropologists often find that elite ideas are questioned and resisted (see Scott 1990). Though usually very simple in design, ideologies are always open to complex and contested interpretations. A modern political doctrine is most likely to succeed when it meshes well with long-established cultural ideas and practices. It is not difficult to present socialist ideology in this form, since the core ideas of equality and mutuality are very widely distributed in human communities. This resonance is the key to understanding how an ideology with very specific origins in Europe in the early phase of industrialization could later be adapted, at least superficially, in virtually every part of the world. This also suggests that the recent collapse of socialist ideologies must be distinguished from the continued vitality of the ideals and values on which the ideologies were based. Gerald Creed (1998) shows that socialism in Bulgaria has a "robust history." Postsocialist governments often pursued more dogmatic ("ideological") versions of capitalist society than Westerners themselves possessed or would uphold as their ideal. Hence, it is unsurprising that many recent studies (e.g., Bridger and Pine 1998) report that the core ideas of socialism are being reasserted by millions of citizens as angry as the Bulgarian villager quoted above.

SOCIALISM AS AN IDEOLOGY

More than one hundred and fifty years have passed since Marx and Engels in the *Communist Manifesto* urged the workers of the world to unite. They offered a comprehensive philosophy of history, focused on the emergence and development of capitalism but engaging with earlier periods and, since they were committed revolutionaries, with the future as well. Their successes in the industrialized countries of Western Europe were limited. In Russia, however, the Bolshevik Party, playing the vanguard role theorized explicitly by Lenin, was able to seize power in dramatic circumstances in 1917. Marxism-Leninism became the political ideology according to which the Soviet Union and its allies organized their societies until the sudden collapse of the bloc more than seventy years later.

This ideology was imposed by elites who rejected the bourgeois institutions of party political competition and freedom of association. Power was concentrated in the state, or rather in the ruling Communist Party. But how was this power to be exercised and justified? The personalizing of power in the hands of old men and the capriciousness of its exercise were sources of weakness rather than strength. In the early phases of socialism, this was accompanied by much political violence; in later phases, by the stench of political corruption.

Given these features, questions of moral justification became imperative. While Western democracies decentralize power through the market and through regular contested elections, socialist states had to develop alternative forms of legitimation. The quasi-religious elaboration of Marxism-Leninism as a political ideology was an attempt to meet this need. It is much more than a body of political doctrine. It forms part of a system of cultural symbols that provides images, often highly idealized, not only of the organization of society but of the very nature of human beings and the scheme of the universe.

How is this ideology disseminated? First, ideological language tends to differ from everyday speech. It is often formulaic, based on a few central slogans, though initiates may obtain greater access. Ideological oratory is frequently incomprehensible to many of those obliged to listen to it. In this respect the language of Marxism-Leninism resembles the formal language of powerholders in many "traditional" societies (see Bloch 1989). Much in its repertoire was drawn from the works of the founding fathers. Concepts such as Lenin's "democratic centralism" were presented as science but taught with the old methods of the catechism. Selected texts were available in lavish complete editions. They might even decorate the living quarters of farmworkers (where it was just as well that few were capable of reading them, since they might have drawn the wrong conclusions from comments such as those of Marx on "the idiocy of rural life"). Ideological language was constantly monitored. On occasion new terms had to be introduced: the language of armed struggle eventually gave way to the language of "peaceful coexistence." But the shift away from ideological language that marked the years of *glasnost* and *perestroika* led swiftly to the collapse of the entire edifice.

Secondly, ideologies are disseminated through many kinds of rituals and symbols. Lenin was a rationalist and an atheist who would doubtless have deplored the construction of his Mausoleum in Red Square and the deliberate fostering of a cult with distinct overtones of more conventional religious cults. But he was also a hard-nosed politician, and there is little doubt that his cult, together with the widespread adoption of new symbols such as the hammer and sickle and the construction of a new ritual calendar, had long-term political payoffs in the Soviet Union. These innovations helped ordinary people to make sense of their social order. People learned that they had a system of which they could be proud. Whatever economic or political difficulties they might face, at some deeper level they had the consolation that they were morally superior to the degenerate imperialists of the West. In the Soviet case ritual creativity was extended from the public sphere of flags and Mayday parades to encroach deep inside the private sphere of life-cycle rituals, including name-giving ceremonies and funerals (see Lane 1981).

Throughout Eurasia there was remarkable uniformity in the symbols used by powerholders to justify the rule of the working classes. From Peking to Prague, the same photographs of Marx and Lenin were carried in the same sort of parades, and the same quotations from the *Communist Manifesto* appeared on the front page of the party newspaper. Similar techniques and inventions have been successfully deployed in other parts of the world. In Hanoi and Havana the similarities to the original Soviet model remained strong; indeed they outlived the original. Elsewhere, socialism is often more variable and elusive. The *Green Book* of Libya's Colonel Qaddafi is quite different from the *Red Book* of Chairman Mao, and different also from other models of socialism in the Islamic world. Postcolonial states such as Tanzania and Zimbabwe have been attracted by the emancipatory rhetoric of socialism, but it is difficult to generalize within such a broad category. The most common unifying elements are a rejection of certain "Western" institutions, including free markets and party political competition, and a concomitant assertion of indigenous alternatives. It is not, however, self-evident that socialism, especially when it is presented by Western-educated leaders, is any more in tune with indigenous ways (see Hann 1993).

COMPLEX RECEPTIONS

How successful were the social engineers of Marxism-Leninism? There is no easy answer, any more than there is an easy answer to questions about the strength of religious belief in modern societies. Some people, from diverse social groups, became very devout believers in the socialist church. Some became radical opponents. The great majority were somewhere in between. This is reflected in the fate of socialism's invented rituals, some of which were more successful than others. Many people in Eastern Europe had little difficulty in adapting to secular, socialist weddings, though some preferred to combine the secular ceremony with a traditional church service; this option was not open to some people who worked for the state, and this could create social tensions. However an entirely secular funeral presented greater problems. In the Hungarian village where I did fieldwork in the 1970s, the Communist Party secretary admitted to feeling uncomfortable when carrying out this ritual. He was seldom called upon to do so. Yet secular funerals became entirely normal in much of Bulgaria.

The public socialist rituals of the old Eastern Europe seem to have been most successful when grafted on to other, nonsocialist elements. Despite the internationalism of the founding fathers, the most powerful such elements were those related to the nation and to nationalism. For example, USSR rituals which commemorated the sacrifices made for the Fatherland in the Great Patriotic War undoubtedly struck deep chords throughout society because they managed to link the larger solidarities of nation and state to personal and familial meanings.

I found very mixed responses to socialist ideology in my comparative work in Hungary and Poland between 1975 and 1982. By this time more and more people were judging their system by its own ideals and finding it to be deficient. The core moral values of socialism were usually tied by ordinary people to a high degree of social equality (even though this feature was seldom highlighted in the official ideological publications). Faced with increasing corruption and a failure to maintain the rising living standards and the social mobility which characterized most socialist countries in their early decades, many people began to lose whatever faith they had had. The interminable speeches at the Party Congresses were boring: people preferred to watch other things, usually Western, on their newly acquired televisions.

Relatively few people formulated explicit challenges to Marxism-Leninism. While the number of "true believers" was declining, there remained enough diverse elements in the ideology for most people to be able to select some that they found attractive. Socialism succeeded in developing a body of diverse ideas which had something to offer to most social groups. For example, young people could value the emphasis on sport and outdoor training, while ignoring more obviously political messages. Intellectuals and artists profited from the encouragement given by socialist regimes to many branches of the arts. People in all walks of life showed a measure of critical detachment from their regime in everyday life, without necessarily calling its ideals into question. For example, they told jokes that turned on central political dogmas of the ideology (e.g., What is the definition of capitalist society? Capitalist society is based on the exploitation of man by his fellow man! And what is the definition of socialist society? Under socialism it is precisely the other way around!).

In only a few cases was there a more comprehensive rejection—for example, among churches and sects that were the objects of persecution. Gypsies frequently resisted socialist efforts (even when well-intentioned) to turn them into disciplined factory workers, because this was so antagonistic to their traditional values and culture. But these were the exceptions: in general socialism was not so explicitly rejected. Even those with an unambiguous aversion to the political dogmas were not immune to the influence of socialist values. How could they have been, given the conditions in which they lived, the air that they breathed?

Beneath the superficial uniformity of Eurasian socialism, Marxism-Leninism was everywhere refracted by specific cultural and institutional factors. Hungary and Poland are neighbors in east-central Europe, and their political and cultural traditions have many common features. Yet by the 1970s the differences seemed more striking than the similarities. In Hungary, the legitimating role of ideology declined following the introduction of the "new economic mechanism." One anthropologist was told definitively that "there was no role for socialist ideology in Hungarian society" (Lampland 1995, 245). Instead, greater emphasis was placed on individualism and economic opportunities, as in most capitalist countries. The party secretary I mentioned above was by training an agronomist, but he was not employed in the socialist sector of the cooperative. His job was to help its members maximize their private production, for the benefit of the national economy. He rationalized this as a pragmatic adaptation of traditional socialist policies toward agriculture. After all, collectivization was not mentioned by the founding fathers, so there was no need to be too rigid in repressing private farmers. Hungary remained a one-party system, but the market-oriented modifications were generally welcomed, and the regime was stable.

In Poland no such pragmatic adaptations proved possible. Collectivization was never fully implemented, though the peasantry remained suspicious of regime intentions. The Communist Party leaders were afraid to experiment with "market socialism" and continued to dominate the media. Economic hardships were caused at least in part by ideological rigidity, and the population became far more disaffected from powerholders than was the case in Hungary. Opposition was regularly mobilized by a powerful institution with deep historical roots among the people, which socialist ideology in Poland simply could not contain: the Roman

FIGURE 1 Hungarian farmer. (Mikkel Ostergaard/Panos)

Catholic Church. An image of the Black Madonna of Czestochowa usually adorned the lapel of workers' leader Lech Walesa, and she was a much more potent symbol than any that the socialists could devise.

If neighboring socialist countries in Central Europe could develop in such different directions, what can we say about the export of socialist ideology to other parts of the world? One fruitful approach is to consider how socialist ideas connect with other elements in the culture. For example, when socialism came to a country such as Laos, it necessarily became entangled with the specific cultural traditions of Buddhism, including ideas about personal "merit making." The constraints of this well-established religious ideology made it extremely difficult for the peasantry to accept a collective basis for the organization of agriculture. However, there were fewer constraints to inhibit relatively smooth adaptations to collectivization in the case of Russian peasants or Siberian reindeer herders. These groups have experienced severe problems since the collapse of socialism, since they had little precedent for the concepts of private ownership and entrepreneurship on which their survival has come to depend.

Often the appeal made by socialist leaders to the collectivist traditions of the people is romantic and simplistic if not just plain false and self-serving. In Tanzania, for example, elite efforts to construct a distinctive African socialism were not notably successful, especially when they implied, as in *ujamaa* villages, a tradition of working the land on a communal basis. The reality, here as in most agricultural societies, is that while land was in some sense under collective ownership, it was very seldom *worked* communally. While certain activities often required labor cooperation, most plots were the responsibility of just one household. Socialist policies that overlooked such complexity were likely to provoke resistance. In East Africa and elsewhere, field studies have shown that, behind a rhetoric of socialist equality, earlier power structures often remained intact, or, alternatively, a "new class" of literate officials became dominant.

Perhaps the clearest illustration of both the ambitions and the limitations of socialism as a modernizing ideology is in the field of gender relations. Many versions of socialism have asserted the desirability of full gender equality, even though Marx himself had little to say on the subject. Realities have been very different. In China, for example, Chairman Mao proclaimed that women held up half the sky. While he was in power women certainly came to undertake more work than previously outside the home, but it is doubtful if they ever lost their subordinate position within it, and only rarely could they exercise equal power in the public sphere. Although the government of China still styles itself socialist, it has in recent decades largely dropped those elements that were in conflict with centuries of patriarchal custom. On the other hand it has tried to integrate others that are not usually associated with socialism but have a firm basis in Chinese history, notably entrepreneurship. On the whole, as in late socialist Hungary, political ideology has been largely displaced by more economistic emphases.

Comparable adaptations may also be noted in Britain, where self-styled socialists have from time to time formed the party of government. For a long time the dominant version of socialism here was based on ideas which had at least a superficial resemblance to those in the Marxist-Leninist countries: for example, British socialists too talked about an abstraction they called "the working class." However this rhetoric came to seem increasingly inappropriate to the structure of British society. Under Tony Blair, the Labour Party completed a "renewal" of its old ideology, which to some critics only confirmed an old academic thesis about the "end of ideology." New Labour was clearly a very different package, not only from the ideologies served up under Stalin and Lenin, but also from those professed by previous Labour Party leaders. Nevertheless, the party found it expedient to identify continuities, for example, in its rhetoric about social justice. Like ideologists everywhere, the "spin doctors" made clever and creative use of language and symbols to get their messages across.

THE GERMAN IDEOLOGIES

Germany provides an excellent case to illustrate the main themes of this chapter: not only the power of socialist ideology to shape minds and to change society, but also the constraints upon this power and the ideology's variable diffusion.

After the Nazi period, in which the political, cultural, and, indeed, racial unity of the German *Volk* was the primary ideological principle, with Dr. Josef Goebbels its best-known expositor, Germany was partitioned by the victorious allies. For almost half a century, until 1990, the German Democratic Republic espoused a rigorous version of Marxism-Leninism with highly centralized political and economic controls and all the usual ritual symbolism. The controls extended to Orwellian language: for example, the wall erected in Berlin in August 1961 to prevent East Germans from defecting was called the Anti-Fascist Protection Wall. Meanwhile the Federal Republic operated in the general style of other Western pluralist democracies.

Even though East Germany performed well in comparison with other socialist countries, the Federal Republic was always much more powerful economically. This was probably the principal factor which led the majority of East German citizens to vote in favor of reunification when given the opportunity in 1990. However the early enthusiasm soon gave way to disillusionment on both sides. The former East Germans were labeled *Ossis*, and they became objects of criticism, pity, and ridicule for *Wessis*. They were perceived as greedy in wanting to receive all at once the privileges of a higher standard of living, which could only come in the form of federal subsidies, since large sectors of the old socialist economy were uncompetitive in the new context. The *Ossis* were in turn bitter about what they perceived to be the arrogance of the *Wessis*. They resented being cast as second-class citizens, and many continued to draw on an egalitarian socialist ideology to assert their dignity.

The economic, social, and political problems of German reunification have been studied by many social scientists, but the extent to which the values of the old ideology have been preserved and continue to influence behavior can only be revealed through in-depth anthropological studies. For example, ideas of personhood and kinship practices developed in very different ways in the two Berlins (see Bornemann 1992). The institutions of socialism had radical effects on life courses. The most important was the provision in East Germany of childcare facilities which enabled women to return to work very soon after giving birth and put them in a much better position to pursue careers on equal footing with men. These women do not feel that their rights and capacities have been enhanced by reunification, which has led to an erosion of these distinctive socialist institutions in the family sphere. (This does not mean that earlier gender models were entirely swept aside under socialist ideology in East Germany. On the contrary, the women who went out to work in factories and offices continued to bear the primary responsibility for cooking, cleaning, and general household maintenance when they went home. As in China, this element in socialist ideology certainly had some impact on divisions of labor, but the deeper structures of power and value in society could not be so readily altered.)

FIGURE 2 Celebrations at the Brandenburg Gate, Berlin Wall, New Year, 1989–90. (Tony Taylor/ Panos)

A population such as that of East Germany, addicted to relatively high doses of ideology over a long period, is liable to suffer "withdrawal symptoms" when the treatment is suddenly interrupted. Where new political and economic opportunities have opened up, people have hurried to take advantage of them, but in areas where the transition has proceeded less smoothly, notably in regions of high structural unemployment, people may turn in frustration to other ideologies to explain their predicament. The source to which people most commonly turn is nationalism: right wing extremism and hatred of all foreigners are newly prevalent among the *Ossis*. This pattern is by no means specific to Germany, or even to Europe. In Israel, in Sri Lanka, and in many other parts of the world, the gaps left by receding socialist ideologies have often been filled by similar phenomena.

The vast majority of today's East Germans, however, have not been mobilized in this way. Rather, they have become typical capitalist consumers. From having the highest rates of voter participation in the socialist years, the eastern districts of Germany now have the lowest. Does this mean that capitalism is nonideological? It would be more accurate to point out that the slogans about "private property," "market economy" and "civil society" are used as incantations in much the same way as the jargon of Marxism-Leninism. It is nevertheless clear that the nature of the ideology has changed, that the domination of a narrow political class has been replaced by more diffuse, less visible forms of domination. The ideology of the market is less transparent than a centrally controlled political ideology, and it is therefore harder to oppose.

Was twentieth-century socialism simply everywhere a horrible failure? The anthropological answers tend to be nuanced, partly because even this apparently most universal of ideologies was always subjected to local modifications that the elites themselves could not fully control. Those who document such complexities may be criticized by those who like to see things in black and white, for example, the ideologues themselves, or their intellectual opponents in dissident groups. But the anthropologist who reports that many elements in socialism were widely endorsed is not thereby excusing the violence and hypocrisy of generations of powerholders.

In African and other postcolonial societies, self-styled socialists did not achieve as much as they expected to. Their efforts may nonetheless have resulted in more equal societies than those which followed untrammeled capitalist paths. Cuba, in spite of an American blockade since 1960, has still managed to provide better health, education, and pensions for its population than many European societies. Maoist China offered virtually all of its citizens better nutrition and subsistence guarantees (and also literacy rates) than free market India, which had a much more dynamic economy overall. Yet many millions died in the disruption of the early decades of socialism in China, as they had earlier in the Soviet Union. These balance sheets are complex. Here I simply suggest that anthropological studies which reveal how ordinary people understood the alternatives of socialism and capitalism and how far they internalized their own ideologies may add something valuable to the statistics of economists and demographers, the prejudices of politicians, and the stereotypes of journalists.

Eastern European societies voted against their previous rulers as soon as they were given opportunities to express their views freely in 1989–91. The party secretary I know in Hungary lost his job and was unable to find a new one. However, he still has friends and sympathizers, and he has been able to get by under postsocialist governments, which have not dared to dismantle a welfare net that still commands mass support. Indeed, after brief experiments with "shock therapy" (notably in Poland), many countries in Eastern Europe have voted the direct successors of the Communist parties back into power. Under the impact of a capitalism that often takes on very crude and extreme forms, many people feel nostalgia for the security they had in the past. But it is more than nostalgia. As Caroline Humphrey found in the mid-1990s when she revisited Buryat collective farms in Siberia, "There is a kind of gut loyalty to this former everyday life, which older people especially cannot abandon" (1998, xii).

Some people draw explicitly on the old ideology when commenting on their current predicament. The old socialist condemnation of "speculation" (*spekulacja*) is often heard in Russia whenever a new trader or entrepreneur is thought to be making unreasonable profits, and especially when the profit goes to a dealer rather than to the manufacturer. This could be seen as a long-term success of socialist ideology, one which continues to inhibit the development of new social forms based on more or less unregulated markets. But of course the underlying value here is much older than Marxist socialism and goes back at least to Aristotle. Perhaps, then, we can say that the ideology of Marxism-Leninism was most successful when it managed to insinuate itself into an older stream of values. The labor theory of value is not a socialist invention, but its incorporation into socialist ideology helped powerholders to justify their programs to peasants who were also deeply committed to a work ethic and to some elements of collectivism. Understood in this way, socialism is more than a modernist political current deriving from Enlightenment ideals of emancipation and progress. It embodies some of the deepest aspirations of all human communities. This is why it is likely to influence minds and to have material consequences in many parts of the world for a long time yet— not only for 1.3 billion Chinese citizens who are still nominally socialist, but also for billions elsewhere who have been touched in one way or another.

REFERENCES AND SUGGESTIONS FOR FURTHER READING

Bloch, Maurice. 1989. *Ritual, History, and Power: Selected Papers in Anthropology.* London: Athlone Press. [Stimulating discussions of ideology in "traditional" societies, with rich Madagascan examples.]

Bornemann, John. 1992. *Belonging in the Two Berlins: Kin, State, Nation.* Cambridge: Cambridge University Press. [Intriguing comparisons of how contrasting ideological systems affected everyday lives in East and West Berlin before the wall came down.]

Bridger, Sue, and Frances Pine, eds. 1998. *Surviving Post-Socialism: Local Strategies and Regional Responses in Eastern Europe and the Former Soviet Union.* London: Routledge. [Contains several studies showing the extent of people's dislocation after the collapse of communism.]

Creed, Gerald R. 1998. *Domesticating Revolution: From Socialist Reform to Ambivalent Transition in a Bulgarian Village.* University Park: Pennsylvania State University Press. [Detailed local case study, focusing principally on the socialist period but with useful 1990s updating.]

Eagleton, Terry. 1991. *Ideology: An Introduction.* London: Verso. [Sharp, radical, and stimulating survey by a leading literary theorist.]

Hann, C. M., ed. 1993. *Socialism: Ideals, Ideology, and Local Practice.* London: Routledge. [Includes a survey of work on Eastern Europe and a good selection of non-European studies.]

————. 2002. *Postsocialism: Ideals, Ideologies, and Practices in Eurasia.* London: Routledge. [A decade after the collapse of Soviet socialism, these case studies assess the extent to which it has been replaced by a new dominant ideology from the West.]

Humphrey, C. 1998. *Marx Went Away, but Karl Stayed Behind.* Ann Arbor: University of Michigan Press. [An updating of an outstanding study of Siberian collective farms, showing how socialist ideology was essentially integrated into a specific cultural system.]

Lampland, Martha. 1995. *The Object of Labor: Commodification in Socialist Hungary.* Chicago: University of Chicago Press. [This fine case study emphasizes how "economistic" motivations prevailed over political ideology in socialist Hungary.]

Lane, Christel.1981. *The Rites of Rulers. Ritual in Industrial Society: The Soviet Case.* Cambridge: Cambridge University Press. [A comprehensive guide to Soviet rituals that includes some useful comparative discussion.]

McLellan, David. 1995. *Ideology.* 2d ed. Buckingham, U.K.: Open University Press. [Excellent survey covering all the contemporary social science uses of the concept.]

Scott, James C. 1990. *Domination and the Arts of Resistance: Hidden Transcripts.* New Haven, CT: Yale University Press. [Good analyses of the limits of ideological power and the subtler forms of resisting it.]

Wolf, Eric R. 1999. *Envisioning Power: Ideologies of Dominance and Crisis.* Berkeley: University of California Press. [Excellent analyses of Kwakiutl, Aztec, and Nazi cases, combined with stimulating general reflections on key concepts, including ideology and culture itself.]

5.

On Conflict and Violence

MICHAEL GILSENAN

ANTHROPOLOGY AND THE MURDEROUS CENTURY

Why are forms of conflict and violence crucial to anthropology? Because they tell us much about the ways in which groups and persons organize and imagine themselves, constitute relations of power and hierarchy, and create social identities and meanings. Both are central to the world in which we live and to our understanding of our places in that world.

And what a world. We are at the end of what the historian Eric Hobsbawm has called "the most murderous century of which we have record." The first half of the twentieth century alone witnessed two world wars, wars of a newly industrialized kind in terms of discipline, order, and technology, the concentration camps and the gulags, as well as systematic colonial violence across the globe. State (rather than "private") armies, navies, and later air forces were organized in supposedly rational and efficient ways and fought in the name of the nation with ever-developing weapons whose range and power have not ceased to increase. Militia or other organizations such as the Taliban in Afghanistan are taken to be signs of primitive and irrational social life, however high-powered the technology.

Millions of people in the twentieth century have been persuaded, coerced, or mobilized in the name of "the people," "the homeland," religion, and other transcendental values, to destroy millions of others, and to die themselves in the effort if need be. Ceremony, religious invocation, emblems, uniforms, rituals of parade, disciplines that include procedures designed to transform the recruit's body and social being within a total institution of hierarchy and rank, all go into producing persons ready to respond to orders to kill others under specific circumstances (figure 1).

FIGURE I British soldier carrying plastic bullet gun. (Howard J. Davies/Panos)

At the same time, we have become all too accustomed to linguistic changes and euphemisms for state violence: "collateral damage" for civilian deaths, "smart bombs" implying some scientific precision that avoids unnecessary casualties. Images of force and war are constantly generated in ever more explicit forms and with ever more high-tech special effects, and are used in powerful media such as film and television as essential to the economics of pleasure and leisure. All these processes are taken to be "normal" in the modern state. By and large, apart from some protests by political candidates at election time, they are perceived as nonproblematic and, in a curious way that requires sustained analysis, innocent.

At this point in world history, the rise of more global economic and political systems has profound implications for both global and localized violence of different kinds. Markets dominated by international companies have grown on a huge scale. Millions can be pauperized virtually overnight. Forced migrations sweep up more millions, while state structures and national institutions seem precarious and less powerful. Small wonder if identities that are conceived as ethnic, linguistic, religious, and historically authentic (even if they are not) become more fiercely important while being ever more precarious. Small wonder if violent relations with other "groups" identified as ancient enemies become more intense, even if in fact "they" have not really been "groups" at all until relatively recently. All sorts of symbols, rites, memories, places, imagined and real wrongs and injuries are cobbled together. And the most terrible acts against neighbors and friends with whom one has intermarried become possible.

Such relations of conflict and violence have defined both prewar and postwar history. Indeed, war helped in powerful ways to form what Emile Durkheim and Marcel Mauss, the great French nineteenth- and early-twentieth-century thinkers who had such an effect on anthropology, called our collective consciousness and representations. They wondered what might socially and morally hold something called "society" (increasingly linked to the institutions of emerging nation-states) together in the age of capitalism, industry, and modernity if people no longer shared the same sense of the sacred, of the gift, of common values, and of what Durkheim called "mechanical solidarity" in the premodern division of labor. In its own grotesque ways, the violence of war has been one part of the answer.

This cultural and political aspect of violence, and the ways in which violence is euphemized and made into "defense" or truth or sacrifice, is the sort of issue that concerns anthropologists. For we always have to address the links of the symbolic, of language, and of power in societies, including our own.

Violence also helps to define our landscapes and sense of place, as well as our temporal sense of history. Towns and villages, churches and schools, have their memorials to those who gave their lives in the sacred cause of country and duty. The cause, the dead, are seen as noble even if there may also be terrible ambiguity about the suffering. So our positive sense of our identity in a community and the world, our memory and powerful emotions of engagement, may owe much to the direct experience and representations of state violence in monuments, memorials, photographs, films, books, museums, television, and in a world of commodities in which forms of violence are now sold.

War is part of the enchantment of the state, of what makes it appear magical and worthy of the sacrifice—that powerful religious term—of one's own and others' lives. At the same time, the enchantment works to make such violence part of a taken-for-granted, natural world for many people, though it may also stimulate strong opposition.

MULTIPLE MEANINGS AND ANTHROPOLOGICAL PROBLEMS

Whether in the Gulf War, Chechnya, Liberia, Somalia, in the high rhetoric of the war against drugs, or in agonized debates in the United States after random school killings, we are confronted with multiple realities of violence against individuals and whole peoples. Sometimes it is easier to speak of some supposed primordial essence that "makes people like that over there," always "over there." Sometimes scapegoats are hunted down. Stereotypes abound, from "Islam is a violent religion" or "It's a Jewish plot," to "Africa is primitive."

Anthropology tries to resist such failures of mind and imagination. It insists on interpreting violence and conflict in all the detail of social and cultural contexts, contexts which they also powerfully shape. Violence and conflict have to be historically situated in the full complexity of very different forms. We have to show that they are formative of sociopolitical relations on the widest as well as the smallest scales.

Anthropologists have learned that what is conceived of as "violence" and "conflict" in one society or section of a society may not be so conceived in another. The languages, metaphors, and images in which violence is communicated and represented may vary enormously. Legal categories in national codes of law—murder and manslaughter in different degrees, grievous bodily harm, crimes against humanity, rape, violations of human rights—are differently conceived and much argued over. Punishment for categories of violence arouses fierce emotion as well as debate in which religion, moral values, and deeply opposed viewpoints are expressed. Is state-inflicted death retributive? redemptive for the victim's family? murder?

Whatever those variations, conflict and violence in word or deed, or the potential and capacity for it, may be integral to group boundaries and personal identities, as well as to relations among "ourselves" and with "others." So violence may be constructive and destructive; required or prohibited; ritualized or relatively unpredictable; hymned in poetry, music, art, and building as the source and summit of glory, honor, and supreme sacrifice, or lamented as degrading, shameful, and a mere waste.

We have also learned that the study of violent conflict requires the greatest sensitivity in the way in which it is carried out, and in the way in which it is written. Anthropology, so often close to the ground and so involved in intimate aspects of personal lives through fieldwork, has a particular responsibility to avoid slipping unintentionally into a pornography or voyeurism of violence.

Anthropologists pay great attention to the framing, defining, containing, or avoiding of kinds of conflict and violence. These processes involve all sorts of informal, everyday tactics and strategies that are so much part of our lives that we do not ourselves perceive them as anything but "the way things are." They may further engage particular, formal, juridical or religious offices, persons acting as mediators or, if they have the power, as arbitrators. Such figures have special claims based on sanctioned social positions such as that of diviner, elder, or judge or holy figure, to be able to produce punishment, resolution, or peace, and they officiate at distinctive procedures and ceremonies. So some conflicts may be treated in routine and predictable ways in which people know what is supposed to happen when it arises (we often say "erupts," a volcanic metaphor which says a great deal about how we like to figure social life as somehow holding down vast subterranean forces that always threaten to become uncontrollable.) Others provoke uncertainty and disagreement.

Societies have elaborate practices, codes, rules, and representations of violence. On closer examination, however, these cultural practices may turn out to have less visible and far more ambiguous links to the realities of social life than people themselves say. Anthropologists look for those cracks in the social surfaces, those breaks in meaning and inconsistencies in accounts and practices. Points of conflict and violence may signal such crucial fault lines.

VIOLENCE, CONFLICT, COLONIALISM

The first anthropology book I read as a student concerned violence, religion, and political conflict between a European state and Arab tribal groups in a part of what was to become modern Libya. E. E. Evans-Pritchard's *The Sanusi of Cyrenaica* is a study of the Italian colonial wars of conquest, from the invasion of 1911 to their expulsion during the North Africa campaigns of World War Two. The book sets out an analysis of tribal and religious structures in this particular context of violence from outside and by a different kind of political entity, a modern nation-state.

Evans-Pritchard was studying processes that were part of more global patterns of violence that emerged over the years of the various colonial conquests. The period of his study included two world wars, heavily industrialized conflicts we still struggle to explain, with increasing scientific and organizational "development," including atomic weapons and the concentration camps. Whole societies were militarized; new forms of the means of coercion became paramount; old technologies and patterns of conflict were transformed; new colonial and eventually postcolonial states emerged, states often profoundly marked by the central place of the army in power.

The Sanusi of Cyrenaica fascinated me. Here was an anthropology that plunged into an analysis centered on colonial violence and the sociopolitical responses to it rather than artificially isolating a tribe or village from wider political and historical processes for examination. That Evans-Pritchard was himself a British military officer serving a major colonial power at the time of doing his fieldwork/active intelligence service in Libya and Egypt during the Second World War gave the text an additional, concealed complexity.

The cultivator and nomadic tribes of Cyrenaica had always had their own capacities for different forms of violence from feud to warfare in competition over vital resources such as water and flocks. "Honorable" violence had been traditionally highly valued in Cyrenaica (as it is in so many societies, including our own, when socially sanctioned by authoritative groups). Carried out in the course of tribal life in what were defined as appropriate ways (rather than by treachery and mere theft for instance), it demonstrated the core values of fearlessness, enforcement of respect for the group, and admired patterns of manhood. Violence and values were closely related. Conflict, who joined with whom against whom in what circumstances, was critical for the social definition of the group.

Violence had its own aesthetics of form, gesture, and language, an important point to which anthropologists continue to give attention. Raiding and feud in Cyrenaica, as elsewhere, were the subject of orally recited poems that were a crucial part of tribal culture. These verses, some remembered over many years and some more ephemeral, gave shape and pattern to tribal history and heroic memory and defined the group, triumphantly, against others. Opponents, of course, might have very different versions of the same events, or ignore them altogether and ridicule their enemies' boasts.

The mediation and resolution of conflict might well involve the intervention of a neutral tribal group of sufficient prestige to command the necessary respect, or oaths sworn at the shrine of a holy man or a lodge of the Sufi Brotherhood. Peace might be made under the aegis of a respected religious sheikh who, if he were important enough, might himself be a learned man who had studied in North Africa or the Hejaz in the holy cities of Mecca or Medina. Shrines were places of purity where blood might not be shed, people's safety could be guaranteed, flocks might be left without guards. God's violence struck those who violated the sacred territory, and weapons had to be left outside its bounds. The offerings of sacrificial animals, a form of sacred violence that consecrated the peace, marked the fulfillment of religious duty and signified participation in a moral community bound by common religious and customary practices and values.

In short, this anthropological account showed how violence and conflict entailed a whole range of social and cultural practices: expectations and explanations of what people might do and why they might do it; histories and narratives structuring those expectations and tribal identities; statements of rules and codes that might nonetheless be violated; sacred spaces and persons, who had themselves to be sensitively aware of balances of force and negotiating strategies to attain reputations as "really" holy persons and places; acts considered to be purifying, as in the making of sacrifice or taking of "proper" vengeance, or polluting, as in being wounded in one's person or honor. The making of peace or the avoidance of conflict involved considerable social skill and negotiation, which might fail.

Yet as the whole African continent became the object of French, Spanish, British, Belgian, Portuguese, and Italian colonial invasions in the nineteenth and early twentieth centuries, the tribe-religion relation took on a specific form around armed resistance to the invading European powers. The colonial campaigns were of a quite different nature from the conflicts the tribes had previously known, defined by the wish for conquest and settlement by an alien people, forced population transfers and many executions, and by the Italian use of the advanced weapon technology of the time. Warfare changed, as it did across the globe. For the tribes, it became a matter of bare survival and, finally, total defeat under the domination of a different kind of social order. Poetry memorialized heroic resistance, suffering, and loss in a new kind of struggle with a new kind of enemy.

Evans-Pritchard showed how a Muslim religious brotherhood, the Sanusiyya, an international association with many lodges spread in oases and on trade routes all the way from West Africa to Cyrenaica in northeastern Libya, became a banner under which tribal groups that otherwise competed with each other might come together to fight long guerilla wars against a technologically superior enemy. The Sanusi were in key positions on the trade routes and in the oases. Their lodges were often established in the boundary zones between tribal sections. They were strategically as well as morally and symbolically placed to give a focus and overarching cause to the fight.

The tribes were, indeed, fighting what was proclaimed a *jihad*. Violence became a sacred, Muslim, moral imperative as well as a matter of sacred tribal honor, and thus doubly sacralized. But far from being the wild and fanatical aggression the term *jihad* falsely conveys in Western media, this was an anticolonial war in which it was the European state, itself still quite young, that behaved, even by European standards, with remarkable cruelty and ruthlessness.

Violence thus played a crucial role in the practices and imagining both of tribal life, the imperial enterprise itself (though that was not Evans-Pritchard's subject, good British colonial officer that he was), and, more important here, of "being Libyan"; it structured and was the substance of the histories of struggle, displacement, death, and what came to be "the nation," histories which were also still significantly tribal.

It took another war, that of 1939–45, before the Italians were driven out of Libya and the head of the Sanusiyya became king of an independent state. Ironically, the new monarchy was effectively under foreign (British) protection, a protection ultimately based on the balance of military and political forces in the Middle East as a whole. Neo-Empire replaced Empire. A more indirect violence, less obviously dependent on visible physical coercion, such a relation was transparent enough to be radically opposed by new nationalist regimes.

SYMBOLIC VIOLENCE, ENCHANTED RELATIONS, AND SOCIAL ORDER

The word *indirect* brings me to an important dimension of the study of violence and conflict. Anthropological writings on these subjects do not focus simply on conquest and military or individual force, rich though such events also are in symbolic and cultural import and in constituting personal or collective memories. For, of course, overt physical coercion is only one aspect of violence and conflict in human relations. Symbolic or euphemized violence, to use the terms of the French thinker Pierre Bourdieu, confronts us with more subtle issues. As the terms indicate, violence and conflict may be masked, mediated, and represented in forms which conceal the relations of violence in society, whether we think of that society as "modern" or "traditional."

In capitalist societies, for Bourdieu, underlying realities of domination and social hierarchy are hidden and misrepresented by the workings of more impersonal, objective mechanisms of social distinction, such as the education system or other forms of social, cultural, or economic investment. In socialist societies party membership and ideological mobilization may serve similar functions. In precapitalist societies, on the other hand, patterns of domination and social relations have to be continuously created through personal links which tie together, say, client and patron. There are rituals of relationships such as godparenthood, specific modes of address, and gifts or debts which are the idiom in which people acquire and maintain their "disguised and transfigured" hold over others. In both cases violence is thus present but "misrecognized." Social relations are "enchanted." Under the spell, we do not see the violence at the foundation of all relations of power. (Bourdieu's argument is closely linked with Marxist writers' understandings of the nature of ideology).

Some writers define modernity itself in part as a process in which explicit, coercive violence became the legitimate monopoly of the state alone. And the modern state developed modes of ordering and discipline which depended on what emerged in the nineteenth century as new models of rational and efficient organization—drawn from the army, the factory, the school, the prison—for their effectiveness, not on physical violence in spectacular events such as public hangings, for example. Physical violence became an individual "problem" to be resolved by law and order. Violence in modern societies, in this way of thinking, is both institutional and symbolic, though no less real and omnipresent. It is in precapitalist societies that personal and group violence plays a more overt, structuring role.

Steven Spielberg's *Raiders of the Lost Ark* makes a joke about this contrast. The Western, white archaeologist figure, played by Harrison Ford, is confronted by a snarling brown "native" brandishing a sword, who makes a great performance of how he is going to kill his enemy. Ford, fed up with this performance, draws a gun and shoots his posturing assailant dead. The audience laughs. The modern hero is not going to play by the rules of "the primitive." So where the swordsman is a kind of parody figure of old-fashioned, personal violence through the sword, weapon of a long-vanished age, the university archaeologist-adventurer just dispassionately, and comically, destroys his opponent with technologically advanced means and no performance.

CENSUS, SURVEY, AND SCIENCE

Let me give an important general example of euphemized violence in which what is defined as modern and what is defined as traditional are mutually constituted by the dominant powers. One crucial colonial instrument of order was to take censuses and surveys of defined tribal, or caste, or religious groups with the aim, among other things, of making them counted and accounted for parts of the political order. The imposed procedures were scientific and statistical, a sign and constitutive element of progress. Who could possibly argue with that?

Yet these seemingly neutral and impersonal terms and procedures euphemized (in Bourdieu's sense) the forcible definition of collective social units as bureaucratic categories to be administered and controlled. The French in nineteenth-century Algeria, for example, may have used military force for some three or four decades to smash resistance. But they also explicitly intended the cadastral land surveys of conquered territories to be used to break up tribal solidarity by fragmenting tribal collective land holdings into individual properties. Apparently impersonal practices which were "scientific" and "progressive" were nonetheless a form of violence that pervaded and disciplined Algerian society more efficiently than mere military controls. Instead of naked conflict, there was the impersonal legitimacy of new ways of systematizing society.

Moreover, such entities, *created* through the census, were seen, not as constructions of the census categories and procedures, but as if they were unchanging and "traditional" identities that had existed since time immemorial. They were "simply" being measured. But the procedures helped to make colonial rule, and the practices of independent states, seem a *natural* historical evolution of objective classification and science rather than of the particular practices of power. Anthropologists and scholars in other disciplines have come to see that "social order," an apparently innocuous phrase, covers a multitude of not-so-innocuous routines and ways of organizing society in which violence and conflict seem to vanish.

What anthropological approaches help us to understand here are the relationships between state policies and the histories of local identities that people themselves may now take to be natural but which were constructed in and through conflict and violence. They also expand our sense of what kinds of violence may be at play in social life in all societies in ways that are relatively unseen.

CUSTOMS, CONFLICT, AND DEVIANCE

The ways in which anthropologists have analyzed various kinds of violence and conflict differ greatly. Marxist anthropologies of the 1950s and 1960s, for example, focused on the centrality of dialectical relations between opposing forces in social worlds. *Custom and Conflict* is the title of a well-known book by Max Gluckman, himself a Marxist and a South African committed to African independence movements. *Schism and Continuity*, by Victor Turner, at that time on the political left, also emerged from the "Manchester school" of anthropology. Both very similar titles point towards one central idea: that conflict is fundamental to social processes which produce it, and are produced by it; that it is patterned and closely related to questions of "custom and schism"; that you must not, cannot, consider them separately.

Gluckman and Turner were writing against functionalist anthropologies. The latter saw violence and conflict as, by definition, dysfunctional elements in what were conceptualized as stable, isolated, and "primitive" social systems outside history. For functionalists using these ideas, conflict could only be treated either as a "breakdown" or as "pathological," an idea which still often surfaces in contemporary media and politics in all societies. This is a major point, as governments and authorities of every stripe tend to stigmatize certain groups such as "gypsies" or "unemployed youth" (often with a racial bias) as "problems" because of their alleged and real violence or offences against law and order. Gays may be classified as an offence to moral order, a classification that itself constitutes a form of violence, and permits multiple forms of prejudicial treatment in which the victim, in a reversal of reality, will have been said to have "asked for" or "deserved" it.

"Violence" is thus identified as a characteristic of "the dysfunctional," "perverse," or "dangerous," some essential quality of "them" against whom it is possible to mobilize opinion and virtuous force. Such a language of functional, conflictless social order disturbed only by the irrational or deviant, conceals the creation and development of greater social inequalities. It also helps to sanctify the state as the sole legitimate user of "good" violence (through the police and prison services on the one hand, and the armed services on the other).

VIOLENCE AND CONFLICT AS PLAY

A quite different anthropological perspective was proposed in a celebrated article on the Balinese cockfight by the American anthropologist, Clifford Geertz. He argued that we could interpret the cockfight as a cultural and social microcosm for understanding Balinese society as a whole. It is a drama of conflict and violence containing the key elements of the Balinese world of *meaning*, a key term for Geertz.

In the cockfight, rivalry, struggle, natural, cultural and economic forces all come together in a performance that is both play and deadly serious. In the blur of action as the cocks strike viciously at each other with their spurred claws, urged on by supporters who have bet on them and by owners whose standing and masculinity are momentarily at stake, uncontrolled conflict and violence are intensely expressed in a controlled setting.

For Geertz, the cockfight is a text which the anthropologist can learn to read, deriving powerful, interpretive insights into the place of violence and conflict in the wider culture. Such insights are far more difficult to achieve in ordinary Balinese life, where courtesy and carefully managed performances of "face" and status are the rule. The cockfight makes a drama out of what is otherwise masked and avoided by the subtleties of politesse.

Though Geertz's work has its critics, his focus on complex, ritualized play and violent contests fought out by masculine creatures of the wild is challenging. It suggests that a specific and highly bounded arena of violent play can be taken as a condensed frame and "text" in which are revealed, to the trained reader, otherwise elusive cultural and social patterning. The drama of the cockfight, for Geertz, gives insight into the seemingly ordered world of everyday Balinese life.

NARRATING VIOLENCE

Geertz's work is based on what he called "thick description." That description is based on hearing as much as on the seeing which the phrase "participant observation" makes us think of. In fieldwork, anthropologists try to listen with acute critical attention to what people say and, just as significantly, don't say, about conflict and violence. Our own anthropological listening leads us to examine in great detail people's own narratives of violence within and among communities and persons. How do people speak about what they may also feel is the unspeakable, explain what they may also sometimes consider inexplicable, or represent the unrepresentable? How does violence structure memory and identity, or seem to obliterate key aspects of what happened?

Anthropologists focus, not so much on the analyses by official spokesmen, intellectuals, or leaders, as on the accounts that emerge at wider levels of society. Very often, we try to elicit the images and memories of those who do not necessarily have a public voice and are not directly recorded on television, in newspapers, or in archives. Such accounts may be less carefully organized than more official versions, and in many ways both richer and more fragmentary. The ambiguities, ambivalence, and even incoherence these voices express or hint at can only be understood after deep attentiveness to people frequently ignored. Such inquiries run the risk of voyeurism and a kind of pornography, of probing acute personal and collective traumas only to write in a way that appeals to a reader's uneasy sense of exploitation.

To illustrate what I mean about narratives of violence, let me turn to my own work on north Lebanon (based on fieldwork in 1971–72 before the Lebanese wars). I wanted to examine a world in which physical violence seemed to be the key principle of social and economic hierarchy. Indeed, I had gone to the region because it was spoken about as one of "naked violence," as a place of "feudal," "unchanging," and "traditional" authority. Landlords coerced landless peasants through rape, arbitrary beating, and constant threats of harassment or loss of the means of livelihood. In this universe of status, honor, and force, where masculinity was integrally associated with a capacity to compel others to do one's will, I wanted to see how the "tradition" and pure violence, of which newspapers and everyone I met talked, actually worked in practice. Lebanon, after all, was a country of enormous wealth, with immensely sophisticated financial and service sectors. Beirut was a capital world-famous for its consumption chic, its cosmopolitanism, and its lively intelligentsia. How could this isolated and traditional zone in the far north (only two hours from the capital by car) have remained so violently "feudal"? Was it possible that people up there really would "kill you as soon as look at you"? Were the people just "violent by nature"? Was coercion so self-evident that it did not really need any analysis at all?

Initially, that was exactly how it looked. The region was indeed a world of hierarchy: great landowners who were often leading national political figures; middle owners and retainers, who were also proud bearers of arms and, as the lords' overseers, controlled the third group of laborers and cultivators. When I began my fieldwork, I very quickly heard the names of the great landlords, who were renowned for their cunning, ruthlessness, and use of force. Woundings and killings, famous confrontations, violations of others' honor, land seizure, and the driving off of others' laborers, it was all there and all retold time and time again. Some described such lords as tyrants who killed at a whim to test a new rifle or to show their supreme indifference to normal values. But others spoke of them as "great men," "men of value," "men with true honor and status" who were "good" and "generous." That was one immediate lesson: there were radically opposed accounts of such men and the way in which they ran their estates.

The second lesson was even more striking. These backward, feudal landlords turned out to have been educated men who sent their sons to law schools in Paris or for chemistry Ph.D.s to America if they could, and invested in the stock market and in property in Beirut. The major figures had transformed agricultural practices by introducing new cropping patterns, machinery, and fertilizers, and, finally, they were not infrequently deputies, even ministers, in the National Assembly.

Moreover, there were many minor lords' families who had been ruthlessly squeezed out by their relatives and now lived on reduced means and diminished status, or none at all.

A third lesson emerged more slowly. I began to realize that behind the boasting of glorious and fearless deeds, the claims to status and the capacity to eliminate opponents, the assertions of the superiority of one family and its history over another, an enormous amount of unspoken effort went into *avoiding* direct physical violence and conflict. People were acutely aware of the dangers and unpredictabilities of confrontation. Rifles such as the Kalashnikov had flooded the market, and even a man of very limited income could buy one or be given one by a lord to whom he was attached as bodyguard or chauffeur. But who wanted to get dragged into major shootouts that might have heaven only knows what consequences?

Even after killings or woundings, which in any case happened as often within family groups as between them, or between lords and their own followers because of some dispute over cash, people actually looked for ways to arrange compensation rather than revenge. They shouted, swore, held solemn meetings debating the rules of just who could be killed in retaliation or who could not, and generally kicked up a storm. But on the quiet, everyone decoded these obligatory displays of outraged honor in terms of just what the group was "really" bargaining for in terms of money, or a taxi license, or some land. Opponents might sneer at what they proclaimed to be false displays of manhood, but they would usually do the same thing in turn if the occasion arose. Family members would be lobbied for support, but they often did not really give it, whatever pious phrases of solidarity and outrage they used. After all, "a man has to live," people said. Everyone had a family to feed, the job market was very tough, and nobody by the 1970s could do without wages and work.

As I listened, all these ambiguities and concealments that lay behind the public performances of violence and honor came to seem fundamental to social life in much less self-evident ways. I became very interested in the stories people told about violence, as well as in the events themselves. These narrations, which were often repeated and which I came to recognize from many tellings, were ways in which personal and social identities were negotiated and reproduced. Men drew on very familiar repertoires of stories in which they or their fathers had played roles presented as heroic. At social evenings, such tales would be a central part of the entertainment, together with wildly comic versions of the humiliations of opponents told with huge relish and much laughter. And then a friend might murmur sardonically to me, "You know Michael, all this is just talk, nothing but lies really. He's just a taxi driver. All this boasting is just empty words. What can you do? In this world, you have to lie." A conspiratorial smile, and then we would be off on another great performance of how a great daring deed had been done.

Moreover, for many of those who had been brought up to be the strong-arm men, bodyguards, and estate managers, the realities of the labor market in Lebanon had come to take priority. The agriculture sector was far less significant than it had been. Consumption patterns had changed enormously, and locals had a sense of being what one sardonically described to me as "useless bastards," on the edge of the burgeoning Lebanese center of Beirut with its ostentatious displays of wealth and class.

People needed to earn money in construction, panel-beating, peddling, taxi-driving, tractor and harvester operating. They did not necessarily want to contribute hard-earned cash to blood money contributions, nor did they wish, whatever the obligatory rhetoric might be, to rush off on some expedition to menace a group with whom an unthinking cousin had got into a fight. "A man has his interest," they said, "he has to look after his own family" and could not always yield to the claims of the wider lineage honor, even if he made a great show of solidarity. "Peasant" families were getting jobs, some had cars, and, not least, they also had rifles. Hierarchy was shifting.

Men even began to speak about "being in the house," normally regarded as archetypally the realm of women, and "not mixing with others out there with all those lies. Nothing comes of it." That certainly challenged local understandings of masculinity and violence. Others insisted scornfully that a "real man" had to be "outside," in the public view, showing that he "needed no one" but that he also had a group of brothers and cousins who would instantly rally around him. To be "at home," for them, was an admission of defeat and of having no "station in life," no "value." So if some young men still sought positions with the lords and swaggered around with their rifles or Belgian revolvers, others talked about work instead. The apparent certainties of force and coercion were thus mined by ambiguity, irony, and unease.

Such subtleties of violence and avoidance, conflict and complicity, talk and silence, taught me to be extraordinarily wary of easy generalizations, particularly in this area of social life. Anthropologists often focus on some intense and small-scale set of relations to explore in real depth how people really live out, perform, deny, ignore, or exalt forms of violence and conflict that are central to their worlds. Patterns may be new and unstable, even if they are spoken about as traditional and authentic. Self-deception and *anomie* may be as fundamental as truth and social coherence. In our contemporary world no one is exempt from grappling with such tensions.

SUGGESTIONS FOR FURTHER READING

Bourgois, Philippe. 1995. *In Search of Respect: Selling Crack in El Barrio.* Cambridge: Cambridge University Press (paperback 1996). [An anthropologist works among the crack dealers in East Harlem at a time when the "crack wars" dominated much American news. Illuminates both the wider social structures of American urban life in a very specific setting and participants' apprehensions about their own lives and deaths; vivid but not sensationalist.]

Das, Veena. 1990. *Mirrors of Violence: Communities, Riots, and Survivors in South Asia.* New Delhi and London: Oxford University Press. [A subtle and delicate study of the forms and significance of violence in South Asia, alert to all the problems of description, voice, and interpretation which anthropologists face in talking to participants and victims.]

Edwards, David B. 1996. *Heroes of the Age: Moral Fault Lines on the Afghan Frontier.* Berkeley and London: University of California Press. [A fascinating study of a social world often taken to be the epitome of the "violent society." Edwards probes the histories, conflicting forces, and accounts of three key persons: a tribal khan, a Muslim saint, and a prince who became the king of Afghanistan. He shows how a nuanced anthropological reading of narratives and genealogies can illuminate even the most complex patterns of violence.]

Gilsenan, Michael. 1996. *Lords of the Lebanese Marches: Violence and Narrative in an Arab Society.* Berkeley: University of California Press; London: I. B. Tauris.

Daniel, E. Valentine. 1996. *Charred Lullabies: Chapters in an Anthropography of Violence.* Princeton, NJ: Princeton University Press. [A complex book about the violence in Sri Lanka. The theoretical sections require real knowledge of semiotics, but the book also offers rich accounts of the world of Tamil estate laborers, of caste, and of language and music. The reader becomes vividly aware of Daniel's intense struggle for understanding.]

6.

Imagined but Not Imaginary: Ethnicity and Nationalism in the Modern World

RICHARD JENKINS

When Yugoslavia disintegrated, new states emerged. Some of those new states had old names, names that had vanished from the international map more than fifty years earlier. In some of those new states, new ways of talking about similarity and difference within the region emerged also. An ugly civil war turned, in places, into something even uglier, something that was perhaps difficult to talk about in a post-Holocaust Europe. Where "race" or similar markers of lineage and descent might once have been evoked, "ethnicity" became the word of choice to identify friend and enemy, and to dramatize lines of alliance and conflict. In the process, a novel obscenity—"ethnic cleansing"—entered the vocabularies of both protagonists and observers. Events in Kosovo since the mid-1990s are a stark reminder, if one were needed, that the genocidal impulse remains a present danger, not to be dismissed as the barbarism of previous generations or "the uncivilized." Kosovo is also a reminder that problems of this nature can never be seen as local. In some respects, there is no such thing as "local" any more.

Other things, in other places, also seem to have become less easy to say. In central Africa, for example, the murderous mass violence between Hutu and Tutsi would certainly once have been called "tribal," as if to describe it thus rendered further explanation unnecessary: *they* have tribes, not *us*. Now, however, following the example set by anthropologists decades earlier, it is likely to be represented in the Western news media as "ethnic" . . . as if to describe it thus renders further explanation unnecessary.

At the other side of the globe, in the context of significant popular support for a new republican constitution and the world media stage offered by the 2000 Olympic Games in Sydney, the issue of Aboriginal land rights and living conditions has dramatized the complex, multiethnic, political reality of the Australian state. This has tempted out from the shadows a taken-for-granted, popular white supremacism to which the state seems not to have a ready response, perhaps because it has also turned a harsh light on the foundations of Australia in bloodshed and large-scale extermination. A consensual name for that history has yet to been found.

Closer to home, for me at least, Northern Ireland during my childhood there was a place in which ethnicity, Protestant and Catholic, was perhaps the major identificatory theme—apart from gender—organizing everyday life (see figure 1). But it was not, at that time, a place in which people talked much about "ethnicity," "culture," or similar abstractions, although matters of nation, background, religion, and sect were, and still are, visible, audible, and tangible. Today, however, even though the word "ethnicity" itself may not be a staple of everyday speech, appeals to "identity," "culture," and "tradition," to excuse violence, to drum up external support, or to euphemize shared histories of violence, are stocks-in-trade of the local political scene. Whether the 1998 Good Friday agreement can change this, founded as it is on ethnic categories and constituencies, still remains to be seen.

Less dramatically, in many places around the world—from the transnational arenas of the European Union to the internal politics of the People's Republic of China and the orderly municipalities of social democracies such as Denmark—ethnic and national identity are among the most crucial bases of claim and counterclaim about who gets what, and how much. Ethnicity, origin, and cultural difference seem, at least for the time being, to have replaced class conflict as the motor of history.

Ethnicity is not, however, only a matter of violence or the politics of collective entitlement. For many people it is simply a source of the intangible collective good offered by "community." But it can also have many other meanings. When the new young star of American golf, Tiger Woods, appeared on the Oprah Winfrey TV show in the United States in 1997, he used the opportunity to insist that, despite being claimed and fêted as such, he was neither black nor African-American. He was, he suggested, "Cablinasian," a mixture of *Ca*ucasian, *Bl*ack, north American *In*dian, and *Asian*. His tongue was at least partly in his cheek, but there was also something serious in his rejection of a crude category of identity—black—and his insistence that, if descent in these terms matters, and in American society it surely does, it is anything but a simple matter.

Sport offers other pertinent illustrations of the salience of ethnic and national identity in the modern world. There is an increasing flexibility of national identification in terms of sponsorship or team membership. The pursuit of individual career advantage and prestige, combined with the quest for national sporting success, has produced, for example, an Irish international soccer squad most of whom

FIGURE I The visual representation of division in northern Ireland: Republican mural, Derry, and Loyalist mural, south Belfast. (Photo from Derry, Mark McEvoy/Panos; from Belfast, Alain le Garsmeur/Panos)

were born outside Ireland and some of whom have, at best, one Irish grandparent. Several players who participated in the 1998 football World Cup competition had to choose which national team to play for. Similarly, Greg Rusedski, one of Britain's top men's tennis players, speaks with the soft Canadian accent of his "native" province of Quebec.

These examples suggest two—apparently contradictory—conclusions. On the one hand, ethnic and national identities mean a great deal to the individuals who claim them, and offer enormous potential for collective mobilization. Attachments of this kind are something for which, and about which, humans remain prepared to fight. They are, literally, calls to arms, imbued with their own imperatives: they impel people to do things. On the other hand, however, ethnicity and nationality appear to be flexible, capable of transposition and transplantation. They seem to be on the move, resources to be constructed or manipulated rather than forces before which we must bend or break. From this point of view, their meaning is not dictated by history or the blind passions of the "blood" but made by us, as individuals or collectivities, in response to our needs and interests.

Thus there are two interpretations of ethnic—or national—identity. On the one hand, it is seen as a fundamental, even an irrational, psychosocial, emotional force. On the other, it appears to be a negotiable, perhaps even superficial, personal resource. These opposing points of view begin to converge, however, if we recognize that my examples all suggest that ethnic or national attachments, far from withering away in the face of increased internationalism, are at least as important in the global arena of the late (Christian) twentieth century as they have ever been. Even in the supposedly "advanced" Western world of Europe and America it is still acceptable to claim and identify with ethnicity. It is still acceptable to do so despite the collective guilt inspired by a history of slavery, colonialism, and genocide that has, for the moment anyway, consigned "race" and "tribe" to an uneasy quarantine of disreputability (if not final oblivion). Neither the progress of modern "rationality" nor the shape-shifting of postmodernism's celebration of infinite difference have undermined the power of ethnicity and national identity to move people and to shape their lives.

WHAT IS IDENTITY?

Similarity and difference are the touchstones of human social identity, which position us with respect to all other people. They tell us who we resemble and from whom we differ. They provide us with at least some idea of what we can expect from others and what they can legitimately ask of us. They are the latitude and longitude that provide us with a functioning, if somewhat imprecise, orientation to the social environment that we must daily navigate.

It makes both logical sense and social sense to say that without similarity there can be no difference, and vice versa. This is one of the basic principles of all classification systems. It should not, however, be understood as merely a version of the static binary oppositions so beloved of structuralist approaches to language and culture. It is, rather, a dynamic relationship between two complementary aspects of a social process (identification) and its product (identity). Within this ongoing relationship of call and response—and call and response again, and again, and again—neither difference nor similarity is determinate or dominant.

Each of these axes of identification is imagined, a product of the human imagination. This does not mean, however, that they are imaginary in the sense that an illusion or a fantasy is imaginary. Far from it. Identification—similarity and difference perpetually feeding back on, and emerging out of, each other—is massively consequential, both in our mundane everyday individual experience and in the historical, social construction of human collectivities. Depending on the context, identification affects everything from which side of the street we can walk on to what we can eat and what we like to eat; from who we can mate with to how we understand our place in the cosmos; from how we live to how we die. Everything. To paraphrase a deservedly famous remark of the American sociologist W. I. Thomas, if we define situations as real, then they are real in their consequences. We define identity as real. Without the work of the imagination that is identification, we could not relate to each other consistently or predictably, and human society as we understand it would be impossible.

One of the central themes of social identification is membership, what the British anthropologist Anthony Cohen talks about as "belonging." This is not the lumpen togetherness of "potatoes-in-a-sack" but the shared *sense* of belonging that comes about through participation in a common symbolic world (in other words, culture). The feeling of similarity which this participation conjures up creates the space within which individual and other differences may coexist under a symbolic umbrella of community: community and belonging are thus imagined but not imaginary.

Whatever its roots, "belonging" immediately conjures up positive, warm images of inclusion, mutuality, and security. These may have their foundations in a range of social contexts: in the emotional hothouse of kinship and family; in more negotiable friendship or economic networks; in a local sense of shared residence and place; in more impersonal and formally defined citizenship; in a common history; or in a more diffuse sense of an apparently shared "way of life" (language, religion, technology, cuisine, etiquette, and the myriad other things that constitute everyday, practical, cultural competences). All of these and more may contribute, in different contexts—and to differing degrees of significance depending on the context—to the idiom of identification that we call ethnicity.

But of course something else may also be evoked when we talk about ethnicity. Inclusion breeds exclusion. It cannot be otherwise. As with similarity and difference, logically and socially the one entails and requires the other. We know who we are—Us—at least in part because we know that we are not Them. This does not mean that conflict is inevitable, or that They must provide the negative to Our positive, but it does generate a fertile field of fraught possibilities. It is therefore not surprising that conflict and ethnicity can be seen feeding off each other as far back as there is a historical record to consult: the Old Testament story of the Israelites' invasion of the Promised Land is, for example, as much a catalogue of ethnic conflict as the Vinland Saga's report of the first encounters between the Vikings and native North Americans.

Ethnicity—much like social identification more generally—is neither a "good thing" or a "bad thing." It simply is. It is difficult to posit a human social world without it. For better or worse, processes of ethnic identification appear to be integral to the frameworks of meaning and significance—culture—that allow humans to know the world, to conjure up that world's meaning, and to recognize themselves in the process of doing so. If this is true, the most promising approach is not to cast a superior eye over ethnicity's apparent irrationality or bemoan the obstacles to progress and civility that it presents but to attempt to understand it on some, at least, of its own terms.

WHAT IS ETHNICITY?

When the ancient Greeks talked about *ethnos*—the root of our modern word *ethnicity*—they had in mind a community living and acting together in a manner which we usually translate today as "people" or "nation." This evokes an image of a collectivity with at least some manners and mores, practices and purposes—a "way of life"—in common. In other words, a group whose members share something in terms of culture. Thus the Norwegian anthropologist Fredrik Barth has defined ethnicity as "the social organisation of culture difference." Ethnicity is not, however, an abstract, collective phenomenon. As we have already seen, it matters personally, to individuals. In this sense, to quote another anthropologist, this time Clifford Geertz, an American, ethnicity is "personal identity collectively ratified and publicly expressed."

Ethnicity is thus one way—perhaps, after kinship, the most ubiquitous way—of classifying humans into collectivities. This necessitates judgments that certain people are similar to each other and, in this way, different from others. Ethnicity draws on the cultural differences and similarities that the participants in a situation regard as significant, in order to build and dramatize these social boundaries. However, the ways in which culture is socially organized into ethnicity are neither obvious nor straightforward. People may appear to differ enormously in terms of culture and yet be able to identify themselves as ethnic fellows: think, for example, about the variety that is subsumed within Jewishness. Nor does apparent cultural similarity preclude strong ethnic differentiation. Viewed by an anthropologist from Mars, I have no doubt that Protestant Anglo-Americans and Protestant Anglo-Canadians look very similar; I have even less doubt, however, that they do not see things this way (not yet, anyway).

These examples suggest a need for selectivity, that our understanding of ethnicity cannot simply depend upon a crude model of cultures seen "in the round." Some cultural themes or identificatory criteria offer more grist to the ethnic imagination's mill than others: language, notions of shared descent, the inventiveness of tradition and history, locality and co-residence, and religion have all proved to be particularly potent ethnic markers. Even so, a common language, for example, or shared religious beliefs and practices, don't necessarily do the trick in themselves. Nor do shared space and place. Although living together may be a potent source of shared identification, space and place can also divide people. They can be a resource to compete for. Even the minimal interaction that is necessary for a sense of difference to emerge takes up space: it needs a terrain. Thus it is that lines may get drawn in the sand; that borders and boundaries may come to constitute arbitrary and culturally defined group territories.

These points suggest an important insight: that ethnicity is not a matter of definable degrees or obvious kinds of cultural similarity or difference. It is not possible, for example, to offer a check list that would enable us authoritatively to determine whether or not members of Group A are *really* ethnically different from members of Group B, or whether Group C, for example, is an ethnic group or some other kind of collectivity. Enumerating cultural traits or characteristics is not a useful way to understand or identify ethnic differences. The world of humans cannot be classified by anthropologists in the same way, for example, that lepidopterists might classify butterflies. Our subjects have a voice, and the baseline is whether a group is *seen* by its members to be different, not whether it "really" is (whatever that might mean).

Self-definition is not *all* that matters, however. It is also necessary that a group should be seen to be distinctive—itself—*by others*. In at least two senses there can be no such thing as unilateral ethnicity. First, ethnicity involves ethnic *relations:* connections and contacts between people who are seen to be different, as well as between those who are seen to be the same. A sense of ethnicity can only arise in the context of relationships and interaction with others. As I have already argued, without difference, there is no similarity. Defining *us* implies—if nothing stronger—an image of *them*. This is true of all social identities. Second, it is difficult to imagine a meaningful identity—ethnic or whatever—that is not accepted and recognized by others. To return to Tiger Woods, it seems unlikely that Cablinasian will ever catch on as an authentic ethnic identity in its own right, if only because it is unlikely to be accepted by others as such. This was not, of course, the point he was trying to make in coining the name, but it makes the point here. It is not enough to assert, "I am an X," or "We are Xs," for either of these things to become so.

VARIETIES OF ETHNICITY

So what kind of thing does count as "being an X" in the contemporary world? What kinds of social identities are ethnic? If we look at actually existing situations, many of the answers to this question appear to be pretty straightforward. In the United States, for example, Chicanos, Sioux, Irish-Americans, African-Americans, Italian-Americans, Jews, Koreans, Chinese, Navajo, Mexicans, Cajuns, Aleuts, Hawaiians, Pennsylvania Dutch, Chippewa, and Ukrainians—arbitrarily chosen from many possibilities—are all recognizably "ethnic," in one sense or another. But what, for example, about the Amish, or the Mennonites, or the Mormons? Or, perhaps even more interesting, what about New England Yankees, or Texans, or people from New Orleans, or southern whites in general? Are they ethnics? My answer, looking from outside, would in all of these cases be differing degrees of the affirmative. But given the strong association in the United States and elsewhere between the words *ethnic* and *minority*, their own answers—certainly in the case of the Yankees, the Texans, and the southern whites—might be a resounding no.

Looking at a range of relationships of similarity and difference may help to clarify matters. Take, for example, the somewhat unsubtle and incomplete sequence shown in figure 2, which draws its general inspiration from a range of anthropological and other studies of Sicily and the *Mezzogiorno*, the "barbaric" south that, in the eyes of many northern Italians at least, is the nearest available Other between them and north Africa. Similar hierarchical models could be drawn up for anywhere in the world. There is nothing particular about Italy in this respect: it has been chosen somewhat arbitrarily here, reflecting my own ethnographic reading. You may like to try the exercise for wherever you live or "come from"; in the process, you might also like to think about what it means to "come from" somewhere.

What does the model mean? Most immediately, it attempts to capture on the page something of the situational variability of identification: in one context my village provides my most important identity; in another it is that I am from the

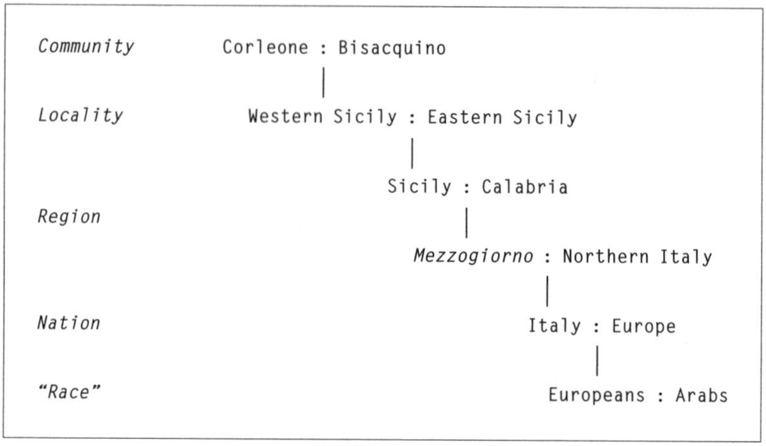

```
Community        Corleone : Bisacquino
                             |
Locality         Western Sicily : Eastern Sicily
                                  |
                          Sicily : Calabria
Region                       |
                          Mezzogiorno : Northern Italy
                                        |
Nation                         Italy : Europe
                                        |
"Race"                       Europeans : Arabs
```

FIGURE 2 Hierarchies of similarity and difference: Varieties and levels of Sicilian identity

south; in yet another it is that I am an Italian. I may be able to emphasize this or that facet of my identity, depending upon what is to my advantage; on the other hand, however, I may not wish to or be able to. And if I come from Corleone, say, I can, depending on the context, mobilize all of the identities represented by the left-hand poles of the oppositional pairs in the model. Those that I differ from at one level, I can share something with at the next. Exclusion becomes inclusion.

The next point to note is that the words "ethnic" or "ethnicity" do not appear anywhere in the above scheme. And yet, in terms of the broad definition offered above—and in terms of our everyday understandings—much of the similarity and difference that is represented here looks, to say the least, something like ethnicity. The diagram thus suggests some questions. Where does ethnicity end and communal identity, or local identity, or regional identity, or national identity, begin? What is the relationship between community and locality, or locality and region? And what are the differences between all of these things? Where does "race" fit in with them?

As I have already suggested, context is important, but in each of these cases, it is difficult to define exhaustively and precisely the characteristics of the identificatory idiom in question. Criteria such as language, religion, descent, territory, and history or tradition have more or less salience at different "levels" of identification. Sicilian community identity—the village and the town—depends for its boundaries largely upon territory, family and descent, and tradition or history (which may all be combined in the local institution of the feud, or *vendetta*). By contrast, although such things undoubtedly serve to signify the difference between western and eastern Sicily, this difference is also very publicly visible in the daily use of language, that is, dialect. Even more marked linguistic differences provide a fault line of identification with respect to the regions of Calabria and Sicily, and the north and the south more generally. But here, at the regional and subnational levels, other factors such as shared cuisine, public interactional etiquette, and a nebulous notion that there are different "ways of doing things," are also significant.

At a greater degree of collective abstraction, national identity involves, in the first instance, a formal package which includes citizenship, a passport, political rights and duties within and without the national borders, and so on. Where the informal powers of others to accept or reject identity have been important previously, this is the unambiguous domain of formal power and authority. And even here, other things are involved too: language, food, and in the Italian case a contrast with much of the rest of the European Union on the basis of, among other things, religion. This recedes in significance, however, beside the dramatic sense of religious difference—embedded in a powerfully symbolized and inventive historical tradition—which serves to draw a line between Europeans and Arabs. Nor is it just religion that is believed to matter in this case. Putative descent reenters the frame in the shape of "race," the belief in distinctive populations sharing common ancestors in the remote past, human stocks with their own characteristics. From this point of view, Italians are very different from Libyans, for example. They are not the same "kind" of people. And although "racial" categories draw upon the visible features of bodies to assert the "naturalness" of particular similarities and differences, let us remember that "race" is culturally defined, not natural. Hence my use of quotation marks, to remind the reader that it is a contested and problematic concept.

In this respect, and in others, this diagram represents, of course, only part of the hierarchical model of identification that could be constructed with respect to Sicilian identity. One could, for example, add in the relationships of similarity and difference between Italians and the other "Latin" peoples of the Mediterranean basin, between the peoples of the western and the eastern Mediterranean, between southern and northern Europe, between Sicilians and Sicilian-Americans, and so on. This would begin—but only begin—to give us a picture of the multidimensional relationships of ethnic identification that are involved in "being Sicilian."

Further complexity emerges if we turn the model on its head. As presently presented, the eye proceeds down the page. In effect, this means beginning at the Sicilian town or village level and thus implicitly adopting the point of view of a very local Sicilian Us. There is another way to do it, however. We could begin from a Northern Italian perspective and go in the other direction, up the page, in which case everything appears in a different light. A member of the Northern League, or a Padanian nationalist, for example, would doubtless emphasize the similarities

FIGURE 3 Immigrant from Burkina Faso in the Villa Literno ghetto near Naples. The camp was burned down shortly after this photo was taken. (Rhodri Jones/Panos)

between Sicilians rather than the differences, and have a different understanding of what they are. Such "external" categorizations of Sicilian identities are important in that they are part of the social terrain and environment within which those identities arise, change, and have their meaning. These categorizations have political, economic, and other consequences which contribute in no small part to whatever it means, in any context and at any point of time, to be Sicilian. Thus, in order to understand the complex social processes of Sicilian identification, it is necessary to adopt many points of view other than those of Sicilians themselves.

Community, locality, region, nation, and "race": are they even the same kind of thing? The answer is no, and yes. No, in that they appear to be about different things, with each evoking its own particular combinations of criteria of similarity and difference. No, in that some of these criteria are easier to negotiate around or away than others; locality or citizenship, for example, are more flexible than versions of the criterion of descent, such as family or "race." No, in that some of them find expression through organized ideologies such as nationalism and racism—political philosophies which assert how the world is and how it ought to be—while some do not. But yes, in that the criteria of similarity and difference in each case are definitively cultural. Yes, in that they all contribute to the social organization of a broad and distinctive genre of collective identification, which is not reducible to either kinship or social class, to pick only the most obvious (gender seems to me to involve altogether different principles of individual and collective identification). And yes, in that they all offer the potential for political organization and ideologizing.

So, instead of searching in vain for ever more exclusive and exact definitions and distinctions, perhaps we should keep our options as open as possible. A more satisfactory approach may be to suggest that communal, local, regional, national, and "racial" identities can all be understood as locally and historically specific variations on a general and ancient theme of collective identification: ethnicity. Each of these variants says something about "the social organization of culture difference": even closely neighboring villages may have some small differences—with respect to patron saints, perhaps, special items of food, the use of particular words, festivals—between them. In the process, each contributes to the symbolization and imagination of belonging and similarity. Each of them also says something about "the cultural organization of social difference." They are, if you like, culturally imagined and socially consequential, a way of putting things which recognizes that distinguishing between "the cultural" and "the social" makes only limited sense, at best.

Communal, local, regional, national, and "racial" identities also offer the possibility of "collectively ratified personal identity." In Sicily, as elsewhere, it may make a considerable difference *personally* to people which village they belong to. It is, after all, individuals who belong. It may also make a considerable difference to people in their judgments of others *as persons:* as potential partners in whatever enterprise is in hand, as adversaries, or merely as objects of safe indifference. Even at the most abstract level of identification, "being Italian" involves more than the possession of a passport and voting rights (and to judge from recent Italian political history the latter may not be very significant at all). Indeed it is possible to be a citizen of another country—the United States, Australia, the United Kingdom—and still "be" an Italian.

WHY ETHNICITY MATTERS

A broad understanding of ethnicity can thus encompass and deal with social identifications which reflect and express similarity and difference defined according to community, locality, region, nation, and "race." Adopting an anthropological point of view encourages and requires us to generalize in this way. As an intellectual enterprise, anthropology tries to take the broadest, the most holistic, view of whatever social situation or context is the focus of attention. As a characteristically comparative enterprise, anthropology also needs sensitizing concepts which travel well—kinship and religion are other good examples—rather than concepts which are too locally specific.

But anthropology has other emphases too: on culture and meaning, on local perceptions and knowledge—viewed from a generalizing and comparative perspective—and on the routines of everyday life. This means that an anthropologist's ideas of "what is going on" must, at the very least, be forged in a process of dialogue with the local people whose social universe is being studied. What *they* think is going on must be taken seriously; it is the baseline from which we proceed. This is the main reason why anthropologists continue to insist upon long-term fieldwork involving face-to-face contact as the mainstay of our research.

So far in this chapter I have concentrated upon the ways in which ethnic identification is a contextually variable and relative process. If we listen to people, this is one of the most important things that we learn about ethnicity: that it may be negotiable and flexible from one situation to another. But this is not the only thing that we learn: depending on cultural context and social situation, ethnicity may not be negotiable. There may not be a choice. And when ethnicity matters to people, it has the capacity to *really* matter, to move them to action and awaken powerful emotions.

This returns us to my opening theme of two contradictory images of ethnic and national identification. We are now in a better position to understand that these images are only apparently contradictory. On the one hand, that ethnicity may be negotiable or flexible does not mean that it is *infinitely* negotiable or flexible. Some aspects of ethnic identification are less malleable than others. It is one thing to get a new passport, change one's religion, move and live somewhere else, or even adopt a new way of life; it is quite another thing to disavow one's family or shuck off the physical attributes that may embody a particular identification. And lest the latter be misunderstood, this careful choice of words does not necessarily refer to the "natural" characteristics of "race": it could just as easily mean a tattoo, male circumcision, or some other ethnically significant body modification.

And this is before we consider whether or not a change of self-identification will be validated in its appropriate context. The power of other people may be decisive. In the north of Ireland, for example, it is one thing to "turn"—as changing one's religion is described locally—on marriage to a member of the "other side." It is quite another, however, for that to be accepted by one's spouse's family and community. Hence the well-known phenomenon of individuals converting under these circumstances, only to become more enthusiastically "bitter"—to use another local expression—than their spouse, in-laws, and new neighbors. There are some kinds of identity that it is no one's *right* to change.

On the other hand, that ethnicity can be a source of powerful affect and meaning does not imply that it is either "primordial" or "natural." This common misunderstanding has been a source of some futile debate, in anthropology and elsewhere, between "primordialists" and "constructionists," between what Marcus Banks has evocatively described as models of "ethnicity in the heart" and "ethnicity in the head." There are several important things to bear in mind about arguments of this kind. First, how much ethnicity and its variants matter, and to whom, differs from epoch to epoch and place to place. There is no human consistency with respect to the strength of ethnic attachments, although that there are ethnic attachments—according to my general definition—does seems to be consistent. Nor do we need to resort to notions of essence and nature to explain why, when ethnicity matters to people, it matters so much: the nature and content of primary socialization—the affective power of symbols, local histories, and the local consequences of identification—are probably sufficient to account for this.

What matters, anyway, is not actually whether ethnicity is a personal and cultural essence with which we are born and about which we can do nothing. What matters is that many people, in many situations, fervently believe this to be so and behave accordingly. That national feeling and identity are of this noble order—rooted in language, collective psychology, culture, and place—is the central tenet of many local brands of nationalism with philosophical roots in the European Romantic tradition and practical political roots going back at least as far as the 1848 bourgeois revolutions. Whether it is true or not, this is certainly consequential.

This brings us to the final important thing. Nationalism—for example—something so apparently timeless that it can be described as primordial, often turns out on closer inspection to be, at least in part, decidedly modern. This is only in part because some versions of nationalism arguably have a long history, while the general collective idiom of ethnic identification is positively ancient. But modern ideologies of nationalism, which argue that nationhood and national sentiment are governed by natural law and justice, are precisely that, modern ideologies, whose usefulness in legitimating domination, appropriation, and mass violence sits uncomfortably alongside their potential to inspire liberation.

This is perhaps the real contradiction at the heart of any discussion of ethnicity and nationalism in the modern world. It is certainly the most consequential. It is why it matters that we should continue to approach these things on their own terms at the same time as we think critically about them. It is a powerful argument for an open-ended anthropological understanding of processes of ethnic identification that can accommodate their fluidity as well as their intractability. That they are imagined but not imaginary.

ACKNOWLEDGMENTS

Although I am responsible for the shortcomings of this chapter, these would have more numerous without the careful attention and advice of Simon Holdaway, Jenny Owen, and David Phillips, to whom I am most grateful.

REFERENCES AND SUGGESTIONS FOR FURTHER READING

Banks, M. 1996. *Ethnicity: Anthropological Constructions.* London: Routledge. [Introduction to the academic literature on ethnicity and nationalism.]

Barth, F. 1969. "Introduction." In *Ethnic Groups and Boundaries: The Social Organisation of Culture Difference*, ed. F. Barth. Oslo: Universitetsforlaget.

Cohen, A. P. 1985. *The Symbolic Construction of Community.* London: Routledge.

Cole, J. 1997. *The New Racism in Europe: A Sicilian Ethnography.* Cambridge: Cambridge University Press. [A good place to start for the reader interested in looking further at the Sicilian case.]

Cornell, S., and D. Hartmann. 1998. *Ethnicity and Race: Making Identities in a Changing World.* Thousand Oaks, CA: Pine Forge. [Introduction to the academic literature on ethnicity and nationalism.]

Eriksen, T. H. 1993. *Ethnicity and Nationalism: Anthropological Perspectives.* London: Pluto. [Introduction to the academic literature on ethnicity and nationalism.]

Geertz, C. 1973. *The Interpretation of Cultures.* New York: Basic Books, chapter 10.

Jenkins, R. 1996. *Social Identity.* London: Routledge. [This and the next work by Jenkins include the general theoretical arguments about social identification on which this chapter is based.]

———. 1997. *Rethinking Ethnicity.* London: Sage.

Schneider, J., and P. Schneider. 1976. *Culture and Political Economy in Western Sicily.* New York: Academic Press. [Another good study for the reader interested in the Sicilian case.]

7

Fighting the Good Fight: Fundamentalism and Religious Revival

WILLIAM O. BEEMAN

FUNDAMENTALISM: ORIGINS

The term *fundamentalism* has rapidly entered the vocabulary of social science in the past two decades as a general designation for revivalist, conservative religious orthodoxy. Though it was originally applied only to Christianity, Gananath Obeyesekere theorizes that the extension of the term to other religious traditions dates from the time of the Iranian Revolution in 1978–79. Today it is used to describe Evangelical Christians, Iranian revolutionaries, ultra-orthodox Jews, militant Sikhs, and Buddhist resistance fighters, among others. Its categorical use is so widespread and so easily applied that the misperception persists that it has always been with us.

The specific origin of the word *fundamentalism* dates to an early-twentieth-century American religious movement. The movement took its name from a compendium of twelve volumes published between 1910 and 1915 by a group of Protestant laymen entitled: *The Fundamentals: A Testimony of the Truth*. These volumes were circulated in the millions and served as the concretization of a cross-denominational set of traditions with roots in previous centuries. It owes its existence particularly to the same evangelical revivalist tradition that inspired the Great Awakening of the early nineteenth century and a variety of early millenarian movements. Spurred on by reactions to Darwin's theory of evolution, the original Fundamentalist movement was seen as a religious revival. It came to embody both principles of absolute religious orthodoxy and evangelical practice which called for believers to extend action beyond religion into political and social life.

These four qualities—*revivalism, orthodoxy, evangelism, and social action*—are the basis for the discussion of fundamentalism presented below. As a number of social scientists have noted, the term has come to have pejorative connotations. Nevertheless, it does seem to serve a useful purpose as a characterization of a repeatedly occurring and nearly universal human social phenomenon. The deeper comparative understanding of fundamentalism may forestall the frequent dismissive attitudes exhibited by groups sharing common beliefs toward other groups whom they see as antithetical to those beliefs. As Lionel Caplan, editor of a prominent collection of essays on the subject has noted, "an adequate understanding of fundamentalism requires us to acknowledge its potential in every movement or cause. . . . We are all of us, to some degree and in some senses, fundamentalists."

REVIVALISM: THEORIES OF SOCIAL PROCESS

Laymen, including government officials and journalists, commonly make the mistake of viewing fundamentalist movements as localized, recent phenomena. This misperception always leads to shock and surprise when these movements emerge to challenge a dominant social order. Nowhere was this more evident than in the Iranian revolution of 1978–79. Despite many decades of antimonarchist activity and an even longer period of Islamic revivalism throughout the region, universal surprise was expressed at the victory of Ayatollah Ruhollah Khomeini and his supporters.

The key to understanding fundamentalist movements lies in the careful investigation of their history combined with investigation of the specific contemporary conditions that bring about their emergence at particular times. This revivalist character of fundamentalist movements may be their most salient aspect. Clear historical and doctrinal precedent seems to inspire confidence in movement members, who must often exhibit great courage to stand apart from the wider society. Just as the original early-twentieth-century Fundamentalist movement sprung from the Great Awakening, which in turn sprung from English and American Puritanism, all fundamentalist movements have such deep historical roots.

In essence, all such movements are a natural consequence of human processes of cultural change. In every society on earth change proceeds at an uneven pace. Some society members embrace change with relish. Others find it oppressive and troubling. When people feel that change is being imposed on them, some find it necessary to resist—sometimes violently. The dynamics of revitalization thus are tied to intergroup dynamics. When a group in society perceives itself as having its power and authority usurped in the course of social change, the group comes to see both internal and external causes as responsible for its fall from power.

Internally, the group may blame itself for its decline. Its leaders often point to internal decadence as the principal reason. They accuse members of becoming weak and irresolute to the point where they let others oppress them. This invariably results in the creation of physical and mental training programs to strengthen the character and resolve of those who want to become the vanguard to restore the group to its former idealized state. These practices are extremely varied. They range from prayer and meditation to ascetic practices and physical or military training.

Externally, the group objectifies an Other, and identifies it as an oppressor. Usually the movement advocates resistance—sometimes violent—to that oppressor. The core operations of the fundamentalist movement may be varied, ranging from guerrilla warfare and attacks on public figures or facilities to more peaceful protests and nonviolent action. Occasionally, these movements embrace the perceived oppressors and direct their energies toward becoming more like them or attracting their attention. Large-scale religious conversions throughout history have often had this quality.

Members of fundamentalist movements see themselves as saviors of society. For this reason they are able to justify almost any action, however extreme, and any personal sacrifice, however great, for their cause. There is a tendency to see the world in black and white terms. People are clearly either enemies or friends. Actions are either good or bad. The unrelenting commitment and conviction of the members of the movement often eventually lead the larger society to see them as a social threat, even when their methods and strategies are peaceful.

All of these movements invariably create a dual myth that links a supposed Golden Age in the past with a Utopian future. The past Golden Age is seen as a time when the members of the movement or those they identify with were strong, vital, and in control of the world. The Utopian future presages a time when movement members will return to that sense of group strength and wholeness. In seeking to do this, they adhere to a clearly specifiable orthodoxy but no easily predictable political ideology. They are as likely to be liberal as conservative in their solution to the problem. Religious belief is the most frequent motivating and organizing principle, although purely secular concerns may also dominate. Most cultures have seen a number of fundamentalist revival movements throughout their history, and all such movements appear to have common features which bear a resemblance to general human ritual practice.

Theories of Revivalist Process

Contemporary anthropological understanding of these movements has been shaped by the work of Anthony F. C. Wallace on *revitalization movements*, which are conceptually equivalent to the fundamentalist revival movements that are the subject of this discussion. Wallace was deeply impressed by the history of an important Native American movement in the late eighteenth century centering around an Iroquois prophet who bore the leadership title Handsome Lake. This prophet drew on preexisting religious traditions. He claimed to have had a supernatural vision warning the then demoralized Iroquois against alcohol, witchcraft, love magic, and abortifactants. His preaching and other miraculous events gained him great credence with the Iroquois, mobilizing and revitalizing their flagging society.

Wallace took Handsome Lake's history as a model for other, similar social movements. He suggested that all revitalization movements go through several stages. Wallace's original analysis is reformulated here in slightly updated terminology:

1. Social change produces cultural tension among members of society.
2. The cultural tension produces an attempt to accommodate, leading to distortion and change in social patterns, causing social disruption.
3. As a response to cultural tension, fundamentalism emerges in the form of an orthodox restatement of cultural patterns. This new doctrine is spread through evangelism, often through the office one or more charismatic figures.

Wallace's analysis of revitalization bears a good deal of similarity to the structure of "social dramas" as described by Victor Turner. Turner's account is drawn loosely from Arnold Van Gennep's analysis of *rites de passages*. Turner likens all social change to a ritual process. In ritual, individuals are transformed from one status to another by first being removed from society to a "liminal space" (from L. *limen*, "threshold"). In this betwixt-and-between state they receive special training and instruction pertinent to their new status. Normal rules of social life are suspended in this liminal period. The transformed members are then reincorporated in the larger society in their new status.

In social dramas, society undergoes transformation when a "social breach" occurs. The social breach can be seen as the first stage of Wallace's analysis as presented above. In Turner's view this leads to a period of liminality when change takes place. During this period normal social rules are suspended or even reversed. This period corresponds to Wallace's second stage. In the final stage, for both Turner and Wallace, a new social order is established.

Turner developed his schema to explain events of more limited duration than the revitalization movements analyzed by Wallace. Nevertheless, the similarities are clear. Religious revival is actually a kind of double process in Turner's sense from the perspective of the participants in the religious revival. Society is seen as undergoing a Turnerian social breach as tension from social change increases.

Liminality occurs as society is seen as unsuccessfully trying to accommodate to change, thereby suffering a breakdown of its social institutions. Finally, a fundamentalist movement emerges which aims to reinstate social order through evangelical action.

Fundamentalist movements are themselves liminal. Normal social rules are suspended within the movement. Members undergo special rituals and training. Their goal is usually to enact an extended social drama, leading an entire society into a liminal state that will eventually bring about total change. Because of the intensity needed for such activity, and because it is usually undertaken by a minority group, the goal of total social transformation is only rarely achieved; but when it is, it is a form of social revolution.

A similar structure to explain the rise of fundamentalism was suggested by the religious scholar Eric Sharpe. Sharpe posits three phases of development of fundamentalist movements. The first is that of *rejection*, when traditionally accepted authority is challenged. In the second phase, *adaptation*, an attempt is made to accommodate the old philosophy with the new. During the third phase, *reaction*, fundamentalist practice arises. Sharpe's schema, which has been widely used in recent studies of fundamentalism, owes a great deal to Wallace's earlier analysis.

The Islamic Fundamentalist Revival Movement

The Middle East offers a wide spectrum of examples of fundamentalist revivalist movements, of which the contemporary "Islamic movement" is perhaps the most important. The movement originated around 1875. Throughout the previous century, European powers, fueled by wealth of the Industrial Revolution, had usurped economic and military power throughout the region. This change in the political and economic order of the world was devastating to Muslims. The leaders of the consequent Islamic movement spurred their followers with idealizations of the Golden Age of the great Islamic Empires stretching from the eighth to the eighteenth centuries when Muslims were wealthy, independent, pious, and militarily strong.

The principal originator of the Islamic movement was Jamal al-Din al-Afghani, an Iranian political leader who aroused Muslims throughout the Middle East and North Africa. He saw the governments in the Middle East as hopelessly corrupt—undermined by Western forces and Western values. His solution was a three-pronged effort consisting of a renewal of personal religious piety, reform and modernization of Islamic law, and resistance to foreign influence.

Al-Afghani's movement was widespread. His successors have included a variety of movements and social groups. Given his broad revivalist agenda, it is not surprising that these successors have manifested a remarkable variety of methods for accomplishing the Islamic revivalist goal. They include far-sighted legal and social reformers, such as the eminent Egyptian jurist Muhammad Abduh. They also include relatively moderate reform groups such as the Islamic Brotherhood, now active throughout the Middle East. More violent fringe groups include the assassins of Egyptian President Anwar Sadat and Palestinian nationalist groups, such as Hamas, a group responsible for a series of devastating suicide bombings of Israeli citizens.

The Islamic movement had at least one full realization of successful fundamentalist revival in the Iranian Revolution of 1978–79. The shah of Iran was toppled from power by a coalition of religious and political forces with a pedigree dating back to Al-Afghani. The revolution emphasized martyrdom in the service of the higher cause of moral and political reform. Its explicit message was to return Iran to a period of harmony and religious strength like the one preceding the secular government of the shahs (see Beeman 1983a, 1983b, 1986, 1996). Although Muslims in the rest of the Islamic world do not necessarily agree with the religious and political agenda of the Iranian revolutionaries, they have been inspired by the revolution as proof that a fundamentalist Islamic revival can take place and can involve a whole society.

ORTHODOXIES

A different kind of analytic scheme to account for fundamentalist movements has been suggested by Niels C. Nielsen Jr. Nielsen's schema draws on the idea of *paradigm shift*, inspired by Thomas Kuhn's important work *The Structure of Scientific Revolutions*. Kuhn promulgated the thesis that a given set of axioms and beliefs constitute a paradigm, which dominates thought in a scientific community until successfully challenged by changed cultural circumstances. Nielsen points out that fundamentalists have a distinct, orthodox paradigm which is the only one allowed their believers. Kuhn himself acknowledged the similarity between his scientific paradigms and religious paradigms in a discussion with the religious scholar Hans Küng, who likewise sees the development of religion in terms of paradigmatic periodization.

Nielsen sees religious orthodoxies to be like Kuhnian paradigms because they constitute all-encompassing worldviews with set assumptions and theories of how the world operates. In fundamentalist movements, orthodoxies are more than theory. They are bodies of inviolate belief to which all members must subscribe to remain in good standing within the movement.

Kuhnian paradigms also imply praxis—a body of procedures and methods that follow from the basic theories and assumptions. In the scientific world, this praxis is made up of the experimental procedures of laboratory testing operations in which hypotheses are tested and theories generated. In fundamentalist movements praxis is made up of the expected conduct of members of the movement that flows from the underlying beliefs of the group.

A model for the specific body of orthodox belief of Christian fundamentalists was proposed by James Barr. In his influential study, *Fundamentalism*, Barr identifies four basic fundamentalist "characteristics" paraphrased here:

1. Inerrancy of scripture
2. Individual salvation
3. Personal witness to belief, abstracted from social context
4. Invalidity of hermeneutic exegesis of scripture.

Barr's study of Christian fundamentalism has served as a model for the study of fundamentalist orthodoxies outside of Christian tradition and is widely acknowledged in contemporary studies.

Orthodoxies for different fundamentalist traditions reflect the character and history of the religions which they represent, but they are generally an amalgam of doctrinal beliefs and specific practice flowing from those beliefs that are unassailable and incumbent on believers. The Chabad Hasidic movement, better known in the United States as the Lubavitch Hasidic movement (Chabad Lubavitch), embodies such a mix. Lubavitchers, who are centered in the Crown Heights section of Brooklyn in New York City, combine a fervent belief in absolute scriptural truth with an equally fervent belief in the imminent coming of the Messiah, who will subsequently establish his kingdom on earth. In this belief, they see the world Zionist movement and the establishment of the State of Israel as transitional. The Commandments of Moses as well as the full set of Noahide laws are not only alive for this group, but are seen as incumbent on all people for the maintenance of social order in the world. Lubavitchers are encouraged to make every encounter with other Jews, and theoretically with non-Jews as well, an opportunity to bring them closer to observing these laws. Consequently, within the Jewish community the Lubavitchers see themselves as the guardians of rabbinic law. They spare no expense, using modern publication and electronic media to supplement direct personal confrontation as a means of bringing errant believers back to orthodox ritual practice. This fascinating mix of traditionalism and willingness to embrace the technology of the modern world to achieve their religious goals is a hallmark of the group's orthodoxy.

Orthodoxy can often engender unusual paradigm shifts as the assumptions of a particular worldview are played out and strengthen over time. One example is the evolution of Shinto in Japan from a medieval reification of feudal relations between the ruling classes and their serfs and vassals to a full-blown state religion in the twentieth century (Bellah 1970). In their earliest forms in the eighth and ninth centuries the deities of Shinto seem to have been derived equally from animistic personifications of local objects and forces of nature such as mountains, streams, forests, the sun, moon, and wind coupled with deific representations of deceased personages of importance, such as feudal lords. The doctrine that the emperor was directly descended from the most sacred deity, the Sun Goddess, combined with these beliefs and eventually created the base for a revivalist religio-political state in the nineteenth century. By World War II this doctrine had evolved into a state orthodoxy in which a divine emperor was seen to reign over a sacred land. All warriors dying in defense of the emperor and Japan were themselves recognized as specially designated deities residing in a special state shrine in the afterlife. The orthodoxy of this period continues to be a controversial force in Japanese life today, despite the fact that the United States forced the emperor to renounce his divinity after the war. The majority of Japanese followed suit and rejected state Shinto, but it continues as a strong force among the most conservative sectors of society. As recently as May 2000 Japanese prime minister Yoshiro Mori faced angry calls for his resignation (figure 1) after one month in office following a speech in which he said: "We hope the Japanese people acknowledge that Japan is a divine nation centering on the emperor" (Kageyama 2000).

FIGURE 1 Women in Japan calling for Prime Minister Yoshiro Mori's resignation following his nationalist remarks in Parliament. (Courtesy of the AP Archive)

EVANGELISM

Fundamentalist movements generally are spearheaded by one or more charismatic leaders who take the lead in gathering believers and delivering the central message of the movement. Moreover, the fundamentalist movement attempts to evangelize a broader population and convince them of the truth of the group's orthodoxy. This population may be circumscribed, as is often the case with Jewish fundamentalist groups who largely limit their evangelism to Jews; or broad-based, as with movements that attempt to address all of humanity.

In the Christian fundamentalist movements in recent years television preachers—sometimes called *televangelists*—such as Billy Graham, Oral Roberts, Jerry Falwell, and Pat Robertson—have been instrumental in evangelistic efforts, reaching millions with their message. The contemporary fundamentalist movement in the United States is so widespread and comprehensive that it supports many charismatic leaders.

Famous evangelists abound in other religions as well. A touchstone for the contemporary Native American movement in the United States was the Ghost Dance religion that swept Native American peoples of the plains in the late nineteenth century. A Paiute evangelist prophet, Wovoka (originally named Jack Wilson), told Native Americans that if they practiced the Ghost Dance, a hypnotic spiritual ritual, the white man would disappear, and Native American civilization would be restored. His message spread from the Great Basin area in Utah and Nevada, north and west to California, Oregon, and Washington, and east throughout the Great Plains. The Lakota Sioux in South Dakota were influenced by the teachings of Wovoka, and established the Ghost Dance among themselves. The practice created fear and distrust among the white soldiers stationed in South Dakota. Eventually a confrontation between the two groups led to the famous massacre at Wounded Knee on December 29, 1890, where two hundred Native American people were killed. This massacre is one of the most important events in Native American history, and is still cited as an essential remembrance in Native American religion.

Another evangelist, Elijah Mohammad, established the Nation of Islam, also known as the Black Muslims, in North America following World War II. This group appropriated Islamic religious ideals in a fundamentalist revival movement designed to help African Americans recover dignity and empowerment in their lives. For three hundred and fifty years African Americans had been oppressed, first through slavery, and later through discriminatory social practices. Elijah Mohammad as messenger of the Nation of Islam, prescribed separation of the Black Muslim community from dominant white society. Members of the Nation of Islam adopted orthodox practices, which liminalized them with regard to general American society, based on standard Islamic belief, including specialized dress, family practices, and dietary restrictions. The current leader of the community, Louis Farrakhan, continues the evangelical tradition. He has been a powerful galvanizing force for the community, helping African-Americans find added dimensions to their lives. Articulate and powerful as a speaker, Farrakhan has predictably disturbed many Americans outside of his community through his separatist rhetoric.

SOCIAL ACTION

Fundamentalism strives to change the world through evangelistic promulgation of its belief structure. Therefore social action, beyond the observance of religious orthodoxy, is a regular feature of the behavior of movement members. At times such social action can be the principal activity of the group. Such social action can take many forms, ranging from informational efforts to political participation, active or passive social resistance, and violent struggle. At this point the actions of fundamentalist religious revival groups blur and begin to resemble the behavior of political activists.

Indeed, a small amount of reflection will confirm that there is no absolute separation between fundamentalist movements and other kinds of social movements and civil struggles. Elements of fundamentalist thinking can be seen in almost all struggle—armed and peaceful—against standing governmental bodies. The Irish Republican Army, the Naxalite movement in India, and the Tamil nationalists in Sri Lanka are just a sampling of groups that are willing to use extraordinary action to achieve "justice" for the societies within which they live. Such groups frequently justify their actions in moral terms verging on religious orthodoxy.

Often fundamentalist groups are driven to social action when their orthodox evangelical goals are frustrated by the events of changing social and political environments in the broader society. Fundamentalist Christians have seen themselves forced into extreme social action as a result of legislation legalizing abortion. These actions have included assaults on physicians performing abortions and bombings of abortion clinics.

An oppressed population defending itself from an oppressor is favorably viewed by most people. For this reason, fundamentalist movements often gravitate toward creating martyrs or emphasizing their oppression by the larger society in order to increase the appeal of their objectives both for their members and for the outside world. In today's world, where finance and information have become globally pervasive, good press is essential for the continuance of any movement, and fundamentalist movements have proved masterful in presenting themselves as underdogs.

Operation Rescue, an important American activist group fighting abortion, has reacted to criticism of its work even by other fundamentalist Christians by pointing up the bravery of its adherents as crusaders for God. This group is opposed to the traditional pastors and televangelists, whom movement founder Randall Terry likens to "pillars of jello." Another group, the Traditional Values Coalition, a fundamentalist Christian organization headed by Reverend Louis Sheldon that claims to represent thirty-six thousand churches in the United States, opposes abortion, homosexuality, and sex education in the schools (figure 2). In 1998, when President Clinton proposed to extend legislation to prosecute "hate crimes" in the United States to include sexual orientation, Sheldon's organization issued the following statement: "The administration's effort to expand the definition of a hate crime is nothing less than a premeditated assault on religious Americans who oppose homosexuality."

The Gush Emunim (Bloc of the Faithful) are an example of a nonmilitant Is-

FIGURE 2 The Rev. Lou Sheldon after having been spat upon by gay rights supporters. (Courtesy of the AP Archive)

raeli Jewish fundamentalist group that felt itself driven to violent social action for theological reasons. The Gush Emunim began as an ideological and nonviolent movement with theological roots in pre-Israeli Palestine. It regards the Zionist movement as sacred, and the occupation of traditional Jewish homelands by Jews as a fulfillment of prophecy leading eventually to the coming of the Messiah. Gush members were greatly encouraged by the capture of West Bank territories from Jordan in 1967. As long as progress was made toward the occupation of Palestinian territory by Jews, no violent political action was contemplated by the group.

The first militant actions by the Gush Emunim occurred following the Yom Kippur War in 1973, when the Israeli government seemed likely to return the Sinai and the Golan Heights to the Egyptians and Syrians. Gush members engaged in civil disobedience and protest to forestall this action. The rise of the Likud party in Israel in 1977 resulted in the opening of West Bank territories captured in 1967 to settlement by Jews—another encouragement to the Gush Emunim. Palestinians in the region were alarmed and reacted with violence toward the settlements. The Gush Emunim then reacted with what has been termed *settler vigilantism* against the Palestinian Arabs; they maintained that if the Israeli government was unable to provide adequate defense for the settlers, it was their obligation to defend themselves—even to the point of using deadly violence. The group's commitment to violent action as a means of achieving its religious goals was underscored in a plan following the 1978 Camp David accords between Israel and Egypt. This plan was to enact *messianic violence*, or cataclysmic action of such magnitude as to facilitate the coming of the Messiah. In this case, the plan was to blow up the Muslim sacred shrine, the Dome of the Rock, located on the Temple Mount in Jerusalem. This plan took several years to create, but was shelved at the last minute for lack of rabbinical support. The Palestinian uprising in 1987 known as the Intifada heralded more attacks on Jewish settlers. This drew Gush Emunim members into more intense violent action, and vigilantism was religiously sanctioned by the group's rabbis.

FUNDAMENTALIST MOVEMENTS AND THE BROADER SOCIETY

Fundamentalist movements can be both positive and negative in their consequences for broader society. They can turn the downtrodden and disillusioned into productive, forward-looking individuals and give them purpose in life. A fundamentalist revival movement can serve as a check against negative tendencies in society as a whole and can eventually serve as a focus for beneficial, directed social change. On the other hand, because such movements often objectify the larger society as Other and oppressor, they can produce participants who defy civil authority and are difficult to predict or control. They often operate on the edge of the law, creating automatic tension with the society in which they exist.

Because of this mixed set of effects, it is sometimes difficult for public officials to decide how to interact with fundamentalists. Their mere separation from society at large can seem threatening to public order. Zealous officials may seek prophylactic action against a given movement for no better reason than that they appear secretive and suspicious. Often the line is drawn at violence. No matter how justified the cause of a movement, or how beneficial its activities, in most societies it will meet official resistance when it espouses violent action. Additionally, in societies like the United States, the government frequently intervenes with force to protect individuals from harm even when they seem to be willing participants in their own destruction by participating in the actions of the movement.

The unintended consequence of this kind of police action is frequently a strengthening of the resolve of the fundamentalist movement to resist. Two government actions in the United States in recent years directed against fundamentalist movements attracted widespread criticism because the members of the movement, while behaving in a decidedly asocial manner, did not manifest violence and yet were killed. The first of these incidents was an action taken by the police of the city of Philadelphia against a communal, urban, political and spiritual organization called MOVE in May 1985. The group was living in abandoned buildings and refused to vacate when ordered. The police then set fire to the buildings, resulting in a number of deaths. Critics claimed that the police took the action they did because the group was largely black, and because they were secretive and defiant. The repercussions of this action continue to be a potent force in politics in Philadelphia today. The second case was a Federal Bureau of Investigation (FBI) assault on a Christian religious-political movement, the Branch Davidians, in Waco, Texas, in 1993. The group lived in cultlike isolation and advocated the destruction of the U.S. government. They also had a large arsenal of weapons but had not manifested any violent actions. The FBI laid siege to the group's compound for many days and eventually drove them to mass suicide.

The demise of the Branch Davidians became a *cause célèbre* with a small fraction of Americans as an example of extreme government interference in individual religious liberties and civil rights. Eventually, a great tragedy ensued. On April 19, 1995, the United States Federal Building in Oklahoma City, Oklahoma, was bombed, killing 168 innocent adults and children. This was the worst terrorist action ever committed in on American soil to that date. The convicted perpetrators of this crime, Timothy McVeigh and Lawrence Nichols, apparently were associated with a paramilitary "militia" group based in the state of Michigan. Testimony at their trial revealed that they believed that the bombing would trigger the overthrow of the U.S. government and lead to a public awakening resulting in a new social order. This new order would embody the values and principles of an imagined earlier age when government exercised minimal control over individual liberties. The perpetrators of this crime espoused an extreme action—in this case the bombing of innocent citizens—in order to further what they believed to be a spiritual and moral cause.

Members of the American militias are undoubtedly a fringe group at present. With an estimated fifteen thousand members, their fundamentalist movement is not widespread enough to ensure its eventual success throughout American society. Nevertheless, despite their outlying position in American social and political life they, like extremist fundamentalists elsewhere, depend on a base of supporters who are sympathetic but not personally activist. If the overall national climate of opinion shifts toward accepting their ideology, their perceived mandate for action will also increase.

In the meantime, like many of their fundamentalist counterparts in other parts of the world, the American militia members will see arrest and punishment at the hands of the government as proof of the value of their actions and gain encouragement from their repression. Thus, violent actions such as the Oklahoma City bombing may increase, even as they are decried by the larger society.

REFERENCES AND SUGGESTIONS FOR FURTHER READING

Barr, James. 1977. *Fundamentalism*. London: SCM Press. [The starting work for most modern investigations of fundamentalism. Subsequent researchers of this topic may disagree with Barr, but their debt to him is great.]

Bellah, Robert. 1970. *Tokugawa Religion: The Values of Pre-Industrial Japan*. Boston: Beacon Press (reprint of 1957 edition published by Basic Books).

Beeman, William. 1983a. "Religion and Development in Iran from the Qajar Era to the Islamic Revolution of 1978–1979." In *Religion and Global Economics*, ed. James Finn. New Brunswick and London: Transaction Books.

———. 1983b. "Images of the Great Satan: Symbolic Conceptions of the United States in the Iranian Revolution." In *Religion and Politics in Iran*, ed. Nikkie Keddie. New Haven, CT: Yale University Press.

———. 1986. *Language, Status, and Power in Iran*. Bloomington: Indiana University Press.

———. 1996. "The Iranian Revolution of 1978–79." In *The Encyclopedia of the Modern Islamic World*. Oxford: Oxford University Press.

Caplan, Lionel. 1987. "Introduction." In *Studies in Religious Fundamentalism*, ed. Lionel Caplan, 1–24. Albany: State University of New York Press. [A good collection of essays on a variety of religious traditions that can be labeled fundamentalist. These include Wahhabism in Africa, Protestant Christians in India, Turkish Muslims, and Sikh fundamentalists in the Punjab. The volume is the result of a conference held at the School of Oriental and African Studies of the University of London in the spring of 1985.]

Cohen, Norman J. 1990. *The Fundamentalist Phenomenon: A View from Within: A Response from Without*. Grand Rapids, MI: William B. Eerdmans Publishing. [A collection of thoughtful essays by a number of prominent religious studies scholars. The bulk of the essays focus on Christianity, but Islam and Judaism are also addressed.]

Deloria, Vine, Jr. 1969. *Custer Died for Your Sins*. London: Collier-Macmillan. [The classic statement on the contemporary Native American movement, including an insider view of the Ghost Dance movement.]

Easton, Nina J. 1995. "America the Enemy: Their Politics are Light Years Apart, but the Bombers of the '60s and '90s Share Volatile Rhetoric, Tangled Paranoia, and a Belief That Violence Is a Legitimate Weapon." *Los Angeles Times*, June 18, 8.

Ginzburg, Faye. 1993. "Saving America's Souls: Operation Rescue's Crusade against Abortion." In *The Fundamentalism Project*, vol. 3, *Fundamentalisms and the State*, ed. Martin E. Marty and R. Scott Appleby, 557–87. Chicago: University of Chicago Press.

Halpern, Thomas; David Rosenberg; and Irwin Suall. 1996. "Militia Movement: Prescription for Disaster." *U.S.A. Today*, January 1, 16 ff.

Holland, Judy. 1998. "NOW Picketing Condemns 2 Anti-Gay Bills in Congress." *San Francisco Examiner*, July 23.

Kageyama, Yuri. 2000. "Mori Sorry for 'Divine Nation' Remark." *San Jose Mercury-News*, May 18, 5A.

Kehoe, Alice Beck. 1989. *The Ghost Dance: Ethnohistory and Revitalization*. Ft. Worth, TX: Holt, Rinehart & Winston. [An authoritative work on the Ghost Dance movement with a useful chapter on other revival movements.]

LaBarre, Weston. 1971. "Materials for a History of Studies of Crisis Cults: A Bibliographic Essay." *Current Anthropology* 12, no. 1: 3–44.

———. 1972. *The Ghost Dance*. New York: Dell. [Classic work on Native American revivalist movements.]

Marty, Martin E., and R. Scott Appleby. 1994. "Introduction." In The *Fundamentalism Project*, vol. 2, *Fundamentalisms and Society*, ed. Martin E. Marty and R. Scott Appleby, 1–22. Chicago: University of Chicago Press. [This massive, five-volume work, edited by two distinguished religion scholars, is the culmination of a multiyear scholarly study involving dozens of researchers, including a number of anthropologists. The project has also inspired a video series for public television. The individual contributions are exceedingly variable in quality, but all contain useful descriptive information on fundamentalist movements in many societies.]

Obeyesekere, Gananath. 1995. "Buddhism, Nationhood, and Cultural Identity: A Question of Fundamentals." In *The Fundamentalism Project*, vol. 5, *Fundamentalisms Comprehended*, ed. Martin E. Marty and R. Scott Appleby, 231–55. Chicago: University of Chicago Press.

Ravitzky, Aviezer. 1994. "The Contemporary Lubavitch Hasidic Movement: Between

Conservatism and Messianism." In *The Fundamentalism Project*, vol. 4, *Accounting for Fundamentalisms: The Dynamic Character of Movements*, ed. Martin E. Marty and R. Scott Appleby, 303–27. Chicago: University of Chicago Press.

Sprinzak, Ehud. 1993. "Three Models of Religious Violence: The Case of Jewish Fundamentalism in Israel." In *The Fundamentalism Project*, vol. 3, *Fundamentalisms and the State*, ed. Martin E. Marty and R. Scott Appleby, 462–89. Chicago: University of Chicago Press.

Turner, Victor. 1974. *Dramas, Fields, and Metaphors*. Ithaca, NY: Cornell University Press.

Wallace, Anthony F. C. 1956. "Revitalization Movements: Some Theoretical Considerations for Their Comparative Study." *American Anthropologist* n.s. 58, no. 2: 264–81.

———. 1961. "Cultural Composition of the Handsome Lake Religion." In *Symposium on Cherokee and Iroquois Culture*, B. A. E. Bulletin, ed. William N. Fenton and John Gulick, 139–51. Washington, DC: Smithsonian Institution.

8.

Unraveling "Race" for the Twenty-First Century

FAYE V. HARRISON

As a social/cultural anthropologist, I have studied comparatively forms of social inequality in which "race" is a significant marker of positioning and power. At a juncture when its status as a biological concept—or, in some circles, even as an anthropological concept—is seriously contested, race can be understood as an ideologically charged distinction in social stratification and as a social and often legal classification applied to people presumed to share common physical or biological traits. Racial categories may be used to mark so-called natural differences even in contexts of ostensible homogeneity. In these cases, the racially designated populations are believed to share, at least in part, some socially salient ancestry (and, hence, presumed heritable characteristics transmitted through the "blood") construed to be of social significance and consequence to the dominant social order. Racialized societies vary in the extent to which socially salient ancestry, appearance, and sociocultural status (e.g., education, income, wealth) are used as criteria for assigning race.

Anthropological studies of the intellectual and social construction of race have proliferated over the past decade, partly as a response to the intensification of racialized tensions and identities in a number of settings around the world. The topic of race has proven to be particularly significant in my career because my ethnographic area specialty is in the Caribbean and the broader African diaspora. In settings such as these, where peoples of African descent predominate or figure prominently in other ways, social definitions and legal codifications of racial and related color distinctions have historically played a major role in "naturalizing" or representing as naturally produced and unchangeable the markedly unequal and unjust distribution of wealth, power, and prestige over the past four centuries of colonial—and now postcolonial or, more accurately, neocolonial—order. Of course, any sense of "order"—and the structure of domination supporting it—has favored the interests, worldview, and structural location of the most privileged strata of people descended mainly from northwestern Europeans and their allies around the world. From the vantage points of the subordinate segments of racially stratified societies, the orderliness, lawfulness, and "natural" guise of structured racial inequalities are often experienced as profoundly problematic assaults against their dignity, life chances, and human rights. For them, "race" is frequently experienced as a form of symbolic as well as materialized violence. However, they may also experience "race" as an identity they embrace and mobilize in everyday life as well as in more broadly based struggles for civil rights, socioeconomic mobility, and political empowerment.

In some contexts, "race" is an unmarked and, in some cases, adamantly denied dimension of lived experience and social identity whose subtlety and unsystematic quality disguises its injuries and displaces them onto more socially acknowledged and politically charged axes of difference such as class, religion, or ethnicity. Especially at a postcolonial—or neocolonial—juncture, when racism has been widely discredited and its heinous human-rights consequences exposed, "race" is often the ugly, embarrassing undercurrent of ethnic conflicts that rises to the surface only when tensions explode.

The more I reflect on my work, the more I realize that my decision to study anthropology as a university student and then later on to become a professional anthropologist may well have been influenced by the profound impact of race and racism on my formative experiences and my subsequent social identity as an American of African descent. Stigmatized in an especially dehumanizing manner, African origins and "blood" have symbolized to many Euro-Americans the social bottom and an ever-threatening contagion to white purity. In my case as well as that of many other black people, the greater social salience of my African heritage relative to my other ancestral origins is consistent with a cultural logic that anthropology has helped me understand. According to "hypodescent," a culturally specific mode of reckoning descent, individuals with any sub-Saharan African heritage have historically been incorporated into the category to which their racially subordinate ancestors were assigned. This classificatory praxis has relegated people of any known African origins to precarious life chances and structural positions.

As I reflect upon who I am, what I do, and what my lived experience has been, I cannot escape the hard "social fact" that I, like many of the anthropological subjects whom I have researched in the field and in the library, live a racially marked existence. The invidious racial distinctions around which my natal community's life was organized and constrained impelled me to think critically about social and cultural differences, and being a particularly inquisitive youngster, violated by "Jim Crow" segregation and inspired by the movement that dismantled it, I yearned to be able to think beyond the limits of folk theory and common sense. Moreover, I yearned to see and travel—both physically and metaphorically—beyond the local, state, and national boundaries that restricted most people's, including my own kinfolk's, gaze.

As a child, my curiosity and hunger to understand race and racism prompted me to raise questions about how the United States fit into the larger world of diversity. Why had one of the most rigid systems of race relations developed in the United States? Does the "racial democracy" that Brazilians and other Latin Americans tout really exist, and, if so, does it represent a model that Americans or South Africans should emulate? I eventually learned that these questions as well as the many others I would eventually ask are amenable to the kinds of inquiry that social and cultural anthropologists undertake, which, for the most part, are modes of investigation that take ordinary people's voices and everyday experiences seriously.

A BRIEF HISTORY OF THE CONCEPT AND SOCIAL PHENOMENON
The only "race" is the human race!

Ironically, while my youthful interrogation of race and racism may have led me to anthropology, the anthropology I encountered in the 1970s and 1980s was largely silent on the question of racial inequality and the ideological and material relations that constitute and sustain racism. However, a few anthropologists continued the tradition of antiracism that had been so much a part of the Boasian school of thought that defined prominent trends within the discipline during the first half of the twentieth century. Franz Boas and his associates and students played a strategic part in dismantling scientific racism and defining the parameters for an antiracist mode of inquiry. Boas's work was probably informed by his experience as a German Jew, whose stigmatized "subracial" status was marked and problematized by anti-Semitic folk ideologies that were eventually elevated by Nazism. The German anthropology of that time played a role in legitimating those unconscionable ideas. In addition to the work of Boas and its legacy, in both the United States and in Europe anthropological inquiry has also been influenced by other antiracist and anticolonial projects, including those advanced by intellectuals of color whose contributions were too frequently unrecognized. (See Drake 1987 and Harrison 1995 for reviews of this intellectual history).

Just before I discovered anthropology as a university student, a vigorous debate on the biology and social significance of race occurred during the 1960s, perhaps paralleling and informed by the struggles for and against racial discrimination and its alternative, desegregation, or integration. Due to its operational ambiguity, arbitrariness, artificiality, and erroneous and harmful assumptions, the concept declined in usage. The intense debates over race's scientific status led many anthropologists to adopt a devout "no-race" position which, unwittingly, resulted in a failure to investigate racism along with race as a socially constructed phenomenon deeply grounded in experiential and material realities. To rid the field of its problematic biological baggage, those anthropologists, with Ashley Montagu (1942) in the lead, jettisoned any notion of race and embraced the culture-centered concepts of "ethnicity" and "ethnic group" as alternatives. Interestingly, although many biological anthropologists attempted to make a conceptual shift away from species- and subspecies-centered thinking to clinal approaches (which examine cross-cutting gradients of populations varying in gene frequencies), they were not completely successful. A sizable minority of physical anthropologists continue to use the race concept, and, for the most part, even those who do not use it have, nonetheless, failed to generate new terminology and a substantial body of research acknowledging the complex nature of human population variation and biohistory. The complete break from the legacy of scientific racism is also being blocked by formidable societal influences, among them the impact of neoconservative foundations such as the Pioneer Fund, which encourage research seeking genetic determinants for academic achievement (notably IQ), upward mobility, and violent crime.

By the early 1990s race as a social and an intellectual construction reemerged as a major focus in anthropological analysis, especially in the United States. Perhaps it is better understood today that, as a dimension of socially defined difference intersecting with and often indistinguishable from ethnicity, race encodes social and cultural differences presumed to be unbridgeable and unchanging, and to have pathological effects on the dominant national body. Ethnicity and race can be thought of as interrelated but distinct dimensions of identity formation, and, depending on the context, one dimension can modify or take precedence over the other. Anthropological analysis now recognizes that, despite the present state of considerable biological knowledge disproving the existence of natural races, *racism*, as an oppressive structure of inequality and power, remains prevalent and persistent with the resilient capacity to alter and disguise its form in response to changing social, political, and economic conditions. Despite an absence or a suppression of race-centered prejudice, racism can be the unintended outcome of everyday discourses, behaviors, and institutional arrangements (Wetherell and Potter 1993). Racism is not only an ideology, discourse, or set of attitudes; it is a system of material relations with ideas, meanings, and sentiments embedded in those relations (Frankenberg 1993, 70).

There is some agreement among many anthropologists and historians that racism arose in the historically specific context of Western colonial expansion and world capitalist development and is not a transhistorical phenomenon existing in all societies and cultures at all times (Williams 1966; Wolf 1982). While racism may assume nearly global proportions today, these far-reaching perimeters derive largely from the roots and routes of international capital's tumultuous history. This is not to say that ideas and prejudices about physical differences were insignificant before the rise of the transatlantic slave trade and the historically unprecedented racial slavery that emerged in the hemisphere that Europeans labeled as the New World. Evidence suggests that folk classifications stereotyping physical traits existed in some precolonial societies; however, it seems that those categories were largely local and particularistic in their significance and impact. In other words, they did not operate in contexts of sustained racial stratification. With the emergence and consolidation of colonial empires, particularly colonies of exploitation, and the modern world-system, the salience and scope of classification systems based on phenotype, or appearance, grew and changed into global racial taxonomies with concrete implications for denying the humanity of whole segments of the world's population. At that juncture in world history and human social development, phenotype (or color) prejudice came to be institutionalized through its convergence with slavery and the formal elaboration of ideas by intellectuals, particularly "scientists," who accounted for social differences in terms of inherent biophysical differences (Drake 1987). As Eric Wolf illuminated in his now classic anthropological history of the world-system, racial classifications were used against targeted peoples who "were made to labor in servitude to support a new class of overlords" (Wolf 1982, 380). In his view, racial categories "mirror" the political processes that alienated populations of whole continents from their lands and transformed them into a supply of coerced labor. Contemporary racial classifications continue to invoke presumed descent from those colonially subjugated populations and thereby deny their descendants access to the more privileged and secure segments of the labor market as well as to organizational power.

RACE RECONFIGURED IN AN ERA OF GLOBAL RESTRUCTURING

Many scholars are observing that during this age of globalization human societies are becoming more tightly integrated into a nexus of intercultural and transnational fields of power, knowledge, and commodification. Advanced telecommunications, the increased mobility of capital and labor, and rapid flows of culture and commodities compress time and space across an uneven political and economic geography, giving the impression that, in some respects, the world is becoming smaller and more accessible. The world as "global village," however, is not set against an idyllic background. Unlike the principles of reciprocity and redistribution which once governed everyday life in the typical village of the ethnographic record, the global community is marked by, among other things, a decentralization of capital accumulation and an upward reconcentration of wealth in the hands of a few. Within this global community we also find a heightening of differences and a deepening of identity politics, often along life-threatening lines of conflict. In many instances, these volatile lines of differentiation relate to shifting dynamics of race as they interact with and mediate those of class, ethnicity, nationality, and gender. Jonathan Friedman explains this pattern of deepening differentiation in terms of the cultural processes that economic forces have engendered. He argues that along with the global system's economic fragmentation there is a tendency toward cultural fragmentation and its concomitant crisis of identity, as exhibited in "the weakening of former national identities and the emergence of new identities . . . based on [the] primordial loyalties [of] ethnicity, race, local community, language and other culturally concrete forms" (Friedman 1994, 86). Movements organized around these distinctions have increased all over the world, in both the "center" and "periphery."

Today, racial meanings and practices are changing, becoming less stable and more contradictory, and ranging in visibility from subtle, hidden subtexts to flagrant acts of hate speech and genocidal violence. Racial tensions and politics are not at all confined to societies, such as those of the United States and South Africa, in which the most blatant and rigid forms of racial formation developed in contexts of white supremacy. As anthropological studies of intergroup tensions in Fiji, Sri Lanka, and Rwanda illustrate, racialization, or *the social processes that give rise to new racial identities or the transformation of old ones*, is not limited to social orders structured around the (immediate) dominance of "whites" (Howard 1991; Daniel 1996; de Waal 1994). While in the overall global scheme of things, whiteness in its cross-cultural varieties has certainly come to be a principal locus of domination, it is important to note that there are also other racisms—subordinate racisms—which, nonetheless, ultimately feed into the structural power of whiteness.

To underscore the severity and far-reaching scope of the problems caused by deepening disparities and conflicts around the world, some researchers have used the concept of *global apartheid* to characterize the troubling gaps in wealth, power, military control, and life expectancy that are widening as neoliberal, free market, global integration proceeds. This state of affairs unleashes considerable *structural violence*—symbolic, psychological, and physical violations emanating from situations and institutional configurations structured in dominance. Structural violence disproportionately assaults impoverished people in the Third World—that is the "South" or Southern Hemisphere where structural relations and processes that also produce uneven and unequal development in the "North" are most concentrated. For the most part, those most adversely affected are peoples of color whose subordinate positions within international fields of power and political economy have historically been rationalized in terms of class and nation as well as race. Even at this neocolonial juncture, as race theorist Howard Winant points out, virtually all over the world dark skin still correlates with the brunt of social inequality and structural violence. However, despite race's global reach, he warns us not to assume any overarching uniformity in patterns of racial formation, for "each nation-state, each political system, each cultural system necessarily constructs a unique racialized social structure, a particular complex of racial meanings and identities" (Winant 1994, 123). Anthropologists, with their comparative research orientation, are likely to contribute a great deal to our understanding of the diversity of racial formations.

North Asian Ambiguity

Since much of the scholarship on race and racism colors racial domination white, correlating it with European descent, it is important to signal the collaborative role that Japanese capital plays in racializing the international division of labor. Aihwa Ong's ethnography of female industrial workers in Malaysia implicates Japanese economic interests in helping to create conditions under which Third World women have become model racialized subjects within a new colonial frontier for capital accumulation (Ong 1987, 1991). Anthropologists have also begun to examine the liminal location—between the "Civilized White" and the "Barbarous Black"—that the Japanese occupy in the global racial hierarchy. For instance, by denigrating the black Other in their mass culture, the Japanese align themselves with whiteness and all it symbolizes in terms of wealth, power, cultural capital, and racial supremacy (Russell 1991). This bias against blackness and other stigmatized forms of racial difference has informed business leaders' assessment of workforce performance in Western economies such as the United States, the United Kingdom, and Germany, where workers are becoming increasingly ethnically and racially heterogeneous due to the international migration of workers from semiperipheral and peripheral economic zones of southern Europe and the Southern Hemisphere. A few years ago, considerable controversy arose over public statements by Japanese business leaders about the disadvantages accrued from employing cognitively inferior workers (e.g., racial minorities) in the United States. According to them, the "mongrelization" of labor within the West is an economic liability.

New Immigrants as Racial Others

Under conditions of postmodernity, postcoloniality, and the post–Cold War era, once-established cultural relations, boundaries, and distances are being disrupted and renegotiated. Extensive economic restructuring, political realignments, and policy shifts in both the North and South are rendering race relations a more volatile front of power and cultural struggle. In the increasingly multiracial nation-states of the North, the meanings and practices of contemporary forms of racism are being used to mobilize xenophobic attacks against immigrants and foreign students. Particularly across northwestern Europe and North America, immigrants, especially "visible immigrants" from the Third World, have come to represent destabilizing, disorderly, and parasitic racial outsiders whose place within Europe's nations and "imagined communities" is tenuous.

According to Jeffrey Cole's ethnographic study of southern Italian workers' everyday reactions to African and Asian immigrants, even within a single European country the extent to which immigrants are perceived as threatening and are subjected to racism varies across regions with divergent patterns of economic development, modes of political organization, and histories of emigration. As emigrants to the industrial north, Sicilians are relegated to the bottom of the labor market and stigmatized as "lazy, rude, and dangerous." Given this experience, they are less inclined than their northern counterparts to express "working-class racism"—to "assert white superiority, denigrate immigrants, or blame them for the countless ills and indignities suffered by the poor and unemployed" (Cole 1997, 131). Indeed, Cole explains that in the north *terroni* (the derogatory term for southerners) as well as foreigners are targets of racist graffiti and gang violence. Derided as Italy's "blacks" and "Africans," Sicilians occupy an ambiguous position, "being 'black' in relation to Italy's north but 'white' in relation to new immigrants" (20). While this ambiguity does not immunize them from anti-immigrant racism, racist expressions in the south tend not to exhibit an explicit political character as they do in the north, where gangs of neo-Nazi skinheads are on the attack and anti-immigrant sentiment is highly politicized. This level of politicization is largely absent in the south, where a patronage system thwarts grassroots political expression, and immigrants have been integrated into the job and housing markets along basically noncompetitive lines. Southern racism occurs in the form of a "brutally exploitative labor market" (124).

The Racial Othering of European Targets

In postcommunist Eastern Europe, economic restructuring has led to widespread unemployment and widening disparities in income and wealth. One consequence of this is the high levels of resentment shown towards foreign students from Latin

America, Africa, and Asia, some of whom become targets of racist violence. However, those most vulnerable to racist discrimination and violence are Europeans themselves, branded as "Orientals" because of their religious affiliation (e.g., Jews and Muslims) or their reputed cultural origins in Asia (e.g., the Roma, or Gypsies, who originate from northern India). Within the last few years in the Czech Republic, Rom have suffered attacks by skinheads, while more than a third of the country's population has supported confining them to isolated reserves. In 1993 a law was passed disenfranchising half of them from citizenship.

Further south, the newly drawn boundaries of the nation-states of the former Yugoslavia (e.g., Bosnia and Herzegovina) have been established in a context of catastrophic inter-ethnic conflict. This war zone, reminding us of the European atrocities of World War II, focuses world attention on the extent to which violently competing nationalisms, defining certain peoples as outsiders to newly defined nations, draw upon assumptions and meanings that are, by implication if not by direct admission, raced. Through a militarized discourse underscoring ethnic and national identities, differences are imagined to be so fundamental and irreconcilable that they somehow justify genocidal campaigns of "ethnic cleansing." In this conflict-laden context, cultural differences are not viewed as amenable to change. On the contrary, they are naturalized as heritable essences so threatening that they demand to be, at best, physically banished or, at worst, eliminated so that the security of national sovereignty can be achieved. Feminist observers have made us aware that in this struggle the battlefield has been extended to the racially marked bodies of women and girls, through whose rape the assaulted nations' respectability is violated, undermining the prospects for preserving national patrimony (Kesić 1996, 51; Williams 1996, vii).

Neo-Racisms

While biodeterminist conceptions of race, whether nineteenth-century or contemporary variants, emphasize natural and biological differences, many current perspectives on race are couched in a language of culture, ethnicity, and nationalism. Consequently, in many settings around the world today, there is "racism without race"; that is, there are public discourses on irreconcilable, unchangeable, and virtually heritable sociocultural differences without any explicit acknowledgment that "races" exist or that "racial" distinctions continue to be socially and politically significant. In these supposedly color-blind, raceless contexts, which are often difficult to interpret or decode, a concept of culture (whether linked to ethnicity or nation) and a broader, culture-centered idiom within which it is embedded serve as an ideological device that defines social differences as essential or natural and, hence, reconfigures racial boundaries (Balibar 1991).

Anthropologists debate whether the xenophobic, anti-immigrant situations in Western European countries such as France and Germany represent instances of "neoracism," in which race is masked but remains a vital subtext, or cases of "cultural fundamentalism," in which a real shift in the conceptual structure of difference-making has been made to usher those societies into a truly "postrace" era (Stolcke 1995). The latter argument perhaps has some appeal, because traditional racist discourses—biologizing discourses—no longer have legitimacy in those political contexts, not even in the eyes of right-wing activists. These politicos tend to conceptualize difference in terms of bounded, incommensurate, and spatially segregated cultural entities that cannot be evaluated in terms of strict hierarchy or explicit relations of superiority and inferiority. In the United States, a comparable, race-evasive, color-blind discourse has gained popularity among growing sectors of conservatives, while others still cling to ideas about the determinative role of IQ and genes in leadership, class mobility, and academic achievement.

In the recent U.S. context, race-evasive idioms highlighting culture and even class—that dimension of social stratification about which Americans usually have little to say—have gained considerable political utility. Increasingly, color-blind conservatives acknowledge the existence of race and racism only when they think whites are the target of a "reverse racism" emanating from government policy and racial minorities' insistence on "making race an issue." Whereas a language of cultural deficits and pathology frames arguments about the problems impoverished blacks and Latinos supposedly impose on American society, a limited notion of class is being used to privilege the legal personality and give a competitive edge to working-class whites over racial minorities situated across the class spectrum. This discursive tactic evades the persistent obstacles that racism presents to blacks and other racial minorities, regardless of their class position. It ignores the fact that the class privileges enjoyed by upper- and middle-class blacks do not immunize them from institutional and cultural racism. For instance, recent studies document that racial redlining deprives African Americans of mortgages that whites of comparable economic circumstances have no difficulty getting. The new, class-focused discourse, then, marginalizes racial oppression by privileging the injuries that whites suffer from class subordination. The injuries that blacks—who are disproportionately represented at the social bottom—suffer from class tend to be attributed to the absence of appropriate "family values," "personal responsibility," or a "culture of achievement" rather than to the outcome of structured class disparities mediated by race. There is little recognition in U.S. public discourse that class intersects with race and that the constraints or opportunities, oppressions or privileges, associated with class are exacerbated or enhanced by race's structural power. Race-evasive discourses, whether centered on notions of culture or class, divert public attention from the persistence of racial oppression while serving to reproduce it.

The discursive shift away from conceptions of racial hierarchy to those of cultural nationalism or class, however, has not been accompanied by parallel changes in material conditions. While American neoconservatives may argue that post–Civil Rights U.S. society is free from racism, that public policy should be completely color-blind, and that racial minorities have no constitutional right to the government protections and sponsorship encompassed within affirmative action policies, disparate outcomes in infant mortality, incarceration and death-penalty sentencing, wealth accumulation, and many other domains of everyday life demonstrate that racial inequalities persist as a concrete reality warranting careful examination and explanation.

In Europe, xenophobic discourses may depart from representing "stranger cultures" in explicit terms of inferiority or superiority, but in the larger international arena, immigrants' homelands and home cultures are clearly positioned in a hierarchical global system that ranks nations and ethnic populations according to disparities of structural power, political economy, and culture. Thus, though Britain and France no longer retain the stature they once held as colonial powers, within the contemporary, neocolonial world order, the European Community undoubtedly has a superior structural position compared to the nation-states of, for instance, sub-Saharan Africa. Since geopolitical power and wealth are now being reconcentrated in the North rather than the South (from which most racialized immigrants come), the modern reality of global apartheid belies any notion of separate but comparable cultures.

A CLOSER LOOK AT IDEOLOGIES OF RACIAL DEMOCRACY AND MIXEDNESS

Given the apparently castelike ascriptions and boundaries of the most systematically oppressive racial formations, it is instructive to examine the more fluid socioracial orders of Latin America and the Caribbean. In many of these settings appearance and social markers such as class and acculturation to Eurocentric norms weigh as much as or, in some situations, even more than ancestry in determining sociocultural status. Particularly in the Caribbean and in those parts of Central and South America where there was an African presence historically, tripartite racial classifications (differentiating white, brown, and black) and variations of a more complexly graded color continuum have represented intriguing contrasts to the largely bipolar definition of race in the United States. The comparative study of those New World societies in which racial slavery has been an important chapter of economic history has revealed a diversity of sociocultural experiences and identities among peoples who share African origins. These varying socioracial identities have been constructed according to varying contexts of demography, language and culture contact, social structure, power structures, and patterns of colonial and postcolonial economic development. As a result of these differences, it is possible for an African American from the United States to be classified as something other than "black"—and perhaps even "white"—in some Caribbean and Latin American contexts.

The region south of the United States has long been represented as a home of "racial democracy" and *mestizaje* (mixedness), presumed to be an alternative to racism. However, as anthropologist Peter Wade argues, though many Latin Americans continue to deny that racism exists, "three polar categories [black, white, and Indian] retain their integrity and . . . meaning" (Wade 1993, 22) despite the existence of ambiguous and blurred boundaries between graded color categories. In other words, just because it is difficult for locals to determine who should be categorized "black" and which physical features are "racially" significant does not diminish race's social significance.

Recent research shows that racial democracy is largely discursive; that is, it is the outcome of nationalist ideologies which marginalize both Indianness and blackness to the extent that they fail to melt into these nations' exaltation of *mestizaje* and *blanqueamiento* (whitening). The privileging of the European contribution to the "mixed" nation has clearly been key. Thus, Wade argues that *mestizaje*, rather than being the democratizing agent it has been claimed to be, coexists with and mediates discrimination and exclusion.

According to Arlene Torres and Norman Whitten, *mestizaje* is a "master symbol of the nation" that reveals "an uneasiness about [and, at worst, a revulsion toward] black and indigenous ethnic-bloc formation" (Whitten and Torres 1992, 20). An associated concept is *indigenismo*, a celebration and commemoration of the indigenous contribution to the nation, not to be confused with *autodeterminación indígena* (native self-determination). A key symbol of local nationalisms, *indigenismo* reflects, on one hand, "a search for the creative dimensions of nationalism through the symbolism of an indigenous past and, on the other hand, a social-political literary symbol that conveys the mood of remorse over the living conditions of contemporary 'acculturated Indians'" (Torres and Whitten 1998, 7). The ideology of *mestizaje*, which is informed by white/mestizo (and therefore non-Indian) constructs, embraces both these aspects of *indigenismo* while paradoxically excluding native peoples from national affairs. This exclusion, along with the violent repression that often accomplishes it, has created, at worst, patterns of racial conflict and, at best, fragile forms of racial rapprochement that inhibit progress toward establishing multicultural democracies. The most graphic instance of *mesti-*

them investigate how everyday racism and racial identities are experienced and interpreted among people for whom racism is often a taboo topic of discussion, even within their families.

Twine studied an agricultural town in the coffee-growing region northwest of Rio de Janeiro, where she observed that racial egalitarianism and "the mulatto escape hatch" (the notion that racially mixed people are whitened and therefore not targets of antiblack racism) were myths that even Afro-Brazilians themselves played a major part in sustaining (figure 1). Although recent legal reform has codified racism as unconstitutional and criminal, Brazilians' understanding of racism is rather limited in that they believe that it must assume the form of formal policies of discrimination and segregation, as once existed in American Jim Crow and South African apartheid. To them, racism entails the complete exclusion of blacks from white homes, even as servants and casual friends. More subtle, de facto practices—be they discursive, socioeconomic, or institutional—are construed only in terms of class inequalities and are not considered at all relevant to the phenomenon of racism. However, based on her observations and the stories Euro-Brazilians and Afro-Brazilians shared with her, Twine found that Afro-Brazilians—both blacks and mulattos (from black-white mixture)—are commonly excluded from positions of community leadership, discouraged from participating in predominantly white middle- and upper-class social clubs, avoided or rejected in many so-

FIGURE 1 Coffee pickers, Brazil. (Maria Luzia M. Carvalho/Panos)

cial situations, represented pejoratively in the media and in popular projections of beauty, and seen as undesirable candidates for marrying whites. (Nonetheless, whites are quite willing and eager to have sexual relations with them and to establish cross-racial relations of Godparentage [*criacão*], which involves the adoption of black children.) Blacks are even rejected as potential marital partners by other blacks and mulattos who have bought into the hope of whitening their children and grandchildren. Several Afro-Brazilians admitted to Twine that when registering their children's birth, which is typically done well after the event without children being present, they register them as "white" and, hence, contribute to a gross inflation of the number of whites in the official records.

Twine reveals the covert racism embedded in the widespread practice of *criacão*. Within the adopting households, these children assume the role of unpaid domestic workers denied the opportunity to attend school regularly because of heavy work responsibilities. Yet Brazilians see the institution of *criacão* as altruistic and as a measure of the absence of racism. Twine explains how the sentimental, power-evasive idiom of fictive kinship "transforms racial hierarchies of domestic labor into unremarkable multiracial households." For Brazilians located across the color spectrum, living in the same household (regardless of how exploitative the division of labor is) and erotic desire across racial lines are taken as key symbols of racial egalitarianism.

As Twine demonstrates, Afro-Brazilians do not completely deny the realities of racism. They acknowledge the hurtful rejections they experience in social situations, and they avoid those painful incidents through patterns of self-seclusion which protect them from being humiliated by "mundane forms of racism" such as verbal abuse. However, experiences with racism are usually interpreted as individual problems not to be openly discussed or confronted. Unfortunately, this avoidance allows the fallacy of racial democracy to be sustained.

Whereas Twine paints a troubling picture in which there is no discursive or political space for making sense of racism or transmitting the conceptual and practical skills for confronting it to the next generation of Brazilians, Burdick's work in Rio and its suburbs paints a more complex and more hopeful picture. Although he concurs with Twine that ordinary black folk are certainly alienated from the black movement's framing of issues, he questions the implication that "false consciousness" is the reason ordinary black folk are not more involved in the new black identity politics. By focusing on popular religious groups, he illuminates how these "groups and informal networks also create pools of people predisposed to act upon the world, but away from social movement organizations" (1998, 200).

Burdick (1998) portrays black women's predicament and their struggle against the cruel emotional wounds that they in particular suffer from pervasive prejudices regarding skin color and hair texture. His demonstration of the gendered basis of raced experience uncovers the emotional impact of Eurocentric beauty standards and constructs of femininity on black women and the psychosocial consequences that those standards have in the domains of love, dating, and marriage. Examining color dynamics in these social arenas, he shows that there are significant gaps between the experiences that black and racially mixed women (*mulatas* and *morenas*, whose nonwhite background appears to be Indian rather than black) have in love, at work, and when participating in popular religious groups. According to him, these differences are being understated or altogether denied within the black movement.

Burdick unravels the ways in which Afro-Brazilians in three different arenas of popular Christianity interpret and reconstruct the meanings of blackness and Afro-Brazilian womanhood. In the male-centered, Africanized mass of the black pastoral movement within Brazilian Catholicism, women's bodies are made into spectacles through liturgical dance and musical performances which display black women's sensual beauty while directing it toward marriage and having children in families in which strong black men are household heads. Black women's problems in love and marriage are silenced, so that a heroic image of black masculinity can prevail.

Although black movement activists are extremely critical and suspicious of Pentecostalism, which they see as hostile to black culture and as a religious mechanism of whitening and self-negation, Burdick argues that black women who convert to this religion experience a form of self-valorization that has nothing to do with their color and outside appearance. An alternative vision of physical beauty is fostered by theological tenets emphasizing the beauty of the soul and respect for natural beauty over both prevailing standards of beauty that glorify white femininity and a *morena/mulata* mystique that sacrifices black women's self-concept and emotional security. Significantly, this new spiritual aesthetic has resulted in a more even playing field for courtship and marriage than black women experience outside Pentecostal churches, and *negras* enjoy a sense of personal triumph for being accepted for their souls rather than being treated primarily as sexual objects. Older black women are also achieving alternative identities that depart from the popular stereotypes of self-effacing, subservient eager-to-please, black maids found on Brazilian television. Burdick illuminates the complex relationship of Pentecostal faith with black identity, showing that the religion's "belief and action form a field of contradictory forces that can both stimulate and hold in check the development of racial identities" (1998, 122).

Finally, Burdick examines the popular devotion to blessed Anastácia, the slave saint who was muzzled and tortured by her master for not submitting to him.

Black movement activists are critical of this set of practices and its imagery for its fatalism toward racism, its focus on individual health and miraculous healing, and its endorsement of "facile racial reconciliation" (Burdick 1998, 151). In contrast, Burdick claims that the devotion helps black women in their everyday life "to value themselves physically, challenge dominant aesthetic values, cope with spousal abuse, and imagine possibilities of racial healing based on a fusion of real experiences and utopian hope" (1998, 149–50). Black activists feel uncomfortable with the image of a black woman in face-iron, silenced, and victimized as a slave. But devotees see Anastácia and her life in different terms. Depending on their location in the socioracial continuum, they see her as a *negra, mulata,* or *morena* who experienced a tragic romance with her master, or a rape, or a refusal to submit for the sake of her dignity and honor. While *morenas* and *mulatas,* following the prevailing ideology of mixedness, are apt to focus on romance, black women interpret Anastácia's predicament in terms of her resistance against rape. This particular interpretation helps them recover a sense of honor they have been denied by the stereotype of the slave woman ready to submit her body in exchange for a little better treatment. These religious devotees, unlike most of the black women Twine describes, have not forgotten the indignities of slavery, and actively invest positive, enabling meanings in the iconography of their black female saint. Burdick concludes that, at least in some cases, the devotion to Blessed Anastácia contributes to "the development of stronger, more self-valorizing, and more critical black consciousness" (1998, 179).

In sum, Afro-Brazilians as well as other Latin Americans negotiate and manage the ambiguities of race and color in ways that vary by gender, age, religious arenas, regional geographies, and exposure to and participation in global circuits which circulate North American (as well as Caribbean and African) models of blackness. Indeed, across Latin America the cultural struggle over the meanings of race as they are being reconfigured today has become more visible, making it difficult to deny the significance of race, black and indigenous movements, and the potential expansion of democratic participation by the formation of identities more rooted in visions of racial, class, and gender justice.

Whether in arenas of academic research, public debate within nation-states, or the deliberations within the UN's human rights committees over states' obligations under the International Convention on the Elimination of All Forms of Racial Discrimination (ICARD), it is imperative that the confusion over what constitutes something as "racial" or "racist" be offset by conceptual tools that anthropological inquiry can provide, at least in part. More scholars and activists have come to recognize that the models of race and racism that evolved from the North American and Southern African experiences do not exhaust the discursive and material structures of racial formation that developed in the past and are still developing and redeveloping in the present world. To the extent that race intersects and entangles with other dimensions of inequality, power, and identity, it commonly ebbs and flows as an invidious undercurrent that gains greatest visibility when tensions heighten and, as E. Valentine Daniel says, "get really nasty" (1996, 15). However, even "nasty" intergroup situations may be rationalized in idioms that deny the relevance, the power, or the existence of that invidious social distinction called race. Current reconfigurations of racism demand careful scrutiny with investigative tools that anthropologists can help offer as a public intellectual service to the world of the twenty-first century.

REFERENCES AND SUGGESTIONS FOR FURTHER READING

Anderson, Benedict. 1983. *Imagined Communities. Reflections on the Origin and Spread of Nationalism*. New York: Verso.

Baker, Lee D. 1998. *From Savage to Negro: Anthropology and the Construction of Race, 1896–1954*. Berkeley: University of California Press. [This book analyzes the social construction of race in U.S. society by focusing on anthropology's role in making and remaking race. The author examines the discipline's interactions with major political currents, legal struggles culminating in Supreme Court decisions, popular cultural representations, and wider intellectual trends.]

Balibar, Etienne. 1991. "Is There a 'Neo-Racism'?" In *Race, Nation, Class: Ambiguous Identities*, by Etienne Balibar and Immanuel Wallerstein, 15–28. New York: Verso.

Banton, Michael. 1966. *International Action against Racial Discrimination*. Oxford: Clarendon Press.

———. 1983. *Racial and Ethnic Competition*. Cambridge: Cambridge University Press.

———. 1988. *Racial Consciousness*. London and New York: Longman.

Brodkin, Karen. 1998. *How Jews Became White Folks and What That Says About Race in America*. New Brunswick, NJ: Rutgers University Press. [In this provocative book, a cultural anthropologist contributes to the current trend of studying whiteness as a historically contingent social construction. This research adds American Jews (of Eastern European origins) to the growing literature on how particular European immigrants and their descendants (particularly the Irish) became "white" in the United States.]

Burdick, John. 1998. *Blessed Anastácia: Women, Race, and Popular Christianity in Brazil*. New York: Routledge.

Cole, Jeffrey. 1997. *The New Racism in Europe: A Sicilian Ethnography*. Cambridge: Cambridge University Press.

Contemporary Forum: Race and Racism. 1998. *American Anthropologist* 100, no. 3: 607–731 (special issue: Faye V. Harrison, guest editor). [This special issue contains essays that examine "race" from the perspectives of anthropology's subdisciplines, population biology, and ethnic studies. Also included are the official statements on race from the American Anthropological Association and the American Association of Physical Anthropologists.]

Daniel, E. Valentine. 1996. *Charred Lullabies: Chapters in an Anthropography of Violence.* Princeton, NJ: Princeton University Press.

de Waal, Alexander. 1994. "Genocide in Rwanda." *Anthropology Today* 10, no. 3: 1–2.

Drake, St. Clair. 1987. *Black Folk Here and There: An Essay in Anthropology and History.* Vol. 1. Los Angeles: Center for Afro-American Studies, University of California, Los Angeles.

———. 1990. *Black Folk Here and There: An Essay in Anthropology and History.* Vol. 2. Los Angeles: Center for Afro-American Studies, University of California, Los Angeles. [In this two-volume work, a distinguished Africanist and African diaspora scholar presents a magisterial study of the Old World African diaspora before the era of colonial expansion. By examining the meanings of blackness (specifically negroidness) in the Nile River Valley, the Middle East, the Mediterranean, and northern European Christendom, the author argues that slavery and skin color prejudice were distinct phenomena before their intersection in the racialized slavery systems of the New World.]

Frankenberg, Ruth. 1993. *White Women, Race Matters: The Social Construction of Whiteness.* Minneapolis: University of Minnesota Press. [A highly nuanced discourse analysis that illuminates white women's experience of whiteness and the gendered dimensions of racial identity. An important feminist work that exposes the raced character of white folks' normative status.]

Friedman, Jonathan. 1994. *Cultural Identity and Global Process.* London: Sage Publications.

Gilroy, Paul. 1991. *"There Ain't No Black in the Union Jack": The Cultural Politics of Race and Nation.* Chicago: University of Chicago Press. [An important exploration of racial politics in Britain, this book interrogates the relations among race, class, and nation. The analytical focus is on black Britons.]

Gregory, Steven, and Roger Sanjek, eds. 1994. *Race.* New Brunswick, NJ: Rutgers University Press. [A collection of essays that interrogate the social significance of race from the perspective of a diversity of cultural experiences, mainly within the United States. Several of the contributors are anthropologists in this multidisciplinary volume coedited by anthropologists.]

Harrison, Faye V. 1995. "The Persistent Power of 'Race' in the Cultural and Political Economy of Racism." *Annual Review of Anthropology* 24: 47–74.

———. 1998. "Introduction: Expanding the Discourse on 'Race.'" *American Anthropologist* (special issue: *Contemporary Forum: Race and Racism*), 100, no. 3: 609–31.

Howard, Michael. 1991. *Fiji: Race and Politics in an Island State.* Vancouver: University of British Columbia.

Kesić, Vesna. 1996. "Never Again a War: Women's Bodies Are Battlefields." In *Look at the World Through Women's Eyes: Plenary Speeches from the NGO Forum on Women, Beijing 1995,* ed. Eva Friedlander, 51–53. New York: Women, Ink.

Montagu, Ashley. 1942. *Man's Most Dangerous Myth: The Fallacy of Race.* New York: Columbia University Press.

Oliver, Melvin L., and Thomas Shapiro. 1997. *Black Wealth/White Wealth: A New Perspective on Racial Inequality.* New York: Routledge.

Ong, Aihwa. 1987. *Spirits of Resistance and Capitalist Discipline: Factory Women in Malaysia.* Albany: State University of New York Press.

———. 1991. "The Gender and Labor Politics of Postcoloniality." *Annual Review of Anthropology* 20: 279–309.

Russell, J. 1991. "Race and Reflexivity: The Black Other in Contemporary Japanese Mass Culture." *Cultural Anthropology* 6, no. 1: 3–25.

Sarduy, Pedro, and Jean Stubbs. 1993. "Introduction: The Rite of Social Communion." In *AfroCuba: An Anthology of Cuban Writing on Race, Politics, and Culture,* ed. Pedro Sarduy and Jean Stubbs, 1–33. Melbourne: Ocean Press; New York: Center for Cuban Studies; and London: Latin American Bureau.

Segal, Daniel. 1993. "'Race' and 'Colour' in Pre-Independence Trinidad and Tobago." In *Trinidad Ethnicity,* ed. Kevin Yelvington, 81–115. Knoxville: University of Tennessee Press.

Smedley, Audrey. 1999 [1993]. *Race in North America: Origin and Evolution of a Worldview.* 2d ed. Boulder, CO: Westview Press. [Winner of the Gustavus Myers Center's Outstanding Book Award, this is an authoritative study of the sociohistorical construction of race as a folk classification, a "scientific" concept, and a worldview within U.S. society and culture.]

Spears, Arthur, ed. 1999. *Race and Ideology: Language, Symbolism, and Popular Culture.* Detroit, MI: Wayne State University Press. [An engaging collection of essays on ideologies of race as reflected in popular culture, diverse linguistic and institutional situations, and nonverbal symbols.]

Stolcke, Verena. 1995. "Talking Culture: New Boundaries, New Rhetorics of Exclusion in Europe." *Current Anthropology* 36, no. 1: 1–24.

Torres, Arlene, and Norman Whitten Jr. 1998. "General Introduction: To Forge the Future in the Fires of the Past: An Interpretive Essay on Racism, Domination, Resistance, and Liberation." In *Blackness in Latin America and the Caribbean: Social Dynamics and Cultural Transformations,* ed. Norman E. Whitten Jr. and Arlene Torres, 3–33. Bloomington: Indiana University Press.

Twine, France Winddance. 1998. *Racism in a Racial Democracy: The Maintenance of White Supremacy in Brazil.* New Brunswick, NJ: Rutgers University Press.

Wade, Peter. 1993. *Blackness and Race Mixture: The Dynamics of Racial Inequality in Colombia.* Baltimore, MD: Johns Hopkins University Press. [This ethnography marks anthropology's resurgent interest in race and blackness in Latin America. Taking a critical view of popular assumptions concerning *mestizaje,* the book presents a rich picture of Afro-Colombian experience across Colombia's diverse sociocultural geography, from locales with heavy black concentrations to sites where blacks are a dispersed minority.]

———. 1997. *Race and Ethnicity in Latin America.* London: Pluto Press.

Wetherell, Margaret, and Jonathan Potter. 1993. *Mapping the Language of Racism: Discourse and the Legitimation of Exploitation.* New York: Columbia University Press. [This study of New Zealand's social discourse on multiculturalism demonstrates how apparently nonracist and antiracist language can, nonetheless, legitimate white dominance and indigenous Maori subjugation. The analysis elucidates the shift from a blatant form of racial hierarchy to the current ideological battlefield in which persistent material inequalities are normalized by a democratic rhetoric of equal opportunities.]

Whitten, Norman E., Jr., and Arlene Torres. 1992. "Blackness in the Americas." *North American Congress on Latin America* 25, no. 4: 16–22, 45–46.

Williams, Brackette F. 1996. "Introduction: Mannish Women and Gender under the Act." In *Women Out of Place*, ed. Brackette F. Williams, 1–33. New York: Routledge.

Williams, Eric. 1966 [1944]. *Capitalism and Slavery*. New York: Capricorn.

Winant, Howard. 1994. *Racial Conditions: Politics, Theory, Comparisons*. Minneapolis: University of Minnesota Press.

Wolf, Eric. 1982. *Europe and the People without History*. Berkeley: University of California Press.

Yelvington, Kevin. 1997. "Patterns of Ethnicity, Class, and Nationalism. In *Understanding Contemporary Latin America*, ed. Richard S. Hillman, 209–36. Boulder, CO: Lynne Rienner Publishers.

Yon, Daniel A. 2000. *Elusive Culture: Schooling, Race, and Identity in Global Times*. Albany: State University of New York Press. [A thought-provoking ethnographic analysis of the cultural struggles involved in multicultural schooling and the formation of diasporic identities among Caribbean as well as other ethnic adolescents in Toronto. The book offers a cogent case study of the contradictory and ambivalent processes of race-making in a hybrid, global context.

9.

Interpreting Gender and Sexuality: Approaches from Cultural Anthropology

ALMA GOTTLIEB

Does an American woman know what it means to be a Japanese woman just because the two are both women? What is a "woman"—is it any person capable of bearing and breastfeeding children, or something more? Something else?

Contemporary Western ideologies often assume the self-evident nature of the terms *woman* and *man, boy* and *girl*. In particular, sex and gender are frequently elided, so that the biological inevitability of the sex organs comes to stand for a perceived inevitability of social roles, expectations, and meanings associated with gender. Yet investigation of people's lives in other places and other times leads us to question this assumption. In this essay we explore how anthropology can help us to reimagine the meanings we often take for granted of seemingly obvious concepts related to *male* and *female*. We will focus on several key issues concerning gender and sexuality as they are conceived in a variety of cultural spaces. We begin by endeavoring to disentangle the two concepts of "gender" and "sexuality," which themselves are so often conflated. To do so, we will problematize the very nature of gender identity. We then explore the issue of power as it relates to constructions of gender and gender identity. We end by considering the cultural construction of sexual desire itself—that seeming bastion of biological urge that, like gender identity, may nevertheless be analyzed through a cultural lens.

GENDER AND IDENTITY

For many people, the most obvious thing to be said about gender is probably that there are two of them. By kindergarten, most schoolchildren know that people come, like the animals in Noah's ark, in pairs—boys and girls—and they easily classify both themselves and everyone else they know into this binary system.

Adults do so too, often beginning with the tiniest people: on hearing of a new arrival to this life, the first question that friends and relatives ask is typically, "Is it a boy or a girl?" Having heard the answer, we may easily assume that we understand something of the baby and his or her future. At the immediate consumer level, we know what sort of present to buy for the newborn; at a less conscious level, we may have an idea of how to communicate with the creature. For example, if it's a baby girl, many Westerners are more likely to speak directly even to a newborn; with a baby boy, many Westerners are more likely to gently roughhouse. Put differently, the infant's sexual identity comes easily to stand for what we assume will become— or perhaps what already is—its gender identity. From there, it is a small step to imagine the child's identity overall.

But how much do we really know about someone once we have identified her or his gender? Much as we may assume otherwise, gender is not an inevitable predictor of a given person's life experience For one thing, the experience of gender is not the same from place to place, nor from time to time. Cultural variability reduces considerably the reliability of using gender to foretell the future texture of individual lives. Moreover, one's own experience of gender may change through one's life. Indeed, it is possible that one might experience both genders at different points in the life cycle. Gender identity itself is variable, both in time and in space. This leads us to what is perhaps the most counterintuitive question of all: Do all people everywhere classify each other into two and only two genders? This is an especially unsettling question—some might even think it absurd. After all, isn't the answer self-evident?

Many cultural anthropologists would say that it is not. What we "know"—or, rather, what we think we "know"—is very much shaped by what is available to us in the way of knowledge. Anthropology is constantly challenging the bounds of our knowledge by uncovering new ways of being, thinking, feeling that someone, somewhere, experiences. Just when we think we "know" what it means to be a man, another "man" comes along, say, serving milk and cookies at a children's party, or organizing a fiction readers' book club, or leaving work early to take a sick child to the doctor, or doing any number of other activities with which we may (stereo)typically associate women and not men, and we are forced to reconsider our definitions—however implicit—of "manhood."

Gender identity, then, is not as fixed, determinate, predictable as we may assume. Indeed, it is the supposition of this essay—and of many practitioners of cultural anthropology—that gender identity is so decisively shaped by cultural effort—the mandate of values, the whims of history, the weight of economy, the power of politics—that it may be a task doomed to failure to delineate where "nature" ends and "culture" begins. Our identity is shaped by our gender, yes—but only insofar as we acknowledge that our gender is, in turn, shaped by everything and everyone around us, and how those around us themselves interpret our gender, the expectations they bring with them to understanding our gender.

If all this seems abstract, let us take a real-life situation as an example: the case of women and men who choose work that is unconventional for their gender, as judged by the common norms in their society. In most postindustrial nations, we might think of male secretaries, pediatric nurses, or preschool teachers, or then again, of female firefighters (figure 1), executives, or construction workers. All these tend to be professions that require a gendered qualifier before them when describing the unexpected gender reversal. Unless a "female astronaut" is specified, for example, one tends to envision a male when reading about an "astronaut"; by the same token, it would be surprising to hear of a "male astronaut," since the default value of "astronaut," as it were, is male, hence a "male astronaut" is culturally redundant. Female surgeons, male midwives, female engineers—all work against the gendered grain of most contemporary Western societies, challenging gender stereotypes insofar as these individuals embody gender contradictions, defy common expectations. How do such people perceive themselves and their

FIGURE 1 Female firefighter. (Photo by Georganne Rundblad)

relations with other (gendered) people? How do others perceive them? Do they have a single identity, and if so, is it the one that is implied by their biology, or the identity that is associated with their chosen career?

To explore these questions, let us examine the case of female bullfighters in the Spanish region of Andalusia. Over the past century, women began to insert themselves in multiple ways into the Spanish bullfighting arena. Some Andalusians—traditionalists who feel comfortable relying on classic gender norms—reject the move wholesale. Among this group are male bullfighters who refuse to fight in the same ring with female bullfighters, parents who discourage their daughters from pursuing a bullfighting career, trainers who refuse to train women bullfighters, and spectators—both men and women—who avoid attending bullfights at which female bullfighters are present. For these Spaniards, the association of bullfighting with masculinity is so strong and single-minded that no challenge to the association will be tolerated.

Yet at the same time, another slice of contemporary Andalusian society is willing to breach convention, expand the bounds of the profession, and permit the possibility of female bullfighters. Among this group there is, of course, the group of women themselves who are training to become bullfighters; their trainers, who may endure criticism or ridicule from their colleagues for training women as bullfighters; and spectators who happily buy tickets to see women fight in the bull ring. Here we see the easy notion of bullfighter-as-embodiment-of-masculinity being contested, and social change—the rush of feminism (whether or not acknowledged as such), with its insistence that women can pursue any profession available to men—changing long-standing notions of professional appropriateness.

The situation is even more complex. In Andalusia, viewers themselves offer a range of opinions and interpretations of the phenomenon of female bullfighters. Some may be sexually aroused by the tight-fitting, bejeweled costume worn by the bullfighters; ironically, this puts the maverick bullfighting woman, who shows both tremendous social courage and tremendous physical courage, in the traditional role of passive sex object, subject to the sexualized male gaze. Other onlookers admire the physical control expressed in an aesthetically pleasing way that female bullfighters demonstrate (qualities these spectators may admire in male bullfighters), playing up the athletes' professionalism and playing down their sexuality. The female bullfighters themselves say they appreciate this latter attitude. Still other spectators maintain that women are doomed to fail at bullfighting because, they allege, women's biology—their fundamental nature or makeup—does not permit them to experience the same bravery and strength that bullfighting demands and that only men by nature fully enjoy. Such fans of the bullfight may feel anything from pity to contempt for women bullfighters.

Examining this range of reactions, we are led to question the long-standing, exclusive association of bullfighting with the masculine. At the same time, we are forced to consider the ways in which the image of a female bullfighter stretches our conventional notions of what it means to be a woman. Can't a female bull-fighter be as much a "woman" as is a woman who chooses, say, teaching, nursing, or motherhood as her profession? Yet at the same time that the female bullfighter may opt for the hypermasculinized image in the bullring, she may adopt a more conventionally feminized image outside the ring. And in her late twenties, as many male bullfighters do, she typically renounces the extreme rigors of the bullfight—and may well marry and raise children. In other words, she herself may play with her own insertion into gender identity to the point of experiencing gender identity in the plural. For the contemporary, Spanish, female bullfighter, we might say, gender identity becomes gender identities.

The case of the female bullfighter is, admittedly, a dramatic one. What about the vast majority of people who (at least appear to) lead more ordinary lives, conforming (more or less happily) to conventional gender roles? Recent studies have begun to suggest that the sort of gender flexibility, ambiguity, and controversy characterizing the situation of Spanish female bullfighters may also apply, if more subtly, to others engaged in less public and less controversial professions. For example, the female office secretary who is sexually harassed by one male superior while being treated respectfully and professionally by another surely experiences her gender differently with her two male bosses from hour to hour on a given day. The woman who suffers from PMS does likewise at different points in the month. The male trucker may similarly experience his gender identity in different ways when talking to fellow male truckers, to waitresses, to the odd female trucker, and to his wife on the phone, all at the same truck stop along the highway. Such examples could be multiplied endlessly. They suggest that "identity" itself is not only a multifaceted construction from place to place, but a construction whose contours may change from situation to situation for any one of us.

This brings up a related issue: Is it justifiable to assert that the very difference between male and female is itself a universally acknowledged one? In fact, many non-Western societies have allowed for a gender role that is either a combination of male and female, or that is neither male nor female. In recent years, such an in-between category has sometimes been called a "third gender." The "berdaches" of many Native American communities—men who dress as women and take on some (but not all) typically female roles in society—have long confounded anthropologists trying to classify them via the dual-gendered system that is prevalent in Western thought. Variations on this theme abound in many non-Western societies. Among the Igbo of Nigeria, for example, "female husbands" and "male daughters" are adults who are biologically female but, by playing typically male roles (husbands and sons), rise to high levels of wealth, power, and status in their society.

In urbanized, postindustrial societies, communities of gays and lesbians may similarly play with gender roles in ways that challenge the commonly held notion that gender is determined by biology. Lesbian parents may tell their children that they have two mothers, for example, but one mother may perform more tradition-ally "maternal" roles in housekeeping and child care, while the other may main-tain a greater, more stereotypically "masculine" commitment to her career.

To date, studies of such alternate gender systems have not had much impact on public discussions of the issue beyond the narrow confines of anthropology. Per-haps one of the contributions that anthropology can make is to keep reminding us that it is just when we are most sure of ourselves and our opinions—when we are convinced that our way of doing things, of arranging our society and our lives, is the most commonsensical, the most "natural"—that social roles such as a "third gender" can productively unsettle comfortable assumptions about the "nature" of gender identity.

GENDER AND POWER

Are women and men fundamentally equal or unequal? Do any societies exist whose members have achieved partial or even full gender equality? Are there limits—whether biological or cultural (or both)—to achieving such equality? In recent years, most feminist scholars have asserted that a significant majority of all known societies, both past and present, exhibit at least some degree of patriarchy—the dominance of women by men in socially significant spheres of life—and that many societies exhibit a high level of gender inequality. Nevertheless, feminist scholars assume that male dominance, although widespread, is not inevitable, because its roots lie in cultural practices rather than in any hypothesized biological mandate. Anthropologists are in an especially powerful position to address this enduring is-sue because of their investigation into the variety of lives as lived around the globe.

Authors have proposed several theories to account for the widespread exis-tence of men's dominance of women. Some have stressed the idea of male domi-nance as an ideological system to emphasize its symbolic components. Feminist psychologists and psychoanalysts propose child-rearing styles or scenarios as es-sential to the development of patriarchal attitudes in adulthood. Models derived from Karl Marx's theories have tended to look at the rise of the state and private property as responsible for the fact that in many societies women have fewer legal, economic, and political rights than do men. One variation on this theme suggests that in prestate societies, women's roles as sisters remained critical after marriage;

this allowed a married woman to retain a degree of authority vis-à-vis the clan into which she was born, which continued to support her rights within her marriage. But over time, states have tended to erode the authority of the clan system itself. According to this theory, women's roles as (clan) sisters have become eclipsed by the importance of their roles as wives. This shift would have brought about a precipitous decline in women's status overall, accounting for the fact that most contemporary societies exhibit some degree of male dominance at least in the political and economic arenas.

Other authors have cited the restrictions that pregnancy, nursing, and continual care of infants and young toddlers seem to place on women everywhere as the preeminent factors that limit women's access to socially valued resources. Nowadays some middle-class women themselves may view motherhood as a hindrance and may delay or even avoid motherhood so as to further career goals. Yet, ironically, archaeologists have hypothesized that the requirement to carry and care for very young children may have led to the invention of the most significant early technological innovations in human history: the baby sling (freeing women to work and walk while holding a baby) and the hunting net. Moreover, scholars are beginning to question the degree to which the mobility of a given woman may in fact be hampered by pregnancy, nursing, or childcare. The long-standing dominance of many traditional West African markets and farms by women shows the extent to which mothers can maintain active work lives, including critically important economic lives, while retaining a commitment to raising children. In these West African settings, children either accompany their mothers to work or stay behind in villages, where they join in multi-age play groups that are typically supervised by grandparents or other adults remaining in the village.

In contemporary, postindustrial societies, increasing pressure to provide both sufficient maternity and paternity leave for new parents, and comprehensive day care for children of working couples, means that more mothers of babies and toddlers can enter the work force on a full-time basis. Many leaders in a variety of Western nations are now looking for models in the Scandinavian countries, which have been at the forefront of government-supported efforts allowing families to combine successful parenthood and successful work lives.

Indeed, many women around the world are no longer content to remain in "second-class citizen" roles. In recent years, feminism has moved from a small movement of middle-class, Euro-American women to a far more global movement, with international meetings at which women from around the world regularly make their voices heard. Engaging in such consequential activities as lobbying to change unequal inheritance laws that disenfranchise widows in many African countries, Third World feminists are setting their own agendas and reorienting previously dominant paradigms of the relations between gender and privilege. At the same time, in some Western nations, a growing "men's movement" is encouraging men to question both traditional and current gender arrangements with which they may earlier have felt comfortable—or perhaps felt uncomfortable.

Issues relating to power differentials—including both the power to compel or coerce another to follow one's dictates, as well as the power to define and represent another's perceptions of reality—not only mark relations between women and men, they also mark relations among men and among women. Thus it is important to avoid "essentializing" the category of women (or of men) into a single, homogeneous group—not only across societies, but within a given society as well. This is so because the differences that divide women from each other, like those that divide men, are at least as great as the ties that bind them. Ethnic affiliation, class, religion, language, marital status, and age all rupture the seemingly unified or "essential" categories of male and female. Like all other means of defining identities, gender identity is created and recreated by changing circumstances.

Let us consider, for instance, the range of experience that characterizes the lives of women who belong to one apparently homogeneous category: fundamentalist Muslim women in the contemporary era. In Afghanistan, as of this writing, the ruling Islamic Taliban party excludes girls and women from all public spheres and professions, including schools, medical services, and the judiciary. At the same time, in Iran, Egypt, and Turkey, fundamentalist women are creating new brands of Islamic feminism as women reinterpret the Qur'an to claim new rights and freedoms in the spheres of education, work, and family. Although both these groups of women veil themselves, the covering has drastically different effects. In Afghanistan, the veil bars women from the public sphere, whereas in Turkey, Egypt, and Iran, it accords women the comfort to work side by side with men in public without feeling shame or fear.

To complicate matters even more, in Turkey, Egypt, and Iran, the contemporary appearance of veiled working women follows on earlier reforms in the 1920s and 1930s in which women in these three countries were either encouraged or obliged by the state to remove their veils, in a governmental effort to modernize and liberate Muslim women. Ironically, some scholars now claim that this earlier removal of the veil coerced women into conforming to men's positions, and that this in turn eroded women's own social networks, which were traditionally a source of power to them. The contemporary decision to "re-veil" among young Muslim women in Turkey, Egypt, and Iran is thus a significant step filled with multiple, historically layered meanings. It serves at once to affirm a deep devotion to Islam; to critique what these women perceive as depraved Western (especially North American) values and practices; and to provide a visual image that renders acceptable their insertion into the modern workplace. In this case, gender intersects with religion, education, history, and nationalism in complex ways that resist easy associations and predictions.

In the Muslim world, as elsewhere, differences in class and culture are also critical in shaping the experiences of children, both girls and boys. For example, whether among Bedouins in Egypt or Pathans in Pakistan, authoritarian and patriarchal elders in the clan strictly control the day-to-day activities of Muslim boys and girls throughout their youth and adolescence, limiting exposure to activities from soccer to marrying for love, as a means of ensuring continuity of values from generation to generation. Yet elsewhere, elite Muslim men transcend the usual boundaries of both religion and state by jetting in and out of European capitals, where they enjoy the pleasures of wealth, all the while retaining a commitment to Islam. Clearly, class and education radically divide the texture of the lives of men and of women around the globe, even men and women who devoutly espouse the same religious faith. Collectively, these examples of the varied lives of contemporary Muslim people in a variety of cultural spaces compel us to consider the possibility of multiple "masculinities" and multiple "femininities" that lie behind simple notions of male and female.

Moreover, intragender relations are by no means necessarily benign. Differences that divide the members of one gender can produce bitter conflict. A dramatic case of women actively pitted against one another by difference concerns relations among mothers-in-law and daughters-in-law. China provides us with the paradigmatic case. Here, the specific place that one occupies in the life cycle is what determines a woman's experience far more than does the simple fact of her being a "woman." As girls and young brides, Chinese females typically wield no authority in any sphere, but if and when they begin to produce sons, Chinese women slowly but inevitably gain prestige and authority. Acquiring a daughter-in-law to dominate—as she was dominated as a new bride—is the ultimate reward to a mature Chinese woman. Ironically, in this system, women gain power and authority only at one another's expense. In this patriarchal structure, women who are barren, or who produce only daughters, traditionally led tragically restricted and belittled lives; in earlier times, such a fate often led to suicide. Here, one observes both the existence of extensive male privilege and the possibility of female authority, albeit in a restricted context.

As this discussion suggests, the interplay of gender with other features that are critical in a local landscape goes a long way to define both our sense of who we are and other people's senses of who we are. Reducing our identity to gender alone is an unrealistic move that postulates identity as composed essentially of a single factor, when it is far more multiplex than that.

Although feminist anthropologists generally agree that most of the world's societies have exhibited, and continue to exhibit, some degree of domination by men over women, nevertheless scholars have begun recently to document the existence of societies that exhibit a significant measure of gender equality. This is especially the case among some small minority groups living on the fringes of large states. For example, among the Lahu of southwest China, an ideology of gender complementarity dominates virtually all (traditional) spheres of social life. A male and female village chief wield power collectively, and each household is headed by a heterosexual married couple. Men and women perform as much labor collectively as they can. Husbands take over much of their wives' labor load during pregnancy, they serve as midwives during childbirth, and they share with their wives all the tasks of childrearing other than breast-feeding from the first days after the birth (see plate 4). Some Lahu villages have maintained these practices more or less intact even in the face of efforts by the Chinese state to institute socialism—efforts that, in some Lahu villages, have inadvertently undermined the indigenous system of gender relations. This unintended effect is especially ironic, given the ideological commitment to gender equality espoused by the Chinese Communist Party. In such places, the tangle of competing models of (top-down, if unintended) patriarchy and (bottom-up) gender equality challenges us to avoid characterizing the society at large before looking at significant regional variations and contestations.

In general, the way that "gender equality" will look may surprise, taking on features in one place that seem far from what prevails as "equality" in another. As Western feminists struggle to achieve consensus over what an appropriate structure of gender equality might look like in postindustrial societies, feminists elsewhere pose their own answers that challenge us to expand our very definitions of power and equality.

THE CULTURAL CONSTRUCTION OF SEXUAL DESIRE

Anthropologists have a unique ability to argue for the cultural foundations of sexuality as well as of gender identity, having documented an astounding variety of practices and ideologies around the world concerning both sex and gender. If our own sexual practices and our own gender ideologies, whatever those may be, are all demonstrably nonuniversal, what claims can we make for their "naturalness"?

Let us consider a celebrated case in the anthropological literature. Among the Etoro people of Papua New Guinea, every adolescent boy must serve regularly as the "passive" partner in oral sex with his maternal uncle throughout his teen years.

This obligatory practice is explained by the Etoro as a method to build up a supply of semen in the young man that will enable him later to prove fertile with a future wife. In this society the biological substance of seminal fluid, far from being seen as the natural outcome of hormonal development, as it is in the scientific model, is instead seen as a constructed creation—one that must be produced actively by the sexual efforts of closely related men. Without such efforts, the Etoro maintain, adult males would never become "real men," and their sterility would prove catastrophic, preventing the society from reproducing itself. Ideas and sexual practices such as this remind us that much as we might find it reasonable to envision sexuality itself as a natural aspect of our identities, it is—like gender identity—as much a cultural as a biological construction.

The model implied in the Etoro practice is, of course, far from the dominant Western model of sexuality, which has a notion of "naturalness" at its very core. Earlier in the century, Sigmund Freud convinced readers of the "naturalness" of sex as an "instinct" or "drive," and of gender roles as outgrowths of the postulated urge. Before Freud, many Westerners endorsed their own folk models of sex as an unavoidable impulse in humans, and many still maintain this position today. Recently, this "naturalness" has been invoked in politicized arenas—for example, in the increasingly public debate about the origins of homosexuality. Thus in the United States, many gays and lesbians insist on a "natural" foundation to their sexual orientation as a reason to grant them equal rights and legal protection, while Christian opponents of gay rights may instead claim that homosexuality is "unnatural." In both arguments, we are far from the Etoro model of sexuality, which instead emphasizes compulsory male homosexuality as a cultural practice that is necessary to create the later possibility of normative heterosexuality.

In many Western societies, a commonly espoused folk model of sexuality insists not only that sexual desire itself is an immutable and/or irrepressible, natural urge, but that it is naturally stronger in men than it is in women. In the United States, men and women alike often attempt to explain the high rape rates prevalent in the nation as the outcome of an unbridled sexual impulse in men that society has not effectively tamed. Sometimes the frequency of rape is accepted as a tragic but inevitable result of the widespread conviction that "boys will be boys."

Yet the existence of an irresistible sexual urge in men concerning women is not a universal perception. For example, Muslims often maintain that women have a greater sexual urge than do men. Indeed, in the views of many Muslims (especially Muslim men), it is precisely to protect women against their own strong desires for sex (which, it is feared, could lead to adultery and other culturally unacceptable transgressions) that the extreme practices of female seclusion (*purdah*) and female circumcision have come about. By contrast, Dani people of Irian Jaya, Indonesia (West New Guinea), would likely repudiate the common proposition that the urge for sex is a natural one in either men or women. Married Dani men and women alike claim that they refrain from all sexual activity for a period of between four and six years after each child is born to them, and a Western ethnographer who reported this was convinced that no infractions occurred. The contrast is stark when we compare the reported infrequency of sex among the Dani with the frequency of sexual activity in the contemporary United States, where "the average . . . couple has intercourse two or three times per week in their twenties and thirties" (though somewhat less frequently as they age; Masters, Johnson, and Kolodny 1986, 326–27).

Even the very private feelings of sexual pleasure that we may experience are themselves shaped—subtly yet decisively—by cultural factors. Let us consider one controversial case: female genital operations performed on some African and Muslim girls. Today, some outspoken leaders are challenging the tradition for myriad reasons—relating not only to medical and ethical issues, but also to sexual pleasure. These critics lambast the practice as destroying any possibility of experiencing sexual pleasure for the women who have undergone the procedure. At the same time, defenders of the practice, including women—in some places, especially women—offer a different scenario. For example, some Pokot women of Kenya report that the pleasure they experience during sex with their husbands is heightened by the fact that their clitoris was ritually removed during their adolescent initiation ritual—a surgico-ceremonial procedure that the girls were told would ensure their fertility. One can surmise that knowing that they are fertile may make these women feel attractive to their husbands, which would in turn produce in them feelings of erotic arousal. Such claims and counterclaims—and the increasingly lively, even explosive internal debate about this issue that is wracking many African and Muslim societies—must surely unsettle any easy dismissal or condemnation we may be prone to espouse regarding a practice that occasions such extreme reactions. At the least, it suggests that the outsider's ability to imagine what circumstances foster private sensations of sexual pleasure in others is limited.

LEGITIMATE SEX, ILLEGITIMATE SEX: VIRGINITY / ADULTERY / INCEST

The social construction of sexuality is not limited to the experience of desire. Every known society also makes clear to its members when it is permissible—or forbidden—simply to have sex, and with whom.

For example, many socially stratified societies that have well-developed distinctions between commoners and elites have required young women (though not young men) to remain sexual virgins before they marry. Nevertheless, the concept of virginity itself is not self-evident: far from being a simple biological fact, the notion has as much of a cultural as a biological foundation. Among the Trobriand Islanders of Papua New Guinea, for instance, the category of "virginity" is extended to adult women whom Westerners would surely not classify as virgins: mothers who have given birth to children that are said to be sired by family spirits rather than by mortal men—even though such women may be married and lead active sexual lives. This ideology is consistent with the matrilineal organization of Trobriand society. In this type of society, women are structurally more critical to the reproduction of the society than are men, who are somewhat peripheral both genealogically and symbolically.

Distant though it may seem to the Westerner, the Trobriand ideology that it is possible for a woman to be impregnated by a god or spirit rather than by a mortal man, is not as "exotic" as it may at first glance appear. How far is it from the Trobriand conception of "virgin birth" to the "virgin birth" that is said to characterize the conception of the major deity that Christians worship around the world? By contrast, other societies do not recognize the category of "virgin" at all. In such settings—Samoa is one example made famous by Margaret Mead's study in the last century—some boys and girls may be permitted to engage in sexual experimentation from a very young age. In such a setting, local sexual practice makes any concept of "virginity" essentially irrelevant.

Even though sex is encouraged or at least permitted early in some societies, nevertheless all societies restrict sexual access to some people. Minimally, a few closely related family members are universally considered taboo as sexual partners. Sex between parent and child is forbidden virtually everywhere, as it is almost everywhere between siblings. Going beyond the "incest taboo," the idea of who is considered an acceptable sex partner and/or an acceptable marriage partner is variable indeed when we look at the gamut of societies cross-culturally. Indeed, just how "incest" is defined is not as easily foreseen as we might imagine. Thus, whereas most Western countries forbid all first cousins and sometimes all second cousins as spouses, many non-Western societies find another distinction far more relevant: cousins who are the children of two sisters or of two brothers are in many societies forbidden as marriage partners, but in many of these same societies, the children of a brother and a sister are not only permitted but are encouraged or even required to marry one another. Here, the definition of "incest" looks different indeed from the shape it typically takes in Western societies, where people tend to insist on the extent of genealogical or genetic difference as the relevant criterion.

At another level, some societies make a clear distinction between an acceptable sex partner as opposed to an acceptable spouse. For one thing, whereas marriage often implies sex, it does not necessarily require it. In some contemporary countries, the case of foreigners who marry natives for citizenship purposes (in the United States, "to get a green card") includes many such sexless marriages. Other circumstances produce complex marriages in contemporary Indonesia. There, gay men generally conceal their homosexual identities; but if they are discovered to have male partners, their sexual habits are usually tolerated so long as the men also marry women, sire children, and lead seemingly conventional—if secretly bisexual—lives. Closer to home for Western readers, many gays and lesbians, including well-known artists, have found it useful to remain in heterosexual marriages as a screen for their homosexuality—though in many of these cases, unlike in Indonesia, their marriages may well be childless and perhaps sexless as well.

In complex societies with significant ethnic and class divisions, the choice of a suitable marriage partner often includes considerations of social background. Marrying (or trying to marry) the "wrong kind of person," or a person from the "wrong kind of family"—however that is defined—can result in ostracism from the family or community, or even in suicide. Marriage is frequently a contentious issue for many religious groups, especially minority groups whose members have had difficult relations with the locally dominant religion. Such is the case of Jews in the contemporary United States, for example, where high rates of intermarriage between Jews and Christians frequently cause disputes in Jewish families. Marriages that are considered inappropriate from the perspective of the prospective couple's families have long been the staple of great art, from *Romeo and Juliet* to Spike Lee's film, *Jungle Fever.* Even as contemporary Western couples typically covet the right to choose their own spouses, families may intervene in subtle but decisive ways to shape the marriage decisions their children will one day make—at the least by teaching certain values that will give their children a conceptual grid through which to evaluate possible mate choices.

In many societies, patriarchy further complicates the picture of who marries whom. Typically, in class-stratified societies, men are permitted to marry downward in class, status, education and age, while women are forbidden or at least discouraged from doing so, being allowed or encouraged only to marry upward in class, status, education, or age (a practice that social scientists term "hypergamy"). One important consequence of these rules is that male dominance within the marriage is generally reinforced. This is so because when a man of high standing and/or wealth marries a woman of low standing and/or wealth, his authority over his wife is generally strengthened by his higher general status. By contrast, if a man of low standing marries a woman of high standing (termed "hypogamy"), his authority over his wife might well be undermined by her higher general status, thus challenging the overall patriarchal structure of the society. Surprisingly, women themselves may avoid such marriages, anticipating that they may cause trouble for their potential husbands. Only in unusual circumstances does hypogamy become attractive. For instance, in recent years some well-educated, Euro-American women in their thirties have begun to perceive that they have a shrinking pool of eligible, unmarried men from whom to choose as spouses; as a result, some of these women are opting to marry men who are significantly less educated than they are (hence occupying positions of lesser prestige), although previously these women (and their families) would have ruled out such a marriage.

When different ethnic groups are systematically (and unjustly) accorded variable levels of prestige in a given society, class factors may be further intensified when it comes to choosing a marriage partner. For instance, in the United States, many (racist) Euro-Americans are more perturbed by the thought of a "white" woman marrying a "black" man (hypogamy) than by the thought of a "black" woman marrying a "white" man (hypergamy).

Once married, adults are generally expected to obey relevant laws concerning sexual fidelity to their partners, whatever those laws may be. In many societies, gender and power intersect to produce a "double standard": women are expected to remain sexually faithful to their husbands at the same time that those husbands are permitted to have extramarital sexual liaisons. In recent years, the political scene in the United States has revealed the extensive occurrence of powerful men's extramarital affairs, culminating recently in the near-toppling of Bill Clinton's presidency.

Ironically, women themselves may excuse their husbands' transgressions (as Hillary Clinton did publicly) and in some cases may even refrain from critiquing the existence of the sexual double standard, rationalizing that "it's in men's nature." In parts of Greece, a woman who discovers that her husband is having an adulterous affair typically blames the other woman rather than her husband, whom she likely sees as incapable of controlling his sexual urges. In some societies that subscribe to this sexual double standard, the existence of polygyny (which permits men but not women to remain married to two or more spouses simultaneously) goes hand-in-hand with this ideology. In this case, which characterizes many traditional African societies, "philandering" men may view extramarital liaisons as an attempt to locate a second or third wife, rather than as adultery.

Still, the sexual double standard, while common, is not universal. Elsewhere, far different mores may prevail. In traditional Nuer communities in southern Sudan, for example, certain women were permitted to have multiple lovers while remaining married. Any children such a woman bore would have considered their mother's husband as their legal father, whether or not he was genetically related to them. Elsewhere—as in south India, the Himalayas, and on the Jos Plateau of Nigeria—the practice of "polyandry" permits women to remain married simultaneously to two or more men (who are sometimes brothers). While rare, this marriage system nevertheless demonstrates the non-inevitability of the admittedly far commoner practice of polygyny.

Although transgressing locally upheld rules about sex—whether concerning incest, adultery, or otherwise—may result in punishment, many rules themselves are now being contested. For example, the gay liberation movement, which is increasingly active in non-Western nations as well as in the West, is challenging traditional notions of acceptable sexuality even as its activists are still frequently harassed. The struggle over the commonly accepted definition of legitimate sex continues in arenas as diverse as conference planning and book fairs. For example, many academic organizations have declined to hold their annual meetings in any of the North American states that continue to maintain antisodomy or antihomosexuality laws, and a book fair in southern Africa was wracked by controversy over its decision first to ban and then (by court order) to allow a gay rights group to have a stand at the fair. In such ways, social traditions concerning sexuality are subject to revision, redefinition, and negotiation.

SEXUALITY IN OLD AGE

In urbanized, contemporary, Western societies, sex is typically seen as a monopoly of the young. Advertisements using sex as a lure for consumers to purchase a product almost inevitably hire young actors and actresses to seduce viewers. Even if old people are not secluded in nursing homes (as is common enough in the United States), their sex lives are rarely considered by others. Some societies carry this to an extreme. For example, in contemporary Japan and Taiwan it is considered shameful for even middle-aged, let alone elderly, women to be interested in sex. Routinely sleeping with (some of) their grandchildren is likely to promote long-term celibacy in older Japanese women.

Nevertheless, discomfort with elderly sexuality is not universal. For example, among the !Kung people of southern Africa, women as they age are said to become both more sexually active and more sexually attractive to men. Indeed, it is not uncommon for young !Kung men to have affairs with elderly women, many of whom dress more and more scantily, revealing more and more of their legs, with each passing year. While the idea of geriatric sex may unsettle our stereotypes about the aging process and the appropriate deployment of sexuality, it encourages us to acknowledge the cultural construction of sexual desire itself.

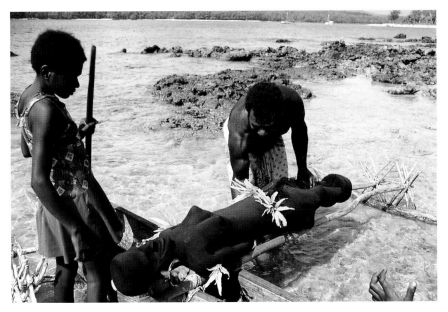

PLATE 1 Entering the global market: a recently bought artifact is laid on a canoe before being paddled to the main island and, ultimately, sold in either Europe or America. (Vao islet, Malakula Island, Vanuatu, February 1980; photo by Jeremy MacClancy)

PLATE 2 Anti-drug slogan painted by Leroy at his crack sales spot. (Photo by Philippe Bourgois)

PLATE 3 Jovellanos, Matanzas Province, is the site of a nineteenth-century sugar plantation where the current residents' ancestors were enslaved workers. In Cuba, conditions of economic austerity and related shortages of construction materials have resulted in dilapidated housing in both rural and urban settings. Black Cubans tend to be overrepresented in the most dilapidated neighborhoods. (Photo by Faye Harrison, July 2000)

PLATE 4 Lahu man preparing dinner for his family while carrying his sleeping toddler on his back. In this part of southwest China, Lahu men and women traditionally share childcare and domestic responsibilites equally. (Photo by Shanshan Du)

PLATE 5 A women's fishing group in Sierra Leone, enacting ideas about the links between the female bodily processes and fishing productivity, early 1990s. (Photo by Melissa Leach)

PLATE 6 Web page (adapted) of Igloolik Isuma Productions. (Courtesy of Igloolik Isuma)

PLATE 7 Praise singer, Tamale, Dagbon. (Photo by John Chernoff)

PLATE 8   Assembled drummers, Karaga, Dagbon. (Photo by John Chernoff)

PLATE 9   Picasso, *Les Demoiselles d'Avignon.* Paris (June–July 1907)
Oil on canvas, 8' × 7' 8" (243.9 × 233.7 cm). The Museum of Modern
Art, New York. Acquired through the Lillie P. Bliss Bequest.
Photograph ©2001 The Museum of Modern Art, New York. ©2001
Estate of Pablo Picasso/Artists Rights Society (ARS), New York

PLATE 10 Jimmie Durham,
Pocahontas's Underwear, 1985.
Feathers, beads, fabric, fasten-
ers. Part of installation piece
*On Loan from the Museum of the
American Indian*. (Courtesy of
Nicole Klagsbrun Gallery,
New York)

PLATE 11 Chris Ofili,
The Holy Virgin Mary, 1996.
Paper collage, oil paint,
glitter, polyester resin, map
pins, and elephant dung on
linen. 244 cm × 183 cm,
96 in. × 72 in. (Courtesy of
Victoria Miro and the Saatchi
Gallery, London)

PLATE 12 One of the last divers in the 1981 land-dive performed by the "custom villagers" of Bunlap, Pentacost Island, Vanuatu. Note that the platforms of all the previous divers have collapsed as they have dived. (Photo by Jeremy MacClancy)

PLATE 13 Jeff Koon's floral sculpture, *Puppy*, at the entrance to the Bilbao Guggenheim, quickly became a favorite spot for tourist photos. Here, a group of visiting businessmen commemorate their stay in the city, February 1999. (Photo by Jeremy MacClancy)

Attitudes about the appropriateness of sexuality through the life cycle are also shaped by the power structure of the society. For example, in a given society, is a widow, especially a young widow, free to remarry? Or, by contrast, is she obliged to remarry a particular man—for example, the brother of her deceased husband, as is (or was) common in some early Western and contemporary, non-Western societies? In India, one sign that women lack autonomy was the traditional rule that prohibited a widow ever to remarry. In classic times, the Indian rule against widows' remarriage even extended to infant girls, who were classified as widows if the infant boys to whom they were betrothed as part of an arranged marriage agreement happened to die as children. As an adult, the highest respect an Indian widow could show her just-deceased husband was to join the funeral pyre with his corpse. Although this practice of *suttee* was outlawed by the British in 1829, it has on occasion been revived in local villages, especially in Rajasthan. These incidents have generated enormous controversy in the Indian press in recent years as Indians (feminists and otherwise) rethink ways of being both Indian and modern. As these examples show, sex, gender, and power continue to be deeply implicated in one another as humans progress through the life cycle.

In this essay we have explored the gamut of possibilities for our lives as gendered and sexual beings. While Western discussions tend to "naturalize" both these components of the human experience as being rooted in biologically immutable structures, cultural anthropologists have long argued that both sex and gender have powerful cultural roots, making it difficult—perhaps impossible—to say where "nature" leaves off and "culture" begins. If anthropology can have any impact on our society as we endeavor to create a more egalitarian set of opportunities for all people regardless of gender, perhaps it is through the realization that gender arrangements and sexual practices alike have an astounding variability as we look around the globe, reminding us that no pattern, however much it may appear to be "natural," is inevitable.

ACKNOWLEDGMENTS

For having given me my start long ago in the scholarly study of gender and sexuality, I remain grateful to my early teachers, Gerda Lerner and Sherry Ortner. For a careful reading of this chapter and many insightful comments, I am thankful to my life partner, Philip Graham. For usefully challenging comments concerning contemporary Muslim experiences, I am grateful to Zohreh Sullivan. For valued advice with a variety of sources used in the preparation of this chapter, I am much obliged to Shyamala Balgopal, Matti Bunzl, Al Kagan, Janet Keller, Jeremy MacClancy, and Beth Stafford. I also thank two anonymous readers of this essay for very helpful suggestions. Finally, many thanks to Bertin Kouadio for much appreciated help in the library.

REFERENCES AND SUGGESTIONS FOR FURTHER READING

Abu-Lughod, Lila. 1993. *Writing Women's Worlds: Bedouin Stories*. Berkeley: University of California Press.

————, ed. 1998. *Remaking Women: Feminism and Modernity in the Middle East*. Princeton, NJ: Princeton University Press.

Amadiume, Ifi. 1987. *Male Daughters, Female Husbands: Gender and Sex in an African Society*. London: Zed.

Ardener, Shirley, ed. 1993 [1978]. *Defining Females: The Nature of Women in Society*. Oxford: Berg.

Arens, William. 1986. *The Original Sin: Incest and Its Meaning*. Oxford: Oxford University Press.

Ashe, Geoffrey. 1976. *The Virgin*. London: Routledge & Kegan Paul.

Berreman, Gerald D. 1975. "Himalayan Polyandry and the Domestic Cycle." *American Ethnologist* 2, no. 1: 127–39.

Boddy, Janice. 1989. *Wombs and Alien Spirits: Women, Men, and the Zar Cult in Northern Sudan*. Madison: University of Wisconsin Press.

Boserup, Esther. 1970. *Woman's Role in Economic Development*. New York: St. Martin's Press.

Brumberg, Joan Jacobs. 1992. *The Body Project: An Intimate History of American Girls*. New York: Random House.

Buckley, Thomas, and Alma Gottlieb, eds. 1988. *Blood Magic: The Anthropology of Menstruation*. Berkeley: University of California Press.

Butler, Judith. 1990. *Gender Trouble*. New York: Routledge.

Caudill, William, and David W. Plath. 1966. "Who Sleeps by Whom? Parent-Child Involvement in Urban Japanese Families." *Psychiatry* 29: 344–66.

Chernin, Kim. 1993. *The Obsession: Reflections on the Tyranny of Slenderness*. New York: HarperCollins.

Chodorow, Nancy. 1978. *The Reproduction of Mothering*. New Haven, CT: Yale University Press.

————. 1989. *Feminism and Psychoanalytic Theory*. New Haven, CT: Yale University Press.

Clark, Gracia. 1994. *Onions Are My Husband: Survival and Accumulation by West African Market Women*. Chicago: University of Chicago Press.

Connell, R. W. 1995. *Masculinities*. Cambridge, U.K.: Polity Press.

Cornwall, Andrea, and Nancy Lindisfarne, eds. 1994. *Dislocating Masculinity: Comparative Ethnographies*. London: Routledge.

Davis-Floyd, Robbie. 1992. *Childbirth as an American Rite of Passage*. Berkeley: University of California Press.

Davis-Floyd, Robbie, and Carolyn F. Sargent, eds. 1997. *Childbirth and Authoritative Knowledge: Cross-Cultural Perspectives*. Berkeley: University of California Press.

Delaney, Carol. 1991. *The Seed and the Soil: Gender and Cosmology in Turkish Village Society.* Berkeley: University of California Press.

del Valle, Teresa, ed. 1993. *Gendered Anthropology.* New York: Routledge.

Dickerson-Putman, Jeanette, and Judith K. Brown. 1998. *Women among Women: Anthropological Perspectives on Female Age Hierarchies.* Urbana: University of Illinois Press.

di Leonardo, Micaela. 1997 [1992]. "White Lies, Black Myths: Rape, Race, and the Black 'Underclass.'" In *The Gender/Sexuality Reader: Culture, History, Political Economy,* ed. Roger N. Lancaster and Micaela di Leonardo, 53–68. New York: Routledge.

Du, Shanshan. In press. *"Chopsticks Only Work in Pairs": Gender Unity and Gender Equality among the Lahu of Southwest China.* New York: Columbia University Press.

Ehrenreich, Barbara, and Deirdre English. 1978. *For Her Own Good: 150 Years of the Experts' Advice to Women.* New York: Doubleday.

Etienne, Mona, and Eleanor Leacock, eds. 1980. *Women and Colonization: Anthropological Perspectives.* New York: J. F. Bergin.

Evans-Pritchard, E. E. 1951. *Kinship and Marriage among the Nuer.* Oxford: Clarendon Press.

Foucault, Michel. 1978 [1976]. *History of Sexuality.* Vol. 1. *An Introduction.* Trans. Robert Hurley. New York: Pantheon.

———. 1985 [1984]. *History of Sexuality.* Vol. 2. *The Use of Pleasure.* Trans. Robert Hurley. New York: Pantheon.

"Gay Zimbabweans Win Fight to Open Booth at a Book Fair." 1996. *New York Times,* August 2, A4.

Geertz, Clifford. 1983. "Common Sense as a Cultural System." In *Local Knowledge,* by Clifford Geertz, 73–93. New York: Basic Books.

Gottlieb, Alma. 1988. "American Premenstrual Syndrome: A Mute Voice." *Anthropology Today* 4, no. 6: 10–13.

Gough, Kathleen. 1955. "Female Initiation Rites on the Malabar Coast." *Journal of the Royal Anthropological Institute* 85: 45–80.

———. 1959. "The Nayars and the Definition of Marriage." *Journal of the Royal Anthropological Institute* 89: 23–34.

Hastrup, Kirsten. 1993 [1978]. "The Semantics of Biology: Virginity." In *Defining Females: The Nature of Women in Society,* ed. Shirley Ardener, 34–50. Oxford: Berg.

Heider, Karl. 1976. "Dani Sexuality: A Low Energy System." *Man* 11: 188–201.

———. 1979. *Grand Valley Dani: Peaceful Warriors.* New York: Holt, Rinehart and Winston.

Herdt, Gilbert, ed. 1994. *Third Sex, Third Gender: Beyond Sexual Dimorphism in Culture and History.* New York: Zone Books.

Hirschon, Renée. 1993 [1978]. "Open Body/Closed Space: The Transformation of Female Sexuality." In *Defining Females: The Nature of Women in Society,* ed. Shirley Ardener, 51–72. Oxford: Berg.

Howard, Richard. 1996. *Falling into the Gay World: Manhood, Marriage, and Family in Indonesia.* Ph.D. diss. Department of Anthropology, University of Illinois at Urbana-Champaign.

Johnson, Michelle C. 2000. "Becoming a Muslim, Becoming a Person: Female 'Circumcision,' Religious Identity, and Personhood in Guinea-Bissau." In *Female "Circumcision" in Africa: Culture, Change, and Controversy*, ed. Bettina Shell-Duncan and Ylva Hernlund, 215–33. Boulder, CO: Lynn Rienner.

Kelly, Raymond. 1976. "Witchcraft and Sexual Relations: An Exploration in the Social and Semantic Implications of the Structure of Belief." In *Man and Woman in the New Guinea Highlands*, ed. Paula Brown and Georgeda Buchbinder. Washington, DC: American Anthropological Association, Special Publication no. 8.

Kessler, Evelyn, and Suzanne McKenna. 1978. *Gender: An Ethnomethodological Approach*. New York: John Wiley and Sons.

Kilbride, Philip L. 1994. *Plural Marriage for Our Times: A Reinvented Option?* Westport, CT: Bergin & Garvey.

Kimmel, M. S., and M. A. Messner, eds. 1995. *Men's Lives*. 3d ed. Boston: Allyn and Bacon.

Kratz, Cory. 1994. *Affecting Performance: Meaning, Movement, and Experience in Okiek Women's Initiation*. Washington, DC: Smithsonian Institution Press.

LaFontaine, Jean S. 1985. *Initiation: Ritual Drama and Secret Knowledge across the World*. Harmondsworth, U.K.: Penguin.

Lawrence, Marilyn, ed. 1987. *Fed Up and Hungry: Women, Oppression, and Food*. New York: Peter Bedrick Books.

Leacock, Eleanor Burke. 1972. "Introduction." In *The Origin of the Family, Private Property, and the State*, by Frederick Engels, 7–67. New York: International Publishers.

Lee, Richard B. 1992. "Work, Sexuality, and Aging among !Kung Women." In *In Her Prime: New Views of Middle-Aged Women*, ed. Virginia Kerns and Judith K. Brown, 35–46. 2d ed. Urbana: University of Illinois Press.

Lepowsky, Maria. 1993. *Fruit of the Motherland: Gender in an Egalitarian Society*. New York: Columbia University Press.

Levine, Nancy. 1981. "Perspectives on Love: Morality and Affect in Nyinba Interpersonal Relationships." In *Culture and Morality*, ed. Adrian C. Mayer, 106–25. Oxford: Oxford University Press.

———. 1988. *The Dynamics of Polyandry: Kinship, Domesticity, and Population on the Tibetan Border*. Chicago: University of Chicago Press.

Levine, Nancy, and Walter H. Sangree. 1980. "Asian and African Systems of Polyandry." *Journal of Comparative Family Studies* 11, no. 3: 385–410.

Lewin, Ellen. 1993. *Lesbian Mothers: Accounts of Gender in American Culture*. Ithaca, NY: Cornell University Press.

Lichter, D. T. 1990. "Delayed Marriage, Marital Homogamy, and the Mate Selection Process among White Women." *Social Science Quarterly* 71, no. 4: 802–11.

Lock, Margaret. 1993. *Encounters with Aging: Mythologies of Menopause in Japan and North America*. Berkeley: University of California Press.

Lu, Hwei-Syin. 1991. *Self-growth, Women's Power, and the Contested Family Order in Taiwan: An Ethnographic Study of Three Contemporary Women's Groups*. Ph.D. diss. Department of Anthropology, University of Illinois at Urbana-Champaign.

Lugo, Alejandro, and Bill Maurer, eds. 2000. *Gender Matters: Rereading Michelle Z. Rosaldo.* Ann Arbor: University of Michigan Press.

Maher, Vanessa, ed. 1992. *The Anthropology of Breast-Feeding: Natural Law or Social Construct.* Oxford: Berg.

Malinowski, Bronislaw. 1929. *The Sexual Life of Savages in North-Western Melanesia: An Ethnographic Account of Courtship, Marriage, and Family Life among the Natives of the Trobriand Islands, British New Guinea.* New York: Harcourt, Brace & World.

Mani, Lata. 1990. "Multiple Mediations: Feminist Scholarship in the Age of Multinational Reception (on the Practice of Suttee, Widow Burning, in India)." *Feminist Review* 35 (summer): 24–41.

Martin, Emily. 1987. *The Woman in the Body: A Cultural Analysis of Reproduction.* Boston: Beacon Press.

———. 1991. "The Egg and the Sperm: How Science Has Constructed a Romance Based on Stereotypical Male-Female Roles." *Signs* 16, no. 3: 485–501.

Masters, William, Virginia Johnson, and Robert C. Kolodny. 1986. *Masters and Johnson on Sex and Human Loving.* Boston: Little, Brown.

Mathabane, Mark, and Gail Mathabane. 1992. *Love in Black and White: The Triumph of Love over Prejudice and Taboo.* New York: HarperCollins.

Mead, Margaret. 1928. *Coming of Age in Samoa: A Psychological Study in Primitive Youth for Western Civilization.* New York: Blue Ribbon Books.

———. 1935. *Sex and Temperament in Three Primitive Societies.* New York: Dell.

———. 1949. *Male and Female: A Study of the Sexes in a Changing World.* New York: William Morrow.

Meggitt, Mervyn J. 1964. "Male-Female Relations in the Highlands of New Guinea." *American Anthropologist* 66, no. 4, part 2: 202–24.

Mikell, Gwendolyn, ed. 1997. *African Feminism: The Politics of Survival in Sub-Saharan Africa.* Philadelphia: University of Pennsylvania Press.

Moran, Mary H. 1990. *Civilized Women: Gender and Prestige in Southeastern Liberia.* Ithaca, NY: Cornell University Press.

Mukhopadhyay, Carol, and P. Higgins. 1988. "Anthropological Studies of Women's Status Revisited: 1977–1987." *Annual Review of Anthropology* 17: 461–95.

Müller, Jean-Claude. 1973. "On Preferential/Prescriptive Marriage and the Function of Kinship Systems: The Rukuba Case (Benue-Plateau State, Nigeria)." *American Anthropologist* 75: 1563–76.

Newton, Esther. 1993. *Cherry Grove, Fire Island: Sixty Years in America's First Gay and Lesbian Town.* Boston: Beacon Press.

Okonjo, K. 1976. "The Dual-Sex Political System in Operation: Igbo Women and Community Politics in Midwestern Nigeria." In *Women in Africa: Studies in Social and Economic Change*, ed. Nancy J. Hafkin and Edna G. Bay, 45–58. Stanford, CA: Stanford University Press.

Ortner, Sherry. 1996. *Making Gender: The Politics and Erotics of Culture.* Boston: Beacon Press.

Pellow, Deborah. 1977. *Women in Accra: Options for Autonomy*. Algonack, MI: Reference Publications.

Pink, Sarah. 1997. *Women and Bullfighting: Gender, Sex, and the Consumption of Tradition*. Oxford: Berg.

Potash, Betty, ed. 1986. *Widows in African Societies: Choices and Constraints*. Stanford, CA: Stanford University Press.

Rapp, Rayna. 1999. *Testing Women, Testing the Fetus: The Social Impact of Amniocentesis in America*. New York: Routledge.

Richards, Audrey. 1956. *Chisungu: A Girl's Initiation Ceremony among the Bemba of Zambia*. London: Faber and Faber.

Riley, Denise. 1988. *Am I That Name? Feminism and the Category of "Women" in History*. Minneapolis: University of Minnesota Press.

Rosaldo, Michelle Zimbalist. 1974. "Woman, Culture, and Society: A Theoretical Overview." In *Woman, Culture, and Society*, ed. Michelle Zimbalist Rosaldo and Louise Lamphere, 17–42. Stanford, CA: Stanford University Press.

Rosaldo, Michelle Zimbalist, and Louise Lamphere, eds. 1974. *Woman, Culture, and Society*. Stanford, CA: Stanford University Press.

Roth, Denise. In press. *Managing Motherhood, Managing Risk: Fertility and Danger in West Central Tanzania*. Ann Arbor: University of Michigan Press.

Sacks, Karen. 1982. *Sisters and Wives: The Past and Future of Gender Equality*. 2d ed. Urbana: University of Illinois Press.

Sanday, Peggy. 1990. *Fraternity Gang Rape: Sex, Brotherhood, and Privilege on Campus*. New York: New York University Press.

Sanday, Peggy, and Ruth Goodenough, eds. 1988. *Beyond the Second Sex: New Directions in the Anthropology of Gender*. Philadelphia: University of Pennsylvania Press.

Shostak, Marjorie. 1981. *Nisa: The Life and Words of a !Kung Woman*. Cambridge: Harvard University Press.

Slocum, Sally. 1974. "Woman the Gatherer: Male Bias in Anthropology." In *Toward an Anthropology of Women*, ed. Rayna Rapp Reiter, 36–50. New York: Monthly Review Press.

Steinem, Gloria. 1983. "If Men Could Menstruate." In *Gloria Steinem, Outrageous Acts and Everyday Rebellions*. New York: Holt, Rinehart, and Winston.

Stone, Linda. 1997. *Kinship and Gender: An Introduction*. Boulder: Westview Press/Harper-Collins.

Sudarkasa, Niara [Gloria Marshall]. 1973. *Where Women Work: A Study of Yoruba Women in the Marketplace and in the Home*. Ann Arbor: University of Michigan Museum of Anthropology, Anthropological Papers no. 53.

Sullivan, Zohreh T. 1998. "Eluding the Feminist, Overthrowing the Modern? Transformations in Twentieth-Century Iran." In *Remaking Women: Feminism and Modernity in the Middle East*, ed. Lila Abu-Lughod, 215–42. Princeton, NJ: Princeton University Press.

Tavris, Carol. 1992. *The Mismeasure of Woman*. New York: Simon and Schuster.

Weston, Kath. 1991. *Families We Choose: Lesbians, Gays, Kinship.* New York: Columbia University Press.

———. 1996. *Render Me, Gender Me: Lesbians Talk Sex, Class, Color, Nation, Studmuffins.* New York: Columbia University Press.

Whitehead, Harriet. 1981. "The Bow and the Burden Strap: A New Look at Institutionalized Homosexuality in Native North America." In *Sexual Meanings: The Cultural Construction of Gender and Sexuality,* ed. Sherry B. Ortner and Harriet Whitehead, 80–115. Cambridge: Cambridge University Press.

Wolf, Margery. 1975. "Women and Suicide in China." In *Women in Chinese Society,* ed. Margery Wolf and Roxane Witke, 114–42. Stanford, CA: Stanford University Press.

Yanagisako, Sylvia J., and Carol Delaney, eds. 1995. *Naturalizing Power: Essays in Feminist Cultural Analysis.* New York: Routledge.

Zihlman, Adrienne. 1989. "Woman the Gatherer: The Role of Women in Early Hominid Evolution." In *Gender and Anthropology: Critical Reviews for Research and Teaching,* ed. Sandra Morgen, 21–40. Washington, DC: American Anthropological Association.

10.

Medical Knowledge and Body Politics

MARGARET LOCK

Among the most famous of the paleolithic cave paintings at Lascaux in the Dordogne is that of the "sorcerer," as he is known today. This image of a masked, leaping figure in costume with antlers on his head is thought by most experts to represent a shaman. In the same cave appears a second masked shaman holding a curious instrument shaped like a bow that appears to be coming out of his mouth. These figures, created fourteen thousand years ago, suggest that shamanism, one function of which is the diagnosis and healing of disease, has been practiced for a very long time. Indeed some experts argue that there may be much earlier signs of elementary medical knowledge. In the Shanidar cave, in what is now Iraq, pollen samples from several kinds of flowering plants, many of them with known medicinal properties, have been found in association with the burial of a Neanderthal man approximately sixty thousand years ago. It is just conceivable that some awareness of the healing properties of plants was already in existence at that time.

As far as we can ascertain, peoples everywhere have amassed knowledge and practices designed to preserve health, account for the occurrence of illness, and provide therapeutic relief. Anthropologists started to record such knowledge during the latter part of the last century, but not until the 1920s did the physician/anthropologist W. H. R. Rivers argue that medicine in nonliterate societies is not simply a random assortment of practices based on custom and superstition. On the contrary, Rivers insisted, medicine is an integral part of society at large, and the form that it takes reflects widely shared values. Anthropologists working in numerous societies and building on the insights of Rivers, particularly since the late 1960s, have shown how medical knowledge and practices, whether those of health care professionals or of the public at large, are culturally informed. This is the case even in complex societies where sophisticated medical technologies are readily available.

With the development from the middle of the twentieth century of antibiotics and other effective technologies, it was assumed that biomedicine would soon eclipse other forms of medical knowledge. This hope was short-lived, once it became clear that chronic and degenerative diseases were not amenable to the "magic bullets" that proved to be so effective in dealing with bacterial infections. Today it is abundantly clear that the infectious diseases have not been vanquished, as we had thought, and that biomedical therapeutics do not always provide cures or even relief of symptoms for a whole range of problems that come under the umbrella of modern medicine. It is also clear that monetary interests at times force drugs and other technologies into the market with insufficient testing, on occasion leading to terrible consequences, as was the case with thalidomide.

Even so, biomedicine is usually taken as the gold standard against which other types of medical practice are measured; however, in addition to the problems noted above, caution is in order for other reasons. Although biomedical knowledge is grounded in science and is in theory thoroughly rational, it is a relatively new science undergoing extraordinarily rapid changes, so that many of its activities are provisional until such time as the workings of the human body are better understood. "Fashions" exist in medicine: technologies, medications, and practices come and go. Even the classification of diseases is regularly revised and modified in light of new knowledge. This expansion and refinement of medicine is assumed to be an entirely logical endeavor, but value judgments and unexamined assumptions are inevitably embedded in these processes.

For example, our unshakeable belief in the powers of technology has led us down a path where illness and distress that cannot be made visible in test tubes, at autopsies, or on screens and monitors, are often reckoned as nonexistent. Arguments about disease classification and what should count as bona fide diseases arise in part as a result of a medical epistemology that limits itself to what are assumed to be universal, measurable facts. Subjective reporting from patients that does not "fit" within biomedical convention is too often deemed to be imaginary or due to indefinable stress. An example of this type of dispute is currently being played out in connection with Gulf War Syndrome.

THE FORMATION OF BIOMEDICINE

Biomedicine is in large part a product of the emergence in the nineteenth century of a systematic human biology in which nature is understood for the first time as constituted by a set of laws entirely independent of both society and culture. This new biology permitted the hardening of certain ideas that had been in the air for many years in pre-Enlightenment Europe. The human body, in contrast to other types of medical systems, came to be understood as a universal entity. By extension, what is normal and what is pathological were similarly assumed to be distributed about a universal norm and fully comprehensible through physical examination of the body and individual behavior. In other words, disease and health can be assessed and controlled independently of the circumstances in which individuals are situated.

A concern about "final" causes is characteristic of biomedicine, that is, a concern with specific, identifiable factors located inside the body, whether they be viruses, genes, or physiological malfunction, all of which factors produce detectable changes in the material body that are then labeled as disease. Currently, vast amounts of funding are directed toward research in which attention is focused on pinpointing genetic predispositions and genetic abnormalities as causal of, or contributory to, a wide range of diseases. Such an approach reinforces the idea that diseases are isolable entities, found everywhere, and without moral or social significance. This approach is associated with several assumptions: that health and illness are located in individual bodies; disease and health are a dichotomous pair; illness and disease are best managed by medical specialists; and preservation of health is primarily the responsibility of individuals.

This reductionistic approach of biomedicine is very unusual; no other medical system has systematically focused so exclusively on final causal explanations internal to the body. Two examples of ways to conceptualize health and illness alternative to biomedicine must suffice here. The concept of health as it was understood by the majority of indigenous peoples of North America prior to colonization was one in which individual health is intimately related to the land on which people subsist. For example "being-alive-well," is the concept used by Cree who reside in northern Canada, This concept implies that individuals must be correctly situated or "balanced" with respect to the land. For the Cree a "sense of place" remains inherent to the continuance of family and community health and, by extension, individual health. This concept is, of course, an ideal, but valued highly.

Today, the Cree are self-consciously mobilizing this concept of health for political ends. The building of the enormous James Bay hydroelectric dam in northern Québec over two decades ago caused massive disruption and dislocation in Cree communities, leading to widespread ill health. This was followed for many years by threats to build a second dam, although it seems that this plan has now been abandoned. The Cree participate fully in the movement that has spread across North America in recent years among indigenous peoples to take back full political and even legislative control of their own communities. Such efforts to eradicate the postcolonial situation of forced dependence, discrimination, and chronic ill health, so evident for many years, are intimately associated with the idea of community healing. For participants in this movement, settlement of land claims and unlimited access to environmental resources are thought of as essential to the restoration of both community and individual health.

A second, very different, example comes from East Asia. In China and Japan the macrocosm of the social and political order, and not the individuals who constitute it, has been recognized for many hundreds of years as the fundamental unit of social organization. Historically, society was understood as constituting more than the sum of its individual parts, and social relations among people formed the basis for continued human existence and moral order. Such thinking is still evident today in post-Maoist China and in the industrial superpower of Japan.

A dominant metaphor of long standing in both China and Japan is that of harmony, sustained through the self-conscious contribution by individuals to social and political order. Even though weakened today by concerns about the rights of individuals—an ethical principle that originated in Europe—the idea that individual interests should be subordinated to families, communities, or even to the nation remains strong. In contrast to biomedical theory, the East Asian philosophical and medical tradition understands health as being in a continuum with illness, not diametrically in opposition to it. Moreover individuals are recognized as having *relative* amounts of health depending on such factors as the season of the year, their occupation, age, and so on, as opposed to a finite presence or absence of health or disease (figure 1).

Illness is conceptualized predominantly as a condition in which the microcosm of the individual is out of balance with the macrocosm of the social order. Both the physical and mental condition of individuals are conceptualized as inextricable from that of their surroundings, social and environmental. Although generalizations about sets of recognizable symptoms common to many patients are made frequently that assist in the selection of the right type of treatment, in East Asian medicine patients are nevertheless understood as having their own individual illnesses. Until recently no claims were made to knowledge about diseases or therapies that could be applied universally, as is characteristic of biomedicine (over the past half century this has changed somewhat because practitioners of East Asian medicine, many of whom are also medical doctors, are knowledgeable about biomedicine).

Because health is believed to depend upon the context in which an individual is located, East Asian medicine is often described as "holistic" by its aficionados; in theory attention is paid to more than the workings of the physical body. In practice, however, individual bodies are manipulated, often to their detriment, in order that they may readjust to the social order. Even though the demands posed by society on individual health are freely acknowledged, they are considered unavoidable and remain essentially unchallenged. Responsibility for keeping healthy rests

FIGURE I Japanese physician applies moxa mixed with oil at an acupuncture pressure point for a baby who is fretful at night, 1974. (Photo by author)

with individuals. Thus in early Chinese history the health of the state, for which the emperor's body was a living microcosm, was dependent upon the moral and healthy behaviors of the emperor's subjects. Individual concerns and interests are by definition suppressed in a Confucian ideology for the sake of society, and this attitude extends to the management of bodies. People are expected to "bend" to fit society and, should illness occur, resort is made to herbal medication, acupuncture, and other therapies to bring the mind/body back into harmony with the macrocosm, with the objective of returning to active participation in society.

In its own way, East Asian medicine is reductionistic in that it focuses on the removal of symptoms, usually without exploring more than superficially what might have caused individual sickness. However therapies are designed to boost the body's inbuilt defense mechanisms, rather than to eradicate pathogens or cut out diseased body parts, and are directed at improving the condition of the whole body. In this sense this system is radically different from the reductionistic, invasive approach associated with biomedicine.

MORAL ORDER AND HEALTH

Within any given society, a large number of people, sometimes the great majority, participate in a shared concept of what constitutes a well-functioning social, political, and moral order, an order that is intimately associated with the continued well-being of individuals who make up the society. A notion of a "sick society," one in which the moral order is under threat, is also widespread and is frequently associated with a perceived increase in the occurrence of disease and disruptions of various kinds. As the examples cited above show, causal explanations for the origins of disease and distress vary through time and space and often depend upon the particular circumstances and form in which a disease is manifested. Such explanations range from supernatural retribution to theories of contagion, a loss of balance between the microcosm of the body and the macrocosm of the environment, ideas about diseases transmitted over generations (whether by spirits, blood, or genes), and disease resulting from toxic environments.

Allocation of responsibility for the occurrence of illness and disease, whether it be with the sick individual, society, or the supernatural, is intimately associated with specific causal explanations and frequently includes a moral dimension in which a search for the source of the problem—misdeeds, misadventure, or bad luck—is usually pivotal. In theory, this is not the case with biomedicine, in that diagnostics and therapeutics are decontextualized, limited to the condition of the interior of the body or occasionally to individual behavior, and thus largely removed from the realm of morals. Nevertheless, tobacco, alcohol, and drug users, people labeled as overweight, individuals with sexually transmitted diseases, and pregnant teenagers, to name a few, are unlikely to escape moral censure.

Despite the availability everywhere of explanations to buffer feelings of helplessness in the face of illness, the question of why some people fall sick while others remain healthy is never far from people's minds. In attempts to quell such concerns, governments, communities, medical experts, and individuals have two options. They may assume that chance is at work, that someone's body has simply gone wrong. The second, and much more frequently chosen option, is to undertake locally recognized procedures to locate reasons and allocate responsibility for the unequal distribution of distress and sickness in society. Those procedures range from divination or consultation with oracles, such as that practiced, for example, by the Azande of Sudan, to genetic testing and screening of pregnant women in increasing numbers in wealthier parts of the world.

Epidemiologists, whose work it is to account for why some people have higher rates of morbidity and mortality than others, usually focus on human populations and not on individuals. Their research has revealed again and again how poverty is associated with higher rates of virtually all types of disease, and how class, gender, and occupation are intimately linked to disease incidence. It is noteworthy that much less funding is apportioned to this type of research than for basic biomedical research.

Some anthropological research also focuses on the relationship of politics and economics to disease and distress, but anthropologists often spend more time than do epidemiologists paying attention to small communities of individuals rather than to whole populations. They frequently emphasize firsthand narrative accounts given by individuals in connection with illness and highlight discrepancies between the subjective experience of illness and objective assessments made by health care professionals. Anthropological research has also shown that among practitioners trained in biomedicine, local culture shapes their knowledge and practices to such an extent that we must talk of cultures of biomedicine to account for the various forms that it takes in different parts of the world.

An increasing number of medical anthropologists have recently joined a group of medical sociologists who challenge the hegemony of a wide range of biomedical claims. Such a challenge does not deny the power of biomedicine or the remarkable successes that it can justly claim. However, the assertion that biomedicine is free of cultural and moral evaluation is itself a moral position, one that can be highly misleading. First, as noted above, this is patently not the case with certain types of patients whose behaviors and habits lead many physicians to make moral judgments. Second, physical distress and disease, the origins of which are so often due to social and political conditions, are liable to be inadequately treated when understood wholly as pathological problems located in the body. This is not to deny that medication often relieves physical symptoms, but the causes of those symptoms, especially those that are chronic, including pain, headaches, fatigue, depression, and so on, remain unexplained, unresolved, and untreated. In some cases an unknown virus may be to blame—this *may* be the situation in some instances of what has come to be known as chronic fatigue syndrome, for example— but even in these cases one must question why certain people are more vulnerable to specific pathogens than are others.

Most nonspecific distress and suffering is not the result of contact with biological pathogens, however, but has social and political origins associated with war, forced migration, working conditions, exploitation, inequalities, violence, and racism. These factors, linked to what has been termed "structural violence," that is, exclusion of people from the basic needs for life and from the assets provided by an equitable society, are neither acknowledged nor relieved through the administration of medication. The following case study illustrates the importance of ethnographic research in exposing political and economic factors associated with a great deal of physical distress. It also shows how medicalization of such problems transforms them into problems located inside individual bodies and thereby depoliticizes them.

IMMIGRATION, NERVES, AND NOSTALGIA

The majority of immigrants from Europe who arrived in the 1960s and 1970s on the East Coast of North America were from small towns or of rural origin, many of them from southern Italy, Greece, and Portugal. In Montréal many of these immigrants who were women, particularly those from Greece, went to work in garment factories that are notorious for their exploitation of the labor force. The hours are long, there is no security, being laid off for long periods of time is common, pay is often below the minimum wage, noise and dust levels are very high, and the ventilation is poor. Managers still parade, as they have since early in the twentieth century, up and down in front of the women as they labor at their sewing machines, reprimanding them for slack and slovenly behavior. Given these conditions, many immigrants opted to work at home, in which case they had to purchase their own machines, pick up the "pieces" to be sewn, and then deliver the completed articles back to the factory door. In the 1980s there were estimated to be about twenty thousand such workers in Montréal. Today the numbers are considerably larger, but the women come for the most part from South America or Asian and African countries, not from southern Europe.

While doing research among Greek immigrants in Montréal in the late 1980s I found that complaints about ill health most commonly expressed by women, particularly those working in the garment industry, were described as *nevra* (nerves). *Nevra* is associated with a frightening loss of control, and is described as feelings of "bursting out," "breaking out," or "boiling over"—in other words, a sense of breaking down of body boundaries. Once the condition becomes more than an odd, isolated episode, then headaches, chest pain, and other pains radiating out from the back of the neck also characteristically become part of *nevra* symptomatology. This illness is so common that at least one major Montréal hospital makes use of *nevra* as a diagnostic category. Some women when they visit the doctor are diagnosed as clinically depressed and given antidepressants, but most do not meet the usual clinical criteria for depression. There is a tendency among physicians to dismiss patients' complaints as hypochondriacal, or simply as fantasy, or to send the patient to see a psychiatrist.

The Greek concept of *nevra* is part of a larger family of similar conditions commonly experienced in the southern Mediterranean, North Africa, and the Arab world, and in Central and South America (where it appears to have been transported from Europe as part of classical European Galenic medicine). The condition is also present in isolated parts of North America, including the Appalachians and Newfoundland, suggesting that it was formerly widely spread throughout Europe. The terms "culture-bound" or "culturally interpreted syndromes" have been used to gloss the plethora of conditions located around the world not recognized by biomedicine, of which the condition of *nevra* or *nervios* (in Spanish) is just one among many. Such conditions are usually characterized in the medical literature as "somatization" and treated as evidence of psychological disorder that manifests itself physically. Anthropologists, on the other hand, attempt to situate *nevra* and conditions like it in the larger cultural and political realities of the lives of sufferers, something that few medical practitioners find necessary, focused as they usually are on symptom relief. Nor do they usually have the time to do so.

Among Montréal immigrants, it is considered normal to have *nevra* in daily life; only when symptoms become very disabling will a woman visit a doctor. Some women are believed to be more constitutionally vulnerable to attacks than others, and men are not entirely immune. Moreover, *nevra* is associated by all women with the immigrant experience, and many women, when interviewed, additionally linked its incidence explicitly to work conditions:

There is more pressure in Montréal. . . . I come from a city of forty thousand in Greece, but they don't have the same pressures that we have here. My aunt works in a factory there, and she works hard, but not like here. Here you have someone on top of your head all the time pressuring you to work harder and harder. That's when you get *nevra*.

Another woman elaborated on problems at home as well as work:

Women get *nevra* because they have many responsibilities. The house and the boss at work. At home there are the household responsibilities and the children, and the woman does everything. The Greek man doesn't wipe the dishes or do anything.

This ever-present background of stress is punctuated by precipitating events ranging from crises such as being fired or laid off from to work, to family quarrels, or even spousal abuse. It is in situations such as these that *nevra* is used to describe the conjunction of destructive social events, uncontrolled emotional responses, and culturally characteristic disabling physical symptoms. In order to better appreciate the cultural significance of *nevra* and its intimate association with individual identity, we must turn very briefly to examine the structure of Greek family life.

In common with many other societies of the world, until recently, the majority of Greeks related a healthy and "correct" human body to a clean and orderly house, and this in turn is associated with moral order in society at large. The house is the focus of family life, not only because it furnishes all the physical and social needs of family members, but also because it is a spiritual center, replete with icons and regular ritual activity, where family members seek to emulate the Holy Family. Management of the house is the special responsibility of the woman, and cleanliness and order in the house are said to reflect her character.

Discussion of private, family matters should not cross the threshold into the threatening domain of the outside world. Ideally, a woman should never leave the house for frivolous or idle reasons, and if she spends too much time outside, where dirt and immorality abound, she can be accused of damaging the all-important social reputation of her family. While men must protect the family honor in the outside world, women have been required to exhibit modesty; their bodies are symbols of family integrity and purity. Emotional stability is valued in this situation, and any loss of control on the part of women is worrisome.

Just as a distinction is made between inside and outside the house, so too is a distinction made between the inner and outer body. Contact between what enters the body and what leaves it must be avoided. Dirty clothes and polluting human products must be strictly segregated from food preparation. Although fulfillment of male sexual needs is considered imperative, a woman's life is hedged with taboos in connection with menstruation, marriage, the sexual act, and childbirth, designed to constrain her behavior and contain the polluting nature of her bodily products.

Of course I have described the normative state, an idealized situation that in daily life is often not lived up to or may be deliberately flouted. Nevertheless, this has been the value system that has shaped the lives of the majority of Greek women until recent times. As is usual among immigrant populations, such values tend to persist after migration, and the uncertainties produced by a new way of life actually promote them at times. For example, in Montréal, Greek immigrant women complain that they seldom have an opportunity to go out of the house unaccompanied by their husbands unless it is to go to work. A Greek-Canadian physician described many of his patients as suffering from what he called the "hostage syndrome," the result of vigilant husbands protecting their family honor in unfamiliar surroundings.

Abiding by traditional codes of conduct can become crippling after immigration. When a harsh climate, cramped apartment life with few friends or relatives nearby, language difficulties, and debilitating working conditions are taken into account, it is hardly surprising that so many women experience acute isolation, physical suffering in the form of *nevra*, and serious doubts about the worth of their lives. The majority of women live with a powerful nostalgia for the life they left behind in Greece. Many were married by their families at a very young age to Greek men on return visits to their native villages in search of brides, and were then brought directly to Montréal. Over the years a large number of these women come to despair of ever having much pleasure in their own lives, and most indicated when interviewed that they had transferred all their hopes for the future onto their children. As one woman put it, "It's too late for me; my dreams are broken."

We see in this example of *nevra* the shaping by shared values of physical symptoms and emotions. *Nevra* is a manifestation of the particular problems raised by migration to a new physical location in which social organization, family life, and working conditions are entirely transformed, creating uncertainty, exploitation, and enormous hardship. The children of Greek immigrants are unlikely to suffer in the same way as did their parents because they are for the most part well integrated into mainstream North American society, and they think of *nevra* as an "old-fashioned" problem that they associate with their parents.

Circumstances similar to those of the Montréal Greek immigrants, but often much more traumatic, in which structural violence forecloses all options for a decent life, is common in the globalized world of today. The numbers of people whose everyday lives are irrevocably disrupted is increasing rapidly due to a burgeoning rate of involuntary migration, wars, drug trafficking, internal strife, development projects, and so on. Increased exposure to infectious diseases and chronic food shortages are common, and millions of people are confronted routinely with trauma and violence, often on a daily basis. Many others are subjected to the indignities and overcrowding of refugee camps for years on end.

In addition to high rates of TB (often resistant to many drugs), AIDS, and other infectious diseases, much of the chronic, unrelieved distress that these people experience is expressed in the form of symptoms and syndromes not unlike those of *nevra*. Very often these symptoms are diagnosed as post-traumatic stress disorder (PTSD). While this diagnosis can be useful in that the gravity of symptoms are recognized, the problem is individualized as both a psychological and medical matter. All too often the inequalities and violence that precipitated the trauma are obscured, while attention is devoted to symptom relief.

It has been shown, for example, that in the burgeoning field of trauma counseling for developing countries devastated by war, emphasis is too often placed on the relief of individual trauma and distress. Counseling is provided in which people are encouraged to "talk through" their personal experiences of loss. However, in the case of Somali refugees, and no doubt for many other people, attention to personal or private loss, even the death of close relatives, is considered inappropriate. What should come first, it is believed, is restoration of moral order in the community, and the reintegration of individuals into social life. In many locations where everyday violence is a way of life, reconnecting individuals with appropriate social networks is regarded as the most appropriate form of care. Excessive attention paid to individual feelings of grief heightens the experience of loss among

Somali refugees, for example, and of being cut off from their land and community. Giving serious attention to what victims of trauma perceive to be in their own self-interest is surely not too big a step for international agencies providing assistance to take, rather than imposing trauma counseling across the board. This can be done while at the same time supplying medications, food, and clean water in order to meet the basic needs of the body.

TAKING CONTROL OF FEMALE AGING

An entirely different example, that of the female life-cycle transition of menopause, highlights the complex relationship among biology, individual subjectivity, medical practices, and culture. Although passage through the life cycle is simultaneously a social and a biological process, the focus of attention within medical circles in recent years, not surprisingly perhaps, has been confined with increasing intensity to changes in the physical body. This situation is widely reflected in turn in public discourse, which also focuses intently on the pathology of female (and more recently male) aging.

Of course, not all women have cooperated with the medicalization of menopause. On the contrary, the aging female body has become the site for ever more contentious debate among both medical practitioners and involved women about its representation and the medical practices performed upon it. Medicalization of the female body, whether young, middle aged, or old, is not due entirely to changing medical interests, knowledge, and practices. It is also a manifestation of potent, never settled, partially disguised political contests that contribute to the way in which the female body is "seen" and interpreted by women themselves, in the popular domain, by policymakers and professionals working in the health care system, and by the pharmaceutical industry invested in the medical management of the female body.

Even though disputes and debates exist about how this stage of the life cycle can best be managed, a common assumption exists that menopause is a universal phenomenon that affects all women in essentially the same way. However, the concept of menopause was first invented early in the nineteenth century in Europe, and only gradually since that time has it become closely equated in the minds of both the public and the medical profession with the end of menstruation. In recent years another transformation has taken place, and menopause is now often classed as a diseaselike state—an "estrogen deficiency." Dominant medical accounts are currently concerned with the postulated long-term effects of lowered estrogen levels on the health of women throughout the latter part of their life cycle. The category "postmenopausal" is applied to all women past reproductive age, who are, by definition, deemed to be at an increased risk for heart disease, osteoporosis, and other diseases associated with aging. Attention has shifted away from any short-term discomfort that may occur around the time of the end of menstruation, as was formerly the case. It is now the specter of aging baby boomers and the burden they are likely to place on the health care system in old age that is of primary concern.

Medical literature on menopause often bemoans the fact that the proportion of women past middle age in the population is rapidly increasing; governments too, not surprisingly, are intently concerned about postmenopausal women and make calculations about their future medical expenses. If popular literature, medication use, and the popularity of local sports complexes are any indication, a large number of women of middle age apparently live with a diffuse anxiety about aging. This state is fueled by professional and media rhetoric; many women think of themselves as being "at risk," and their internalized image is, it seems, one of living with an estrogen deficiency. Despite the presence of a health-conscious population and a widely accessible health care system, the situation is very different in contemporary Japan. A brief examination of some of these differences permits us to reexamine certain common assumptions made in North America about aging.

AGING AND JAPANESE SOCIETY

The "graying" of Japan has taken only a quarter of a century, whereas the equivalent demographic changes occurred over the course of about one hundred years in Europe and North America. Some official estimates calculate that, if present trends continue, by the year 2025 people aged sixty-five and over will make up a remarkable 24 percent of the population, and among the elderly, more than 53 percent will be over seventy-five years of age. Japan will be the "oldest" society in the world. It is notable that the health and aging of women in their forties and fifties has, until very recently, received little attention in Japan; it is only as potential caregivers for their elderly relatives that they appear in professional and popular literature. This is particularly evident when compared to the number of publications on the elderly themselves.

Since the early 1970s, when the question of the elderly first began to capture the attention of Japanese policymakers, it has been stated repeatedly, following a Confucian value system, that it is preferable for the aged to be taken care of in their own homes. Family members should be the primary caregivers, although some money has been set aside by the government to train paramedicals to assist with the elderly in the home. However, politicians are concerned that the government is increasingly "expected" by the public to play a larger role in the care of the aging population, and several policy changes have been implemented to reverse this trend.

In contemporary Japan the "homebody," or "professional housewife," is idealized; her lifestyle and behavior are made into the standard by which all Japanese women are measured (despite the fact that over 60 percent of women are in the labor force; figure 2). However, the assumption is that once she becomes middle-aged the homebody, living in a nuclear family, will become a social anomaly because her children have left home. No longer of obvious productive use, aside from occasionally feeding her husband, a middle-aged woman is free to be prevailed upon, as was the norm in times past, to carry out her lifelong duties to the extended family. Nuclear families are expected to become extended, and elderly parents should reside with their adult children, preferably their firstborn son, so that their daughters-in-law may care for them until death.

Because financially secure, middle-class women are assumed to represent Japanese women as a whole, the situation of the majority who must give up work to look after their relatives, often at great cost to the well-being of the entire family unit, is all but erased from national consciousness. Moreover, many Japanese, with the longest life expectancy in the world, live to be well over ninety years of age, and daughters-in-law in their seventies find themselves bound over to caring for one or more incontinent, immobile, and sometimes senile relatives. Furthermore, since stroke is the most usual cause of disability among the elderly in Japan, intensive nursing is often required, and men assist very rarely with this onerous duty. It is, therefore, a concern about home nursing and living together as a three-generation family that takes up most of the energy of activist women in Japan to-

FIGURE 2 A cake-factory assembly line in southern Kyoto, Japan. (Photo by author)

day, much more so than does the question of *kōnenki* (the term that glosses as menopause). Together with the politically active among the elderly themselves, middle-aged women question the intransigence of national and local governments regarding the social impact on the family of an aging society.

In Japan, the idea of an autonomous individual has never taken hold to a great extent, despite more than a century of exposure to European and North American philosophy. Movement through the life cycle continues to be subjectively experienced for most people largely in terms of how one's relationships with others shift through time. For women particularly, life is expected to become meaningful according to what they accomplish for others rather than for themselves, and the expectation that middle-aged women will devote their time to the care of the elderly is deeply internalized. It appears that the end of menstruation has never been a potent symbol for Japanese women. Today, a few individuals, as they grow older, mourn the loss of youth and sexual attractiveness, but most emphasize what is described as the inevitable process of aging itself: graying hair, changing eyesight, faulty short-term memory, and so on. Furthermore, these marks of aging, while they obviously represent the irretrievable passing of youth, are primarily signposts to the future—for what may be in store for a woman as her body becomes ever more feeble, making her dependent on others and, most important of all, unable to work or contribute to society.

FIGURE 3 Elderly people enjoying a lively discussion, Kyoto, Japan. (Sean Sprague/Panos)

This understanding of female aging in Japan is reinforced by further contributing factors. Perhaps the most important was revealed by survey research carried out in the mid 1980s which shows that, compared with Americans and Canadians, Japanese women experience remarkably few symptoms at the end of menstruation, including those considered to be universally characteristic of menopause, namely hot flashes and night sweats. It is notable that there is no word that specifically signifies a "hot flash" in Japanese. On the basis of this finding, it can be argued that discourses on aging are shaped not only by unexamined beliefs about the female body and its function in society, but also in part by "local biologies." In other words, there is sufficient variation among biological populations that the physical effects of lowered estrogen levels on the body, characteristic of the female midlife transition, are not the same in all geographical locations. There is evidence from other parts of the world in addition to Japan of considerable variation in symptom reporting at menopause. This variation, to which genetics, diet, environment, and other cultural variables no doubt contribute, accounts for differences in subjective, embodied experience. The different experiences that dominate in North America and Japan respectively are sufficient to produce an effect on (but *not* determine) the creation of knowledge, both popular and professional, about this life-cycle transition. *Kōnenki* has never been thought of as a diseaselike state, nor even equated closely with the end of menstruation, even by Japanese medical professionals. The symptoms most closely associated with *kōnenki* are shoulder stiffness and other similar, culturally specific sensations, including a "heavy" head. Clearly menopause is not a universal event, but a culturally constructed concept.

Japanese physicians keep abreast of the medical literature published in connection with menopause, and so one might expect, living as they do in a country actively dedicated to preventive medicine, that there might be some incentive for them to make use of hormone replacement therapy (HRT). This is the medication widely recommended by health care professionals in Europe and North America for life-long use with virtually all postmenopausal women. However, this is not the case because, as we have seen, symptom reporting is low, and very few Japanese women go to see physicians in connection with distressing symptoms such as hot flashes. In addition, local biology plays a part in other ways. Mortality from coronary heart disease for Japanese women is about one quarter that of American women. It is estimated that although Japanese women become osteoporotic twice as often as do Japanese men, these rates are approximately half of what they are in North America. These figures, combined with a mortality rate from breast cancer about one quarter that of North America and the longest life expectancy in the world for Japanese women, have meant that there is relatively little pressure for gynecologists in Japan to enter into the controversial international arena of debate about the pros and cons of long-term use of HRT. This debate is in any case something about which many Japanese gynecologists are decidedly uncomfortable because of a pervasive concern about unwanted side-effects from long-term use of powerful medication. The first line of resort of Japanese doctors when dealing with healthy, middle-aged women is usually to encourage good dietary practices and plenty of exercise. For those few women with troubling symptoms, herbal medicine is commonly prescribed.

Increasingly, certain Japanese physicians, directly influenced by trends in North America, are currently seeking to medicalize *kōnenki* and to treat it much more aggressively as a disease of aging. It will be interesting to see not only how successful is this move, but also whether the symptoms reported by Japanese women change as a result of this new medical interest in the aging of women. It seems unlikely that this will happen unless simultaneous widespread and massive transformations in dietary and behavioral practices bring about radical changes in the embodied experience of the end of menstruation for large numbers of women. On the other hand, fears on the part of Japanese women about becoming dependent on the younger generation, like certain of the parents-in-law whom they care for, may well promote the medicalization of menopause. This may be so even though at the current time several key medical "experts," the majority of them North American, are having second thoughts about blanket recommendations for long-term use of hormone replacement therapy.

The politics of aging, an urgent matter in both Japan and North America, is constructed in these two cultural spaces, therefore, in very different ways. Although both discourses are in part the product of a rhetoric about biological change, with its associated risk for distress and even major disease (particularly in North America), this rhetoric is shaped by local biologies, historically informed knowledge, culturally influenced medical knowledge and beliefs, government interests, and situated social exigencies. Women's experiences at the end of menstruation, including unpleasant symptoms, are also informed by this complex of situated variables and are not universal. These findings suggest that it is important to decenter assumptions about a biological universalism associated with aging. Obviously aging is unavoidable, but the power of both biology and culture to shape the experience of aging and the meanings—individual, social, and political—attributed to this process demand fine-grained, contextualized interpretations.

CULTURE, POLITICS, AND THE LOCAL CONFIGURATION OF BIOLOGIES

Very recent work on the origins, geographical distribution, and evolution of HIV shows clearly that attention has to be paid not only to the social context and sexual practices of communities, but to local configurations of biologies. The form that HIV takes, the presence of other diseases, especially sexually transmitted diseases, malnutrition, and available medical technologies must all be taken into consideration. Molecular epidemiological studies of HIV have demonstrated the emergence of recombinant strains in different parts of the world that are exceptionally difficult to control. These recombinant strains are most marked in geographical areas undergoing massive breakdown, where nutritional status is poor, other types of sexually transmitted diseases are rampant, violence, including rape, is widespread, education is limited, condoms are lacking, and biomedical treatment is unavailable or completely ineffective. This is a horrific example of the way in which diversification of local biologies, in this case viral evolution, is accelerated and intensified by social forces, so that the AIDS epidemic in the developing world, in stark contrast to that in North America and Europe, spins further and further out of control.

The examples of *nevra* and other conditions associated with trauma, of menopause, and of HIV, each in their own way make clear that the challenge is to dislodge the familiar assumptions of universality made in Europe and North America about health, illness, disease, and life-cycle transitions. What appear to be the exotic anomalies associated with other parts of the world are made intelligible through anthropological research. At the same time the contribution of social inequities, politics, and violence to the incidence of so much disease and distress is brought into focus. Furthermore, the way in which biology, society, and cultural values are coproduced—how they are inseparable from one another and mutually malleable—is made abundantly clear.

SUGGESTIONS FOR FURTHER READING

Hogle, Linda. 1999. *Recovering the Nation's Body: Cultural Memory, Medicine, and the Politics of Redemption.* New Brunswick, NJ: Rutgers University Press. [An ethnography based in Germany about the disputes and practices associated with the procurement of body tissues and organs for therapeutic and scientific purposes.]

Lindenbaum, Shirley, and Margaret Lock, eds. 1993. *Knowledge, Power, and Practice: The Anthropology of Medicine and Everyday Life.* Berkeley: University of California Press. [This collection of essays covers a wide range of topics in medical anthropology, with emphasis on the relationship of power embedded in medical knowledge and practice.]

Lock, Margaret. 1990. "On Being Ethnic: The Politics of Identity Breaking and Making, or Nevra on Sunday." *Culture, Medicine, and Psychiatry* 14: 237–52. [A discussion of the body as a medium for the expression of social and political inequalities.]

———. 1993. *Encounters with Aging: Mythologies of Menopause in Japan and North America.* Berkeley: University of California Press. [A comprehensive ethnography of the politics of female aging that also shows how the cultural construction, medicalization, and subjective experience of menopause differs in Japan and North America.]

———. 2001. *Twice Dead: Organ Transplants and the Reinvention of Death*. Berkeley: University of California Press. [An examination of the creation of the concept of brain-death and the contradictions and anxieties associated with the procurement of organs from brain-dead bodies in North America and Japan.]

Nguyen, Vinh-Kim. 2001. "Epidemics, Interzones, and Biosocial Changes." In *Entangled Histories*, ed. Wolf Lepenies. London: St. Martin's Press. [A discussion of globalization and the interrelationship of politics, culture, and biology in the HIV/AIDS epidemic in West Africa.]

Scheper-Hughes, Nancy. 1992. *Death without Weeping: The Violence of Everyday Life in Brazil*. Berkeley: University of California Press. [An exhaustive exploration of the exploited existence of slum dwellers in northeast Brazil and its effect on affiliation, health, and physical survival.]

Young, Allan. 1995. *The Harmony Of Illusions: Inventing Post-traumatic Stress Disorder*. Princeton, NJ: Princeton University Press. [An examination of the creation of the concept of trauma with emphasis on its contemporary psychiatric management as post-traumatic stress disorder.]

Zarowsky, Christina. 2000. "Trauma Stories: Violence, Emotion, and Politics in Somali Ethiopia." *Transcultural Psychiatry* 37: 383–402. [An ethnographic account of the experience of war-related distress among Somali refugees in Ethiopia.]

11.

Anthropology, Culture, and Environment

MELISSA LEACH AND JAMES FAIRHEAD

Environmental concerns are now highly prominent in debates about global development and futures, whether in international policy circles or among populations influenced by increasingly global media. International agendas are being set to address problems such as desertification, deforestation, biodiversity loss, greenhouse gas emissions, and climate change. Environmental degradation threatens "sustainable" development which would—in the widely repeated terms of the Brundtland Commission—"meet the needs of the present without compromising the ability of future generations to meet their own needs" (WCED 1987, 8). The extent to which similar environmental problems appear to recur across the world, the transnational nature of many environmental problems, and the ultimate sanction that there is "only one earth" on which we all face a tragedy of the commons, might suggest the truly global nature of the environmental crisis and the need for universal scientific values and a global environmental ethics to respond to it. More than any other important, contemporary discourse, the debate on the environment has adopted the concept of the global perspective as both motive and motif.

Yet global environmental problems have local origins and impacts. Anthropologists demonstrate the cultural diversity with which any globalized aspirations must contend. In this they also show, and have succeeded in bringing to international attention, that "traditional" forms of knowledge and organization have contributed to environmental sustainability in many localities. They can be learned from and built upon. Contemporary anthropology also examines the multifaceted character of environmentalism in the West and its constitution both in specific popular cultures and policy institutions. It thus explores the spectrum of sites in which environmentalisms are produced and their effects felt.

The perspective that anthropology takes highlights the significance of social relations and culture in mediating people-environmental relations. Hence it reveals the problems in approaches, still present, which view environmental issues in purely technical terms, or which conceive of environmental problems simply in terms of imbalances between sheer numbers of people and overall resource availability. Yet anthropological approaches have been many. While endorsing the growing attention to "culture" in environment-development debates, this chapter also questions the ways in which it has been incorporated.

Furthermore, diverse cultural perspectives have been harnessed selectively, and with distortion, to suit globally defined environmental agendas which, rather than being shared or universal, actually reflect the priorities of those in positions of power. Yet local realities and alternative cultural perspectives can offer very different views of change from the orthodoxies on which global environmental agendas rest. In this respect anthropology reveals global agendas, and the science and notions of environmentalism with which they are associated, to be equally partial, cultural perspectives. This poses a challenge not only for the ways that "culture" is used, understood and defined, but also for approaches to the governance of environment and development processes.

To set the scene for this argument, we begin by illustrating how people interact with local environments—with their "surroundings," as the environment can be broadly defined—in culturally grounded ways. With the focus largely on rural settings, selected examples are used first to show the significance of cultural diversity in the ideas and knowledges through which people comprehend and work with ecological processes. Second, we discuss anthropological perspectives on the social institutions which shape people-environment interactions.

LOCAL CULTURAL KNOWLEDGES

Much anthropological research now illustrates the culturally diverse and creative ways in which people interact with their environments. In many rural and urban localities, people are directly dependent on environmental resources and services for their lives and livelihoods, so many local environmental concerns and representations are technical; they are about manipulating the environment for day-to-day survival and prosperity. Yet as work on local people's conceptions of their ecology (ethnoecology) has shown, technical concepts are not merely utilitarian, but embedded in broader sets of ideas and beliefs—ways of thinking about and understanding the world. Whether or not environmental processes and phenomena have a material existence in and of themselves, anthropology stresses that the meanings which people impose on them are always socially and culturally shaped.

For instance, when African farmers describe and manipulate the soils and vegetation which are basic to agricultural livelihoods, they use culturally embedded concepts. Kinship terms such as "companionship" or "brotherhood" may be used to describe situations in which particular trees, crops, or weeds coexist; equally, terms such as "killing" or "struggle" can be used to describe competitive suppression, whether in fallows or crops. Soil fertility may be described in terms of heat and cold, damp and dry, hard and soft, with farmers managing these attributes to balance their qualities. Such vocabularies find echoes and gain their meaning in the broader frames in which people understand their world and their place in it, which might include phenomena—such as kinship and social relations—that Western science would not treat as "environmental." For example, Kuranko-speaking farmers in West Africa use the term *tombondu* to refer to a soil which has acquired softness, "oiliness" and "maturity" through prolonged, intensive cultivation. Literally meaning "abandoned settlement," the term makes metaphorical reference to the way old village and hamlet sites acquire such characteristics through habitation, gardening, and rubbish disposal. The concepts of oiliness and maturity are also applied to girls who have completed their initiation rites, establishing them as fertile women; within this broader frame of reference, then, *tombondu* soils are "initiated" through work into a newly fertile, productive status.

Because of their cultural embeddedness, local idioms used to categorize and explain ecological phenomena frequently do not translate easily into those of Western environmental science. For example, scientists have often assumed that farmers do not manage for crop diseases, because when presented with diseased specimens, they sometimes neither distinguish diseases, nor consider the poor health of crops in terms of disease. It was thus presumed that they could not see the disease vector. However, farmers may have other frameworks for understanding and influencing crop health. Farmers in the Bwisha area of Kivu, in DRC, formerly Zaire, for instance, consider rain, dew, and humidity to have particular cooling and putrefactory qualities, and manage for these—the conditions in which disease develops—in their cropping, through altering sowing time, weeding, variety selection, and so on. Understandably, within this cultural framework, they refer to fungicides as "medicines against the rain."

Equally, people may consider agencies and processes which have little place in the classificatory schemes of contemporary Western thought and science as important influences on environmental processes. They may think land and vegetation retain enduring links with those who worked it in the past, so that maintaining correct relationships with ancestors is essential to current land productivity. The environment may be inhabited by numerous spirits or deities, perhaps associated with particular trees, rock complexes, water bodies, or animals, and maintaining correct relationships with these is considered important to people's livelihoods and prosperity. Many African agricultural peoples seem to view their relationships with such entities as one of necessary respect and mutual accommodation. For instance, among Kuranko-speakers, interfering with *djinn* spirits by felling the forest patches which are their homes can prompt death and ill-fortune for the feller's family. For these reasons, they carefully conserve "djinn villages." In contrast, a number of peoples with primarily hunter-gatherer economies, including the Nayaka in southern India and groups in the rain forests of Central Africa, seem to understand their environments as "giving freely" to them, as part of a "cosmic economy of sharing" which also ideally permeates social relationships. This sort of view of the environment is very different from the Western one, common since the Enlightenment, of the environment as the subject of control by society and technology.

In many cultural settings, the concepts used to describe ecological processes are also used to describe aspects of people's health and fertility. Thus, where Western science conventionally draws its boundary between body and field, local beliefs may draw causal links which cross-cut such boundaries. For example, several West African peoples believe that if a woman who is menstruating or in the early stages of pregnancy enters a stream or pond as part of a fishing group, both the fishing and her future fertility will be ruined (plate 5). Equally, a hunter's fortunes can be influenced by his wife's sexual activities; if she engages in adultery while he is hunting, a hunter in Sierra Leone's forests will say that "the bush will close," and he will kill nothing.

Such examples begin to indicate how, within particular cultural understandings, people's behavior and relationships can have direct consequences for the "natural" environment and vice versa. In this sense, a network of conceptually linked processes and causal relationships cuts across the division between "nature" and "society" or "culture" that is so basic to European thought. Unsurprisingly, claims to authority over these sorts of linked ecological and social processes can be central to local political dynamics. The power of the leaders of territorial cults in Central and Southern Africa earlier this century rested strongly on their claims to manage environmental and human fertility concerns. Along Africa's Upper Guinea coast, power relations in women's and men's initiation societies rest on claims to gender-specific knowledge and on claims to power over respective ecological domains.

Knowledge, ideas, and beliefs concerning ecological relations are neither static nor necessarily shared by all the members of a particular society. Knowledge may develop through a creative interplay between theory and practice, and through interaction with ecological processes that are themselves dynamic. It may also develop through local processes of debate between people whose opinions reflect their positions in local society. For example in the forest-savanna transition zone of Guinea, West Africa, elders of landowning lineages tend to associate the existence of large trees in peri-village forests with the foundation of settlements by their ancestors, reflecting a domain in which they have relative authority. In contrast, young women tend to explain them as the overgrown fence poles of kitchen gardens, reflecting their relative powerlessness in lineage affairs and their more everyday concerns with kitchen gardening.

At one level, therefore, anthropology is well placed to show how particular environmental understandings might be associated with a particular "culture": with a particular society, or with a broad regional tradition encompassing subtle local variations on common themes. But anthropologists have also emphasized the diverse cultural perspectives which may coexist within any given local setting. These may be associated with local axes of social difference (e.g., determined by gender, age, caste, kinship position, socioeconomic status, or occupation) and can be the stuff of local debate. But the anthropological notion of cultural perspective also allows for the recognition of commonalities, coalitions, and alliances across localized cultures. This is especially pertinent in a globalizing world in which the idea of "cultural boundaries" has become even more problematic. Such alliances may be grounded in aspects of common experience: for example, those engaged in commercial logging from urban and rural backgrounds, in southeast Asia and in Latin America, might share similar perspectives on forests as a source of valuable timber. Alliances can also be forged around environmental phenomena as shared political symbols, as when forest dwellers in Malaysia's Penan unite with Western environmental activist groups to valorize medicinal plants, deploying this value symbolically in campaigns for rain forest preservation. Because they are produced through, and supportive of, particular relations of power, these cultural perspectives can usefully be seen as "discourses" on environment; this argument becomes clearer later in the chapter when discussion focuses on the relationship between environmental knowledge and material practices.

Much international attention has focused on cultural diversity in ecological knowledge. It is sometimes argued that nonindustrial societies possess a "primitive ecological wisdom" which could offer pointers towards sustainable future ways of life, or that detailed indigenous knowledge of soils, plants, animals, and so on offer vital resources for global struggles to develop sustainable food-production systems, conserve biodiversity, and so on. Alternatively, localized, culturally specific knowledge is seen as important to fine-tune or adapt generalized technologies to local settings. Such arguments underlie the creation of international networks and centers to record and preserve indigenous knowledge. However, these efforts frequently portray knowledge as static and "traditional," associated with particular cultures. They ignore the intracultural and transcultural diversity and dynamism discussed above. Equally, these arguments often take an evaluative perspective: culturally specific knowledge is selected and valued insofar as it is recognizable in the terms of Western science, or insofar as it is seen as useful to address globally defined environmental agendas or the goals of externally defined campaigns. At the extreme, local knowledges may be repackaged in scientized terms, or within romanticized notions of "sacred wisdom," to such an extent that they become un-recognizable to those who spawned them and thus suppress local creativity in the process. Taking cultural diversity seriously requires a far more balanced, comparative approach.

CULTURE, INSTITUTIONS, AND SUSTAINABILITY

Work on environmental knowledges treats culture largely in terms of ideas and beliefs. Arguments from this work are often coupled with the perspectives from a second area of anthropological inquiry, emphasizing how local organizations and institutions can promote environmentally sustainable practices. This work has tended to subscribe to a slightly different view of culture, referring to whole ways of life and lifestyles. This view is problematic because it glosses over the relationship between knowledge and practice and the many factors which influence it, and also over the processes and relations of power which produce particular forms of organization.

Nevertheless, this strand of work has been highly influential in bringing cultural concerns into international environment and development debates. In some formulations, including the ecosystems approaches to cultural ecology which became popular during the 1960s, culture is seen as having adaptive value in the maintenance of the environment. Thus, it is argued, culturally defined norms about cooperation, religious institutions, and so on serve to regulate the human impact on surroundings, so that people-environment relations remain harmonious. This perspective has been criticized within anthropology for two reasons: first, for its static and inaccurate portrayal of homogeneous, structure-driven "societies" with common ecological concerns; other approaches have instead emphasized social difference and power relations, the diversity of resource concerns in any local setting, and the playing out of resource struggles through history. Second, conventional cultural ecology—in its emphasis on "unconscious" adaptive regulation—downplayed people's understanding, knowledge, and reflection concerning aspects of ecology and environment. As we have seen, these issues have been key themes of other anthropological work—for instance, on "ethnoscience," "indigenous knowledge," and cross-cultural comparisons of how "nature" and "society" are understood.

Nevertheless, these older anthropological arguments about organization have been taken up within international debates. Linked with views of environmentally benign knowledge systems, they have contributed to or rejuvenated a concept of "ecocultures": that certain peoples, principally nonindustrial, possess forms of knowledge and organization which make their ways of life more harmoniously integrated with their environments and thus sustainable. Such claims are often made for remote "forest peoples," "hunter-gatherers," and "tribals" in particular. Other societies may "traditionally" have maintained such harmony, but have seen it ruptured by external economic or political forces: the imposition of inappropriate state regimes and the undermining of traditional authority; commercialization; modernity; or new urban aspirations. Defenders of these arguments then go on to claim that (1) certain local culture-environment systems are adaptive or sustainable; (2) the world has much to learn from these; (3) those which are adaptive should be conserved; and (4) on the precautionary principle (similar to arguments used about biodiversity), it is important to retain cultural diversity to avoid the loss now of systems which, in the future, might be valued. Some of these ideas are already embodied in national and donor policies and programs—for instance, in "cultural reserves" created for indigenous peoples to occupy within biodiverse rain forest areas, or in community-based sustainable development which seeks to support or rebuild traditional, environmentally sustainable institutions.

However, some of the same problems found in the treatment of ecological knowledge also apply here. First, there are problems with the view of "cultures" as shared, bounded wholes, relating to single, static environments. For instance, in one area, there may not be a community of homogeneous interests, but an assortment of people who, with different livelihoods and different socially defined responsibilities, give priority to different environmental goods and services within ecologies that are also diverse and variable. In a watershed in Rajasthan, for example, the same hillsides are valued by women of scheduled castes for gathering saleable wild foods; by Rajput women as a convenient source of fuelwood; by men to plant trees for cash sale of poles, and by livestock-raising groups as common grazing grounds. Evidently, such diverse values can come into conflict.

Second, how people use and manage environments depends on the ways they can come to access and control particular resources and services, and perhaps struggle with others to do so. Many social and political relationships and institutions, both local and not-so-local, are involved in these processes and shape their ecological outcomes. To focus on "culture" as knowledge and ideas is to ignore these and thus assume falsely that environmentally benign beliefs translate into environmentally benign practice. Adopting a definition of "culture" so broad and holistic as to conflate all within "ways of life" is to lose analytical insight. For instance, it may be important to recognize that people fell trees or knowingly allow soils to degrade because they are only tenants on the land with insecure tenure. Broader processes—state policies, changes in market prices, and so on—interact with these local institutional dynamics in affecting patterns of environmental change. Such processes have a profound impact which tends to be underplayed by analysis framed in terms of static ideas of culture and by images of past environmental harmony ensured by community-level organization, now disrupted by external forces. Instead, highly charged resource politics have been features of most societies, past and present, albeit played out in culturally shaped ways.

Finally—but crucially—an evaluative perspective has dominated international debates about the cultural determinants of environmental change and the value of "conservationist" cultures where knowledge and organization are seen to ensure harmonious environmental relations. Policymakers have tended to value these "ecocultures," as they are sometimes called, selectively and to the extent that they support environmental values and trajectories of change which are compatible with those in global debates. Thus ecocultures are judged according to their contribution to combatting the problems which global and Western debate have highlighted, such as tropical deforestation, biodiversity loss, or desertification. Equally, many studies of the social and cultural dynamics of environmental change—of deforestation or soil degradation, for instance—frame their analyses in terms of these problems uncritically, without questioning their "reality." In this way, studies of social and cultural change support a view of these broad environmental problematics as shared, global preoccupations, and of the science that underlies them as universal, objective, and neutral. But as the following cases show, serious attention to diverse cultural perspectives can question these global orthodoxies in fundamental ways, showing them, and their underlying science, to be partial cultural perspectives grounded in particular relations of power.

Forests in West Africa

The forest-savanna transition zone of West Africa has, since early colonial times, been portrayed as undergoing rapid deforestation. "Islands" of forest in a sea of grassland, they are assumed to be relics of once-extensive natural forest cover, the climax vegetation for the zone's humid climate, progressively destroyed by local farming and fire-setting for hunting and pastoralism. This supposed human disturbance to natural vegetation has led government policies and international aid programs to restrict land use practices thought to be environmentally damaging through regulations and fines, while state agencies have taken control over threatened "natural" trees. Some forest patches have been singled out for more community-based forms of conservation, on the grounds that they are "sacred" forests culturally preserved amid secular destruction around them.

But at least in forest Guinea, local cultural perspectives strongly contradict this view of progressive savannization, presenting an opposed, even reversed, reading of the landscape. Villagers describe how forest patches, far from being relics of destruction, have been created by themselves or their ancestors in savannas. Elderly men frequently emphasize the effects of tree planting, settlement foundation, and the role of forests as early war fortresses, while women tend to focus on the gradual vegetation-enhancing effects of gardening, household waste, and the grazing of domestic animals. Many forest-building and expanding practices are of an extremely common kind, grounded in villagers' practical ecological knowledge and the fundamental idea that land is improved through use and work. Forests are not "sacred" in local thought, even though they can be sites for initiation activities and ancestral veneration. Many local farming and early burning practices have enhanced the progressive expansion of forest into savanna over the last century; a change confirmed by historical sources such as comparative air photographs and archival descriptions. Yet scientists and administrators have repeatedly overlooked such evidence in favor of data supporting their conviction of deforestation. The latter both conforms with dominant scientific theories and supports particular economic and political interests, not least the revenues to be derived from government-controlled trees.

Environmental Degradation in the Himalayas

The Himalayas have been portrayed as a region of environmental crisis par excellence. Dominant views hold that local farming and fuelwood collection practices lead to the depletion of tree cover (figure 1). Encouraged by rapid population growth, the deforestation frontier is pushed further and further out from settlements onto more mountainous and marginal land, where it leads to soil erosion. This progressive degradation is felt not only locally, but downstream as well, with soil erosion and landslides blamed for flooding on the Nepalese and Indian plains below. This crisis has provided the justification for a variety of government interventions aimed at restricting shifting cultivation and halting deforestation, and for large inputs of international aid into mountain Nepal.

However, detailed research among mountain farmers reveals some very different perspectives. Farmers generally do not interpret the region's ongoing environmental change as degradation or crisis caused by their practices. Rather than degrade land in response to population growth, they have, through active agricultural innovation and tree planting, been able to intensify production on parts of their land in sustainable ways. While donors and scientists have treated landslides as an indicator of ecological collapse, some farmers consider them advantageous—and even trigger them deliberately—to fertilize valley bottom lands.

FIGURE 1 Carrying home dry fuelwood gathered from the forest floor, Nepal. (Photo by Ben Campbell)

Furthermore, many of the erosion processes attributed to careless farming can be reinterpreted as due to long-term tectonic changes. Indeed, a critical review of empirical evidence for and against environmental degradation reveals a vast diversity of possible measurements and interpretations. Depending on the data selected, the Himalayas can appear to be about to become totally denuded, or about to experience a vast increase in tree cover, or anywhere in between. Farmer-induced ecological collapse is only one possible interpretation among many; nevertheless, it has commonly been selected by many aid organizations and governments because it matched their own policy objectives.

Rangelands and Desertification

"Desertification" has long been a powerful concept in international and national policy arenas addressing dryland degradation, and was given renewed vigor following the Desertification Convention discussed at the United Nations Conference on Environment and Development at Rio in 1992. Within the term's original sense as a progressive expansion of desertlike conditions, pastoralists are frequently blamed for ecological damage: persistent tendencies for individual herders to overstock their herds leads to a tragedy of the commons in which rangeland carrying capacity is exceeded, resulting in overgrazing and vegetation decline.

Yet there is considerable scientific doubt over, and very little hard evidence for, the ongoing, long-term expansion of desert margins. Cultural perspectives found among herders point instead to the inherent variability of dryland systems and to cycles of desert expansion and retreat linked to rainfall variation. Their herding strategies are logical in this context, making opportunistic use of heterogeneous and risky rangeland conditions, whether through mobility, cycles of herd-building and decline, or other strategies aimed at living with, rather than overriding, uncertainty. Local cultural perspectives gain support from non-equlibrium perspectives in ecological science which now recognize the inherent "patchiness" of dryland systems over space and time, and the sudden and unpredictable ecological transitions which can occur within them. Nevertheless, perspectives emphasizing rangeland degradation and "desertification" have proved useful to governments and donors, for instance, in providing neutral, technical grounds for aid interventions, and in enabling governments to take politically desirable control over the movements of pastoralists on the grounds of their degrading activities.

ANTHROPOLOGICAL PERSPECTIVES ON GLOBAL SCIENCE
AND ENVIRONMENTALISM

Cases such as these suggest that the orthodox views of environmental change which currently dominate international policy debates are, themselves, particular cultural perspectives. Notions such as desertification or deforestation, and the perception that they are occurring in particular places, rest on evidence which fails to describe the whole of a problem, and which may be open to falsification.

The perspectives which inform these dominant positions in international science and policy are just as cultural as the local perspectives which sometimes prove to counter them. Two themes in anthropological research address this: first, a growing engagement by anthropologists in the relationship between scientific knowledge and policy; second, research on environmental movements in popular culture. Both bodies of work necessitate multisited ethnographies, straying from more classic, locale-grounded approaches in anthropology. Equally, they engage with other disciplines (such as the sociology of science and media studies) as earlier anthropological genres shade into a postdisciplinary style. Both bodies of work show how, like the perspectives of land users, science and popular environmental movements are cultural: partly rooted in experience of ecological processes; embodying particular ideas, beliefs, and values concerning the environment and people-environment relations; and employing particular concepts, vocabularies, and theories of causation. That a relatively small number of orthodoxies have come to dominate in international circles—including among scientists, donors, governments, the northern public, and their environmental movements—seems to reflect significant convergences in, for instance, economic and funding interests, and education and training.

The scientific ideas which underlie these perspectives are clearly not universal or neutral. Formal science is itself culturally produced, as shown by anthropological research which takes the approaches once used to study the cultural perspectives of remote rural peoples into the world of laboratory scientists and climate or land use modelers, or into the meetings in which they debate their findings. Indeed, critical studies of science now emphasize that all attempts to understand ecological processes will reflect cultural ideas or social or political agendas. Different, and partial, scientific knowledges not only theorize environmental change in different ways, but also carry very different implications for how human agency in environmental change is understood and hence for resource claims and policy. Particular scientific theories have underpinned dominant positions in international policy debates. For instance, the notion of "carrying capacity" (and thus of overstocking by pastoralists) has been used as a justification for conventional rangeland policy and for controlling the movement of pastoralists. Equally, theories of island biogeography, compounded by use of the precautionary principle, have underpinned orthodox approaches to the protection of biodiverse areas involving the exclusion of local inhabitants. Alternative scientific theories can suggest very different policy approaches and uphold very different claims over resources.

Formal science is not just culturally grounded; it is far from consensual as well. While an empirical contrast between the perspectives of formal science and those of lay publics may be evident, formal science, too, is clearly not consensual. Many global environmental problems, involving long and distant causal chains and complex processes, are the subject of debate within the international scientific community. Major shifts in the theoretical underpinnings of ecological science have also given rise to new debates and opposing positions in understandings of ecological systems. In particular, there is a divergence between conventional, linear perspectives on change and dynamic, non-equilibrial perspectives which emphasize uncertainty, conjuncture, and contingency. Non-equilibrial perspectives—what some have heralded as the "new ecology"—theoretically open the way for a greater pluralism in environmental science—a pluralism in which diverse cultural perspectives and local knowledges may find a voice. In practice, however, the extent to which older ecological theories continue to dominate in administrative and policy circles is striking.

Implicit in culturally specific representations of the environment are particular notions of the environment's "value," as derived from prevailing priorities in natural resource exploitation or from the biases of particular scientific disciplines or popular concerns. A good example concerns the way professional foresters and ecologists in Africa have conventionally valued closed-canopy, or gallery, forest (almost defining "forest" in these terms), so that any conversion of this type of vegetation community is seen to constitute "degradation." Yet the same conversion may be viewed positively by local inhabitants, for whom the resulting fallow vegetation provides a greater range of gathered plant products and more productive agricultural land. A third set of values, upheld by certain Western environmental organizations and the publics who provide their funding, gives priority to the aesthetic and moral connotations of "wilderness" or to large wildlife species. Thus the same landscape changes can be perceived and valued in different ways by different groups; what for some is "degraded and degrading" may for others be merely transformed or even improved.

The cultural perspectives which drive current environment-development agendas are produced through particular political and economic relations. Frequently, these perspectives reflect the institutional histories of colonial and donor regimes, and they clearly have material effects, justifying control over the land and resources of others in the name of national or global patrimony. Such external claims over resource management and control can have deleterious consequences for local livelihoods. They can marginalize or alienate people from natural resources over which they previously enjoyed access and control, perhaps directly undermining their ability to secure food or income. This has sometimes been the case, for instance, with policies to exclude people from externally managed forest or wildlife reserves, or to confine pastoralists to fenced paddocks. Where inhabitants must, out of necessity, continue to use resources claimed by external agencies, they often find themselves subject to taxes or fines which render them more resource-poor. In some cases, the assertion of professionalized claims over land and resources has also had adverse ecological consequences. For example, external prohibitions on the setting of bush fires in Guinea undermined inhabitants' early burning strategies, risking greater fire damage by late, dry-season fires. Cultural perspectives on environment, in this light, are perhaps best understood as shaped by discourses. The notion of discourse draws attention to the ways that particular ideas come to embody relations of power and reproduce them. It emphasizes that power-knowledge has real practical consequences, or "instrument effects"—enabling control over resources or people, for instance.

The growth in global environmentalism as a form of discourse involving large sections of the world's population is significant both as a phenomenon and in its effects. Broadly defined as a concern to protect the environment through human responsibility and effort, environmentalism can itself be seen as a cultural perspective in the sense that it reflects particular ways of understanding the world and one's place within it. Forms of environmentalism participate in a transcultural discourse *par excellence*, emerging through, and in turn playing a role in, globalization by reducing social distance and compressing the world. Yet, in the globalization of environmentalist discourse, through a range of complex processes and forms of alliance-making, whose perspectives are represented and whose are excluded?

The globalization of environmental discourse has, for instance, been strongly assisted by growth in global information flows, including international conferences, information technology, and the mass media. The mass media do not simply transmit messages to their audiences about "the real world." Rather, they participate in constructing environmental issues in particular ways, by embodying culturally specific "messages" which are interpreted by their audiences according to their preexisting cultural frames of reference. These communicative processes appear to have an inbuilt tendency to generate "crisis" narratives with respect to environmental issues. Equally, as the geographer Jacqueline Burgess (1990) argues, the capacity to give meaning to the environment is being contested in novel forms of cultural politics through the mass media. The alliance between actors, musicians, Brazilian Indians, pop music promoters, conservation organizations, the media industry, and the consumers who buy records to support the campaign against the destruction of the Amazonian rain forest provides a case in point.

A dominant strand in global environmental discourse emphasizes more global integration as the best way to protect the environment. It is here that the notion of a global "common future" and the role of international conventions find their place. This discourse has a number of particular effects. It legitimizes the need for international, global mechanisms to address environmental problems; it justifies the assertion of global rights and claims over resources such as biodiversity, rainforests, and so forth on the grounds that they are global patrimony, over and above local claims; and it supports a reliance on development and Western science as solutions to environmental problems. While arguments for public participation and for support of cultural diversity may be made from within this discourse, they are seen as part of—and as means to achieve—agendas already set by global agencies.

Although the inhabitants of local environments may themselves participate in the production of ideas about environmental change, they now do so with even less power to define the terms of debate. As token participants in global and national forums, they may have little chance to express alternatives to the dominant viewpoint. Equally, it is not uncommon for rural inhabitants in their interactions with development fieldworkers to confirm outsiders' preconceived ideas, given the power relations which operate at such "interfaces." Such confirmation may arise out of fear, suspicion, or a desire to remain on good terms by accepting what is being offered. Confirmation can also reflect the relations of authority and the memory of past experience which structure these interactions. More significantly, land users may also selectively adopt outsiders' environmental idioms and turn them to their own advantage in struggles over identity and resource control. For example in Guinea, externally derived images of forest loss are invoked by villagers in discourse about ethnicity to identify themselves respectively as "forest people" or "savanna people" in ways which, in colonial and now modern Guinea, have political significance. Yet in other contexts they invoke very different practical ecological knowledge which contradicts these external stereotypes.

Localized discourses which counter, or resist, these globalized environmental perspectives already exist. Indeed, many of the diverse cultural perspectives found among land users, discussed earlier in this chapter, contain the seeds of such discourses. Some strands of radical environmentalism would seem to support such localized perspectives, generalizing from evidence of local knowledge and organization to create broad arguments that advocate eco-friendly localism. In contrast with the dominant views outlined above, radical environmentalist perspectives hold that development is a Western conspiracy which has damaged the environment. They suggest that the replacement of local cultural perspectives by Western science is ecologically destructive. And they advocate opting out of globally defined agendas for sustainable development in favor of local self-determination and forms of development grounded on communal values, subsistence perspectives, and indigenous knowledge, with women's knowledge and perspectives (ecofeminism) frequently seen as key.

But these broad, antiglobalist positions can in themselves be seen as defined by dominant global discourse, having developed in opposition to it. And many of the positions that they uphold, such as the myth of "primitive ecological wisdom," equally risk imposing globally defined values on local cultural diversity, overriding people's own experiences and realities.

To sum up, anthropological work shows that cultural perspectives on ecological processes and people-environment relations are as diverse as the world's ecologies and the historical experiences of their inhabitants. Cultural perspectives are diverse in the concepts and vocabularies through which ecological processes are understood; in the institutions and forms of sociocultural organization through which environmental goods and services are accessed, controlled, and struggled over; in the ways in which particular aspects of the environment are valued; and in how "nature" and "culture," or people and environment, are categorized and bounded. Cultural perspectives are discourses in the sense that they are produced through and supportive of power relations, and can have material effects, supporting particular positions in struggles for control over environmental goods and services.

But in the context of globalization, and through convergences in information flows, scientific ideas, and economic and political concerns, international debates about environment and development have come to be dominated by a powerful set of global orthodoxies. In keeping with the ideas of Western science and contemporary environmentalism, these orthodoxies frame environmental problems and set agendas for sustainable development in such a way as to admit cultural diversity only on their own terms. In this process (and, paradoxically, sometimes through the very conservation and development programs which claim to build on and encourage local environmental knowledge and organization), localities are reproduced within global discursive images. Land users' own perspectives and creativity are thus silenced or pushed into reformulation as discourses of resistance.

Much current discussion of the cultural dimensions of globalization values the apparent spread of consciousness of a shared earthly ecosystem as an important manifestation of an emerging global culture. Science and the scientific ethos of grounding policies and decisions on empirical evidence and proof are also gaining global ground and are frequently seen to provide a neutral, universal basis on which political decisions can proceed. Yet these trends risk contradicting a third important element of a global ethics—democratic participation and support for a global civic culture—if the supposed "global environmental consciousness" and universal, neutral science are not themselves subjected to cultural critique. For if the arguments and evidence presented in this chapter are valid, then global environmentalism and its supportive science can be seen, at least in part, as the products of particular, Western-dominated cultural traditions and relations of power. The imposition of global orthodoxies and analysis upon different environmental values and notions of sustainability can infringe not only on local livelihoods, but also on cultural freedom, in a deeply decivilizing process.

No single culture or set of cultural perspectives holds the key to understanding and addressing the complex environmental challenges which the world faces now or will face in the future. Achieving environmental sustainability—and certainly, an environmental sustainability which is compatible with livelihoods and citizenship for the world's populations—will require a democratization of expertise in the very definition of environmental issues and problems. It will require the bringing together of diverse knowledges into "hybrid" forms that shed light on problematics from diverse angles. And it will require a science-policy process that, while acknowledging the existence of independent biophysical processes, embraces the plurality of partial, cultural perspectives through which people come to understand these processes and the environmental issues linked to them, with explicit recognition of the political or economic agendas which may inform them. This highlights the challenge to develop greater understanding of the culture and politics of global science and policy institutions, with a view to defining where room for maneuver or space to recast debates might lie. And it recasts citizen participation and the sustenance of cultural diversity in far more political terms, with self-determination in knowledge, ideas, and organization at their core.

ACKNOWLEDGMENT

An earlier version of this chapter appeared as chapter 6, "Culture and Sustainability," in *World Culture Report: Culture, Creativity and Markets* (Paris: UNESCO Publishing, 1998).

REFERENCES AND SUGGESTIONS FOR FURTHER READING

Agrawal, A. 1995. "Dismantling the Divide between Indigenous and Scientific Knowledge." *Development and Change* 26: 413–39. [Incorporates some of the critical perspectives taken in this paper.]

Bird-David, N. 1990. "The Giving Environment: Another Perspective on the Economic System of Hunter-Gatherers." *Current Anthropology* 31, no. 2: 189–96.

Brosius, J. P. 1997. "Endangered Forest, Endangered People: Environmentalist Representations of Indigenous Knowledge." *Human Ecology* 25, no. 1: 47–69.

Burgess, J. 1990. "The Production and Consumption of Environmental Meanings in the Mass Media: A Research Agenda for the 1990s." *Transactions of the Institute of British Geographers* n.s. 15: 139–61

Croll, E., and D. Parkin, eds. 1992. *Bush, Base, Forest, Farm: Culture, Environment and Development.* London: Routledge. [Reviews the breadth of anthropological perspectives on environmental issues.]

Descola, P., and G. Palsson, eds. 1996. *Nature and Society: Anthropological Perspectives.* London: Routledge. [Reviews the breadth of anthropological perspectives on environmental issues.]

Fairhead, J., and M. Leach. 1996. *Misreading the African Landscape: Society and Ecology in a Forest-Savanna Mosaic.* Cambridge: Cambridge University Press. [Incorporates some of the critical perspectives taken in this paper.]

———. 1998. *Reframing Deforestation: Global Analyses and Local Realities: Studies in West Africa.* London: Routledge. [Incorporates some of the critical perspectives taken in this paper.]

Foucault, M. 1971. "The Order of Discourse." In *Untying the Text: A Poststructuralist Reader,* ed. R. Young. London: Routledge and Kegan Paul.

Haraway, D. 1988. "Situated Knowledge: The Science Question in Feminism and the Privilege of Partial Perspective." *Feminist Studies* 14, no. 3: 575–99.

Ives, J., and B. Messerli. 1989. *Himalayan Dilemmas: Reconciling Conservation and Development.* London: Routledge and New York: United Nations University.

Latour, B., and S. Woolgar, with J. Salk. 1986. *Laboratory Life: The Construction of Scientific Facts.* Princeton, NJ: Princeton University Press.

Leach, M. 1994. *Rainforest Relations: Gender and Resource Use among the Mende of Gola, Sierra Leone.* Edinburgh: Edinburgh University Press; Washington, DC: Smithsonian Institution.

Milton, K. S. 1996. *Environmentalism: The View from Anthropology.* London: Routledge. [Reviews the breadth of anthropological perspectives on environmental issues.]

Nyerges, A. E. 1997. *The Ecology of Practice.* Amsterdam, the Netherlands: Gordon and Breach (especially the overview in chapter 1). [Reviews the breadth of anthropological perspectives on environmental issues.]

Peet, R., and M. Watts, eds. 1996. *Liberation Ecologies: Environment, Development, Social Movements.* London and New York: Routledge. [Incorporates some of the critical perspectives taken in this paper.]

Scoones, I., ed. 1995. *Living with Uncertainty: New Directions in Pastoral Development in Africa.* London: Intermediate Technology Publications.

Swift, J. 1996. "Desertification: Narratives, Winners and Losers." In *The Lie of the Land: Challenging Received Wisdom on the African Environment,* ed. M. Leach and R. Mearns. Oxford: James Currey; New York: Heinemann.

Thomas, D., and N. Middleton. 1994. *Desertification: Exploding the Myth.* Chichester, U.K.: John Wiley.

Thompson, M.; M. Warburton; and T. Hatley. 1986. *Uncertainty on a Himalayan Scale.* London: Ethnographica, Milton Ash Publications.

WCED (World Commission on Environment and Development). 1987. *Our Common Future.* Oxford and New York: Oxford University Press.

12

Hunger in Africa: Untangling Its Human Roots

ELLEN MESSER AND PARKER SHIPTON

Since early recorded history, both environmental and human causes have been implicated in the etiology of hunger. The Old Testament cites drought but also siege warfare and lack of administrative foresight to store food for bad years as sources of starvation, while ancient Chinese texts blame famines not only on bad weather but also on bad emperors. In spite of the vagaries of the weather, European peoples since about 1800, and others elsewhere in this century, have managed to remain mostly free of widespread starvation. Yet we continue to witness dramatic mortality from hunger and malnutrition-related illness at the turn of the millennium, most visibly in Africa, and less visibly but still to a significant extent in Asia.

The droughts and famines that culminated in 1972–73 and 1984–85 in the Sahel and in the Horn of Africa were some of the worst of the past century. Parts of Angola, Burundi, the Congo Democratic Republic (formerly Zaire), Liberia, Mozambique, Rwanda, Sierra Leone, Somalia, and Sudan, lately mired in civil war, have been experiencing severe food shortfalls, and chronic hunger and malnutrition persist in many other parts of the continent, where postconflict countries suffer the legacy of destruction. Hunger persists despite, and sometimes partly because of, the efforts of hundreds of specialists and often well-intentioned workers of aid agencies to illuminate the causes of African hunger and help bring about its end.

It has become conventional wisdom that the causes of hunger and malnutrition in Africa are complex, variable, and dependent. In a continent so vast (more than thirty million square kilometers, just over three times the land mass of the United States), so diverse in ecosystems and livelihoods (foraging, farming, fishing, herding, mining, wage working, and trading—in countless combinations), so rich in cultures (three hundred to a thousand or more languages, depending on how you count them), and so varied in political regimes (from Marxist Guinea Bissau to staunchly capitalist Côte d'Ivoire), hunger clearly can have no single root.

Moreover, as anyone who has looked into the topic knows, the causes reinforce each other in vicious circles. Drought, flooding, and civil war disrupt transport and communication; transport blockages give rise to hoarding; hoarding raises food prices; rising food prices encourage speculation and more hoarding; hoarding and deprivation encourage sudden, unplanned migration and family division; sudden migration contributes to grazing shortage, water source overuse, disease, and ethnic and religious tensions and political instabilities, leading to more civil war, and so on. Poverty, malnutrition, and illness can all worsen each other in loops. High human fertility contributes to crowding and land shortages, which may in turn give rise to competition and conflict. Such gloomy observations as these are familiar enough.

Complexity, variability, and the entanglement of things are always safe conclusions. They make the writer or speaker look smart enough to discern the differences and trace the interconnections; and any adversary in a debate risks looking like a simpleton. Recent journal issues suggest that "it's complex," "it varies," and "it depends" have indeed been the orthodox conclusions about all subjects in social science and humanities in the past decade or two (perhaps a function of tight academic job markets and risk averseness). Many articles in the journals conclude little more. This tendency to gravitate to these conclusions and not move beyond them—one might label it "complicationism"—has reinforced itself in a way inimical to practical action. Just as serious, from an intellectual point of view, is that it seems to stifle bold questions about causes and effects. We do *not* wish to argue that the world isn't complex, variable, messy, or tangled (decidedly, it is), but only that to repeat these mantras to each other as if every thinking person didn't know them already (and as though it weren't possible to complicate or simplify any problem) does little good. Every African who has suffered hunger or malnutrition knows that some causes and effects matter more than others.

Ironically, the complexity and interdependence of the causes of hunger and famine—the very things that seem to make it so intractable—are the very features that may bring hope for a broader improvement of nutrition in what has come to be known as the "troubled continent." For just as the causes can contribute to each other in tangled, subtle ways, so might the solutions. Moreover, some of the very processes that seem so often to be part of the problem—exogenous crops, ethnic (or "tribal") loyalties, and migration, for instance—are just as often part of shorter-term remedies or longer-term adaptations that alleviate the problems they may have helped cause.

RESOURCE POOR OR DISENTITLED:

TWO COMPLEMENTARY APPROACHES

Two schools of thought influential in the analysis of poverty and famines over the past several decades have been the "shortage" school and the "entitlement" school. The first school, exemplified by geographer Michael Mortimore and his collaborators, places the main blame on environmental factors: poor soils, drought, flood, bugs, and so on. This line of explanation is congenial to Malthusian demographers and economists, who argue that human population in Africa threatens to grow beyond the limits of the environment to sustain it, and that famines and food shortages are evidence that these limits are already being reached.

The second points the finger more at human agents and their individual or aggregate thought and action: at the cultural, economic, and political processes that lead to what economist and philosopher Amartya Sen (1981) has called "entitlement failure," or inability of some persons to gain access to what food (or water) there is. Poor or otherwise disadvantaged persons or groups find themselves unable to command adequate intake of food, whether or not food might be available in the region, because they lack good land, labor power, or health, or because they suffer from unfavorable conditions of exchange, basically low income or inadequate savings relative to the costs of food. Poor nations, like poor households or homesteads, may find that they lack the power and wealth to achieve sufficient nutrition as their own resource endowments, as allocated, do not produce sufficient food, and as the relative value of their export commodities and command over additional food security aid declines.

The very debate is political, since it can seem to lead to big conclusions about whether there's anything that leaders, policymakers, or revolutionaries can do at all about hunger and famine. It is also academically political, because it leads to important implications about (say) whether those concerned should bother learning, or awarding grants for, material science or instead devote their attention to the social studies, including the close linguistic study of economic and political rhetoric. Such debates have been instructive in the past several decades. They have shaken some out of fatalistic complacency and attuned others to enduring regional differences in resource endowments.

But recent studies have shown that areas judged by development economists to be high in population, "resource poor," and ripe for conflict and hunger are capable of improving their lots—especially when political-economic policies don't unduly interfere. Ukerewe Island in Lake Victoria, now in Tanzania, is a classic historical case of indigenous agricultural intensification (with terracing, irrigation, etc.) despite, or because of, crowding in a confined space. Mary Tiffen and colleagues (1994) show how, in Kenya, farmers in the densely settled central high-lands and comparably crowded parts of the western provinces kept their lands highly productive by symbiotic intercropping, and by careful crop rotation and other means of conservation. Farther west, Jane Guyer has documented how peri-urban Nigerian women, acquiring customary land-use rights, have elevated garden crop production for market, simultaneously improving income for producers and diets for urban consumers. Other African peoples, from the Swahili-speaking people of the Kenyan and Tanzanian coast to the Moorish Mauritanians and im-migrant Lebanese, having little or dwindling agricultural resources, have pros-pered over the past two centuries by long-distance travel and trade. Crowding does not necessarily mean resource exhaustion, nor does local scarcity of material resources necessarily lead to enduring economic poverty.

Both sides of the shortage/entitlement debate are right in their own ways. Moral, economic, and political causes of hunger and malnutrition exacerbate ma-terial ones and are aggravated by them in turn as regimes and companies in charge of "resource-poor" polities see little hope in developing taxable, long-term pro-duction and enterprise, and instead opt to extract what material and human re-sources they control while they are still in power. Scientific explanations of the problem, whether based in material or social realities, have tended to ignore or discount the kinds of questions about divine or other ultimate causes that many people inside Africa have posed to explain progressive land degradation, low yields, or other disappointments—and if not to solve the problems, then to try to transcend them.

Among the questions that anthropologists, as insider-outsiders, have asked are, What sources of self-perpetuating misery link resource poverty to hunger and conflict, and how can these vicious circles be reversed? How do indigenous people understand the problem, and do their views on it differ from those of various out-siders? Given communication gaps and often competing interests, what are the appropriate roles of "developers" (people with ideologies of modernity to com-municate or impose), "policymakers" (people in power), and "local people" (some of whom turn out not to be so local)?

DISPELLING A FEW MYTHS

First we attempt to correct a few misconceptions about Africa and the nature of hunger, famine, and chronic malnutrition.

Africa is not a starving continent. Its appearance in newspapers, on television, and on the electronic web mainly at times of food emergencies belies the ingenu-ity of rationing and resilience, and the ironic combinations of feasting and fasting that are almost everywhere evident to one who lives there. It also belies cruel inequalities. In many African contexts people who have excess food rotting in their granaries may live close by others who are hungry and malnourished. Moreover, there is no reason to suppose that Africa will inevitably be a continent with famines. In the twentieth century, the former Soviet Union, colonial India, and pre-reform China all took their turns as world regions of dire famine.

Hunger does not necessarily mean general food shortage, but often maldistribution of what food there is at all levels: global, regional, national, local, or even familial. As Jean Drèze, Amartya Sen, and collaborators have shown, hunger can hit not just in economic slumps but also in boom times. What matters is both how much food there is to go around and who has what powers to get it.

Famines are not just about food, and hunger is not what kills. Rather, in famines, it is violence and disease that kill. Disease follows as a consequence not only of malnutrition, but also of the migration of desperate victims of drought and warfare to crowded, unsanitary feeding stations and water points.

Here it may help to distinguish between hunger, malnutrition, and famine. Hunger, strictly speaking, is a subjective sensation, not a biological condition, but the term is sometimes used synecdochically (as we use it in this essay) to stand for broader complexes of problems that include biological ones. Hunger is not necessarily a problem, though. It can be voluntarily entered into or embraced, as in the month-long daytime fast of Ramadan in which the Muslim population of the northern half of Africa (and bits of the southern) engages every year as one of the five "pillars" of Islam—an institution many Muslims deem healthy for body, mind, and spirit. In some non-Muslim parts of Africa, too, the familial self-rationing of diets and some resulting hunger and thinning seem to be voluntarily accepted as part of a strategy of conserving resources through lean seasons—a process that can merge into, and easily be confused with, true destitution.

Malnutrition is a biological condition with many forms. It can refer to shortages of calories, protein, enzymes, vitamins, or minerals, or to malfunctions of complex, interactive processes involving bodily capacities to process these. Malnutrition is not always accompanied by hunger as a sensation, since many bulky foods—like cassava, one of Africa's most important emergency crops as well as a staple (in some areas) and snack food (in others)—can fill the stomach and sustain life without well nourishing the body.

Famine too is given many definitions, but the best of these convey the possibility that vital solid *and/or* liquid ingestibles are lacking *or* inaccessible in some relatively severe and widespread way, *without* necessarily implying that everyone in a population starves to death. For that is not usually what happens.

Famine does not affect all people in a famine zone equally. Ironically, famine in Africa has been predominantly rural and often affects food producers themselves, who in most of the continent are also predominantly female. Within affected populations, those who are most likely to suffer are the young children and the elderly, who are least likely to be able to move to where there is food or paid work, or to command food on the basis of their work. Outside of famine areas, difficult access to land, to multiple sources of income, and to education (affecting child care) also determine who will suffer hunger, even when food is not short.

Someone usually profits by famine. It is done by buying land, animals, or jewelry from the destitute, by speculating in grain, by lending at high interest, by hiring cheap labor, or by other means. Wealthy men with urban connections, traders with liquid capital, and large landholders with police or government protection are most likely to prosper. So are local powerbrokers who can insert themselves as intermediaries for relief supplies, selling (or smuggling and selling) what donors expected them to distribute for free. Famine drives social classes farther apart, and such effects can outlast a famine itself.

People who suffer hunger or malnutrition do not just do so as passive victims. Active strategies that rural African people use to prevent and minimize food problems are too numerous to attempt to list. They variously include subtle social measures like age-mate co-initiation where there are age sets; incest taboo and exogamy (out-marriage); redistributive feasting and gift-giving; and animal loan partnerships—all of which create wide-ranging networks of contacts that can be activated in times of need and serve other functions too. They include crop diversification among farmers and, among herders, "overstocking" to leave a self-reproducing herd after periodic catastrophic loss that experience has taught them to expect, or keeping jewelry to trade. They include intensifying productive efforts early in a crisis, finding ways to conserve energy later when the body has weakened, substituting foods, pledging property, and migrating to the homes of kin or to towns and cities where food supplies may be more diverse and regular. They include passing on oral history and legend with advice on how their forebears coped, and how it might be done again.

Hunger and malnutrition don't go away when they disappear from our newspapers and television screens. In a continent heavily dependent on rainfed farming—and large parts of Africa have only one growing season per year—seasonal hunger for whole populations, and chronic malnutrition for parts of them, continue year in and year out. A process of enfamishment in a population can take decades or much longer to aggravate to the point of attracting journalistic notice, and its effects on health and economic well-being can linger long after the more dramatic images of bloated bellies and vacant eyes have vanished from the printed page or the screen. Hunger is more pervasive and complicated than the famines that take over the headlines. Although we tend to think about African famine as linked to conditions of drought or warfare that absolutely prevent food from reaching the hungry, poor people—and by extension, poor peoples—go hungry because they lack the wealth and power to acquire food even when national and global food supply appears sufficient. Many lack the political voice to declare themselves needy and to demand other humanitarian aid, especially in nations with no free press. Political leaders on government and antigovernment sides of civil conflicts not only may have no political interests in ending their suffering, but may even find it to their own advantage, as some did, for instance, in eastern Nigeria (Biafra) in 1967–70 and others have done recently in southern Sudan, to use hunger as a weapon of war.

Individuals may also go hungry where distribution rules militate against their getting an adequate share, where maladapted habits of consumption do not provide an adequate mix of nutrients, or where individuals are health-deprived and unable to ingest, metabolize, and benefit from the nutrients potentially available. Hunger, then, is a problem of food poverty and deprivation that can persist even in the presence of adequate food in a region. Efforts to bolster food production are therefore in themselves insufficient actions against hunger.

QUESTIONS OF QUANTIFICATION

African food problems are hard to quantify, and most numbers about African hunger and malnutrition are unreliable. Hunger numbers roughly estimate food problems in three ways: food shortage (food production plus imports, minus exports), food poverty (the balance of income and expenditure relative to the costs of adequate food), and malnutrition (human incapacitation related to inadequate nutrient intake, malabsorption, and nutrition-related disease). While all figures confirm that the magnitude is great—approximately three-quarters of a billion people around the world, according to the Food and Agriculture Organization of the U.N., lack access to adequate food—these and less global numbers vary, and all are suspect. It is even hard to know whether local, national, or regional statistics are more reliable, because numerical aggregations that may dilute local enumeration errors remain subject to manipulation by small numbers of individuals in power in national regimes.

The reasons why reliable statistics on African food and hunger are so hard to produce and so likely to mislead are technical, cultural, and political. Discouraging figures for a normal year on aggregate or *per capita* food production and on income or consumption expenditures conceal much guesswork about both the production and population figures, and they also miss regional and local differences in terminology and translation significant for counting the numbers of hungry or malnourished. Production figures are suspect because reporting relies on surveyors' being able to reach representative samples of people, which is problematic in parts of the continent where fuel is short and roads wash away in rainy seasons. Government officials rightly perceive that control of the food supply is critical to their staying in power and so skew numbers for their own purposes. Regimes interested in acquiring food aid, which their members can siphon and sell privately or dispense where they need voters or supporters, tend to underestimate food production. So do farmers who wish to pay lower taxes, to give up less to government agencies and so have more to distribute elsewhere at higher prices, or to qualify for special assistance targeted at underproducers. But experts also find it hard to count and measure the food value of all the different plants growing on intercropped fields.

Diversified occupational practices and household or homestead membership, which give African people flexibility in pursuing livelihood, also make enumeration difficult. Surveyors counting heads and income ask about "families" or "households," but where people live in multihouse compounds, such words may translate into terms meaning people sleeping under the same roof, working in the same field, or eating from the same storage unit or pot—and none of these groups need be the same. Moreover, foreign-derived economic concepts like "income," "investment," and "employment" don't translate easily into many African languages. Local etiquette in much of the continent forbids counting people or animals and may discourage prying into another's granary. African rules of conversation often favor yes as an answer for agreeability's sake, particularly where the questioner is perceived as senior. Marketed produce may not be "surplus" as foreign researchers have often assumed; those who sell it after harvest may well need to repurchase it, or its equivalent, more expensively before the next harvest. Finally, malnutrition numbers that compare individual food intake or growth (in children under five years of age) to some universal or national standards not only present on-the-ground problems of measurement but also suffer from the experts' disagreements on what constitutes adequate nutrition for health. Such difficulties notwithstanding, international nutrition experts, producing background numbers for the International Conference on Nutrition in 1992 and the World Food Summit in 1996, seem to have agreed that neither economic production, including food production, nor food availability per capita was keeping up with population growth in Africa; that in Asia hunger numbers were still large, but politically stable countries showed impressive improvements; and that in Latin America nutrition and economies were stagnating.

POLITICAL-ECONOMIC CAUSES OF FAMINE

Wars have lately been the main human cause of African famine, and they contribute to other forms of hunger here and in other parts of the globe. Armed conflict almost anywhere in Africa disrupts food production and distorts food distribution. National governments that divert resources to armaments and military activities have less to spend on peaceful development of economic and environmental resources and on public health. In the narrower sense, hunger continues to be used as a weapon, particularly in ethnically pitched conflicts where one side purposely destroys the food supplies and future food capacity of the opposition—as British forces did in the Nandi campaign in Kenya in 1905–1906, or as government forces from Rhodesia (now Zimbabwe) did in that country, Mozambique, and Zambia during the guerrilla war in the late 1970s—and sometimes may actually attack humanitarian assistance that appears channeled in its direction. Alex de Waal (1997), Ellen Messer and colleagues (1998), and others have analyzed these disturbing processes.

Ethnicity, or "tribalism," is indeed a key to understanding African hunger, but *not* in the sense of inbred proclivities or mental disabilities of races or cultures. Rather, ethnicity, along with religious, occupational, or class divisions, has been *used* by some actors to purposefully design and justify civil wars in many African states, which are themselves a legacy of, among other things, violently contested colonial boundaries. Political tensions arising from the exaggeration and manipulation of ethnic regional differences are compounded by religious ones as partisans of Islam, Christianity, and indigenous African faiths compete for control of national law and resources.

Sometimes genealogical, ethnic, racial, and religious schisms align coterminously as regional interests compete for control over key strategic resources such as water and petroleum. The compounded acrimonies have been most intense in the zone south of the Sahel, where Islamic northern Africa shades patchily into a more heavily Christianized southern half of the continent. To return to Nigeria and Sudan, both their civil wars have pitted national governments against ethnic groups or internal alliances of them. In the Nigerian case, since the country's independence in 1960, an unstable mix of a Muslim-dominated, northern, Hausa-speaking population and a religiously more mixed Yoruba and Igbo population (to name only the largest three groups) has produced over a dozen coups-d'état and, in oil-rich Igboland, a failed (Biafran) war of secession characterized by the use of food blockades. In the Sudanese case, the struggle for hegemony by a northern, Arabic-speaking, Islamic people and their government over southerners who speak indigenous tongues and practice Christian and indigenous African religions (including Dinka, Nuer [or Nath], and other Nilotic groups, among others) combine racial, ethnolinguistic, religious, and economic animosities in the same civil war. Across the border, in Ethiopia, the politically motivated, forced resettlement from rebel-held northeastern to government-controlled southwestern parts of the country in the early and mid-1980s was a major contributor to continuing famine.

The flows of refugees back and forth between Ethiopia, Eritrea, and Sudan have been both a cause and an intermittent solution to the hunger and other hardships on both sides.

Civil strife is also a response to misplaced development policies that make African hunger not just a local or national phenomenon but an international one. Contributing to hunger and malnutrition are African nations' international debt and unfavorable terms of trade for cash crops. Ironically, these together often motivate leaders to take even more of the best land out of food crops to produce more export crops for foreign exchange. Other international development choices like removing subsidies and raising food prices—favorite strategies of the World Bank and International Monetary Fund in the 1980s and 1990s—have also proved politically destabilizing, particularly in cities, even though they are meant to improve production and income in the countryside.

Misguided development aid contributes to hunger. Donor and lender agencies seeking to intensify production often make disruptive choices. The "white elephants" of large grain-storage structures and large machinery that no longer function lie strewn over the landscape of African nations. Water rights are central to irrigated farming and the functioning of agricultural communities, but even where technical structure is appropriate, social and political structure rarely allows for the water's smooth distribution in newly irrigated or resettled zones. Ethnic conflict, as on the Senegalese-Mauritanian border, sometimes erupts as different peoples compete for land, as well as water, that becomes more valuable with such technical interventions. Large-scale, mechanized farming schemes may choke on the costs of expensive fuels and the scarcity of spare parts; or, as in parts of Sudan, they may "mine" the soils of nutrients as owners enjoy short-term gains at the expense of long-term, sustainable yields.

Green revolution schemes that promote agricultural packages of improved seeds, fertilizers, and pesticides have achieved only spotty success in boosting African food production. They may not fit microclimate and soil conditions. Farmers may not be able to afford unsubsidized inputs, such as fertilizer—that are necessary for optimum yields. And even a potentially appropriate package may not reach many of the farmers because agricultural extension does not, particularly where extension agents are male and farmers are female. Even favorably disposed farmers know seeds and chemicals may not reach them on time: a frequent shortcoming where interagency or interministerial committees are in charge, where irregular cash flows and fuel supplies disrupt transport, and where chain lenders sometimes divert funds they are expected to convey to farming people. For all these reasons, the more risk-averse farmers often choose to use potentially "high-yielding" inputs incompletely or not at all.

Additional issues are the food producers' motivations. As Audrey Richards (1939) documented for the British colonial office in Northern Rhodesia in the 1930s, African rural producers often appear to be underproductive not because they are "slothful" but because they are undernourished and embedded in continuing seasonal cycles of undernutrition. In addition African farmers may have their own sense of dignified labor and reject intensive farming plans that demand unaccustomed strenuous exertion and regimentation. Project assumptions often fail to take into account gender-based division of labor and household economy. As Jennie Dey (1981), Judith Carney (1992), and others have documented in the Jahally-Pachar Irrigated Rice Scheme and other projects in the Gambia, female farmers limit their work on men's fields where they do not control the product and the income from their labor.

Most such failures are associated with foreign aid. But this is not to say that national efforts—for example, compulsory resettlement schemes in Mengistu's Ethiopia or tea cooperatives in pre-1994 Rwanda—have led to happier or more humane outcomes. Among the most harmful have been attempts to move scattered populations into villages for convenient government control (sometimes glossed as "rationalization") or for access to public services. Unhappy outcomes have attended both brutalizing and benign policies, as witnessed in the punishing initiatives of Ethiopia's Mengistu government and the benevolent but still impoverishing *ujamaa* cooperative efforts of Tanzania's President Julius Nyerere. However they may have differed in the motives behind their plans, both these programs dramatically disrupted rural production, income streams, and food security.

Programs that are big successes in one way are often big failures in another. In western Kenya, tobacco-growing programs that have proved highly lucrative to small farmers growing the crop on contract have also contributed to deforestation through cutting of trees to fuel the drying barns—thus quickening dangerous soil erosion over the longer term. There too, irrigation that has boosted agricultural productivity on flatlands has also created new habitats for mosquitoes (vectors of malaria) and snails (vectors of schistosomiasis). Programs to remove weeds from maize fields may eliminate essential seasonal nutrients that the poorer populations glean from "wild" greens that grow there. All point to the general conclusion that developmental planning is rarely ecologically holistic or farsighted.

Agricultural and food-related interventions from Europe and North America have tended to focus on crops and animals of interest to people in those parts of the world. Maize (corn), wheat, and rice have received far more attention until recently than indigenous African staples like sorghum and millet, let alone cowpeas or cocoyams. Research on potatoes is still far ahead of research on cassava, a bulky source of calories (but not of other major nutrients) on which many of Africa's poor, and others in times of hunger, depend. Similarly, livestock "upgrading" programs have concentrated on cattle, sheep, and goats, but not on camels and donkeys used over large parts of northern Africa for transporting food. European and American-interbred varieties have lacked the resistance to local diseases that naturally selected, indigenous breeds often have. African herders have also been shown, as in Chad in the 1980s, to resist dairying and meat-increasing schemes that channel milk into calves and away from humans. New agricultural biotechnologies that promise crop and livestock varieties genetically engineered against local diseases might help stem some crop and livestock losses. But to achieve such improvements, there must first be investment in agricultural infrastructure in order to put the appropriate genes into the appropriate local plant and animal varieties, to get them to farmers or see that they can procure them themselves, to monitor coevolution of pests and breakdown in resistance, and to be ready with resistant replacement varieties.

Most, but not all, of the successes have been small in scale. They have usually drawn on local initiatives, often involved private or nongovernmental organization (NGO) activity, and taken unglamorous forms. Small-scale well-digging and irrigation, dry-season market gardening, appropriate crop storage, and development of markets for particular crafts and crops have all contributed to livelihood in many varied settings across Africa. Grassroots saving and credit associations have improved local capital mobilization in many places with no international help, although there is a current boom in NGO "poverty-lending" or "microcredit" program schemes, especially aimed toward increasing the resources and entitlements of women. Programs for rural access roads (capillary or feeder roads) and flood-control dikes using local labor for maintenance have met with some success.

"Participation" is sometimes honored more in lip-service than in practice, for it always sounds nice—and at worst it can be just an empty development buzzword or a smokescreen for authoritarian planning. Nor is it so easy to achieve: rare is the case where all people whose lives are to be affected by a program or policy can realistically be actively involved in its planning, even if they wish to be (something not to be assumed).

Yet participatory projects and programs, when they integrally involve intended beneficiaries in background assessment, priority-setting, program design, implementation, monitoring, and correction, do seem to produce more successful and enduring outcomes. Using "participatory rural appraisal"—which need not and ought not be as rapid as sometimes attempted—researchers involved in program design assemble focus groups of community members who represent the different factions, occupational interests, religions, ethnicities, and gender categories salient

FIGURE I A young Somali fills a water container from a pump
installed by Oxfam, Wajir, Kenya. (© Adrian Arbib/Survival)

within a community. With them, they discuss and determine community-based
perceptions of natural resources, social units, and priority problems—such as access to clean, potable water. With the community, they then set priority projects,
help organize the activities, acquire outside materials, information, and resources
where necessary, so that the community can proceed. Such focus groups often
identify seasonal sources of hunger problems or constraints on the successful
implementation of health programs—as where they conflict with peak seasonal
loads—and lead to corrective actions.

Participatory modes of doing research have also contributed to successful
plant-breeding efforts, as where an innovative, USAID-sponsored Collaborative
Research Studies Bean-Cowpea Program in Malawi, including anthropologist
Anne Ferguson (1994), had local female farmers, not only "experts," identify the
salient characteristics of crop varieties and help select improved cultivars. Before

and during the fighting in Sierra Leone, anthropologist Paul Richards (1986) continued to work with rice farmers to select varieties appropriate for both their ecological and social—especially labor—constraints. Such programs build on local or "indigenous" knowledge. Usually they involve not only the local people, but also an interdisciplinary team of social and life scientists.

Successful programs also tend to begin with community demand. An important feature of African social life is that institutions introduced from overseas have often evolved to serve purposes quite different from their ostensible ones, in addition or instead. Churches serve as farmwork groups, soccer matches and funerals serve as political rallying points, and women's groups double as savings associations, while government offices often serve as places of private enterprise. Private aid agencies, among others, have discovered that channels for influencing hunger will be found through schools, religious centers, sporting clubs, and other community or intercommunity organizations. Seldom can one tell from the label whether an organization will be useful for development or food relief or is active in them already. Local people's roles in demanding, planning, and implementing development and relief programs—and their feeling they have a stake in them—are likely to be critical to their success.

History mocks the claims of some that Africa is a region of endemic cultural backwardness or ecological ignorance needing to be remedied by outsiders. Most rural Africans have a detailed knowledge of their environment in some way and have developed a variety of risk-averse production and consumption strategies. Unfortunately, outside agricultural development aid usually fails to build on local expertise, and interventions meant to be helpful may actually interfere with traditional modes of coping with stress. Foreign development aid may also play into the hands of leaders who, knowing that their time in power may be short, seek to advantage their own kin, cronies, and ethnic groupmates while they can—or are pressed by these into doing so. Unbalanced and selective development assistance appears to have been a factor in Rwanda's civil war between Hutu and Tutsi, as a president and his inner circle diverted land and funds to their friends, ignoring growing inequality and, in one instance, regional famine, thus fanning ethnic competition for resources and potential for violence. Even successful and praiseworthy efforts, such as the Botswanan government's decentralized early warning and response program for famine, have sometimes been criticized by anthropologists, such as Jacqueline Solway (1994), for strengthening the government at the expense of local communities and undercutting, rather than building on, local coping capacities and their moral economy.

The question throughout Africa is not just how to ensure that Africans produce more food (far less, how to get more food to Africa), but how to help ensure that people in Africa have the means to acquire food and other necessities by their own chosen means.

Hunger is a symptom of more general poverty, and food crises are not just failures of crops or animals, but failures of livelihoods. In almost any African setting, individuals and domestic groups patch together multiple ways of producing food and earning additional income. African hunger is not just a matter of failing rains and leaching soils, but of people lacking the means to acquire food even where it exists.

Isolation is a problem, but market involvement has proved a double-edged blade. Ironically, local as well as national responses to hunger sometimes carry the seeds of new hunger. Changes in land use patterns that reduce areas where wild foods can be gathered during a hungry season or year, and famine-relief policies that keep people in a fixed location where they cannot support themselves in a bad year or season, may eventually become stressors themselves.

Men's migrations to cities, plantations, and mines are common responses to hunger and poverty. These movements can provide much-needed cash remittances—useful not least for buying food—for women, elders, and children left behind. But they can sometimes have negative consequences on local production at the same time, as they may leave women overburdened with farm and household duties. They can leave women temporarily lacking technical knowledge or contacts for bulk marketing that have been traditionally male prerogatives.

Exchanging labor, crops, or animal products in the market so one can then purchase food may relieve the stress of seasonal hunger, but sometimes at the risk of replacing it with chronic undernutrition later. Whether it does so depends not just on the amounts of food those who remain at home are able to produce for their own subsistence. It also depends on conditions of exchange, including wages and other income that poor workers are able to demand, the ease of remittance and absence of competing temptations for individual spending (and expensive borrowing), and the relative prices of market food and nonfood crops—prices over which rural people usually have little control.

Although integration into a wider market increases risk for rural Africans by making them dependent on expensive fertilizers, fuels, and spare parts, it is also the market, particularly for labor, livestock, or durables, to which these people may have to turn in a crisis. While cash crops such as sugarcane and coffee render farmers vulnerable to blights and to price slumps over which they have little control, these same crops can also provide income for people who can choose to spend it on nutrition. None of these changing forms of economic integration is good or bad in itself. What counts is how each plays out in particular climates and ecosystems, under particular regimes of access to land, water, and other resources, and under particular conditions of market, labor, and currency.

Emergency relief must be combined with longer-term planning to be effective. Un-questionably, food aid and other relief from abroad have saved many thousands of rural Africans' lives. But as de Waal (chapter 13 in this volume) indicates, emer-gency aid can also be misdirected and harmful. Relief tends to come too late and too slowly, and it may not arrive where it is needed or be provided on the same free or easy terms of exchange its senders intended. Even if it arrives, food aid may not suit local tastes or even be edible according to local standards.

Where relief is supplied year after year, it can also become part of the continu-ing food problem. Dependency on relief aid is demoralizing and may sap local incentive and initiative to produce. Moreover, as "entitlement" scholarship has shown, money hastily dumped on one community can sometimes end up inflating food prices for others around and worsen their hunger. Demands for relief crisis after crisis can also demoralize donors, who experience "compassion fatigue" after seemingly never-ending bursts of giving.

Nor is it always clear where to send aid. Large and thinly spaced relief camps have commonly become sinkholes of perpetual dependency, despondency, crowd-related illness, and death for those strong enough to travel to them in the first place. Where prolonged, they also may become the hatching ground for new rounds of violence, as in the Hutu-Tutsi conflict that spread in the 1990s from Rwanda and Burundi into eastern Zaire. Relief agencies accept in principle that aid should be distributed as closely as possible to recipients' homes. But this too presents a contradiction, as continued relief without additional economic devel-opment may keep people trapped in environments unsuited for their long-term sustenance.

"Food-for-work" programs, requiring unskilled labor (in road or canal main-tenance, for example) in return for food and supply handouts, can help needy rural African people maintain minimal nutritional status while contributing also to in-frastructure. But time allocated to work for food, and for travel to where it can be performed, competes with alternate responsibilities in family and farm care.

Other relief with development programs, including efforts to improve garden-ing, food processing, water management, and health conditions, are managed by private aid agencies with mixed success. Funding for such community develop-ment initiatives often comes from agencies that support mainly sponsorship pro-grams for individual children. Individual child sponsorship does not hurt, but neither is it a main answer for African rural poverty, and the organizations know it. Hungry little doe-eyed Tina is usually not as isolated as she looks in the magazine ad, nor is it sure that a windfall from overseas would help her get along with her neighbors. But these programs do appeal to a public that seems to yearn for person-to-person contact over long distances, and agencies use donations for many other community microcredit, production, and health initiatives.

All this points toward the big question: What ought to be done, or how might it be done differently, to alleviate or, better, to prevent the problems of hunger and malnutrition that have beset so many African people? No single answer can suffice, but we propose three pieces of a solution, concentrating on ways in which outsiders to the continent might recognize and join together with the already considerable efforts of insiders.

WHAT NEEDS TO BE TURNED AROUND

First, aid agencies and governments can stop trying to "reform" landholding and other basic property rights to fit their own ideologies. Neither capitalism nor socialism has proved to be the answer to Africa's food problems. Africans have starved and suffered from chronic malnutrition in "free-market" economies like Babangida's or Abacha's Nigeria and Mobutu's or Kabila's Congo Democratic Republic, just as they have under socialist regimes like Mengistu's 1980s Ethiopia and Nyerere's late 1970s and early 1980s Tanzania. Some of the most spectacular failures to address Africa's rural poverty and food problems have been attempts to collectivize or individualize land ownership, and to replace rural people's complex systems of interlocking group and individual rights (and claims to access) into publicly or privately owned lands on European-American models. Socialist "villagization" like Tanzania's of the 1970s produced settlements that quickly exhausted the soils around them. Privatization schemes like Kenya's since the mid-1950s have concentrated land into the hands of individual males and have opened doors for rash mortgaging, for speculation, and for absentee landlordism. Such attempts at planned change in the landholding systems of rural cultivators have produced mainly unhappy surprises—not more food—as foreign ideologies prove inapplicable ecologically, economically, politically, or culturally.

Second, aid agencies can rethink credit, which has been a main strategy of international aid since the founding of the Bretton Woods institutions. World Bank projects and programs still revolve around lending, albeit usually at low interest. Bilateral aid such as USAID projects, which enter as country-to-country grants, often become loan projects within the country. Credit schemes, which may involve technical assistance, training, marketing support, or other extras, have been based on the assumption that rural Africans have little of their own to work with, that intermediary channels will pass loans on to farmers, that the farmers will use "farm loans" for farming, and that a lack of temporary capital is the main obstacle keeping rural people poor. These old assumptions have gradually proved unfounded; programs based upon them have yielded disappointing outcomes for nearly all concerned. Credit means debt. It also saps incentives to produce: the more one has borrowed, the more one is working for someone other than oneself, and the less one is likely to care about the yields. Experienced farmers and herders know, as Shakespeare's Polonius told Laertes in *Hamlet*, that "borrowing dulls the edge of husbandry." Most rain-fed agriculture in Africa is too risky to allow reliable repayment on loans whose interest mounts steadily. Where land is used as mortgage collateral, farm credit can be treacherous. But it is always tempting, and if nothing else, needy relatives often press would-be borrowers into accepting money that they hope they will be able to manage wisely. Rural Africans want and need to save. But rural people variously tend to invest in livestock, trees, jewelry, trade goods, and so forth—more than in money—and with good reason, where currency inflation rates are high. Those who have been designing economic programs involving credit might explore nonmonetary options, as in the example of the Heifer Project, which "lends" animals, the principal of which is repaid with interest, as participants pass on offspring of these animals to additional participants. Such initiatives have at least some local counterparts, as in the indigenous stock loan partnerships of Fulbe in the Sahel, or Jie and Turkana in East Africa.

Microfinance, emulating or grafted onto traditional, rotating saving and credit associations, shows inconclusive results in Africa to date. While it can help in fostering some kinds of trade and small manufacturing enterprises, it seems to work less well in agriculture, where people in a given locality tend to need money at the same times of year. It seems to work best when tied to saving. But the broader point is that credit is not the panacea it was once supposed to be, and in large programs that end in recurring debt, anxiety, and demoralization for their ostensible beneficiaries, it may have done at least as much harm as good.

Both land allocations and financial credit connote patronage, whether at international, national, or local scale. They are political tools: doling out land or loans is a way to secure military favors, placate dissenters, or launch political careers, and not necessarily the route to political democracy and economic growth that supportive donors envisage.

Third, governments can free up labor migration. Over almost all rural Africa, people are kept alive partly by the remitted earnings of nonresident kin. In many instances, people have devised elaborate systems of pooling contributions from extended kin and neighbors to sponsor schooling and labor migration overseas, in the hope that when a promising son (or, less commonly, daughter) of a family, lineage, or community finds compensated work, he (or she) will help support either the sponsors or their children. Labor migration and remittance are both a fervent hope and a hard social reality to which families (however defined) have had to adjust, along with rising rural population and changing land use patterns. Before they move across borders, they need to make sure they can exit their countries, enter others, and either remit money or reenter with it when they want; but these can all pose stiff problems for African migrants.

This is not the place for an extended critique of the nation-state as the focal unit of aggregation in the world's policymaking and politicking. But it is at national borders, and at nations' checkpoints at ports and airports, that African people encounter the stiffest resistance to their movements. The illogical placement of borders, relative to the distribution of ethnic, linguistic, or religious groups, leads us to ask whether nations whose borders were initially imposed by Europeans are, or must be, the political and economic units with which Africans most closely identify, or whether it might be possible for economic programs to build on the more complex, real social and cultural mixture of groups, networks, and categories with overlapping and cross-cutting loyalties.

Whatever the relevant units of aggregation—family, community, ethnic group, nation, continent—it is undeniable that among the factors prohibiting free movement of Africans, and thus one of the human roots of African famine, are conscious and unconscious racism. While anthropologists have tended in recent decades to denounce the concept of race as analytically problematic or even useless—and to conclude therefore that there can be neither any right answer to how many races there are, nor any sure, single method of pegging anyone into one of them—all can agree that "race" is relevant to the extent that people actually form judgments upon what they perceive race to be. Whether expressed in terms of skin color, hair texture, stature, bone structure, or undefined combinations of bodily, attitudinal, and aptitudinal traits, racial perceptions matter to migration—both within Africa and between Africa and outside. If racial prejudice doesn't close a physical or legal portcullis to opportunity-seekers or refugees, it can yet make life so miserable among autochthonous members of a host society or country as to be just as effective a barrier.

African people need better and more accessible markets for their labor and talents, both at home and overseas. Nearly everywhere on the continent, one may find some young men and women clamoring to travel, study, and work in richer countries. If people in these privileged countries are really serious about helping Africans, their own nations' travel and immigration barriers will simply need to be eased up.

IN THE MAIN

Hunger—even in Africa—is not always directly linked to food shortage, so technical solutions, whether on the side of agricultural technology to increase food supply or of fertility control to decrease demand, will not suffice by themselves. People who persistently suffer hunger lack political, and not just technical, capacity to overcome hunger and poverty. Recent decades' advances in technology for advanced early warning of and response to famine, impressive as they are, are also insufficient without commensurate mechanisms of cooperation on the ground. Present-day famines are found exclusively where information cannot move freely or where the political stability needed in order to produce and distribute essential foods and medicine is absent. Moreover, the downturn in per-capita food production in Africa in recent decades likely would not have occurred in the absence of war. Over the past twenty-five years—since the World Food Conference and energy crisis of 1974—African peoples and nations have learned much about management of famine *from each other.* A challenge now is to learn how to calm the political instability and violence that continue to plague the continent, recognizing that these are linked also to the vestiges of colonial economies, neocolonial continuities, and the political-economic systems of the current world and African states that refuse to put food at the top of their human development agendas.

To minimize involuntary hunger, fresh coalitions will need to be forged among "public" and "private" agencies—at multiple social levels. They will need to involve those who are the intended beneficiaries right from the beginning, and eliminate obstacles to these people's self-motivated and directed problem-solving. Too often efforts to "develop" Africa have been based on assumptions that aid recipients are passive, or worse yet, a problem to be eliminated. Instead of treating recipients as obstacles to development, aid donors and lenders—and these, now under heavy scrutiny, may themselves have to evolve radically in coming decades—might seek ways to strengthen these peoples' own food-security strategies, individual and collective, and pay special attention to ways to bolster, and not interfere with, the locally adapted modes of livelihood. In agriculture, animal and range management, rural finance, and small industry, African ways of living and producing have turned out to be wiser and more productive—and harder or more dangerous to reform—than foreign experts anticipated. The hardest part of intervention remains the listening.

Among the widest communication gaps to be bridged is the chasm between people who are content to base their etiology of hunger and famine—and their prescriptions for action—more on material science (soils, weather, crop strains), and those who base theirs more on spiritual considerations, including ancestors, witchcraft, divinity, and the role of appropriate human behavior in bringing about products and processes of interest. This is *not* a simple distinction between foreign and African modes of thought. Both are readily found within and outside the continent, and most people in most places are capable of thinking in more than one of these ways, depending on the context. In different parts of the world distinct ethnicities, religions, and classes differ in their prevailing modes of explanation for health or illness, socioeconomic success or failure, and the deserved pleasures or unfair hardships in the life of an individual or community. To dismiss as illogical the different modes of reason and rationality informing such judgments, etiologies, and eschatologies is to miss the chance to grow through understanding. To reject as false the premises different from one's own is to ignore the reality of prayer, sacrifice, or witchcraft to those who practice it, talk about it, hide from it— or conversely, to disregard all talk of molecular structures, drainage rates, or drought resistance as unreflective scientism. It is the sharing of unanswered questions, as well as the sharing of answers, money, and material, that may prove the biggest challenge of all for those seeking betterment of the human condition in Africa through whatever means.

If there has been a single missing ingredient in intercontinental efforts to address African food problems so far, it has been time. Problems of food and hunger are always urgent. Yet it takes time to accommodate alien customs and the subtle reasons and passions behind them; time to learn languages and ask questions in terms familiar to the asked, or to vary translation and to back-translate; time to wonder whether our most sacred assumptions might be turned inside out; time to try, fail and back off, to try the opposite, to wait and see. There is also a fundamental gap in reasoning between the appeal of "timeless" or cyclical tradition and time-tested wisdom, on the one hand, and the modern agricultural or social scientist's quest for ever more rapid, timely, and efficient social, agricultural, and nutritional change on the other. The tools of information technology and biotechnology, as valuable as they might be, shall never be substitutes for the sober reflection and open-minded communication that makes them a part of effective strategies for African people and those who would assist them into a more evenly provident era.

If poverty is a tangle of processes contributing to each other in vicious circles, small successes can surely contribute to other successes in equally systemic fashion. Gains in nutrition and health can add to gains in mobility, information sharing, and political cooperation, which can add to domestic production, purchasing power, and in turn nutrition. A more stable politico-economic environment, perhaps less tightly tied to the nation-state and less dependent on international aid apparatus, is likely to reduce the land grabbing, border blockages, and overborrowing that render the most vulnerable destitute. Evening out price swings should help reduce the hoarding that makes them more extreme. Solving one of these problems is likely to help solve the others. The ratchet of poverty is a reversible one.

In this web of cause, effect, and ratchets, anthropologists working on food and famine have mostly continued to pursue understandings that are ecologically grounded without necessarily being deterministic and, while rooted in local facts, are more animated by local voices and more respectful of local categories of thought than those of most other disciplines. We attempt to understand the "whole" food system or process in local terms, but also to integrate these understandings within the larger view of regional and global politics, religion, and trade, and thus to add something to the more measured perspectives of economists, agronomists, plant breeders, and engineers. Anthropologists no longer have a monopoly on ethnographic fieldwork and method, or even on "cultural studies." Even as political scientists increasingly talk about culture, and rural sociologists and geographers do "participatory" development research, it is this thinking and engaging of the whole, and the linking of many different spatial and temporal scales and levels of social analysis, that at least in theory set anthropology apart. But holistic analysis, alas, is also easier said than done. This may be why so many carry it out so incompletely—or why, in their quest to avoid essentializing, many forestall action or constructive policy engagement. There is no simple formula. But mere complexity, the most conventional conclusion of our age, is perhaps no longer enough of an answer.

REFERENCES

Bonfiglioli, A. M. 1989. *Dudal: Histoire de famille et histoire de troupeau chez un groupe de Wodaabe du Niger.* Cambridge: Cambridge University Press.

Carney, Judith. 1992. "Peasant Women and Economic Transformation in the Gambia." *Development and Change* 23, no. 2: 67–90.

Clay, Jason, and Bonnie K. Holcomb. 1986. *Politics and the Ethiopian Famine, 1984–1985.* Cambridge, MA: Cultural Survival.

Cole, David, and Richard Huntington. 1997. *Between a Swamp and a Hard Place: Development Challenges in Remote Rural Africa.* Cambridge, MA: Harvard University Press, for Harvard Institute for International Development.

Copans, Jean, ed. 1975. *Sécheresses et famines du Sahel.* Vol. 1. *Écologie, dénutrition, assistance.* Vol. 2. *Paysans et nomades.* Paris: Maspero.

Dahl, Gudrun. 1979. *Suffering Grass: Subsistence and Society of Waso Borana.* Stockholm: Studies in Social Anthropology, University of Stockholm,

de Waal, Alexander. 1989. *Famine That Kills: Darfur, Sudan, 1984–1985.* Oxford: Oxford University Press.

———. 1997. *Famine Crimes: Politics and the Disaster Relief Industry in Africa.* London: James Currey; Bloomington: Indiana University Press.

Dey, Jennie. 1981. "Gambian Women: Unequal Partners in Rice Development Projects?" *Journal of Development Studies* 17: 109–22.

Dongmo, J.-L.; A. Franqueville; M. Jeannin; G. La Cognata; G. Mainet; and C. Seignobos. 1976. *Recherches sur l'approvisionnement des villes.* Memoir, Centre pour l'Étude Géographique Tropicale. Paris: Éditions du Centre National de Recherche Scientifique.

Downs, Richard, and S. P. Reyna. 1988. *Land and Society in Contemporary Africa.* Hanover, NH: University Press of New England.

Downs, Richard; S. P. Reyna; and Donna Kerner, eds. 1991. *The Political Economy of African Famine: The Class and Gender Basis of Hunger.* London: Gordon and Breach.

Drèze, Jean, and Amartya Sen, eds. 1995. *The Political Economy of Hunger.* 3 vols. Oxford: Clarendon.

Ferguson, Anne. 1994. "Gendered Science: A Critique of Agricultural Development." *American Anthropologist* 96, no. 3: 540–52

Ferguson, James. 1990. *The Anti-Politics Machine.* Cambridge: Cambridge University Press.

Garine, I. de, and G. A. Harrison, eds. 1988. *Coping with Uncertainty in Food Supply.* Oxford and New York: Oxford University Press.

Guyer, Jane I., ed. 1987. *Feeding African Cities.* Studies in Regional and Social History. Manchester, U.K.: Manchester University Press, for International African Institute.

Hart, Keith. 1982. *The Political Economy of West African Agriculture.* Cambridge: Cambridge University Press.

Huss-Ashmore, Rebecca, and Solomon Katz, eds. 1989–1990. *African Food Systems in Crisis.* 2 vols. London: Gordon and Breach.

Hutchinson, Sharon. 1996. *Nuer Dilemmas: Coping with Money, War, and the State.* Berkeley: University of California Press.

Iliffe, John. 1987. *The African Poor: A History.* Cambridge: Cambridge University Press.

Linares, Olga. 1992. *Power, Prayer, and Production: The Jola of Casamance, Senegal.* Cambridge: Cambridge University Press.

Messer, Ellen. 1984. "Anthropological Perspectives on Diet." *Annual Review of Anthropology* 13: 205–49

Messer, Ellen; Marc Cohen; and Jashinta D'Costa. 1998. *Food from Peace: Breaking the Links between Hunger and Conflict.* Washington, DC: International Food Policy Research Institute.

Morgan, Dan. *Merchants of Grain.* Harmondsworth, U.K.: Penguin.

Mortimore, Michael. 1988. *Adapting to Drought: Farmers, Famine and Desertification in West Africa.* Cambridge: Cambridge University Press.

Pottier, Johan. 1985. *Food Systems in Central and Southern Africa.* London: School of Oriental and African Studies, University of London.

———. 1999. *Anthropology of Food: The Social Dynamics of Food Security.* London: Polity Press.

Raikes, Philip. 1989. *Modernizing Hunger: Famine, Food Surplus, and Farm Policy.* London: James Currey.

Richards, Audrey I. 1939. *Land, Labour, and Diet in Northern Rhodesia.* Oxford: Oxford University Press.

Richards, Paul. 1986. *Coping with Hunger: Hazard and Experiment in an African Rice-Farming System*. London: Allen and Unwin.

Sen, Amartya. 1981. *Poverty and Famines*. Oxford: Clarendon Press.

Shipton, Parker. 1990. "African Famines and Food Security: Anthropological Perspectives." *Annual Review of Anthropology* 19: 353–94.

Solway, Jacqueline. 1994. "Drought as a 'Revelatory Crisis': An Exploration of Shifting Entitlements and Hierarchies in the Kalahari, Botswana." *Development and Change* 25, no. 3: 471–95.

Tiffen, Mary; Michael Mortimore; and Francis Gichuki. 1994. *More People, Less Erosion: Environmental Recovery in Kenya*. Chichester, NY: John Wiley.

Vaughan, Megan. 1987. *The Story of an African Famine*. Cambridge: Cambridge University Press.

Watts, Michael. 1983. *Silent Violence: Food, Famine, and Peasantry in Northern Nigeria*. Berkeley: University of California Press.

World Hunger Program, Brown University. 1995. *The Hunger Report*. Providence, RI: World Hunger Program.

13

Anthropology and the Aid Encounter

ALEX DE WAAL

In March 1985, at the nadir of the Ethiopian famine, while journalists and aid agencies were counting the numbers of people at risk of starvation in the millions, a group of Ethiopian refugees in a camp in neighboring Sudan went on a hunger strike. They demanded that the refugee authorities and aid agencies permit them to leave the camp, to take their children out of the feeding centers and clinics, so that they could return home to the Ethiopian highlands. Aghast, relief workers said that this was a suicidal plan: how could starving people turn their backs on food and medicine to face an arduous trek into the perils of war and famine? "The march of death" they described it. But the refugees insisted, refusing food rations until at least the men and some families were permitted to begin their journey home.

Fifteen years later, no experienced or informed aid worker—let alone a social anthropologist—would be surprised by such a turn of events. Anthropological research on famine "coping strategies" has revealed the rationale of the refugees' decision. For them, the flight to a refugee camp was not their last act of desperation, throwing themselves on the mercy of foreign charity. Rather, it was part of a calculated strategy which, if successful, would enable them to cultivate for the coming year and return to a degree of normalcy after the famine. Land, seeds and plough oxen awaited them in the highlands, and in March the rains had come. Meanwhile, some family members could remain dependent on relief until the time came for them to rejoin the household.

This striking case illustrates just one of the uses of empirical, fieldwork-based social anthropology in relief and development. It dictates a radically different approach to the design of famine relief programs—one which is slowly and incompletely being adopted by many aid agencies. More widely, anthropological research in various elaborate or rapid forms is now recognized as a sine qua non for effective, community-oriented aid programs. Anthropological methods are increasingly being used to develop and refine the "social technologies" of grassroots development and relief: assessing food needs in a famine, establishing mechanisms so that assistance reaches the most needy, ensuring that community development programs are equitable and sustainable—all these require an anthropological input.

Meanwhile, the anthropologist's reflex—to turn critical scrutiny toward the exercise of power in all its forms—has enabled a different and more subversive theme to emerge. The anthropologist is well placed to study the "developmental" and "humanitarian" modes of power whereby the transnational institutions whose business is to deliver relief and development sustain and justify themselves, exercising political, economic, social, and cultural power over the lives of millions of poor and vulnerable people. What preconceptions and interests dictated that aid workers would try to stop refugees from voluntarily leaving a camp? What made them believe that the refugees should only accept aid on the terms dictated by foreign aid agencies? In turn, such analysis often raises questions about the roles of anthropologists themselves in the aid encounter. The reciprocally ambivalent relationship between aid institutions and social anthropologists will be a recurring theme of this chapter.

SUDAN: COLONIALISM, DEVELOPMENT, AND ANTHROPOLOGY

Sudan, as one of the ancestral sites of the anthropological discipline, is also a fascinating case for examining the roles of anthropology in relief and development. I use it as an example throughout this chapter. Africa's largest country and one of its most complex, Sudan has been both a laboratory for various forms of development and relief and the location of a particularly productive school of anthropological inquiry, both Sudanese and foreign (chiefly British).

In its formative years, social anthropology often served the colonial state as an intelligence system for the administration of native peoples. Sudan, with its bewildering variety of "tribes," many of which had no identifiable rulers, was a challenge to a colonial order that preferred to rule through local notaries. But some of the anthropological research that was commissioned from this puzzlement proved rather more challenging than the authorities had anticipated. A notable case is Prof. E. E. Evans Pritchard's trilogy on the Nuer, which celebrated the virtues of statelessness. Many succeeding anthropologists, professional and amateur, have found themselves treading much the same path. Called upon by a powerful institution to help them understand (and thereby control) some recalcitrant tribe, the fieldworker has ended up with more sympathy and understanding for the subjects of her research than for the commissioning power and has written a report accordingly. Anthropology is perhaps the only discipline that is so inherently subversive.

After Sudan's independence in 1956, anthropologists were also called into service in support of ambitious plans for state-led, planned development. At the University of Khartoum, a variant of the British empirical, fieldwork-oriented school of anthropology quickly matured, producing studies that often combined theoretical insight with relevance to the developmental challenges of the day. Whether they were absorbed and acted upon is a different question.

The dominant development theories of the 1960s and 1970s emphasized the need for resource injections and state planning. From the viewpoint of the development scientist, the anthropologist's role was to improve the efficiency of planning, to be a technician, identifying the social and cultural snags that might slow down development. Any more far-reaching critiques were filed away. This is an approach that still prevails in some quarters. Many development agencies prefer to hire anthropologists as consultants only, for the purpose of producing the social impact assessments required by their donors' contracts. Such studies, often rushed and usually undertaken when the main decisions about project design and implementation have already been made, rarely have much influence. Also, the scarcity of full-time posts for anthropologists in both universities and development agencies has forced many, usually reluctantly, into the consultancy business. But rigorous anthropology always retains its tendency to critical reflection: the anthropological challenge to "development" is as old as the practice of development itself.

Development, as envisaged during these years, simply did not work. In the case of Sudan, the country's "development decade"—the ten years of peace following the 1972 agreement to end the first civil war—concluded with a crippling foreign debt, a country littered with unfinished or collapsed megaprojects, environmental decay, famine, and renewed war. Elsewhere in Africa the failure was equally clear, albeit less spectacular. This crisis of "development" was a spur for a more constructive relationship between anthropology and development.

ANTHROPOLOGY AND GRASSROOTS DEVELOPMENT

The 1980s and 1990s have seen a focus on various forms of "grassroots" development, centered on communities, especially rural communities whose livelihoods derive from smallholder agriculture, pastoralism, crafts production, and fishing. Governmental donors in Europe and north America have increasingly switched their funding to nongovernmental organizations (NGOs), whose approach stresses "participation," "partnership," and "empowerment," concepts that require extreme cultural sensitivity if they are to be meaningful or operational. The empiricism and versatility of anthropological methods have proved extremely valuable for this approach. A substantial number of grassroots development practitioners have anthropological training, and many of those who do not have acquired informal anthropological skills.

Anthropology is now an acknowledged partner in development practice. Practical development anthropology has gained recognition and has developed its own corpus and methodologies. These are empirical, fieldwork-oriented, holistic, and respectful of local people's concepts, priorities, and views. Socially aware and sensitive development practitioners, who may not have formal training in the social sciences, and who may not regard themselves as "doing" social anthropology, have produced reports on the social and economic realities of poor (mostly rural) communities. Tested against the brute reality of what works, this seam of "gray" literature is a rich source of anthropological raw material, which may yet become source texts for future Ph.D. theses.

Of more immediate interest to development practitioners, and still more so to the recipients of aid, is the question of what anthropologists actually do, how this feeds into the development process, and whether it helps to alleviate the lot of poor and vulnerable people. The development economist Robert Chambers is one of the most enthusiastic exponents of the anthropological approach to development. In Chambers's hands, "anthropology" is less an academic discipline or profession than an attitude of mind. He may be theoretically naive (deliberately so), but his fieldwork eclecticism, responsiveness to the needs and insights of poor people, and readiness to challenge any disciplinary or theoretical framework that fails to work—that is, deliver tangible benefits in terms of power, income, and resources to poor people—are all refreshing. His work is imbued with a moral agenda of encouraging, enabling, and empowering poor and marginal people; an outlook that is instinctively attractive to social anthropologists. Chambers examines and argues for some interesting social technologies which have arisen from the heterodox conjuncture of social science and the frank puzzlement of development planners.

One exemplar of a broadly "anthropological" approach to development is farming systems research (FSR, and its siblings, pastoral and forest systems, and the like). Conventional agricultural research concentrated on increasing the yield of certain varieties of crops; however, having developed "improved" varieties, agronomists were frequently faced with the puzzling question of why poor farmers were reluctant to use them. FSR by contrast focuses on the entire productive environment of the farmer: it is a holistic approach that integrates the range of decisions a farmer must make. A high-yielding variety of grain crop may, for example, not be attractive because it produces less straw for domestic animals, requires more labor at a critical time of year, or cannot be intercropped with another valued product such as oilseeds.

Another case of the convergence between social anthropology and rural development is in the field of credit. Surveys of rural poverty consistently find that respondents' most common demand is for cash loans. Small-scale credit is rapidly becoming one of development's fastest growth areas. In some countries, variants on standard banking practices have proved highly successful: the Grameen Bank in Bangladesh is an example. Elsewhere, options such as revolving credit associations have been developed out of traditional institutions. Successful support to such institutions requires at the very least some anthropological understanding. Another variant is "Islamic" banking. Islam prohibits usury, so rather than lending at interest, the bank enters into a business partnership with the client, sharing the profit. Islamic banking has been used by political Islamists in Sudan and elsewhere to build a political constituency, but it also has encouraging possibilities for developmental use. Again, anthropological as well as economic skills are called for.

A third example is respect for indigenous technical knowledge. The wealth of rural people's practical (and sometimes theoretical) knowledge about their environment has never been a secret to ethnographers, but it took until the 1980s for this to be recognized by the development industry and, characteristically, to be given its own acronym (ITK).

Of equal importance, anthropological techniques have been absorbed into the basic lexicon of development research. Rapid rural appraisal (RRA) was created as a short-cut attempt to introduce economists, agronomists, environmental scientists, and others to basic anthropological methods. Anthropologists will recognize RRA methods as formalizations of standard fieldwork techniques for getting people to talk about the issues that most concern them. A simple example is asking villagers to put households into categories according to wealth and then provide the criteria for the categorization. The results are usually more meaningful than any survey of household income and expenditure, as well as more reliable, not to mention quicker. RRA has since been developed into participatory rural appraisal (PRA), which goes further in involving the subjects of development (both the rural and the urban poor) in creatively defining their own predicament and needs. A range of gamelike methods has been developed. There is now a thriving niche industry of PRA methods and findings: some professional anthropologists may be surprised (and perhaps a little galled) to discover just how powerful the techniques have proved to be. However, there is also a tendency among some development practitioners to use very rapid appraisal techniques that amount to little more than wandering around and chatting to a few people randomly encountered on the road: the anthropologist's painstaking approach and skeptical eye will always be needed as a quality control.

RELIEF ANTHROPOLOGY

A new branch of development anthropology has emerged since the mid-1980s, with research in Thailand and Sudan leading the way. Relief anthropology began with studies of refugees, whom Sudan hosted in large numbers and with generous asylum laws in the 1970s and 1980s. It further developed in response to drought and famine, establishing some technologies which have relied heavily on anthropological method and insight.

An example of these technologies is the creation of famine early warning systems based on the use of social and economic survey data. The argument is that if food shortages can be predicted reliably and early enough, then governments and aid agencies can take timely and effective measures to prevent them from deteriorating into famine. Given the complexities of rural economies, the monitoring of weather patterns and agricultural production alone (provided by satellite imaging and the like) will not generate sufficiently reliable early warning data: these must also come from monitoring the market prices of basic foods, unusual migrations of seasonal laborers, unusual patterns of sale of assets, and the like. Setting up such mechanisms for collecting socioeconomic data and interpreting the output requires anthropological expertise.

The idea of "smart relief" is another social technology with anthropological parentage. In response to the repeated and usually correct allegation that relief aid is "sticky" and tends to become attached to the hands of officials, contractors, and soldiers through whose hands it passes, the idea of self-targeting or "smart relief" has been developed. The idea is that, by using the existing networks and strategies of the poor as the mechanisms for distribution, the stickiness of relief need no longer be a problem. Informal trade networks using market women could, for example, become a mechanism for relief distribution. Identifying and using such mechanisms clearly requires anthropological expertise.

One of the central concepts in understanding and responding to famine is "coping strategy." Research on coping strategies investigates how rural people respond to food deficits: by searching for wild foods, migrating in search of casual labor, selling livestock and assets, taking loans and gifts from neighbors and kin, and a range of other social and microeconomic activities that enable them to acquire food and, where possible, keep their social networks intact and retain sufficient assets (seeds, land, animals) to return to a viable livelihood after the crisis (figure 1). "Coping strategies" have been celebrated as a demonstration of rural people's re-

FIGURE 1 This young refugee from Chad tried to make money by selling catfish he dug up from the mud; photographed at a refugee camp in Geneina, Darfur, western Sudan, 1985. (Photo by author)

silience and skill and as an antidote to the paternalism entrenched in the relief in- dustry, which had assumed that drought victims merely threw themselves on the charity of aid agencies. The example which opened this chapter, of the Ethiopian refugees who abandoned their camp in Sudan, preferring the calculated risk of short-term hunger while they cultivated to a future of perpetual pauperism in a camp, is a case in point. Analysis of coping strategies has since become the founda- tion for improved early warning systems, smart relief, and other culturally sensitive responses to famine. It has also been used to deflate some of the wildly exaggerated predictions of disaster, among them the absurd claim made in November 1996 that a million refugees in eastern Zaire faced imminent death, a claim forwarded in sup- port of a campaign for international military intervention in central Africa.

These concepts derived by relief anthropologists have often proved constructive, but they can also be abused. The case of coping strategies is one instance. At various times in the 1990s, aid donors have invoked coping strategies as a pretext for cutting their relief food pledges to famine-stricken countries, arguing that the people will survive anyway. This has occurred repeatedly in Sudan. In addition, the Sudanese government has abused the concept in its own counterinsurgency in the war zones of the South. People facing destitution are drawn to towns, where casual, income-generating opportunities are available. Sudanese military planners aim to collect the rural southern population around garrisons in what they call "peace camps," thereby denying a civilian base to the rebel Sudan People's Liberation Army (SPLA), while simultaneously providing raw human material for conscription and labor on mechanized farms. Speaking of "coping strategies" (as the Sudanese Government and its apologists do) rather than of destitution following military-made famine gives this strategy a spurious legitimacy.

ANTHROPOLOGY IN "COMPLEX EMERGENCIES"

In many cases, relief and development programs are implemented against a background of civil war. In a number of African countries, protracted conflict has become the norm, and anthropologists, along with relief and development practitioners, have been obliged to live with this unfortunate fact (figure 2). Most internal wars in Africa have not resembled the Clausewitzean clash of regular and professional armies, but the mobilization of militias, often along ethnic lines, to pursue irregular warfare for a mixture of ends, including the creation of local business empires, removal of minority ethnic groups, and so on. Social anthropology is essential to make sense of what would otherwise appear as simply anarchic or mindless processes of violence and decay. As these wars are generally fought among the civilian population and at their expense, relief agencies have found that most of their work occurs in what they euphemistically call "complex emergencies." Understanding the context for their operations and practically responding to the challenges they face demand an anthropological approach.

Sudan is a case in point. Since 1983, southern Sudan has been the location of a long-running, bloody, and intractable war. Another distinctive anthropological approach to relief, partly initiated and implemented by non-anthropologists, has developed there. Since 1989 there has been an extensive relief program on both sides of the battle-lines under United Nations auspices, known as Operation Lifeline Sudan. In response to the enduring inability of the SPLA to build civil institutions that can administer relief for the civilian populations it controls, UNICEF and other Western relief agencies have experimented with their own "capacity

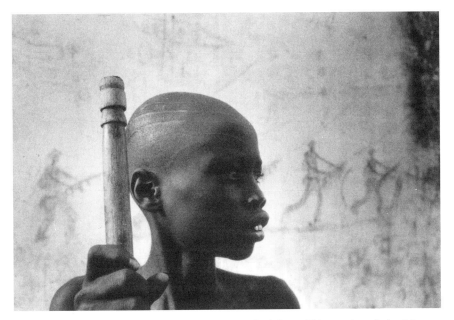

FIGURE 2 Dinka youth displaced far from his home by the fighting, Thiet, southern Sudan. Note graffiti on the wall depicting the war. (© Adrian Arbib/Survival)

building," an attempt at social engineering in order to establish the minimum social structures essential for the administration of relief. It is an exercise in applied anthropology, implemented with varying degrees of skill and success. Under capacity-building programs, southern Sudanese have witnessed a succession of forms of relief committees, "Sudanese indigenous NGOs," quasi-autonomous relief administrations, and the like. Some small-scale solutions have been snatched from the teeth of adversity. One example is the resettlement of Uduk communities, displaced several times by the spread of the conflict, to small farming settlements in Ethiopia (this with the assistance of their long-time ethnographer, Prof. Wendy James). Faced with the prospect of the mass death and dispersal of her subjects of study, morality impels the anthropologist to become more participant than observer.

More widely, the context of the war, with its continual forced migration, social disruption, and lawlessness, along with the threat of looting by armed factions, has made such experiments in enlightened social technology hazardous. Aid workers, journalists, and human rights monitors, Sudanese and foreign, have been attacked and robbed, and on occasion lost their lives. An interesting response to these threats has been a UNICEF-led program of developing "humanitarian principles" to govern relief work. This is a different enterprise in applied anthropology. It is an attempt to elaborate the relevant parts of the Geneva Conventions in line with southern Sudanese customary laws and the prevailing circumstances. There may be something absurd in a young aid worker lecturing Sudanese bishops and elders on "humanitarian principles," but the exercise itself is an interesting one. UNICEF, at least, has something to learn. (It is a variant of the International Committee of the Red Cross's project of "dissemination" of international humanitarian law, using simplified teaching materials adapted to the cultures of warstricken societies across the world. The ICRC generally finds that the core concept of the "warrior's honor" and associated principles of restraint and humanity in warfare are more immediately recognized across the world than are comparable concepts of individual human rights.)

Meanwhile, under the auspices of the National Islamic Government in Khartoum, social science has been pressed into service in pursuit of Islamic social planning. In one respect, the Civilisation Project (as its architects label it, a term with imperial echoes) and one of its more ambitious strands, the Da'wa al Shamla (Comprehensive Call to God) are remarkable and innovative approaches to the problem of state and society in an impoverished country. Breaking down the Western distinctions between public and private, religious and secular, state and society, civil and military, commercial and philanthropic, Sudan's rulers have sought to build a range of "Islamic" institutions that will create a new form of society. Some of the initiatives have been creative. For example, the extension of "Islamic" credit into small-scale agriculture and artisanship has fused traditional mechanisms with the insights of recent development anthropology. Similarly, official recognition of migrants' associations in towns has proved an interesting means of mobilizing community resources. Along with some social anthropologists, the Sudanese Government and its quasi-governmental institutions have employed economists and town planners with some anthropological training to help design their programs.

The fatal flaw in this project has been the lack of popular consent and the authoritarian and militaristic means of implementing it. Jihad (Holy War) encompasses both the struggle for an Islamic society and the war against the SPLA. Where the Islamist social and political project has encountered non-Islamic societies—notably in the South—it has fused with counterinsurgency. Here, anthropology has been occasionally brought in to serve in its old role as an adjunct to military intelligence, identifying chiefs (colonial-style "native administration" has been revived) for cooption and exploring the cultural essences of southern tribes so that they can be more effectively controlled and, if possible, "civilized" and evangelized. Whether Sudanese anthropology under a militant Islamist government can also play a subversive role remains to be seen.

FIGURE 3 While a Western aid truck is unloaded, a boy underneath gathers up spilled food for later personal use, Darfur, western Sudan, 1985. (Photo by author)

ANTHROPOLOGY AND THE AID ENCOUNTER

It is evident that high theory is not an enduring priority for most anthropologists working in Sudan today. The practical morality of poverty, famine, and war dictate a rather old-fashioned, empirical bent to fieldwork. But the combination of empathy with the subjects of study and a critical awareness of the power relations manifest in the aid encounter has contributed to another strand in the anthropological corpus. The aid industry itself—its institutions, its morality, its symbolism and logic, and its interaction with those whom it calls "recipients" or "beneficiaries" (or sometimes even "partners")—has become a rich and important subject for anthropological inquiry. And, arguably, the products of participant-observation fieldwork have proved just as subversive to the aid industry as to more ambitious theoretical critiques.

Robert Chambers's model of "rural development tourism" was an early attempt to analyze (and discount) the institutional and perceptual biases that outsiders bring to the observation of poverty in the Third World. Chambers argued that aid officials commonly underestimate the extent and depth of rural poverty because of their selective exposure: they travel on tarmac roads, during the dry season, visit aid projects, talk to aid recipients, and meet chiefly with men. If by contrast they chose to leave main roads, travel during the rains, visit unaided areas, talk to those who never receive assistance, and meet with women, their assessments might be much less sanguine. In the twenty years since this critique was first made, development agencies have made a serious attempt to overcome these biases.

My own model of "disaster tourism" was a variant on this, developed to explain why the opposite process—an exaggeration of suffering—occurs during declared famines. For example, aid workers, journalists, and economists (among others) overestimated imminent deaths in the 1984–85 Sudanese famine by a factor of ten or twenty. The explanation lies in a combination of factors, including visiting at the worst times of year, visiting famine camps, where the worst suffering is to be found, and meeting the most destitute, combined with a failure to understand coping strategies, a failure to understand the epidemiology of famine mortality, and an inappropriate concept of "famine" based on neo-Malthusian assumptions. Subsequent anthropological study has illuminated how this selective exposure and understanding is further exaggerated in the media and in aid agencies' representations of famine (of which more below).

The internal culture of aid institutions provides an interesting and sometimes bizarre contrast with local society. Terje Tvedt has examined the operations of a Scandinavian NGO in Torit, Southern Sudan:

For some of the NGOs, money was not the decisive constraint on their scope of activities. What affected project size and project components was usually not the purse, but arguments about what was morally right and most conducive to local development. Generally, the NGOs acted within a culture of absolute affluence, in which services and goods were not costed. . . . It was difficult to question the principle that aid was free and in some mysterious way outside the realm of economic realities and the emergence of governmental systems. (1998, 192)

In the context of a deeply impoverished rural society, this was a strange logic indeed. It is a logic that has continued—and become more extraordinary—as peacetime development has been replaced by wartime relief. Throughout southern Sudan, villagers who rarely saw a wheeled vehicle have been busy clearing bush airstrips in order to attract the World Food Program's heavy-lift cargo aircraft or the smaller planes used by NGOs to supply their clinics and rehabilitation projects. This interaction with Westerners, their technology, and their aid culture is not only strange, but prolonged. At the time of writing, the air deliveries have been going on for more than a decade. The social and cultural legacy of this will prove an interesting subject for future ethnography. Will southern Sudan develop its own versions of cargo cults? Will future local administrators who arrive by land rover be for ever compared, unfavorably, with the white people, each of whom seemed to possess an airplane?

The transnational developmental and philanthropic industries operate within their own, relatively closed worlds of self-reinforcing assumptions. Since the late 1970s, the International Monetary Fund (IMF) has had a key role in running the Sudanese economy: for much of the 1980s the entire Sudanese ministry of finance was geared toward meeting IMF conditions and deadlines. But empirical economic research—using simple anthropological methods—has shown that the statistical foundation of the IMF's analysis was fundamentally flawed. Notably, the national economic statistics omitted the huge but unrecorded remittances of Sudanese expatriates working in the Gulf states. The IMF believed that Sudan's priority was to balance its foreign exchange books by importing less and exporting more. In reality, the country was awash with hard currency that had escaped the official banking system: the challenge was to tap this wealth in the informal sector. It required some straightforward community-level surveys to discover this rather significant fact.

Sudan is not exceptional. In many African countries, most of the economic activity escapes official measurement or even recognition. Studying the "real economy" of Zaire (now Democratic Republic of Congo) requires anthropological investigation. The economic dynamics of rebel-held enclaves in Sierra Leone and Liberia demand similar methods of study. In Somalia, arguably, the entire national economy is informal.

The anthropologist or social historian will also be surprised to read much of the World Bank's analysis of Sudan, which presents the country largely as virgin territory crying out for "development." From the earliest days of the colonial conquest a century ago, Sudan—or rather the most favorable parts of it—were aggressively developed by the colonial state and the cotton industry. The Gezira Scheme, begun in 1905, is not only the world's largest irrigated farm, but in its early years was attracting migrant labor from as far away as Nigeria. In contrast to the Bank's assessment, a long line of left-leaning social anthropologists and political scientists have argued that Sudan's problem has not been the absence of "development," but too much of the wrong sort of "development."

Anthropologists have taken this analysis further in other countries. A notable case is James Ferguson's study of Lesotho, a country that has historically served primarily as a labor reserve for its immensely bigger neighbor, South Africa, and whose economy only makes sense in the context of this basic fact. Its economy is strikingly different from that of Sudan, but World Bank analyses of Lesotho construct a similar picture of a country demanding a comparable dose of "development." It will scarcely come as a surprise to find that Bank-funded rural development projects do not have a good record of success—at least according to their stated aims and objectives.

Rather than simply rebutting the World Bank's claims, Ferguson (1990) asks why they are made and so consistently repeated. He concludes that these strikingly ahistorical analyses have served the Bank's own institutional purpose—justifying itself and its programs—while also assisting the common aim of successive governments, namely extending bureaucratic control over rural areas. Development projects may "fail" according to the social and economic criteria contained in their justificatory documents, but despite this they "succeed" both for the development industry and the bureaucratic state. Adapting Foucault, they extend the "developmental mode of power" and its associated apparatus.

Development institutions come in many guises. Each has its own particular interests and identifiable logic. The population and family-planning agencies, for example, locate a crisis of population almost everywhere they cast their institutional gaze. Environmental agencies are comparable. The food aid business is a classic example of a solution searching for problems.

There is also a "humanitarian mode of power." The "humanitarian international"—the cosmopolitan elite of relief workers in the United Nations and NGOs, their donors in government aid departments, attendant journalists, consultants, academics, peace and reconciliation specialists, and the like—also has its internal culture and logic. It too justifies itself. Its fund-raising has its own genre. The "famine story," whether told by a television journalist or an NGO commercial, is instantly recognizable. It has a similar symbolic structure to a fairy-tale, with a victim (usually a black child), a villain (the weather, a frightening warlord, a complacent bureaucrat) and a savior (a white aid worker equipped with Western technology and traditional Judeo-Christian compassion). The bureaucratic functioning of the relief industry has its own rules: needs assessments, statistics for populations "in need" and "malnourished" (their apparent precision belying the extraordinarily uncertain statistical methods used in their generation), concern with access and logistics, monitoring and finally program evaluations (rarely thorough, even more rarely taken note of).

Important subtraditions in the humanitarian international can be identified. Anthropologists are only recently beginning to subject these to study: Jonathan Benthall's *Disasters, Relief, and the Media* (1994) is an auspicious beginning. At the risk of peddling caricatures, we can identify several different institutional cultures. The United Nations' specialized agencies, with their formal bureaucratic structures and internecine struggles for prestige, warrant a monograph of their own. The International Committee of the Red Cross has a unique culture, a mix of Geneva haute bourgeois Protestant philanthropy, diplomatic secretiveness, and a readiness to allow a trusted delegate to take almost any initiative. British and secular American relief agencies have a tradition of practical empiricism. The group that Benthall dubs the "French doctors" have their own ideal of "humanitarianism," in which symbolic action to exemplify their principle of "sans-frontierism" plays a leading role. Among religious-based organizations there is the hands-off "partnership" of the north European Protestant agencies, various brands of Christian zealots, and the emerging Islamic humanitarianism in both its "Jihadist" and more tolerant versions. The latter, with its idiom of rights and obligations, may prove an interesting challenge to the Western emphasis on charity, pity, and "neediness."

Taking the aid industry as a whole, ever more elaborate language codes are also developing, with specific dialects for each different branch. These serve the familiar purpose of creating "citadels of expertise" that are impenetrable to the layperson, unless he goes through a prolonged apprenticeship. Aid workers have sometimes casually compared their institutions to churches (especially missionary societies): one of the parallels is the demand that ordinands learn arcane language codes and master essentially theological concepts. These specialized codes are essential for allowing aid practitioners to communicate with one another, establish common definitions of the situations in which they find themselves, and write proposals to get money from their governmental funders. They justify the existence of the aid profession and create barriers to the entry of new organizations into the club.

AID: TOWARD AN ANTHROPOLOGICAL EVALUATION

Anthropology can contribute to the practical alleviation of poverty and famine. It can examine the internal logic of the aid apparatus—and perhaps help it become more effective. But what of the empirical benefit or otherwise of the aid encounter? Can social anthropology pass any judgment, however preliminary, on whether aid is a worthwhile enterprise? Any conclusions must of course be case-specific and tentative, so let us focus on Sudan.

What of the interaction between the contrasting worlds of rural Sudan and the cosmopolitan aid industry? Returning to Tvedt (1998), in Torit (dubbed "Little Norway" by aid workers) some of the myriad possibilities for unintended consequences can be drawn out by a preliminary anthropological analysis. Our focus is not on roads and health posts built, or farm incomes increased, or rural women trained in bookkeeping, but on wider questions of social and political change. Power relations—an issue markedly absent from conventional evaluations of aid programs—will be a central concern. In South Sudan in the 1970s, the local administration was virtually bankrupt, and over time it is unsurprising that many governmental functions and attributes came to be transferred to the aid industry. Tvedt's study—along with others—shows that there was a reorientation of legitimacy away from government toward aid agencies, and the redirection of governmental accountability from constituents to external funders.

The relief agencies' ethics of supplying immediate human need and thinking about the political ramifications afterward also contributed to this trend, especially after the descent into civil war in the 1980s. Many soldiers (on both sides) have been fed by international humanitarian relief, and much of the current government's so-called Comprehensive Call—social engineering meets colonial-style pacification—has been premised on the availability of relief food and the gullibility of some of the aid practitioners.

The aid apparatus, operating in planned settlements (whether "peace camps," irrigation schemes, or resettlement sites) tends to produce new forms of social organization and political authority. The extension of bureaucratic power, especially when its logic is overtly philanthropic, may weaken or dismantle former hierarchies and create the conditions for the emergence of new forms of political mobilization. The SPLA's militarist centralism emerged in its strongest form in refugee camps which formed its bases in its early years. Islamic extremists have found that rural populations in planned settlements are the easiest to mobilize. The draconian urban replanning of Khartoum, involving the forced removal of hundreds of thousands of squatters (chiefly southerners) to new "peace cities" at a distance from the capital, is also prompting new forms of sociopolitical organization. (But contrary to the government's expectations, Christian revivalism has played a leading role in these communities.)

At a different level, the IMF's erroneous assumptions about the functioning of the Sudanese economy contributed to disastrous policy errors that not only squeezed the national economy but left successive governments with virtually no leeway for any socially benign policies. The imposition of austerity measures, insisted upon by doctrinaire IMF economists, contributed to both the 1985 and 1989 coups d'etat. At all levels, the implications of the loss of legitimacy for the government were disturbing. Anthropological analysis can make a powerful argument that one of the contributory factors in the decline of Sudan to a state of famine and war has been the aid encounter.

Can relief and development play a more constructive role in the future? Can the specific material benefits delivered by aid agencies be matched by a genuine "empowerment" of the Sudanese people? There is a challenge to social anthropologists, both to address this question and to contribute to creating more democratic forms of relief and development.

Social anthropology is increasingly important to the transnational enterprises of relief and development. To the extent that relief and development are concerned with assisting poor and vulnerable communities, especially at the grass roots, the anthropological approach has proved to be invaluable.

Relief and development work is an important niche for trained social anthropologists. But much of the most academically interesting and practically valuable work has come from people who are not professional anthropologists at all—administrators, economists, development and relief workers, both local and foreign. Anthropological method and outlook in skilled amateurs is just as important as the presence of trained anthropologists in aid institutions.

Anthropology's contribution will continue. Its foundations in empirical fieldwork, open-mindedness, and readiness to embrace heterodox method, along with its responsiveness to the demands and insights of its subjects, repeatedly prove its relevance.

Meanwhile, the enduring contradictions of the anthropologist's position in relief and development should continue to provide a creative spark for the study of the "humanitarian international" and the transnational development industries themselves. Institutions as powerful as these, operating transculturally, must never escape the anthropologist's critical gaze.

REFERENCES AND SUGGESTIONS FOR FURTHER READING

African Rights. 1997. *Food and Power in Sudan: A Critique of Humanitarianism*. London: African Rights. [Analysis of the politics of aid in Sudan, including a rare analysis of Islamic humanitarianism in theory and practice.]

Benthall, Jonathan. 1994. *Disasters, Relief, and the Media*. London: I. B. Tauris. [Analysis of the internal culture of the humanitarian industry and its relationship with the media.]

Brokensha, D. W.; D. M. Warren; and O. Werner, eds. 1980. *Indigenous Knowledge Systems and Development*. Lanham, MD: University Press of America. [The key text for the "indigenous technical knowledge" business.]

Chambers, Robert. 1997. *Whose Reality Counts? Putting the First Last*. London: Intermediate Technology Publications. [Wide-ranging and eclectic synthesis of approaches to development; radical in both methods and political orientation.]

Collins, Joseph, and Bill Rau. 2000. *AIDS in the Context of Development.*, Geneva: UN Research Institute for Social Development. [A rare synopsis of the HIV/AIDS pandemic, and responses to it, in a political and social context.]

de Waal, Alex. *Famine That Kills: Darfur, Sudan, 1984–1985*. 1989. Oxford: Clarendon Press. [Analysis of famine coping strategies and mortality in the Sudanese famine.]

———. 1997. *Famine Crimes: Politics and the Disaster Relief Industry in Africa*. London: James Currey. [Analysis of the politics of creating and preventing famine, focusing on both national and international interventions, and critical of many of the latter.]

Escobar, Arturo. 1995. *Encountering Development: The Making and Unmaking of the Third*

World. Princeton, NJ: Princeton University Press. [Theoretical deconstruction of how the aid industry plays its role within north-south economic and political relations.]

Edwards, Michael, and David Hulme. 1995. *Non-Governmental Organizations and Accountability: Beyond the Magic Bullet*. London: Earthscan. [Critical analysis of the roles of NGOs from an insider perspective.]

Ferguson, James. 1990. *The Anti-Politics Machine: "Development," Depoliticisation, and Bureaucratic Power in Lesotho*. Cambridge: Cambridge University Press. [Classic analysis of how aid bureaucracies can "succeed" in their own terms while failing to deliver any material benefits to their supposed "beneficiaries."]

Hobart, Mark, ed. 1993. *An Anthropological Critique of Development: The Growth of Ignorance*. London: Routledge. [A highly stimulating and wide-ranging collection of essays, analyzing the aid industry and its impacts.]

Howell, Paul; Michael Lock; and Steven Cobb, eds. 1998. *The Jonglei Canal: Impact and Opportunity*. Cambridge: Cambridge University Press. [A classic of social and environmental analysis applied in the service of development.]

Keen, David. 1994. *The Benefits of Famine: A Political Economy of Famine and Relief in Southwestern Sudan, 1983–1989*. Princeton NJ: Princeton University Press. [How national and international policies can "succeed," but famine can be created and not relieved.]

James, Wendy. 1990. "Kings, Commoners, and the Ethnographic Imagination in Sudan and Ethiopia." In *Localizing Strategies: Regional Traditions of Ethnographic Writing*, ed. R. Fardon. Edinburgh: Scottish Academic Press. [The historical roles of anthropologists in relation to the political authorities in Sudan and Ethiopia.]

Leach, Melissa, and Robin Mearns. 1996. *The Lie of the Land: Challenging Received Wisdom on the African Environment*. London: James Currey. [Anthropologists and historians critically reanalyze orthodoxies about environmental decay in Africa.]

Lewis, I. M. "Anthropologists for Sale?" 1995. In *The Future of Anthropology: Its Relevance to the Contemporary World*, ed. Akbar Ahmed and Cris Shore. London: Athlone. [Anthropology in the service of development planning: an apologia.]

Mair, Lucy. 1984. *Anthropology and Development*. London: Macmillan. [Now somewhat outdated; nonetheless, an excellent overview of anthropologists' roles in the development industry.]

Malkki, Liisa. 1995. *Purity and Exile: Violence, Memory, and National Cosmology among Hutu Refugees in Tanzania*. Chicago: University of Chicago Press. [Is Hutu extremism in Burundi one of the unintended consequences of ambitious but misguided social planning by refugee development agencies?]

MacGaffey, Janet. 1991. *The Real Economy of Zaire: The Contribution of Smuggling and Other Unofficial Activities to National Wealth*. London: James Currey. [How anthropological analysis can turn economic orthodoxy on its head: an early example.]

MacGaffey, Janet, and Remy Bazenguissa-Ganga. 2000. *Congo-Paris: Transnational Traders on the Margins of the Law*. Oxford: James Currey. [A late example of the above, focusing on entrepreneurism in the Congolese diaspora in Europe.]

Moorhead, Caroline. 1998. *Dunant's Dream: War, Switzerland, and the History of the Red*

Cross. London: HarperCollins. [Authoritative but critical history of the International Committee of the Red Cross.]

Tvedt, Terje. 1998. *Angels of Mercy or Development Diplomats? NGOs and Foreign Aid.* Oxford: James Currey. [One of the most incisive analyses of the difficulties inherent in the aid industry, focusing on NGOs, particularly strong on Sudan.]

14

The Refugee: A Discourse on Displacement

E. VALENTINE DANIEL

"The world is awash with refugees." "Waves of refugees arrive in Europe." "Refugee stream swells into the millions." "First a trickle, then a flood." "Tens of thousands seek asylum." "The camps overflow with refugees." Such are the typical media headlines in Europe and America. Minimally, it appears that embedded in such phrases, the word *refugee* itself does not swell with a sense of warmth, safety, succor, or welcome but seethes with menace and foreboding. It is also clear that its connotations far exceed its denotation in significance. My interest in this essay is, however, not limited to the denotation and connotations of the word *refugee* but extends to the discursive field within which *refugee* as a phenomenon is embedded and the practices it entails. I would like to raise and, to the extent possible, explore a set of related questions: What does *refugee* represent in official and public discourse? What are some of the other related words, institutions, practices, prejudices, assumptions, and histories that together constitute a field of meaning in which the representation of *refugee* is *real*-ized? And finally, if we take anthropology as a an exercise in critical inquiry, what ought to be its relationship to such a representation?

THE REFUGEE: FROM RELIGION TO RACE

Ari Zolberg, an eminent political scientist, traces the origin of one of the persisting meanings of *refugee* to 1573, when its French antecedent, *refugie*, was employed to describe foreigners (they happened to be Calvinists) who fled into France from the persecution of the Spanish rulers of the Low Countries. A century later, the word was adopted from French into English when the Calvinist Huguenots, in their turn persecuted by Louis XIV, fled to England. Hence, Zolberg's definition: Refugees are persons whose presence abroad is attributable to a well-founded fear of violence against them in their own country because of membership in a certain group—however defined—and who can only be assisted in a country other than their own. No one is a refugee in the full sense of that term without recognition: the recognition by another country's political authorities that the person in question is deserving of asylum and refuge. If this much about a refugee has remained the same, there is much that has changed.

That which was shrouded by the cloak of religion in the sixteenth and seventeenth centuries became more explicitly political by the late eighteenth century. The revolutions of the century—the French and the American—created refugees marked more by their political ideology than by their religious beliefs and practices. With the rise of scientific racism in the nineteenth century and the establishment of colonialism as one of the most envied forms of domination, the stage was set for the racialized refugee of the first half of the twentieth century and the ethnicized refugee of the late twentieth century. This is not to say that religious identities have not played a role in the formation of refugees—consider the religion-based partition of India and Pakistan in 1947 that generated fourteen million refugees. And it would be absurd to claim that the part played by explicit political ideology in the production of refugees diminished in the twentieth century—consider the two Russian revolutions of 1905 and 1919 and the Chinese revolution of 1949. The political was and is ubiquitous. But racism (most grotesquely expressed in the holocausts during World War II) and its more recent transformation, ethnicism (to wit: in the Balkans, Rwanda, Ethiopia/Eritrea, the Sudan, Sri Lanka, and Palestine), has been the distinctive feature in the formation of refugees in the twentieth century. Even where religion, language, or politics constitute the effective prejudices (for example, between the Bosnian Muslims and the Orthodox Serbs or the Tamil-speaking Hindus and the Sinhala-speaking Buddhists of Sri Lanka), and physiognomic differences are hard to find, racial markers are imagined, given paramount significance, and then integrated into the other differences so effectively as to constitute them. During the Kosovo crisis, an American "expert" on National Public Radio attempted to distinguish for the listener the swarthier Kosovars from the fairer-skinned Serbs, while television footage all the while kept showing a goodly number of blonde and blue-eyed, anything-but-swarthy Kosovars. So powerful, indeed, is the need to racialize difference.

Anthropology's own entry into "refugee studies" is—relative to its sister social sciences of sociology, political science, and economics—recent. In the division of labor in the academy, anthropology has been seen as the study of the radical other, who in the racialized scheme of things appears to always inhabit the form of the nonwhite. It is no accident then that anthropological interest and assistance was not summoned during the inflow of refugees from Europe after World War II, but entered the picture with a sense of purpose and appropriateness only after the Vietnam War, when Southeast Asian refugees started seeking asylum in Europe and the United States. The major event that inaugurated refugee studies as a bona fide interest of anthropology was the establishment of the Refugee Studies Programme at Oxford University in 1982. Sadly, for the most part, in these early years, anthropologists played the role of the expert state functionary of the racialized other, serving as cultural and linguistic mediator to the medical, legal, and social institutions of the host country. Following the end of the Vietnam War, the fear in parts of America of an influx of refugees from Asia and of "illegal immigrants" crossing the Mexican border was expressed as fear of "the browning of America." Among the "illegal immigrants" were a large number of "unrecognized" refugees fleeing from the violence of U.S.-supported despotic regimes of Central and South America.

The anxieties surrounding the influx of refugees in Western Europe was even more marked (figure 1). Germany, because of its wartime history and postwar spirit of atonement, instituted the most liberal of official policies towards refugees and asylum seekers. Writing of the 1980s and 1990s, the Germanicist Jeffrey Peck observes, however, that in Germany—where such matters are always finely delineated—racialized hierarchies proliferated. The anxiety regarding the "foreigner problem" appears to have ordered itself in the following hierarchy, ranked from the least to the most "problematic": (1) "Germans"—all citizens of the former GDR; (2) "almost German"—ethnic Germans from Poland, Rumania, and the Soviet Union; (3) "noble foreigners"—white Americans, French, English, Dutch, and Scandinavians; (4) Eastern European "Auslander"—primarily Poles; (5) "Auslander"—Turks, Roma, and Sinti, Indians, Pakistanis, and Sri Lankan Tamils; (6) Asian "Auslander"—Vietnamese in the former GDR. The overt definition of *refugee* may be a sanitized and juridico-politically correct one; in its covert counterpart, race is an inextricable component. Racist xenophobia directed at the refugee is no stranger in other Western European countries either; they just undergo different inflections.

The literary critic, Edward Said, and others have observed, that *refugee*, unlike *exile*, has no aestheticizing connotations, no "touches of solitude and spirituality." Whereas *exile* does not invoke an image of the racialized other, *refugee* almost invariably does. *Refugee* is also a bureaucratic, international-humanitarian term, which *exile* is not. The exile in his aestheticized aloneness poses no threat. He is exempted from discussions about immigrants in general, for it is hopefully believed that, unlike the immigrant, the exile forever hopes to and someday will return home. When issues regarding refugees become entangled with concerns

FIGURE 1 Demonstration of refugees and German citizens after the arson which destroyed a refugee hostel, killing five people. At first a few young Nazis were suspected. Later the police arrested a Lebanese man, a resident in the hostel; Luebeck, Germany. (Rob Huibers/Panos)

about immigration in general, "hydrophobic" metaphors—trickles, flows, streams, waves, and tides—yield to military and violent ones: *The Immigration Invasion, The Path to National Suicide: An Essay on Immigration and Multiculturalism, The Immigration Time Bomb, The New Ethnic Mobs,* or more delicately, *Peaceful Invasions.*

ALTERNATE HISTORIES OF THE DISPLACED

This history of *refugee,* the word and the phenomenon, is by and large a Western history. And because of the West's dominance since the sixteenth century, in the subsequent creation of nations, and in the founding of colonialism and neocolonialism—all three being major complicit forces in the production of refugees—this history has become assimilated into a generic world history. And most significantly, an integral part of this history is also the history of nations. Alternate histories of those displaced by violence can, of course, be written. One example comes from the Islamic world. The 5.5 million Afghanis who fled into Iran and Pakistan during the Soviet occupation are numbered among the world's refugees by the United Nations High Commissioner for Refugees. But the Afghani anthropologist Nazif Shaharani informs us that the term *refugee,* with its unique connotations bequeathed by Western history and civilization, becomes, in the Islamic worldview, a significant misnomer. The appropriate word, he asserts, is *mujahirin,* which

translates as "those who leave their homes in the cause of Allah, after suffering oppression." Unlike the Calvinists of the Low Countries (and later, France) who
brought material wealth and many skills which benefited the host countries, the
Afghani *mujahirin* had little more than their faith. And yet, one keen and well-in-
formed observer quoted by Shahrani states "that nowhere in the world have
refugees been received as well as Afghans in Pakistan." The word *mujahirin* has not
been assimilated into the history of the term *refugee* and therefore does not carry
the latter's menacing meanings. The refugees of the nineteenth and twentieth centuries are defined by the nation and, in its details, are unimaginable without it.

For instance, when the Tamil equivalent of the word *refugee* was sought to describe the inflow of refugees from Sri Lanka into South India (figure 2), there were
two contenders: *saranadaivor* and *ahathi*. The first comes from the Sanskrit word,
saranam, which means refuge and shelter, but it also refers to a place where one
truly belongs, and in this sense is one's true or ultimate home. But the latter meaning would conflict with the international meaning of the word *refugee*, with its uni-
versalized but uniquely Western genealogy, which refers to someone whose home
is elsewhere, in another nation, and who is therefore, by definition, in her displaced location, in her "receiving country," essentially a stranger (figure 3). Therefore, the modern and more appropriate choice was *ahathi* which, even if not a
perfect gloss, carried, among other connotations, the important one of victim-
hood, and thus served the master concept of the Latinate *refugee* far more faith-
fully than the Sanskrit-derived *saranadaivor*. Furthermore, by being a word not of
Sanskritic but of Dravidian origin, the choice of *ahathi* is also a gesture in favor of
Tamil subnationalism and against a superordinate Indian nationalism that privileges Hindi (a language of Sanskritic/Indo-Aryan origin) as the national language.
In this mini-contest for the *mot juste* we witness a far mightier drama of the genealogy of the refugee phenomenon being acted on a stage of history where the
forces of colonialism, racism, and (sub)nationalism converge.

For the anthropologist Liisa Malkki, not only might there be no continuity
between the word *refugee* and its equivalents in non-European languages and
cultures, but any continuity claimed, even for *refugee* in its European context, is
patently false. In a commendable essay (1995a) on refugees and exile, she proposes
that the refugee, as we understand such a person in the late twentieth century—as
a legal entity and problem of national and international scope—is a relatively recent social category, brought into being only at the end of World War II. Even
though it may be difficult to see no continuity whatsoever between populations
displaced by the fear of violence in previous ages and the years following World
War II, it is indeed immensely instructive to focus on the reconfiguration of
refugee after World War II and thereby appreciate its novelty.

FIGURE 2 Tamil returnees who have been refugees in India
since 1990 have emotional reunions with relatives and friends,
many of whom they have not seen for over five years; Pesalai
Open Relief Center, Mannar Island, Sri Lanka, March 1995.
(Howard J. Davies/Panos)

THE REFUGEE AS DISCOURSE

The postwar *refugee* is embedded in an encompassing discourse of attendant
terms, as well as various technologies of power, that did not exist before the world
was confronted with thirty million Europeans displaced by six years of war. Not
only did the ubiquitous refugee camp come to occupy the center of this new discursive field, but so did an entire class of specialists—doctors, therapists, bureaucrats, social workers, lawyers, reporters, photographers, and teams of various
other functionaries. In this field, a new thicket of an interconnected vocabulary
grew. A casually assembled sample of such a vocabulary includes words, acronyms
and phrases such as *asylee, asylum policy, the asylum question* (mainly in Germany),

FIGURE 3 A displaced fisherwoman from the island of Kayts
wanders through ruins in Jaffna's Old Town, Sri Lanka. (Martin
Adler/Panos)

non-refoulement—the right of refugees not to be returned to a country in which
they would suffer persecution—*repatriation, returnees, receiving country, country of
asylum, national boundaries, countries of origin,* the Cartegena Declaration, *statutory
refugee, a well-founded fear of being persecuted,* the 1951 Geneva Convention Relating to the Status of Refugees (GCRSR), the Refugee Relief Act of 1953, the
Refugee-Escapee Act of 1957, the 1967 Protocol Definition, UNHCR, *internally
displaced persons (IDP),* and *boat people.* It has also generated a series of contrasts
such as, economic refugee vs. political refugee, pull vs. push factors, a-status and
b-status asylum seekers, refugee versus exile, Auslander vs. Aussiedler, refugee
proper vs. internal-refugee (also IDP). The last dyad returns us to the role of the
nation-state in the formation, forms, and transformation of the refugee as a dis-

cursive fact; for without the construction of well-bounded sovereign nations, the distinction between an internal refugee and a refugee proper would be meaningless.

In order to understand refugee discourse, a few words must be said about discourse itself. A discourse is not to be taken as something purely verbal. A discourse includes signs in general: gestures (say of pity or contempt), structures (e.g., boundaries or shelters), material things (like passports and visas), silence (e.g., the silence of the media about the fact that the financial burden for refugees is disproportionately borne, not by the wealthy nations of Europe and North America, but by the poor nations of Asia and Africa), and, not least of all, ignorance (regarding such facts, for instance) itself. As signs, not only do they communicate messages, they create a reality "that comes without saying and goes without saying." Above all, a discourse determines who will speak for what, where, when, and to whom. In short, discourse creates the conditions of authority and truth. Witness, for example, the power vested in psychiatric social workers in refugee camps who determine, after a brief interview, whether a given asylum seeker qualifies for resettlement in one country or another, or merely deserves deportation. These functionaries, along with guards, the police, immigration officers, Immigration and Naturalization judges and lawyers, State Department and Home Office bureaucrats, congressmen, and parliamentarian policymakers, and scores of other constituents of the refugee discourse, through their practices, create the conditions that make possible the separation of truth from falsehood, the deserving from the undeserving, the criminal from the victim, and tens of other such distinctions.

THE INDIVIDUAL IN REFUGEE DISCOURSE

Who is a refugee? The question calls for a definition. To define is to draw a real or imaginary line around an entity, so as to bound it, and thereby prevent it from blending into some other entity. The ideal refugee as defined by the United Nations and the various member nation-states is, like these very same nation-states, imagined to be bounded and sovereign. In court hearings all over North America and Europe, the asylum seeker, in order to qualify for asylum, must prove that he or she, as a *(sovereign) individual*, has a well-founded fear of persecution. The semantic import of the word *in-dividual* (literally, that which cannot be divided) is mostly hidden. The assumption that all selves are by definition *in*dividual selves goes unquestioned. The myriad ways in which the covert meaning of *in*dividual causes overt confusion and misunderstandings may be witnessed in every court in Europe and North America where petitions for asylum seekers are adjudicated. The applications by many Third World refugees founder on the point of the individual applicant trying to prove that she has reason to fear persecution as an individual and not merely because her kinsman was tortured by the regime, or because his ethnic group or village had been threatened by a terrorist group. For instance, just being a Mayan in Guatemala, where the persecution of Mayan Indians in general is as ubiquitous as it is well documented, is not a sufficient cause for the granting of asylum to a Mayan Indian. The asylum seeker must show why she, personally and individually, has a warranted fear of persecution; even the fact that a close relative may have been killed by agents of the state may not be sufficient reason for granting her asylum.

At a more subtle level, take the case of a Tamil mother from Sri Lanka seeking asylum in Canada. Her only son, who was a refugee in Canada, dies and is cremated. Many years later, after her two daughters are grown, married and have sought and received refuge in Australia, this mother seeks asylum in Canada. Why? Because she wishes to live on the soil with which her son's ashes have combined and where when she dies she wishes her own ashes to become part of the same soil. Attempts by attorneys to persuade her to make her case on other, more "acceptable" grounds (e.g., she was a witness to her husband's murder by the armed forces; that she was a potential witness against them in a future investigation; therefore, she had reason to fear that she might be killed) failed. What was culturally "true" to her was the sense of self that did not end at the boundary of the skin but extended to a relationship with the soil—but no longer the soil of her land of birth but the soil in which her only male progeny was buried. This represents a *dividuated* sense of self rather than an *individuated* sense of self, and the cultural need to recover a deeply disequilibriated sense of self by rejoining a part of her that was lost.

A social scientist who has not worked outside the West may not appreciate the fact that the person who seeks asylum is first and foremost a human being quite apart from whether or not he is an *in*dividual, sovereign or otherwise. There are many ways of being human; being an individual is just one of them. The juridico-political definition of an individual is a product of Western modernity, arguably only as recent as the modern nation-state, and by no means universal. This is of no concern to the officials who determine the future of the refugee, nor is the unwarranted equation of personhood and individuality, an equation that might undermine some people's sense of what it is to be truly human. An anthropologist who has lived and studied in the society and culture from which an asylum seeker or refugee comes could help facilitate the needed appreciation of this fact, and point out the adverse consequences of failing to appreciate it. This is an instance of local knowledge being brought to bear on the dictates of translocal knowledge in a courtroom that is both local and translocal at the same time.

Even in the West, the juridico-political definition of a refugee—as bounded and sovereign—is undermined, in several ways, by the commonsense use and understanding of the term *refugee*. This commonsense usage has productively fuzzy boundaries. It does not tell you the difference between an asylum seeker and a refugee, or when a refugee ceases to be a refugee. Long after an asylum seeker is recognized as a refugee, granted her entitlements, and subsequently naturalized in a new country and home, it is not uncommon to hear references to that person as a "refugee." New York City is filled with an older generation of Jews who escaped the holocaust who sometimes refer to themselves and are referred to by others as refugees. This leaves the identity of a refugee much more open and tenuous than that contained by the definitions proffered by the United Nations and the legal status conferred by the nation-states of the world. It is the anthropologist's task to negotiate among these different understandings of *refugee* and not necessarily force all variations to fall into line with the politico-juridical definition of the term.

REFUGEEHOOD AS A CRISIS OF TRUST

Daniel and Knudsen (1996), minimizing the nation-state-generated distinction between an "internal refugee" and a proper refugee, argue that from its inception, the experience of a refugee puts trust on trial. The trust in question pertains to the state, its structure, and its functionaries. The moment the nation-state that is supposed to protect fails to do so, or even worse, colludes in inflicting suffering on a person in its care, the germ that constitutes a refugee is formed. In a profound sense then, one becomes a refugee even before fleeing the society in which one lives, and could continue to be a refugee even after one receives nominal asylum in a new place among a new people. Such an understanding of what constitutes a refugee may be too broad and too narrow at the same time, vis-à-vis the juridico-political definitions offered by such international organizations as the UN, and yet the mere kernel of its truth in a refugee's experience is incontrovertible. The loss of this trust in question is triggered by a radical and violent disjunction between a person's familiar way of being in the world and a new reality of sociopolitical circumstances that not only threaten this habitual way of *being in the world* but also force the affected person to *see* his world differently. To the extent that the various juridico-political definitions of *refugee* try to foreground flight from life-threatening circumstances as the qualifying feature of a refugee, then "life" can and must be understood in this wider sense of something being not only physical, but also cultural and even spiritual. It is only because life becomes significant in this wider sense that a sentiment as simple as trust becomes so crucial.

ANTHROPOLOGY'S PLACE IN REFUGEE STUDIES

Even so brief a sketch of the discursive range and practices that constitute the refugee phenomenon makes clear how vast the field is, how dense its microlegitimations, how many its misrecognitions and misunderstandings. What is, or might be, the place of anthropology in such a field? To borrow a phrase from the philosopher Ian Hacking, an anthropologist begins by observing "at the level of tiny local events," and then asks the little question that engages with multiple levels of the discursive field. For this is precisely what anthropologists do best. Such "local events" may be encountered in a Red Cross refugee camp in Sri Lanka, a drunken brawl in a half-way house in Denmark, an INS detention center in Seattle, a court hearing in London, a little church in the Netherlands, on an internet chat group discussing Kosovo, or a chance discussion among fellow travelers on a train. In fact, just such a chance discussion recently on Ethiopia served as a "local event" of significance to one of my students who, was led to ask herself: Why is it "news" to the average citizen of the West to learn that the poorest countries of the world in Africa and Asia bear the greatest burden of caring for refugees and not the rich countries of Europe and North America? Its newsworthiness is made possible by prejudices that are part and parcel of refugee discourse. Such prejudices (or prejudgments, in the etymologically strict sense), which lie mostly below the surface of awareness, are made up of acts and assumptions whose consequences, among other things, are to reinforce and reproduce the very prejudices that sustain them. It is at the level of local events that the discourse on refugees takes content and shape, and eventually determines what is counted as "true," "just," and "deserving." And anthropologists, by their training and their commitment to fieldwork, ought to be among the most qualified to analyze such local events for what they may betray. Not only do local events reveal global prejudices, but, to an anthropologist who is deeply steeped in the life of a community and is at ease with its language—in the widest sense—they also reveal local prejudices that are embedded in barely articulated sentiments. Thus, it is the anthropologist's task to understand, interpret, and convey to a wider world the full import of what a "life," in this full sense, means to those who are subject to the trauma of displacement and the collapse of trust. Such an understanding can only be acquired by a deeper-than-normal appreciation of a people's lived experiences, for which extensive and intensive fieldwork in a community is indispensable.

No sooner, however, do we invoke the notions of "community" and "field" than new questions are generated. For we can no longer—especially in refugee studies—take the meaning of community for granted; we cannot take it to be a community in stasis, fixed in time and place. A community of refugees is paradigmatic of a community in motion presenting the kind of field site and fieldwork that until recently did not fall within the scope of anthropology. Such a community expands and contracts, concentrates and dissipates, adjusts and adapts, all the while redefining itself demographically and culturally according to the times and places through which it moves. The anthropologist, as fieldworker, commentator, translator, and—if called upon to be one—advisor, cannot harbor any essentialized and static notions of community and culture but must be attuned to the shifts and shift accordingly, unremittingly questioning and reevaluating her ethnographic authority in light of this dynamic community and shifting field.

Over the last two decades, fieldwork and the accompanying claim to ethnographic authority on the part of the anthropologist have come under much criticism. Some of the criticism is justified, while some merely calls for throwing out the baby with the bath water. Were we to preserve the best of the conceivable consequences of fieldwork as the sine qua non of the discipline—even though the concept of "the field" in fieldwork itself has undergone major changes—then it will be noted that in no other human science, including journalism, can one find the importance given to the injunction to observe painstakingly, closely, sympathetically, critically, and repeatedly whenever possible—and to observe always in context. Add to this injunction the value given in anthropology to the full participation in the life of a community, and you have in a nutshell the distinctiveness of anthropological field research. For it is in the field that one has the possibility of witnessing the formation of the refugee in her nascent state, as it were.

READING THE FIELD

If one of the consequences of the critique of ethnographic authority has been to prod ethnographers into becoming more reflective about writing—regarding its authority, veracity, style, responsibility, and so on—then an accompanying, albeit unintended, consequence has been the cultivation of keener ways of reading. The primary reading material for the fieldworker/ethnographer is not literature in the conventional sense of that term but the text and texture of social and cultural contexts, called the field, in which she immerses herself just as a reader of a riveting novel might immerse herself in her book. Refugee discourse is such a text that merits immersion. But the text that the ethnographer reads—here, refugee discourse—is most productively read if it is read as what the philosopher Michel Foucault called "genealogy": a text that is gray, meticulous, patiently documentary, scribbles on a field of entangled and confused parchments, on documents that have been scratched over and recopied many times, a site wherein one encounters the union of erudite knowledge and local memories of historical struggles, dissentions, and disparities. The psychiatric social worker or the immigration judge looks for a coherent autobiographical narrative from the refugee. Deviations from this ideal are interpreted as contradictions and untruths and cause for denial of refuge. The life of a refugee, following the moment of the collapse of trust to which I have referred, is itself rarely a simple narrative that leads to one truth. It too is a genealogy: gray, scribbled over by a mess of memories and experiences, differently valued, variously arranged, and shaded over by a range of emotions that keep shifting like the sand beneath the tide. Genealogy—in the sense given to it by Foucault and Nietszche, from whom he derives and adapts the concept—cannot be diagrammed as a neat descent of ancestors and progeny as in a kinship diagram nor as a straightforward history of causes and effects. Rather, genealogy is more akin to the combined working out of genetics, with all its internal complexities— environment and pure chance. In genealogy, events are selectively remembered and forgotten, and interpretations selected out and selected in. And the agent that does the selecting is usually not the individual but culture and history.

Of course, refugee discourse can be read as a story in a novel just as a novel could be read genealogically. But that would be to "read" refugee discourse poorly. One of the "keener" ways of reading that I have referred to is to read against the grain of the text, and that is the only way to read genealogically. From poststructuralism—and deconstruction in literary study in particular—anthropologists may learn to read against the grain. But such lessons can only be learned and applied analogically. For the text that the fieldworker reads is not a text made up of written signs on parchment—though it may include that too—but a far wider range and variety of signs that are embodied in and surround human beings within their ordinary and extraordinary lives. In the instance being considered, reading against the grain of refugee discourse is to read the formations, forms, and transformations of the refugee, not as dispensed for us by the idea and the reality of the nation-state but as revealed to us in the tiny local events and sideshows of history—always remembering, of course, that to read against the grain is to be able to simultaneously read " along the grain." It is only through such a reading, for instance, that one discovers that many of the laws and statutes pertaining to refugees established and enforced by nation states and the United Nations are there more to serve the interests of states than those of human rights.

The call to "read" the field of refugee discourse against the grain even as one gets to know the prevailing writing along the grain, requires the anthropologist to understand the "context" of fieldwork somewhat differently than it has been understood over the greater part of the life of the discipline. Even as we recognize the power of fieldwork, which is a highly localized art, it cannot be practiced without the acknowledgment of the reality of a thoroughly globalized world. To acknowledge this reality is to realize that "context" is as much translocal as it is local, as much transpresent as it is present. For how can one understand a Kosovar refugee without knowing the history of empire and the history of World War II, the politics of the U.N. and the politics of Yugoslavia, the geography of the Balkans and the religion of the Serbs? The text is thick not only with words but with human suffering that defies words or is expressed in nonverbal signs that may range from a gesture to the organization of space or a composition of a piece of music. And the context in which the refugee is formed is shaped by the dialectic between the locally and the translocally shaped human experience.

DISPLACEMENT AND PRODUCTIVE HOMELESSNESS

A refugee is a displaced person, displaced by violence directed against her, violence for which she is not responsible. If a refugee is a displaced person, she is also decentered. Both displacement and decentering are spatial orientations relative to a place called "home." Home in the case of displacement connotes something physical whereas in the case of decentering it connotes something psychological, moral, and even spiritual. When refugees are repatriated, they may find "home," in both senses of the term, unavailable or missing. But even if a change of party, policy, or heart on the part of a government or the intervention of an international organization can remedy displacement, it is much harder for a refugee to recover her center, her home, in the moral sense. Once again, when the presence of both these senses in *refugee* is realized, the juridico-political definition is left wanting.

In a little under two decades, anthropology itself has undergone a certain measure of displacement and decentering. It has been forced to give up the comfort and conceit of working in a sequestered place among relatively sequestered peoples in a distinctly demarcated elsewhere called "the field." In short, it has had to give up the conceit of its own "centers" of expertise and in so doing undergo a certain decentering itself. Two main factors brought about this change. First, anthropologists came to realize that all peoples of the world have always been part of the global and never exclusively local. Second, as the century comes to a close, global flows—be they of peoples, goods, or information—have dramatically increased in volume and frequency. Most important, anthropologists have come to realize that the marginal—be they peoples, spaces, or processes of the world—that served as anthropology's center for almost a century are just as likely to be found in the interstices of the metropolitan centers of New York, London, Geneva, and Bangkok as in the non-Western(ized) elsewheres. The refugee is such a "marginal." The detention center where he or she may be held is an interstitial space where tiny local events tend to happen. It is a field where one can find the dialectic between the local and the translocal at work. It may serve as a context where an "instruction manual" of how to "read" a text or a life according to official dictates comes into contradiction with an alternate reading, a reading against the grain, offered by local voices and local experiences.

Even though at very different registers, the homelessness of the decentered anthropologist and the homelessness of the displaced and decentered refugee have helped to create what Max Weber called an elective affinity between the two and I hope the grounds for a better understanding of the refugee's plight and possibilities. The recognition of globalization, the translocation of "the field" and "community," the transformation of fieldwork, and the "discovery of the marginal in the center and the center in the margins" are some of the factors that have contributed to this productive homelessness in anthropology. Conversely, one could say that thanks to anthropology's emphatic entry into refugee studies, it has been able to make its homelessness productive. I would like to close this essay by pointing out two such productive effects. The first concerns time and space; the second concerns place.

Some anthropologists began their work among settled communities, witnessed their crises of trust under conditions of persecution and terror and their becoming internally displaced, and followed their escape and transient lives in refugee camps and eventually in the countries of resettlement. Some have pursued the study of the "homelessness" of those who came to the host country as adults, whose formative years were in the countries of their birth, and those who came as children and have grown up away from the countries of their birth. In conventional fieldwork, most anthropologists spend a year or two of intense fieldwork in a community, return home and write a monograph; in a few instances, they make one or two return visits to the same "field." In this new kind of field research, where the interest in a people persists over space, time, and generations, one finds an unprecedented depth of commitment to inquiry and a check on premature claims to expertise. Such a study does not seek to essentialize the refugee into a "thing" but persists in sketching out its perpetual transformation.

Anthropologists working among refugees have also found it necessary to do ethnographies of the state (for example, the study of the Immigration Naturalization Service or the Home Office) as a means to better understand refugee discourse and the "homelessness" of the refugee. This too is relatively new, a move to a new place of field research. More work in this last area has to be done by anthropologists; it cannot be left to its sister social scientists—the political scientists, economists, and sociologists—who have a much longer history of working nearer the centers of power and feel at home there. Being "at home," these social scientists are more disposed to read refugee discourse along the grain as scored over and over again by these centers of power, whereas the homeless anthropologist, one hopes, is likely to be disposed to read otherwise, and in so doing understand the dynamic experience of refugees and other forced migrants differently.

Finally, if the "homelessness" of the anthropologist can be productive, so can the "homelessness" of the refugee. In fact, to read the refugee only as victim is another instance of failing to read against the grain. Refugees are also creators of new worlds and new possibilities; they embody the "traumatic kernel" of a better world.

REFERENCES AND SUGGESTIONS FOR FURTHER READING

Appadurai, Arjun. 1992. "Global Ethnoscapes." In *Recapturing Anthropology: Working in the Present*, ed. Richard Fox, 191–210. Santa Fe, NM: School of American Research. [This is a fine introduction to the dynamics of globalization and ethnicity in the late twentieth century.]

Daniel, E. Valentine. 1984. *Fluid Signs: Being a Person the Tamil Way*. Berkeley: University of California Press.

———. 1997. *Charred Lullabies: Chapters in an Anthropography of Violence*. Princeton, NJ: Princeton University Press. [Especially relevant is the chapter, "Nation and Alienation," which is an account of Sri Lankan Tamil immigrants and asylum seekers in the United Kingdom and their ambivalent relationship to the idea of "nation."]

Daniel, E. Valentine, and John Chr. Knudsen, eds. 1996. *Mistrusting Refugees*. Los Angeles: University of California Press. [This collection of essays, written from a range of disciplinary perspectives, deals with the issue of trust in the lives of refugees from a range of countries. Especially pertinent to the present essay, in addition to the editors' introduction, are the chapters by Jeffrey M. Peck on Germany and its racist accommodation of refugees and immigrants; Michael J. Fischer on Iranian refugees in the United States and the creative ways in which they intersect with different diasporic flows; John Knudsen on Vietnamese refugees in Norway and the conflict between generations; Beatriz Manz on the state of the Guatemalan Mayan and the difficulties of fostering trust in a climate of fear where displacement seems endemic; Nazif Sharani's chapter on Afghani *mujahirin* ("refugees") in Pakistan; and Alexander Aleinikoff's analysis of refugee laws and their partiality towards statist interests over human rights.]

Foucault, Michel. 1971. "Nietszche, Genealogy, History." In *The Foucault Reader*, ed. Paul Rabinow, 76–100. New York: Pantheon.

Fuglerud, Oivind. 1999. *Life on the Outside: The Tamil Diaspora and Long Distance Nationalism*. London: Pluto Press, 1999. [A study by an anthropologist who also works for the Norwegian government in the department that handles the petition of asylum seekers. This is a fine example of an ethnography of the state.]

Hacking, Ian. 1986. "The Archaeology of Foucault." In *Foucault: A Critical Reader*, ed. David C. Hoy, 27–40. New York: Basil Blackwell.

Journal of Refugee Studies. Oxford, U.K.: Oxford University Press. [Published since 1982, this is an influential journal that helps institutionalize and consolidate "refugee studies" as a distinct discursive domain.]

Malkki, Liisa H. 1995a. "Refugees and Exile: From 'Refugee Studies' to the National Order of Things." In *Annual Review of Anthropology*, vol. 24, ed. William H. Durham, E. Valentine Daniel, and Bambi Schieffelin. Palo Alto, CA: Annual Reviews. [The best overall review essay on the anthropology of refugees to date. Her bibliography of 177 titles is exhaustive.]

———. 1995b. *Purity and Exile: Violence, Memory, and National Cosmology among Hutu Refugees in Tanzania.* Chicago: University of Chicago Press. [An analysis of the complex dynamics among colonialism, nationhood, and sovereignty in Africa.]

Reimers, David M. 1998. *Unwelcome Strangers: American Identity and the Turn against Immigration.* New York: Columbia University Press. [An incisive study of the current debates on immigration in America and the race factor. The author is a historian.]

Zolberg, Aritide R. 1989. "Who Is a Refugee?" In *Escape from Violence,* ed. Aristide R. Zolberg, Astri Suhrke, and Sergio Aguayo. New York: Oxford University Press. [A landmark book, and one of the best reviews of the field of refugee studies from a political science point of view.]

15.

Our Own Way:
On Anthropology and Intellectual Property

Nemo dat quod non habet
(No one gives what he does not have).
Roman legal phrase

A. DAVID NAPIER

ORDINARY COMMODITY, UNCOMMON ODDITY

I have come to believe that if history were recorded by the vanquished rather than by the victors, it would illuminate the real, rather than the theoretical, means to power; for it is the defeated who know best which of the opposing tactics were irresistible. —Maya Deren, *Divine Horsemen* (1953)

Not long ago, while attending a conference held in the former family home and vineyard of the great French physiologist Claude Bernard, I had a singularly moving experience. On my way to the second-floor seminar room of this remote and tranquil country home, I noticed in the estate's small museum a display case containing two quivers. Approaching the case, I thought it likely, given Bernard's famous interest in curare, that these were ethnographic artifacts, probably of Amazonian origin. Yet I was at great risk of missing that day's meetings when I read that one of the two contained the very curare arrows that had been given to Bernard and that, in turn, had aroused his curiosity (figure 1). Here, in other words, were the very things—the intellectual property of an Andean Indian whom we will *never* know—to which the modern discipline of anesthesiology and its great consequence (namely, the pharmacological amelioration of suffering) are indebted.

The year was 1844. The arrows and quiver had been collected from an unidentified Amazonian two years earlier by a man named Goudot. We know nothing of the individual who, by giving them, helped shape the field of anesthesiology. Every patient undergoing open-heart surgery is indebted to him. Indeed, what modern medicine might look like without this discovery is hard to imagine.[1]

But what is also remarkable about this exhibition is its empirical concreteness.

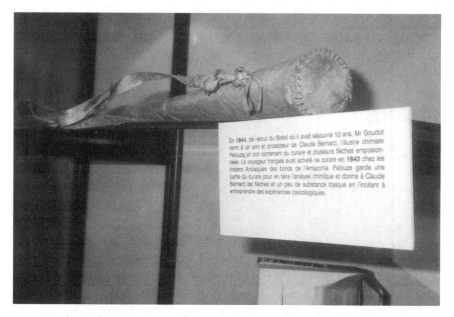

En 1844, de retour du Brésil où il avait séjourné 10 ans, Mr Goudot remit à un ami et protecteur de Claude Bernard, l'illustre chimiste Pelouze, un pot contenant du curare et plusieurs flèches empoisonnées. Le voyageur français avait acheté ce curare en 1842 chez les Indiens Andaquies des bords de l'Amazonie. Pelouze garda une partie du curare pour en faire l'analyse chimique et donna à Claude Bernard les flèches et un peu de substance toxique en l'incitant à entreprendre des expériences toxicologiques.

FIGURE I Amazonian curare quiver and arrows, Museé Claude Bernard, Villefranche, France. (Photo by author)

Were curare to be discovered today, its molecules would immediately be synthesized and patented (as those of curare eventually were), and the messy and still dangerous arrows discarded. But the quiver and arrows belong here in rural France; for here, both the history of modern medical practice *and* the abuses of indigenous intellectual property rights remain quite humbly and starkly embodied.

Today, more than one hundred and fifty years later, we are finally asking why the Amazonian who gave us curare and those who shared his knowledge of its use were never even thanked, let alone rewarded or reimbursed. Is simple human greed the reason, an unwillingness to share the profits of such a discovery? If so, are there ways of protecting the disadvantaged from the oppressive strangulation of multinational corporations and the individuals they hire to expropriate indigenous knowledge? If not, why have we neglected to compensate him? Is it because our notions of property are incommensurable with indigenous forms of knowledge? If so, why have his given way to ours? If not, why has he continued to lose out? Is it because we know his dilemma, but have no clear way of reciprocating? In such an instance, what can "reimbursement" mean? And how do we reimburse? Does our confusion about how to do this arise from the fact that the process of globalization homogenizes our views of what matters? If so, how can indigenous peoples resist the temptation to comply with these overwhelmingly seductive trends? If not, how may we learn to see what can be morally gained by an appreciation of what is unique about them?

These are major questions of our era—all of which come into focus when we imagine that Amazonian holding out his curare arrows to the waiting hand of one Mr. Goudot. How may the outcome of such gift-giving be bettered for the giver? And what can anthropology offer toward its betterment? To answer these last questions, we must first understand what we ourselves are doing when we commodify knowledge as property; for even the most basic anthropological assessment will reveal that our universal assumptions about the ownership of knowledge are themselves eclectic and culturally driven.

As Coombe (1998b) and Strathern (1999) have both clearly shown, facilitating some awareness of how culturally peculiar are our own property practices is *the* fundamental contribution that anthropology can make to any and every discussion of intellectual property rights; and, if one is tempted to think this a rather nonspecific goal, one need only recall just how late those politicians and environmentalists have been in attending to the issue of indigenous rights. Time after time the colonial records have remained completely silent on the mere existence of indigenous inhabitants within colonial territories; and any examination of the romantically motivated environmental literature will readily show how recent is the inclusion of indigenous peoples into the environmentalist's view of the landscape.

GLASS BEAD GAMES

Capital is a term for assets, whether in the form of money or otherwise, which are used for the purpose of making more money.—Cheryl Payer, *Lent and Lost*

Before one can buy and sell knowledge, one must first find some means of quantifying it; and to quantify it, one must first give it a name, establish a provenance, and at least suggest a range of experiences to which it might apply. Failure in any of these endeavors can undermine both a claim to own that knowledge and, in turn, its marketability.

In some indigenous systems of thought the buying and selling of ideas—even putting them out to bid—is not only a familiar activity, but also one that is morally acceptable. More often, however, this is not the case. Increasingly vocal indigenous groups have rejected the concept of intellectual property outright, claiming that it is based on ways of thinking that are unfamiliar and, indeed, immoral.[2] Musing, not long ago, over this problem of incommensurability—of what ideas are and how they may be exchanged—I came across a description of the first encounter between Rudyard Kipling and Mark Twain that seemed perfectly to encapsulate this predicament.

Kipling had journeyed from his new home in Brattleboro, Vermont, to Twain's home in Elmira, New York, to pay a visit to one of his favorite literary heroes. As Stuart Murray points out in his wonderful book on Kipling's Vermont, Twain later wrote of the encounter with Kipling: "I believe that he knew more than any person I had met before, and I knew that he knew that I knew less than any person he had met before. . . ." Twain told his wife: "Between us we cover all knowledge; he knows all that can be known, and I know the rest."

Like most else of which Twain made humor, there is a dark message here that makes the absurdity of his remarks the more tragic: we all know that there are modes of understanding that are not easily given over to the sort of schoolboy fact-knowing that Twain saw in Kipling's control of knowledge. Is "the rest" that Twain claimed as his own a kind of wisdom that comes of experience, or just the plain ignorance allowed for by his typically ironic turn of phrase? At one level, his comment is just funny. At another, it's an extraordinary insight that carries with it the implicit awareness of so much that cannot be known, in the sense of being spoken of or written about—let alone labeled, classified, or owned.

So what, one may say? If indigenous peoples have ways of knowing that escape the myopic views of hardened capitalists, it is unlikely that those same capitalists would ever be in a position to steal traditional knowledge. Things are, however, not so simple. The fact that a Balinese friend of mine allowed me to photograph a sacred piece of wood (on the grounds that the god would [as it did!] jamb my camera if it did not approve of photography), would not keep me or anyone else from seeking patent rights for a product derived from that species of tree were we to explore its medicinal properties. One does not, in other words, have to understand the indigenous view of some plant or animal to profit from its efficacious by-products. In fact, to benefit, one need not at all be aware of the broad levels of symbolic and metaphysical integration that are part of what gives that thing indigenous meaning. Nor need one see that those same levels of integration also bind that indigenous person to his or her landscape in ways that make commodifying the natural world both conceptually problematic and morally unacceptable.

It is these broader domains of knowing that philosophers refer to when they speak of embodied knowledge, and looking at how people embody and value what they know in different cultural settings is what social anthropology is all about—how, in particular, our beliefs about what moves the cosmos influence our daily practices and the cultural artifacts (the "knowledge") we create to give presence, and a sense of permanence, to those beliefs—how understanding what someone is trying to do is so deeply connected with what that individual believes holds the world together.

Here, then, we come to anthropology's first, and perhaps its central, contribution to the issue of how indigenous peoples might be honored for what they know: for the anthropologist, like the increasingly world-wise indigenous person, is positioned at the threshold that separates what is locally known and what exogenous information must be known for survival. Only here is it possible to establish the degree to which specific indigenous ways of knowing advantage or disadvantage individuals and groups as they attempt to make their way in a monolithically capitalistic world. Here, in other words, is where we must begin if we intend to gain some grasp of why indigenous peoples have not been better positioned to claim what would be, under more favorable circumstances, rightfully theirs.

So, thinking about such mysteries of human difference, I found myself having great sympathy for Twain in his encounter with the young and precocious British author, as, in the same vein, I could not help also feeling sympathy for so many indigenous groups that have never subscribed to the idea that knowledge can be commodified, or at least have never subscribed to that notion in a way that would allow them a modicum of success today. And what constitutes success, exactly?

This is an enormous problem, and one that is all too frequently left out of discussions of the procuring of intellectual property rights for indigenous peoples. Part of the reason for this lacuna is the top-down perspective of policymakers and even advocates who, themselves, are immersed in the legitimization of their own organizations. It doesn't take deep reflection to see that it is not only the World Intellectual Property Organization (WIPO) that is caught up in getting those who ignore it to accept its authority: any day at an international meeting at which vested political and economic interests are represented will reveal that the reason the emperor has no clothes is because he has given them to his brother who is attending in the guise of that country's Minister for the Environment.

When an international organization's own credibility hinges on accepting the sometimes bogus claims to sovereignty made by those so-called "leaders" who have bought into the international status quo, it is we who reify and legitimate those international systems by allowing them to negotiate and legislate morality at such a remove; for it is we who read newspapers, watch television, and waste countless hours discussing the private habits of those very politicians who have enslaved themselves to various forms of institutional life that are patently unhealthy. These activities increasingly occupy us, moreover, at the expense of the kind of daily interactions that might otherwise have sensitized us to what is really feasible when we set out to think up the world anew.

Whether or not an indigenous group is properly represented, then, is crucial; but determining this is complicated by our endorsement of international rules of entitlement that overlook the diverse, sometimes problematic, ways in which authority is recognized and secured. How, then, do indigenous peoples come to learn the nuanced, self-legitimizing language that is spoken at international congresses? How might they understand the degree to which those same international groups "are mutually recognizable, produce similar documents, speak a common language" (Strathern 1999, 197) and collectively reify their identities as experts?

While those who attend international conferences may actually be legitimating the transnational institutions they believe to be responsible for undermining indigenous autonomy, their mere presence also, if passively, endorses the process by which the diverse moral worlds of indigenous life are homogenized. Even anthropologists who find themselves defending indigenous rights must, like those who lead delegations and represent their countries in the highest capacities, kowtow to their so-called peers in other countries because they need those peers to legitimate what they themselves are doing. As I said to a deeply committed friend in one such setting, the problem with these meetings is that they have become so "immunological": now that diversity is fashionable, one can no longer distinguish the antigens from the antibodies. Clothing, alas, still goes a long way toward inducing certain behavioral responses, which is why a photograph of a loin-clothed indigenous delegation strikes us as so tragic. And there is no reason to think that certain indigenous values about property are any less different than what is or is not worn in the courtrooms where "rights" are negotiated.

But there are even more complex reasons for suppressing indigenous modes of thinking in intellectual property debate. If "tradition" is not understood monolithically, it becomes very difficult to identify the group one is meant to be defending.[3] The Sierra Club may be unwilling to subsidize Native Americans who have opted for life in a Phoenix plug-in trailer park over their relatives who are willing to remain at home on the candle-lit range.[4] But how, we may ask, might that Native American seeking out intellectual property rights avoid the double-bind in which any choice is a losing one? Stay at home and have one's resources taken, or get a degree at the local university and risk losing one's "traditional" epithet?

Alas, anthropologists might have been more help here than they have been; for it is both disgraceful and disheartening to find us quibbling over how best to assist the less fortunate in procuring their intellectual and cultural rights—especially those who, in calmer times, were the object of a more remote fascination. One almost hesitates to put to print a record of the sad battle that ensued for years between the American-based organization, Cultural Survival, which promoted the development and management of indigenous resources in the hope of promoting a fairer participation in the market economy, and its British-based parent, Survival International, which saw such activities as "at best a money-making gimmick and at worst a harmful idea" (Corry 1993, 2), the effects of which may be precisely the

opposite of those intended. Indeed, the very existence of a movement for traditional resource rights (Posey and Dutfield 1996) is a testament to the fact that
many indigenous groups now see in intellectual property and the commodification of indigenous knowledge "only the spread of Euro-American forms of property that will legitimate the extractors of resources and make it more not less difficult to promote indigenous claims" (Strathern 1999, 186).

To feed up a laundered notion of indigenous peoples as in themselves harmless
and by us harmed,[5] especially while some sponsored groups apply their profits to
the purchase of chain saws, aircraft, and even automatic weapons, might give one
pause when reflecting on "our" role as protector of "their" rights.[6] But indigenous
peoples who have witnessed their peers being shot by loggers and gauchos can
only have a diminished sense of the world's longevity and their participation in it.
Apocalyptic images throughout the history of Western art and literature have am-
ply illustrated the human tendency to seek immediate gratification in the face of
imminent annihilation. Ronald Reagan, too, believed that the sale of America's
natural resources was justified by the coming Armageddon (Vidal 1988); how,
then, can we blame indigenous peoples for exacting what they may perceive, in a
precarious moment, to be their just rewards? Who are we, anyway, to say what
constitutes "just remunerations"?

If, however, we reject a rarified description of indigenous life, what then? The
practice of using demeaning terms to justify the most appalling forms of oppression is widely documented (Leach 1964), and even hinting that members of another society might also suffer from their own tyrants—that is, to describe them as
we might one another—will do nothing if not erode the novelty that makes possible our fascination in the first place. Even more troubling, ought one instead
mount "a worldwide outcry demanding respect" (Corry 1993, 2) for the rights of
indigenous groups while knowing full well that seeking distant alignments between do-good organizations and oppressed "fourth-world" peoples[7] can actually
advance their victimization by local power brokers who, once advocates disappear
back to the city, punish locals the more severely for having spoken out (Stoll
1995)?

Let us remember that these culprits may well be those same "leaders" who appeared at last week's international meeting claiming that the indigenous problems
of the world were sorted out long ago by the vague language of the Biodiversity
Convention signed by 126 heads of state;[8] moreover, codes of professional behavior that have been independently developed, signed, and publicized[9] have had a
very limited impact on the "cultural cleansing" of indigenous peoples by their economically driven oppressors. If one cannot even get the United States government
to ratify the convention, imagine what the average gaucho might think were he to

read its recommendations during a siesta from tree cutting. In the vicious throes of survival and human greed, he now must contemplate some way to

> respect, preserve, and maintain knowledge, innovations, and practices of indigenous and lo-
> cal communities embodying traditional lifestyles relevant for the conservation and sustain-
> able use of biological diversity and promote their wider application with the approval and
> involvement of the holders of such knowledge, innovations, and practices and encourage
> their equitable sharing of the benefits arising from the utilization of such knowledge, inno-
> vations, and practices. (Article 8[j])

Well, yes, this is a start; but common sense tells us that the likelihood of such language having *any* impact on human behavior in the rainforest is, for the moment, exceedingly remote.

Show me a single indigenous group that has fairly benefited by multinational exploitation and has, in turn, successfully redistributed among its members the rewards of that arrangement, and I will be the first to say that this transcendence of the socioeconomic problems that plague the rest of the world might be swiftly remedied by a careful examination of those indigenous institutions that made this equitable transference of assets possible. The problem, in other words, with seducing indigenous groups to transform their natural resources into commodities is that the process itself often so disrupts their lifeways that even they themselves may be caught between the preservation of those lifeways and what is required to succeed in the arenas of international exchange. How, in short, can indigenous peoples both exist in "local communities embodying traditional lifestyles" and in international settings where they must compete with multinationals for the preservation of their intellectual property? Who, in fact, could manage at all under such expectations?

Without painting too depressing a picture here, I need to remind myself of what it was like to be a member of a committee convened to assess a draft of the first-ever intellectual property accord between a major corporation (The Body Shop) and an indigenous group (the Kayapó of Brazil). The very language of the document—and indeed its very title—got weaker and weaker with age: at first a contract seemed likely, but a contract is a legal document, and the Kayapó, being neither a corporation nor a politically autonomous body (Moustakas 1989; Brush 1993, 1996; Napier 1997), were in no position to enter into a binding contract that might be at odds with existing Brazilian policies and that, in any case, could almost certainly never be policed for them by their national government. To the contrary, where the presence of indigenous peoples on exploitable land provides de facto tenure and entitlement, "removal" of those individuals by homesteaders is all too often pursued clandestinely. Indeed, almost any kind of proposal for international agreement could similarly erode an already tenuous relationship between indigenous groups and their overlords; and those who feel that enough visibility in the media might guarantee the safety of indigenous peoples who demand their rights need only channel-surf now and again to find that yesterday's heartbreaking vignette has been replaced today by an infomercial on food-rendering products, or by a new episode of *The Simpsons*.

So, shelf-life is a real dilemma facing fourth-world peoples—one, furthermore, that goes broadly unrecognized: first, because we rarely question either the source or the longevity of our own enthusiasm for novelty; second, because a respect for another nation's autonomy (including its right to oppress its own minorities) seems always to remain the *sine qua non* of international relations.[10] And who were these representatives of The Body Shop anyway to meddle in the affairs of a sovereign country (Coombe 1998a)? So, instead, we were left, for that moment at least,[11] with the word *covenant*—a word of no legal consequence, but one which, so we hoped, might perhaps embarrass other, less considerate, corporations into feigning a concern for the rights of indigenous peoples.[12] In the meantime, as we congratulated ourselves for behaving morally, indigenous groups around the globe were being daily eradicated for their unwillingness to accept the world's view of them as helpless and needy. Indeed, those who actively resisted colonialism continued to be the most aggressively humiliated, and those who shunned international congresses were simply ignored.

So, what good is anthropology, then, in promoting the intellectual property rights of indigenous peoples? What do we learn here that is at all encouraging? What we learn, in the first instance, is why it *is* important to embarrass corporations[13]—why it is immediately necessary to call attention to those silenced indigenous voices by insisting on a covenant, if not a contract. But this is not all; what we also learn through attending to differences of culture is just how important it is now and then to leave behind the bright lights of those international meetings in favor of local indigenous initiatives that are better tuned to some specific moral world. For so often between that candle-lit dwelling and the big university there exists a small community college struggling to meet the needs and to better the lives of its indigenous poor. These settings, without doubt, can also be morally and politically complicated, but at least one's involvement at such a level may be adjusted on a daily basis in light of some real sense of what may be feasible. At least one is aware of the meaningfulness or meaninglessness of gestures made by all of those people in expensive suits who yearn to be seen at conferences, in hotels, over long dinners, behind the closed doors that protect them from the kind of real life that they so much fear living. For one thing is quite clear: left to their own devices, corporations will always seek to extract the greatest possible profits. So why should they inherently be at all capable of policing themselves either morally or ethically?

Take, for example, the following passage from the Harvard Medical School's 1990 "Policy on Conflicts of Interest and Commitment," which begins by claiming that moral scrutiny is essential, and ends by washing its hands in wishful thinking:

Public trust in the enterprise of academic medicine and the legitimacy of its powerful role in society require a constant amenability to public scrutiny. Consequently, it is necessary at this time to ensure the continued confidence of the public in the judgment of researchers and clinicians and in the dedication of academic research institutions to the integrity of the scientific enterprise. The strength of this assurance is based on two assumptions underlying the explicit rules and implicit norms governing faculty behavior at the Harvard Medical School: (1) that the vast majority of scientists are honest and conduct their research with the highest standards of integrity; and (2) that for the vast majority of cases, self-regulating structures and processes in science are effective.

Based on these assumptions . . . cooperation between industry and academic medicine is consistent with the highest traditions of the medical profession and can energize scientific creativity.

Indeed! One need only place this statement in the context of the Medical School's huge indirect cost surcharge for faculty grants (up to 88 percent) and the fact that industrial laboratories daily tempt away its researchers, to perceive the school's own potential conflict of interest and to imagine just how much suspension of judgment is actually required to sustain this particular cultural myth about the superabundance of human good will within a bastion of self-interest. Where so much of what people do depends upon the profits secured through ownership of intellectual property, it is no wonder that institutional review boards are so busy. This is in an esteemed setting of presumed integrity—imagine what it must be like in the gold-mining camps of the Amazon basin.

MINDING THE GAP

> *Sin is for one man to walk brutally over the life of another and to be quite oblivious of the wounds he has left behind.*[14]—Shusaku Endo, *Silence*

One need not make the topic of modes of thought the exclusive subject of this chapter to realize that one cannot make too much of the topic itself. In light of the complex turf that now constitutes what is and is not intellectual property, it is easy to see that an indigenous person is unlikely to negotiate successfully the sale of his rights to his own genes if he cannot manage to succeed in the market for Brazil nuts. For even among those who ought to know better—namely, among bench scientists who make their livelihoods patenting the molecules they have synthesized—what actually may and may not be patented is rarely understood with any precision. This, after all, is why so many tax dollars are spent on the salaries of patent and copyright attorneys and on the government examiners who award these privileges.

In order, in other words, to own something, one has to know what the ground rules are for establishing what the word *own* might mean. *Nemo dat quod non habet*, "No one gives what he does not have." While the simple Calvinist reading of this Roman legal phrase translates something like "You can't give what you don't have," the original Latin also makes possible a wonderful play on words: for the singular noun, *nemo*, allows us, as it did Jules Verne in *20,000 Leagues under the Sea*, to personify this "Mr. Nobody" (this Captain Nemo) who loses his identity in attempting to give what is not his, or to offer something that is actually nothing.[15] In Latin, in other words, there is deeply embedded in this saying the idea that it is both impossible to get "something for nothing" and wrong to think that one should: "A 'no one' tries to give what he doesn't have"—or, even more damning: "One who has acquired immunity (legally or by deceit) from giving a part of him/ herself in what is given, risks losing all means of reciprocating with his/her fellow citizens": "If you don't know how to give part of yourself in what you give, you are nothing, an outlaw (without the law)."

Though this final interpretation seems far-fetched to modern-day capitalists, it was very much understood in the context of the social obligations of Roman citizens—citizens for whom the *nexum*, the institutionalized exchange relation of two people, was predicated on a fundamental idea: namely, that the process of giving and giving back could not survive if the giver was not "somebody," somebody willing to stand behind what was offered by becoming a literal part of it. "Civilization" in other words, could survive much, but not trickery in trade, and certainly not the cynical elevation of tricky dealers to culture heroes. Odd, then, that we should find the Late Roman Empire an emblem of society's dissolution, especially since the social rights our corporations enjoy would have, in the absence of social responsibilities, seemed outrageous to those same classical forbears. Let's face it, the reduction of the fourth world to a permanent service sector is not going to be reversed by allowing a corporation to move abroad every time citizens ask it to improve its benefits program.

Were it only possible for those very Romans to view us as we glorify Wall Street cheaters who export themselves, their flight capital, and their corporate identities to wherever they may extract the greatest trade advantage, what sad paragons of nothingness our businessmen would appear; for they have not only absolved themselves of the responsibility of creating good will in society at large, but, more tellingly, they have absolved themselves of liability for what their corporations do. In fact, this is the explicit meaning of the British "Ltd."—a limiting of personal liability for a corporation which, itself, has become a person. In America such protection for executives had, by 1886, been made official when the Supreme Court ruled that those who ran corporations should be exempted from what the corporation did, and that the business itself should enjoy all of the rights granted to people—which, incidentally, is why a corporation can own intellectual property, whereas an individual cannot if the art is known to more than one person (i.e., is in the public domain). Corporations are, as it were, slaves of their executives who themselves remain largely protected when the drone misbehaves or goes bottom up. The corporation, then, is now a "person," while its chief executive officer becomes a "nobody."

So, how do traditional peoples compete in a game where the deck of cards remains this unfavorably stacked? Well, in short, they don't; for, ironically, the identification of a corporation as a legal person also means that it has personal rights that indigenous collectivities do not. Corporations are, for instance, permitted "to spend unlimited sums to defeat environmental initiatives, because campaign spending limitations have been ruled to interfere with their right to free speech" (Pope 1996, 14).[16] Because of their individuality, companies can, furthermore, possess rights to trade secrets that groups of traditional peoples cannot, because the ideas of the latter are in the public domain whenever those ideas can be shown to be known by more than one person. A corporation, in other words, has individual rights without social duties, a fact which has led it to be described as a person "without a soul" (Perkins 1999, 6).[17] And if one really persists in thinking of them as the socially responsible players they claim themselves to be in all of those public radio advertisements, a healthy discussion about the merits of NAFTA (North America Free Trade Agreement) with any citizen of an American "motor city" (e.g., Flint, Michigan) would provide a proper, if not an edifying, reality check.

Combine the corporate "person" with an increasingly flight-driven notion of capital,[18] and one can see that it might, were it not for the advocacy of certain anthropologists and social activists, be time for all indigenous peoples to throw up their hands and surrender. Where market success for indigenous groups rests both on alien definitions of knowledge and on competing against the "personhood" of a corporation, one can see how the issue of indigenous rights procurement begins to look, as we say, rather "academic." And remember that these conditions will continue to prevail regardless of what we do to address the practical matter of how rights might be concretely procured and regulated in the unlikely event that an indigenous person decides against all odds that he or she wishes to pursue them.

BODY SHOP OR CHOP SHOP?

So out of the ground the Lord God formed every beast of the field and every bird of the air, and brought them to the man to see what he would call them; and whatever the man called every living creature, that was its name.—Genesis 1:19

One of the primary dilemmas faced by indigenous peoples in the procurement of intellectual property rights is that so many of the precedents for the rights of indigenous peoples to their heritage stem from cultural property—and particularly from cultural return—cases in which entitlement to heritage is a function of its inalienable connection to a group of people who collectively value it. This issue has been addressed by a number of anthropologically oriented researchers who have called attention to the disjunction between cultural property (the ownership of which depends upon collective knowledge over generations) and intellectual property (the ownership of which depends upon showing that what one knows is new).[19] Groups' rights to knowledge (except, of course, for our personified corporations) run against the grain of what we mean by invention. In patent law, for instance, the main criteria (in America, at least) for awarding patent rights to an individual are that his or her invention be new, that it be useful, and that it be nonobvious. It is, of course, the last of these that is most problematic for indigenous groups, since shared knowledge (except, again, for corporations) is, as it were, always obvious to those who share it. Non-obviousness is, therefore, the trickiest criterion, but essentially it means that the idea would not be obvious to anyone normally skilled in the art in question.

By current patent law, then, the fact that more than one Guyanese native knows that the greenheart nut induces estrus in mammals (i.e., that it is a "natural" means of birth control) automatically places that knowledge in the public domain and, therefore, outside the reach of any potential owner. Of course, the individual who synthesizes a molecule of greenheart so that it may be marketed as a pharmaceutical product can and will succeed in controlling its manufacture and sale, which is why corporations are so well positioned to make huge profits on indigenous knowledge. Setting aside the enormously complex issue of how one translates "remunerations" into a local system of value,[20] this is also, of course, why no Amazonian is likely to receive a single penny for any of the successful open-heart surgeries that were the outcome of one Amazonian's having given his curare arrows to Mr. Goudot. It will do no good to take your native recipe, chants and all, to a court of law—unless, that is, you have adopted the sort of swan's-song lingo one regularly hears on National Processed Radio, or you have benefited enough from affirmative action training to enable you to synthesize your own molecules, to seek out patents for them, and to defend them vigorously against transgressors.

This last idea—beating capitalism at its own game—is a difficult, though not always an impossible, task. Where the political incorporation of an indigenous people becomes feasible, advantages may, in fact, be collectively realized. Many Native American groups, for instance, have (to the dismay of outsiders of many political persuasions) used their political autonomy to reap significant financial gain in markets excluded to others. Gambling is one example; gaining concessions for harvesting natural resources is another. Though the odds are greatly unfavorable, they are, sometimes at least, not insurmountable.

Yet even the most autonomous and powerful political bodies have difficulty competing with corporations that are not burdened by geographical allegiances. A multinational is just that—American, say, when it comes to needing military escorts to transport its oil; Liberian when it comes to avoiding expenses on the tankers that transport it. One could wonder how willing the Liberian army might be to protect those tankers, as, equally, one could wonder how the taxes otherwise levied on those tankers might be put to some use in America. The Gulf War, that is, made much more apparent than precision bombing.

Add to their ability to change national allegiance the fact that multinationals can shift capital with even greater ease, and one has no trouble imagining why indigenous groups repeatedly find themselves at the mercy of corporations. After all, if rich multinationals are able to bring politicians begging shamelessly on their knees, those corporations should have no difficulty subjugating the indigenous groups to whom those same politicians have denied basic human rights.

Against such odds, one favored response of indigenous peoples has been to remain silent about what they know; for while making lots of noise can call attention to their predicament, it does little to afford real assistance to those who have been disadvantaged, and may, in fact, attract more predators who hear from a distance the cries of the wounded. Though many indigenous groups, and their anthropologist friends, protest unfair trading practices, the grotesque profits made by big business often make the greed of industrial shareholders that much greater.[21] Simply demanding justice, therefore, will probably have little or no effect, and may actually work adversely. While one is unlikely to halt military fly-overs of indigenous lands because they shake the very bones of the spirits that reside in the clouds, an anthropologist can at least draw attention to the dilemma, and do so in a way that is artful enough, as Margaret Mead once put it, that any person with an ounce of good sense might plainly see its significance. A simple map of Australian Aboriginal dream strings (figure 2) or a totemic map of their Uluru (figure 3) will

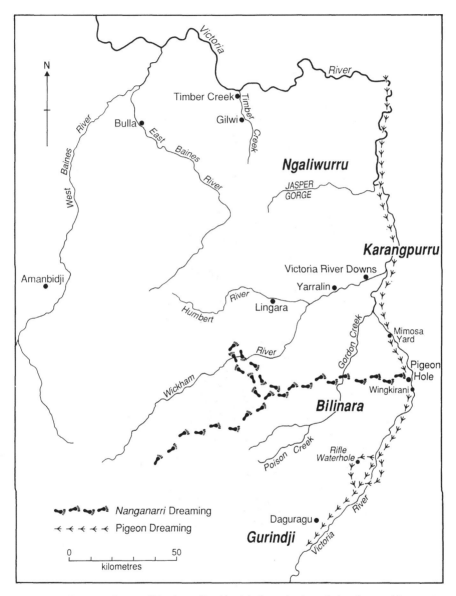

FIGURE 2 Dreaming "strings." For Australian Aboriginal peoples, boundaries of ownership are not legal lines that divide one autonomous space from another, but tracks that unite points of symbolic significance—time-honored webs of embodied relations that define both rights and obligations. (Rose 1992, 54; reprinted with the permission of Cambridge University Press)

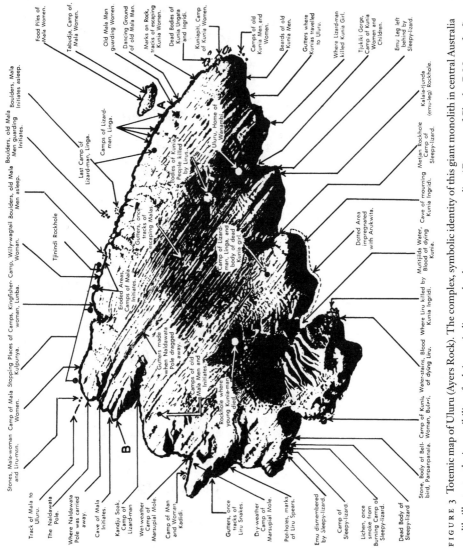

Track of Mala to Uluru.

The Naidawata Pole.

Where Naidawata Pole was carried away.

Cave of Mala Initiates.

Kandju Soak, Camp of Lizard-man.

Wet-weather Camp of Marsupial Mole.

Camp of Man and Woman Kadidi.

Gutters, once tracks of Liru Snakes.

Dry-weather Camp of Marsupial Mole.

Pot-holes, marks of Liru Spears.

Emu dismembered by Sleepy-lizard.

Camp of Sleepy-lizard.

Lichen, once smoke from Burning Camp of Sleepy-lizard.

Dead Body of Sleepy-lizard.

Stones, Mala-woman and Liru-man.

Camp of Mala Women.

Stopping Places of Camps, Kulpunya.

Kingfisher- Camp, woman, Lumba.

Willy-wagtail Boulders, old Mala Woman.

Boulders, old Mala Men guarding Initiates.

Boulders, Mala Men guarding Initiates asleep.

Food Piles of Mala Women.

Tabudja, Camp of. Mala Women.

Old Mala Men guarding Women.

Dancing Ground of old Mala Man.

Marks on Rock, tracks of escaping Kunia Women.

Dead Bodies of Kunia Ungata and Ingridi.

Kuniapiti, Camp of Kunia Women.

Camps of old Kunia Men and Women.

Beards of old Kunia Men.

Gutters where Kunias travelled to Uluru.

Where Lizard-man killed Kunia Girl.

Tjukki Gorge, Camp of Kunia Women and Children.

Emu Leg left behind by Sleepy-lizard.

Kalaia-Ijunda (emu-leg) Rockhole.

Last Camp of Lizard-man, Linga.

Camps of Lizard-man, Linga.

Tjininidi Rockhole.

Eroded Areas, Camps of Mala. Initiates.

Gutters, once tracks of escaping Malas.

Gutters made when Naidawata Pole dragged away.

Camps of old Mala Men and Initiates.

Rockhole where young Kuniaman died.

Gutters of Kunia People killed by Liru.

Bodies of Kunia People killed by Lirus.

Camp of Lizard-man, Linga, and body of dead Kunia girl.

Uluru, Home of Wanambi.

Meljan Rockhole Camp of Sleepy-lizard.

Dotted Area impregnated with Arukwita.

Multjilda Water, Blood of dying Kunia.

Cave of mourning Kunia Ingridi.

Stone, Body of Bell- bird, Panpanpanala.

Camp of Kunia. Woman, Bulrri.

Water-stains, Blood of dying Liru.

Where Liru killed by Kunia Ingridi.

FIGURE 3 Totemic map of Uluru (Ayers Rock). The complex, symbolic identity of this giant monolith in central Australia readily illustrates the impossibility of valuing an indigenous landscape as a commodity. (Courtesy of Charles P. Mountford)

do more to show how unamenable are indigenous notions of ownership to modern concepts of property than will any political rally or beautiful photograph (figure 4).[22] As Benthall points out in a recent editorial, "The game is for high stakes, but cool and trained attention to the rules and to ways of changing them is likely to be more effective than moral indignation" (1999, 3).

We will get more specific in a moment, but first one must be aware that copyright, in addition to secrecy, is a major means of protecting what one knows. The problem with copyright, and it is a problem that *all* self-promoting academics must be aware of, is that to copyright something does not protect the ideas about which one writes; it only protects the way those ideas are made public. How many ethnobotanists know, for instance, that publishing one's field notes as a book may actually strip the rights of the knowledge described from those whose knowledge they profess to honor? While one cannot plagiarize a document or a trademark, what one *tells* in one's writing is placed within the public domain by virtue of its copyright. I can, for instance, talk to you about the greenheart nut without acknowledging its main proponent, Conrad Gorinski, but I may not cite without quotations his manner of describing its use.[23]

Because of the potentially disastrous implications of making knowledge public, secrecy remains the time-honored way of protecting ideas—both in modern and in traditional societies. The problem, of course, with secrets is that they may be

FIGURE 4 The aesthetic beauty of Uluru suggests a wholly different meaning to non-Aboriginals who seek to preserve the "natural" landscape. (© John Mills/Survival)

stolen and their rights awarded to the thief herself. The other problem, especially for traditional peoples, is that secrets more often than not die with their owners. On the other hand, secrets may also be collectively shared and policed—which is why covens of shamans may so effectively be compared to modern-day patent-pooling cartels. Here, the advantages for those who have access to resources and to knowledge are obvious: new, patentable discoveries may, through license or through deceit, be built upon another's recent invention without actually having to understand or untie that earlier knowledge.[24] Furthermore, the same invention may be remade in a different way that allows for the procurement of a separate, new patent. This process—called "reverse engineering"—is what has made so many electronics manufacturers wealthy. Just take it apart and rebuild it in a different way. Let us not, therefore, forget the real consequences of simply having or not having access to recent knowledge, even to recent knowledge that resides within the public domain.

In England, for instance, a company named Oxford Analytica has done very well for itself by regularly convening academic experts from the university to offer up-to-date assessments and feasibility studies for corporations planning business ventures in the most favorable locations around the globe. This is, of course, business as usual for companies that (who?) need to know just how cheaply they are likely to build and operate that soft drinks plant in West Africa; but not being a player at this level means that Third World countries—despite their rich base of knowledge—become effectively reduced to an enslaved work force for the First World. While some countries have laws that are meant to prohibit the importation of goods made by slaves, we have few ways of knowing when goods that appear to be the outcome of fair labor practices are actually slave-produced and then laundered through front companies. The problem, moreover, will only escalate when buying into these front companies has boosted the American economy and made the rich so much richer. Though Oxford Analytica will now gladly sell its knowledge to so-called Third World Countries, the political reality persists: every policymaker who applauds NAFTA and the GATT (General Agreement on Tariffs and Trade) for creating financial health in the West should at some point in her political career be required to abandon the air-conditioned hotel and escorted fact-finding tour in favor of an honest day in the field. For I know of no anthropologist who would dare argue that a laborer in America or Europe ought to be capable of succeeding in markets where the ground rules in human dignity are negotiable.

One must remember here that market success in patentable knowledge functions no differently. Indeed, in some ways it is more viciously contested, since courts may overrule a person's right to his own patent if he fails to pursue his idea in a timely way. Not only has "free trade" now created more false-fronted shops than a Colorado mining town, but if you decide not to mine your own claim in a timely manner, someone else may be rewarded handsomely for extracting your very ideas from under you. Even assuming, in other words, that indigenous peoples learned all the ropes of international trade and patent law,[25] it would be unlikely in the extreme that they might recruit the necessary resources to halt the reverse engineering of a legitimately awarded patent.

And then there are the flagrant violators. We promote the myth that laws are enforceable across national boundaries,[26] but how many visitors to Taiwan built marvelous libraries out of bootlegged books? And how many Americans, knowingly or otherwise, buy "genuine GM" auto parts that have been illegally fabricated abroad? While trademark owners spend millions pursuing counterfeiters, what free trader, after all, will aggressively pursue such violators when windfall profits accrue to merchants who turn a blind eye to the origin of counterfeit goods? Violators even boast that "piracy is the best form of foreign aid." Is it any wonder that something as innocuous as a trade meeting in Seattle could lead to such anger and hostility? Open competition, we all know, never rewards reticence, except, of course, if you are dead sure that you own something that others cannot obtain. This, after all, is why Sotheby's has traditionally done so well on the upper East Side and in Mayfair.

UNEASY RESISTANCE
Taking [for the oppressed] means in nearly every case being taken.—Frantz Fanon

While the odds against indigenous peoples may have been more or less stacked since the days when Europeans first thought it profitable to trade with them (and fully cemented against them by the Age of Discovery), the record of indigenous resistance is equally as old, even if we tend to ignore it.

When Caesar entered the Lowlands for the second time in 53 B.C. to try bringing down the resistant tribes, he was not prepared to fail. Like American forces in Vietnam, the Roman militias, despite their ingenuity and sheer size, were unprepared for indigenous forms of resistance. Caesar demanded allegiance; yet what happened? His plan was as it had been elsewhere: bring tribal leaders together; impress them with the fact that they will cooperate; offer them a piece of the power if they do so; even offer to eliminate their local enemies. But in Gaul this did not happen: for when Caesar invited local leaders to a summit, some representatives *just didn't come.*[27]

Every time an indigenous person knowingly ignores the rhetoric of domination, she may indeed be exercising her freedom; for to liberate oneself from the oppressor one must ignore rather than resist. This is what social theorists mean by the term *hegemony*. And understanding hegemony as it works on the ground may be one of anthropology's greatest contributions to the intellectual property debate; for it doesn't take a fool to sense when one is being coerced, though many fools fail to appreciate the effects of their own coercion. This is a big claim, but it has its merits in the realm of truth; for, as we have seen, nostalgia about a romanticized native past repeatedly provides no real solution for indigenous groups because it requires an ossification of native identity that by definition disempowers indigenous peoples from adapting to ever-changing circumstances. Similarly, the righteous protests mentioned earlier may often produce effects opposite to those intended. These outcomes are a function of what Gramsci first meant by hegemony—the dynamic "combination of force and consent variously balancing one another, . . . an active and practical involvement of the hegemonized groups, quite unlike the static, totalizing and passive subordination implied by the dominant ideology concept" (quoted in Forgacs 1988, 423–24).

Because political commentators and journalists have widely taken up the word *hegemony* as a fanciful replacement for the word *domination*, even social theorists now fail to understand how hegemony functions. Few realize that in exercising this failure they too are actively participating in Gramsci's "hegemonizing" process, since equating the terms, without attributing any volition to the oppressed, actually cements the very idea that oppression is inevitable and that the oppressed will always be subject to oppression—hence, Deren's epigraph for the first section of this chapter.

Those who participate in contests or structures where status terms are recognized by both oppressor and oppressed, are not challenging hegemony; they are acknowledging it. The Hell's Angel who affiliates himself with a "congress" of gang members—including a president, a sergeant at arms, and various elected representatives, may be undermining what the white-collar crooks in Washington are up to—but the action also functions to acknowledge the power that these ruling crooks possess.

To ignore the call of a reciprocity that is, by nature, self-stigmatizing, is to be a nobody in the eyes of those who stigmatize. This is the most dangerous form of liminality; for what the nameless stand for is a breach of the sort of heroic and egotistical values that are otherwise everywhere to be seen in society at large. This is precisely why some indigenous peoples have called for a refusal to accept the terms laid out by Western governments (no matter how favorable), of the corporations that sponsor those governments (no matter how lucrative),[28] and even of the advocates who seek intellectual property protection for indigenous peoples (no matter how loudly those advocates claim to own the moral high ground).

Native Americans are probably best positioned (given their autonomy relative, say, to Amazonian tribals) to attempt this line of free thinking.[29] Indeed, since pursuing legal rights to knowledge one already owns "forces indigenous people to play the dominant society's game" (Greaves 1994, 6), some indigenous spokespersons call for an outright refusal to accept the economically driven terms of legal ownership that have been invented by capitalists for their own benefit. However, even at its best—that is, where freedom can mean the ecstatic pleasure of creative liberation—the tactic of denying the authority of an oppressor is very dangerous, particularly in an age of cultural homogenization in which the ability to respect real difference of viewpoint becomes about as rare as the desire of most Americans to learn a foreign language. For the extreme arrogance of thinking one can live without capitalism, the most ruthless forms of punishment are often exacted.[30]

The more political autonomy a group has, the more it can claim its own corporate rights, and the more it is empowered to ignore the status demands of social and political hegemony. When the Dalai Lama refuses to comply with an interview request from television personality Diane Sawyer, he does much more than make sure he still meets a group of anonymous people in Ohio to whom he had already committed himself that day. By ignoring requests from important people in favor of talking with commoners, he both transcends the bleak realities of the everyday and offers some hope to the disadvantaged that they too may find transcendence. What we see in such behavior is, therefore, complex: on the one hand, an expression that transcends the otherwise inevitable oppression of a punishing world; on the other, a creative realization of the joy and liberation to which successful transcendence gives rise.

This is why the freedom to create is actually more basic than a bill of rights, and why creativity can never itself be fully measured by any single set of intellectual property terms. This is, moreover, why many anthropologists feel that the first step to securing intellectual property rights for indigenous peoples is to secure their political autonomy. The problem is that Brazil is no more likely to offer such freedom to the Kayapó than is the United States to return to the State of Vermont its former status as an independent commonwealth.

AN HONEST DAY'S FIELDWORK

A woman generous with both her friendship and her ideas, she left the latter lying around like pencils, she said, in the hope they would be stolen.—William Mitchell (on the ideas of Margaret Mead)

Just a dozen or so years ago I set out to learn if certain medicinal plants that had been brought to my attention during research on other matters had either been previously studied or might be studied to good humanitarian effect. In writing this chapter, I therefore had an excuse to dig through old and fading files; my interest in so doing stemmed from a distinct impression I still carry around that I had failed in my effort to call attention to the potential medical value of what had been openly offered to me by "indigenous" friends. At the time, I naively believed that creating new and useful knowledge could only have a beneficial outcome.

Today I am very thankful for not having gone down that road (especially after I discovered that a university scientist I knew had been clandestinely mining my fieldsite), but reading over a typically disinterested response from a pharmaceutical company, I at least know now why it is a good idea not to throw away every old letter. Though ethnobotany is itself an old discipline—indeed, as ancient as the specialization of healing itself—one cannot make too much of just how recent is the surge of interest in the subject and in its related intellectual property concerns. The overinflated expectation that Merck, Sharpe & Dohme's molecular prospecting agreement with Costa Rica's National Institute of Biodiversity (InBio) will result in a true canvassing of the economic potential of that country's botanical resources (Sittenfeld and Gamez 1993) must be placed against the background of what I was then told: namely, that there was a time back in the 1950s—that is, before computer-based molecule building and testing—when companies had a go at canvassing the rainforest; but the results had been very disappointing.

Part of the reason for that disappointment, of course, was the fact that research then was no more ethnographically informed than were most of the World Bank's development projects in the Third World during the same era. The hideous concept of "cultural" (or "social") capital—an invention of management specialists that was meant to quantify and to corral local ways of behaving (i.e., indigenous habits) into economically productive forms of behavior—had yet to be thought up, and corporations were just as out of touch then with indigenous knowledge as they are today. Indeed, given the homogenizing effects of technology and of the English language on all of the earth's inhabitants, it is probably safe to say that the potential outcomes of what might be learned are actually far less today than they were in 1950. And despite all of the treaties and international conferences, it is probably also fair to say that even the most enthusiastic racists who now want to patent other peoples' genes so as to preserve (read "own") them will not equal what was learned by one man named Goudot who took a curious interest in the knowledge of a single Amazonian native.[31]

Against the idea of cultural capital, anthropology has offered the notion of "indigenous knowledge for development," or IK. While this concept will still raise the ire of those who believe that such intervening measures seek to make indigenous peoples into unsuccessful capitalists, at least the idea has enough of the ear of those who work in international development to indicate some need to understand the extraordinary diversity of indigenous ways of thinking (e.g., Sillitoe 1998). To date, the idea has been favorably received by a number of government and non-government organizations,[32] and it suggests at least that anthropology is being recognized as the only real mechanism for avoiding future disasters of insensitivity.

This is not just a boastful call for recognizing the importance of anthropology in intellectual property debate or, more important, for developing human respect and genuine cooperation among diverse peoples. Nor is it simply an attack on the culturally unadventuresome and methodologically sterile predispositions of bench science.[33] Corporations will continue to sign contracts with other corporations or governments rather than create bonds with unincorporated indigenes for reasons that we have already considered, and those same corporations will, if they are at all concerned with their images, refuse (at least publicly) to deal with vigilante ethnobotanists who see indigenous knowledge as the best thing since the California Gold Rush.

Politically correct acquaintances who think that they are supporting native peoples merely by buying stock in corporations that attempt to work with indigenous groups (e.g., the Body Shop, Ben and Jerry's Ice Cream, or Shaman Pharmaceuticals) should ask themselves whether or not their money wouldn't be better spent on a college-level course in political economy; for the shareholders in Shaman are also, if they one day find themselves in bankruptcy, equally capable of attacking their corporation for its failure to behave in financially responsible (read economically aggressive) ways.[34] What is more important still is that even the most altruistic relationship between a corporation founded by a venture capitalist (e.g., Shaman Pharmaceuticals) and an indigenous group will, as it becomes increasingly profitable, create havoc. Shaman's early losses made it, at first, an ideal focus for the watered-down sympathies of humanitarian capitalists, but the problem looks more complex when the USDA finally gets around to allowing a darling company its monopolies on plant- or animal-derived drugs that may (like Taxol) have a real impact on cancer or (like Salagen) reduce the negative side effects of cancer therapy. The staggering financial outcomes will, in other words, eventually be apparent without attending to how far they are from the conceptual framework of those Ecuadorian natives who gladly sold their oil concessions for just one tin roof on the old grass hut.

Even Shaman's 20 percent local contribution to indigenous peoples was apparently figured on their prospecting budget (Burton 1994, 1) rather than on future royalties. And to whom would they give the profits anyway? Certainly not directly to the shaman who offered them the indigenous knowledge, for he is (as this same favorable article politely acknowledges [ibid.]) feared for his deadly powers by his own neighbors; and his case is anything but anomalous.[35]

While Shaman commendably builds schools, purifies water, and promotes social welfare, such outcomes, we must remember, will only be as good as that, or any other, corporation's commitment to a local moral world whose very human rights are not otherwise, or only minimally, protected. Indeed, access to a working knowledge of what is locally feasible may not only allow for more realism among award-winning environmentalists who wear their badges so proudly down the stuffy hotel corridors of their international meetings, but facilitate a genuine capacity on the part of indigenous peoples to respond most appropriately to an inevitably changing world. Access to knowledge is critical, and certainly much more important than being patronized by me, by you, or by Shaman.

Though what anthropologists do may so often be imperfect, our discipline—as practiced by us or by indigenous people themselves—may, in the end, have the only monopoly on the translation of cultural categories of thought. And though translating categories, in itself, may strike us as an abstract and academic predilection, its real implications are everywhere to be seen when we get down to the basic business of not walking over one another's lives. Humble though working at ground level may appear to high-flying policymakers, that is where even those policymakers will contribute most.[36] As Posey says, the anthropological contribution toward indigenous control of indigenous knowledge will only be realized "when anthropologists become researchers for and consultants to indigenous peoples and traditional communities" (quoted in Sillitoe 1998, 242).

Anthropology's contribution, then, to the future of what intellectual property might mean—both for indigenous peoples and for transnationals—is critical: first, in demonstrating what sorts of initiatives may actually be feasible; second, in using knowledge of what is feasible to become a good advocate for indigenous peoples who have less access to all of those pompous international conventions; and third, in showing how advocacy must be situated in a dynamic notion of culture which allows for indigenous groups to be as much or as little like us as they themselves wish to be, and in which we wish more for them than that they be what we are not.

What indigenous peoples need to protect their intellectual property, then, is a better understanding of the merits of reciprocity on the part of those who have benefited from them—whether those beneficiaries be corporations that have synthesized indigenous therapies or anthropologists who have gained professionally by illuminating indigenous forms of knowledge. Since there is no way to reciprocate without reciprocating, a willingness to "marry in" is essential. One need only look at the difference between French and English attitudes toward indigenous peoples in colonial New England to see that what the English desperately lacked was any desire to live with, and to marry, those they preferred to enslave.

The schools built today on the international charity of Shaman Pharmaceuticals, or The Body Shop, or anyone else will, in other words, only be as successful as the quality of the intellectual property courses taught within them, and the commitment, intelligence, and compassion of those who teach those courses. This, then, is the main role of anthropology—to show how essential it is to live and love not only in places where the lights are not very bright, but in places where they, at least as yet, do not exist.

ACKNOWLEDGMENTS

I am grateful to the many individuals who patiently assisted me in formulating the arguments I present in this chapter. In particular, I would like to thank the following people for commenting on previous drafts: Jonathan Benthall, Margaret Donlon, Marc Garcelon, Francis Huxley, J. Thomas McCarthy, William Mitchell, Rodney Needham, Ghillean Prance, David Stoll, and Marilyn Strathern. Obviously, my thanking them for their help is not meant to reflect their wholesale endorsement of what I argue.

NOTES

1. "From extensive pharmacological studies of curare, Norman Bisset at King's College has found that curare carried in calabashes is typically made from species of *Strychnos* [Loganiaceae], whereas curare carried in bamboo tubes is made from *Chondrodendron* [Menispermaceae] or *Curarea* [Menispermaceae]. Unlike the African *Strophanthus* poisons, curare does not affect the heart but instead is a muscle relaxant that kills by paralyzing the muscles required to breathe. Tubocurarine, so named because it was isolated from curare carried in bamboo tubes, and toxiferene, isolated from curare carried in calabashes, have both become crucial anesthetic drugs for use in surgery; some surgeries, particularly open-heart surgery, would be impossible without these compounds or synthetically modified derivatives" (Balick and Cox 1996, 118–19).

2. See, for example, Posey 1994, 235; Native Americans have been especially supportive of this position. Richard Deertrack of Taos Pueblo is such an advocate (Greaves 1994, 6), as is Enrique Salmon, a Tarahumara Indian who runs the Baca Institute for Ethnobotany in Crestone, Colorado (personal discussion).

3. See, for example, Brown 1998, Conklin and Graham 1995; Kane 1993; Ramos 1987, 1991, 1994a.

4. One may get a taste of this dilemma in a brief and pointed editorial published some years ago in *The Village Voice* (Conason 1986). For a discussion, see Napier 1992.

5. Such a notion is expressed, for example, in the commercially sponsored and oddly romantic, *Millennium* television series; see Beidelman 1992.

6. As one would expect, the press has made a feast of Indian resistance and expressions of self-determination. See, for example, "The Savage" 1993. The Kayapó, because of their commercial connections, were among those most heavily criticized for their spending.

7. That is, peoples who have few if any rights that derive from the laws of the countries within the borders of which they may live.

8. This was the United Nations Conference on Environment and Development (U.N.C.E.D., or so-called "Earth Summit") held in Rio de Janeiro in June 1992, out of which came the Rio Declaration, the Convention on Biodiversity, and "Agenda 21," in particular, which concerns indigenous knowledge and sustainable development. For a discussion, see Posey 1994. See also Brown 1998 and references therein for a sense of the scope of this and other such declarations (e.g., the Julayinbul Statement on Indigenous Intellectual Property Rights [1993], the Mataatua Declaration [1993], and the Suva Declaration [1995]. For a summary of the involvement of the United Nations in the domain of indigenous rights, see Suagee 1994.

9. For a summary of these initiatives, see, for instance, Colchester 1994; Cunningham 1992; and Posey 1994.

10. This fact was made glaringly obvious by the recent riots in Seattle, Washington during a meeting of the World Trade Organization and by such actions as the Clinton administration's elimination of human rights as a criterion for most favored nation trading status for China.

11. For the later permutation of this document, see Posey 1994 (appendix A).

12. And, yes, alas, these were the same rain forest crunchers who had been applying their profits in ways that appeared alarmingly exploitative—especially to The Body Shop, which found itself in the uneasy position of having to defend activities it might otherwise have found objectionable.

13. To see what the most active monitoring organization advocates, log onto www.rafi.org.

14. For a discussion, see Napier 1986, 43.

15. A "man named Nemo," a Mr. No One, an embodied nothing.

16. "If we're going to grant standing to fictitious entities, we could make the law a more reliable protector of everyone's long-range interests by opening the courthouse doors to the salmon and the sequoia" (Pope 1996, 14).

17. See Roland Marchand's *Creating the Corporate Soul* (1998).

18. This shifting identity is most apparent in the recent debates over what the claim, "Made in America," actually is allowed to mean. Can, for instance, corporations that manufacture products abroad (e.g., shoes, car parts, electronics) and then assemble them locally actually claim to be making them at home?

19. Though I have written elsewhere about this problem (1994, 1997), thorough examination of this double-bind may be found, for example, in Moustakas (1989) and Strathern (1999).

20. On the complexities of so doing, see Napier (1997); see also any of the ethnographic films that focus on this problem (e.g., *N!ai*, or *Broken Rainbow*).

21. The catalyst for Benthall's editorial (1999) was an article in the *Times* that warned corporations against being sued by irate shareholders who felt that the companies they invested in had not moved aggressively enough in beating the competition.

22. Though a discussion of mnemonic systems and indigenous forms of mapping boundaries is beyond the scope of this chapter (see, e.g., Fairhead and Leach 1996), an examination of the magisterial work of Woodward and Lewis (1998), or Thrower's thought-provoking study (1999) will provide some intimation of the complexities of adjusting modern concepts of property ownership to traditional forms of controlling access to land. For fascinating accounts of Aboriginal systems, see, for example, Mowaljarlai and Malnic 1993, and Rose 1992. On the colonial mapping of aboriginal lands, see Ryan 1996.

23. The distinction between copyright and patent is more dramatic than one might at first suspect. In the early 1990s, for instance, Craig Venter, then a scientist at the National Institutes of Health, intended to use patents to control the rights to new genetic "tags" which he and his colleagues had been identifying "at the rate of 50 to 150 per day" (Hubbard and Wald 1997, 125): "Bernadine Healy, the director of the NIH, says that, although the sequence tags are now meaningless pieces of DNA, the NIH had to seek patents in order to be able to publish the sequences without them falling into the public domain. . . . Opponents, even within the biotechnology industry, say that, on the contrary, patenting at this stage is likely to limit both scientific and entrepreneurial interest" (ibid.). As Hubbard and Wald point out, the arguments are over the impact of copyright on the protection of ideas, not over issues of morality: "No one here is fighting for the purity of research, or insisting that scientists avoid commercial entanglements" (ibid.).

24. Can an American patent an ancient tree by-product (Neem) used in India to clean teeth, or the aquatic resources of a national park (Yellowstone) simply because no one has yet done so? No, not if it is a natural product; but let him or her name its efficacious molecules, and control over any by-products, even to the detriment of those who formerly marketed such by-products, can be obtained.

25. Which is exceedingly unlikely, since most university researchers can't identify what constitutes a patent.

26. See, for example, Benko (1987) and Brownlie (1992).

27. One such clan was the Menapiers, from which I am happy to have been provided a surname!

28. In America, the hideous level of political "sponsorship" is evidenced, for instance, by the fact that on average a U.S. Senator must make more than $10,000 per day to refinance her next election. Is it any wonder that incumbents are so rarely defeated in any election year? The favored method of "earning" these funds comes from honoraria for so-called speeches that are given over breakfast with those seeking favors.

29. This is why Amazonian advocates have long campaigned for indigenous park lands. For an excellent argument for advocacy, see, for instance, Colchester 1994; for a polemically described disaster story, see Kane 1993.

30. Even in relatively peaceful Vermont, Abenaki leader Homer Saint Francis can find himself surrounded by armed police for driving around in a car "registered" under his homemade tribal license!

31. Though the Human Genome Diversity Project has endorsed the collection of genetic information from the blood of some 722 populations, the fact that this is meant to uncover valuable genetic information that "must lie hidden within such unexplored genomes" (Hubbard and Wald 1997, 177) has led to justified suspicion and fear among indigenous populations. Indeed, the absence of any moral catalyst for this initiative has led to its being dubbed the "vampire project" (ibid.).

32. These include the World Bank, the UN (and its branches, UNDP, UNESCO, WHO, and UNECA [United Nations Economic Commission for Africa]) and the following NGOs: "1. CIRAN/Nuffic. Centre for International Research and Advisory Networks, part of the Netherlands Organization for International Cooperation in Higher Education . . . which publishes the Indigenous Knowledge Systems Monitor.
2. CISDA. Centre for Information Society Development in Africa. . . . 3. IDRC. International Development Research Centre. . . . 4. ITU. International Telecommunications Union. . . . 5. SANGONet. Southern Africa's Nonprofit Internet Service Provider. . . . 6. WIPO. World International Property Organization" (Green 1999, 20).

33. For reasons that have more to do with the nature of bench science than the subject of this chapter, it is not surprising that scientists have come very late to the notion that plants, like other molecular organisms, are sometimes like factories and sometimes like people: like factories in the sense that they go through regular cycles of productivity and inactivity, and like people in that they are often no less diverse within their respective species than we are in ours.

34. Drug giant Eli Lilly & Co. had, for instance, invested millions in Shaman, which it presumably intended not to lose; but, at the time of writing, Shaman was fighting to forestall collapse through the introduction of new products marketed by its main operating division, ShamanBotanicals.com.

35. For a comparable and rather more famous case, see Napier 1997.

36. Examples of those who have feet planted in more than one world are rare. There are few individuals who can function—as, for instance, does Everett R. Rhoades, M.D.—both as an indigenous healer and as director of the Indian Health Service (Rhoades 1996).

REFERENCES

Aoki, Keith. 1996. "(Intellectual) Property and Sovereignty: Notes Toward a Cultural Geography of Authorship." *Stanford Law Review* 48: 1293–1355.

Balick, Michael J., and Paul Alan Cox. 1996. *Plants, People, and Culture: The Science of Ethnobotany*. New York: Scientific American Library.

Beidelman, T. O. 1992. "*Millennium:* Tribal Wisdom and the Modern World" (review article). *Cultural Anthropology* 7: 508–15.

Benko, R. P. 1987. *Protecting Intellectual Property Rights: Issues and Controversies.* Washington, DC: American Enterprise Institute for Public Policy Research.

Benthall, Jonathan. 1999. "The Critique of Intellectual Property." *Anthropology Today* 15, no. 6 (December): 1–3.

Bisset, N. G. 1991. "One Man's Poison, Another Man's Medicine?" *Journal of Ethnopharmacology* 32: 71–81.

Boyle, James. 1996. *Shamans, Software, and Spleens: Law and the Construction of the Information Society.* Cambridge, MA: Harvard University Press.

Brown, Michael F. 1998. "Can Culture be Copyrighted?" *Current Anthropology* 19, no. 2 (April): 193–222.

Brownlie, I. 1992. *Treaties and Indigenous Peoples.* Oxford: Clarendon Press.

Brush, Stephen B. 1993. "Indigenous Knowledge of Biological Resources and Intellectual Property Rights: The Role of Anthropology." *American Anthropologist* 95, no. 3: 653–72.

Brush, Stephen B., and D. Stabinsky, eds. 1996. *Valuing Local Knowledge: Indigenous Peoples and Intellectual Property Rights.* Washington, DC: Island Press.

Burton, Thomas M. 1994. "Magic Bullets: Drug Company Looks to 'Witch Doctors' to Conjure Products." *Wall Street Journal,* July 7: 1, 8.

Clifton, James A., ed. 1990. *The Invented Indian: Cultural Fictions and Government Policies.* New Brunswick, NJ: Transaction Publishers.

Colchester, Marcus. 1994. *Salvaging Nature: Indigenous Peoples, Protected Areas, and Biodiversity Conservation.* Discussion paper (DP55). Geneva: United Nations Research Institute for Social Development (in collaboration with the World Rainforest Movement, and the World Wide Fund for Nature).

Conason, J. 1986. "Homeless on the Range: Greed, Religion, and the Hopi-Navajo Land Dispute." *Village Voice,* July 29: 19–26, 73.

Conklin, Beth A., and Laura R. Graham. 1995. "The Shifting Middle Ground: Amazonian Indians and Eco-Politics." *American Anthropologist* 97, no. 4: 695–710.

Coombe, Rosemary J. 1998a. "Intellectual Property, Human Rights, and Sovereignty: New Dilemmas in International Law Posed by the Recognition of Indigenous Knowledge and the Conservation of Biodiversity." *Indiana Journal of Global Legal Studies* 6, no. 1: 59–115.

———. 1998b. *The Cultural Life of Intellectual Properties: Authorship, Appropriation, and the Law.* Durham, NC, and London: Duke University Press.

Corry, Stephen. 1993. *Harvest Moonshine Taking You for a Ride.* London: Survival International.

Cunningham, A. 1992. *Ethics, Ethnobiological Research, and Biodiversity.* Gland, Switzerland: WWF International.

Deren, Maya. 1953. *Divine Horsemen: The Living Gods of Haiti.* London: Thames and Hudson.

Endo, Shusaku. 1969. *Silence.* Trans. William Johnston. Rutland, VT: C. E. Tuttle.

Fairhead, James, and Melissa Leach. 1996. *Misreading the African Landscape: Society and Ecology in a Forest-Savanna Mosaic.* Cambridge: Cambridge University Press.

Florio, Maria, and Victor Mudd. 1986. *Broken Rainbow*. Film/video, 70 min. Dir. Victor
Mudd and Thom Tyson. Earthworks/Direct Cinema.

Forgacs, David, ed. 1988. *An Antonio Gramsci Reader: Selected Writings, 1916–1935*. New
York: Schocken.

Greaves, Tom, ed. 1994. *Intellectual Property Rights for Indigenous Peoples: A Source Book*.
Oklahoma City: Society for Applied Anthropology.

Green, Edward C. 1999. "Indigenous Knowledge for Development." *Anthropology News*
40, no. 7: 20.

Harvard Medical School. 1990. *Policy on Conflicts of Interest and Commitment*. Boston: Harvard University.

Hubbard, Ruth, and Elijah Wald. 1997. *Exploding the Gene Myth: How Genetic Information
Is Produced and Manipulated by Scientists, Physicians, Employers, Insurance Companies, Edu-
cators, and Law Enforcers*. Boston: Beacon Press.

Kane, Joe. 1993. "With Spears from All Sides." *New Yorker*, September 27: 54–79.

Leach, Edmund R. 1964. "Anthropological Aspects of Language: Animal Categories and
Verbal Abuse." In *New Directions in the Study of Language*, ed. Eric H. Lenneberg.
Cambridge, MA: M.I.T. Press.

Marchand, Roland. 1998. *Creating the Corporate Soul: The Rise of Public Relations and Corporate Imagery in American Big Business*. Berkeley: University of California Press.

Marshall, John, and Sue Marshall-Cabezas. 1980. *N!ai: The Story of a !Kung Woman*. Film/
video, 59 min. Dir. and ed. by Adrienne Miesmer and John Marshall. Documentary
Educational Resources.

Mitchell, William E. 1996. "Communicating Culture: Margaret Mead and the Practice of
Popular Anthropology." In *Popularizing Anthropology*, ed. Jeremy MacClancy and
Chris McDonough. London and New York: Routledge.

Mountford, Charles P. 1965. *Ayers Rock: Its People, Their Beliefs, and Their Art*. Honolulu:
East-West Center Press.

Moustakas, J. 1989. "Group Rights in Cultural Property: Justifying Strict Inalienability."
Cornell Law Review 74: 1179–227.

Mowaljarlai, David, and Jutta Malnic. 1993. *Yorro, Yorro: Everything Standing Up Alive:
Spirit of the Kimberley*. Broome, Western Australia: Magabala Books.

Murray, Stuart. 1997. *Rudyard Kipling in Vermont: Birthplace of the Jungle Books*. Benning-
ton, VT: Images from the Past; Hanover, NH: Centinel.

Napier, A. David. 1997. "Losing One's Marbles: Cultural Property and Indigenous
Thought." In *Contesting Art: Art, Politics, and Identity in the Modern World*, ed. Jeremy
MacClancy. Oxford: Berg.

———. 1994. "Saving or Enslaving: The Paradox of Intellectual Property." *Journal of the
Anthropological Society of Oxford* 25, 1: 49–58.

———. 1992. *Foreign Bodies: Essays in Performance, Art, and Symbolic Anthropology*. Berkeley: University of California Press.

———. 1986. *Masks, Transformation, and Paradox*. Berkeley: University of California
Press.

Parker, Eugene. 1993. "Fact and Fiction in Amazonia: The Case of the Apêtê." *American Anthropologist* 93, no. 3: 715–23.

———. 1992. "Forest Islands and Kayapó Resource Management: A Reappraisal of the Apêtê." *American Anthropologist* 92, 2: 406–28.

Payer, Cheryl. 1991. *Lent and Lost: Foreign Credit and Third World Development.* London and Atlantic City, NJ: Zed Books.

Perkins, Harold. 1999. "Soul Food for the Boardroom." *Times Literary Supplement*, January 22, 6.

Pope, Carl. 1996 "Corporate Citizens." *Sierra* 8, no. 6: 14.

Posey, Darrell A. 1990. "Intellectual Property Rights and Just Compensation for Indigenous Knowledge." *Anthropology Today* 6, no. 4: 13–16.

———. 1994. "International Agreements and Intellectual Property Right Protection for Indigenous Peoples." In *Intellectual Property Rights for Indigenous Peoples: A Source Book*, ed. Tom Greaves. Oklahoma City: Society for Applied Anthropology.

Posey, Darrell A., and Graham Dutfield. 1996. *Beyond Intellectual Property: Toward Traditional Resource Rights for Indigenous Peoples and Local Communities.* Ottawa: International Development Research Centre.

Ramos, Alcida Rita. 1994a. "From Eden to Limbo: The Construction of Indigenism in Brazil." In *Social Construction of the Past: Representation as Power*, ed. George C. Bond and Angela Gilliam. London: Routledge.

———. 1994b. "The Hyperreal Indian." *Critique of Anthropology* 14, no. 2: 153–71.

———. 1991. "A Hall of Mirrors: The Rhetoric of Indigenism in Brazil." *Critique of Anthropology* 11, no. 2: 155–69.

———. 1988. "Indian Voices: Contact Experienced and Expressed." In *Rethinking History and Myth: Indigenous South American Perspectives on the Past*, ed Jonathan D. Hill. Urbana: University of Illinois Press.

———. 1987. "Reflecting on the Yanomami: Ethnographic Images and the Pursuit of the Exotic. *Cultural Anthropology* 2, no. 3: 284–304.

Rhoades, Everett R. 1996. "Two Paths to Healing: Can Tradition and Western Scientific Medicine Work Together?" *Winds of Change: American Indian Education and Opportunity* 11, no. 3: 48–51.

Rose, Deborah Bird. 1992. *Dingo Makes Us Human: Life and Land in an Aboriginal Australian Culture.* Cambridge: Cambridge University Press.

Ryan, Simon. 1996. *The Cartographic Eye: How Explorers Saw Australia.* Cambridge: Cambridge University Press.

Sillitoe, Paul. 1998. "The Development of Indigenous Knowledge: A New Applied Anthropology." *Current Anthropology* 19, no. 2 (April): 223–52.

Sittenfeld, Ana, and Rodrigo Gamez. 1993. "Biodiversity Prospecting by INBio." In *Biodiversity Prospecting: Using Genetic Resources for Sustainable Development*, ed. Walter V. Reid et al. Washington, DC: World Resource Institute.

Stoll, David. 1995. "Guatemala: Solidarity Activists Head for Trouble." *Christian Century*, January 4–11: 17–21.

Strathern, Marilyn, 1999. *Property, Substance, and Effect: Anthropological Essays on Persons and Things.* London: Athlone Press.

Suagee, Dean B. 1994. "Human Rights and Cultural Heritage: Developments in the United Nations Working Group on Indigenous Populations." In *Intellectual Property Rights for Indigenous Peoples: A Source Book*, ed. Tom Greaves. Oklahoma City: Society for Applied Anthropology.

Suchman, M. C. 1989. "Invention and Ritual: Notes on the Interrelation of Magic and Intellectual Property in Preliterate Societies." *Columbia Law Review* 89, no. 6: 1264–94.

"The Savage Can Also Be Ignoble." 1993. *Economist,* June 12: 76.

Thrower, Norman J. W. 1999. *Maps and Civilization: Cartography in Culture and Society.* 2d ed. Chicago: University of Chicago Press.

Turner, Terence 1993. "The Role of Indigenous Peoples in the Environmental Crisis: The Example of the Kayapó of the Brazilian Amazon." *Perspectives in Biology and Medicine* 36, no. 3: 526–45.

———. 1992. "Defiant Images: The Kayapó Appropriation of Video." *Anthropology Today* 8, no. 6: 5–16.

———. 1991. "Representing, Resisting, Rethinking: Historical Transformations of Kayapó Culture and Anthropological Consciousness." In *Colonial Situations: Essays on the Contextualization of Ethnographic Knowledge*, ed. George Stocking. Madison, WI: University of Wisconsin Press.

Vidal, Gore. 1988. *At Home: Essays, 1982–88.* New York: Random House.

Woodward, David, and G. Malcolm Lewis, eds. 1998. *The History of Cartography.* Vol. 2, bk. 3. *Cartography in the Traditional African, American, Artic, Australian, and Pacific Societies.* Chicago and London: University of Chicago Press.

Wright, Robin. 1988. "Anthropological Presuppositions of Indigenous Advocacy." *Annual Review of Anthropology* 17: 365–90.

16.

Anthropologists in a World with and without Human Rights

ELLEN MESSER

On New Year's Day, 1994, Zapatista rebels in Chiapas, Mexico, confronted the Mexican government with demands for basic human rights. Appealing for land, livelihood, adequate food, and access to health care and education, they demanded the essential human right to subsistence as well as an end to discrimination, which denied them access to government social programs. By framing their demands in terms of universal human rights, these indigenous Maya demonstrated how the concept and rhetoric of "human rights" have penetrated grassroots politics and enabled grassroots communities to reach out to international human-rights institutions and advocates. But the human-rights demands of these Zapatistas also highlight the persistent and multiple violations of human rights by governments, even those which have signed human-rights covenants and conventions.

As George Collier and others (1994, 1997) have documented, the Zapatista rebellion originated as a response to state-sponsored (or state-protected) violence against peasants who were demanding rights to land and to state-sponsored welfare and economic development programs from which they had been excluded. These exclusions denied them equal access to state benefits and violated their economic and social rights to adequate food, health care, and a decent standard of living. Subsequently, the Mexican government's brutal repression of the Zapatistas further violated their civil-political rights, first by forcing Zapatistas and their supporters to flee into the mountains and then by denying them access to livelihood or Non-Governmental Organization (NGO) aid. These events demonstrate that the protections and practice of human rights are still very limited, even in countries such as Mexico, which are legally obligated to safeguard them.

On a larger scale, human rights abuses occur and persist as a consequence of development agendas implemented by international development banks and agencies. These organizations are usually charter-bound (and party to United Nations summits) to protect human rights. Over the years some, like the World Bank, have spawned special protocols to review proposals. These protocols were designed to prevent or offset damages of large projects, such as river development for hydroelectric power, that would result in human-rights violations such as involuntary resettlement of indigenous peoples and destruction of environmental resources. Other agencies, such as the United Nations Development Program (UNDP), have added human rights to the protocol of annual state-level reporting on development progress. In 1997, UN Secretary General Kofi Annan directed all UN agencies to mainstream human rights into their agendas, programs, and practices. Nevertheless, in 1998 the American Anthropological Association (AAA) Committee for Human Rights (CfHR) was asked to consider several cases of alleged displacement and discrimination against indigenous people and damages to their environments associated with development lending, especially by the World Bank and its sister institutions in Latin America. Although "human-rights" rhetoric is now widespread and a point of reference both at the grassroots level and at world summits, human-rights concerns frequently appear to have no impact on development decision making. Such behaviors illustrate a principal paradox of the past fifty years (1948–1998) of "progress" in human rights. Human beings and human rights are supposed to be at the center of development efforts, yet human rights concerns frequently take a back seat to competing political and economic interests.

Addressing this contradiction between human-rights principles and practices, anthropologists since the 1940s, in the course of academic fieldwork and on assignment by NGOs such as Amnesty International and Cultural Survival, have monitored compliance with human-rights standards and criticized violations and abuses. In Africa, confronting emergency relief and development policymakers and NGO field practitioners, anthropologists such as Alex de Waal both "study up" the institutions and discourse of human rights and development professionals and "study down" grassroots social movements to discover how they incorporate human rights into their ideological and practical agendas. In the Americas, working with indigenous leaders who formulated the Declaration(s) of Barbados and Americanist human-rights codes, anthropologists have helped establish channels through which indigenous peoples and others suffering human-rights abuses can protest violations and demand protections directly. In Asia, challenging traditional and state authorities, nutritional and feminist anthropologists demand human-rights protections for the lives and livelihoods of women and children. Internationally, joining with NGOs in the 1990s UN development summits, anthropologists have helped negotiate the substantive contents and added cross-cultural understandings of human rights, especially those of women, children, refugees, and indigenous and other minorities.

In the process of interpreting questions such as "What are rights?" and "Who is counted as a full 'person' or 'human being' eligible to enjoy them?" anthropologists have moved between practice and theory. Responding to questions originally posed in the 1960s by human-rights experts but never satisfactorily answered, they offer cross-cultural insights on the ways particular cultural concepts of rights, obligations, or nurturance and codes of behavior correspond to UN universal human-rights standards. These studies also show how different notions of personhood can create categories of privileged (protected) or underprivileged (denied protection) under customary or national law; they also identify the duties of the more fortunate to improve the conditions of the less fortunate. Ethnographic evidence also lends substance to abstract human-rights standards, such as what quantities or types of nourishment constitute "adequate food," or what level of well-being constitutes "health."

Longitudinal anthropological studies of communities which adopt human-rights standards and rhetoric and make them their own should also prove important, particularly for policymakers and advocates interested in understanding the local contexts of human-rights compliance and adherence. Methods to study these global-to-local linkages are suggested by Elizabeth Colson and Conrad Kottak (1996), who are developing ways to monitor the local-level changes associated with the global spread of ideologies and political practices. Barbara Johnston (1994) and other "engaged anthropologists," draw on Roy Rappaport's holistic anthropological ideas of the social impacts of environmental change. They are slowly penetrating the policy-making arena (at least in the United States) and having some impact on decision making, for example, in the locations of off-shore oil drilling and of nuclear waste depositories. As highlighted in Emilio Moran's (1996) and Richard Wilson's (1997) edited volumes, human rights are transforming societies and also anthropology. These developments signal both a growing willingness by anthropologists to use anthropological theory and methods to engage in policy and mainstream political action and also some new openings in policy circles for them to be heard. The first section below reviews the historical phasing of human rights against a background of development rhetoric and theoretical and applied work by anthropologists. The second summarizes the major human-rights emphases characterizing the different world regions (Africa, Asia, Latin America). The third briefly considers some of the institutional settings in which anthropologists pursue human-rights agendas, including a 1997 case study of the CfHR's response to Chilean energy interests' abuses against the indigenous

Pehuenche. The final section explores how anthropologists advocating human rights move from action to theory, and some of the key controversies remaining for human-rights-centered anthropology.

HUMAN RIGHTS, DEVELOPMENT PARADIGMS, AND ANTHROPOLOGY

Modern human rights are part of an international legal system first promulgated in 1948 with the adoption of the Universal Declaration of Human Rights (UDHR) and later supported by binding instruments. The UDHR offered a synthesizing umbrella document, which voiced aspirations for human dignity and decency, and constituted a point of reference that all UN members could agree on. However, the American Anthropological Association's Executive Board in 1947 officially rejected the notion of universal human rights as ethnocentrically Western. Instead, they championed protection of indigenous rights and emphasized that different peoples have different rights concepts; they refer to different authorities, and usually suffer further marginalization in what Western development experts call "progress." They furthermore questioned the framework of national sovereignty that was to be held accountable for human-rights enforcement. Additionally, theoretical purists opposed participation in human-rights debates on the grounds that advocacy, policy-oriented, or interventionist anthropology was inconsistent with scientific rigor. Their more applied colleagues favored more direct social and economic actions over abstract discussions of rights to improve the negotiating strength of smaller-scale societies. And anthropologists also worried about the political sensitivity of criticizing human-rights abuses by states in which they desired to continue fieldwork, and about the appropriateness of anthropologists, whose comparative advantage had always been small-scale ethnographic studies, devoting time to study human-rights political processes and institutions, which tended to be the conventional domains of political scientists and sociologists. It was not until the 1980s that these critical viewpoints were significantly overturned and human rights became a legitimate if not mandatory issue for anthropological scrutiny.

Over the interim decades (1948–88), the chronology of more specific and legally binding UN covenants, treaties, and conventions, usually described in terms of four generations of human rights, roughly paralleled both the shifting economic-development paradigms which arose during this period and the changing roles of anthropologists who worked in settings of development and contributed to human-rights constructs.

In the 1950s and 1960s, the main human-rights emphasis centered on civil-political rights. Political-economic development was meant to be achieved and measured in terms of economic growth (GNP), the benefits of which were supposed to "trickle down" to the economically disadvantaged. Despite official AAA objections to the very idea of universal rights, Margaret Mead, Lévi-Strauss, and some of their colleagues (especially those associated with UNESCO), contributed to conceptualizations of universal human rights and also introduced anthropological perspectives into programs of planned cultural and technological change, public health, and nutrition. Although international human-rights covenants stressed obligations to share the benefits of Western technology with the developing world, anthropologists already emphasized the need for greater respect for cultural diversity, indigenous rights, and indigenous knowledge, a perspective that was to achieve wider prominence in the 1980s.

Over the 1970s, economic-social-cultural rights received more attention as development rhetoric shifted to growth-with-equity. Experts recognized that the "trickle-down" effect was not uplifting the poor and that more should be done to meet "basic needs" for food, health, education, and housing of the impoverished and disadvantaged segments in developing countries. Conferences followed: in 1974, the World Food Conference, advocating "freedom from hunger," and in 1977 the Alma Ata summit, heralding "health for all." Both linked human-rights rhetoric to development goals, but in what remained their grave weakness, offered no enforceable framework of government obligations to meet human rights and development goals. During this period, the anthropologies of medicine, nutrition, and development all expanded and contributed to development paradigms and practice, but mostly outside of a human-rights framework. Anthropologists also contributed ethnographic and political-economic insights to official UN discussions about genocide and discrimination against women, and about ways to prevent both kinds of abuses (the UN Convention on the Prevention and Punishment of the Crime of Genocide had been entered into force in 1951; the UN Convention on the Elimination of All Forms of Discrimination against Women in 1979). Increasingly, such expanding human-rights formulations demonstrated three things: the interdependence and indivisibility of civil-political and economic-social-cultural rights; the need to consider collective as well as individual rights; and the linkages of human rights to development processes.

These three concerns coalesced during the 1980s when less industrialized countries formulated a code of development rights. This code was in part a protest against the burdens of debt and structural-adjustment policies which were forcing governments to eliminate nutritional and health subsidies and streamline social services. Third World leaders promulgating the people's right to development emphasized that (1) the human being is the subject of development; (2) civil-political and economic-social-cultural rights are interdependent and indivisible;

and (3) peoples of the world can legitimately demand a peaceful and just social and economic order that provides freedom from extreme want and also protects the environment. Over this period, anthropologists spoke out against the human-rights abuses of political dictators in specific countries of Africa and Latin America, the complicity of U.S. and European aid, and also the human-rights contradictions of development assistance.

In Africa, Jason Clay and fellow anthropologists at Cultural Survival, an NGO, exposed the highly publicized Ethiopian famine in the mid-1980s as not strictly a natural disaster, but a mainly man-made, political one, which implicated food-relief agencies such as CARE and CRS in keeping the genocidal leader, Mengistu, in power. Assessing this situation, Clay suggested that anthropologists were human-rights activists by default. The Ethiopian experience catapulted anthropologists into debates over the use and abuse of aid, debates which continued to rage over the next decade, particularly with regard to famines and conflicts in neighboring Sudan and Somalia (see the discussion by de Waal, chapter 13 in this volume).

In Central America, U.S. anthropologists such as Martin Diskin and Carol Smith both challenged the economic and political human-rights records of local dictators, as well as the terms of U.S. foreign assistance. Diskin publicly opposed U.S. policies in El Salvador and Nicaragua that restricted economic opportunities for the poor but supplied military elites with arms. Smith and others brought to light the ways in which official U.S. economic aid for community-development projects in Guatemala had been cynically used to identify and eliminate community leaders. They also criticized the ways in which NGOs, ostensibly helping communities to develop economically, usurped and postponed the necessary political negotiations between communities and the state in Guatemala.

The 1990s have seen an increasing number of formulations by states of indigenous rights, as well as UN development summits that express rights-based concerns for peace, economic justice, and a sustainable environment. Over this period anthropologists have been at the forefront—documenting abuses in Central America, Africa, and Asia; protesting against discrimination and economic injustice in the United States, Europe, Japan, and Australia; and suggesting ways to expand human-rights concepts so that they can connect with local ideas of rights and measures of their fulfillment.

For example, in Latin America, which has been the focal point for organizing peoples to demand indigenous rights, the right to land, and to self-determination in development (figure 1), Rodolfo Stavenhagen (1991) has elucidated the historical and cultural rationales underpinning the ideologies and dynamics of elite cultures that marginalize and abuse indigenous peoples. These studies have been fol-

FIGURE 1 First international Indian conference, Altamira, Brazil, February 1989. (© Ken Taylor/ Survival)

lowed up by Jennifer Schirmer (1998), whose disturbing interviews and analytical commentaries with elites, including the head of the Guatemalan military largely responsible for that country's 1980s massacres, suggest that old orders die hard, even in the face of competing and more humane ideologies and political platforms. In such reports, anthropologists clearly confront the limits of cultural relativism; marginalizing indigenous people and killing them and other peasants is intolerable. So is the elite cultural ideology that rationalizes such brutality in the name of elite cultural survival. Indigenous anthropologists (Guatemalan Maya are a case in point) also enter into this discourse by presenting academic papers that reinterpret their cultural histories in the light of European (or anthropologists') distortions and by preparing and disseminating, for their own peoples, educational materials on authentic indigenous language and culture.

The merits of competing (good vs. bad) cultural orders are less easily defined or reconciled, however, in cases where multiple indigenous collectivities each claim (1) authenticity and sovereignty to negotiate control over land and resources, and (2) the political autonomy to decide which people have the right to remain within their native community or to exile nonconformists. The incendiary writings of David Stoll (1993), who witnessed and analyzed the ways in which the Guatemalan military played off one indigenous group against the other in their struggle for land and livelihood, implicated both anthropologists and human-rights NGO activists in partisan and sometimes violent standoffs. Less controversially, Diskin and other anthropologists (1991) have shown how the legal structures and rhetoric of human and indigenous rights present local peoples with opportunities to claim land and resources. These opportunities have influenced local identities and leadership struggles among indigenous groups. In the process, foreign anthropologists speaking for native peoples are being replaced by indigenous leaders organizing their own struggles. These leaders demand legal and development advice and networking assistance, but they speak in their own indigenous voices.

Other anthropologists document the plights of local peoples who are transformed, displaced, or otherwise marginalized by economic development that also destroys or appropriates their environment. For instance, the California-based Barbara Rose Johnston (1994, 1997) and colleagues, who have written extensively on this topic, consider the question, "Who pays the price?" when alleged development efforts conflict with human rights, and economic ends trample environmental resources. Their analyses show that the negative human and environmental impacts of 1980s development efforts are "life-and-death matters." Alongside these development disasters, there is a class of policies and projects orchestrated by the environmental movement, which, in the best of all possible worlds, seeks alliances with indigenous groups and does not work at cross-purposes. At times, however, the movement functions more like a predatory transnational corporation. For example, Robert Hitchcock has exposed animal-rights activists who sometimes favor preservation of wildlife over human life and injure or kill people as part of antipoaching and conservation campaigns in southern Africa. He documents also that African hunters in Botswana, Zambia, and Zimbabwe may face violence or be forcibly resettled if they try to take game for subsistence where their governments want to protect wildlife.

Environmentalists and indigenous peoples also come into conflict over who should control development of forests and waterways. In South America, Cultural Survival and other indigenous-rights organizations have tried to promote viable economic strategies in the rain forests, such as the tropical forest nut mixture, Rainforest Crunch. These strategies have multiple purposes: they can protect biodiversity, safeguard indigenous people's claims over land and resources, and help them make a living. But such efforts are usually small-scale; they also demand some investment capital and marketing savvy—entrepreneurial dimensions which may be in short supply among both the untested rain forest producers and the do-good NGO distributors. Moreover, some anthropologists and human-rights organizations (e.g., Survival International) question the wisdom of promoting projects which tie indigenous peoples more closely to capitalist forces and global markets that they cannot control.

REGIONAL CULTURAL RELATIVISM AND UNIVERSALS

As part of their continuing efforts to trace evolving human-rights and development paradigms, anthropologists have also introduced distinct regional perspectives. In Africa, debate centers over whether human rights are individual or collective, and whether the rights to development and to freedom from hunger take precedence over Western political emphasis on individual political-economic freedoms. African political leaders in 1981 produced their own regional African (Banjul) Charter on Human Rights, which asserts that in African societies "peoples," not individuals, have rights and that individual freedoms may have to be sacrificed, at least in the short term, to support subsistence and development rights. These leaders leverage the term "peoples" here to mean nations, not ethnic collectivities, the rights of which may be brutally suppressed in the state-building process. Critics counter that exploitation and deprivation of political freedom are not African cultural characteristics but social structural ones, and that national "peoples" are an abstraction. Moreover, ethnographic examples are able to demonstrate that individuals in many African systems of thought enjoy pan-human as well as collective identity; for Sudanese Dinka, for example, all are "children of God" (Deng 1990), and for the Kenyan Luo, "a man is a man for all that" (Cohen and Odhiambo 1989).

Nevertheless, native and non-native anthropologists continue to seek distinctive African interpretations of personhood, multiple allegiances, and social connectedness, over and against universal formulations of individual rights. In these anthropological accounts it is possible to detect a desire to document and discuss the convergences and divergences between customary and UN notions of persons and rights. It is also possible to perceive in them anthropologists' wish to privilege small-group rights, although individuals living under African state rule surely desire to enjoy the human-rights protections promulgated in UN covenants.

It is thus still a challenge for anthropologists to understand how a diversity of rights and obligations can be articulated so as to protect individuals who are simultaneously members of several social groups. To promote human rights in Africa, advocates need better information on how traditional societies ascribe and how individuals achieve human dignity, full social adulthood, and community membership. What are the standards for treating those not yet considered to be full human beings or social persons, such as children or strangers? What are the basic rules of nurturance and teaching for transforming them into fully socially responsible adults? For example, the American anthropologist Elizabeth Colson, who worked in rural Zambia, demonstrated how strangers have traditionally been turned into group members and how state bureaucracy and economic change are now undermining such processes. Her study (Colson 1970) also raises instructive questions about local tolerance for cultural diversity.

A related special case is the local, state, and international interpretations of the rights of refugees (on this, see de Waal, chapter 13 in this volume). Also of special interest for the understanding of local concepts of human rights is the phenomenon of outcasts—those former or would-be members of a group who failed to meet minimum standards of behavior which define group membership and personhood. Under what circumstances do particular African groups revoke the rights of those (otherwise protected by birth or social history) whose aberrant behavior is judged too egregious and destructive to the social fabric? Increasingly, Africans may have to resort to the individual human rights defined in the international legal sphere (1) because rights and attendant responsibilities are loosening, as are the geographical and cultural ties that traditionally bind, and (2) because traditional rights and responsibilities atrophy in new urban contexts and with greater mobility. In particular, women and children may find themselves denied protections in both customary and national law. Although African nations are slowly dismantling the discriminatory legacy of apartheid, there persist special human-rights concerns over forced labor, slavery, genocide, and ethnocide; involuntary genital surgery performed on women; and clashes over Islamic versus UN notions of political rights and women's rights. All have long been anthropologists' concerns.

Similar issues arise in Asia, where questions of cultural relativism have also centered on which rights take precedence—subsistence and development or political freedoms—and whether the real struggle is for self-respect and political human rights or for food and some relief from extreme poverty. From an Indian perspective, the question of whether the cultural and religious language of duties and obligations can be reconciled with universal human-rights notions, rigorously pursued by Schweder and colleagues (1991), is not strictly academic. The practical question of socioeconomic justice or "the right to be human," wrestled with by U. Baxi (1989) and others who are continually rethinking human rights in the Indian context, is how best to protect the rights of individuals or partial peoples still subject to discrimination and destitution in duty-based contexts of caste and class equality. Anthropologists working in Asia also seek to understand better the circumstances under which caste or gender distinctions lose their strictness or shed particular kinds of deprivation. Martha Chen (1986), who works extensively with women's organizations in South Asia, points to the influence of NGOs, foundations, and international agencies such as UNICEF, particularly for improving the lives and rights of women and children.

Additionally, in Asia, as in Africa, anthropologists seek to unravel and sever cycles of violence predicated on mythical dehumanization of "the other" in multi-ethnic contexts where more tolerant pluralism is likewise indicated in the traditional sources. For instance in Sri Lanka, the anthropologist Stanley Tambiah (1992) has attempted to understand the mythologies used by the dominant Sinhalese to justify violence against Tamils and other non-Sinhalese. He shows their cycles of violence to be the consequences of conscious, selective, cultural constructions of an alleged heroic past, which is used to serve destructive, modern, political-economic ends. Since there is nothing culturally inevitable about this process, Tambiah believes that with human-rights education to promote human understanding and tolerance, along with political good will, the cycles of violence might be stopped.

Other anthropologists seek understandings that can help to end discrimination and violence against women, especially in India. For instance, Helen Papanek (1989) traced step-by-step the actual behaviors by which women get less of available resources. She then evaluated the material consequences of this discrimination. The next step was to examine the local ideas behind such behaviors (women are of lesser value; the particular resources are "bad" for women; or it is believed that women tolerate and thrive on less). These steps allow measurement in both local cultural and scientific terms of the possible multiple layers of causation. They also invite reflections by the individuals: do they feel discriminated against and want to mobilize to change cultural practices or complexes that, at least from an outsider's perspective, are abusive? Investigations such as Papanek's often reveal that customs potentially abusive to women have neither great historical depth nor central cultural importance, but instead are adjustments to scarce resource conditions. Such customs persist, not because they are necessary, economically or ideologically, to authentic cultural survival, but because they benefit members of certain privileged groups (usually males in power). Moreover, improving economic conditions may eliminate the original rationale for such customs without destroying the culture.

In Latin America, the focus of human-rights organizing is to protect the rights of local collectivities struggling for autonomy and survival. Central American anthropologists have perhaps been the most personally involved, sometimes at the cost of their lives. Particularly in Mayan regions, indigenous groups are organizing to bear witness and document massacres, but also to assert leadership. Across Latin America as a whole, indigenous peoples press vocally for their rights to land, culture, and self-determination in development. Since Spanish colonial times, Latin America has witnessed a continuing debate over "who is a human being" with full rights before the law. It has also experienced never-ending gaps between constitutional guarantees of rights to citizens, and violations against indigenous peoples and political dissidents. Rodolfo Stavenhagen leads the efforts by anthropologists and legal scholars to understand and overcome the sources of discrimination, and to advocate rights for collectivities and communities. His comparisons of customary community law versus human-rights codes in Mexico present a practical research agenda for discerning and reconciling community and universal concepts of rights, persons, and justice. His service on UN and Inter-American human-rights drafting groups maintains an anthropological voice, which emphasizes the need to protect collective rights, especially the rights of indigenous peoples (e.g., Stavenhagen 1991).

Thorny and as yet unresolved issues in Latin America involve freedom of religion and religious authority. At least since Vatican II, the Catholic Church has been at the forefront in promoting political and economic rights. Some anthropologists argue that the particular form of Catholic grassroots organizing in Christian Base Communities (Catholic Action), affirming local empowerment (Liberation Theology), contributed to consciousness-raising and rebellion by Guatemalan indigenous communities, who then suffered terribly under the military. At least one, the priest-anthropologist Ricardo Falla, joined the struggle; as an active member of a Guatemalan community in resistance, he reported on the military's brutalities, the community's attempts to organize resistance, and subsequent competition for land and other economic resources by different feuding groups. Concerned with righting social and economic injustice, the Church and anthropologists also confronted the inroads of Protestant missionaries, whose programs of conversion and economic assistance arguably destroy native cultures. (The missionaries, at least one also an anthropologist, however, protest that they are saving lives and that they, themselves, are subject to human-rights abuses.) Complicating local religious contexts and notions of religious freedom are internal community power struggles. Here traditional authorities who benefit from the status quo may oppose those who resist traditional religious service and desire to break out of its constraints, which stifle their individual economic advance.

INSTITUTIONAL INVOLVEMENTS

Concerns about human rights since the 1940s have propelled anthropologists into policy contexts. UNESCO's annual reports, yearbooks, and special publications offer evidence of anthropologists' pioneering work conceptualizing race, the rights of the child, and religious and other cultural perspectives on human rights. Most recently UNESCO's *World Culture Report*, directed by Mexican anthropologist Lourdes Arizpe, explores local-to-global linkages connecting human rights, economic development, and environmental policy.

Since the 1950s UNICEF has endeavored to formulate and establish programs to plan, implement, and monitor the rights of the child (see chapter 17, by Judith Ennew, in this volume). Following UNICEF's lead, advocates for children's rights assert that children have a right to be free from violence and to enjoy adequate food and nutrition. They prod governments to set goals for child health and establish programs to fulfill them. Certain anthropologists criticize UNICEF and NGOs for universalizing norms touching on children's well-being. Nancy Scheper-Hughes, for example, faults UN agencies for seeing the problems of child survival in terms of medicine, when their main sources are in fact poverty, powerlessness, and injustice. More commonly, however, anthropologists elect to work with nutritional and medical personnel, helping them to connect more effectively to communities and to formulate not just needs-based assessments and programs but rights-based ones as well. Others, turning to indigenous medicine, help to negotiate community rights over plants and their genes. For example, ethnobotanists associated with UNESCO, FAO, IPGRI, and NGOs have drawn out the important connections between indigenous biological knowledge, intellectual property rights, and the conservation of plant genetic resources. Anthropologists involved in this kind of work have suggested that in the future FAO might coordinate much more closely indigenous rights, economic rights, and issues of environmental protection. All are examples of the ways anthropologists can use the framework of human rights to increase coordination among agencies and to facilitate the connecting of initiatives from UN summits to grassroots communities.

Counterbalancing this constructive role, anthropologists also persist in their critic's role, monitoring UN agencies and international financial institutions to establish if they actually promote a human-rights agenda. In the 1980s, they spoke out against the negative nutritional and health impacts of structural adjustment programs, largely implemented by the World Bank and IMF. In the name of human rights, they savaged proposed river development and large dam projects (with an occasional success, as in Senegal). And into the 1990s, anthropologists criticized especially World Bank lending operations that caused involuntary resettlement and environmental destruction, and failed to respect human rights.

Partly in response, the World Bank began to hire anthropologists to help evaluate and devise ways to replicate factors contributing to successful projects, and also to deal with public relations surrounding potentially volatile issues such as indigenous rights and the environment. With the bank's encouragement, World Bank anthropologist Michael Cernea published a series of essays by anthropologists pressing for development "as if people matter," advising the World Bank this was a good development strategy. Indigenous-rights advocate Sheldon Davis and the Brazilian development anthropologist Dan Gross also were hired to give advice and be spokespersons for World Bank programs in their politically sensitive areas of expertise.

Despite its hiring of anthropologists and its "people matter" rhetoric, the World Bank's chief and only criterion for lending remains economic. Among the World Bank family of institutions, the International Finance Corporation (which, in developing countries, arranges loans to the private sector rather than to governments) is not held strictly accountable to guidelines on indigenous rights and the environment. In the mid-1990s, communications between the World Bank family and the CfHR indicated that the bank is still implicated in actions by governments (such as that of Brazil) and by the private sector (in countries such as Chile) that deny indigenous peoples their rights to land or adequate representation and compensation. In the case of the Bío Bío River dam in Chile, indigenous Pehuenche were removed from their land, not compensated for their losses, not allowed their rightful share of profits from forest cutting on what had been their lands, and restricted from participation in the discussions and evaluations of the Pehuen development foundation. All this was done although the foundation allegedly had been set up to benefit them and so meet criteria for protecting the rights of indigenous people who might be involuntarily resettled! Anthropologists investigating this case discovered that for all its inadequacies, however, the World Bank may be the only lender over which concerned citizens have leverage. Private lenders (with whom loans were negotiated by the Chilean developer as a result of the human-rights protests) have no legal obligation to consider human-rights impacts, and only do so if political pressure can be brought to bear by citizens' groups or NGOs.

Partly as a result, anthropologists increasingly find themselves working with NGOs on human-rights, development, and environmental concerns. International networking, assisted by new electronic technologies, makes possible immediate information-sharing on abuses, legal frameworks for protest, and techniques for mobilizing grassroots action to an extent never before possible. In the case of the Zapatistas, the Mexican government's use of starvation as a weapon against the insurgents was broadcast all over the world by NGOs. Networking elicited an international response, which was able to document abusive behaviors by the Mexican government and pressure the government to seek a rapid settlement.

In the United States, anthropologists are also developing more forceful institutional mechanisms to address human rights. Since the 1990s, human-rights violations have been monitored, reported, and protested through the CfHR, now a permanent committee of the American Anthropological Association. Its "Declaration on Anthropology and Human Rights," accepted by the general membership, declares, "[A]nthropologists . . . should . . . be concerned whenever human difference is made the basis for denial of basic human rights, where 'human' is understood in its full range of cultural, social, linguistic, psychological, and biological senses." In practical terms, the human-rights activities of anthropologists build on, and are "consistent with international principles, but not limited by them. Our understanding of human rights is constantly evolving as we come to know more about the human condition."

BETWEEN ACTION AND THEORY

Such statements and expanding activities suggest that, in contrast to fifty years ago, universal human rights are now as widely embraced by the anthropological community as they are by the peoples they study. Collective and indigenous rights are today part of the human-rights framework, and instead of opposing them to each other, anthropologists endeavor to make indigenous and human rights mutually reinforcing. Action-oriented and policy-engaged anthropology often begins with attention to the human-rights dimension. With respect to this issue, anthropologists have crossed the divide separating theoretical, applied, and advocacy anthropology. They have also learned to study human rights at multiple social levels, from the grassroots to UN summits, with the associated rhetorics and cultures of the UN agencies. But all this does not mean that anthropologists or others have dropped the idea that rights are culturally relative or that they have become less politically sensitive. Indeed the human-rights experts as well as the anthropologists finally seem to recognize that to be effective, rights must be adopted by communities that already have their own notions of rights and persons. Consequently, a growing area of anthropological research and action is the analysis, communication, and translation of human-rights language and behavior across communities, and between communities and states or international agencies. As de Waal and other anthropologists so eloquently articulate, human rights is a persistent struggle, pitting local communities against states and sometimes against each other. In such contexts, the role of the anthropologist appears to be to protect, to give technical (including legal) and social assistance to oppressed people, and to lobby the (U.S.) government or the World Bank for policies that affirm human rights. In international contexts, the role of the anthropologist may also be to provide guidance to find culturally appropriate institutional mechanisms that can break cycles of violence and permit survivors some return to normalcy. This includes evaluating possible structures through which violators might be allowed amnesty or brought to justice.

Exploring human rights in cross-cultural practice also has much to teach anthropologists studying human classification, political rhetoric, culturally diverse understandings of "the good life" (or the contents of economic-social-cultural rights), and the basic rights and obligations underlying social structure and social relations. Ultimately such analyses promise to elucidate fundamental questions of social transformation. In other words, they promise to clarify the circumstances under which modern universal values (such as human rights) are adopted by individuals and peoples who until now embraced (1) restrictive notions of who exactly is a human being deserving of protection and (2) alternative notions of rights and obligations. Human-rights and development experts still need anthropologists to raise such questions: to explicate what it means to be "human" in different cultures; to explore the contexts in which people from very different backgrounds make human rights a common creed and standard for interaction; and to discover how individuals in collectivities learn to tolerate and respect "difference" in other human beings.

REFERENCES AND SUGGESTIONS FOR FURTHER READING

The journal *Human Rights Teaching*, published over the 1980s, provides an account of UNESCO's activities in human rights.

There are also a number of good regional sources. For Central America, reports by anthropologists are published in the *Cultural Survival Quarterly*, the *Guatemala Scholars Network News*, and the North American Congress on Latin America's *Report of the Americas*. At the end of the 1980s, anthropologists at Cultural Survival also put together an internet resource guide. These resources showed that a growing corpus of activities indexed under other terms, such as violence and discrimination, also addressed human-rights issues.

For Asia, a research and advocacy literature is published in *Reports* of Asia Watch, *Bulletin of Concerned Asian Scholars*, and *Cultural Survival Quarterly*.

For Africa, see *African Rights* and additional suggestions for reading in de Waal's chapter 13 in this volume.

Baxi, U. 1989. "From Human Rights to the Right to Be Human: Some Heresies." In *Rethinking Human Rights: Challenges for Theory and Action*, ed. S. Kothari and H. Sethi, 151–62. New York: New Horizons.

Cernea, Michael. 1991. *Putting People First: Sociological Variables in Development*. New York: Oxford University Press.

Chen, Martha A. 1986. *The Quiet Revolution. Women in Transition in Rural Bangladesh*. Cambridge, MA: Shenkman.

Cohen, D. W., and A. E. S. Odhiambo. 1989. *Siaya: The Historical Anthropology of an African Landscape*. London: Currey.

Collier, G., and E. Quaratiello. 1994. *Basta! Land and the Zapatista Rebellion in Chiapas*. Oakland, CA: Food First.

Collier, G., and L. Stephen, eds. 1997. "Ethnicity, Identity, and Citizenship in the Wake of the Zapatista Rebellion." *Journal of Latin American Anthropology* 3, no. 1.

Colson, Elizabeth. 1970. "The Assimilation of Aliens among Zambian Tonga." In *From*

Tribe to Nation: Studies in Incorporative Processes, ed. R. Cohen and J. Middleton, 35–54. Scranton, PA: Chandler.

Colson, Elizabeth, and Conrad Kottak. 1996. "On Linkages Methodology for the Study of Multi-level Systems." In *Transforming Societies, Transforming Anthropology*, ed. E. Moran. Ann Arbor: University of Michigan Press.

Davis, Sheldon. 1988. *Land Rights and Indigenous Peoples: The Role of the Inter-American Commission on Human Rights*. Cambridge, MA: Cultural Survival.

Declaration of Barbados. 1971. International Work Group for Indigenous Affairs Doc.1. Copenhagen: IWGIA

Deng, Francis. 1990. "A Cultural Approach to Human Rights among the Dinka. In *Human Rights in Africa: Cross-Cultural Perspectives*, ed. A. A. An Na-im and F. Deng. Philadelphia: University of Pennsylvania Press.

de Waal, Alexander. 1997. *Famine Crimes: Politics and the Disaster-Relief Industry in Africa..* Bloomington: Indiana University Press.

Diskin, Martin. 1991. "Ethnic Discourse and the Challenge to Anthropology: The Nicaraguan Case." In *Nation-States and Indigenous Indians in Latin America*, ed. G. Urban and J. Sherezer, 156–80 Austin: University of Texas Press.

Downing, T., and G. Kushner, eds. 1988. *Human Rights and Anthropology*. Cambridge, MA: Cultural Survival. [A pioneering set of essays, predominantly focused on Latin America, with an excellent bibliography.]

Executive Board, American Anthropological Association. 1947. "Statement on Human Rights Submitted to the Commission on Human Rights, United Nations." *American Anthropologist* 49: 539–43.

Glean, M. 1966. "Introduction to Human Rights in Perspective." *International Social Science Journal* 18, no. 1: 7–10.

Gossen, G. 1994. "Comments on the Zapatista Movement." *Cultural Survival Quarterly* 18: 19–21.

Heggenhoughen, K. 1995. "The Epidemiology of Functional Apartheid and Human Rights Abuses." *Social Science and Medicine* 40: 281–84.

Hitchcock, R. 1997. "African Wildlife: Conservation and Conflict." In *Life and Death Matters*, ed. B. Johnston, 81–95. Walnut Creek, CA: Altamira Press.

Johnston, B., ed. 1994. *Who Pays the Price? The Socioeconomic Context of Environmental Crisis*. Washington, DC: Island Press.

———. 1997. *Life and Death Matters: Human Rights and the Environment at the End of the Millennium*. Walnut Creek, CA: Altamira Press. [Offers a stimulating set of essays by anthropologists working in different world regions and environmental contexts.]

Kapferer, B. 1988. *Legends of People, Myths of State: Violence, Intolerance, and Political Cultures in Sri Lanka and Australia*. Washington DC: Smithsonian Institute Press.

Kuper, Leo. 1985. *The Prevention of Genocide*. New Haven, CT: Yale University Press.

Lévi-Strauss, C. 1952. *Race and History*. Paris: UNESCO.

Marchione, T. 1984. "Approaches to the Hunger Problem: A Critical Overview." In *Food as a Human Right*, ed. A. Eide, W. B. Eide, S. Goonatilake, J. Gussow, and Omawale, 117–38. Tokyo: United Nations University Press.

———. 1996. "The Right to Food in the Post–Cold War Era." *Food Policy* 21, no. 1: 83–102.

Martinez, S. 1996. "Indifference with Indignation: Anthropology, Human Rights, and the Haitian Bracero." *American Anthropologist* 98: 17–29.

Mead, M. 1950. "World Culture." In *Anthropology: A Human Science*, ed. M. Mead, 134–45. Princeton, NJ: Van Nostrand.

Messer, E. 1993. "Anthropology and Human Rights." *Annual Review of Anthropology* 22: 221–49. [Reviews the global history of anthropology and human rights by region and topic.]

———. 1996. "Anthropology, Human Rights, and Social Transformation." In *Transforming Societies, Transforming Anthropology*, ed. E. Moran, 165–210. Ann Arbor: University of Michigan Press.

———. 1997. "Pluralist Approaches to Human Rights." *Journal of Anthropological Research* 53: 293–315.

Moran, Emilio. 1996. *Transforming Societies, Transforming Anthropology*. Ann Arbor: University of Michigan Press.

Nash, J. 1994. "Global Integration and Subsistence Insecurity." *American Anthropologist* 96: 7–30.

Nations, J. D. 1994. "The Ecology of the Zapatista Revolt." *Cultural Survival Quarterly* 18, no. 1: 31–33.

Nigh, R. 1994. "Zapata Rose in 1994: The Indian Rebellion in Chiapas." *Cultural Survival Quarterly* 18, no. 1: 9–13.

Papanek, Helen. 1989. "Socialization for Inequality: Issues for Research and Action." In *Samyi Shakti*. New Delhi: Center for Women's Development Studies.

Richards, P., and G. Ruivenkamp. 1997. *Seeds and Survival: Crops and Plant Genetic Resources in War and Reconstruction in Africa*. Rome: International Plant Genetic Research Institute.

Safa, H. 1990. "Women's Social Movements in Latin America." *Gender Sociology* 4: 354–69.

Scheper-Hughes, N. 1997. "Demography without Numbers." In *Anthropological Demography: Toward a New Synthesis*, ed. D. I. Kertzer and T. Fricke, 201–22. Chicago: University of Chicago Press.

Schirmer, Jennifer. 1998. *The Guatemalan Military Project: A Violence Called Democracy*. Philadelphia: University of Pennsylvania Press.

Schweder, R. A., ed. 1991. *Thinking through Cultures: Expeditions in Cultural Psychology*. Cambridge, MA: Harvard University Press.

Smith, C. 1996. "Development and the State. Issues for Anthropologists." In *Transforming Societies, Transforming Anthropology*, ed. E. Moran, 25–56. Ann Arbor: University of Michigan Press.

Sponsel, L. 1996. "Human Rights and Advocacy Anthropology." In *Encyclopedia of Cultural Anthropology*, ed. D. Levinson and M. Ember, 602–6. New York: Henry Holt.

Stavenhagen, R. 1989. "Indigenous Customary Laws in Latin America." *America Indigena* 49: 223–43.

———. 1991. *The Ethnic Question: Conflict, Development, and Human Rights.* Tokyo: United Nations University Press. [Offers an eloquent discussion of people's and indigenous rights.]

Stoll, D. 1993. *Between Two Armies in the Ixil Towns of Guatemala.* New York: Columbia University Press.

Tambiah, Stanley. 1992. *Buddhism Betrayed? Religion, Politics, and Violence in Sri Lanka.* Chicago: University of Chicago Press.

Turner, T. 1997. "Human Rights, Human Difference: Anthropology's Contribution to an Emancipatory Politics." *Journal of Anthropological Research* 53: 273–91.

UNESCO. 1981–1987. *Human Rights Teaching.* Vols. 2 (1981), 3 (1982), 4 (1985), and 6 (1987).

Wilson, R., ed. 1997. *Human Rights, Culture, and Context: Anthropological Perspectives.* London: Pluto Press.

17.

Future Generations and Global Standards: Children's Rights at the Start of the Millennium

JUDITH ENNEW

Shortly after the forces of Saddam Hussein invaded Kuwait, the largest meeting ever held of heads of state took place in New York. Yet the seventy-one world leaders had not gathered to discuss strategies in the face of almost certain war. The meeting, in September 1990, was entitled "The World Summit for Children" and was convened by the United Nations Emergency Fund for Children (UNICEF). One of the aims of the summit was to obtain the signatures of heads of state to new United Nations human-rights legislation, the Convention on the Rights of the Child. In this objective the meeting was supremely successful. No other piece of human-rights law has come into force so rapidly, nor received quite so much public attention.

The other objective of the meeting was to ensure that children actually enjoy the rights provided in the Convention. The summit ended with agreement on a plan of action that included twelve broad goals to be achieved before the year 2000. All signatories promised to develop national plans of action to this end and to report on progress at five-year intervals. Yet, as a new millennium dawns and a global follow-up meeting is planned, it is clear that in this respect the summit was unsuccessful.

Legally, in the words of the Universal Declaration of Human Rights, children are "entitled to special care and assistance" and to "grow up in a family environment, in an atmosphere of happiness, love, and understanding." Yet, in reality, children the world over are abused, neglected, and exploited. Many fail to reach adulthood. Although technology and medical knowledge have increased at an unprecedented rate in the past century, five million children still die every year from easily preventable diseases. In nations affected by conflict, such as Afghanistan,

Angola, Mozambique, and Sierra Leone, up to a third of all infants die. As civilians are increasingly affected by modern warfare, more children are killed in armed conflict than in previous centuries. Moreover, it is clear from national reports on the summit goals that they have not, in general, been achieved. From the point of view of children, the twentieth century was a disaster.

It is ironic to reflect that, around 1900, a Swedish reformer, Ellen Key, claimed that this would be a "century of childhood," in which both women and children would be freed from the control of men and change the world for the better. The twentieth century indeed saw women's role change in many countries. Where they were formerly valued mostly for their ability to bear and raise children, they are now expected to join men as equals in education, politics, and the workplace. Yet this means that child rearing, language development, education, and socialization are increasingly in the hands of a battery of new professions. Instead of being a century of children, it became a century of child experts.

CHILDHOOD

The idea of childhood now common in the North is fairly recent. French historian Phillipe Ariés argues that during most of European history children were considered to be the same as adults and had a range of family and social duties by the time they reached the age of six or seven. The change in our current ideas about childhood came alongside changes in family life and work, when manufacture started to take place in factories rather than in homes or small workshops where adults and children had worked side by side. Social reformers throughout the nineteenth century fought to keep children out of factories—and ensured that women stayed at home to care for them. Compulsory schooling ensured that the future workforce was educated in both the skills and work habits needed by industry. The result is that a particular image of childhood has come to appear normal and natural. According to this, children are by definition incapable, and childhood requires specially trained professionals to support parents. Children are effectively separated from adults, and their responsibilities are reduced to obeying orders; playing and learning in protected environments; and consuming special foods, belongings, clothes, and amusements.

Studies of other cultures show that childhood not only varies across different historical periods, it also varies among places and cultures. Children are not as incapable as northern models suggest, and childhood is not always separated from adulthood in the same way. In the North children remain dependent on their parents until well into their teens or even twenties. Yet, in many other parts of the world they are expected to be fully independent from an early age. Many Northern teenagers do not have the social skills to cook, clean, and take responsibility for their own behavior, much less to be trusted to look after a younger child. Yet in the South quite young children often take a virtually full parental role with respect to younger brothers and sisters so that parents can go out and earn the family livelihood. There are many recorded cases of children who are heads of the family and main breadwinners, increasingly so in countries where many parents die as a result of HIV infection. Paradoxically, in developing countries many small girls working as maids are looking after older children in richer families where the northern model of prolonged childhood has been adopted. The majority of children in the South work from an early age in order to bring their family income up to subsistence level; many carry what would be regarded in the North as adult-sized burdens of responsibility for household tasks and child care. For most of them, the ideal standards of northern child development experts are unthinkable luxuries. Intellectual stimulation, playful learning, personal space, and the development of self-awareness are meaningless in practical terms

The Convention on the Rights of the Child does not ignore children's developing capacities. In several places it refers to the need to listen to children's opinions, taking into consideration their "age and maturity." But it does not spell out exactly what is meant by this phrase. This is probably wise. Ideas about age and maturity are not just measured by physical and psychological tests, they are also related to cultural meanings. What is expected of children at different ages varies from one society to another. Age is a heterogeneous meaning system that, like time, is both arbitrary and negotiable. Industrial societies use clock time and chronological age to structure social relationships. Exact ages are known, births and deaths are recorded, and birth date is an inalienable attribute of all citizens, whether young or old, alive or dead. Yet, in many other societies, age is not the most relevant characteristic used to allocate duties and to allow involvement in decision making. In any case, a considerable number of births are not recorded, and large numbers of people the world over do not know their exact age. The relevant social construct in these societies is not age but stage—an idea more logically tied to maturity than age can ever be. In Tanzanian law, for example, what is important is the "apparent age" of a child, for purposes such as deciding whether sex has taken place "under the age of consent." This is a value judgment that is based, on the one hand, on the reality that few young people have birth certificates and, on the other hand, on an assessment about whether the girl involved was able to give informed consent to sexual intercourse. At community and family level, how people are categorized with respect to their social duties and the responsibilities of others toward them is a function of observed, socially agreed, maturity. Thus a boy does not become a man until he is a husband and father with the economic means to support his wife and children. Just being able to impregnate a girl is insufficient proof of manhood.

The Convention on the Rights of the Child defines children by chronological age as human beings under the age of eighteen. But this means that there is no distinction between, for example, a newborn baby and a sexually mature teenager. Yet clearly there are different stages to the progress through childhood. These are formally or informally marked by rituals in all parts of the world, but, as with other aspects of childhood, there are no universals. In addition, growing up is different for boys and girls, not only because they develop different physical features, but also because the social stages are different. To a certain extent this can be based on the clearer physical marker of puberty for girls provided by their first menstruation. For boys, puberty is a less focused event. Yet, in societies in which women and children are economically and socially dependent on men, a girl often becomes a woman at a far earlier age than a boy can become a man. Girls may be married off as soon as practicable after their first menstruation, in order to ensure that they do not become pregnant outside marriage and produce children for whom no father can provide economic support. Boys, on the other hand, may have to wait long after they reach physical maturity before they are recognized as men who can support their own wives and children.

In many societies, this difference between boys and girls is explicitly recognized in the progressive stages boys and girls pass through on the way to adulthood. The Sereer of West Africa provide a typical example. They differentiate very little between boys and girls below the age of seven or eight years. Then, according to the traditional scheme, boys become *sisim*, or the "young of the tribe," and begin to learn the behavior expected of them, largely through being told what not to do. As they approach puberty, probably around the age of eleven years, they become shepherds, or *gaynak*, who are prepared for circumcision, which takes place as part of a ritual process of initiation when they become *pes*, or youth in their early twenties. Young adulthood, or *wayabane*, comes with marriage in the late twenties and early thirties but is not accompanied by the political status of elder or decision maker, which comes with full maturity. Girls, on the other hand, are first educated in the duties and correct behavior of young girls, or *fu ndog*, mostly through numerous prohibitions, until they are about ten years old. The serious business of learning how to behave as a young women is accompanied by tattooing during their adolescence *(nog we)*. They become adult women *(muxolare)* through initiation, which includes education about sexual behavior, and marriage, which occurs for them about ten years earlier than it does for young men.

All societies use ritual to mark stages in the lives of their members, the most universal being those associated with birth, the transition out of childhood to youth or adulthood, marriage, and death. Baptism, marriage, and funeral rites are important social ways of recognizing physical facts. One of the most important functions of the activities that usually accompany initiation is teaching. The knowledge passed on, often while young people are in seclusion and always in separate groups according to gender, involves not only values but also information about sex, sexuality, parenthood and (in the case of girls) childbirth, as well as economic skills such as animal husbandry and agriculture. It may also include secrets related to magic and ritual. Traditional initiation ceremonies are now becoming less frequent and take less time to complete, because they have to be fitted in with the school year. They are increasingly separated from learning and becoming simply public ceremonies. This means that older generations may feel ineffectual because their ancient knowledge no longer appears useful. Young people learn medical facts of sex and reproduction in school, divorced from the cultural understandings and rules of their own communities.

So the position of children in all societies is changing, and they are beginning to be valued in different ways. In the North children are usually seen as a financial cost to society and their parents. Their value is largely sentimental or emotional. Elsewhere they are valued because they work when they are young and can be relied on to provide for their parents when they grow old. All member states of the United Nations, with the exception of the United States and Somalia, have now ratified the Convention on the Rights of the Child, which means that they are bound to observe universal standards. Yet even within each country children experience childhood in many different ways, according to whether they are rich or poor, boys or girls, urban or rural, members of certain ethnic or religious groups, and so forth. Thus the application of global standards is challenged by a complex array of childhoods, each of which appears to be natural to a child's own community. Moreover, even the notion of human rights is not universal, and children's rights often appear to threaten parental authority.

The Convention does not mean that children should be allowed to run riot outside adult control. Its main concern is the recognition that children must enjoy all the rights modern societies acknowledge for all human beings and also those catering to the special vulnerabilities of childhood. One way of understanding this is dividing children's rights into three broad categories that are sometimes referred to as "the three *P*s": provision, protection, and participation. Because children are dependent, they require services that *provide* for their developing needs, such as health and education. They need to be *protected* from abuse, exploitation, and other harm. As they gradually mature they have the right to *participate* by stating their opinions and having them taken into account by adults. This last right is one of the innovative features of the Convention and, although it has raised considerable interest, there are as yet no criteria for assessing what it means. For example, it is sometimes claimed that children participated in the World Summit for Children by singing songs and handing out agendas to the heads of state. Yet some children's-rights activists have referred to this as mere decoration, claiming that visibility is not the same as participation. With respect to provision and protection, however, recent research has provided considerable information about making realities of children's rights.

PROVISION RIGHTS

Provision rights concern children's rights to survive and develop to the maximum of their potential. High infant and child mortality is one of the primary obstacles to social and economic development in many countries and continues to be a massive drain on both human and economic resources. Infants and young children are highly dependent on the care they receive from parents and other caretakers. National and international agencies have invested extensive resources in the management and improvement of mother and child health. Yet, although considerable progress has been made, death and illness rates in the first twenty-four months of life remain higher than for any other age group, except the very old. In some places, health education programs have had little or no impact on eating habits, family planning, and use of immunization services. One problem is that these topics tend to be thought of by planners as purely medical issues. It is true that food intake directly affects bodily processes, but economic and cultural issues determine what is eaten, by whom, in what quantities, when, where, and how.

Breast-feeding, for example, constitutes part of a process of nutritional, social, and emotional care, in which the overall welfare of mother, family, and community are all involved. The process of transition from breast to family fare, from being carried to independent movement, is not only a matter of physical growth. Child development is linked to social and cultural aspects of mother-child relationships, families, communities, and national policies. Poor nutrition may be the result of food availability, but also of beliefs about breast-feeding, weaning processes, and the different social value of girls and boys, as well as of the dynamics of family relationships. These can all be affected by public policies on child rearing and nutrition. From infancy onward a society passes on its most basic ideas through the way it teaches language and early social skills. It is not for nothing that we talk of a child learning its "mother tongue." Even an infant's needs and the ways these are felt, expressed, and responded to are not simple biological factors but are subtly fixed by cultural and societal rules.

These ideas are far from universal. Symptoms such as apathy and listlessness,

which northern medicine might take to be indicators of poor health, may be socially acceptable, or even welcomed as good behavior, and thus not alert parents to
a child's malnutrition. In addition, a demanding baby may be put more frequently
to the breast, or given extra tidbits, and thus fare better in times of crisis than a
passive infant, whose needs may be overlooked by preoccupied parents or other
caretakers. A study of infant temperament among the Maasai (figure 1) during the
sub-Saharan drought of 1973–74 showed that babies could contribute to their
own development and survival. Although it might be supposed that children who
constantly call for attention might be more vulnerable to abuse in a situation of environmental catastrophe, this study found that "difficult" children, who cried and
fretted, were more likely to survive than quieter, more undemanding, children.
Similarly, women in Brazilian shantytowns appear to distinguish sickly children
whose survival is unsure and who will require too much emotional and material
involvement from their mothers. These children seem to be subjected to passive

FIGURE 1 Maasai mother and child in a village close to the
Maasai Mara Game reserve, Kenya. (© Adrian Arbib/Survival)

neglect. If they survive, all well and good, and mothers will gradually become attached to them and care for them, but if they die they are just fulfilling expectations.

Where family food supplies are inadequate, children often progress well while they are being breast-fed and then deteriorate after they are weaned. In one rural area of Vietnam, for example, the percentage of children who are malnourished in the first year of life is around 12 percent, rising sharply to 37 percent between one and two years of age. This is linked to the fact that children tend to be weaned around the age of two years. Many cultures acknowledge that this is a risky time for children. Weaning is frequently associated with the arrival of a new baby and feelings of resentment in the supplanted older brother or sister. Among the Ga of Southern Ghana, jealousy toward a newborn baby is expected. Parents and grandparents are expected to make a special fuss over the displaced sibling to prevent irritability, refusal to eat, loss of bladder and bowel control, and loss of weight. The Ga term *kwashiorkor*, which refers to this mix of psychological and physical symptoms, has been appropriated by modern medicine to refer to a purely physical condition of severe protein deficiency often associated with weaning.

The severe wasting condition known by the Greek term *marasmus* in northern medicine is not so closely associated with weaning. The Samia of Western Kenya distinguish clearly between this and *kwashiorkor*. Both conditions are seen as having social origins. *Marasmus* is viewed as being the result of breach of moral values, known as *ekhira* and associated particularly with adultery by the child's parents or others in its social environment, even the midwife. *Kwashiorkor*, on the other hand, is associated with witchcraft or "the evil eye," particularly before a child is weaned. Both these ideas tend to emphasize the importance of breast-feeding. Thus traditional beliefs and practices enhance the survival chances of both child and mother. By the same token national child-rearing policies and health education programs need to harness such beliefs if they are to be successful.

Traditional learning also needs to be taken into account when state education systems are planned. Yet this is seldom the case, and children often experience a contradiction between the knowledge and values of their homes and the things they are taught at school. If schools fail to take community values into account when they teach sex education, for example, confusions about what is acceptable sexual behavior may result in disruptions in families and even activities that could further the spread of HIV infection. Thus it is particularly important that the Convention not only insists on the right to education, but also makes provision for children to be taught in their own languages and with respect for their own cultures.

Education does not only take place in schools. Children need to learn how to be full members of their communities. This informal learning occurs through the ways they are treated by adults. They learn by watching and copying, through explanation, example, discipline, and play in the course of sharing work and relaxation with adults. As children become increasingly separated from adults in the modern world, so children's games and toys have become specialized commodities that are generally associated with frivolous pastimes. By contrast, when adults are not working, they are said to indulge in leisure, recreation, and competitive sport—they never merely play. Yet play is not trivial. It is a form of learning through experience that is important throughout life, and children's toys have a function in this process. They do not have to be expensive designer commodities, however, for the learning to be successful. "Cat's cradle" games with string have been reported from places as far apart as the Arctic and the Great Australian Desert. Throughout his life, Alfred Haddon, one of the fathers of British social anthropology, stressed their value as a way of making friends in strange societies and he advised new researchers to master the art before setting off to the field. The function of these apparently innocent games in other societies is not simply that they keep children occupied. Nor are they regarded as trivial pursuits. Children in subsistence societies have a good deal of work to do, and adults also "play" at cat's cradle. String figures are fun of course, but in the societies in which they originate, they also serve to remind players of features of their environment: birds, beasts, plants, and the topography of the natural world. Thus they may represent the shapes of nearby mountains, showing that a form of geography lesson can take place, passing information between generations without writing or pictures, but nevertheless in three dimensions. In European history too, adults and children frequently shared the same games, often associated with festivals, such as Christmas, Twelfth Night, and harvest festivals that united communities.

PROTECTION

In an ideal world all adults would provide all children with an environment in which they could develop their full potential and become healthy, useful members of society. Unfortunately this is not the case, and it is not sufficient to provide health and education services and to support families as they bring up the children in their care. Children also have to be protected from adults—even sometimes their own parents—who abuse, neglect, and exploit them. In the decade since the World Summit for Children, this has been increasingly recognized, and a number of issues, such as child labor, child sexual abuse, and exploitation, have become topics of widespread public concern as well as new international legislation and programs. In each of these cases it is increasingly clear that immediate reactions of shock and the desire to rescue children have to give way to considered responses based on understanding different cultural perceptions and gathering good information.

For instance, the past two decades have seen a marked increase in media reports about the sexual abuse and exploitation of children. These have ranged from often hysterical reports about long-term abuse of children by their families in the Shetland Islands to tales of children used by sex tourists in Thailand and teenage prostitutes in the streets of New York. It is often claimed that sexual abuse is growing at an extraordinary rate, yet, according to most clinical and social work practitioners, the increase is more likely to be an effect of an increase in recognition and reporting. In addition, many misunderstandings influence statistical accounts of child abuse.

There are three levels at which abuse can be understood. In the first case there are cultural practices that seem to be abusive when viewed from outside. In the second place, certain actions are regarded as abusive within a culture, because they depart from normally accepted rules. Slapping a child is regarded as abusive in Sweden, but as proper socialization in many countries. In Hawaii it is regarded as preferable to verbal punishments that last longer and affect a child's self-esteem. The third level of abuse, which is beyond the control of those who care directly for children, is societal neglect, in which there is no money left over for child health, welfare, and education because a government is spending the bulk of its income on arms and defense.

Similarly it is sometimes argued that scandals and exaggerations about abuse and exploitation draw public attention away from poverty-related neglect. According to this, media and welfare authorities have allowed the relatively small group of street children to dominate programs that would do better to address problems of urban poverty in general. The most common assumption about children who live on the street away from their families is that they are malnourished, and a frequent project intervention is of the soup-kitchen variety. While malnutrition may be a problem for poor children in general, the available evidence indicates that street children are sometimes better nourished than their rural or slum-dwelling contemporaries. This may be because it is the better-fed, stronger children who have the energy and enterprise to espouse street life (figure 2). Or it may indicate that, once they are on the street, children have better access to food. There is ample anecdotal evidence to indicate that where there is an urban restaurant culture (as in Latin America), street children are able to beg a variety of high-quality, leftover food from restaurants and cafes. A comparative study of the

FIGURE 2 Street children, Calcutta. (Sean Sprague/Panos)

nutritional status of homeless Nepali boys in Kathmandu and rural and urban children living with their families found that in terms of physical growth, and despite exposure to infections, the street boys fared better than both village and slum-dwelling children.

Many organizations providing for street children claim in their fund-raising publicity that street children lack concentration and are aggressive. These characteristics are frequently attributed to the stress of street life, the lack of self-esteem felt by "abandoned" children who are stigmatized by society. Yet in most cases children have chosen to leave home and live on the street, and the majority return home to their families from time to time, especially for family festivals. It is also often asserted that street children have lost all moral values and are incapable of feeling or giving affection. However, an increasing number of well-grounded research projects are showing, as with nutrition, that the psychosocial profile of street children is by no means simple. A study of the street children of Johannesburg not only provided anecdotal evidence of altruistic behavior but also showed that their moral attitudes were those of mainstream society. Another study of street children in Cali used a battery of psychological tests, concluding that the street children surveyed were far from being universally damaged in terms of neurological functioning and self-esteem. A team of medical and social scientists in Nepal tested stress levels of street children in Kathmandu, using cortisol levels in saliva samples and comparing them with control groups of children living with their families. The results showed that stress levels of the street children were "surprisingly low."

GLOBALIZING CHILDHOOD

Representatives of northern countries in which childhood is commonly considered an especially vulnerable and incapable state were largely responsible for drafting the Convention on the Rights of the Child. Through international welfare organizations, ideas of childhood are exported to the South. Northern-trained psychologists perform experiments on intellectual development, sometimes with no adjustment to allow for the effects of culture and variables such as malnutrition. Governments in countries where children live in extended families, encouraged by foreign funding, promote the notion that correct parenting takes place only in a family with two parents, two children, and one pay packet. Even in the North, childhood is something of a mirage. The realities of childhood innocence and happiness are far less frequent than the myths about them.

Early debates on the Convention on the Rights of the Child tended to be dominated by legal standard setting. Now that policy goals and interventions for implementing these standards are being drawn up, it is important to explore the meanings they have in different cultural contexts. One danger of accepting the idea that other systems of concepts and beliefs can be equally rational is that this can suggest that universal standards cannot be set. Local cultural ideas and practices might always be used to counter them. Corporal punishment is a case in point. International human-rights law defines beating a child as a violation of human rights. Local perception may be that it is a child's right to be disciplined and that beating is the traditional way to do this. It is all too easy to end in an impasse in such discussions, with culture being used as a trump card and often being purloined and rewritten to suit political arguments that have nothing to do with the welfare of children. Yet international standards can be set, not through establishing which system is "best," nor by negotiating some kind of lowest possible denominator, but by moving the debate to another level in which different activities are viewed as serving the same social necessities. This can be easiest to demonstrate at a practical level. For example, children traumatized by war in Zimbabwe and Mozambique have been demonstrated to recover better through the use of traditional methods of healing than through psychological counseling imported by foreign aid workers. Traditional healing is certainly cheaper and probably restores children more effectively into the lives of their communities, in which such healing methods are a natural part of the way people think. Those who plan policies and programs for children would be well advised to take into account detailed information about the ways children actually live in their communities, as well as local beliefs about childhood. Otherwise they may not only waste resources on projects that do not last because they are not meaningful in the context of children's daily lives, they may also put children at risk of violations of their rights.

SUGGESTIONS FOR FURTHER READING

Alston, P. 1994. *The Best Interests of the Child: Reconciling Culture and Children's Rights*. Oxford: Macmillan.

Connolly, M., and J. Ennew, eds. 1996. "Children Out of Place." *Childhood* 3, no. 2: 131–45.

Corsaro, W. 1997. *The Sociology of Childhood*. Thousand Oaks, CA, London, New Delhi: Pine Forge Press.

Ennew, J. 1986. *The Sexual Abuse of Children*. Cambridge: Polity Press.

James, A., and A. Prout, eds. 1990. *Constructing and Reconstructing Childhood*. Brighton, U.K.: Falmouth Press.

Kenyatta, J., 1938. *Facing Mount Kenya*. London: Martin, Secker & Warburg.

La Fontaine, J. 1994. *Child Sexual Abuse*. Cambridge: Polity Press.

Scheper-Hughes, N., ed. 1987. *Child Survival: Anthropological Perspectives on the Treatment and Maltreatment of Children*. Dordrecht, Holland: D. Reidel.

Scheper-Hughes, N., and C. Sargent, eds. 1999. *Small Wars: The Cultural Politics of Childhood*. Berkeley: University of California Press.

Van Bueren, G., ed. 1998. *Childhood Abused: Protecting Children against Torture, Cruel, Inhuman, and Degrading Treatment and Punishment*. Aldershot, Hampshire, U.K., and Brookfield, VT: Ashgate.

18.

The Anthropology of Science

SARAH FRANKLIN

As anthropology has come to be more focused upon contemporary Western culture and society in the twenty-first century, one of the major new fields to emerge as an important ethnographic site has been the investigation of science and technology. This has taken a number of forms and has led to significant theoretical challenges for anthropology (itself also a science), including how to define what science is and does. While some anthropologists have worked alongside scientists in the laboratory as a means of conducting an ethnography of scientific practice, others have examined science as a cultural system, tracing its meanings and effects more widely. Still other anthropologists have examined science as a cross-cultural, or transnational, practice. In the process, anthropologists have asked how science emerges as a specific form of cultural activity, both in the West and elsewhere, and how it both shapes and is shaped by the broader currents of society. They have also asked what science is and how it may change in the future.

The production of scientific knowledge is a highly valued activity, and it has long been argued that Western scientific knowledge holds a privileged form of authority in modern industrialized societies. Indeed the entire project of modernity is deeply rooted in a post-Enlightenment ethos of rationality, progress, and innovation epitomized by scientific, medical, and technological advances. At the same time, science has also been increasingly at odds with modernity in the second half of the twentieth century and at the turn of the new millennium. While modern, industrialized societies remain highly dependent on scientific and technological innovation, this is also seen to have potentially destructive effects, in the form of environmental damage, effects on human health, or disasters such as the one at Chernobyl. While scientific accomplishments are still held in high esteem, growing public distrust of science and increasing awareness of scientific uncertainty has created what some sociologists call the "risk society," described by Ulrich Beck (1992) as "a phase of development of modern society in which the social, political, ecological, and individual risks created by the momentum of innovation increasingly elude the control and protective institutions of industrial society" (27).

On the one hand, science is described as a means of objective description, based on the experimental method as a means of discovery and dedicated to improved and more accurate, rational understandings of the natural, chemical, and physical properties of the world around us. On the other hand, science is clearly a particular way of knowing, and while it is premised on an objective relationship to the phenomena it describes, this relationship is neither as fixed nor as straightforward as it might appear. Both in terms of how scientists who conduct scientific investigations understand their work, and in terms of how scientific ideas and imagery permeate other dimensions of social life, it is clear that science means many things to many people. From an anthropological perspective, this is neither surprising nor problematic, as science is in this respect no different from any other social activity. Indeed, it is the very diversity encompassed within the relations of science and society which has made it such a productive site of anthropological inquiry.

Anthropologists who work alongside scientists in the laboratory have taken a number of approaches to the practice of "ethnography in the lab." For Stefan Helmreich, who studied artificial-life (A-life) scientists at work in the Institute for the Study of Complexity in Los Alamos, New Mexico, the opportunity to examine scientific narratives of the creation of artificial life produced findings which evoked very traditional anthropological themes. Helmreich (1998) found, for example, a close correspondence between Biblical ideas of creation and paternity and the origin narratives of A-life scientists, whose accounts of the "genesis" of virtual life bore striking resemblances to Judeo-Christian models of genealogy, divinity, and paternity—despite the avowed atheism of many A-life researchers. Science fiction, another potent source of imaginative inspiration for A-life researchers, appears in Helmreich's account not as the opposite of science but as an integral part of it. Contrary to the view of science as neutral, objective, and shaped by a disciplined encounter between the experimental method and the "real world," Helmreich's account reveals the extent to which scientists also create the conditions they study. Arguing that the high-tech world of scientific innovation in A-life communities reproduces very specific idioms of kinship, gender, and sexuality which shape core elements of A-life science, Helmreich's ethnography emphasizes how deeply cultural values and beliefs shape even the most objective aspects of research science.

Other anthropologists have similarly mapped the ideological worlds and specific rationalities of scientists based on detailed ethnographic studies of highly specialized scientific professionals at work. For example, Hugh Gusterson's study of a post–Cold War nuclear weapons laboratory contrasted the rationalities and belief systems of nuclear scientists against those of antinuclear protestors in a study which foregrounds the diverse positions informing relationships to modernity, progress, and the politics of arms control. Gusterson (1997) argues that such studies are crucial to the "repatriation of anthropology," claiming that

in an era when our understanding of what it means to be human is increasingly being transformed by the men and women in white lab coats who splice genes and split atoms, in an era when the practice of daily life is increasingly mediated by such technologies as the internet, Prozac, and television, we need more anthropologists to explore the complex articulations and disjunctures between science and society. (226)

In his ethnographic account of the development of polymerase chain reaction (PCR), the genetic engineering technique for which Kary Mullis won a Nobel Prize in 1993, anthropologist Paul Rabinow (1996a) provides a detailed portrait of scientists at work in the rapidly expanding biotechnology industry. Like Gusterson, Rabinow examines the specific rationalities guiding scientists' efforts, locating these within "styles of life" of young scientists who chose to work in industry rather than pursue academic careers. Rabinow describes the biotechnology industry as "a distinctive configuration of scientific, technical, cultural, social, economic, political, and legal elements, each of which had its own separate trajectory in the preceding decades" (19). Describing the context of innovation as itself like an experiment of sorts, Rabinow provides an account of science-in-the-making as a set of movements and swerves whereby "the concept [of PCR] became an experimental system; the experimental system became a technique; the techniques became concepts" (169).

For Rabinow, such changes in the production of scientific knowledge, which are instrumentally driven by technical innovations rather than a more abstract "search for truth," exemplify wider forms of cultural change. He uses the term "biosociality" to describe the ways in which the new genetics are reshaping not only ideas about science and innovation, but about the future of humanity, individual identity, and society. Rabinow claims that

in the future the new genetics will cease to be a biological metaphor for modern society and will become instead a circulation network of identity terms and restriction loci, around which a truly new type of autoproduction will emerge which I call "biosociality." . . . In biosociality nature will be modeled on culture understood as practice. Nature will be known and remade through technique and will finally become artificial, just as culture becomes natural. (1996b, 99)

In Rabinow's account, science is a form of material culture as well as a potent source of cultural meaning, combined in ways that both reflect and reshape changing cultural values and "styles of life" at the same time as the new genetic sciences also produce new life forms.

Studies such as those by Gusterson, Rabinow, and Helmreich raise new questions for anthropologists at a number of levels. Studying scientists involves working with elite professional groups who are by definition experts in their respective fields. This creates a situation for the anthropologist of "studying up," as Laura Nader has described it, whereby the usual power relation of the anthropologist to his or her informants is reversed. Rather than confronting questions about the colonial legacy, which has positioned anthropologists as more powerful than the groups they have traditionally studied, the anthropology of science frequently requires the ethnographer to assume a subordinate position in pursuing fieldwork. The innovation thus required of the ethnographer in such a situation to devise strategies to become accepted, trusted, and integrated into the working groups they study is considerable and adds a unique dimension to studies of this sort.

A similar challenge attends the task of revealing science to be as culturally based a social activity as anything else. In contrast to the view of science described by Sharon Traweek (1988) in her pioneering study of physicists in the United States and Japan as a "culture of no culture," ethnographers of science are attentive to the personal, cultural, and professional values which shape the production of scientific knowledge and the pursuit of technological innovation. Thus the anthropology of science offers a critical perspective on a uniquely privileged sphere of activity, revealing it to be shaped by very distinctive cultural forces, even as it also exerts a powerful determining influence on the rest of society.

Just as anthropologists have studied both the sciences of life and the sciences of death, so too have they examined everyday controversies over scientific authority as it enters into the most quotidian aspects of life. Christopher Toumey's work on scientific meanings in everyday life examines scientific authority as a source of important symbols which are mobilized in very different ways by actors in a range of social contexts. Examining contestations over scientific authority in diverse contexts—from debates over evolutionary theory to uncertainties about water flouridation—Toumey (1996) considers science from the point of view of "how we borrow bits and pieces of science, loose and jagged, to aid our existential efforts to make sense of our lives" (9). He argues that in American society a considerable gap separates scientific and popular understandings of science, and that this gap produces a number of paradoxes in terms of how scientific authority is used—for example, the amount of authority that is invested in scientific explanations at the same time they are very poorly understood.

From an anthropological standpoint, such paradoxical relationships to scientific authority are hardly surprising, as ethnographic studies frequently reveal the shifting and contradictory aspects of people's lives in relation to all social structures and norms, such as the family and kinship, political authority, wealth and property, or institutionalized religion. To discover that science is not "properly" understood by the general public is therefore only surprising in relation to the expectation that we are all fully rational, logical, and predictable in our thoughts and our behaviors, which, as any ethnographer can quickly tell you, is happily not the case. While this understanding of science may appear unfamiliar, such a perspective is part of the process of "making the familiar strange" for which anthropology is often best appreciated. What science stands for, and the authority it holds as a form of expert knowledge, are issues that arise from the premise that scientific "facts" can mean quite different things in different contexts and to different people. Scientist's own understandings of science are diverse as well and have different shaping influences on the "swerves" and directions that scientific research follows in the course of experimental discovery.

Interventions into human reproduction and genetics are not surprisingly the subject of several studies by anthropologists, given the profound implications of projects such as the Human Genome Initiative and the considerable public debate surrounding innovations such as cloning. While such developments are hailed as evidence of scientific progress and celebrated as triumphs of human ingenuity, they also engender considerable public unease—a discomfort often associated with the image of scientists "playing God" with the facts of life. Recent research by the Medicine and Society program of the Wellcome Trust (1998) in Britain, for example, has yielded further insight into public perceptions of cloning by identifying one of the primary sources of public distrust as the scientific community itself. The Wellcome report offers the intriguing finding that public acceptance of cloning is not enhanced by increased understanding of the new genetics. In fact, the more focus-group participants understood about the science of cloning (which they proved very adept at assimilating), the more distrustful they became: "As participants' awareness increased, so did their concern and apprehension," the study concludes (Wellcome Trust 1998, 25). Participants in the focus groups viewed regulation with skepticism, and "were unconvinced public opinion would have any effect on what research was done" (35). While their expectations of medical research were described as "high," the study revealed frequent turns to "conspiracy theory" and found that "suggestions that secret research was taking place were common" (37). One of the main conclusions of the Wellcome report is that members of the British public believe they are largely ignorant of what is going on in science laboratories. They are distrustful and do not believe what they are told by government representatives, policymakers, or regulatory bodies. They feel that scientists are themselves high-handed and dismissive of their concerns, and they feel their own opinions matter very little in debates over controversial subjects such as cloning.

Anthropologists have an important role to play in relation to findings such as those contained in the Wellcome report. In writing of the new reproductive technologies, for example, Marilyn Strathern (1992) has argued that technological assistance to human reproduction makes explicit a significant transformation of the very meaning of nature or of "natural" facts, such as the "facts of life." In rendering processes such as conception amenable not only to technological intervention but also to increased consumer choice, what were formerly the "biological facts" of human procreation are displaced by new knowledges and techniques, introducing an insecurity into a domain of social activity integral to the definition of social relations through kinship, parenthood, family, and genealogy. As Strathern notes, "Developments in reproductive medicine do not just comprise new procedures; they also embody new knowledge. In redefining the conditions under which it is possible to live or die, reproductive technology puts people in the position of making new kinds of choices in the context of new kinds of information" (1995, 347).

As a consequence, "there is no vacuum in people's practices and habits of thought" (Strathern 1995, 348). For, "If new knowledge takes away old assumptions, it will have put new assumptions in their place" (348). Strathern argues that new technologies of human reproduction make explicit a contingency in what were formerly understood as the intractable, natural, universal foundations of human procreation. Consequently, such technologies have a displacing effect, whereby previous assumptions about the inviolability of "the facts of life" are replaced by other assumptions—for example, that technology can transcend such limitations. The effect of this substitution, Strathern argues, makes explicit not only the content but the formal qualities of Euro-American knowledge practices. The importance of "natural facts" to Euro-American kinship thinking reveals a particular model of knowledge, and indeed a particular cultural logic, through which the world is understood. In sum, the interventions into reproduction occurring in the context of new reproductive technology can show us how "Euro-American kinship was always about a kind of knowledge" (360).

Research such as that undertaken by Strathern on new reproductive technologies thus refigures traditional anthropological interest in kinship to examine the kinds of uncertainties surrounding new technologies such as those outlined in the Wellcome report on cloning, described earlier. For example, the finding that public confidence in science is not ameliorated by greater scientific literacy can be widened to suggest that the displacing effects of scientific intervention engender fundamental questions about relationality, sociality, and the domain of the natural. Part of the repatriation of anthropology described by Gusterson, then, is the effort to examine the particularity of Western, or Euro-American, knowledge practices. This has implications not only within the production of science, as Gusterson, Traweek, Rabinow, and Helmreich have shown; it also has consequences for spheres of social interaction and personal identity, such as kinship, which may seem unrelated to highly specialized work in scientific laboratories. It is in the interconnections between these diverse approaches to "science as culture" that a uniquely anthropological portrait of science has begun to emerge.

REFERENCES

Beck, Ulrich. 1992. *Risk Society: Towards a New Modernity*. London: Sage.

Edwards, Jeannette; Sarah Franklin; Eric Hirsch; Frances Price; and Marilyn Strathern. 1999. *Technologies of Procreation: Kinship in the Age of Assisted Conception*. 2d ed. London: Routledge.

Franklin, Sarah. 1995. "Science as Culture, Cultures of Science." *Annual Review of Anthropology* 24: 163–84.

———. 1997. *Embodied Progress: A Cultural Account of Assisted Conception*. London: Routledge.

Franklin, Sarah, and Helena Ragoné, eds. 1998. *Reproducing Reproduction: Kinship, Power, and Technological Innovation*. Philadelphia: University of Pennsylvania Press.

Gusterson, Hugh. 1997. *Nuclear Rites: A Nuclear Weapons Laboratory at the End of the Cold War*. Berkeley: University of California Press.

Heath, Deborah, and Paul Rabinow, eds. 1993. *Bio-Politics: The Anthropology of the New Genetics and Immunology*. Special issue of *Culture, Medicine, and Psychiatry* 17: 1.

Helmreich, Stefan. 1998. *Silicon Second Nature: Culturing Artificial Life at the Turn of a Millennium*. Berkeley: University of California Press.

Hess, David. 1992. "Introduction: The New Ethnography and Anthropology of Science and Technology." *Knowledge and Society* 9: 1–28 (special issue: *The Anthropology of Science and Technology*, ed. D. Hess and L. Layne).

———. 1997. "If You're Thinking of Living in STS: A Guide for the Perplexed." In *Cyborgs and Citadels: Anthropological Interventions in Emerging Sciences and Technologies*, ed. G. Downey and J. Dumit, 143–64. Santa Fe, NM: School of American Research Press.

Rabinow, Paul. 1996a. *Making PCR: A Story of Biotechnology*. Chicago: University of Chicago Press.

————. 1996b. *Essays on the Anthropology of Reason*. Princeton, NJ: Princeton University Press.

Rapp, Rayna. 1994. "Risky Business: Genetic Counseling in a Shifting World." In *Articulating Hidden Histories*, ed. J. Schneider and R. Rapp, 175–89. Berkeley: University of California Press.

————. 1995. "Heredity, or Revising the Facts of Life." In *Naturalizing Power: Essays in Feminist Cultural Analysis*, ed. S. Yanagisako and C. Delaney, 69–86. New York: Routledge.

Strathern, Marilyn. 1992. *Reproducing the Future: Anthropology, Kinship, and the New Reproductive Technologies*. Manchester, England: Manchester University Press.

————. 1995. "Displacing Knowledge: Technology and the Consequences for Kinship." In *Conceiving the New World Order: The Global Politics of Reproduction*, ed. F. Ginsburg and R. Rapp, 346–64. Berkeley: University of California Press.

Toumey, Christopher. 1996. *Conjuring Science: Scientific Symbols and Cultural Meanings in American Life*. New Brunswick, NJ: Rutgers University Press.

Traweek, Sharon. 1988. *Beamtimes and Lifetimes: The World of High-Energy Physics*. Cambridge, MA: Harvard University Press.

Wellcome Trust, Medicine and Society Programme. 1998. *Public Perceptions on Human Cloning*. London: The Wellcome Trust.

Wynne, Brian. 1996. "May the Sheep Safely Graze? A Reflexive View of the Expert-Lay Knowledge Divide." In *Risk, Environment, Modernity: Towards a New Ecology*, ed. Scott Lash, Bronislaw Szerzynski, and Brian Wynne. London: Sage.

19.

Fieldwork at the Movies:
Anthropology and Media

FAYE GINSBURG

MODES OF IMAGINING

A 1998 piece on the opinion page of the *New York Times* offered this tale of media, late capitalism, and the local meanings of globalization:

John Burns, the *New York Times* New Delhi bureau chief, tells me a delightful story about his seventy-year-old Indian cook. Although John has four different satellite dishes on his roof top ("I'm practically running an uplink station" he says), he still couldn't get the World Cup matches off Indian TV. When he was complaining about this over breakfast, his cook invited John to come over to his house next door. When they entered, John found the cook's illiterate wife watching the BBC. "I said, 'What's she doing? She doesn't even speak English.'" The cook explained that a friend of his had started a "private" cable system and strung cable into his house along the local telephone poles—for $3.75 a month. "Then he hands me the television remote," says John, "and with increasing astonishment I start at Channel 1 and click all the way to Channel 27. He had television stations from China, Pakistan, Australia, Italy, France. With all my satellite dishes, I had only 14 stations. (Friedman 1998: A11)

This anecdote depends for its effect on the assumption that both writer and reader are American and collaborate in the persistence of the smug, if occasionally guilt-ridden, assumptions that media technologies of modernity (cinema and television) or postmodernity (cable, satellites, VCRs and computers) are securely in the hands of the West. Their circulation "elsewhere" (Third and Fourth World settings) has been interpreted variously as the project of development and modernization schemes, or as cultural imperialism that has escalated with the rapid globalization of media distribution. What is meant to surprise in the story is the inversion of those assumptions, as an elderly Indian couple of modest means and apparently limited cultural sophistication have set up an inexpensive and effective cable system that gives them access to a globe's worth of television, while the rich American neighbor, armed with outsize technology, struggles to tune in to a soccer game. It is this world next door to the bureau chief, unanticipated by Western media theory, in which media circulates within and between non-Western countries, that a number of anthropologists (and others) argue has been ignored in contemporary scholarship, despite the strong interest in transnational cultural flows.

In 1993, in a comprehensive review essay, Debra Spitulnik invoked the insights of Stuart Hall and other sociologically grounded media scholars to call for more engagement by anthropologists with "mass media as vehicles of culture, as modes of imagining and imaging communities." Five years later, a fertile domain of study—the anthropology of mass media—has emerged along with a general rethinking of the practice of anthropology. Cultural worlds are growing ever closer due to the ease with which travel and migration now take place and especially due to the spread of media, which send images of other cultures ricocheting around the globe. For many years mass media were seen as almost a taboo topic for anthropology, too redolent of Western modernity and cultural imperialism for a field identified with tradition, the non-Western, and the vitality of the local. As media are becoming more ubiquitous, even in remote locales, an increasing number of anthropologists have recognized the necessity of attending not only to the presence, but also to the significance of film, television, video, and radio as part of the everyday life of people throughout the world, taking up with new interest the study of the production, circulation, and consumption of mass-media forms, as well as visual culture, broadly conceived. People who are studying these forms as vehicles for the mediation and expression of social processes and cultural meanings are working in field sites as diverse as BBC boardrooms, villages in upper Egypt, fan clubs in south India, radio stations in Zambia, or popular talk shows in Bolivia, and even in anthropology classes.

The anthropology of mass media is informed by several intertwined legacies of thought. A number of scholars link their work on media to the field of visual anthropology, often bringing a critical revision of that field through the lens of anticolonial scholarship, especially on ethnographic, documentary, and popular film practices, past and present. Others focus on its empirical counterpart in the production of a variety of alternative, diaspora, and small-media practices made by people who until recently were only objects and never producers in the enterprise of cross-cultural representation.

Another, related, concern emerges among those interested in how processes of modernity, postmodernity, and globalization actually work on the ground. Aca-

FIGURE 1 Family watching television in Upper Egypt. (Courtesy of Lila Abu-Lughod)

demics investigating these themes track the cultural effects of transnational flows of people, ideas, and objects (in some cases mediated by film, video, and television) and how they help create what Benedict Anderson (1983) aptly called "imagined communities" of the nation. Anthropologist Arjun Appadurai (1996) has been influential in pointing to the prominence of media as a central part of public culture. His influential essay on "global ethnoscapes" points to the significance of the spread of film, television, video, and photography throughout the world. Attending to what he calls "mediascapes"—the ways in which satellite, video, and electronic technologies transcend nation-state boundaries that were sustained more easily through print and terrestrial television—he argues for the increasing significance of the imagination in the production of culture and identity in the contemporary world, offering an extraordinary range of possible lives to many people in many different parts of the world.

The significance of media as a dimension of culture crucial to comprehending the contemporary social world is especially clear in number of recent groundbreaking projects that provide models for how claims about media can actually guide research. Lila Abu-Lughod's work on the production, circulation, and impact of Egyptian television melodrama serials is exemplary, tracking how these are intended by the state to operate (if not always successfully) as a means to mold its citizens. In one of her recent articles (Abu-Lughod 1997) on the social life of these narrative forms as they move from producers to audiences, she demonstrates how, by staging heightened emotional display, television melodramas encourage viewers to embrace individuality over kinship—a key transformation in the making of modern subjects.

One might think of these linked processes of the cultural production of media, its circulation as a social technology, and the relationship of mediated worlds to self-fabrication as existing on a continuum. On one end is the more self-conscious cultural activism in which cultural material is used and strategically deployed as part of a broader project of political empowerment. For indigenous and minoritized groups, such work can provide what Homi Bhabha (1994) has articulated as "a third space" (or, more self-consciously, what some have called Third Cinema), in which traditional lines of identity are blurred and political mobilization is incipient. In the middle range are reflexive but less strategic processes in which the imaginative encounter with cinematic or televisual images and narratives may be expressive and/or constitutive of a variety of social worlds such as the transnational links that video, television shows, films, and computer networks provide for diaspora communities. On the other end of the continuum are the more classic formations of mass media such as national cinemas and television. In this case, anthropological research focuses on the complex and divergent ways they operate, tracking the often unstable relation between intention and effect as these media are put to the service of constituting modern citizens in the Third World through a variety of forms, notably in popular soap operas, telenovelas, melodramatic serials, cultural programming, and talk shows, and examining how these are intended and understood from production to distribution to consumption.

Because anthropologists so frequently locate themselves in non-Western and remote places, their research not only offers a thick, vertically integrated , and multisited sense of the social life of media, but also engages with how these kinds of social life occur outside the circuits of First World settings which have provided a West-centered frame for much academic discussion of media until quite recently. Ironically, even those arguing about and against cultural imperialism or researching the exporting of American culture through the circulation of popular film and television programs nonetheless presume the centrality of American media. In an effort to correct that, ethnographers and scholars in media studies are attending increasingly to the circulation of media in settings not dependent on Western hegemonic practices, such as the export of Hindi cinema to other parts of South Asia, or of Mexican telenovelas throughout Latin America. Such work makes clear the insufficiency of bounded concepts of culture as a way of understanding contemporary lives in our own or other societies.

Scholars developing ethnographies of media usually begin with an interest in understanding questions generated by the phenomenon itself, often motivated by a desire to comprehend the popularity, power, and/or passion attached to certain kinds of media production and viewing (e.g., Why is Indian cinema so popular in Nigeria?). It quickly becomes apparent in almost every case that answering these questions leads to an appreciation of the complexity of how people interact with media in a variety of social spaces and of the resulting shifts in the sense of the local as its relation to broader social worlds becomes almost a routine part of everyday life. Understanding the social relations of media production, circulation, and reception in this way entails a grounded focus on the everyday practices and consciousness of social actors as producers and consumers of different forms of media. Their interests and responses shape and are shaped by the variety of possible identities: cultural, generational, gendered, local, national, regional, and transnational. Recognition of this variety forces anthropologists to develop an increasingly complex and plural notion of what constitutes an audience. Indeed, these multiple identities may be part of a single social subject's repertoire of cultural resources, as is clear in the following hypothetical example:

An Egyptian immigrant in Britain, for example, might think of herself as a Glaswegian when she watches her local Scottish channel, a British resident when she switches over to the BBC, an Islamic Arab expatriate in Europe when she tunes in to the satellite service from the Middle East and a world citizen when she channel surfs on CAN. (Sinclair, Jacka, and Cunningham 1996, 25)

While one might focus research around the multiple identities of a single subject, studies are also often multisited, tracking the various social players engaged when one follows the object. Researchers are tracking television serials and films as they move from elite directors to working-class consumers; they might also track the circulation of the physical object itself, such as a cassette recorder, radio, or even radio sound to see how they articulate with (and sometimes oppose) larger hegemonic processes of modernity, assimilation, nation-building, commercialization, and globalization, but in terms that draw attention to how those processes are being localized.

THE ACTIVIST IMAGINARY

The assumption that the center always dominates the so-called periphery too often has meant that scholars have failed to understand what is actually happening in the periphery itself. To correct that problem, much recent anthropological work on mass media addresses counterhegemonic fields of cultural production, most notably in the small but influential study of media—mostly video and low-power television—being produced by minoritized people as a culturally protective response to the introduction of dominant forms of mass media.

In the last two decades, indigenous people have had to deal with the threats and possibilities of mass media entering their lives, primarily through the imposition of satellites and commercial television, and have struggled to find ways to turn that circumstance to their advantage. This point was made effectively by Eric Michaels (1994), who, in the 1980s, worked with Warlpiri people in the Central Desert of Australia to help them develop their own low-power television as an alternative to the onslaught of broadcast and commercial television introduced by the newly launched communications satellite. Michaels's work demonstrated how profoundly different Warlpiri video (and television) was from Western practices of mass media, from the complex ways in which production was organized along kinship lines; to the centrality of sacred landscapes and slow movement that distinguished the formal aesthetics of pieces; to the ways in which Warlpiri watched and interpreted (or were prohibited from watching) certain images, movies, and videos. Since then, other anthropologists, such as Terry Turner (1992), working with different Amazonian groups, have shown how local people may embrace video as part of indigenous projects of cultural revival (see figure 2), how they organize its use according to existing social hierarchies, and how their making of videos is structured by indigenous aesthetic principles (such as repetition with the Kayapó) that guide performance of rituals.

As anthropologists study the impact that media such as video might have on their communities, indigenous media makers are busy using the technologies for a variety of purposes, sometimes as legal documents in negotiations with encompassing states or to assert their presence televisually within national imaginaries. Such works present a kind of Faustian contract, or what Harald Prins (1997) calls "the paradox of primitivism," in which exotic imagery of indigenous people in documentaries about native rights "while effective (perhaps even essential) as political agency, may pervert the cultural heritage that indigenous peoples are committed to preserving." For their own people, these works have multiple aims: cultural preservation through the documenting of ceremonies and traditional activities with elders or the creation of works to teach young people literacy in their own languages; communication among and between communities on issues such as how to confront loggers and gold prospectors; or long-distance communication among relatives separated by vast expanses, such as the Inuit, who are spread across the Arctic (plate 6).

Much of the writing and research on indigenous media has focused on remote communities in the Amazon and Canada's Arctic where media content is produced and consumed primarily by members of the same community (although

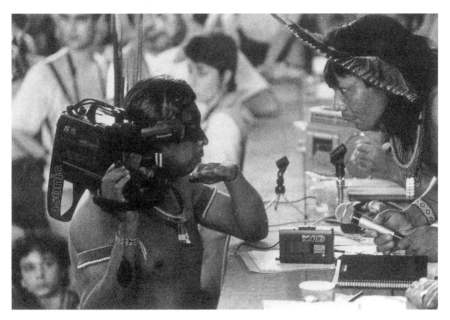

FIGURE 2 The 1989 First International Indian Conference in Altamira, Brazil, demonstrated Amazonian Indians' awareness of the power of the media to create indigenous solidarity and to dramatize their case on the world stage. The Kayapó, who had been working with video locally, were leaders in this effort. The leaders of the Altamira rally, Kuben'i (left) and Payakan (right), had become experienced videocameramen by the time of the conference and planned events partly with an eye toward how visual media, intensifying the combined effect of both traditional dress and videocams, would strategically heighten their display of power. (© Sue Cunningham/Survival)

the work also circulates to other native communities as well as to non-aboriginal audiences via film festivals and broadcasts). Indigenous people who live in or close to metropolitan areas also have been aspiring to be recognized as part of the broader world of media imagery production and circulation, yet they feel that their claim to an indigenous identity within a more cosmopolitan framework is sometimes regarded as inauthentic, as if their comfort with aspects of modernity, including film making, erased their legitimacy. Maori filmmakers were the first to break that barrier with films based on contemporary Maori life such as *Te Rua* (Barry Barclay, 1990) and *Once Were Warriors* (Lee Tamahori), which, in 1994, became the first indigenously made feature to become an international hit. Aboriginal Australian filmmakers Tracey Moffatt (*Bedevil,* 1996) and Rachel Perkins (*Radiance,* 1998) have both shown feature films at the Cannes film festival. Similarly, the opening of the first Native American feature film, *Smoke Signals,* marked an extraordinary moment not only for its distinctive achievement, but as an index of the growth and significance of indigenous media. While such forms of cultural production clearly differ in scale and style from local, community-based video, these media makers insist that there is no absolute dividing line that establishes one arena of indigenous production as somehow "more authentic" than another. These works are all part of the efforts of indigenous people living in a variety of situations to claim a space that is theirs in the world of modernity's representational practices.

This activist engagement with media encompasses not only indigenous work but media being produced by diasporic communities, who use media to create community across dislocation, and by a variety of other minoritized people who have become involved in creating their own representations as a counter to dominant systems. This includes work being done by people with AIDS; Palestinians in Israel's occupied territories; and immigrants and minorities in Europe and the United States. One might think of this creative and self-conscious process of objectification as a form of "cultural activism," a process in which film and video are used by subaltern groups not only to pursue social change but to alter the way in which their cultures are represented. A particularly compelling instance for theorizing the intersection of media, culture, and power is Sreberny-Mohammadi and Mohammadi's (1994) important analysis of the powerful role played by small-scale forms of mass media—audiocassette tapes and leaflets in this case—in the Iranian revolution that deposed the Shah, what some have called "the revolution of the television era." By demonstrating how small-media technologies helped to mobilize people living in a repressive political context, they also challenge mainstream media studies which insist on the continued dominance of the more established media forms.

For these and a number of other scholars, the presence of mass and small media in "cultural peripheries" is more than a part of a global process of the penetration of media. In a way that encompasses contradictions, these technologies signal an increasing awareness and objectification of culture—often stimulating a revival of certain traditional practices—at the same time as they draw local communities into larger processes of social transformation. Appadurai (1996), for example, suggests the word "culturalism" as another way to signify this kind of mobilization of identities, in which mass media and the imagination play an increasingly significant role. Such phenomena, Abu-Lughod (1997) points out, are produced out of unequal cultural encounters with others who may have preconceived notions of their interlocutors as cultural subjects. This work offers an interesting and important perspective on the argument that one of the distinguishing characteristics of modernity is the restructuring of local social relations in much broader frameworks of time and space.

MODERNITY, NATIONAL HEGEMONIES, AND THE UNEXPECTED RESPONSE

Media practices are clearly central to the disjunctions of modernity (or post-modernity) but not necessarily in the ways that we might have expected. The un-predictability and frequent vitality of responses have generated much recent inter-est in what anthropology might offer in terms of an understanding of how such restructuring is taking place. Joining a number of studies by other social theorists theorizing the place of media in the emergence of alternative modernities all over the globe, several recent projects exemplify the value of anthropological research on this topic. In his study of media in northern Nigeria, for example, Brian Larkin (1997a) uses the trope of "parallel modernities" to account for those who are not mobile but who nonetheless participate in the imagined realities of other cultures as part of their daily lives through circuits in which Western media content is only one of many alternatives which might "offer Hausa youth the choice between watching Hausa or Yoruba videos, Indian, Hong Kong, or American films, or videos of Qur'anic *tafsir* (exegesis) by local preachers" (409). The popularity of In-dian cinema is evidenced not only by cinema attendance but also by a burgeoning local culture industry of *littatafan soyayya* (love stories), "pamphlet type books in which the imagined alternative of Indian romance is incorporated within local Hausa reality." The intense interest in the spectacle and plot of Indian films and their indigenization in these *soyyaya* books as well as in locally produced videos (Larkin 1997b) offers Hausa youth a medium through which they can "consider what it means to be modern and what may be the place of Hausa society within that modernity" (434).

The concept of transnational encounters facilitated by mass media in the cre-ation of new social spaces also guides Mayfair Yang's recent work on mass media and transnational subjectivity in Shanghai, and what she calls a Chinese "traveling culture" created through interaction with Hong Kong and Taiwanese popular cul-ture. She tracks how, over the last century, media have played a part in transforma-tions of the Chinese state, first in the development of a new national community and then in the creation of a powerful state subjectivity. Most recently, she is an-alyzing the "reemergence of a transnational Chinese global media public and its effects on the modernist project of the nation-state" (Yang 1997, 287). She joins others in critiquing frameworks of cultural imperialism, popular through the mid-1980s; the point, of course, is not to assume that power is lodged in the West, but to track how and why media are now so closely associated with power and its em-bodiment, so that states everywhere attempt to control the mediation of their own representations and that of others through regulation, censorship, and efforts to contain the means of distribution. In the case of China, it is not Western domination but regional/ethic Chinese capitalist modes of power that are contesting the power of the Chinese state. Yang follows this process through the realignments of satellites, an analysis of programming, and the response of a worker's film criticism group in Shanghai to a popular television show entitled "A Beijing Native in New York" (305). Through their identification with the protagonists who make the journey described in the show's title, they evaluated, vicariously, the costs of being uprooted from family and the familiar against the benefits of exposure to Western modernity and financial opportunities.

Other studies of melodramatic television serials in China, Egypt, and Syria offer helpful cross-national comparisons, suggesting that despite intentions to bolster national sympathies, televisual projects, even when sponsored by a tightly controlled state authority, can in fact foster debate and dissent. In Salamandra's (1998) study of the reception of several different series produced by Syrian Arab Television in 1993 and 1994 for the popular Ramadan period, battles over who controls public representations of history became apparent in the diverse and often critical responses of Damascenes across the social spectrum, despite the ruling Ba'th Party's intention that the series should produce feelings of national pride. Similarly, Rofel's (1994) analysis of "Yearnings" describes how a seemingly innocuous 1991 Chinese television melodrama telling the sagas of two families, the worker Lius and the intellectual Wangs, from the period of the Cultural Revolution to the present, produced considerable debates, in which, she argues, a post-Tiananmen national identity was being worked out, demonstrating the powerful constituencies and interests attached to different narratives of the nation, particularly regarding Chinese womanhood.

PRODUCING AND CIRCULATING CULTURE

In most anthropological studies of media, audiences are varied and situated in a broad social field which strategically includes both producers and audiences in the query, as well as intertextual sources through which meaning is constituted. For example, in her study of Tamil popular cinema—an industry which has a remarkable influence in the creation of political celebrity—Sara Dickey looks at its significance for the urban poor of south India living in the small city of Madurai. Her analysis situates film within a broad social field that includes viewers, filmmakers, film texts, and historical/political circumstances, and sees it as part of a "vast system of popular literature, greeting cards and posters, clothing, fashions, gossip, legends, memories, and activities supporting the stars" (1993, 41), a world in which fan clubs, political activities, and popular opinions play a central role. Seemingly oblivious to this response, middle- and upper-class filmmakers, she argues, view themselves as imparting appropriate cultural ideals to what they regard as narrow and unsophisticated lower classes and unenlightened poor, while these viewers actively participate in creating meaning from images that both represent them and enable them to escape, momentarily, their difficult circumstances.

SELF-REFLECTIONS: ETHNOGRAPHIES OF WESTERN MEDIA

If mass media presented a kind of forbidden object to anthropologists working in non-Western settings, the final boundary was fieldwork in the social worlds and cultural logics of media institutions where "dominant ideologies" are produced. In our own as well as other societies, anthropologists have been bringing new methods and insights to the territory already established by a small but significant body of work by sociologists of media. Recent ethnographies of media as a field of cultural production focus on a variety of institutional sites, including public television production in the United States and the United Kingdom; the use of a variety of media in public relations in the service of human rights as well as capitalism; the practices of war correspondents and *National Geographic*. Other projects are focusing on the world of cinema production, providing a rich set of comparative cases, from the production of culture in the Bombay film industry to the post-Soviet world of film production and the creation of movie stars in Egypt. Ethnographic approaches to these fields provide grounded analyses and critiques of how "technologies of power" are created and contested within such intimate institutional cultures, shaped by ideologies balanced between logics of national public service, audience appeal, aesthetics, and "the audit." Georgina Born, in her study of the BBC (1998), demonstrates how ethnography enables her to break up the apparent unity of public broadcasting into a more complex, fluid, and unstable field governed by different value systems, some aesthetic, some economic, some driven by a concern for audience response. She follows several productions through the system, with attention to other institutional practices of television accountability, such as focus groups, the restructuring of production, aesthetic decision making within genres, and especially the recent importance of (and contradictions created by) new commercial and global distribution imperatives as they bump up against the longstanding ideology of public service.

Ethnographies of cultural production open up the "massness" of media to interrogation as they track the ways in which structures shape the actions of professionals who are in the business of making representations of other cultures, and how structures of power affect image-making practices, an area pioneered by Lutz and Collins (1993) in their study of the history and forms of cultural representation in *National Geographic*. Mark Pedelty's ethnography of war correspondents covering El Salvador's civil war (1995) takes these claims one step further and shows how these cultural producers negotiate among the event, their sources, and their editors, who serve as conduits for expectations of how "exotic cultures" should be framed. He looks at the concrete ways in which American reporters are constrained, for example, by diplomatic sources on whom they depend. News photographers, always interested in the exotic, would focus on the eye-catching images of peasants and Indians in traditional dress but often "as if the person wearing it didn't exist," as the Nobel Prize winning activist Rigoberto Menchu remarked (100). A particularly lively new arena for these kinds of objectifying practices has been the marrying of public relations to social movements for human and cultural rights in spectacles organized to garner glamour and support for their causes. These "nonprofit," intercultural negotiations with the media are often fraught with contradictions and cultural stereotypes on both sides, as Maclagan (1997) elucidates in her groundbreaking study of the strategic deployment of Tibetan "culture," by Tibetan refugees and their Western supporters alike, as they mobilize political support for their cause. Increasingly, these works emphasize that oppositional logics are insufficient for grasping media practices; rather, our models must allow for the simultaneity of hegemonic and antihegemonic effects.

COMPLICITIES

Many ethnographers studying mass media often find themselves implicated in their object of study in a relationship of complicity that places us increasingly in the same social universe as our subjects—if not in an activist relationship, then at times in an unanticipated reversal of authority over the representation of culture. Anthropologists have found themselves working as production assistants, extras in Indian films, or as momentary celebrities on popular talk shows. Anthropologist and filmmaker Jeff Himpele (n.d.) describes how he "got framed as an attraction" for Bolivian television viewers in a rich, reflexive analysis of *Open Forum*, a network TV program (and base for a political party) in which urban Aymara testify as to their problems and receive assistance in return. Initially hoping to do fieldwork there, he went with his Bolivian wife to the studio in La Paz and met with the program coordinator Arturo, who urged him to talk to the host of the show, Compadre Carlos Palenque. "Don't worry. It is the norm that observers also participate in the Forum." As any anthropologist would, Himpele complied. That evening, after seeing himself on television, he recognized an ironic reversal that is one of the hazards of ethnographic work with media.

Instead of the ethnographer representing culture for those back home, here was the local culture-representation business fixing upon my difference in order to promote itself by announcing to people in their homes that a North American anthropologist thought it was worthy of study.

He goes on to describe a growing sense of terror that he had become like the show's host, who exploits the difficulties of Bolivia's poor and indigenous people for his own professional gain.

Anthropologists at last are coming to terms with the inescapable presence of mass media as a contemporary cultural force extending the forms and processes of political expression and the production of identity, including the mediation of hegemonic forms and resistance to them; the growth and transnational circulation of public culture; and the creation of national and activist social imaginaries. Such research has a salutory effect on anthropology as well as media studies, opening up new questions regarding the production and circulation of film and electronic media throughout the world, in non-Western as well as Western societies, potentially resituating the "looking relations"(Gaines 1988) that take place between and among cultures and across boundaries of inequality.

ACKNOWLEDGMENTS

Thanks to numerous friends and colleagues for their helpful discussions and comments, including Barbara Abrash, Lila Abu-Lughod, Annette Hamilton, Brian Larkin, Meg Maclagan Fred Myers, Rayna Rapp and especially to Jeremy MacClancy, editor of this collection, for encouraging me to write this essay and for his expert editorial guidance.

REFERENCES AND SUGGESTIONS FOR FURTHER READING

Abu-Lughod, Lila. 1993. "Editorial Comment: On Screening Politics in a World of Nations." *Public Culture.* 5, no. 3 (spring): 465–69.

———. 1995. "The Objects of Soap Opera: Egyptian Television and the Cultural Politics of Modernity." In *Worlds Apart: Modernity through the Prism of the Local*, ed. Daniel Miller, 190–210. London: Routledge. [These are part of a larger project on questions of modernity, nation-building, gender, and the media which Abu-Lughod has been working on via extensive field research into the production, circulation, and reception of Egyptian soap operas and melodramas. The first reference is a very useful collection of articles on media and nation-building from the journal *Public Culture.*]

———. 1997. "The Interpretation of Culture(s) After Television." *Representations* 59: 109–33.

Anderson, Benedict. 1983. *Imagined Communities: Reflections on the Origins and Spread of Nationalism.* London: Verso.

Ang, Ien. 1985. *Watching Dallas: Soap Opera and the Melodramatic Imagination.* London and New York: Methuen.

———. 1991. *Desperately Seeking the Audience* London: Routledge.

———. 1996. *Living Room Wars: Rethinking Media Audiences for a Postmodern World.* London: Routledge. [Ang's work has been enormously influential in recognizing the complexity of questions of reception. Her concern with cross-cultural work and ethnographic complexity has been influential for anthropologists working in media.]

Appadurai, Arjun. 1996. *Modernity at Large: Cultural Dimensions of Globalization*. Minneapolis: University of Minnesota Press.

Armbrust, Walter, ed. 1998. *The Seen and the Unseeable: Visual Culture in the Middle East*. Special issue of *Visual Anthropology* 10, nos. 2–4.

Banks, Marcus, and Howard Morphy, eds. 1997. *Rethinking Visual Anthropology*. New Haven, CT: Yale University Press. [This is a recent collection that represents how visual anthropology is remaking itself to incorporate topics such as mass media along with the more traditional concerns such as ethnographic film and non-Western art practices.]

Bhabha, Homi. 1994. *The Location of Culture*. New York: Routledge.

Born, Georgina. 1998. "Between Aesthetics, Ethics, and Audit: Reflexivities and Disciplines in the BBC." Talk delivered to Department of Anthropology, New York University, April.

Crawford, Peter, and Siguron Baldur Hafsteinsson, eds. 1994. *The Construction of the Viewer*. Aarhaus, Denmark: Intervention Press. [A yeasty mix of anthropologists and media studies scholars jointly concerned with understanding audiences.]

Dickey, Sarah. 1993. *Cinema and the Urban Poor in South India*. Cambridge: Cambridge University Press.

Dornfeld, Barry. 1998. *Producing Public Television*. Princeton, NJ: Princeton University Press.

Downmunt, Tony, ed. 1993. *Channels of Resistance: Global Television and Local Empowerment*. London: British Film Institute. [Those working with indigenous and other minoritized communities have long seen the embrace of media by such groups as an important resource for local empowerment, as this collection of works by scholars, activists, and media makers demonstrates.]

Friedman, Thomas. 1998. "The Mouse That Roars: A Global Tale." *New York Times*, July 18, A11.

Gaines, Jane. 1988. "White Privilege and Looking Relations: Race and Gender in Feminist Film Theory." *Screen* 29, no. 4: 12–27.

Gallois, Dominique, and Vincent Carelli. 1995. "Video in the Villages: The Waiapi Experience." In *Advocacy and Indigenous Film Making*, ed. Hans Henrik Philipsen and Birgitte Markussen. Hojbjerg, Denmark: Intervention Press.

Ganti, Teja. 1999. "Centenary Commemorations or Centenary Contestations? Celebrating a Hundred Years of Cinema in Bombay." *Visual Anthropology* 11, no. 4 (special issue on Indian cinema): 399–420.

Ginsburg, Faye. 1991. "Indigenous Media: Faustian Contract or Global Village?" *Cultural Anthropology* 6, no. 1: 92–112.

———. 1993. "Aboriginal Media and the Australian Imaginary." *Public Culture* 5, no. 3 (special issue: *Screening Politics in a World of Nations*, ed. Lila Abu-Lughod): 557–78.

———. 1994. "Culture/Media: A Mild Polemic." *Anthropology Today* 10, no. 2 (April): 5–15.

———. 1997. "'From Little Things, Big Things Grow': Indigenous Media and Cultural Activism." In *Between Resistance and Revolution: Cultural Politics and Social Protest*, ed. R. Fox and Orin Starn, 118–44. London: Routledge.

———. 1998. "Institutionalizing the Unruly: Charting a Future for Visual Anthropology." *Ethnos* 63, no. 2: 173–201. [Based on research with Australian Aboriginal communities and a long involvement with ethnographic film, these articles address how and why indigenous media comes to be supported by state interests (1993) and how this kind of work can play an important "decolonizing role" in the field of ethnographic film and visual anthropology.]

Ginsburg, Faye; Lila Abu-Lughod; and Brian Larkin, eds. Forthcoming. *The Social Practice of Media: Ethnography in the Age of Digital Reproduction* Berkeley: University of California Press. [This collection offers the cutting edge of new work being done in the ethnography of media.]

Hall, Stuart. 1992. "Cultural Studies and Its Theoretical Legacies." In *Cultural Studies*, ed. L. Grossberg et al., 277–94. New York: Routledge.

Himpele, Jeff. 1996. "Film Distribution as Media: Mapping Difference in the Bolivian Cinemascape." *Visual Anthropology Review* 12, no. 1: 47–66.

———. Forthcoming. "My Tribal Terror of Self-awareness: An Anthropology of Media Agency in the Bolivian Popular Classes." In *The Social Practice of Media*, ed. Lila Abu-Lughod, Faye Ginsburg, and Brian Larkin.

Jacob, Preminda, ed. 1998. *All Singing, All Talking, All Dancing: Cinema and Society in India*. Special issue of *Visual Anthropology* 11, no. 4. [As more attention is being paid to mass media in different parts of the world, special collections are emerging that bring together ethnographic and neighboring research in particular regions, in these cases on the Middle East and India.]

Juhasz, Alexandra. 1995. *AIDS TV: Identity, Community, and Alternative Video*. Durham, NC: Duke University Press. [An excellent example of engaged scholarship that looks at how mass media stigmatizes a community and how the community has responded with its own mediations.]

Kirshenblatt-Gimblett, Barbara. 1996. "The Electronic Vernacular." In *Connected: Engagements with Media*, ed. G. Marcus. Late Editions, 3. Chicago: University of Chicago Press.

Larkin, Brian. 1997a. "Indian Films and Nigerian Lovers: Media and the Creation of Parallel Modernities." *Africa* 67, no. 3: 406–39.

———. 1997b. "Hausa Dramas and the Rise of Video Culture in Nigeria." In *Nigerian Video Films*, ed. Jonathan Haynes. Ibadan, Nigeria: Kraft Books.

Lutz, Cathy, and Jane Collins. 1993. *Reading National Geographic*. Chicago: University of Chicago Press.

MacDougall, David. 1997. "The Visual in Anthropology." In *Rethinking Visual Anthropology*, ed. Marcus Banks and Howard Morphy. New Haven, CT: Yale University Press.

Mankekar, Purnima. 1999. *Screening Culture, Viewing Politics: An Ethnography of Television, Womanhood, and Nation in Post-Colonial India*. Durham, NC: Duke University Press.

Maclagan, Meg. 1997. "Mystical Visions in Manhattan: Deploying Culture in the Year of Tibet." In *Tibetan Culture in the Diaspora*, ed. E. Steinkellner. Albany, NY: State University of New York Press.

Marcus, George. 1996. "Introduction." *Connected: Engagements with Media*, ed. G. Marcus, 1–18. Late Editions 3 Chicago: University of Chicago Press.

Martinez, Wilton. 1993. "Who Constructs Anthropological Knowledge? Toward a Theory of Ethnographic Film Spectatorship." In *Film as Ethnography*, ed. P. Crawford and D. Turton, 131–63. Manchester: University of Manchester Press. [An elegant study that asks, empirically, how students learn about other cultures through ethnographic film.]

Michaels, Eric. 1994. *Bad Aboriginal Art: Tradition, Media, and Technological Horizons*. Minneapolis: University of Minnesota Press.

Miller, Daniel. 1995. "Introduction: Anthropology, Modernity, Consumption." In *Worlds Apart: Modernity through the Prism of the Local*, ed. D. Miller, 1–23. London: Routledge. [Miller places much of the work on media in the broader framework of the spread of modernity and the increasing objectification and circulation of culture that accompanies this process.]

Miller, Toby. 1998. "Hollywood and the World." In *The Oxford Guide to Film Studies*, ed. J. Hill and P. C. Gibson, 371–82. New York and Oxford: Oxford University Press. [Miller argues for the centrality of distribution to understanding the domination of world media markets by Hollywood cinema, what he calls the "new international division of cultural labor."]

Morley, David. 1992. *Televison, Audiences, and Cultural Studies*. London: Routledge.

Morley, David, and Kevin Robins. 1995. *Spaces of Identity: Global Media, Electronic Landscapes, and Cultural Boundaries*. London: Routledge. [Like Ang, Morley has been influential for anthropologists trying to understand media circulation and reception, opening up audience research to more complex approaches.]

Nichols, Bill. 1994. *Blurred Boundaries: Questions of Meaning in Contemporary Culture*. Bloomington: University of Indiana Press. [Nichols, one of the key cinema studies scholars to engage with ethnographic film, addresses the increasingly complex ways in which cultural difference is represented in film and video.]

Palatella, John. 1998. "Pictures of Us." *Lingua Franca*, July/August, 50–58. [Palatella usefully summarizes the debate that has emerged around scholarship on indigenous media, though he fails to engage any indigenous intellectuals in the discussion.]

Pedelty, Mark. 1995. *War Stories: The Culture of Foreign Correspondents*. New York: Routledge.

Penney, Chris. 1998. *Camera Indica: The Social Life of Photographs*. London: Blackwell. [Penney's comprehensive study of the range of uses of photography in India, from lithographs to wedding photos, is a compelling case for the ethnography of mass-mediated visual forms.]

Pines, Jim, and Paul Willemen, eds. 1989. *Questions of Third Cinema*. London: British Film Institute.

Prins, Harald. 1997. "The Paradox of Primitivism: Native Rights and the Problem of Imagery in Cultural Survival Films." *Visual Anthropology* 9, nos. 3–4: 243–66.

Rofel, Lisa. 1994. "*Yearnings:* Televisual Love and Melodramatic Politics in Contemporary
China." *American Ethnologist* 21, no. 4: 700–722.

Rony, Fatima. 1996. *The Third Eye: Race, Cinema, and Ethnographic Spectacle.* Durham, NC:
Duke University Press. [Rony offers a postcolonial critique and revisionist history of
ethnographic film, from its early origins in living dioramas at world's fairs, through the
work of Flaherty, Hurston, and Deren.]

Roth, Lorna. 1994. *Northern Voices and Mediating Structures: The Emergence and Development of First Peoples' Television Broadcasting in the Canadian North.* Ph.D. diss. Concor-
dia University, Montreal, Quebec, Canada. [An excellent overview of the emergence
of indigenous television in Canada, taking a critical communications approach to the
expansion of the public sphere to include diverse voices.]

Ruby, Jay. 1991. "Speaking for, Speaking about, Speaking with, or Speaking alongside: An
Anthropological and Documentary Dilemma." *Visual Anthropology Review* 7, no. 2: 50–
67.

———. 1999. *Philosophical Toys: Explorations of Film and Anthropology.* Chicago: University
of Chicago Press. [Ruby, a key figure in visual anthropology, takes on some of the
dilemmas posed by "the burden of representation" of other cultures.]

Salamandra, Christ. 1998. "Moustache Hairs Lost: Ramadan Television Serials and the
Construction of Identity in Damascus, Syria." *Visual Anthropology* 10, nos. 2–4 (special
issue: *Visual Culture in the Middle East,* ed. Walter Armbrust): 227–46.

Shohat, Ella, and Robert Stam. 1994. *Unthinking Eurocentrism: Multiculturalism and the
Media.* New York: Routledge. [A comprehensive, intelligent, and engaged overview of
the key issues in the historical and contemporary production and circulation of cultural difference through cinema and video.]

Sinclair, John; Elizabeth Jacka; and Stuart Cunningham, eds. 1996. *New Patterns in Global
Television: Peripheral Vision.* London: Oxford University Press. [These scholars engage
with the Eurocentrism of arguments about cultural imperialism by tracking and analyzing the circulation of media outside of Hollywood, with attention to Mexican and
Latin American cinema and television; Indian (especially Bombay) cinema; and Chinese cinema.]

Spitulnik, Debra. 1993. "Anthropology and Mass Media." *Annual Review of Anthropology.*
Vol. 22. Palo Alto, CA: Annual Reviews.

———. 1999. *Producing National Public: Audience Constructions and the Electronic Media in
Zambia.* Durham, NC, and London: Duke University Press.

Sreberny-Mohammadi, Annabelle, and Ali Mohammadi. 1994. *Small Media, Big Revolution: Communication, Culture, and the Iranian Revolution.* Minneapolis: University of
Minnesota Press.

Turner, Terence. 1991. "The Social Dynamics of Video Media in an Indigenous Society:
The Cultural Meaning and the Personal Politics of Video-Making in Kayapó Communities." *Visual Anthropology Review* 7, no. 2 (fall): 68–76.

———. 1992. "Defiant Images: The Kayapó Appropriation of Video." *Anthropology Today* 8, no. 6: 5–16.

———. 1995. "Representation, Collaboration, and Mediation in Contemporary Ethnographic and Indigenous Media." *Visual Anthropology Review* 11, no. 2: 102–6. [Turner, who has done groundbreaking activist research bringing video to Kayapó groups in Brazil, makes a case for the significance of indigenous media as a medium for cultural revival and political intervention, and as part of a broader process of the objectification of culture.]

Worth, Sol; John Adair; and Richard Chalfen. 1997. *Through Navajo Eyes*, with a new introduction, afterword, and notes by R. Chalfen. Albuquerque: University of New Mexico Press. [This 1972 classic study—in which they taught a group of Navajo how to use cameras without "cultural bias"—was recently reissued with a very helpful contextualizing introduction and afterword by Richard Chalfen, who was an assistant on the original project.]

Yang, Mayfair Mei-H. I. 1997. "Mass Media and Transnational Subjectivity in Shanghai: Notes on (Re) Cosmopolitanism in a Chinese Metropolis." In *Ungrounded Empires: The Cultural Politics of Modern Chinese Transnationalism*, ed. Aihwa Ong and D. Nonini, 287–319. New York: Routledge.

20

Ideas of Culture and the Challenge of Music

JOHN CHERNOFF

It would seem natural that anthropologists, who are students of culture, would be deeply involved with the arts, but anthropologists think of culture within a specialized frame of reference that stands in ironic distinction to widely held ideas that identify culture with art. To be sure, the artistic artifacts of ancient civilizations are a significant focus of archaeological interest, as are any artifacts that seem to be expressions of the mentality of living groups that anthropologists study. By and large, however, in anthropological thought the arts are derivative of other factors of human life that relate directly to evolutionary adaptation and survival. From such a perspective, culture is based on patterns of interaction with the material world, and art is a reflection and affirmation of that level of culture, not even necessarily self-conscious. It is not surprising that in anthropology, the least considered art is the least material one: music.

To many people in the world, music is a universal language. Some have even speculated that music might offer a way to communicate with aliens from beyond the stars. To anthropologists, however, music is something that separates people as much as it connects them—indeed, even connects some people in order to exclude others. The idea that different people have different tastes in music inspires no debate, perhaps because the issue seems of little importance. People can really hate other people's music, but I do not remember the last time anyone fought a war over music. Nor do I know anyone who would argue that we all need to listen to the same music, except maybe on certain special occasions involving sports or patriotism, and then the issue is once again about who we are or are not. For social scientists, especially anthropologists, issues involving different musical preferences are codes for parochial perceptions. Until just recently, Western anthropologists worked mainly in places where, in Western perception, the local music was denigrated in equal measure with the particular locals under investigation. And of course, even with the invention of media that can take sounds from one place to another, the music of those other people has generally been a big stumbling block on the path toward empathy.

Non-Western music: How are anthropologists to talk about it? Whenever an anthropologist stayed in the field long enough to learn to appreciate the music there, the overwhelming fact about the music remained how odd it sounded to European ears. As social scientists, anthropologists have held to two rudimentary ideas about music. First, any particular type of music itself is less important than the various ways people in different cultures deal with it. Second, musical taste is entirely relative because it is a product of culture: music is culturally organized and culturally meaningful sound. Thus, the fact that some people can completely fail to appreciate noise that others find musical, and vice versa, is a good example of cultural relativity, but not much more. Music is significant as an aspect of culture, but music is difficult to talk about, and anyway, music is something like a residue of more fundamental cultural concerns.

Clear enough, one might say, but such ideas are qualified by the ambiguities of culture, in particular the differences between social scientific discussions of culture as a way of life and the more common use of the concept to indicate refined and enlightened development in arts and letters. This division of thought remains as influential today as ever: in a multicultural world where people of diverse heritages mingle, anthropologists have been champions of toleration and have maintained their focus on social customs and group life. Many anthropologists would proudly claim credit for their discipline's role in advancing the idea of cultural relativity, an image of the world as a pluralistic and continuously changing place where all points of view are relative and somehow complementary, where lots of little lower-case truths provide cumulative complexity, a variety of alternatives and thus a presumption of choice. And we should note that asserting the relativity of human experience ironically certifies anthropology's main mission of comprehending the human species—its origins, nature and diversity—as a unified picture. Apparent differences are really variations of a theme, and nuanced cultural portraits reveal the hidden complementarities that can connect cultures. The intellectual agent of anthropological relativism is the sophisticated significance that has accrued to the concept of "culture" as an alchemical term used to straddle the old philosophical problem of the One and the Many.

"Culture" is an amazingly plastic concept, ever ready for further articulation, something somewhat ineffable that characterizes a distinct group of people and is passed down from generation to generation as a medium for growth and adaptation. The root *ethno-* in the words *ethnography* and *ethnology* denotes a folk or a nation or a people united by culture. But whether cultivated from the inside or imposed from the outside, cultural identity is an elusive vision that always degenerates into a muddle at its boundaries. Cultural anthropologists work at these boundaries, germinating their theories out of the muddles. Anthropological writings about culture typically stand as testimony to overcoming boundaries through the face-to-face encounters and relationships between an anthropologist and "other" people who are "different" from the anthropologist. Nevertheless, the anthropologist seeks and finds evidence of a shared humanity. Wherever they are, human beings have to get food, organize their communities, raise children, deal with death, and so on, handling all the imperatives of life amid all the institutional permutations and solutions that their ecology, history, and imaginations can produce. In this cultural laboratory, our common humanity is elevated to truth in various theoretical systems of classification and comparison of cultural responses to basic human needs. Ultimately, though, when everything has become comparable and the hidden complementarities are explained, the last thing to be understood is that which is thought to be farthest from the necessities of life: art. Indeed, in mainstream Western intellectual traditions, the notion of pure aesthetic judgment is defined negatively, that is, by the absence of interest based on need. Thus, within the anthropological agenda, art is normally seen as an expressive and derivative element of culture, something that enhances structures and functions that are already there, and therefore something about as far as possible from real significance. With its emphasis on the physical factors of life, anthropology seems an infertile field for comparative aesthetics.

In the centers of Western civilization, a narrower concept of "culture" dominates intellectual exchange, in which culture occupies its own territory within society instead of permeating the whole. Culture is seen as a refinement of human experience, approaching the spiritual, representing people's identity in an essential way that is separate from what they have to do to survive. Culture in this sense is often associated and appropriated by people of means and power, those seemingly least affected by life's bodily struggles because they are above the nitty gritty and the hoi poloi. They and those who interpret culture for them have not completely forgotten the allusion of culture to ethos, but there are distinctions: real art occupies the elevated realm of "high" culture; other creative expressions that celebrate "low" culture or "popular" culture are understood as "folk" art, folklore, or crafts. Along with the associations of social class, the distinction is poignantly indicated in that the higher art normally has to be subsidized, while the lower forms support themselves with more immediate forms of participation or give and take. What message could anthropology contribute in such an incongruous climate?

Committed to demonstrating what alien peoples have in common by rationalizing their differences into larger systems, anthropology would seem forced into a posture critical of such divisive discourse. Nonetheless, from anthropology's early years, when Western world dominance was being articulated in every way, anthropology did not challenge this competing model of culture, and the discipline has had little to contribute directly to the broader issues pertaining to art.

And so what would anthropology have to do with music? Answering that question is something of a minor project that reflects the character of anthropology's intellectual mission. Because music is the least material of the arts, people can more easily get an idea of other arts that can exist in some sort of physical form: much sculpture and decorative arts can be carried from place to place; poetry, drama and literature can be written; architecture and some paintings and sculpture can be portrayed in drawings or somewhat adequately described in prose. Until recently, however, music could not be heard outside an actual performance context. And in the highly critical world of music appreciation and music scholarship, where even today people are still holding on to belief in a Western canon and defending its accustomed place in Western education, anthropology has had little impact. Perhaps art is the last bastion of parochialism that anthropology could not surmount; perhaps anthropologists have not tried very hard.

Nevertheless, since anthropology's territory is the whole species for the last few million years, then music-making, while not thought particularly important except as an evolutionary marker, is certainly grist for the mill. Thus there is a slightly obscure discipline, "ethnomusicology," that joins anthropology and musicology. Since anthropology's early years, however, the root *ethno-* and the word *ethnic* have had a privative connotation, designating people by what they are not, which was that they are not Western, reserving the more restricted concept of high culture for the West and signaling the application of the broader and lower concept of culture elsewhere. Ethnomusicology conforms to that outdated heritage. Ethnomusicology is usually seen not as the study of music in culture but as the study of music in "other" cultures. The territory comprises any music that is not in the canon of European classical music, a difference that in practice separates Western "art" music from non-Western music as well as folkloric music and popular music.

Accepting this division in fields of study has had broad consequences with regard to the very conception of music per se, reflected in the existence of very different epistemologies, that is, different ideas about methods of studying music and about what constitutes an understanding of music. One can infer that originally such a division separated a type of music—Western—that was to be criticized or appreciated from "other" types of music that required "understanding" validated by objectivity instead of judgment. Today, this latter type of understanding of "other" musical idioms is based on the explanation of the cultural meaning of the music. Indeed, ethnomusicology itself can be defined by the anthropological proposition that musical idioms should be understood in context and that musical meaning is culturally determined. But this central demonstration of ethnomusicology did not happen overnight. A century ago, the matter was not even much of an issue. A few idealists might have viewed music as a universal language, capable of creating bridges across cultural boundaries. For the most part, separating Western art music from other musics merely reflected the way of world, in which almost everything about the former was elevated and refined—the patrons, the presumed aesthetic effects, the discourse, the performance skills, the expensive elite venues. The *ethno* in *ethnomusicology* affirmed a scholarly division of labor that continues to relegate ethnomusicology to a marginal position (if any position at all) in music schools. As scholars, ethnomusicologists remain members of the elite culture of universities and museums. But even today, ethnomusicology is seen as separate from historical musicology or music history, also similarly defined in department guides as the study of music in its wider cultural and social contexts, as if the mainstream historians deal with genuine music and the ethnomusicologists deal with curiosities. Even today, musicologists are naively capable of attending a lecture by an ethnomusicologist and blithely asking, "What does your talk tell us about music?"

One of the problems with the prefix *ethno-* is that it is almost by definition in opposition to the pluralistic and multicultural world that is emerging. The very name of the discipline links it to an inherent and invalid negation that alienates anything non-Western in many subtle ways. In today's world, the existence of such a division is grating in some cases, absurd in others, and quite frequently an embarrassment. The word *ethnomusicology* also seems to link the field to colonialism and to anthropology's role in that historical time as well as to contemporary neo-colonialism and racism. Admittedly, it is a bit risky to use colonialism as an emblem of racism and exploitation: the colonial period was a time when the larger historical movement of humanity toward a multicultural world took major steps forward. Nonetheless, I think most people today would agree that the idea of defining a subdiscipline as the study of non-Western anything is politically loaded. The prefix *ethno-* certainly is a stumbling block that has real impact on just about anybody who is tuned into the kind of soundscape our modern world provides.

There are many complicated and ambiguous reasons why ethnomusicology is studied in music schools instead of anthropology departments. Anthropology departments do not generally teach courses on the music of Africa, India, Indonesia, Native America, or any of the places that anthropologists might think of as their province for social scientific work. Of course, until recently, such courses were not part of any music curriculum either. A century ago, when one could only hear music where it was performed, only a few early travelers had written descriptions of musical events in various parts of the world, and most of these descriptions had not been culled from archives for general scholarly consumption. Not until well into the twentieth century could scholars get samples of non-Western music to listen to, apart from local or staged folk music. By the same token, non-Western music was also inaccessible to the paradigms and terminology anthropologists used. Also, in the not-so-distant past anthropology was not yet promoting relativism but was more concerned with understanding cultural evolution and where different societies should be placed on an evolutionary scale. Non-Western music was therefore something for which they sought material examples for museums, to be exhibited alongside prehistoric bones and stones. It is not clear whether those in the vanguard of European colonialism actually disliked indigenous music. I have not read an account of a district commissioner dancing or doing anything at local festivals except watching. In films set in the colonial era, when we see isolated Westerners made desperate by local music, the music mainly serves a symbol of an ubiquitous and overwhelming presence of the "other" culture; more significant, perhaps, is the implication that music can fittingly represent the "otherness" of a culture and thereby become a symbol of a realm beyond the limits of understanding. Let us not yet talk about missionaries, who have been such a convenient target for concerned intellectuals; everyone is implicated in history.

Nonetheless, while closed-minded people burned sculptures deemed to be pagan idols, a few of the more open-minded who gathered idols to take home must also have gathered musical instruments as if they were accumulating power objects. I once visited the back rooms of the Musée de l'Homme in Paris: uncountable musical instruments were piled to the ceiling, like bones in a Capuchin monastery. I suppose the scene is the same in the storerooms of other museums of former colonial nations. Indeed, musical instruments are still displayed as art and artifacts in contemporary exhibitions, for example, such as one just a few years ago at the Smithsonian Institution's Museum of African Art, where, despite contemporary technology, one could not press a button to hear a recording of any displayed instrument.

But why were these instruments carefully collected and shipped and catalogued at all? Perhaps curators and collectors hoped that African or Native American music could here or there contribute an intriguing motif for refinement in European art music, as other folk traditions had already done. One can assume that the collectors, whether anthropologists or not, had other priorities besides music, but at least they had a regard for cultural acquisitiveness. After all, the same elites who patronized and sponsored European museums also patronized orchestral music in concert halls. As seems always to be the case everywhere, at the centers of power, where the highest artistic expression is achieved, things tend to get a bit stuffy. Folk traditions from the periphery, from the provinces or colonies, or revived from the past, are tapped to provide creative inspiration for the development of sophisticated styles at the center. At the center the folk traditions are both stylized and refined with technical innovation, becoming distinctive and often classical. When the classical tradition becomes too mannered or academic, new ideas from the periphery again infuse the high art of the center and help it reach a further elaboration of style. Those instrumental artifacts in the museums are testimony to some very tentative musical excursions in the vanguard of this process that never came to much.

During the colonial period, the most serious engagement with non-Western music was probably occurring in Christian missions. In the face of varying degrees of contestation, a trend gradually emerged toward the translations of more and more sections of the liturgy into the vernacular. The anthropological subfield of linguistics benefited greatly from the challenges of translating the Bible and from the philosophical subfield of hermeneutics, which featured discussions of the limitations and complexities of translating sacred texts. Along with these undertakings, missions often took the lead in educational and literacy efforts to cultivate leadership and devotion, with two musical consequences. First, indigenous music was gradually adapted and adopted into the liturgy. Second, several products of the local schools became knowledgeable about Western music and were able to contribute to the adaptation of hymns and other works as well as compose significant works on their own for use in local services. If conservative souls were concerned about the effect of indigenous styles within the musical traditions of sectarian worship, indigenous composers for their part worried about preserving what they understood as the defining elements of their traditional styles. All the people involved in these processes made some sort of peace with hermeneutic issues and had hands-on learning experiences at the meeting of musical worlds.

Given the linkage between missions and education, the local academic presence of local music has often reflected the legacy of such composers, whose social and intellectual inclinations were more toward musicology than anthropology. Moreover, their cross-cultural efforts at the edges of Christendom found an occasional audience or forum among their colleagues in music schools, where their compositional idioms conformed to recognized genres. Whatever the extent to which ethnomusicologists see themselves as positioned between musicology and anthropology, the logical extension of initial encounters with non-Western music was toward musicology. It was unquestioned that musical notation could provide a more adequate representation of the music than a descriptive text. The problems the early ethnomusicologists faced had much to do with responding to the challenges of non- Western music in musical terms, and they saw themselves as working toward the development of music theory, finding ways to enhance their own community of scholars by hammering out a common language. Like anthropologists, they assumed a fundamental universalism, and they sought the conceptions and principles that could encompass additional musical diversity and thus sophisticate comparative musicology.

Far removed from the religious needs of new, non-Western congregations, scholars of music theory found a lot of ready-made data in any available non-Western music, which contained all kinds of unfamiliar ways of structuring sound. The people who created those musical structures had already made their contribution and were of only circumstantial interest: they could fill in circumstantial details about the music, such as how they designed and made the instruments that produced the sounds. Anthropologists could help in this latter area, the study of musical instruments, by collecting them, though—judging from the piles of unused ones in the museums—mainly for others to analyze. Up to now, a weird fetishism seems to have attached itself to musical instruments from far-off places, and people get excited about ones that are older than others or were associated with non-Christian religious rituals. Such estimation resembles the way commodity value is determined for the plastic arts. As for the music itself, nascent ethnomusicology was so specialized—so musical—that anthropologists observing musical events were either intimidated or disinclined. The retrospective consensus among ethnomusicologists is that anthropologists felt they lacked the training, techniques, or skills to work on music. Given the nature of the beast at that time, the anthropologists were right. Ethnomusicology belonged in music schools where people did musical analysis. Anthropologists were peripheral characters who worked in other buildings on campus or in the museums.

By mid-century in Europe and America, the situation began to change, and non-Western music served as a different type of artifact for a different theoretical purpose. Many anthropologists were still attached to museums and still helping to plan displays about material culture in less developed societies, but evolutionary paradigms gradually gave ground because of intercultural encounters documented by trained anthropological researchers, who were only indirectly related to colonial agendas of social administration or religious conversion. Many social scientists who viewed Western chauvinism as a curable disease argued strongly about the relativity of cultural practices, including, by extension, cultural judgments. Musical life also came under the anthropologist's lens, perhaps as something derivative or peripheral to what a social situation was really about, but certainly something there. From this invigorated social scientific perspective emerged a potential anthropology of music. Music-making is a type of behavior, and people interested in music can study the institutionalization of music-making in that light: the recruitment and training of musicians, performance styles, performance venues like festivals and celebrations, religious and political roles of music, song texts, composition, patronage, ecological and instrumental resources, and so on. Information about music was considered complementary to the information about more significant institutions in the economic and political realms. There was a general conviction in social and cultural anthropology that any valid observation was data that could eventually be plugged into a systematic network of information, a permanent store of knowledge that could be codified and correlated in myriad ways. Ethnographers everywhere accepted the idea that their work was relevant to this grand project. Musical activity was an hors d'oeuvre on the smorgasbord at which they feasted.

It is somewhat strange, though, that in the anthropological record, there are many descriptions of events that contain little or no reference to the music that we know was a part of the scene. And indeed, music was very often there. Western observers felt that abdicating aesthetic issues was justified: unlike Western music, which exists in its own bounded world, non-Western music often appears attached to other activities and thus somehow related to institutional functions. The basic assumption has always been that music makes whatever is happening more itself, no small feat when one thinks about it; nonetheless, one can understand whatever is happening perfectly well without needing that extra bit of intensity for one's descriptive palette. Reading ethnographies, you might even think that people in the non-Western world rarely make music. It is an ironic and shocking contrast, no doubt intentional at the time, that Colin Turnbull's classic 1961 book on the people formerly known as pygmies, *The Forest People*, begins with a strange survey of previous cultural portraits, which he assesses with regard to the degree to which the authors note the continual singing, dancing, and music-making that dominated his own perception of the people. Turnbull was skeptical of anyone who did not deal with music. Anthropology would be a far different discipline than it is today if it had been immersed in the same questions about art that have concerned its elite patrons in their own cultural reflections. Missing in the early images of non-Western music was a sense that the music as an art presented evidence of high cultural development. Indeed, there seemed to be no interest in the questions of why music seems so important to so many people, why music refers to so many things beyond itself, or how music could become so highly developed in so many materially impoverished societies. The non-Western world is full of such places where music has been elevated by intensive intellectual and creative energy to levels of sophistication that challenged almost every other image of these societies in the Western agenda.

Mid-century social scientists were likely to reply with knee-jerk relativism, maintaining the significance of context over expression. Aesthetic matters, if they are to be addressed at all, should be framed by ethnographic knowledge of the surrounding cultural context, and knowing the symbolic associations and social significance of any art is the key to understanding it. The idea of a common humanity inspired the modern notion of cultural relativity, but it was generally thought that such affinities could not be reliably extended into the ambiguous realm of artistic sympathy. But then again, getting too involved in ethnographic details pretty much precludes any sense of artistic depth—just the opposite, in effect: all that cerebral mediation can be alienating and dull. The whole matter has always been a real conundrum. In mid-century, it was possible for a leading anthropologist like Robert Redfield to be self-consciously heretical in commenting on the possibility of transcending cultural boundaries at a museum exhibition, by suggesting that Westerners cultivate the immediacy of direct encounters with non-Western art and by arguing against the discipline's inclination toward studied contextual explanations.

Professionally, anthropologists collect information about the social location and social role of art, but it takes a long time. Until recently, anthropologists stayed so long in the field that they really believed that they knew, truly and deeply, the people they studied. That deep knowledge, paradoxically, established their credibility through the systematic intricacy of their writings more than through the replicability of their observations. After all, there are not a lot of anthropologists, and they are spread out. When they have achieved that depth, typically alone in their mission, has it not been their great temptation to believe that they, at least, had transcended the complex and different cultural configurations that their work objectified? Thus tempted, some would become possessive of their empathy and hold it up as a bulwark of authority against anyone else, especially some of their colleagues who worked in the same place. But would not the larger spirits among them hope that others could also achieve it—could move beyond an ideal of respectful relations between strangers toward a true community of humankind? Back in the museums through most of the century, paleontologists were convinced that humankind is a single species, and they were on the track of a single ancestor. The human sentiments through which people could actually recognize themselves in "others" might also allow the possibility of an unmediated appreciation of art.

In the museums, nobody can play the instruments well enough to command a public performance venue, and the instruments have remained on shelves, except for those of exquisite manufacture that can be displayed among the plastic arts. Interest in non-Western art was stimulated by the expanding contacts of the age of imperialism, but that interest had deeper precedents, starting from the Renaissance fascination with the pagan world and the Enlightenment projection of the ideal of natural law and the noble savage. Manifestations of both alienation and quest, these conceptions existed in counterpoint to the dominant history of control and consolidation. As noted, the museums that display the evidence of paleontology and archaeology also participated in collecting evidence of achievements in the realm of culture, and artifacts verifiably collected on location partake of this projected value. Within a notion of cultural evolution, non-Western cultural achievements could be compared, unfavorably, to those of the Western world. However, from another well-grounded Western perspective, in which the way of the world is the corruptor of the human spirit, the value of these artifacts actually increases with their distance from the Western centers of power. It is spurious to compare wood carvings to a Michelangelo sculpture or musical instruments to a Stradivarius violin. In a polarized world of "us" and "others," distance from the Western centers implies closeness to the opposite centers. Documentation of the non-Western artifacts thus has carried the burden of demonstrating the roles of the objects in native life, particularly how much and for how long the objects have played those roles in the institutions of their locales. For anthropological purposes, as comparative criteria moved further toward issues of cultural integrity, the denotation of authenticity has defined the commodity value of any given object.

On its own terms, anthropology came to advocate a contextual approach that did not go as far as the approach evident in other types of modern art criticism, such as, for example, attempting to view a Renaissance painting or a Greek temple with reference to the creative period's cultural milieu as an interpretive tool, a potential pathway toward culturally informed experience and a perspective on the participatory nature of the art's aesthetic mediation. Instead, concerns of tradition and authenticity led to aesthetic perspectives based on form and style and to explanations of mediation based on cognition and knowledge. In promoting this limited type of cultural relativism, anthropologists and ethnomusicologists abdicated broad aesthetic issues of perception and feeling. In mid-century, probably influenced by Western concert-hall performance models, ethnomusicologists accepted a narrow Western definition of aesthetic values as judgments on matters of beauty and feelings about art objects. From a musicological perspective, the task was to study and analyze abstracted forms that were or could be removed from their original creative context. Many ethnomusicologists would have asserted that aesthetic concerns are inaccessible to comparative research and even irrelevant to art that explicitly serves a social purpose in cultures without traditions of artistic criticism similar to those in the West. It would be another generation before scholars would look at a performance context with the idea that the aesthetics of music could be tied to how the music achieved its effectiveness in social situations. We now appreciate how rhythms can be used to establish and coordinate distinctive patterns of interaction among participants in a musical context, and, as such, musical structures and performance dynamics can be interpreted as significant contributors to cultural style and social cohesion. Even well into the 1960s, however, as the colonial period was formally ending and anthropologists were focusing on the transformation of traditional societies, ethnomusicologists pursued their musicological mission in harmonious concert with an increasingly out-of-date anthropological vision that valued precolonial traditions for exemplary cultural integrity. For example, there were scholarly articles taking the position that non-Western popular music played by non-Western musicians using Western instruments in dancehall settings was derivative and not within the scope of the discipline; in contrast to the music of indigenous historical traditions, the popular music lacked depth, symbolic complexity, and cultural inspiration. Even though the local people liked it and gravitated toward the intermingled forms, scholars were unprepared to deal with the music and tried to ignore it.

But at least anthropology had entered the game for real. As the discipline has increased its presence in the Western intellectual environment, many ethnomusicologists have moved toward the anthropological side of their disciplinary axis. In a pattern that continues to remain compelling, the contributions of mid-century anthropology to the study of non-Western music have been made not so much by people with degrees in anthropology as by musicologists and musicians who are influenced by anthropology. Anthropology has always had its share of seekers, but those who have advanced the field of ethnomusicology are basically people who love music. Perhaps the process was a luxury in the twilight of the colonial era, but more and more people have been documenting the stunning variety of musical traditions in the world, and thus has the cumulative record acquired weight. The legacy of the seekers has changed almost every aspect of ethnomusicology except for its usual location in music departments, and despite what some musicologists would prefer, anthropological perspectives have assumed intellectual dominance in the field. Functionalism, structuralism, semiotics, symbolic interactionism, symbolic anthropology, and so on: all have their influence.

More important, perhaps, ethnomusicologists have adopted the anthropological method of participant-observation, and they have spent lots of time with music-makers in other cultures. A musical apprenticeship often provides the framework for their intercultural relationships, a role that often prompts their teachers to offer a more detailed and intimate understanding than could ever have been available from a consistently analytical or objectifying approach. As participants in the musical traditions, disciples of their performance masters, ethnomusicologists gain evidence for a refined understanding of tradition's movement from generation to generation. Early models of non-Western art were based on a rather static image of tradition. These models presumed a stability in style that attributed superiority to earlier forms which preceded cross-cultural contact as definitive—hence the concern with artifacts and their authentication. One correlated idea was that artistic forms were passed down from generation to generation, and performers mainly had to learn or master the idiom of the tradition. As Western apprentices have become involved with living artists and more aware of local critical contexts, they have gained insight into the challenges that various art forms pose to aspiring practitioners, challenges that link the personal and the aesthetic realms and reflect considerably the art's current location in the social environment, including the mind-boggling vicissitudes inherent in the possibility, explicitly accepted by their teachers, that a Westerner can be trained to be a vehicle for the tradition.

Anthropological interests have thus led ethnomusicology further into the study of music as human behavior and into uncharted territory in cross-cultural relationships. Suspended in an uneasy limbo remained the fundamental issue of the difference between anthropology's wide conception of culture and musicology's elitist conception. Although many scholars continue to address theoretical concerns about music as structured sound, the main influence of anthropologically informed studies of music has been to undermine the musicological approach. An effort to ground music in a cultural context does not merely reflect a social scientific inclination to the abandonment of musicological analysis, nor does it merely reflect the belief that issues of musical meaning should be addressed with regard to the references and associations of indigenous people. More than that, the case has been argued persuasively that it is not possible to understand a piece of non-Western music from a score or a recording. Efforts to isolate or abstract so-called musical elements analytically have tended to yield not just one-sided or limited descriptions but have often led to actual mistakes in perception and analysis.

In Africa, for example, the types of musical decisions that musicians make are generally based on the situational or symbolic dimensions of the musical performance. Quite apart from such obvious factors as the relationship of music to language, as both speech and oral art, what a musician plays is generally determined by the specific people who are at a performance, why they are there, what they are doing at a given moment, and even what may be happening in the general society beyond the context of the particular gathering. The dynamics of the performance also reflect the dynamics and pacing of the ongoing event the music enhances. Although African musical performances can often be characterized as improvisational, the improvisation generally has a social or situational reference that may be more important than any reference to generative musical structures. Therefore, without an orientation grounded in a performance's social dimensions, matters as diverse as choice of repertoire or choice of improvisational motif cannot be understood. Both theoretically and practically, Western composers and music theorists interested in cultivating African influences may find this state of affairs frustrating, as most efforts to abstract African musical structures are generally superficial by definition.

For example, at a dance gathering in an African society, what might sound like a complex rhythmic elaboration may rather be a proverbial praise-name articulated on an instrument in recognition of a particular person's lineage, or perhaps represent an invocation for a particular deity or ancestor. What might seem to be creative inspiration in changing a rhythmic or melodic line might turn out to be a musical allusion to another dance, inserted as a joke, as an experiment, or because of confusion. The types of dances played and their stylistic variations may vary from situation to situation as a reflection of the composition of the assembly. Particular pieces or even inserted motifs might reflect mythic or historical allusions, or they might reflect the presence of a particular dancer. Such widely varying contextual elements are the kinds of things many African musicians think about and focus on while making musical decisions, and what they are doing musically cannot be inferred from the musical elements that would be evident from an audio recording or a score. As a result, in-depth studies of African musical idioms must be more ethnographic than musicological in perspective. Some people still venture purely musicological analyses out of allegiance to the old presumed canon asserting the priority of musicology in ethnomusicology's interdisciplinary disposition; later, perhaps, someone who knows more about the social and cultural context of the performance, or who knows the musical repertoire in greater detail, will provide data to demonstrate that the first scholar overinterpreted the musical elements with the aid of an active and hopeful imagination. Occasionally, of course, misinterpretations can serve a useful purpose when transported to other realms of creativity, but they do so as an ironic victim of the relativism they were projected to overcome.

As might be expected, culturally informed approaches to music derive the greater part of their significance in cultural terms more than in musical terms. The most obvious consequence is simply increased respect for non-Western people and cultures. As I noted, music can be the focus of tremendous intellectual and artistic creativity in societies that have been demeaned by various standards—as materially impoverished, as technologically underdeveloped, as historically vulnerable to exploitation and oppression. Whatever music's weight in theories about social structure, people value music: they frequently have a surprising ability to appreciate a foreign musical idiom, and even if they cannot easily appreciate it, they still give it respect as a higher order of achievement. Music, like other arts, does help people establish connections with other people they do not know; as such, music traverses cultural boundaries and plays a role in overcoming prejudice and negative images. Although there is an inherent friction between an unmediated experience and a culturally informed experience of art, there are many cases where the two perspectives work in concert, where people like an unfamiliar music to begin with and like it even more when they understand the creativity involved.

A place where I spent many years, in northern Ghana among the Dagbamba people, exemplifies this point well. The Dagbamba generally were not interested in adapting to the institutions of their British colonizers, many of whom in turn considered the Dagbamba stubborn and backward; the Dagbamba remain somewhat vulnerable to domination by the national government and by economic interests from the more developed southern regions of Ghana. Their musical institutions, however, offer a key to understanding the depth of their cultural life and the validity of any claim they might make for a well-lit place on the world stage. Their music is anchored in epic songs that convey episodes in the history of a six-hundred-year-old dynasty of chiefs, one of the oldest continuous father-to-son dynasties in the world, and perhaps the oldest. Apart from having a performance context reminiscent of pre-classical Greece, the epic history informs other Dagbamba musical idioms which branch out into drumming and singing that bestow proverbial praise-names onto chiefs (plates 7 and 8). These names are applied to descended members of various chiefs' lineages, whether or not the people still have any claim to chieftaincy. The musicians know the family lines of people in their communities, and with the help of musicians, everyone in Dagbamba society can trace his or her ancestry to some point on a chieftaincy line. In effect, music is what lets people know that they are one family. More than that, the rhythms of the proverbial praise- names are used as the foundations of wonderful drum ensemble pieces for social dancing. More than that again, this dancing is done by individuals at events like weddings, funerals, and festivals; people dance to the names of past chiefs and publicly demonstrate their relationship to the dynasty and to other members of their lineage segment. This incredible degree of historical consciousness is thus more than a focus for thought: historical knowledge, instead of being learned cognitively or represented through various symbols, is brought down to the level of social interaction, where people embody their personal relationship to history by dancing in musical contexts while others in their community are looking at them. I know of nothing really comparable in the Western world, but many societies in other parts of the world—Africa, Asia, the Middle East, the Americas, Oceania, Australia—do amazing things within their musical traditions. In all these places, anthropologically informed ethnomusicologists have debunked racial, cultural, and historical stereotypes at the same time as they have enriched people's understanding of the creative and intellectual potentials of human beings, and both these aspects of their work have contributed to discourse on the world's crucial concerns.

It has taken some time, but gradually the documentation and description of cultural achievements in the world's musical traditions have become an impressive body of knowledge, all the more impressive because it only represents a fragment of those traditions. Ethnomusicologists have returned the favor to anthropologists and have demonstrated many ways in which the study of music can yield insight into social and cultural issues, insight that is profoundly humanistic and fundamentally humanizing. This level of awareness about musical meaning relies on possibilities and sensitivities of musical appreciation that formerly seemed unattainable or unproductive. Looking back at the class consciousness and cultural chauvinism of the colonial era, we might wonder how people could not be self-conscious about the seemingly transparent way they used their own music to support their sense of their identity and their ideas of what was best about themselves. We might also wonder why it has been so difficult for members of the intellectual elite, especially those who should know how important music is, to recognize that music could present a similarly elevated view of other societies and to apply alternate standards to counteract the imagery of derogatory views. Certainly, too, scholars have not been quick to see the opportunities for fresh and innovative perspectives on a host of big issues about artistic style, about stylistic boundaries, about influence and change, about craftsmanship and artistry, about distance and meaning and usefulness, and so on. Every idea in art history ever debated by classicists, archaeologists, philosophers, or historians could have been put to a new and intriguing measure with every "other" tradition studied. Today, these opportunities remain only partially explored.

With a few exceptions, it is only recently that ethnomusicologists have truly looked as much at the people who are the world's music-makers as at the merely sonic character of the world's music. For those people, music has served as a positive force to strengthen identity, revealing processes of cultural resistance and potential redemption. In courtly contexts of the colonized, we see reaction and the codification of classical idioms. In less organized places where people have been thrown together from diverse backgrounds, musical activity has been one of the means with which subgroups consolidate their sense of themselves, giving themselves coherence in their relations with other groups similarly defined; the evolution of their musical idioms has been an added means to develop and display a broader or more generalized sense of their combined identity. Examples of this kind of musical contribution are easily found in such cultural processes as the coming together of African cultural groups from the earliest days of the African Diaspora, the Zionist formulation of non-Western elements of Jewish heritage to counter assimilationist trends in nineteenth-century Europe, or the continuous creation of new oppositional youth idioms as earlier idioms are appropriated and commercialized by mass culture. Such processes can be extremely complex.

The insights that reward people who think of music primarily in cultural terms are simply not available to those who think mainly in musicological terms; indeed, the latter are often victimized by a narrow conception of music that practically precludes their understanding the breadth of the artistic conception of many non-Western idioms. The fact that music points to so many things beyond itself is another way of saying that musical contexts pull many things together, and sometimes it is only in musical contexts that certain parts of society come into relationship or that certain social relationships become visible. Thus, beyond the big identity issues of group cohesion and community boundaries, of authenticity and traditional change, of inclusiveness and exclusiveness, or of dominance and resistance, music is also important just because musical contexts are places that people invest with meaning. Many institutional and personal players struggle to realize various benefits around musical performances, where there are stories upon stories of poignance and significance involving money, love, values, work, status, persuasion, visibility, or artistic growth. Isn't it odd that many social scientists still consider music to be derivative of culture when so many people, including Westerners, devise their musical events to bring to unique display that which they feel can represent their culture at its best—and by extension represent what they deem to be best about themselves? It is this territory of cultural imagery and self-portraiture that ethnomusicology is particularly qualified to explore.

In the final quarter of the century, the old ideals about music's capacity to transcend boundaries have reappeared in multicultural settings around the world, and quite a few old perspectives have been inverted. Although a number of prescient musical ethnographies have cleared the ground for a new understanding of older issues, it is mainly the increased movement of people from continent to continent that has challenged the relativist model of discrete musical traditions. Again, too, it is musicians who have taken the lead in exploring and combining diverse musics. To them, there is nothing strange in getting together with musicians from other cultures and expecting to make satisfying music, and it is legitimate to blend samples of sounds or actual musical pieces into their work to add texture or allusion. But to a conservative practitioner of a culturally identified tradition, or to an ethnomusicologist who has elaborated that musician's repertoire, the way that these other musicians use the indigenous music can seem everything from naive to ruinous. Proponents of multiculturalism could maintain that even when music from one part of the world is appropriated based on misperception, the resulting music can still quite adequately serve different expressive purposes in its new context. This kind of transformation has occurred frequently in the history of music, and it is even more prevalent now.

On the other hand, this process is more commercialized than ever before, and non-Western musicians are acutely attentive to potential ways to make their music a commodity. In some cases, their patrons are abandoning indigenous music for imported products of mass media. The younger musicians are caught in multiple ironies. They believe in the intrinsic genius of their local tradition and in its capacity to extend its beneficial effects into the world. They believe that they need to modernize their music to help it attract interest at home and cross cultural boundaries into larger markets abroad, but they are afraid of losing their music's special qualities. They are either dependent upon or willing to trust foreign producers or collaborators who often lack adequate understanding of the deeper structures of the local tradition. They and their patrons become starstruck by the relative wealth or presumed success of local musicians who have worked abroad, or who one way or another gain access to mass media, and they do not learn enough from the generation of more aged musicians who know more about the traditional substance of the idiom. At the extremes, we see musicians in the vanguard of the new age who are ready to hear diverse musics in any combination as beautiful, contrasted with venerable musicians from local traditions who see modernization in all its aspects as a threat that will attenuate the most culturally distinctive and valuable aspects of their style.

In this confusing situation, the cultural perspective that has characterized anthropology as an avatar of a multicultural world also ironically appears to be aligned with forces of conservatism and reaction. From some vantage points, globalization seems an irrevocable process that aims to minimize the importance of culture by reducing it to the role of adding local color in a small, small world. In today's centers of power, the technical-scientific, financial, corporate, and political elites of the world's nations have already defined a conception of the world in which everything is getting hooked up, in which privative issues of otherness, like notions of Western and non-Western, are irrelevant to the new realities that are being established. Culture has become an enigmatic obstacle to this process: when things do not go as intended, the reason usually has something to do with local culture. In a contrasting view, culture's most important function is to link generations as a tool for survival; the loss of cultural perspective is linked to anomie, frustration, and a loss of historical perspective and values that could reflect a long-range, multigenerational view. Some people who resist the new world order are ethnic chauvinists or religious radicals; others allege the shallowness of mass media and assert the richness of local knowledge and its expressive forms. Thus has culture itself become the focus of debate and contestation. With regard to music, the convenient and facile division of cultural territory among musicologists and anthropologists has simply become outdated. There are now many more players involved in interpreting cultural meaning, and now we see more clearly how important music is for people's ideas of themselves. For many people, more than ever, music represents their own cultural distinctiveness and their claim to a place in a multicultural world where issues of ethnicity, race, transnationalism, pluralism, and nationalism highlight culture's meaning in multiple ways. Those whose experience of modernization and whose cross-cultural interactions anthropologists would normally study have themselves brought music into the mix.

What happens to the traditional musical idioms and artists? On the international scene, they are still subsidized, particularly by Western museums and universities. Collectors of non-Western plastic arts are running out of traditional pieces to collect, and they are gradually becoming open to the qualities of modern non-Western art that incorporates different cultural elements in refreshing and intriguing ways. When such art is exhibited, though, the entertainment at the opening is likely to be supplied by an ensemble of traditional musicians and not by a pop band from the promoted region. The new art, like the new music, is fun, but the traditional or older arts still have cachet. On the local scene, the record shows that the traditional musicians of many societies have previously exercised strong influence because of their broad knowledge of social concerns and important social events. They are often among the most conservative in their societies because of their links to older patterns of patronage and reciprocity. As they watch the increasing commodification of their social world reach into the realm of music, they are concerned that the changing scene is incompatible with the dedication and spiritual generosity their art has demanded of them. They are comfortable asserting moral authority because they see themselves as the ones who know what is best in their culture. Despite the ambivalence with which people in some societies view musicians, or possibly as an aspect of that ambivalence, musicians are a kind of elite group resembling intellectuals. They are the ones who know their culture and have a role in events—ritual, ceremonial, communal, festive—that are most significant for maintaining cultural identity and continuity.

These indigenous intellectuals stand in an intrinsic conflict with other groups who would also claim that same cultural knowledge or preservative function in a modernized world: first, those from their own societies who have become intellectuals in universities and other educational institutions, and second, decision makers in their government who are concerned with matters of national identity and wish to control the role of traditional culture within it. In societies where older systems of authority are being replaced, people are status-conscious, and literacy is a definite marker of status; it can be difficult for educated people to humble themselves before their illiterate elders. Nonetheless, the educated people and bureaucrats communicate first with foreign commercial and academic interests, and they can present themselves as insiders, even though they often may not have access to the cultural knowledge of the local elders. Meanwhile, musicians playing in popular idioms have accepted the commercial nature of the system; they are searching their culture for roots they can connect with their own musical mission. And in the powerful centers of international mass media, musicians and culture brokers are ever alert for new ideas and new sounds to energize their music or musical products.

All this contestation about cultural knowledge and authority has shifted one connotation of culture as a heritage toward culture as a specific inheritance from a group's forebears. This idea has informed ethnic perspectives for a long time, but the contestation has expanded this aspect of cultural meaning toward a sense of culture as actual property which people have or do not have. "Culture," that plastic concept of ambiguous reference, is frequently discussed as if it were an objectifiable entity. Cultural interlopers are sometimes accused of stealing culture. People who work with outsiders or share information about customs are sometimes accused of selling their culture. In formerly colonized nations particularly, new intellectual and administrative elites maintain that the nonliterate musicians are naive cultural stewards and need protection against outsiders who are capable of exploiting them. Many local musicians in turn believe that the new elites have no claim on their knowledge and are interfering with their relationships. When cultural influence and cultural transmission imply theft and appropriation, one logical conclusion is the application of legalistic perspectives on intellectual property and copyright, shifting the realm of discourse to the authority of the literate. But how is ownership of culture determined? Is culture—and by extension, identity—something that can be stolen? Could a traditional musician hold a copyright on a piece of music that has been passed down from generation to generation? If not, who holds the copyright and who collects the royalties? Does a Western musician or scholar do the right thing or set a bad precedent in making payment to an organization and thereby validating its representation of indigenous musicians as a class? How explicit could an ownership definition become? Could it apply to a rhythm, a chant, or a dance style? Add courts, position papers, and various commissions to other efforts to define a position of authority over cultural processes. All these efforts are increasingly congruent with contemporary processes of commodification and metaphors of value.

What is amazing is that music, which time and again has been considered superficial, should bring to a unique resolution and display so many variations of the idea of culture, so many cultural problems that have no clear solution, so many relationships that are otherwise unacknowledged. Probably the underlying questions are not supposed to be answered but are raised only to challenge and engage people to respond, to enter a world of players and participants. Even in its most formal venues, music exists in a realm of play. In that realm, discourse is peripheral and tends to be transparently motivated and personal. The ultimate benefit of studying music in context has been understanding the value of musical contexts in themselves over any intrinsic value in the music itself. Music's main value reflects music's impermanence: it accrues mainly to the experience of those who are involved and doing things in musical contexts and only to a lesser extent, if at all, to anything that can be taken away. Music has always been something of a mystery, somehow beyond words, something beyond rational understanding, or, conversely, something that indicates the limitations of understanding. Modern philosophers and theologians discuss divinity in such a manner, by talking around the idea, focusing on effects and manifestations but not attempting to understand their subject in itself. In the same vein, music may partake of qualities considered to be spiritual, but in a secular world, music provides a comparable forum for discourse about things that have no substance but only effects and manifestations.

These effects and manifestations have nourished the cultural perspective that anthropology has championed, and it is now clearly the musicologists who occupy a more bounded world of culturally relative insight. Still, among even the most up-to-date scholars—those who note the multifaceted and relative complexity of the contemporary world and who proclaim its defining characteristic to be irony—most have difficulty accepting and working with ironic concepts as the focal points of their knowledge. When knowledge is ironic, then who is to say who knows what? But what one knows about music is not the main issue. The academic study of music started when intellectuals were peers or adjuncts to the elite, but the cultural influence of the Western elite is fading. Certainly, people from everywhere are moving through the world more than ever before, and there is no shortage of people capable of challenging anyone else's statements about music. More important, though, our ideas about culture have changed. Our understanding of music has reached the point where we recognize that musical performances are momentary events and that music's cultural meaning lies within its potential to transform the people who participate in, or attend, or are involved in musical events. This meaning is not to be abstracted into knowledge but rather recreated and experienced anew. If every aspect of musical meaning seems changed, this one has not changed. Is it possible that intellectuals can grasp this further irony about the abiding nature of impermanence? Could they take the measure of music as a model for their work, striving not to promote an idea of truth but to create a vehicle for participation and transformation?

SUGGESTIONS FOR FURTHER READING

Rather than listing a large number of distinguished ethnomusicological writings, I would recommend the following as an introduction to various ways of interpreting music by linking it to broader manifestations of cultural meaning.

Berliner, Paul F. 1993. *The Soul of Mbira: Music and Traditions of the Shona People of Zimbabwe.* Chicago: University of Chicago Press.

Blacking, John. 1973. *How Musical Is Man?* Seattle: University of Washington Press.

Chernoff, John M. 1979. *African Rhythm and African Sensibility: Aesthetics and Social Action in African Musical Idioms.* Chicago: University of Chicago Press.

Stoller, Paul. 1989. *Fusion of the Worlds: An Ethnography of Possession among the Songhai of Niger.* Chicago: University of Chicago Press.

Thompson, Robert F. 1974. *African Art in Motion: Icon and Act in the Collection of Katherine Coryton White.* Los Angeles: University of California Press.

21.

Art/Anthropology/Museums: Revulsions and Revolutions

CHRISTOPHER B. STEINER

In the first few years of the twentieth century, when social anthropology was slowly coming of age as a professional discipline in Europe, the study of art and visual culture was positioned somewhere at the very distant edge of this emerging new field. In its attempt to differentiate itself from other existing disciplines (such as history, art history, and philosophy), anthropology identified its academic niche as the study of small-scale, nonliterate, non-Western societies with a special focus on social structure. While art and material objects were recognized as playing some role in the organization and cultural life of these so-called primitive societies, their overall significance was thought to rank considerably below more "serious" categories of inquiry, such as kinship systems, modes of production, and political governance. As a result of this overall lack of interest in art and aesthetics by the early practitioners of anthropology, we tend to think of the formation of the discipline as completely separate and unrelated to late-nineteenth- and early-twentieth-century developments in European painting and sculpture. But a closer reading of the histories of anthropology and early modern art reveals an important sphere of confluence, wherein developments in both fields appear to have influenced or, at the very least, rubbed shoulders with each other.

PRIMITIVIST REVOLUTION

When I went to the old Trocadéro, it was disgusting.—Pablo Picasso commenting on his first visit to the anthropology collections at the Trocadéro Museum of Ethnography in 1907

The formation of ethnographic museums in cities such as Paris, London, Oxford, Leiden, and Berlin, beginning sometime in the 1870s, provided not only a material laboratory for anthropological documentation of Europe's expanding colonial empires, but also offered a powerful visual catalyst that led artists like Vlaminck, Derain, Matisse, and Picasso toward an iconography of primitivism. For the art world, this period marked a radical art-historical break with the representational traditions that had previously extended from the Renaissance to the nineteenth century. When Picasso wandered alone into the African and Oceanic galleries of the old Trocadéro ethnographic museum on a fateful day in the spring of 1907, he was initially disgusted by the musty smells, soiled surfaces, and sensory clutter of this exotic and shocking material world. But as Picasso noted years later, in an interview with André Malraux, something in the museum compelled him to stay that day: "I was alone. I wanted to get away. But I didn't leave. I stayed. I understood that it was very important."[1]

At about the same moment that Picasso walked through the turnstile of the Trocadéro, Émile Durkheim, somewhere in another corner of Paris, was pouring through recent ethnographic writings on Africa, the Americas, and Pacific. Durkheim was in search of the primary data out of which he and his associates in the *Année Sociologique* would eventually develop a model of "primitive" society—leading to the formation of the new discipline of comparative sociology. Encounters by Picasso and Durkheim with material and documentary evidence of other cultures yielded, in both cases, revolutionary outcomes. While the writings of the new French sociology (especially Durkheim's *The Elementary Forms of the Religious Life*, published in 1912) paved the road for the founding of modern British social anthropology in the 1920s under the tutelage of such figures as A. R. Radcliffe-Brown and Bronislaw Malinowski, the advent of primitivism in modern art (marked most strikingly by Picasso's painting *Les Demoiselles d'Avignon* (plate 9), which he completed just a few months after his famous museum visit in 1907), would lead to a complete refiguring of both the representation of the human body and the image of so-called primitive societies in twentieth-century art. Born out of similar engagements with the discovery of cultural differences, anthropology and modern art would not only partake in a concurrent birth but would also share interests in a kindred engagement with a complex and still largely unfamiliar world that existed beyond the shores of Europe.

The anthropology of art, which began to emerge several decades after these two monumental encounters between Western and non-Western cultures, developed a discourse of inquiry that was predominantly robed in the fashions of current anthropological theories. Thus, for example, anthropologists who subscribed to the functionalist's view that societies were made up of interrelated parts, approached art by considering it as just one of many other institutions that helped maintain social balance and cohesion. In this sense, the category "art" was treated as no different than say religious ceremonies, marriage customs, or child-rearing; the meaning of art, like the meaning of these other social phenomena, could be ascertained by exploring every situation in which it was used and then tracing out the linkages between its function and the overall structure of the social organization.

Yet, unlike some of the other subfields of the discipline, the anthropology of art was always acutely aware of its filial relations with the broader art history of the modernist period. Both artists and anthropologists, after all, were drawn to the same subjects. But unlike anthropologists, the artists that were inspired by ethnographic collections never sought out indigenous viewpoints on these artworks or material cultures. So, while Picasso and his colleagues may have been moved by the flood of "primitive" objects that were arriving in Europe in the first decades of the twentieth century, they demonstrated virtually no interest in uncovering the interpretation of these pieces in their original cultural contexts. Indeed, in most instances, an ignorance of indigenous meaning appears almost to have been a precondition for what was considered "pure" aesthetic response and appreciation. In the most extreme case, Picasso is reported to have once answered a question regarding the influence of African art on his work with the facetious quip, "Art nègre? Connais pas!"[2] It is precisely this sort of self-fashioned obliviousness—"Negro art? Know nothing of it!"—that typifies the modernist lack of engagement with ethnographic things.

Seen within this context, we might begin to better understand why so much of the early anthropology of art was designed specifically as an effort to recontextualize the material cultures that had been wrenched (both literally and figuratively) from their indigenous social milieus. Missionaries, soldiers, explorers, and colonial administrators all seized objects from their original owners, while modern artists exacerbated the process of estrangement by projecting onto these objects their own peculiar meanings and interpretations. Reacting to these two forms of displacement, one of the principal goals of anthropology has always been to situate the objects in the social or symbolic world within which they were originally meant to be used or seen. While such an anthropology of art usually succeeded in throwing light on indigenous iconography and the social or ritual function of objects in their proper cultural framework, it often failed to properly account for the "life history" of the objects themselves. That is to say, because the anthropology of art grew out of an assumption that the modernist appropriation of non-Western art had to be negated in order to understand the art of other cultures, anthropology largely ignored the migration of "primitive" art into the "civilized" world of museums and collections. Thus, while modernist artists may have infused ethnographic objects with their own eurocentric fantasies and meanings, ethnographers imagined a world in which the very objects they were trying to interpret were represented as though they had never left their indigenous homes.

In his highly acclaimed BBC series *The Tribal Eye*, for example, David Attenborough, one of the great popularizers of the anthropology of art in the 1970s, presents a sequence of Dogon masked rituals which make it appear as though no European, prior to the arrival of Attenborough and his film crew, had ever before set foot in the Bandiagara Cliffs of Mali. The energetic and graceful masked performers that fill the screen are said, in the narrator's voice-over, to be dancing the masks of their forefathers, following an unbroken tradition stretching back into the past to time immemorial. From the perspective presented in the film, which indeed typifies the viewpoint of the anthropology of art from its inception until fairly recently, it would be nearly impossible to know that one of the major collections that drew Picasso's eye in 1907 was a group of Dogon ancestor masks that had just been brought back to the Trocadéro Museum from French West Africa by Lt. Louis Desplagnes in the fall of 1906.

BATTLE OVER THE *PRIMITIVISM* EXHIBITION

> *I came out of the museum with a mixed feeling of exhilaration and also with some anger.*
> —Rasheed Araeen commenting on his visit to the Museum of Modern Art's exhibition, *Primitivism in Twentieth-Century Art*, in 1984

If the advent of primitivism in modern art marks the first point of reference for a history of the anthropology of art, then the second pivotal moment probably does not occur until some eighty-years later on the occasion of a major retrospective of the primitivist movement held at the Museum of Modern Art (MoMA) in New York City. In an exhibition entitled *Primitivism in Twentieth-Century Art: Affinity of the Tribal and the Modern*, which opened in the fall of 1984, art historians William Rubin and Kirk Varnedoe brought together a vast selection of "modern" masterpieces positioned alongside the "primitive" objects that were said to have inspired them. One of the exhibit's highlights was a display of *Les Demoiselles d'Avignon*, which was hung near some African masks that share an affinity of form with the two "masked" women on the far right of Picasso's composition. While the exhibit earned wide public acclaim—heralding the dawn of a new age of museum blockbuster shows in New York City—it also became the battleground for some heated academic debates between anthropologists, art historians, and the museum's curators.

At issue, initially, was the definition of "art" in Western and non-Western contexts, and whether the museum had degraded the material objects of Africa, Oceania, and Native America by presenting them as "works of art" (in the Western sense of art-for-art's-sake) without properly situating them in their historical or social settings. At the heart of the controversy was the following type of question: If a cult object is the focus of intense piety in its indigenous culture, is it then appropriate to ignore its fundamental sacred significance and exhibit that object as a form of pure aesthetic expression with none of its religious or social context in evidence? The museum, on the one hand, took the position that to elevate such an object to the category "art" was indeed the highest honor the West could accord to the material culture of another society. To burden that object under the interpretive weight of didactic ethnographic labels, their argument goes, is to trivialize the "beauty" and intense aesthetic effects of such an artwork. In fact, failure to be moved by the putative universal aesthetic appeal of "primitive" objects was taken by the curators as evidence of cultural bias or—even worse—racism. Thus, for example, in his response to art historian Thomas McEvilley, one of the most outspoken critics of the exhibition, curator William Rubin wrote, "I wonder how many of his readers who saw our show and stood before the monumental Nukuoro island carving of the goddess Kave share McEvilley's conviction that what they were looking at was 'not art.'"[3] Critics of the show, on the other hand, argued that failure to contextualize non-Western objects, such as the contested Micronesian religious statue, was an act of Western arrogance that bordered on cultural imperialism. They pointed out that while the museum took great pains to date and detail all of the European paintings, prints, drawings, and sculptures in the exhibit, the so-called primitive works were displayed without dates or attributions, and with no ethnographic explications whatsoever.

If, up until now, the anthropology of art had been framed largely as a response to modernism's indifference toward the cultural context of non-Western material culture, the *Primitivism* exhibition (though it was indeed seen as upholding these very insensibilities) altered the discourse of the field in a new and dramatic way. Now the problem of anthropology was no longer one predicated on filling in the ethnographic voids that early modernist appropriations had left wide open; rather, at issue was the more troubling question of how a major art museum like MoMA could perpetuate the interpretive deficiencies and myths of the early modernist period. What had the anthropology of art accomplished over the past half century or more if none of its lessons on the meaning of non-Western art in its indigenous settings were included in such a major public forum?

The intensity of the crisis in the discipline which the *Primitivism* exhibit had generated was perhaps not immediately evident. The debate at the time of the exhibition itself centered largely on the status of objects as "art" versus "non-art." But ultimately, it seems, the original debate might have been masking a more profound issue which eventually came to light in later reflections on the MoMA debacle. The important question, which now appears very clear, is the following: Where were the voices of the living indigenous peoples whose ancestors (some of whom are probably indeed still alive) created the works that were put on display in the museum? At stake, then, were not merely the consequences of some bombastic debates carried out by cultural outsiders on the relative aesthetic merits of other people's material objects; rather, at issue was an urgent need for a serious interrogation of the nature of that discussion itself and some reflection on the identity of those whose views on such matters were deemed relevant and authoritative. By presenting modern art's "primitive" counterparts as an embalmed collection of speechless, timeless, ahistorical figures in need of Western curators to act as their arbiters of meaning and art-historical value, the MoMA exhibit perpetuated the colonial myth of non-Western cultures as static, isolated, and backward communities. In a sober and smart critique of the *Primitivism* exhibition, Pakistani-born artist and writer Rasheed Araeen summarized the crux of the new problem: "The point is that those who have been seen as 'primitives' are in fact part of today's society, and to ignore their actual position in this respect is to indulge again in imperialist fantasies."[4]

Ironically, one of the few cracks in the show's facade of Western hegemony was a small, obscure label identifying an object that had been removed from the exhibition in deference to indigenous religious beliefs. In place of a Zuni war god from the collections of the Berlin Museum für Völkerkunde (which would have served to illustrate its influence on Paul Klee's painting *Mask of Fear* from 1932) was a placard that read "The museum was informed by knowledgeable authorities that Zuni people consider any public exhibition of their war gods to be sacrilegious." Clearly, then, there was more to the art/non-art debate than mere academic posturing. Here, in this seemingly innocuous little label was evidence that living tribal peoples still had voice in controlling the fate of their appropriated objects, and that the objects on display "may in fact 'belong' somewhere other than in an art or an ethnographic museum."[5]

As it emerged from the long shadow cast by the *Primitivism* exhibition and its ensuing controversy in the mid 1980s, the anthropology of art appeared no longer able to focus exclusively on the meaning and interpretation of material objects in their indigenous milieus. This approach now seemed sorely artificial and misguided. What had to be accounted for at present was the meaning of those objects in the broader context of a history of Western appropriations and evaluations. While anthropology's vision had been riveted for so long on a singular mission to probe indigenous settings, new concerns that emerged outside the "box" of traditional inquiry would invigorate the field. Topics that were now at issue included the politics of collecting and exhibiting in Europe and North America, the influence of the West on non-Western artistic practices, documenting the presence of living Native and non-Western peoples as active participants in the international art world, and an anthropological discourse on contemporary art that could apply itself as readily to postmodern subjects as it did to the arts of small-scale societies once conventionally studied by anthropologists. In the 1980s, then, boundaries were smashed, categories were dissolved, and histories of the "tribal" and "modern" were fused and revitalized. And, unlike the previous anthropology of art, which prepared its theories with ingredients culled largely from the more staple recipes of the field—models drawn from such subspecialties as the anthropology of kinship, economics, or politics—the new anthropology of art would now emerge as a key player in setting the tone and agenda for the broader discipline itself.

BITING IRONY

As an American Indian, there are only negative places that the art world can put [your art], only disgusting places.—Jimmie Durham (Cherokee)

Just as anthropologists and artists overlapped in their interests and agendas at the beginning of the twentieth century, so too at the end of the century they continue to participate across a shared field of inquiry. However, unlike earlier examples, which involved European artists projecting in art their personal visions of an imagined "primitive" world, recent artistic exercises within the realm of anthropology have been characterized largely by non-European artists commenting through their works on the subjugating practices and effects of primitivism itself. Artists who associate themselves in some way with the societies that have traditionally been the subject of anthropological study are now turning their gaze onto their chief observers—using art as both a vehicle and weapon in their social, political, and academic critiques.

Much of this work draws upon the irreverent power of irony to make trenchant critical points about the anthropology of art, and in so doing yields powerful lessons on transcultural aesthetic appreciation. Consider, for instance, a work from 1985 by Cherokee artist Jimmie Durham, entitled *Pocahontas's Underwear* (plate 10). This piece, which is part of his larger series *On Loan from the Museum of the American Indian*, explores with tremendous wit and parody the status of Native American material culture within the discipline of anthropology and its associated museum practices. Putting on display an invented pair of red, feathered, lacy lingerie allegedly belonging to Pocahontas—an Indian "princess" who has long been subject to Euro-American fantasies involving scantily clad tribal women— Durham undresses the history of anthropology's voyeuristic obsessions with the most intimate details of other people's material cultures. Freudian sexual fetishism bumps hips here with anthropology's museological fetishism—an academic tradition that appears, in Durham's view, as intent on collecting, analyzing, and displaying every conceivable aspect of other people's private lives. Durham once referred to the anthropology of art and the history of its museum practices as collective exercises in necrophilia, since in his view anthropology turns the work of active subjects into "dead" objects by arresting the social life of things and dissecting material culture into disembodied analytical parts. Although *Pocahontas's Underwear* speaks volumes to such bitter issues as social death and cultural rape, its humorous overtones also invite an opening to dialogue which might strip away some of the prejudices and assumptions that have been identified with Western encounters with non-Western material cultures.

Like Durham, but working within the framework of a different social and historical tradition, African-American artist Fred Wilson also offers an alternative engagement with non-Western arts and cultures. Using the museum itself as his palette, Wilson creates exhibits or installation pieces that comment on the relationship between colonial power, the anthropology of art, and the history of ethnographic collecting and display. For instance, in an installation work entitled *The Other Museum* from 1991 at the gallery of the Washington Project for the Arts, Wilson included a section which he called "The Colonial Collection." Here, he wrapped a half-dozen African masks in the flags of their homeland's former British and French colonizers—some with their eyes covered, others with mouths gagged by folded Union Jacks and Tricolors. Because Wilson sees the masks as representing hostages of museum culture it is not surprising that his modifications suggest perhaps the arresting images of the American embassy hostages in Iran who were blindfolded and put on public display in the late 1970s.

In another installation entitled *Primitivism: High and Low*, which was exhibited in New York at Metro Pictures Gallery in 1991, Wilson took aim at the Museum of Modern Art's *Primitivism* exhibition, and more generally at museum representations of what he calls "the cultural other." One stunning piece in that installation, *Picasso/Who Rules?* (figure 1), poses a series of questions that interrogate the relationship between modernity and tradition in Western attitudes toward non-Western arts, and thereby addresses through the medium of art itself some of the key issues in the new anthropology of art. Using a full-scale reproduction of *Les Demoiselles d'Avignon*, Wilson adorned the squatting figure at the bottom right of Picasso's painting with an African mask cut into the canvas itself. A footstool positioned directly below the masked figure enticed gallery visitors to step up to the artwork and peer into the eye holes of the painting's wooden appendage. Viewers were met by the eyes of two Senegalese men and Wilson himself on a video recording asking such baffling questions as "If my contemporary art is your tradi-

FIGURE 1 Fred Wilson, *Picasso/Who Rules?* 1991. (Courtesy of Fred Wilson and Metro Pictures Gallery, New York)

tional art, is my art your cliché?" and, "If your contemporary art is my traditional art, is your art my cliché?"

The work of artists like Durham and Wilson continues to prod the anthropology of art to question its methods, categories, and assumptions. And from such dialogue between anthropologists and artists fresh perspectives on art will begin to emerge. As Fred Wilson once put it, "If the world is so small, how can we come up with a new way of looking at art using all the philosophies, anthropologies, and histories about art to create something really new and vibrant."[6]

CULTURE WARS

I think this show is disgusting. It is a disgusting show.—Mayor Rudolph Giuliani commenting on the Brooklyn Museum of Art exhibit *Sensation*, which opened in New York in 1999

On the eve of the close of a century that was ushered in by Picasso's epiphanic visit in 1907 to the Trocadéro in Paris, New York City Mayor Rudolph Giuliani encountered in 1999 the art of several young contemporary British artists whose works were featured at an exhibition of Charles Saatchi's collection entitled *Sensation* at the Brooklyn Museum of Art. His reaction to some of this art, like Picasso's in a different place and time, was one of initial outrage and disgust. But unlike Picasso, who felt compelled to stay and "understand" the shock of the strange and exotic, Giuliani left in a flap. And on his way out he threatened to suspend $7.2 million in city funding, discharge the museum's board of trustees, and barricade the doors of the building if certain artworks which he considered "deeply offensive to a significant portion of the community" and described in several media interviews as "sick stuff" that "should happen in a psychiatric hospital not in a museum" were not removed from display—including, for example, Damien Hirst's dead animals suspended in formaldehyde and, perhaps most notably, Afro-British artist Chris Ofili's painting of *The Holy Virgin Mary* (1996), a paper collage on linen depicting a Black Madonna in a colorful flowing robe, dabbed with a clump of elephant dung and surrounded with images of women's buttocks and genitals clipped from pornographic magazines (plate 11). In spite of the Mayor's protests, the exhibition opened as scheduled, and attracted a record-breaking audience of some seven thousand people within just the first few hours of the show's debut. While some of these visitors were perhaps drawn to the exhibit out of a genuine interest in contemporary British art, much of the crowd was also probably attracted by the controversy stirred by Mayor Giuliani. Shortly after its opening, the exhibit had already been debated on the floor of the United States Congress, made the subject of countless powwows in the media and tabloids, and argued in legal cases before city, state, and federal courts; in addition, Ofili's controversial painting of the Holy Virgin Mary had been smeared and defaced with white oil paint by an enraged seventy-two year-old retired Catholic school teacher.[7] But *Sensation* remained open and continued to break museum attendance records on a daily basis.

The controversy at the Brooklyn Museum of Art is but the most recent in a whole series of museum battles fought over the past decade or so in the United States—beginning *en force* in 1989 with a condemnation by North Carolina Senator Jesse Helms and other congressional conservatives of Andres Serrano's putatively blasphemous photograph *Piss Christ* (1987), which prompted New York Senator Alfonse D'Amato to proclaim that the federally funded artist who photographed a crucifix submerged in urine "is not an artist, he is a jerk." That scandal was followed only weeks later by the abrupt cancellation of Robert Mapplethorpe's retrospective exhibit *The Perfect Moment* at the Smithsonian's Corcoran Gallery of Art, after one hundred members of Congress criticized government support of certain allegedly homoerotic and pedophilic images in the show which they considered pornography and "not art."

These various battles waged during the past ten years over the exhibition of controversial art in American museums have come to be known collectively as the Culture Wars. If the anthropology of art is founded on the premise that it can interpret art by situating it in the context of its indigenous culture, then surely the discipline must be able to throw some meaningful light on the nature of this most peculiar form of late-modern ritual combat. Indeed, I would suggest that these clashes over the exhibition of contemporary visual culture touch upon some of the most fundamental aspects of *any* anthropology of art and are at the core of understanding the very nature of the social construction of the category "art." Reading the Culture Wars through the lens of anthropology reveals a whole range of critical issues, including such things as the role of museums as ritual sites that shape and define community and cultural values, the function of art as political symbol in a struggle for power and leadership, the economic aspect of art in global systems of commodity exchange, and even the cross-cultural construction of decency and filth.

Museums as Ritual Sites

Anthropologist Clifford Geertz once said that rituals consist of places or moments where societies come together to tell stories "*to* themselves *about* themselves." Today, in the secular context of a modern nation-state, one could argue that museums have largely replaced the traditional sites of ceremonial practice, and it is in museums (perhaps even more so than in temples, kivas, or village squares) where societies now construct and recount their narratives of group membership and identity. Maybe that might account for the astounding rise in recent years of museum and gallery attendance figures throughout Europe and North America. In 1994, for instance, the British press reported that museum visits in England alone had surpassed the combined public attendance at cinema theaters and sporting events during the same year. Recent upsurges in museum crowds cannot simply be explained by greater public interest in matters of fine art, science, or natural history. Instead, it would almost surely appear that museums are viewed increasingly as gathering points for the transmission of collective cultural knowledge, and as sources for the foundation of shared discourse and nationalist identity in the diverse, urban, multicultural societies that much of the world population now inhabits. Viewed in this way, it becomes increasingly clear why the Brooklyn Museum show in 1999 should have stirred such high anxieties and emotions. What is at issue here is not simply someone's right to view or not view a particular set of objects or images; rather, the self-representation and definition of community itself is put under pressure and disputed. In a public site of ritual contestation, supporters of artistic freedom struggle against Christians deeply offended by what they perceive to be Chris Ofili's desecration of the Holy Virgin Mary; animal rights activists and radical vegetarians rally against Damien Hirst's dead and embalmed pig, shark, and sheep to expose wider concerns regarding societal cruelty to animals; politicians scramble to the perceived safety of a moral high ground; and artists and collectors scream foul play against multimillionaire Charles Saatchi's capacity to dominate, control, and even destabilize the contemporary art market economy. On opening day, which was described by one commentator as "a ritual devoted to interpretations of free expression,"[8] and by another as "a bizarre carnival of media coverage,"[9] protesters from the Catholic League for Religious and Civil Rights lined one side of the street carrying rosary beads, reciting the "Hail Mary," and singing Christian hymns, while across the way their detractors wore T-shirts emblazoned with the slogan "I ♥ Sick Art." Meanwhile, a freelance preacher in black denims and white shirt scaled a wall, folded his arms, and advised those clutching $9.75 tickets: "You want to sow a crap? That's what you're going to reap." How different is this really from some of the ritual behavior anthropologists have long studied across the globe? What, for instance, would a visitor arriving for the first time in Brooklyn on a sunny afternoon in early October make of this strange procession of museum-goers snaking their way from the subway station past hordes of protestors handing out "vomit bags" brightly emblazoned with the sword and shield of the Catholic League. Taken out of context, this scene of "ritual" procession might be as baffling to an outsider as the seemingly bizarre ceremonies and magical incantations witnessed by anthropologist Bronislaw Malinowski soon after disembarking in the Trobriand Islands some eighty-five years earlier. Only now the anthropological gaze is not directed into the thatched huts and yam gardens of a small coral island formation in the Solomon Sea, but onto the massive marble steps of a nineteenth-century Beaux-Arts building deep in the heart of Brooklyn.

Art as a Political Weapon
In the Highlands of New Guinea, just southwest of the Trobriand Islands, political leaders, known as Big Men, customarily adorn their bodies with paints, feathers, and shells on collective ceremonial occasions known as *moka*. Drawing upon the art of visual splendor and superb oratory skills, the Big Men hope to attract a constituency of loyal followers and, in the process, crush the political aspirations of their less resplendent challengers. This is a classic anthropological example of how visual culture can be used to satisfy political aspirations and goals. But the relationship of art to politics is of course not limited to the hills and valleys of rural New Guinea. Following the Brooklyn Museum debacle, critics of New York City Mayor Giuliani were quick to point out that in light of his upcoming bid against Hillary Clinton for a seat on the United States Senate, the mayor was profoundly aware of the importance of the Catholic vote, which makes up an estimated 44 percent of New York State's electorate. His outrage over what he alleges to be Chris Ofili's desecration of the Holy Virgin Mary, by associating the Madonna

with pornographic images and elephant dung, may very well illustrate another excellent example of art being pressed in service of political ends. For by slinging criticism toward artworks such as Ofili's, Giuliani (a Catholic) forced his political opponent, Hillary Clinton (a Methodist), to dress herself in the discourse of artistic tolerance, espousing liberal views (perhaps in spite of her own moral or aesthetic judgments) toward an image that was putatively defamatory to the Catholic community. Giuliani entered into a gambit he could not lose, and he emerged from the contest dressed in the dazzling attire of a champion of antidefamation and Catholic virtues.

The Status of Art

One recurring problem in the anthropology of art has been the question of whether the concept of "art" itself is universal or whether it is a distinctive feature of Western cultures that is generally not found in the non-Western societies most often studied by anthropologists. The problem for Africa, at least, has been stated something like this: If there is no word in any African languages that translates into "art," then does this mean that there is no art in Africa? One answer to this rather thorny question is to point out that most African languages also do not possess an indigenous term which translates adequately into the word "music." Does this mean there is no music in Africa? The negative answer to *that* question seems pretty obvious. Yet the issue of how to define visual "art" remains perplexing. I would suggest that perhaps a better approach to resolving the dilemma may be indicated by an anthropological reading of the Brooklyn Museum controversy. By momentarily stepping beyond the domain of African art (or indeed any non-Western tradition), we see immediately that the definition of "art" is just as problematic inside the contemporary Western art world as it is outside. If we acknowledge this point, then the debate over art/non-art which has dominated discussions in the anthropology of non-Western art, suddenly becomes recast in radically different terms. The problem is no longer whether a Dogon ancestor mask and the carved wooden figure of a Micronesian goddess are works of art or religious artifacts; rather, the challenge is to understand the social institutions, agents, actions, and cultural frameworks of meaning that allow such objects to be viewed as "art" at all. From this perspective, the category art becomes much more fluid and reflects the situational positioning of its various definitions. In the context of a masked ritual held high in the Bandiagara Cliffs of Mali, a Dogon mask *is* a religious icon; in the Rockefeller Wing of the Metropolitan Museum of Art the same mask *is*, at least from a certain perspective, a work of Dogon art. A brown paper shopping bag filled with elephant dung, labeled *Bag of Shit* and signed by artist Chris Ofili, sitting on a shiny white pedestal in a spotlighted, white-walled gallery at the Osterwalder's Art Space in Hamburg *is*, from a certain perspective, a work of art. The same container in a sweeper's barrow at the London Zoo *is* a bag of shit. Thus, the anthropological mission is no longer focused on identifying some putatively inherent qualities in Western objects that elevate them to "art"; rather, it is to locate the institutional structures and cultural discourses that construct and frame the category art itself wherever it may be.

The "Western" Conundrum

Another concern which analysis of the Brooklyn Museum exhibit brings to light is the problematic division between such categories as "Western" and "non-Western" art. This conventional division between two world art traditions has become a major concern and sometimes a stumbling block for the anthropology of art. While anthropology traditionally studied non-Western cultures, increasingly many within the discipline have turned their attention to topics in Western societies. This transition reflects an increasing awareness that institutions and individuals are no longer grounded in a particular geographic space, but move across a complex and integrated transnational map of exchange and displacement. The case of the Brooklyn Museum show underscores the difficult nature of such divisions between the "West" and "non-West." How does one classify, for example, the art of Chris Ofili? He is an artist of Yoruba (Nigerian) descent born in Manchester, England, whose patrons include London-based, Iraqi-born, Jewish advertising titan Charles Saatchi. One of Ofili's recent artworks on the subject of the Holy Virgin Mary, described by the artist (who is himself a former altar-boy and practicing Roman Catholic) as "a hip-hop rendition of Old Master paintings,"[10] daubed in shellacked elephant dung collected from a consort of African and Asian elephants at the London Zoo and adorned with pornographic cutouts from international adult magazines creates a political scandal in New York City fueled by the politically inspired wrath of conservative, Republican, Italian-American Mayor Rudolph Giuliani. Is Ofili's style Yoruba? African? British? Catholic? Hybrid? International? Postmodern? Or are these categories now meaningless in a world of swirling global migrations and transnationally forged identities?

Art and Money

If it is increasingly clear that art across the world is a tool of political struggle, it is also evident, particularly since the market boom of the 1980s, that art is an economic commodity as well. Some in the recent anthropology of art have even suggested that we value art in proportion to its economic worth, and that distinctions between the "tribal" and the "modern" are often made according to an artwork's price tag. "The continuum from ethnographic artifact to *objet d'art*," writes anthropologist Sally Price, "is clearly associated in people's minds with a scale of increasing monetary value and a shift from function to aesthetics as an evaluatory basis."[11] The Brooklyn Museum controversy also illustrates the intersection of art and money, and suggests the difficulty we have in associating the two. Many in the museum and art world who advocate artistic freedom of expression nonetheless support Mayor Giuliani's claim that the museum is guilty of engaging in dubious financial arrangements with the collection's owner, Charles Saatchi, who donated $160,000 toward the cost of the show, and with several New York art dealers and galleries from whom the museum is reported to have received thousands of dollars in pledges and support. Christie's auction house, which is gearing up to sell Saatchi's collection after the exhibit closes, is said to have contributed $50,000 to the Brooklyn Museum installation.

The high-finance aspects of art have little to do with traditional concerns for aesthetics or meaning, but much to do with economic speculation, and they are best approached through an anthropology of art that connects seamlessly to an economic anthropology. Critics of art collector Charles Saatchi have referred to his extravagant buying practices as "a sort of voodoo deal, where you can make an image of your demon."[12] Here in this network of exchange, the rationale of the market economy is momentarily suspended while the logic of precapitalist magic appears to take over.

Purity and Danger

Finally, somewhere on the periphery of the *Sensation* debate there has also emerged an interesting discussion on indigenous cultural context and the hermeneutics of elephant excrements in African societies. In championing Ofili's work, some perhaps overzealous supporters have proclaimed that dung might be considered "sacred" in Africa and thus, from Ofili's perspective at least, it may be an honor for the Holy Virgin Mary to be touched by elephant excrement. Michael Kimmelman, art critic for the *New York Times*, for example, reported in his review of the exhibition that "Elephants in Africa represent power. Dung is meant to suggest fertility. African art has always incorporated dung without meaning to be offensive."[13] Another journalist even connected Ofili's artistic medium to the ancient Egyptian reverence for dung beetles or scarabs, and the association of animal excrement with reincarnation.[14] And Arnold Lehman, director of the Brooklyn Museum of Art, speaking to reporters in defense of Ofili's painting, noted, presumably in total seriousness, that "animal dung is venerated in many African cultures." While perhaps well intentioned, such statements also evoke disturbing visual images as repulsive say as some of the notoriously grotesque scenes in Gualtiero Jacopetti's 1963 "ethno-exploitation" film, *Mondo Cane*.

Anthropologists following this debate have been quick to point out that there is no evidence for "dung worship" anywhere on the African continent. Dung is used in some parts of Africa as a source of fuel, as a basic element of house construction, and very rarely as a substance for magical ointments and body ornamentation.[15] Some of these fanciful ideas on the religious significance of dung in Africa may find their origins in the rather vague and fanciful remarks made in the museum's audio tour by pop-star narrator David Bowie. Standing before the dung-anointed Madonna, listening intently to the words spewing forth from their digital audiowands, museum visitors learn that: "Here the exposed breast of the Virgin Mary, traditional nurturing symbol of her generosity and compassion, is made of the manure that nourishes African soil." Comments on the symbolism of elephant waste have also been fueled by Ofili himself, who suggested (albeit in an indirect and somewhat ambiguous way) that the idea of using elephant dung came to him during an eight-week visit to Zimbabwe where, at the age of twenty-four, he traveled to discover and explore his African roots. "There's something incredibly simple but incredibly basic about it," Ofili is quoted as saying about elephant dung, "It attracts a multiple of meanings and interpretations."[16]

Finally, speaking out on the issue of pachyderm waste, Cathrine Acholonu, special adviser on arts and culture to Nigeria's President Olusegun Obasanjo, has been outraged not only by the painting but also by the wild American and British speculations on the culture of dung in African societies. "What faeces is in Africa," she angrily declared at a press conference in Lagos, "is what faeces is all over the world. It is something that is dirty." Acholonu also went on to note that "all over the continent and in Nigeria, African traditional behaviour is distinguished by cleanliness, restraint, and a sense of order and propriety. Africans don't plaster themselves or their environment with faeces, a substance which they view with disdain."[17]

Some years ago, anthropologist Mary Douglas formulated an elegant model of purity and pollution in which she demonstrated quite convincingly that the categories "clean" and "dirty" are culturally constructed and bear little correlation to objective qualities inherent in materials or things.[18] Drawing perhaps upon a "pop" reading of Douglas's work, many interpreters of Ofili's painting have assumed that elephant dung *must* mean something different in Africa than it does in Brooklyn. But how different are these speculations from the "fetishism" and "black magic" that Picasso incorrectly associated with African masks and statues from societies whose works he encountered out of their ethnographic contexts at the Trocadéro? Has anything really changed in the "century of progress" that separates these two encounters? I would suggest that, although misinterpretations of other people's arts continue to spew forth from the font of cross-cultural interpretation, the differences between the beginning and end of the twentieth century are indeed profound. For while Picasso spun his wild fantasies about Africa in the total absence of any indigenous voices, conjectures on Ofili's work are being carried out within earshot of the artist himself. The irony is that unlike Picasso's situation, where Europeans disregarded African perspectives by hiding behind a screen of colonial arrogance and racist stereotypes, today it is Ofili who is resisting engagement with his all-too-eager Western interlocutors—"hunkered down in his central London studio," as the *New York Times* reported shortly after the Brooklyn Museum scandal first broke, "screening the avalanche of phone calls he has been getting for the last few days."[19] In one of the few interviews Ofili has granted since the Brooklyn Museum controversy erupted, he is quoted as saying, "I don't feel as though I have to defend it. The people who are attacking this painting are attacking their own interpretation, not mine. You never know what's going to offend people, and I don't feel it's my place to say any more."

It is against this backdrop of an art world intent on deciphering the meaning of *The Holy Virgin Mary*, and Ofili's reticence to engage in any interpretive dialogue whatsoever, that acclaimed Nigerian artist and art critic Olu Oguibe has put forth his own intervention. Oguibe claims that all of these speculations on the symbolism of dung have in fact largely been orchestrated by Ofili himself, who has quietly played to his advantage Western stereotypes and misconceptions of Africa and her visual cultures. The source of Ofili's interest in elephant waste, according to Oguibe, is neither his distant Yoruba heritage nor his hasty visit to Zimbabwe (where he points out that none of Ofili's fellow travelers, many of whom were also impressionable Afro-British artists, appear to have stepped into a similar epiphany of poop); rather, it is the work of New York conceptual artist David Hammons, who created in the 1970s a series of "Dirty Art" using among other things animal excrement.[20] In 1978, Hammons produced a series of installations entitled *Elephant Dung Sculptures* which incorporated clumps of dung striped with gold paint and placed on toy carts alongside miniature plastic elephants and peanuts.[21] Through these works, Hammons represented black identity in America as something fashioned out of recycled scraps and detritus, and also explored the culture of "dirt" as a metaphor for African American urban poverty.

What Ofili has done by linking elephant dung to his African past and, in particular, to his tour of Zimbabwe, is to construct a brilliant art-historical myth using the basic building blocks of an anthropology of "primitive" art. That is to say, he has exploited the Western art world's expectation that black visual culture must be read within an Afrocentric universe of meaning, in order ultimately to suggest a sort of pseudo-anthropological interpretation of his own work that relies on an invented ethnographic narrative accounting for the "spirituality" and aesthetic power of dung. It is only through a careful analysis of the Brooklyn Museum controversy that the true meaning of Ofili's work begins to emerge, allowing us to catch Ofili's "joke," which is, I would suggest, largely at the expense of the anthropology of art. Wrapped in layers of political symbolism and transcultural associations, *The Holy Virgin Mary* is exactly the sort of artwork that ought to engage those who seek a better understanding of visual culture from the perspective of anthropology. Indeed, it is the kind of work that the anthropology of art *must* consider if it hopes to have any social relevance or meaning in the century ahead.

NOTES

1. André Malraux, *Picasso's Mask* (New York: Holt, Rinehart, and Winston, 1976), 10.

2. "Opinions sur l'art nègre," *Action* 3 (April 1920): 26.

3. William Rubin, "Letter to the Editor," *Artforum* 23, no. 6 (1985): 44.

4. Rasheed Araeen, "From Primitivism to Ethnic Arts," in *The Myth of Primitivism: Perspectives on Art*, ed. Susan Hiller (London: Routledge, 1991), 164.

5. James Clifford, *The Predicament of Culture* (Cambridge, MA: Harvard University Press, 1988), 209.

6. Lisa G. Corrin, "Mining the Museum: Artists Look at Museums, Museums Look at Themselves," in *Mining the Museum: An Installation by Fred Wilson* (New York: The New Press, 1994), 9.

7. Anon., "Vandal Attacks Ofili Madonna," *Art in America* 88, no. 2 (2000): 31.

8. Michael Ellison, "Sensation Seekers Defy Mayor as Show Goes On," *Guardian*, 4 October 1999, 2.

9. Steven C. Dubin, "How 'Sensation' Became a Scandal," *Art in America* 88, no. 1 (2000): 53–59.

10. Peter Plagens, "Holy Elephant Dung!" *Newsweek*, 4 October 1999, 71.

11. Sally Price, *Primitive Art in Civilized Places* (Chicago: University of Chicago Press, 1989), 84.

12. John Davison, "Leading Artist Stages Protest at the Destabalising Power of Saatchi," *Independent* (London), 23 November 1999, 11.

13. Michael Kimmelman, "A Madonna's Many Meanings in the Art World," *New York Times*, 5 October 1999, E1.

14. Natalie Angier, "The Shock of the Natural: Works in Brooklyn Have a Long Tradition," *New York Times*, 5 October 1999, E1.

15. Allen Roberts, in the on-line discussion group for H-AfrArts, 5 October 1999; subscribe to the list at H-AfrArts@h-net.msu.edu, and visit the web site at www.h-net.msu.edu

16. Carol Vogel, "Holding Fast to His Interpretation; An Artist Tries to Keep His Cool in the Face of Angry Criticism," *New York Times*, 28 September 1999, E1.

17. Toye Olori, "Painting of a Black Virgin Mary Sparks Debate in Nigeria," *InterPress Third World News Agency*, 26 October 1999. My thanks to Eli Bentor for bringing this news item to my attention.

18. Mary Douglas, *Purity and Danger: An Analysis of the Concepts of Pollution and Taboo* (London and New York: Routledge, 1991; first published in 1966).

19. Vogel, "Holding Fast," E1.

20. H-AfrArts on-line discussion group, 6 October 1999 (see note 15 above). For more on this and other aspects of the Ofili controversy, see Donald J. Cosentino, "Hip-Hop Assemblage: The Chris Ofili Affair," *African Arts* 33, no. 1 (spring 2000): 40–51, 95–96.

21. Tom Finkelpearl, "On the Ideology of Dirt," in *David Hammons: Rousing the Rubble*, ed. Alanna Heiss, 61–89 (Cambridge, MA: MIT Press, 1991).

SUGGESTIONS FOR FURTHER READING

Ames, Michael M. 1992. *Cannibal Tours and Glass Boxes: The Anthropology of Museums.* Vancouver, B.C.: University of British Columbia Press.

Coote, Jeremy, and Anthony Shelton, eds. 1992. *Anthropology, Art, and Aesthetics.* Oxford: Clarendon Press.

Fisher, Jean, ed. 1994. *Global Visions: Towards a New Internationalism in the Visual Arts.* London: Kala Press, in association with the Institute of International Visual Arts.

Gell, Alfred. 1998. *Art and Agency: An Anthropological Theory.* Oxford: Clarendon Press.

Karp, Ivan, and Steven D. Lavine, eds. 1991. *Exhibiting Cultures: The Poetics and Politics of Museum Display.* Washington, DC: Smithsonian Institutions Press.

Kirshenblatt-Gimblett, Barbara. 1998. *Destination Culture: Tourism, Museums, and Heritage.* Berkeley: University of California Press.

MacClancy, Jeremy, ed. 1997. *Contesting Art: Art, Politics, and Identity in the Modern World.* Oxford: Berg.

Marcus, George E., and Fred Myers, eds. 1995. *The Traffic in Culture: Refiguring Art and Anthropology.* Berkeley: University of California Press.

Phillips, Ruth B., and Christopher B. Steiner, eds. 1999. *Unpacking Culture: Art and Commodity in Colonial and Postcolonial Worlds.* Berkeley: University of California Press.

22

Paradise Postponed: The Predicaments of Tourism

JEREMY MacCLANCY

"Tourism?" the student scowled, when I introduced the topic of next week's class. "*Tourism?* But that's something you just do, and enjoy yourself, and not think about. It's not something you *study*." The attitude is widespread, but still misguided. For tourism and leisure are now the largest industries in the world. And that's no joke. Just because tour operators try to sell us sun, sea, sand, sex, and "fun, fun, fun" does not mean we should not cast a serious eye over the whole business. In fact, the very opposite: all too easy to hide the seamier side of the trade behind the glossy promises of unbridled pleasure in foreign settings. Operators want us to buy into prefabricated dreams, but who is really paying the price?

Hunter-gatherer groups in Thailand know the answer, and it is not a pretty one. Squeezed out of their sylvan homelands by the accelerating deforestation of the logging companies or pushed away by beachside developers, they are forced to enter Thai society at the very lowest rung. There they have the choice of working for local planters or merchants at punitive rates, or joining a human zoo for tourists to gawp at. Uprooted, much of their culture now but a memory, they perform "characteristic" tasks—tree-climbing, corrupted versions of their rituals, pig-killing—for the visitors to video. Some also sell their crafts. Some simply beg.

This sort of story is all too common for indigenous and tribal groups throughout the world. In Jamaica, coastal peoples are banned from their beaches, recently privatized. In Kenya, fishing communities are denied their hitherto traditional access to coral reefs, now parts of government-run marine parks. In Tanzania, the homes of pastoralists are razed and their livestock expelled from their customary grazing areas, all in the name of developing ecotourism. Elsewhere, those who survive by agriculture are turfed off their land for the sake of hotel construction. In the process, water may become a scarce resource as the constant tourist demand for showers and baths overburdens local supplies. In sum, it seems that wherever the needs of locals clash with others' greed for the tourist dollar, it is the locals who lose the contest (figure 1).

The tribulations of tourism are not, however, restricted to embattled indigenes. In Europe, many locals today face similar, though admittedly lesser, onslaughts from the peering eyes of intrusive tourists who now come to their hometowns in massed groups. As shown by the Dutch anthropologist Jeremy Boissevain, many harassed locals choose to resist covertly, by being sullen and obstructive, by parodying or ridiculing the visitors. Resentment towards the interference of affluent outsiders is commonplace. Classifying them into derogatory national stereotypes is one way of assuaging the pain they cause, as are emotional outbursts. In the words of one Maltese woman who complained angrily to Boissevain, "We are used as carpets! . . . The residents have a right to live. We want to live. When we air our views, outsiders tell us that (our city) is not ours, but it belongs to the Maltese population. But we live here! We have a right to our city" (1996a).

In Jerusalem, the tale is similar, though in this case the story takes a slightly different twist. There, Palestinian shopkeepers feel demeaned by the condescending style of affluent visitors to their tourist-goods stores. They compensate by yarning

FIGURE 1 Tourists take pictures inside a Maasai cultural village. (© Adrian Arbib/Survival)

to each other tales of their sexual conquests. More fantasy than reality, these tales serve to reset the moral balance, otherwise so gravely upset by the self-assumed superiority of affluent outsiders only all too well aware of their monetary might. Through sex (albeit more narrative than enacted), the financially exploited turn the tables on their exploiters. Virtual slaves of capitalism, they strive, through their stories, to regain some modicum of mastery over their dominators. But the more insightful of these merchants realize that any success is also a sign of their failure: the sex is fleeting, the structural inequities perdure. The orgasm over, the woman is still a wealthy tourist, and he a petty trader in a saturated market. She can continue to travel, picking up pretty boys as she goes; he remains bound up with the daily struggle in the overcompetitive streets of Jerusalem's Christian Quarter. Her financial clout makes her the potent consumer and his lack of it makes him the consumed, whose only recourses are stories for his peers and the occasional sex for himself. According to Glenn Bowman who studied this trade, in local parlance the men wish to "fuck" the visitors but it is they who, in the end, are truly "fucked."

Some Europeans choose to hide aspects of their culture from the tourist gaze. Though they continue to stage their major festivities, which draw in the crowds and ensure locals' prosperity, they start to concentrate their efforts on previously minor ceremonies, either held away from main tourist areas or outside the tourist season. These revitalized events take on a new significance for their participants, becoming locally private opportunities to celebrate community, free from the stare and questions of inquisitive outsiders. For instance, in the north Spanish city of Pamplona, the annual June fiesta of Sanfermines was made famous by Hemingway, who was fascinated by its daily bull-running, bull-fighting, and sustained ambience of public revelry. Thanks to his writings and the efforts of his imitators however, the fiesta has now become so large, so drunken, and so riotous that many locals who do not profit directly from the presence of the crowds quit town for the period and leave the festivities to the incomers. Instead they prefer to participate in "little" Sanfermines, a late September celebration of one of the areas within the Old Quarter of the town. As locals said to me, this four-day fiesta was so pleasurable because there was such an atmosphere of people enjoying themselves "at home." They do not have to worry about the observations of outsiders and they all know how to behave.

If these strategies of covert resistance, fantasy, and hiding fail to secure local life against the depredations of the intruders, they can always turn to organized protest, active campaigns against unwanted changes. To take but one example from a list of many, in southwestern Spain, many locals are angry that the Coto de Doñana, a former royal hunting ground of marshlands, sand dunes, and pine and eucalyptus forests, has been declared a national park, to be preserved and promoted for ecotourism. To them, the rise of tourist ventures (from which they do not benefit), together with the state and international intervention which accompanies this new business, only serve to restrict their access to the resources of Doñana. In retaliation they persist in their traditional use of the space: hunting there (albeit furtively), collecting its wild vegetables, and leading their animals into its pastures (now done secretly, at night). But even these measures were not enough when the area suffered a prolonged drought in the early 1990s. To safeguard their livelihoods, two hundred locals cut the wire fences and let their horses and cattle through. Police came to shoo them away, but the resulting negotiations between the ranchers, their mayor, and the regional government did result in an agreement allowing the herdsmen to graze their stock in delimited areas of Doñana.

So far, so bad. Worse may be yet to come.

The examples given above suggest that the predicaments of tourism can be drawn in the stark terms of good versus bad, of the upright against the voracious, of locals versus developers. However, closer examination reveals that the encounter with organized tourism cannot always be portrayed in black and white: far more often, the picture must be painted in diverse shades of gray. And it is here perhaps that social anthropology can make its greatest contribution to the study and understanding of tourism and its effects.

Analysts of tourism have convincingly claimed that its market is so vast and so complex, so differentiated and diffused, that generalizations about its nature and process cannot be easily made. Some have tried to argue that because of its commonly exploitative character—of the non-Western poor by the Western wealthy—tourism should be seen as "the new imperialism." But others have counter-argued that the industry is in fact so heterogeneous that terms like *neocolonialism* are not adequate labels for it. True, new kinds of imperialism are emerging with the tourist industry, but many other things are happening within it at the same time. Given this complexity, anthropologists are well placed to tease out the threads of different tourist knots. For their training in long-term fieldwork primes them, in any particular ethnographic setting, to listen to the competing voices of members from different interest groups, to compare their words with their deeds, to disentangle the overlapping realities, and to clarify the various misconceptions and consequent confusions.

Malcolm Crick, who studied the industry in the ancient Sri Lankan city of Kandy, found that some middle-class locals thought tourism was seriously "polluting" their culture. These critics castigated tourists as the cause for apparently increasing levels of heterosexual prostitution, homosexual prostitution of young boys, dishonesty by locals, drug abuse (especially among the young), and irresponsible behavior by youths keen to emulate Western ways. They also complained of the rise of tourism as creating a system of apartheid. They thought their compatriots were being treated as second-class citizens in their own homeland, and they complained about the way hotels employed security guards to keep locals out. The arrival of more and more Westerners brought some money into the country, but it also pushed prices up, making domestic tourism too expensive a prospect for many middle-class Sri Lankans. Members of local elites did profit from tourism, as they had the capital to do so, but most Sri Lankans were powerless to do more than watch the cash flow. In Kandy, the feeling most associated with tourism was "deeply felt resentment and social jealousy."

Sri Lankan critics' claims about the decline in public morals might have appeared cogent. But, as Crick pointed out, they always relied on idealized images of the Sri Lankan past, which could not withstand historical scrutiny. In other words, tourists were being made the scapegoats of a variety of social ills, with critics fabricating a past to suit their purposes. These critics were at the same time ignoring the fact that tourism was only one force for social change among several others. Tourism, when it arises in a particular place, does not spring from nothing, as though the contemporary contexts of that place were irrelevant. The advent of tourism in any one area is deeply affected by the current social and economic situation of that area. The coming of the industry may indeed exacerbate already-established phenomena, such as young women selling access to their bodies, and may transform local morals, such as codes of hospitality to visitors. But these changes may well have already been set in motion by other forces whose arrival predated that of tourism: for example, the expansion of a cash economy, the creation of plantations and factories, the rise of labor migration. Tourism has its sins, but it should not be made to bear all those consequent on more general socioeconomic development. Local elites might be the only Sri Lankans who make substantial money from tourism, but this is not an especial evil of tourist development itself, just part of the general capitalist process in that country.

There is no doubt that tourism can have a devastating effect on local cultures, drowning them in wave after wave of new ideas and new money. But there is also no doubt that the introduction of tourism can have precisely the opposite effect, serving to boost or even revitalize local ways. A pair of very different examples here will illustrate two possible modes of this process. The first and perhaps the most spectacular example comes from the southern end of Pentecost island, part of southwest Pacific archipelago of Vanuatu (formerly the Anglo-French colony of the New Hebrides). There, since at least the early nineteenth century, locals have performed the annual ceremony of *gol*, "land-diving," to celebrate the yam harvest (see plate 12). The male members of each village which chooses to hold the event cut down trees to make poles. These are lashed together to make a tall tower. A series of platforms are constructed down one side of the tower. Each man who elects to dive selects his own pair of lianas. Each pair is then secured to the end of a platform and the other end of the pair tied to the ankles of the diver. To the accompaniment of women and some men dancing and singing at the foot of the tower, the divers then take turns, proceeding from the lowest platform to the highest, to drop. The elasticity of the lianas takes the strain of the dive when the diver reaches his lowest point and the vines are stretched to the maximum. Other men then rush quickly forward to catch the diver and prevent him hitting the ground. According to the Guinness Book of Records the gravitational force experienced by the divers is the highest reached by human activity outside of the industrialized world.

Since the late nineteenth century, missionaries, predominantly Anglicans and Catholics, have worked in the area, in a largely successful bid to persuade the locals to adopt Christianity. Locals who converted were forced to abandon their rituals and to don Western dress. Members of one village (Bunlap), however, stubbornly resisted these changes. Instead they vigorously asserted their commitment to customary ways. They did not let their penis-wrappers or grass skirts rot, and they continued to perform the *gol*. In the 1960s these villagers began to enjoy an unexpected payoff for their cultural resilience. Tourists started to attend the land-diving. In order to control the movements of these Westerners, the chief of the village only allowed them to visit during the days surrounding the event, and entry to the tower area was very strictly supervised, so that no visitor could avoid paying the hefty entrance fee (in 1981—the year I attended—the price was fifty Australian dollars). Well aware of their desires, the chief allowed those with cameras to climb the tower. He knew they liked to take photos from directly behind the platforms as divers let themselves go. These tourists attending the event were expatriates from the minicapital of the archipelago, Australians visiting the islands, and Americans, touring the Pacific on their yachts, who had specially sailed in. The chief of Bunlap, moreover, was quite prepared to solicit actively more tourists when he visited the main town on a nearby island. The money recouped was divided equally among the villagers, with a certain proportion kept aside for spending on communal projects.

In the mid-1970s educated locals began to lead a call, throughout the archipelago, for independence from their colonial masters. In a bid to unite all islanders, they campaigned for a positive revaluation of *kastom* ("traditional ways") and, where necessary, for its revitalization and even for its revival. According to them, *kastom* was no longer to be seen as backward and evil but as a great cultural asset, compatible with Christianity. Once independence was achieved, in 1980, the new government began actively to promote tourism to the country. The number of visitors started to rise steadily. People in villages neighboring Bunlap, seeing that traditions were back in vogue and mindful of the money being made by the land-divers, decided to revive the ceremony in their own territory. But while prepared to put up towers and jump from them, they were not ready to swap their trousers for penis-wrappers, even for a day. The tourists who turned up to their land-dives were disappointed. To them the ceremony, when performed in shorts, was not so photogenic.

In Pentecost a particular kind of cultural tourism, based on brief stays at a certain time of year, has dovetailed very successfully with already-established local ways. It has served to boost the resistant stance taken by the villagers of Bunlap and brought them tangible material benefits without at the same time creating internal division. Carefully controlling the process, they only accept tourists on their terms and at their price-levels. They can now feel, with some justification, that their forefathers made the right decision when they rejected the missionaries' advances. Once they were denigrated by the powers that be. Now they are held forth by the government as an example of how distinctive the country is. Furthermore, their example is so enticing that their neighbors are imitating them. But for these latter-day revivalists, the rewards are lesser, as they are not prepared to go the whole *kastom* way, and so attract fewer tourists.

The second example comes from the Basque Country in northern Spain. In the late 1980s, leading Basque politicians were deeply concerned about the economic decline of their homeland. The heavy industries, on which Basque prosperity had once relied, were closing down. The level of unemployment had risen dramatically, while disaffected nationalist youth entered the ranks of the local terrorist organization, ETA. In a bid to reverse these trends, the Basque government entered into an agreement with the Guggenheim Foundation in New York. The government would commission Frank Gehry, the renowned Canadian architect, to design a world-class building in Bilbao (the economic capital of the area), and the foundation would fill it with a series of top-quality exhibitions of modern art.

To the politicians, the Museo Guggenheim Bilbao was a key component of their strategy to improve the image of their country. It would become an emblematic building for the city, in the same way that the Sydney Opera House had become for Sydney. The politicians planned to revitalize Bilbao generally, by commissioning the erection of not just the Museo but a series of impressive public buildings, all designed by architects of the greatest renown. Their overall aim was to establish Bilbao as a European center for service industries, modern technologies, and upmarket tourism. The Museo was meant to be a central part of this strategy, attracting businessmen with cultural aspirations and cultivated tourists with deep pockets.

The Museo opened in 1997 and was an immediate triumph, attracting a great deal of international attention and stimulating a broad range of effects, many of them unforeseen. In a remarkably short time, the museum substantially changed the external image of Bilbao, with Spanish and foreign journalists alike seeing the building as a major contribution toward the successful establishment, for the city and the Basque Country as a whole, of a new identity: nonterrorist, cultured, creative, modern, and cosmopolitan. Bilbao, previously seen as a gray, dirty city, was suddenly converted into an exciting destination for non-Basque and foreign tourists. So many have started to come that in festive periods it has become difficult to find any hotel accommodation—a phenomenon unimaginable before the Museo's inauguration. The museum has also altered the city's internal image as well. In the words of one prominent local, "The Guggenheim has stimulated our self-esteem in those things in which we thought ourselves weak." Local journalists echo the sentiment: the building has brought the city's inhabitants "a good dose of optimism and self-esteem"; thanks to the Museo, "we have come to believe the miracle. . . . We are the best."

Much of this re-evaluation is due to the tourist gaze. For, to their great surprise, locals have had to become accustomed to their city, its events, and themselves becoming the objects of visitors' scrutiny. Prior to October 1997, the only postcards available were a miserable clutch of tired city portraits lying almost forgotten in the corners of newsagents' kiosks. Now "tourist shops" (hitherto unknown) sell a colorful variety of wide-angle and telephoto shots artfully depicting the Gugu, the Euskalduna (a new convention center constructed one hundred yards down the riverbank from the Museo), and rediscovered "sites" of the Bilbao townscape. One journalist noted that Bilbao has become "an open and admirable space which tourists photograph with passion, as if dealing with a recently discovered treasure." Even *Euskadi Information*, the daily newspaper of ETA's political wing, did not criticize the coming of tourists but detailed their activity in wondrous terms: a Rolls-Royce with foreign number-plates becomes stuck in the narrow streets of the Old Quarter; a horde of American millionaires disembarks from a luxury cruiser. "What things! What things!" was the radical reporter's only comment.

Besides the sheer number of tourists entering the Museo, Basque newspapers also trumpet the visits of an array of more newsworthy visitors: famous actors, dancers, industrialists, film producers, Nobel laureates, rock musicians, politicians, princes, painters, sculptors. These are photo opportunities of mutual benefit to the titanium-sheathed museum and its celebrated visitors, a chance for both to reflect their glory, each off the polish of the other (see plate 13). Even the visit of a renowned but reserved philosopher to the building was given feet of column inches. Paul Ricoeur thought the Museo a vertiginous synthesis of chaos and cosmos.

A certain sector of Bilbao's population has risen to the challenge implicitly posed by the publicized visits of these distinguished tourists. "Society" gatherings, above all held in the Museo, but also elsewhere in the city, have suddenly become popular. The inaugural party for a new exhibition, a Basque government reception, a prestigious firm's launch of its latest product: all become the excuse for local gossip columnists to list and comment on the more noteworthy guests whom the event has been able to attract.

If we follow Carol Duncan's idea that state museums are designed as spaces for the enactment of civic rituals, then the soirées held in the Museo may be regarded as secular ceremonies enabling, and consolidating, the formation of a new Bilbao-based elite. In the late nineteenth century, the rapid industrialization of the area had stimulated the rise of a newly enriched elite. Many of these industrialists were ennobled and, in the first decades of this century, patronized the cultural renaissance of the city. But the Civil War, its immediate Francoist aftermath, and the subsequent decline of heavy industry devastated old fortunes and disturbed established hierarchies. Thus this renovated sense of "Bilbao Society" is an essentially recent phenomenon, one based on the newly grounded elites of hegemonic nationalist politicians, their mandarins, captains of contemporary industries, and various creative artists who like to bask under the bright lights. The transition to democracy now effected, the days of constant demonstration and popular calls for radical change now long past, these latter-day elitists can now afford to parade themselves (and so be defined) at the Guggenheim's gala events.

Now, if the Gugu is to set a novel, *civilizing* standard for a newly rediscovered "Society," then members of that elite have to behave, and dress, accordingly. The soirées thus become key occasions for the nonchalant parading of a vested sophistication and the nocturnal creation of *glamour* (the English word is used in the local press). This striving for an effortless, but all too evanescent, style by those aspiring to high status is a game of high stakes. For, as some are only too well aware, they run the risk of looking like a group of provincials out of place in a world-class building; their attempt at sparkle is outshone by the titanium, their desire to enchant laid bare by the lack of magic. All too easy, in these circumstances, for even the smartest gown to look like the Emperor's New Clothes. In the words of one local commentator, assessing the opening party for the Rauschenberg retrospective at the museum, "It is very true that Bilbao society, in order to achieve glitter for these events, to which it should become accustomed, needs information and social recycling. A gala night needs elegance, glamour and even a touch of extravagance. Thanks to the importation of personages it was possible to find all these key aspects." A year later, at another Guggenheim gala, the society columnist finally felt able to congratulate the self-garlanded: listing the best-dressed women, he pronounced, "A display of graceful ladies, the elegance of a summer Bilbao caught in sultry weather. Bilbao, at last, can show itself off."

The Museo has attracted much criticism. When the project was initially made public, a broad collective of local artists and writers castigated it as another, woeful example of the "Coca-colonization" of non-American culture by American forces, sucking public subsidies away from other, more local, more worthy cultural initiatives. Since its opening, many critics have also denigrated the museum as more theme park than art gallery:

This is like Disneyland. You can't enjoy the works exhibited because immediately you are pushed by a group of pensioners or the typical Anglo-Saxon tourist with sandals and the skin of a crab. This museum has turned into just another tourist attraction. One sees pictures or works of art in the same way that one would visit a souvenir shop in Salamanca.

As one commentator has argued, what some visitors seem to be buying when they pay for their ticket is not so much a culturally enriching occasion, but "the Guggenheim Experience." What they are purchasing is more the sign value of the goods and their connection to ideas of a cultivated lifestyle and a rounded personal identity. The danger in all this is, as one wag put it, "If the Guggenheim is Disney, are all we visitors Mickey Mouse?"

Whether one takes sides with the politicians who backed the project or the local guardians of high culture who condemn it, one thing is clear. The building of the Museo Guggenheim Bilbao has changed Basque life. Locals contemplate pictures they would have never otherwise seen, thousands of tourists peer at what locals had previously disregarded, the affluent and their hangers-on have created a "high society," and a host of ancillary businesses have opened up. The debate about the nature and functions of the Museo shows no sign of ending. Maybe this is the way things should be: an expensively funded museum, filled by locals and tourists, stimulating constant discussion on what kind of culture Basques want. Here tourism has not so much revitalized culture as helped refigure what could be meant by it.

This Basque example underlines how "cultures" must now be seen as permeable and dynamic. Long gone are the days when a culture could be regarded as static, clearly bounded, and uncontested. For tourists, like other travelers such as labor migrants, visit other cultures but take some of their own with them at the same time. Tourists, by their very presence, change what they have come to see. And when they come in large numbers, the changes they can effect may be very large. Their sustained gaze makes locals conscious of their actions, not as appropriate means to certain ends, but as objects of significance and curiosity in themselves. Their example also offers locals new standards of behavior to assess and maybe to imitate. Thus tourists might go to visit another culture, but that way of life is already modified, sometimes slightly, sometimes grossly, by its admission of tourists. What can then occur is that the passage of foreigners through an area becomes an accepted, standard aspect of a broadened conception of local ways. Thus, in places such as Bali, Venice, and other much-visited parts of the traveled world, tourism becomes a "traditional" part of regional life.

In some cases locals, keen to feed the market, may invent traditions to satisfy visitors' desire for seeing cultural difference. But this deliberate fabrication of folkloric custom should not necessarily be seen as a cultural "lie." In Malta, locals did not mind performing novel dance routines for the tourists. In fact, many have come to enjoy them and now regard them as part of their own contemporary traditions. In other words, because of tourism they had exaggerated the distinctiveness of their way of life and found a new source of pleasure, maybe even of pride, in the process.

The problem here is that those travelers who seek an encounter with an "authentically" different way of life will always be disappointed, or mildly self-deluding. This holds true as much for British backpackers keen to outdo their peers by venturing into the more dangerous zones of southeast Asia as it does for middle-class Americans visiting the lesser developed parts of Eastern Europe. The common concept of authenticity held by almost all these wanderers is a mythical one grounded in a pre-tourist world, linked to ideas of unchanging cultures unaffected by the outside. So all today's tourists get to see are performances of "staged authenticity," where the fact that the event has to be put on for, or remain mindful of, the visitors robs it of the very quality so many have traveled to seek. The paradise they search for is forever postponed.

To some tourists, the most acceptable solution to their self-contrived conundrum is to turn postmodernist: to embrace the failure of their search and to revel in contemporary tourism in itself. The "authentic" is then recognized as an impossible ideal and the visitors, having traveled so far, take what pleasure they can from the cultural mishmash they find at their destination. The traveler becomes a tourist of tourism, able to relax in the knowledge that there is no escape from this circle. Following this strategy, it no longer seems quite so absurd to fly from New York to Bilbao to view American paintings in a building designed by a Canadian on the banks of a Basque river. Nor does it seem so silly to make one's long way to Pentecost only to jostle with other camcorder-carrying tourists bent on filming local divers who have just returned from a trip working on a cargo ship between the islands and Sydney. For this is the world we all now live in. Perhaps then best to stay at home, surfing tourist sites on the Web.

REFERENCES AND SUGGESTIONS FOR FURTHER READING

Boissevain, Jeremy. 1996a. "'But We Live Here!' Perspectives on Cultural Tourism in Malta." In *Sustainable Tourism in Islands and Small States: Case Studies*, ed. L. Briguglio et al. London: Pintar.

Boissevain, Jeremy, ed. 1996b. *Coping with Tourists. European Reactions to Mass Tourism*. Oxford: Berghahn. [An informative collection of articles on locals' ways of coping with the coachloads of incomers.]

Bowman, Glenn. 1989. "Fucking Tourists: Sexual Relations and Tourism in Jerusalem's Old City." *Critique of Anthropology* 9, no. 2: 77–93. [A brilliant, incisive, and influential article written in a forceful style.]

Cohen, Erik. 1996. "Hunter-Gatherer Tourism in Thailand." In *Tourism and Indigenous Peoples*, ed. Richard Butler and Tom Hinch. London: International Thomson Business Press.

Crain, Mary M. 1996. "Contested Territories: The Politics of Touristic Development at the Shrine of El Rocío in Southwestern Andalusia." In Boissevain 1996b.

Crick, Malcolm. 1994. *Resplendent Sites, Discordant Voices: Sri Lankans and International Tourism*. Chur, Switzerland: Harwood Academic. [Still, so far, the only ethnography devoted to the anthropological study of tourism.]

Keefe, Jean, and Sue Wheat. 1998. *Tourism and Human Rights*. London: Tourism Concern. [A plain statement of the damage tourism can wreak.]

23

Survival International

JONATHAN MAZOWER

Survival is the only worldwide organization supporting tribal peoples through public campaigns. It was founded in 1969 after an article by Norman Lewis in the UK's *Sunday Times* highlighted the massacres, land thefts, and genocide taking place in Brazilian Amazonia. Like many modern atrocities, the racist oppression of Brazil's Indians took place in the name of "economic growth." Today, Survival has supporters (including many anthropologists) in eighty countries (figure 1). It works for tribal peoples' rights in three complementary ways: campaigns, education, and funding. We work closely with local indigenous organizations and focus on tribal peoples who have the most to lose, usually those most recently in contact with the outside world.

Survival runs worldwide campaigns to fight for tribal peoples. We were the first in this field to use mass letter-writing, and we have orchestrated campaigns from Siberia to Sarawak, Canada to Kenya. Our work forced the Brazilian government to recognize Yanomami land in 1992, and so to fulfill for the first time its constitutional commitment to this people. A few years previously, Botswana's government halted plans to evict Bushmen from the Central Kalahari Game Reserve within weeks after Survival issued a bulletin. There have been many other successes.

Campaigns are not only directed at governments, but at companies, banks, extremist missionaries, guerrilla armies, museums, narrow-minded conservationists, and anyone else who violates tribal peoples' rights. Survival was the first organization to draw attention to the destructive effects of World Bank projects—now recognized as a major cause of suffering in many poor countries. As well as letter-writing—which generates thousands of protests—we use many other tactics,

FIGURE 1 Anthropologist John Palmer with the Wichí, northern Argentina, collecting information for a survey of their lands, to be used in their defense in an upcoming court case, late 1990s. (Courtesy of Jonathan Mazower/Survival)

from vigils at embassies to direct lobbying of those in positions of power; from putting cases at the United Nations to advising on the drafting of international law; from informing tribes of their legal rights to organizing headline-grabbing stunts. All our work is rooted in direct personal contact with hundreds of tribal communities.

Our educational programs, aimed at people in the "West" or "North," set out to demolish the myth that tribal peoples are relics, destined to perish through "progress." We promote respect for their cultures and explain the contemporary relevance of their way of life. We also produce high-quality material for children, for they are the conscience of the future.

We provide a platform for tribal representatives to talk directly to the companies which are invading their land. We also disseminate information to tribal peoples, using both community radio and the written word—telling them how other tribes are faring and warning them about the threats posed by multinationals. In this way, we give them access to the information they need to make their voices heard. We believe that public opinion is the most effective force for change. Its power will make it harder, and eventually impossible, for governments and companies to oppress tribal peoples. Survival also plays a major role in ensuring that humanitarian, self-help, educational, and medical projects for tribal peoples receive proper funding. A good example is the Yanomami medical fund, which succeeded in virtually eliminating malaria in some Indian areas.

Survival is the only major organization in its field which refuses funding from national governments—this ensures our freedom of action but also makes us stretch our scarce resources to the limit. We are also the only international pro-tribal peoples organization to have received the prestigious Right Livelihood Award, known as the "alternative Nobel Prize." Most important, our work has been applauded by countless tribal peoples and their organizations throughout the world.

Since 1969, the "developed" world's attitude to tribal peoples has changed beyond recognition. Then, it was assumed that they would either die out or be assimilated; now, at least in some places, their experience and values are considered important. Survival has pushed tribal issues into the political and cultural mainstream. This, perhaps, is our greatest achievement of all, but there are many barriers of racism, tyranny, and greed which we must still overcome.

If you would like to support Survival's work or find out more about us, please contact us:

Survival International
6 Charterhouse Buildings
London EC1M 7ET
UK

Tel: (+44) (0)20 7687 8700
Fax: (+44) (0)20 7687 8701

General enquiries: info@survival-international.org
Web site: http://www.survival-international.org

Contributors

WILLIAM O. BEEMAN is a professor in the Departments of Anthropology and Theatre, Speech, and Dance at Brown University. He has conducted fieldwork in Iran, Japan, India, Central Asia, and Germany. He is author of *Language, Status and Power in Iran*, and *Culture, Performance and Communication in Iran*; editor of the book series Margaret Mead: The Study of Contemporary Cultures; and author of numerous books and articles dealing with language, religion, performance traditions, and political culture.

PHILIPPE BOURGOIS is a professor and chair of the Department of Anthropology, History, and Social Medicine at the University of California, San Francisco. His most recent book was on the U.S. inner city, *In Search of Respect: Selling Crack in El Barrio* (1995), which was awarded the C. Wright Mills Prize and the Margaret Mead Prize, among others. He has conducted fieldwork in Central America on political violence, ethnic conflict, immigration and labor relations, and street children. In addition to several coedited volumes, he is also the author of *Ethnicity at Work: Divided Labor on a Central American Banana Plantation* (1989). He is currently conducting fieldwork among homeless heroin injectors in San Francisco for a book to be published by University of California Press as *Righteous Dopefiend: Homeless Heroin Addicts in Black and White*.

JOHN CHERNOFF is the author of *African Rhythm and African Sensibility*.

E. VALENTINE DANIEL is a professor of anthropology and director of the Southern Asian Institute at Columbia University. Of all his writings, he is best known for his two books, *Fluid Signs: Being a Person the Tamil Way* and *Charred Lullabies: Chapters in an Anthropography of Violence*. He is currently writing a book on the American philosopher Charles Peirce, to be entitled *Charles S. Peirce's Philosophical Anthropology*.

ALEX DE WAAL has worked in and on the Horn of Africa for twenty years, concerned with issues of refugees, famine, war, and human rights. He is the author of *Famine That Kills: Darfur, Sudan 1984–1985* (1989); *Famine Crimes: Politics and the Disaster Relief Industry in Africa* (1997); and *Who Fights? Who Cares? War and Humanitarian Action in Africa* (2000). Currently he is director of Justice Africa, an advocacy organization based in London.

JUDITH ENNEW is a researcher in the Centre for Family Research, University of Cambridge, and visiting fellow in the Department of Anthropology, Goldsmith's College, University of London. She has been an activist and researcher in children's rights since 1979, specializing in child workers, "street children," and child sexual exploitation. From 1993 to 1998 she was the international coordinator of the Childwatch International Monitoring Children's Rights Project. She has worked in Latin America, Africa, South and Southeast Asia, and Eastern Europe on children's rights issues, and is now involved in various programs to strengthen capacity in child research, especially among grassroots workers.

JAMES FAIRHEAD is a professor in the School of African and Asian Studies at the University of Sussex. He specializes in the social anthropology of agriculture, forestry, ecology, and food systems in Central and West Africa. Together with Melissa Leach, he has written the prize-winning *Misreading the African Landscape* (1996) and *Reframing Deforestation* (1998).

SARAH FRANKLIN is a reader in Cultural Anthropology at Lancaster University, where she is also a member of the Institute for Women's Studies and the Centre for Science Studies. She is the author of *Embodied Progress: a Cultural Account of Assisted Conception* (1997) and coauthor of *Technologies of Procreation: Kinship in the Age of Assisted Conception* (1999) and *Global Nature, Global Culture* (2000). She is the coeditor with Helena Ragone of *Reproducing Reproduction: Kinship, Power, and Technological Innovation* (1998) and with Susan McKinnon of *Relative Values: Kinship Studies Reconfigured* (2001).

MICHAEL GILSENAN holds the David B. Kriser Chair in Anthropology and Middle Eastern Studies at New York University, where he chairs the department of Middle Eastern Studies. He has carried out fieldwork in Egypt and Lebanon and is currently engaged in research on Yemeni migration around the Indian Ocean. He has written *Saint and Sufi in Modern Egypt* (1973), *Recognising Islam* (1982/1995), and *Lords of the Lebanese Marches* (1996).

FAYE GINSBURG directs the Center for Media, Culture, and History at New York University, where she is also David B. Kriser Professor of Anthropology. Her books on anthropology and media include *Media Worlds* (2002), an edited volume, and *Mediating Culture* (forthcoming).

ALMA GOTTLIEB is a cultural anthropologist specializing in Africa. She has contributed articles to many books and scholarly journals and is on the editorial board of several journals. She is the author of *Under the Kapok Tree: Identity and Difference in Beng Thought*; co-editor (with Thomas Buckley) of *Blood Magic: The Anthropology of Menstruation*; coauthor (with Philip Graham), of *Parallel Worlds: An Anthropologist and a Writer Encounter Africa*; co-editor (with Judy DeLoache) of *A World of Babies: Imagined Childcare Guides for Seven Societies*; and co-author (with M. Lynne Murphy) of a *Beng-English Dictionary*. She has recently completed *The Afterlife Is Where We Come From: Infants and the Culture of Infancy in West Africa*. She is a professor of anthropology, African studies, and women's studies at the University of Illinois at Urbana-Champaign.

CHRISTOPHER HANN has been the director of the Max Planck Institute for Social Anthropology in Halle (Saale), Germany, since 1999. Previously he taught social anthropology at the University of Kent at Canterbury.

FAYE V. HARRISON is a professor in the Department of Anthropology, University of Tennessee, Knoxville. She specializes in Caribbean and African diaspora studies and is also interested in the history and politics of anthropology. Her publications include *Decolonizing Anthropology, African-American Pioneers in Anthropology*, and numerous essays. She is currently writing a book on the role of "outsiders within" anthropology's division of labor by race, gender, and (trans)national status.

RICHARD JENKINS trained as a social anthropologist at the Queen's University of Belfast and the University of Cambridge, and has been professor of sociology at the University of Sheffield since 1995. Current areas of interest include social identity theory, European societies, ethnicity and nationalism, the cultural construction of competence and disability, and the dis/re-enchantment of the world. He has undertaken research in Belfast, the English West Midlands, South Wales, and Denmark. Recent books include *Pierre Bourdieu* (1992), *Social Identity* (1996), *Rethinking Ethnicity* (1997), and *Questions of Competence* (1998).

MELISSA LEACH is a social anthropologist and professorial fellow of the Institute of Development Studies at the University of Sussex, where she established the Environment Group in 1990. She has researched and published extensively on social and historical aspects of landscape change and the construction of environmental knowledge, especially relating to West Africa and the Caribbean. Her books include *Rainforest Relations* (1994); *The Lie of the Land* (1996); *Misreading the African Landscape* (1996), and *Reframing Deforestation* (1998), the latter two with James Fairhead. She has just completed a major research project on environmental science/policy processes and society, and is developing new work around citizenship, science, and risk.

MARGARET LOCK is a professor in the Department of Social Studies of Medicine and Department of Anthropology at McGill University. She is the author of *East Asian Medicine in Urban Japan: Varieties of Medical Experience* (1980) and the award-winning *Encounters with Aging: Mythologies of Menopause in Japan and North America* (1993). Her latest book is entitled *Twice Dead: Organ Transplants and the Reinvention of Death* (2001).

JEREMY MacCLANCY is a professor in the Department of Anthropology at Oxford Brookes University and a founding trustee of Chacolinks, which campaigns for the threatened rights of the indigenous peoples of northern Argentina (www.chacolinks.org.uk). He has done major fieldwork in Vanuatu and Basque Spain. Among other works, he has written *To Kill a Bird with Two Stones: A Short History of Vanuatu* (1980/2001); *Consuming Culture* (1992); and *The Decline of Carlism* (1999). He has edited or coedited books on popular anthropology and the anthropologies of sport, food, and art.

JONATHAN MAZOWER is the projects and campaigns officer for Survival International, London.

ELLEN MESSER is an associate professor at Brown University and involved with the World Hunger Program. Her research interests include cross-cultural perspectives on the human right to food; biocultural determinants of food and nutrition intake; sustainable food systems (with special emphasis on the roles of NGOs); the impacts of agrobiotechnology on hunger; and the cultural history of nutrition, agriculture, and food science.

A. DAVID NAPIER is a professor of anthropology at Middlebury College. He is the author of three books on the cultural construction of the self: *Masks, Transformation, and Paradox* (1986), *Foreign Bodies* (1992), and *Age of Immunology* (in press). He has conducted fieldwork in India and Indonesia on indigenous healing and ritual, and has spent several years working in clinical settings. He is the founder and current executive director of Students of Human Ecology, a nonprofit organization that sponsors mentor-apprentice learning in medical, cultural, and environmental studies.

NANCY SCHEPER-HUGHES is professor and former chair of the Department of Anthropology at the University of California, Berkeley, where she also directs the doctoral training program in Critical Medical Anthropology. She served in the Peace Corps in Brazil (1964–66), helping to found a community organization that is still active. In rural Alabama, she worked for a civil rights and legal organization (1967–68), conducting research on hunger and malnutrition. She spent a year during the democratic transition as Chair of the Department of Social Anthropology at the University of Cape Town, South Africa (1993–94). Her numerous publications include *Death without Weeping: The Violence of Everyday Life in Brazil*, and *Small Wars: The Cultural Politics of Childhood* (coedited with C. Sargent). She is working on two new books: *Undoing: The Politics of the Impossible in the New South Africa*, and *The Ends of the Body: The Global Traffic in Human Organs*.

JANE SCHNEIDER is a professor in the Graduate Program at the City University of New York. Among her books, she has coauthored *Culture and Political Economy in Western Sicily* (1976) and *Festival of the Poor: Fertility Decline and the Ideology of Class in Sicily, 1860–1980* (1997), and has edited *Italy's Southern Question: Orientalism in One Country* (1998) and coedited *Cloth and Human Experience* (1991).

PARKER SHIPTON is associate professor of anthropology and research fellow in African studies at Boston University. Author or editor of many publications on Africa and in social and cultural anthropology, he is a former president of the Association for Africanist Anthropology.

CHRISTOPHER B. STEINER is an anthropologist who currently holds the Lucy C. McDannel '22 Chair in Art History and Museum Studies at Connecticut College. His books include *African Art in Transit* (1994), *Perspectives on Africa* (1997), and *Unpacking Culture: Art and Commodity in Colonial and Postcolonial Worlds* (1999).

Index